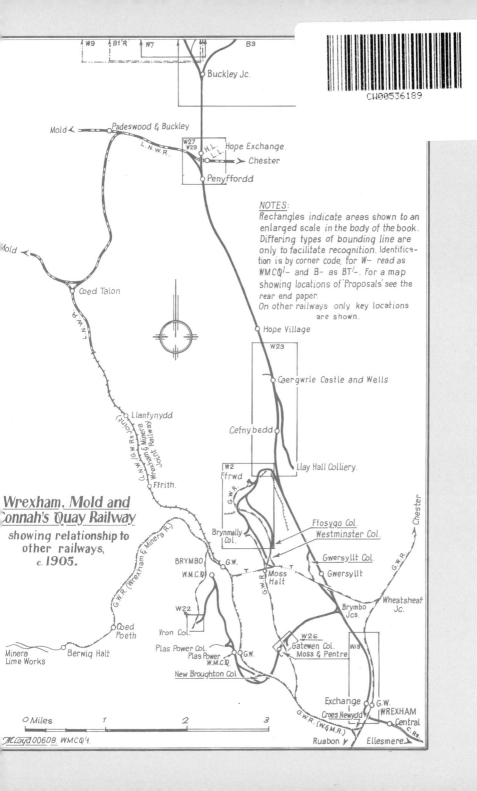

W9   B1'R   W7   B3

Buckley Jc.

Mold ◄

Padeswood & Buckley

L.N.W.R.

W27
W29   H.L.
     L.L.

Hope Exchange.

➤ Chester

Penyffordd

Mold ◄

Coed Talon

L.N.W.R.

NOTES:
Rectangles indicate areas shown to an
enlarged scale in the body of the book.
Differing types of bounding line are
only to facilitate recognition. Identifica-
tion is by corner code, for W— read as
WMCQ'/– and B— as BT'–. For a map
showing locations of 'Proposals' see the
rear end paper.
On other railways only key locations
are shown.

Hope Village

W23

Caergwrle Castle and Wells

Llanfynydd

(L.N.W./G.W. Rs Joint)
Wrexham & Minera
Joint Railway

Cefn y bedd

Ffrith.

W2
Ffrwd

G.W.R.

Llay Hall Colliery.

Wrexham, Mold and
Connah's Quay Railway

showing relationship to
other railways,
c.1905.

G.W.R. (Wrexham & Minera R.)

Brynmally
Col.

Ffosygo Col.
Westminster Col.

BRYMBO
W.M.C.Q.

G.W.

T.   T.

Moss
Halt

G.W.R.

Gwersyllt Col.

Gwersyllt

Chester

G.W.R.

W22

Vron Col.

Brymbo
Jcs.

Wheatsheaf
Jc.

Coed
Poeth

Minera
Lime Works

Berwig Halt

Plas Power Col.

Plas Power
W.M.C.Q.

G.W.

W26

Gatewen Col.
Moss & Pentre

W18

New Broughton Col

Exchange

G.W.

Croes Newydd

WREXHAM

G.W.R. (W&M.R.)

Central
C. Rs.

Ruabon ▼

Ellesmere ➤

0 Miles   1   2   3

M.Lloyd 00608. WMCQ'1.

To the PM and Kathy

From The Senior Man

Christmas 1994

The
WREXHAM, MOLD & CONNAH'S QUAY RAILWAY

including

THE BUCKLEY RAILWAY

by

James I.C. Boyd

"Down in a coal mine
Underneath the ground
Up to your arse in water
Bloody nearly drowned"

(Welsh coal-miner's ditty)

THE OAKWOOD PRESS

© James I.C. Boyd and Oakwood Press 1991
ISBN 0 85361 417 2

Typeset by Gem Publishing Company, Brightwell, Wallingford, Oxfordshire.
Printed in Great Britain by The Nuffield Press Ltd

Abstract

Aston Hall Colliery Railway	AHCR
Buckley Railway	BR
Chester & Holyhead Railway (LNWR)	C & HR
Dee & Birkenhead Committee	D & B Cee
Great Central Railway	GCR
Great Western Railway	GWR
London & North Western Railway	LNWR
Manchester, Sheffield & Lincolnshire Railway	MS & LR
Mold & Denbigh Junction Railway	M & DJR
North Wales & Liverpool Railway	NW & LR
North Wales Mineral Railway	NWMR
Oswestry, Ellesmere & Whitchurch Railway	OE & WR
Whitchurch, Wrexham, Mold & Connah's Quay Jc. Rly	WWM & CQJR
Wrexham & Ellesmere Railway	W & ER
Wrexham & Minera Railway	W & MR
Wrexham, Mold & Connah's Quay Railway	WMCQR

Published by
The OAKWOOD PRESS
P.O.Box 122, Headington, Oxford.

Contents

Principal Acts of Parliament

BUCKLEY RAILWAY

23–4 V.c.lxxxix	14th June 1860	Incorporation
26–7 civ	29th June 1863	Additional Capital
29–30 xli	18th May 1866	Power to carry passengers
29–30 cclxx	23rd July 1866	Agmt. & lease to WMCQR for 999 years
4 Ed.7 c.xcvi	2nd July 1904	Transfer to GCR (GCR Act)

WREXHAM, MOLD & CONNAH'S QUAY RAILWAY

25–6 V.c. ccxxi	7th Aug 1862	Incorporation
27–8 ccxxxiv	25th July 1864	Extn. Whitchurch & Brymbo
28–9 clxxvi	29th June 1865	Dee Valley & Farndon lines
28–9 cclxi	5th July 1865	Extn. Connah's Quay
29–30 ccclviii	10th Aug 1866	Extn. Buckley
29–30 ccclix	10th Aug 1866	Extn. Connah's Quay
30–1 cc	15th Aug 1867	Extn. of time for Whitchurch
32–3 cliii	9th Aug 1867	Financial
36–7 ccxxxii	5th Aug 1873	Lease of Buckley Rly.
45–6 ccxxxii	18th Aug 1882	New lines etc/Financial
46–7 lxv	29th June 1883	Hawarden Loop etc/Financial
46–7 cviii	16th July 1883	Financial
51–2 lxxvii	5th July 1888	New lines etc/Financial
53–4 lix	4th July 1890	Extn. of time (Wirral Rly Act)
56–7 lxxix	29th June 1893	Extn. of time (MS&LR Act)
58–9 cxlviii	6th July 1895	Wirral Rly title (MS&LR Act)
4 Ed.7 c.xcvi	22nd July 1904	Transfer to GCR (GCR Act)

Note on Photographs

The provision of contemporary pictures is an overriding problem with a subject which ceased to exist in 1905 and would not have been an obvious objective for early photographers. Only one 'railway photographer' is known to have visited the WMCQR before the First World War. The Railway was clearly not in a tourist area, nor used by tourists; it had no scenic attractions so is not illustrated – if appearing at all – in local Guide Books. Fortunately, a set of views of the Buckley Railway in the mid-1870s has survived, though in poor condition today. Most negatives have been lost and recourse has been made to copying, with some loss of quality.

In an ideal world, photographs taken after 1905 would not be used but under the circumstances, later ones right up to the present time, and where a feature is not otherwise available, have been included. This step has been taken with reluctance and the indulgence of readers is sought.

Note on Messrs. Beyer, Peacock & Co. Ltd.
  This Manchester-based locomotive manufacturer features frequently herein. The spelling of the title varies officially from time to time, the firm preferring 'Beyer-Peacock' between the First and Second Wars.
  The historic spelling, Beyer, Peacock & Co. Ltd. has been adopted here.

Note on Nomenclature
  The following definitions are used:–

TRAMROAD – A wooden or iron rail route using either plate or edge rails mounted on stone (or) blocks instead of cross sleepering. Not intended for locomotive operation.

TRAMWAY – A narrow gauge railway-type system using conventional edge rails on cross sleepers, and usually of later date than a Tramroad. Suitable if required, for locomotive operation. Such were found hereabouts in more recent times in clay pits, mines and quarries etc.

RAILWAY – A standard gauge railway usually suitable for any form of motive power. Within the present context, a Railway may mean a system existing by right of Statute (e.g. The Wrexham, Mold & Connah's Quay Railway) or one built without statutory authority, by arrangement with local landowners and owned/operated privately in order to link industrial premises with a statutory undertaking.

Index to Tramroad Drawings

(*Note:* Indexing is by Reference No., not Date)

Index to Railway Drawings

(*Note:* Indexing is by Reference No., not Date)

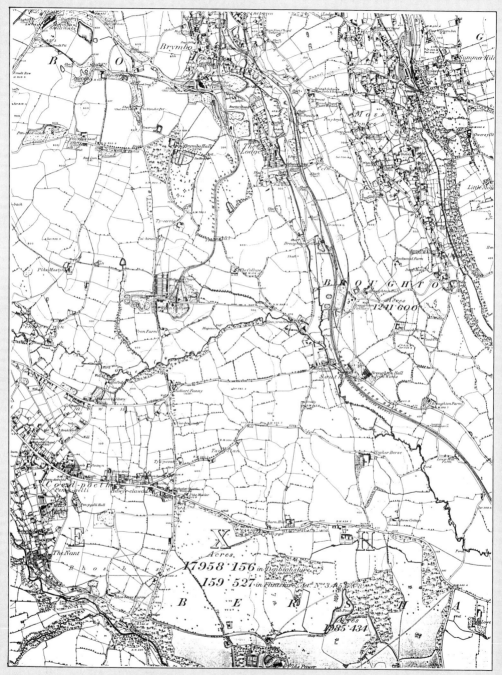

The railway position in the Brymbo district in 1870.

Courtesy First Edition, 1″ Ordnance Survey

Introducing The Wrexham, Mold & Connah's Quay Railway

The arrival of a tubular-shaped packet in the postal delivery pigeon-hole marked 'B' in the vast hall of the late Lord Portman's Dorset residence, (by then Bryanston School) marked the monthly delivery of THE RAILWAY MAGAZINE. Its contents made a pleasant diversion in those academic surroundings. The issue for November 1937 was particularly so, as it contained an article, 'Notes on the LNER in North Wales'. 'Surely North Wales is the home of the old LNWR?', I thought, 'and perhaps, the Great Western?' Clearly, it seemed those two companies did not have all that territory to themselves for the article showed pictures of trains (which were almost identical to those of the Cheshire Lines Committee) which passed our house frequently heading for Chester. It was a revelation that similar tank engines, lettered 'LNER', drawing teak-coloured coaches, should actually operate in a Welsh stronghold of Euston and Paddington. Well, Christmas holidays were nigh and with pocket money permitting after that charitable event, it might be possible to load one's pushbike onto a Chester (Northgate) train and from there, explore the matter. I duly purchased a copy of the Ordnance Survey ¼inch map 'Manchester & North Wales' from the School bookshop (in anticipation) and boldly put down the cost to my School account!

The holidays arrived; as I did in Chester. Once clear of the flatlands which border the Dee west of that city, my cycle led me pleasantly towards Mold with its attractive backdrop of the Clwyd Range. I had noted I would pass over the LNER at Hawarden on a section of railway which had once borne the exhausting title of the Wrexham, Mold & Connah's Quay Railway. Hanging about at Hawarden, the then-frequent train service soon produced a train: expecting I suppose, something akin to those fine green-painted engines which I might see at Manchester Central or London Road, it was a disappointment to find it was hauled by another 4–4–2 tank engine of the GCR type which had brought me to Chester earlier that day and drawing a rake of scruffy teak carriages too.

Despite this deflation and realising that Hawarden had not given me an explanation of what the LNER was doing hereabouts, I pushed on for the map showed me that beyond Ewloe, a branch off this same Seacombe –Wrexham line, meandered curvaceously down to the river at Connah's Quay. If that line proved as dull as the one I had seen at Hawarden, I could return to Chester and catch an earlier train home . . . and consider cancelling my order for THE RAILWAY MAGAZINE as well.

Shortly, a bridge ahead spanned the road. This must be it: to left and right, high up on the bank above the road, tall smoking chimneys spoke of industry. I pushed the bike up a rough track and onto the railway line which was single and shorn of stone ballast, abounding in clinker upon which the sleepers lay proudly. Many sleepers were split, some broken under the rail: some carried tell-tale marks where wagons had derailed and the flanges had scored the sleeper-tops for yard upon yard. The rails were old and had certainly done their duty elsewhere before coming here. Keys in the chairs were often a luxury. I stood on some sort of railway summit: to the north the line fell quite steeply beside a brickworks and toward a silvery streak below which was the Dee. In a southerly direction it also fell, curving away out of sight and throwing off sidings on either hand, their pointwork controlled by simple ground levers, some with 'WMCQR' cast on them. Here and there an iron boundary post (also with those initials) had survived. It was a complicated scene, not to be quickly absorbed. Brick-kilns, chimneys, stacks of tiles and bricks, heaped pipes and sheets of untidy water: clay pits, mud, loading platforms (at which stood rakes of unusual wagons which carried others upon their backs) confused the eye. There was a casual air about the whole system – the rural informality of the Somerset & Dorset which I knew well in term-time was, by the standards in front of me, a pompous undertaking. This place had a carefree atmosphere about it; fencing was but occasional, clearly the railway was used by all and sundry as a right of way and there were no trespassers' signs. I only passed two weary semaphore signals – these proved to be worked off the gate heels at Castle Brickworks. There was no one about, no one shouted at me but then, there were no trains either. Later I learned there never were any on a Saturday, the day of my visit.

I mounted my cycle and rode southwards towards Buckley Junction, then returned to ride down to Connah's Quay. This was a world apart; perhaps everyone was at a football match? I passed no stations, no sign of movement anywhere: the railway was mine for the rest of the day. I explored long sidings, brick-ovens, curious transfer platforms: I coughed in the smoke from the kilns and stared into the murky waters of deep, water-filled and worked-out clay pits. Wagons of coal stood in mud akin to that I had seen in photographs of Flanders during the then-recent war. Here and there the rails disappeared beneath a thick yellow soup. Worse forms of liquid had to be traversed from time to time, undisguised domestic sewage into which old prams, crushed galvanised bins, rags and bottles were thrown. Cycling was hazardous. As I neared Connah's Quay the smells were heightened by those from the river.

On reaching the dreary cluster of buildings which heralded Connah's Quay, I took the left fork and followed the line into the LMSR station's interchange yard. It was full of rotting wagon hulks, only one line being fit to use. In the 1960s, after the Buckley section had closed (but this yard remained) a well-meaning signalman permitted a British Rail 2–10–0 locomotive to work into it. It derailed so completely that recovery took two days. The 'back platform' (apparently for the use of WMCQ section passenger trains), baffled me completely and one may only assume it was put in to anticipate the event of a passenger service being inaugurated.

It was late and time for me to leave 'The LNER in North Wales' for another day. I doubted if THE RAILWAY MAGAZINE's correspondent had made such close an acquaintance with the system as I had in the last few hours.

As one opens an old album of wedding photographs, I came to renew my knowledge (in the late 1960s) and then only because a serious national outbreak of foot-and-mouth disease prevented me from fieldwork in the area I was currently researching. For two decades afterwards I watched the dying throes of industry and railways in the district. Dereliction followed abandonment: today the area is transformed by the input of vast sums of Government funds and its identity lost as a second industrial revolution transforms the landscape once more.

On a brilliant June morning in 1987, I stood in a shallow railway cutting in Buckinghamshire. Pigeons flew in and out of the thickets and rabbits darted to and fro in the early sunshine. A green woodpecker was making a meal out of a Great Central Railway fencing post and there was even a lark in the sky; yet of an actual railway there was nothing but a long stretch of green sward, and the archings of successive overbridges as they stretched into the distance. Tall grasses, stagnant water underfoot . . . Beeching had carried out his brief here. Yet here had lain proud Watkin's Great Central Railway, that arrogant colossus which had snatched the little WMCQR to itself. The victor hereabouts had been picked clean off the face of the earth, yet only the day previously had I ridden in a train along its victim.

The beauty of Israel is slain upon the high places; how are the mighty fallen.

Quantum sufficit.

Background to the WMCQR:
River – Tramroad – Railway

To understand how the Railway came into existence, a little background to the times will be helpful. The River Dee rises above Bala Lake: ultimately it flows into the Irish Sea by a wide-mouthed estuary channel between the North Wales Coast and the Wirral Peninsula. Between these places its course is circuitous and in former days, its lowest bridging point was at Chester: that city became the port for Ireland and for centuries it was the most important shipping place in the northwest of England.* Below Chester the river has changed course frequently, swinging between shores so that seaside villages would be on the water's edge for a time, only to be abandoned by the river which had swung to the other side of the channel and left former small ports with hardly any water at all. Navigating this tricky estuary was extremely treacherous: wrecks abounded. For example, Parkgate on the Wirral was favoured with water at the beginning of the 19th century but in 1821 the river receded and transferred itself to the Welsh shore. The whole railway picture of this area is dominated by the erratic behaviour of the Dee compared with the stability of its neighbour the Mersey on which the ports of Birkenhead and Liverpool developed. In time Chester was abandoned in favour of Flint, because it was nearer the sea. Some of the small Welsh harbours survived because they had a navigable 'gutter' to connect them to the main river.

The Dee was improved by various Statutory Powers dating from 1732 and it became a tidal canal between Golftyn and Chester on 3rd April, 1737. The most westerly anchorage on the Welsh shore was a stone pier named New Quay (later to be named Connah's Quay). This pier at Golftyn was a venerable place mentioned in the Domesday Survey and the Wepre Iron Road was to lead to it from the coal pits at Northop Hall at the turn of the eighteenth century.

Simple tramroads, some made in timber, carried local products down to the river for onward waterborne transport round our coasts, especially across the Irish Sea. Such was the growth in output of local coal that Chester – until then the principal market for that coal – could no longer take

---

*'MANAGEMENT OF THE RIVER DEE'. (G.A. Wright) Clwyd Record Office. [Open Shelf]

it all. By 1800 the Dublin market had become the Flintshire pits biggest customer; by 1873 the tramroads had lost their place to railways and Connah's Quay had become the chief port on the Dee. The first railway hereabouts was the Buckley Railway, a very basic line linking the pottery industries etc. around that place, with Connah's Quay and an export trade; the Company was financed and promoted by local enterprise, the trains were worked by steam locomotives. The course was heavily graded up from the coast and no passengers were carried. Local products were conveyed in the traders' own wagons . . . all the ingredients for making the system one of great interest. Then along came the similarly-inspired WMCQR, conceived and built by industrialists around Wrexham with its heavier industries. This district also wished to gain the Dee and beyond, to reach Birkenhead by a crossing of the river onto the Wirral shore thus by-passing the monopoly of combined GWR/LNWR at Chester.

The WMCQR (disregarding the satellite Buckley Railway which it worked from an early date), was basically a coal carrier. Coal in northeast Wales had been worked for centuries. The coal seams came near the surface so that whilst most of Wales heated itself with turf and wood, inhabitants in parts of Flintshire and Denbighshire simply dug fuel out of their own backyards.

The area was pock-marked with little coal pits, family concerns: outsiders from England saw the potential of this coal and created the larger, underground pits which sent most of their coal away for use, not in Wales, but in England – this was the traffic on which the railways relied. Some pits were very wet (hence the nickname, 'The Slutch') and most produced a quantity of slack coal for which customers were hard to find. Short-time working and poverty were on a scale unknown in South Wales where all coal could be sold. Industrial unrest hit the coal mines and in consequence, the railways too: the big lines could weather the storm, but the small ones fared badly in such times. Some pits had been worked beyond their economical life even before the railways came, and continued in decline.

Against this background however, there were always industrialists who thought expansively, and had the GWR served them in the way they considered it should, the WMCQR would never have come to pass.

So, river, tramroad and railway, each in its turn combined to link this part of North Wales during the Industrial Revolution. Only canal transport failed to play a part, despite an attempt so to do. The earth's natural resources were exploited and then worked out to the effect that today, it is difficult for the mind to comprehend the magnitude, noise, dirt and squalor of this anthill of manufacture and employment. Much of what is described herein has disappeared with deliberate attempt at restoration of acres of industrial wasteland to present-day needs. A skeleton of railways survives and grass waves in the breeze where it covers yesterday's workplaces. The derelict chapel, perched precariously on the lip of the deep, water-filled clay-pit, is even now prey to the bull-dozer: the drone of throaty earth-moving machinery is unbroken, as is the stench of their diesel exhausts. Man is about to create another era which in time, later man will demolish in his turn. For the moment, consider 1905 when the WMCQR lost its identity, and there is today no one alive who can recall it . . . and read on!

The Tramroad Era

Introduction

Before the coming of the railway, the pioneer industries on the south bank of the Dee were served by tramroads; they were the earliest in North Wales. These have been little researched and due to opencast coal mining in the area since the Second World War, and the building of new housing estates and factories in the last decade or so, backed by an effort by Governments to offset unemployment, fieldwork has been hampered. Other difficulties arise from a repetition of proper names and the variation of local titles, for instance, Hawarden Colliery or Mare Hey Colliery were names (with or without prefixes) given to coalpits in quite different parts of the district. Worse still, the name Ewloe covers a wide area and when used in documents it is seldom clear whether the parish, village or collective area is intended: the Tithe Maps are incomplete in this regard, Estate Maps lack names but recourse to the Ordnance Surveyors' Survey Maps produced 1834/5 to a scale of 2 ins/1 mile is a good starting point. Throughout the following there is much which remains unknown and though local historians have published their findings on the courses of the first tramroads, seen through the eyes of a railway historian their suppositions lack knowledge of the type of terrain through which a tramroad, even of most primitive type, could be taken.

The earliest tramroads were of wooden construction, the first being a Sandycroft-linked line whose course or even whole existence is lacking in confirmation. There was an 'Iron Road' from the Northop area to Wepre on the river which reflected the plateway standards found elsewhere in those times (late 18th century) but otherwise the remaining plateways of the district were of very light construction compared with (for instance) those in South Wales . . . this may account for the low esteem in which they were held by their users who found them ill-kept and unreliable. These light plateways were well-established hereabouts before 1800. The coal-carrying Mancot and Wepre lines apart; most of the others were servants of the clay industry around Buckley for, although there was coal extraction there too, it was the products of the claypits which produced the highest tramroad tonnages. Evidence of coal-burning by those involved in pottery, brick and tile making is found in the embankment-work of the tramroads which was composed almost entirely of clinker and ash.

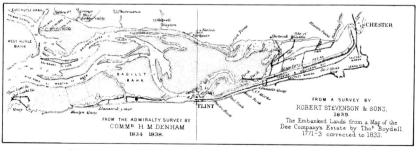

Map of the Estuary of the River Dee; surveyed in 1834, 1838 and 1839.

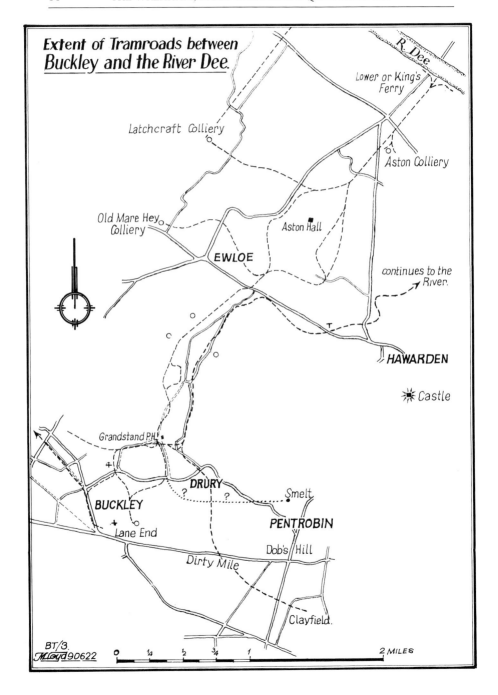

Extent of Tramroads between
Buckley and the River Dee.

R. Dee

Lower or King's
Ferry

Latchcraft Colliery

Aston Colliery

Old Mare Hey
Colliery

Aston Hall

EWLOE

continues to the
River.

HAWARDEN

Castle

Grandstand P.H.

DRURY

Smelt

BUCKLEY

PENTROBIN

Lane End

Dob's Hill

Dirty Mile

Clayfield.

BT/3.
J.M.Lloyd 90622

2 MILES

The Tramroads

LATCHCRAFT (or LATCHCROFT)

A wooden railway connecting Latchcraft Colliery near Wepre with the river at the latter place, the lower section replacing an unreliable 'gutter' or river tributary in which ships would lie. Traditionally 'built by a Chester Company (Sparrows' successors)' about 1740 and said to have been abandoned by 1801. A brickyard later covered some of the course and the site today is unrewarding. No proof of its existence survives.

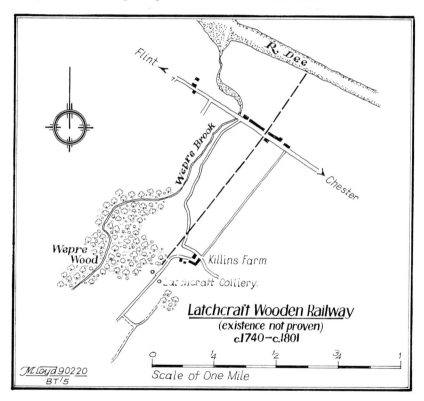

Latchcraft Wooden Railway
(existence not proven)
c.1740–c.1801

Scale of One Mile

MANCOT (or MANCOTT) OLD RAIL WAY

Another wooden railway built about 1740 to link Big Mancot with the river at Mancot Mark (via Pentre) length approx. 1 mile. The system was the outcome of a lease from Glynne of Hawarden Castle for 21 years to George Hope of Chester, to mine coal at Great and Little Mancot; the lease was renewed in 1748 for 'the Mancots and Aston'. The route is shown on old documents as passing alongside the west edge of Mancot Lane, thence over the marsh to reach the Mark where the remains of a wooden jetty survive. The system was replaced about 1793 by the Mancot New Rail Way.[1]

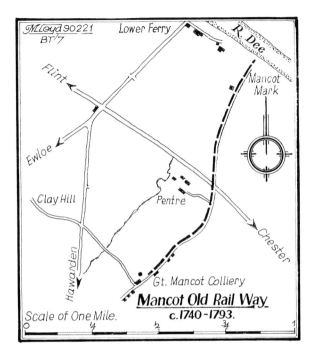

SANDYCROFT WOODEN WAY (or SANDYCROFT RAIL ROAD I)

Under a lease given by Glynne of Hawarden Castle dated 1751, John Dutton and Walter Stubbs of Beckbury, Broseley, Shropshire were permitted to lay tramroads from Sandycroft (Old) Colliery (near Lloyd's Hills), Buckley, past the lead-smelting works at Pentrobin and so northwards along Moor Lane, Hawarden to the river at Fowl Pool Gutter – otherwise known as Sandycroft Mark. Rees Rawson shows the agreed course and more than one attempt has been made to trace it and prove construction. One suggestion is that only the length northwards from the head of Moor Lane at Hawarden ever existed and there is a hint of earthworks along this stretch: if this was so, carting to the top of Moor Lane would take place. A tramroad leading to Sandycroft Gutter existed by 25th March, 1752 but its course southward of here is not known. Lewis suggests that Isaac Wilkinson's account for making 'waggon wheels and waggons' in 1756 could mean the line had been built but local sources hinting that the course included one of the steep entrenchments surrounding Hawarden Castle where the load would be against the hill, would appear to be beyond acceptance. However, an open mind prevails, and the matter remains in doubt.

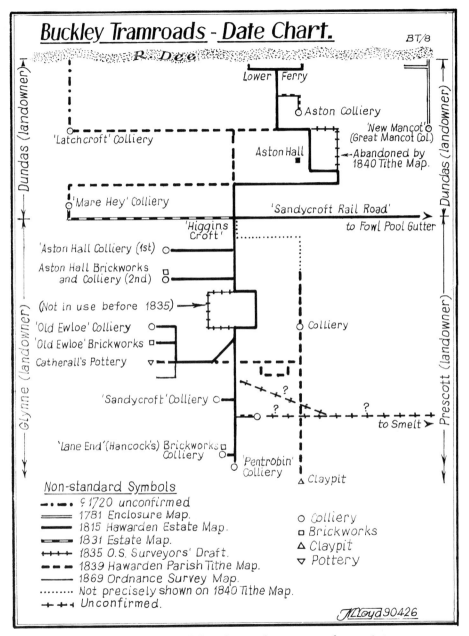

Buckley Tramroads - Date Chart.

BT/8

R. Dee

Lower Ferry

Aston Colliery

'Latchcroft' Colliery

'New Mancot' (Great Mancot Col.)

Aston Hall

←Abandoned by 1840 Tithe Map.

'Mare Hey' Colliery

'Sandycroft Rail Road'
to Fowl Pool Gutter

'Higgins Croft'

'Aston Hall Colliery (1st)

Aston Hall Brickworks and Colliery (2nd)

(Not in use before 1835) →

'Old Ewloe' Colliery

'Old Ewloe' Brickworks

Catherall's Pottery

Colliery

'Sandycroft' Colliery

? ? ?

to Smelt ➤

'Lane End'(Hancock's) Brickworks Colliery

'Pentrobin' Colliery

△ Claypit

Dundas (landowner)

Dundas (landowner)

Glynne (landowner)

Prescott (landowner)

Non-standard Symbols

- ·—·— ς 1720 unconfirmed
- ══════ 1781 Enclosure Map.
- ━━━━━ 1815 Hawarden Estate Map.
- ▬▬ ▬▬ 1831 Estate Map.
- ++++ 1835 O.S. Surveyors' Draft.
- ▬ ▬ ▬ 1839 Hawarden Parish Tithe Map.
- ━━━━ 1869 Ordnance Survey Map.
- ········· Not precisely shown on 1840 Tithe Map.
- +·+·◄ Unconfirmed.

- o Colliery
- □ Brickworks
- △ Claypit
- ▽ Pottery

J. Lloyd 90426

Willett, writing in 1822 and therefore without personal acquaintance, says 'A wooden tramway was built about 1770 to carry coals from the Ewloe Hills'; a sentence also quoted by Dendy Marshall (BRITISH RAILWAYS DOWN TO THE YEAR 1830). Unfortunately the phrase 'Ewloe Hills' is so vague as to be worthless hereabouts.

MANCOT NEW RAIL WAY

Beriah Botfield of Old Park Furnaces near Coalbrookdale, Shropshire, built a line at Mancot in 1793, probably 'plated in the Coalbrookdale manner ... from Little Mancot to the Dee', so avers Lewis. At that time Botfield had leases at Sandycroft (Buckley) and Mancot Collieries. However, both Rees Rawson and Baxter maintain it was the original wooden line at Big Mancot which was plated over with timber, confusion easily arising due to the similarity in place names.

It must be accepted that an iron plateway replaced the wooden line at Mancot on the same course as the Old Rail Way and was used by successive lessees throughout the varying fortunes of the colliery which, like neighbouring ventures, opened and closed under later operators. Its zenith came about 1862 when being worked by Plant, Rose & Plant: in 1864 these lessees were planning to replace the tramroad by a standard gauge siding to the C&HR section, following down the side of Chemistry Lane. However, the Colliery lease for 14 years was surrendered to Dundas (owner of the land at the northern end of the route) on 25th August, 1869.

There is no reference to a siding connection in LNWR records.

ASTON TRAMROAD

At various times and in different documents this plateway was dubbed in accordance with landownership:–

NORTHERN SECTION
    The Aston Tramroad
    The Aston Railway
    The Aston Tramway Co.
    The Admiral's Railway
    The Aston Rail Road
    The Aston Branch Railway
    The Dundas Tramroad

SOUTHERN SECTION
    The Buckley & Aston Tramroad
    The Buckley & Aston Railway
    The Buckley Railway Co.

and therefore great care is needed to identify the precise length of tramroad in question. The system extended from Pentrobin Colliery, near Lane End Brickworks, Buckley, to the south bank of the river at Lower Ferry or King's Ferry as then known. Titles of places were changed during its lifetime, and changes occurred in landownership: it is convenient to refer to the whole as The Aston Tramroad.

As completed the system was made up of two sections: the southern end was built by Rigby (Ironmaster of Hawarden) and Hancock (Brickmaker of Buckley) after they went into partnership in 1792. It was to carry their products – coal, tiles, pottery, bricks, drainpipes etc – from Lane End brickworks and was about 1¾ miles long. At its northernmost point it made end-on junction with the northern section at the Northop–Hawarden road,

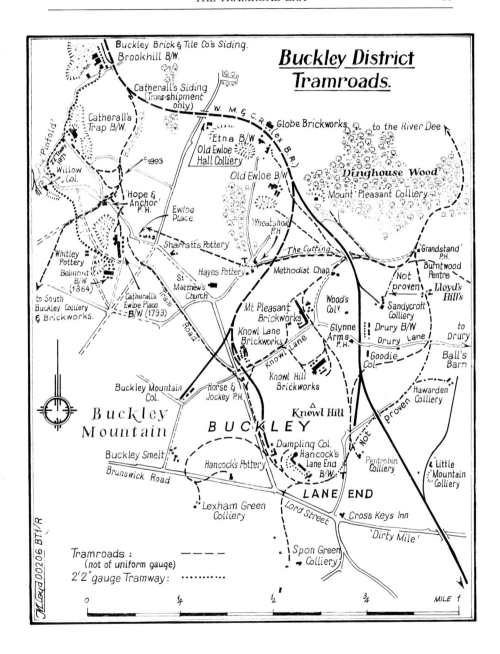

Buckley District Tramroads.

Buckley Brick & Tile Co's Siding.
Brookhill B/W.

Catherall's Siding
(Trans-shipment
only)

W. M. & C. R. (ex B.R.)

Catherall's
Trap B/W.

Globe Brickworks   to the River Dee

Etna B/W.
Old Ewloe
Hall Colliery

Old Ewloe B/W

Dinghouse Wood

'Pinfold'

c.1893

Willow
Col.

Hope &
Anchor
P. H.

Ewloe
Place

Mount Pleasant Colliery

Wheatsheaf
P.H.

Sharratt's Pottery

'The Cutting'

'Grandstand'
P.H.

Whitley
Pottery

Belmont
B/W
(1864)

Hayes Pottery

Methodist Chap.

St
Matthew's
Church

Catherall's Tram
Ewloe Place
B/W (1793)

to South
Buckley Colliery
& Brickworks.

Mt Pleasant
Brickworks

Knowl Lane
Brickworks

Knowl Lane

Wood's
Coly.

Glynne
Arms
P.H.

Burntwood
Pentre

Lloyd's
Hill's

'Not
proven'

Sandycroft
Colliery

Drury B/W

Drury Lane

to
Drury

Goodie
Col.

Ball's
Barn

Buckley Mountain
Col.

Horse &
Jockey P.H.

Knowl Hill
Brickworks

Knowl Hill

Hawarden
Colliery

'Not proven'

Buckley
Mountain

BUCKLEY

Buckley Smelt

Brunswick Road

Hancock's Pottery

Dumpling Col.
Hancock's
Lane End
B/W

Pentrobin
Colliery

Little
Mountain
Colliery

LANE END

Lexham Green
Colliery

Lord Street

Cross Keys Inn

'Dirty Mile'

Spon Green
Colliery

Tramroads :
(not of uniform gauge)
2'2" gauge Tramway :

0   ¼   ½   ¾   MILE 1

J.M.Lloyd 00206 BTI/R

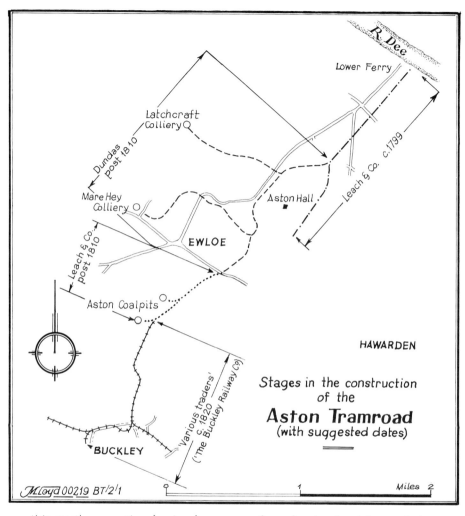

Stages in the construction of the
Aston Tramroad
(with suggested dates)

this northern section having been a southward extension of an existing tramroad, prolonged to the Northop–Hawarden road for the purpose of reaching the southern section there and so forming a continuous route. The southern portion traversed the lands of the Glynnes of Hawarden, and the northern that of Dundas of Aston Hall.

Although by then the Tramroad was almost life-expired, it should be noted that The Dundas Estate was purchased by William Ewart Gladstone (successor to the Glynnes) of Hawarden Castle in 1870. Aston Hall had been Dundas property since 1782. The Hall was built by Adam Aston in 1215 but the later building dates from 1616.

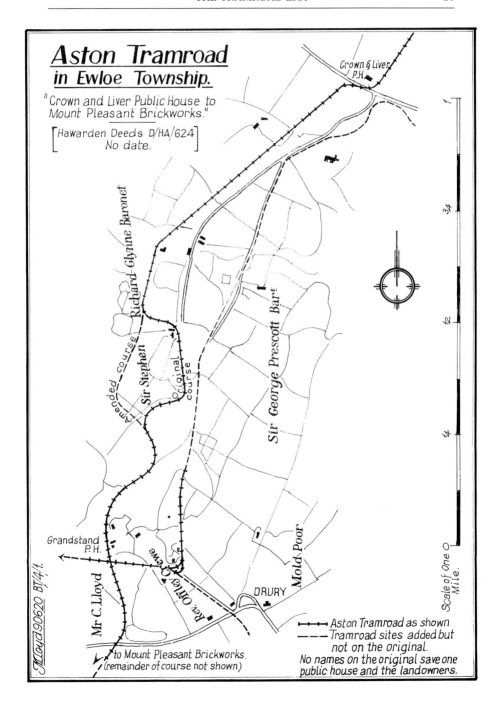

Aston Tramroad in Ewloe Township.

"Crown and Liver Public House to Mount Pleasant Brickworks."

[Hawarden Deeds D/HA/624] No date.

Crown & Liver P.H.

Richard Glynne Baronet

Amended course

Sir Stephen

Original course

Sir George Prescott Bar.

Grandstand P.H.

Mr C. Lloyd

Rev. Offley Crewe

Mold Poor

DRURY

to Mount Pleasant Brickworks. (remainder of course not shown)

Scale of One Mile.

Aston Tramroad as shown
Tramroad sites added but not on the original.
No names on the original save one public house and the landowners.

JLloyd 90620 BT/4/1.

The northern section itself consisted of parts of three earlier tramroads. By 1799 Leach & Co. were lessees for mineral (etc) extraction on The Dundas Estate and were enabled to build 'an iron plateway' from their coalpits and brickworks to the Dee, a length of about 1¼ miles. One such pit was the Aston Colliery, later called Queen's Ferry Colliery which today is a caravan site on Clay Hill. There were numerous small pits hereabouts with tramroad systems linked to the main tramroad line. When in later years the Aston Hall Colliery Railway usurped the Tramroad, a branch of that Railway served pits hereabouts too, but they were not the historic workings which had been exhausted.

This first length is shown on the Hawarden Estate Plan of 1815 and before 1835 (the date of the first Ordnance Survey) a loop line had been made to the east to by-pass these first workings and serve new ones. This loop must have had a short life for though shown on the 1834/5 Survey, it appears on the Hawarden Parish Tithe Map in 1839 as 'Old Railroad'.

To return to Leach's line: its known length would not have extended it southward beyond these workings east of Aston Hall yet the Estate Plan of 1815 shows that line extended by a somewhat circuitous route to reach the Northop–Hawarden road, cross it and make an end-on junction at Higgin's Croft with a tramroad coming north from Buckley. Such must be the fruits of the Agreement dated 1809 between Leach & Co. and Dundas . . . to receive later mention. So, by the date of the Estate Plan there existed a continuous tramroad from Lower Ferry to Higgin's Croft, entirely on Dundas lands, constructed between 1809–15.

The Tithe Map of 1839 shows a new line altogether, making a junction with the original Leach line northeast of Aston Hall and making a detour of the Hall to the west; it rejoins the 1809–15 line a little to the north of the Northop–Hawarden road. From this new piece, westward-stretching branches served Latchcraft Colliery (clearly, still productive) whilst a second branch ran to Old Mare Hey Colliery (confusingly known at times as Hawarden Colliery), alongside the road west of Ewloe. This line features on 1869 edition maps and was the ultimate form. By the late 1860s it only carried the traffic of those who refused to patronise the new Buckley Railway.

The Agreements of 1809 and 1811 confirm the extent of the Dundas-based system as then terminating at Aston Colliery, and the southward extension to Higgin's Croft. There were to be three passing places and 'Dundas will contract and narrow the present rail road now used at Aston from the present width to such narrower width as will not exceed 2ft 6ins, and shall make the intended rail road to the same width instead of the dimensions recited in the 1809 Agreement' . . . so says the 1811 Agreement. Measurements taken recently at various sites including Clay Hill give a plateway gauge of 2ft 6ins–2ft 8ins.

Part of the 1809 Agreement contains additional proposals:

> Dundas has agreed to form and make with or without the aid of a double inclined Plane as may be thought advisable in that respect at his own expence a Rail Road or Way of Cast Iron from the Turnpike leading from Hawarden towards Northop near the Turnpike Gate of Ewloe to communicate with the present Rail

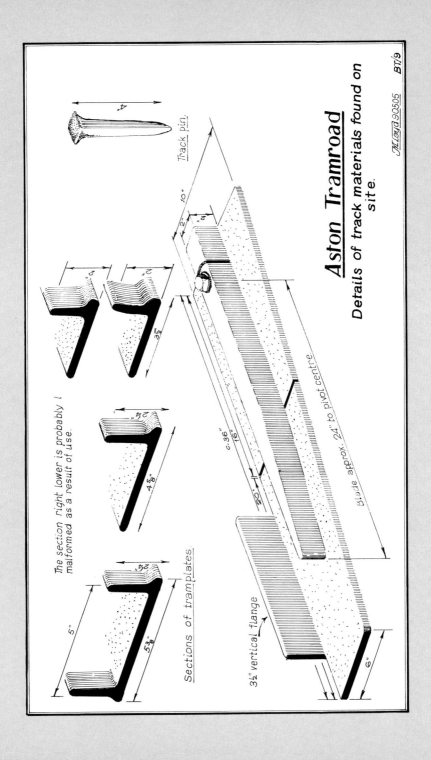

Aston Tramroad

Details of track materials found on site.

Track pin.

4"

2" 10"

3½"

Sections of tramplates.

The section right lower is probably
malformed as a result of use.

2½"

4⅝"

2½"

5"

5⅜"

3½" vertical flange

c. 36"

16"

20"

6"

Blade approx. 24" to pivot centre

BT/9

> Road of the said Charles Dundas at Aston . . . into the River Dee at a certain place situate in the township of Saltney where a stage is now being erected for the shipment of coals from the Aston Colliery . . . for 19 years . . . and allow them (Leach & Co.) make a railway through the lands of Charles Dundas lying south of the same Turnpike Road . . . to be of similar dimensions to the one now used at Aston aforesaid for the conveyance of coals from Aston Colliery . . . (from) . . . a field called Higgin's Croft and over his lands (either upon a regular or gradual descent or upon a double inclined Plane) towards the present Rail Road of Dundas so that there may be a free passage for all waggons laden with coals . . .

The gradient was not to exceed 1 in 30 and the windlasses, ropes etc of such an inclined place were to be kept in repair by Dundas: the wharf was deemed sufficient to handle 90 tons a day. The parties concerned would enjoy the right to build 'other Rail Roads in Ewloe Township . . .'.[2]

The most interesting feature north of Higgin's Croft was a swing bridge to carry the Tramroad across the 'Weppra Road'. In 1857 Charles Davison was Surveyor of Highways to Saltney Township and there is more than a hint in these matters that his relationship with Vice Admiral Sir James Dundas, then landowner, could have been better. Davison had had many complaints about this bridge and had attempted to compel Dundas to rebuild it; Dundas made limited alterations but no more. A case was brought against Dundas but the outcome was but a nominal fine: he was found 'not guilty of neglect' but obliged to alter the bridge to Davison's satisfaction and under his direction. The detail is amusing.

Some fourteen years before a 'Post Boy' (actually an elderly man, drunk at the time) mistook the road on which his vehicle was travelling and was knocked from off the box of the stage coach by the bridge, and was killed. Dundas' defence was that the Tramroad was 'of far more value than the Saltney Road and if it wished to improve the latter then the Turnpike Trust ought to pay part of the cost of raising the Tramway'.

Dundas was charged with obstruction of the 40 ft wide road, ('A Public Road built under the Saltney Award in 1781')

> the tramroad being made wholly on Sir James' side of the road . . . The Swing Bridge was made . . . in the year 1803. The height of the bridge is, and ever has been, 7 ft 9 in. and the breadth across the road 12 ft.* and no serious complaint has been made during the time. The Swing Bridge has always been swung aside for carts etc. at harvest time and care has always been taken to avoid causing inconvenience to farmers.

It took 2 – 3 minutes to swing the Bridge aside so that there was some delay to a highly laden cart or high carriage. Defence maintained that stoppage of the Tramroad could be a serious injury to the district . . . and cause considerable expense to Dundas. (1st December, 1857).

> The present Highway Surveyor has a high carriage. (!)

The Bridge appears to have remained in its rebuilt form until the end of the Tramroad's life.

---

*given elsewhere as 20 ft between the supporting walls.

The recommended course of action at the time was:

1. Raise the span by 2½ feet
2. Put the structure into proper repair (or replace it completely)
3. Place a person in the adjoining cottage to look after the Bridge during daylight
4. The Bridge to be turned in favour of the road at night
5. To complete the work by 1st March next (1858)
6. Dundas to pay costs incurred

Dundas' agent, James Edwards, stated that work had begun in July 1858 to raise the embankment and Bridge by 2 feet and that 'the Railway is in fair condition with a fair average trade this Quarter.'

To appreciate exactly what the plateway was like and how it worked, evidence given at the Committee of Enquiry into the building of the Buckley Railway (held in May 1860) gives enlightening insight. James Davison described the route as from King's Ferry with a length of 3½−4 miles; he said there were branches to six brickworks and two collieries of which two brickworks and one colliery were owned by Rigby & Hancock.* The premises are not listed but may have included Pentrobin (Lane End) and Spon Green Collieries, and Aston Hall, Old Ewloe, Lane End, Knowl Lane and Mount Pleasant brickworks.

(A confusing utterance from Davison was that 'he knew of another tramroad from Austin Quay [sic] to King's Ferry of the same distance.')

He agreed the Aston Tramroad did not serve all the industry in the neighbourhood, as two brickworks, one colliery and one pottery relied on the Turnpike Road, they having no tramway connections 'as the intervening land is in the hands of other parties'. One of these premises had been in business for twelve years and another for twenty. Part of the Tramroad was on Dundas land; Davison rented a wharf from Dundas to which his products travelled by cart. In consequence of Notice for the building of the statutory Buckley Railway appearing in the LONDON GAZETTE in November 1859, Davison gave support for the scheme: Dundas then gave him notice to quit the wharf. As for Rigby & Hancock, they were lessors for a portion of the Tramroad and agents for Dundas. All traders in Buckley save Rigby & Hancock were in favour of building a Buckley Railway.

Davison's firm, Charles Davison & Co. (he was General Manager) carted away most of their output but had to use the Tramroad for a short distance where they were obliged to pay the highest charges as the rates were unequal for all users. Davison had to find his own horses and his own wagons; his total cost was 1/8½d. per ton for the 3½ miles, whereas cartage cost him 1/7d. per ton; if a railway was built the cost would be 9d. per ton from his works.

The condition of the plateway was poor:

> It was bad in construction . . . made of L-shaped rail and gets filled up with dirt and snow − in snowy weather it is impassable; in consequence in 1859 the Tramway was closed by severe weather.

and he had to send 600 tons by road. When asked the age of the line he gave 'as old as I can remember' (but another witness gave '60−70 years old'). The

---

*these figures must be treated with caution . . . there would seem to be at least four collieries if Aston Hall and Eleanor (Deeside) are included.

state of the line was so rough that bricks were badly damaged; this was not so damaging as the breakage of coals which might be refused at the place of shipment.

When George Bellis was cross-examined he confirmed the line had always been made of iron, never of wood, and that the gauge was 3 feet (i.e. 2 ft 8 in.*).

> It is in a very bad state of repairs – it is old-fashioned L-shaped rail . . . they have nothing to keep them in gauge in place but their own weight. I could push my foot against them and put them out of shape.

He said the rails were 12 ft long and had four holes punched through them which took the spikes

> some of the rails have no spikes to keep them in their own place . . . the rails are laid with a barrier on the inside . . . it is one of the most old-fashioned shape.

He added that some curves were as sharp as a chain and a half near the summit and that the steepest gradient is 1 in 16.† Apart from the swing bridge

> giving only 10 ft 10 in. headway and indicted some years ago as a Nuisance at the Quarter Sessions . . . now raised to customary height . . . now required is 15 ft . . . I am sure it is a swivel

there were no other bridges, but three crossings on the level of Turnpike Roads, and of several public roads.

As to William Hancock's links with the Tramroad, he pointed out that Hancock & Co. owned a brick and tile works but that another 'Hancock & Co.' were 'Proprietors of the Tramway. Mr Hancock manages them all . . . he receives money for both'. Bellis thought Hancock shipped 20–30,000 tons a year. The capacity of the line was wholly insufficient.

> We had tremendous smashes last winter – we have lots of waggons broken . . . the road is in such a bad state that the axles broke . . . it cost us pounds and pounds . . . the rails not being laid properly, jolting and jolting down. We formerly complained but there is no use in complaining there is such a monopoly you are only laughed at . . . we formerly complained but found it of no use.

Counsel for Dundas and the Tramway Co. suggested they had intent 'to establish a communication with your (Davison's) works if you desire it', but Davison replied that

> I can tell you Mr Hancock your client has been very desirous to keep the Tramway from us – there was a clause in his last Lease not to make communication for 18 months.

He would not take the Tramway connection if offered . . .

> we have suffered enough from the grinding monopoly.

Much of the time of the Enquiry was spent in considering the superiority or otherwise of Connah's Quay over King's Ferry (or Lower Ferry as it was known previously) as a place of shipment, having regard to the Buckley Railway's intention to terminate at Connah's Quay. It was upheld that when

---

*An approximate figure as the line was a plateway.

†The figure in the Minutes is not clear – it may be 19.

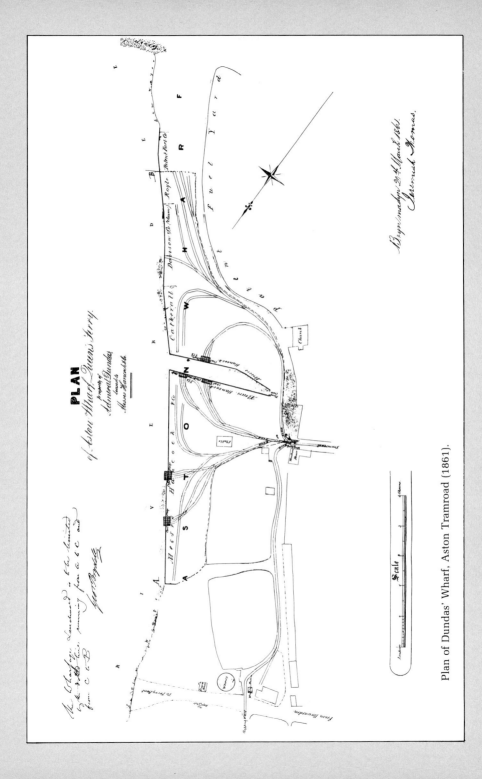

Plan of Dundas' Wharf, Aston Tramroad (1861).

winds and tides were contrary, it might take 24 hours or up to 9–10 days to work a sailing ship the two miles upstream from Connah's Quay to King's Ferry. Davison had had bricks loaded at King's Ferry which were urgently wanted in Swansea but had been held from 10th April to 19th April before the tide could float off the loaded ship; he had two ships, one of 100 tons and the other of 85 tons capacity; water at King's Ferry was 2–3 ft shallower than at Connah's Quay. A ship's captain confirmed there could be 12 ft of water at Connah's Quay when King's Ferry had none.

William Shepherd of Ewloe Barn Brickworks had no tramway; he used King's Ferry wharf and carted 12,084 tons there in 1858; he had his own wharf, an advantage over the others who had none. His works burned 6,042 tons of coal in 1858 and he had no colliery business of his own. He brought in iron ore from Barrow by his own sailing flat and it was often detained off Connah's Quay for seven days awaiting favourable conditions. He had been manager for Hall & Hancock for 22 years, and was currently Hancock's partner in Spon Green Colliery.

When William Hancock was examined he confirmed he had leases from Sir Richard Glynne, Sir James Dundas, Sir George Prescott (and others) and that there were seven partners in the Tramroad venture, the line being 4–5 miles long; the Tramroad served one but not both of Davison's works. 'If connections were made to Buckley Colliery and Kenrick Lloyd's Brickworks, the tramway could accommodate the whole traffic of the district'. Under his lease with Dundas he could build such extensions. Present tonnage over the line was 60–70,000 of which his firm, Hancock & Co. supplied about half. In view of the amount of traffic passing from Hancock & Co. they were given lower rates than others – by Agreement they were bound to send all their products by Tramroad, the cost was $8\frac{1}{2}d.$ for the whole distance. Davison 'has a small line that connects their works with the Tramway, shared with Messrs. Royle's.* They are charged $10d.–11d.$ per ton. No one paid more than $11d.$ per ton which included the Aston wharfage.'

Horse haulage costs varied; Davisons paid $4\frac{1}{2}d.$, Hancocks $6d.$ and some others $7d.$ per ton. Then there was 'waggon hire' which was $1\frac{1}{2}d.–2d.$ He argued that the highest charge to include use of Tramway, hire of waggons and haulage was $1/6d.$ per ton, 'which is quite as low as it would be by this Bill'. Waggon capacity was $3\frac{1}{2}–4$ tons each, and one horse could take 8 tons or two waggons. Some coal was taken by Tramroad to the trans-shipment siding on the Chester & Holyhead line; this cost $1/4d.$ per ton; Hancock had to load the standard gauge vehicles and take them approximately $\frac{1}{2}$ mile to the main line siding. The coal came from his Spon Green Colliery.

Questioned about the condition of the track

> . . . their Lordships will not expect that it is in the same condition as the London & North Western or any great line for passengers.

> Is it in a sufficient state for the safe conduct of the traffic?

> Yes, men are kept on for repairs.

He had had no complaints about the state of the line; there had been no accidents and if the Turnpike Trustees had complained and pulled up some of the rails, then he did not know: 'They threatened some 20 years ago.' He

---

*J. Royle & Son, Etna Brickworks.

thought the Tramroad was more than 70 years of age (this would mean it had been open by c.1790). There was a roundabout reference to the existence formerly of the Sandycroft Rail Road (II); Rigby & Hancock had acquired that line 'over twenty years ago' (suggesting a date around 1840) when 'one rail was taken up and the two trams were united.' This is the only known reference to the abandonment date of that Sandycroft line.

The partners in the Aston Tramroad were: John Rigby, William Hancock, William Highnet, James Hancock and Mrs Rigby. The partners in the works were the foregoing with the exception of Mrs Rigby and the inclusion of William Hancock (Junior).

A branch line to Davison's works would have to be about two miles long and near the works would be on 'Mr Cook's land'. Davison would have to obtain the sanction of Mr Cook though Dundas had offered to make it. (Cook was a promoter of the Buckley Railway scheme and owned some land on which Buckley Colliery stood.)

Hancock gave the surprising information that 'there were two or three inclines on the Tramway in the past, but damage was done owing to the ropes breaking and destroying goods, but in those days inclines were not so well-known or so well managed as they are now . . . it was common hempen rope, no twisted wire then.' The positions of these inclines is not known; they may have been those within works premises leading down into the clay or coal pits.

Samuel Edwards, Harbour Master at King's Ferry, contributed some detail of tonnages received at the wharf 'most of all this traffic is shipped.' He recorded 32,000 tons the previous year – this would entail 8,000 wagon loads in 4 ton capacity wagons or 4,000 trains each with one horse in (say) 308 working days; so in a six-day working week, the line would have to pass seventy-eight 2-wagon trains in each direction. Edwards maintained (naturally) that King's Ferry was a safer anchorage than Connah's Quay as vessels could lie two abreast there. They had no steam tugs of their own, but some were available at Saltney (in fact by this time it was only possible for ships to reach Saltney if in tow); and he confirmed that vessels drawing 10–11 ft of water might be detained 4–6 days.

When Henry Robertson, already firmly entrenched at Brymbo, was examined on 28th July, 1862 he confirmed the Tramway began at Sir Stephen Glynne's clay works: it carried about 70,000 tons a year and he was once in treaty for the purchase of it. He said the gradient was 1 in 30, but an interjector shouted '1 in 18'! Glynne received an annual rent for it of £2–3,000 and Dundas £X.* He added 'The Tramway is a relatively good one and 16 years ago was highly valued by its owner.'

Defending the interests of the owners of the Tramway and their commitment to keep it in repair, Gregory Burnett, Agent to Glynne, said 'The expense of the Tramroad in taking goods down to the river is sometimes more than the royalty.'

A proposition from Messrs. Rigby & Hancock's solicitors (they had leased the whole Tramway c.1858), is not dated:–

> . . . Rigby & Hancock have laid down certain railways some time since, leading from certain Brick & Tile Works at Buckley and elsewhere to join the railway of J.W.D. Dundas, desire exclusive privilege of carrying all coal, canal [sic], slack,

*the figure is illegible.

tiles, firebricks, etc.) at a rate of 3*d.* per ton including wharfage . . . and pay Dundas ¼ part tonnage . . . they would carry *all* goods including their own and would promote increase in traffic except that part, a branch of their road communicating directly with Lodge Croft* Colliery with Dundas' Road . . . Rigby & Hancock to use the railway for all products save those disposed by Land Sale . . . and *at any other* works at Buckley or elsewhere . . . nor build a competing line . . .

Rigby & Hancock would pay £10 a year towards the expense of keeping a man at the Wharf as book-keeper and for clearing their berths there. The proposition must have been acceptable as the burden of their monopoly features consistently at the Enquiry into the building of the Buckley Railway.

Arrangements to be dated 25th March, 1858 for leasing for 16 years of 'The Buckley Railway' (which was that part of the Tramroad between Buckley Mountain and junction with the Dundas line at Higgin's Croft, plus the branch at Queen's Ferry Wharf on Glynne land), allowed for Glynne's use of 'The Aston Railway' at a reduced charge, together with the use of the Wharf for shipment and the siding at Queensferry station on the C&HR. Glynne was not to allow any other railway 'not built under an Act of Parliament' through any part of his Estate as from 21st October, 1855 or any Buckley bricks (etc.) produced . . . for shipment on the Dee or 'for transit along the Holyhead Railway' so as to forestall local competition. On the Plan attached to the foregoing is entitled 'Tramway from Sir John Glynne's Brickwork', and it extends from Lane End, Buckley, to the east of the 'Boar's Head' Public House, Ewloe. The Buckley Railway is defined as 'the property of Sir S.R. Glynne insofar as his ? in the townships of Pentre Robin and Ewloe in the County of Flint from Buckley Mountain to the junction of a railway the property of Admiral Dundas in the township of Ewloe and "also that Branch Railway leading to the Wharf belonging to Admiral Dundas"'.

A detailed account of the 'Buckley and Aston Railroad'† between 1850 and 1856 reveals, to some extent, the relative activity of these concerns.

	Tonnages						
	1850−1	1851−2	1852−3	1853−4	1854−5	1855−6	Totals
Ashton & Co.							
Knowl Lane Brickworks	11,779	11,185	11,838	13,812	11,331	12,003	71,948
Hancock & Co.							
Lane End Brickworks	18,708	18,709	15,107	22,382	18,722	19,744	113,372
Catherall							
Ewloe Place/Trap Brickworks	4,652	3,536	2,825	2,896	2,815	3,420	20,114
Royle & Son							
Etna Brickworks	2,950	2,649	3,443	3,664	2,819	3,162	18,687
Davison & Co.							
Ewloe Barn/Old Ewloe Brick &							
Tile Works	6,359	5,338	7,332	7,041	5,971	6,571	38,612
Mount Pleasant			69		3,816	8,776	12,661
	44,448	41,417	40,614	49,795	45,474	53,676	275,394

(N.B. Some of these companies could also have used other forms of cartage.)

*another name for Latchcroft.
†Ref: BUCKLEY No. 7 (1980) p. 15.

On 25th March, 1858 Rigby & Hancock paid Glynne £2,250 'for themselves and on behalf of the late Buckley Railway Co. in full satisfaction for all claims for rents, royalties in respect of workings, coal and minerals . . .', thus buying up the remainder of the lease.

We must now move ahead to the opening in 1862 of the Buckley Railway when Messrs. Boydell & Powell, solicitors of Chester and representing Rigby & Hancock, wrote to Dundas' solicitors, Messrs. Helps & Parker, also of Chester, on 7th July, 1862:

> You are doubtless aware that the 'Buckley & Connah's Quay Railway'* is now open and ready to convey traffic from Buckley Mountain at a considerably less rate than the above Company (our clients) can do under the present arrangement with Admiral Dundas. Their Manager has, however, seen several of the Manufacturers, now their Customers, and these are willing to continue to custom on the Admiral's Railway, provided the Tolls are reduced. This our clients cannot do unless they are met by the Admiral to whom they now have to pay 4 pence & one eighth per ton for all goods that go over the line. If, however, the Admiral would reduce this, say by one penny half penny, the Traffic could be kept on the line. We now write to know whether the Admiral is willing to make the reduction, if so our clients can make arrangements with, we believe, all their former customers except for Messrs. Davison, to continue for 18 months certain to send their Manufactures down the Tramway otherwise the Traffic must go down the Buckley & Connah's Quay Line. As we must at once give an answer we shall be obliged by your early reply.

Within days of the foregoing letter, a House of Lords Committee of Enquiry was examining (on 29th July, 1862) the case for building a Whitchurch, Wrexham, Mold & Connah's Quay Junction Railway and hearing objections: clearly the Buckley Railway's opening had only dented the tramroad traffic for Mr Gladstone (on cross-examination) said:

> . . . carries a good deal of traffic indeed the bulk of it comes from the district down to the River Dee . . . it is very old and imperfect and is worked by horses . . . of rude construction . . . belonging to a former period . . . several generations since it was made . . . it is so imperfectly constructed that it is as much as the horses and wagons can do to keep upon it.

He ended with the euphemism that 'the Tramway is as a tramway, a relatively good one.'

Hancocks continued use of the Aston Tramroad between his Lane End Brickworks and the river is supported by the publication of the Ordnance Survey six inch First Edition maps in the 1869–71 period: in January 1866 the new WMCQR had made its northern point a junction with the Buckley Railway. Just south of this was their passenger terminal, Buckley (later Old Buckley), situated on Knowl Lane. Hancock now laid out a trans-shipment yard with the standard gauge sidings here, the Tramroad tracks leaving his premises by tunnel, cutting and curve, followed by a passing loop. The Tramroad continued to fall to a loading platform from which numerous plateway spurs fanned out. Trolleys of bricks etc. could be run onto wagons on the standard gauge here.

The continuation of the Tramroad to the river survived the building of the WMCQR which was obliged to make a crossing on the level with the Tramroad; thereby Hancock could enjoy the choice of continuing to use the Tramroad he leased, or send goods away by the new Railway.

*the statutory Buckley Railway Company.

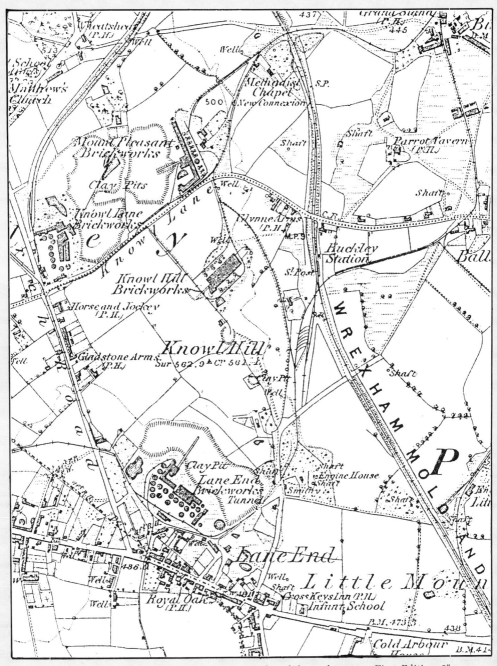

The area around Old Buckley Station reproduced from the 1871, First Edition 6″ Ordnance Survey map.

In the WMCQR (Arrangement) Act 1869 there is reference to

Heads of Arrangement between the WMCQR Co. and the BR Co. in respect of their leasehold interest in the Aston Tramway belonging to Mr Dundas and Messrs. Hancock & Co. in respect of their right of user of the tramway, and Mr Dundas (an infant and a ward of the Court of Chancery) as owner of that tramway, and Mrs Dundas and Mr Houblon as his guardians appointed by the Court.

This Agreement provided for the discontinuance of the Tramroad and for compensation to be paid by WMCQR for its

interference in the rights of the parties interested in the Tramroad and for the lands of Mr Dundas to be taken by the Company, was confirmed and made binding on all the parties to the said Agreement . . .

A payment was to be made to Mr Dundas by a mortgage of the Company under a further Agreement of 31st December, 1866. So it would not seem the Tramroad ceased work until at least the date of the passing of the Act concerned, namely 9th August, 1869. The Act further states:

Agreement for compensation 31st December, 1866 to be paid by the Company to the parties interested in the Aston Tramway should be provided for: (in respect of that section of the line known as The Buckley & Aston Tramway Co.)

Some financial papers in the Clwyd Record Office refer to the decade before the building of the Buckley Railway. (ref: D/HA/1212)

Estimated cost of maintaining the tramway from
Lower Ferry to Buckley Mountain.
11th May, 1852

Annual cost of maintaining tramway when properly laid down but not supplying new rails: per mile	£22	0s.	0d.
Cost. New rails at 20 lbs. per yard, 31 tons at 8 (tons) per mile may be delivered at £5 10s. 0d. per ton = £172 14s. 0d. interest thereon @ 7½% which would allow for diminished value of rails at the expiration of 15 years, then probably the duration	£12	19s.	11d.
Annual interest on laying rails, blocks, fastenings, contingencies etc.	£8	0s.	0d.
Wolverhampton 11th May, 1852 *Henry Beckett*	£42	19s.	0d.

(Ref: D/HA/1217)

The Buckley & Aston Railway Co.

*Copy Statement on their behalf
do. on Sir S.R. Glynne*

Dr.   The Railway Co. in a/c with Sir S.R. Glynne, Bart.   Cr.

31 Dec. 1862	to 1 year's tonnage 36,000 tons; rent as per lease	£150	0s.	0d.	Recd. from Mr. Shepperd being rent on his behalf	£ 12	10s.	0d.
	to 1 year's surface rent of land as per lease	£ 50	0s.	0d.	by tax on £200 @ 9d. 14 July 1862 by cash	£100	7s.	10d.
	to balance	£ 11	14s.	9d.	7 Jan. 1863 do.	£ 91	6s.	0d.
						£ 91	8s.	9d.
		£211	14s.	9d.		£211	14s.	9d.

N.B. The tonnages are calculated from returns made by the B & AR.Coy.

(Ref: D/HA/1217)

Copy of A/C made for Sir S.R. Glynne & Sent to Hancock & Co. 9 July 1863.

Dr.   to Buckley & Aston Rly. Co. in A/C with Sir S.R. Glynne, Bart. for year 1862   Cr.

To first & second qrs. tonnages (19,010 tons) @ 1*d*. per ton as per lease	£ 79	4*s*.	2*d*.	July 12 (1862)	By cash pro tax	£100 £ 3	6*s*. 18*s*. 0*d*. 2*d*.
To first half year's surface rent of land	£ 25	0*s*.	0*d*.			£104	4*s*. 2*d*.
To third & fourth qrs. tonnages (15,962 tons)	£ 66	10*s*.	2*d*.	Jan. 7 (1863)	By cash pro tax	£ 91 £ 3	8*s*. 9*d*. 11*s*. 3*d*.
To second half year's surface rent of land	£ 25	0*s*.	0*d*.		£ 95	0*s*.	0*d*.
To year's Wharfage rent reserved as per lease*	£ 12	10*s*.	0*d*.		By cash pro Tax	£ 12	0*s*. 8*d*. 9*s*. 4*d*.
Balance due to Coy	£ 3	9*s*.	10*d*.				
	£211	14*s*.	2*d*.			£211	14*s*. 2*d*.

*this item deleted – 'from call reserved in pursuance of agreement with C. Lloyd'.

Measurements of gauge at the north end agree with the approximate gauge of 2 ft 6 in. mentioned in the 1810 period Agreements. The surviving material at Hancock's Wharf opposite Buckley (Old) station give an approximate gauge of 3 ft 9 in. on the straight and 4 ft on curves (measured to the centre of the plate): there are (1989) sufficient surviving materials at the Wharf to give a broad outline of their form. It is clear how slight in dimensions were the cast-iron (later wrought iron) plates themselves: unlike the heavier pattern on the Wepre line (more akin to those used elsewhere in the country) the drawing (*page 23*) shows that the plate bases were 3½–4½ in. wide without reinforcement or thickening anywhere, with the vertical flange 2–2½ in. high. Certain verticals were curved 'backwards', presumably to reduce friction. At 36 in. intervals the plate was punched with a ⅝ in. hole at 1¼ in. from the plain edge. Plates at the Wharf vary in length (some are simply broken lengths) but the longest is 27 ft: some are cast in a curve; these are 11 ft long.

There was also a trough section plate; 12 ft long, 5 in. wide and 2¼ in. high, it was strengthened on the outer face at the foot of each vertical and used to guide wheels where the wheels on one side of the vehicle might be without the directional help at all, or for use on level crossings where a vertical flange was needed on both sides of the plate.

Turnouts comprised a double bottom base plate, tapered, the whole approximately 37 in. long; the blade was of 2 in. square cast bar opposite the tip of which there was a vertical plate to keep the wheel from running off the base plate.

The plates were held to burnt clay (not stone) cubic or rhomboidal blocks made at Hancock's premises. These vary in size, the largest having a top surface of 11½ in. × 9 in.; on this surface a hole was drilled centrally to take a wooden plug into which dowel pin(s) were driven; some pins were tapered, 4 in. long. Certain blocks have no hole but a single slot 1 in. deep and ¾ in. wide cut across them to take the edge of the wheel and guide it where no plates were in use.

The platework though light was probably adequate for the wagons which brought products from brick and tile works to the various sidings' wharves: return traffic would have been made in coal to fire the kilns. The construction shows that criticisms of the track and breakages were fully justified.

At Wharf edges the works' trolleys were led onto a flat wagon which traversed the face of the wharf at a lower level than the tramroad yet higher than the railway track below it – a mezzanine position. The traverser track might be laid in bridge rail with a 4 in. width at base, 2 in. high. A typical gauge was 2 ft 6 in.; the trolley wheels were plain tyred with a groove in the centre . . . but not in all examples.

The tramplates were given a brick infill between them, carefully laid with a convex surface to drain it; the result was a work of art in itself, giving a garden path effect with different patterns and sizes of bricks. The bricks themselves often carry 'Wm. Hancock & Co., Chester' (or similar style) and 'Flintshire', 'Buckley' and 'Hawarden' appear on other versions: they vary in size, pattern, quality etc. and may in parts be seconds or stock material no longer in fashion.

The products of Buckley were sent down by tramroad, suitably protected by straw packing to reduce breakages. The Irish market was not in favour of this as the straw was wont to carry Foot and Mouth Disease; straw was ultimately banned and a trade in heather was created in consequence, this being gathered from the hills around Buckley and taken to the brickyards where it was heaped up ready for use – due to this practice there are today patches of heather where it would not normally grow and it can still be found beside the former Buckley Railway course where it flourishes in a friendly environment.

WEPRE IRON ROAD

There was coal under the lands of the Leach family in Wepre and Northop, lying inland from Connah's Quay at about two miles. The oldest surviving lease to work it is dated 12th March, 1789, and this was renewed on 1st July, 1796 for a period of 40 years – taking it to 1836. The land was described as 'on the south side of the Turnpike Road leading from Northop to Hawarden, in occupation of widow Tothy'. This property was duly leased to Marcus Dixon at whose death the residue of the lease passed to Thomas Hewitt of Hook House, Parkgate in the Wirral. The above leases to work coal were given to The Irish Coal Company, an undertaking of Sir John McCartney, Bart. of Dublin, Daniel Bell and James Connolly of Dublin, and John Anderson of Cork city. The area involved was '. . . colliery at Northop . . . at Northop House and at Green Field, and coalpitfields adjoining road from Chester to Holywell'. (The Greenfield working was on Lord Mostyn's land.)

On 31st October, 1800 McCartney and colleagues took out a mortgage of £5,500 ('British Sterling') from Thomas Hewitt but failed to pay the interest; (at 5%). By 24th March, 1808 the Principal was due for repayment after seven years, but only £269 19s. 0d. had been received over the whole period, making £1,778 5s. 11d. due in interest, plus the £5,500. The case was taken

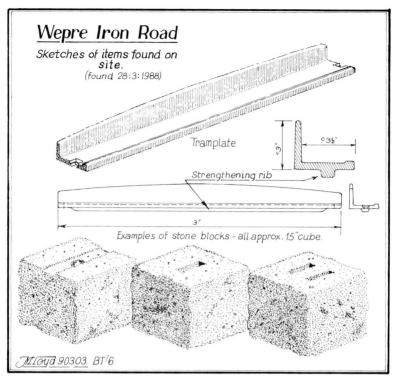

Wepre Iron Road

Sketches of items found on site.
(found 28:3:1988)

Tramplate

Strengthening rib

3'

Examples of stone blocks - all approx. 15"cube.

Lloyd 90303. BT'6.

to the High Court, 'Thomas Hewitt v McCartney & Others': at the hearing on 23rd June, 1807 it was said that the debtors resided at or near the City of Cork . . . 'and are desirous of having a commission for the taking of their examination there . . . the debtors live very remote from each other . . . the said premises and coal works thereby granted in mortgage were a scanty security for the said sum . . . Defendant has expended very considerable sums of money on the entire of the said coal works in the improvements thereof . . .' There was disagreement among the debtors as to what relative portions of the workings each would by then be allotted, Anderson and Connolly maintaining that McCartney had lost his full entitlement by 1806.

Some of the leading names in Dublin were involved in the Chancery Court including George Archer (of Essex Bridge, Dublin) and when support for the debtors was required 'gentlemen of the city of Dublin' were readily forthcoming to that end. The importance of Flintshire coal to that city, and the alleged potential of a source not then evaluated probably encouraged speculation. Of the colliery premises themselves, their 'scanty security' does not support the vision of a place of much substance, while another writes of 'an extensive colliery'. It is likely that in neither case was there personal acquaintance of the place.

The lessees of the undertaking were men of purpose; against the financial background so described they set to work in autumn 1799 to link the colliery by tramway with the Dee. The aforementioned failure made it necessary for the Court to be given a picture of the costs of building the line, a very fortunate state of affairs for the historian! The 1799 figures are given here exactly as in the curious form they appear in the documents.[3]

14th–18th Sept, 1799	*W & J Rigby, Hawarden*					
	878 rails	3T	1C	18Q	Sept	
		12		3	Dec	
		16		1	Jan	
	11	19		1	Feb	
	@ £11.11.0					190 5 10
Sept–Oct	*Coalbrook Dale Co.*					
	5280 rails 110T 15C 2Q					
	@ £10.10.0					1117 15 1
18th Sept, 1799–	*John Harrison & Pearson*					
	@ £11.11.0 ton					689 7 8
23rd May, 1800	for undermentioned rails					
	2886 rails 59T 13C 3Q					

Feb 1800	Cash for 11 weeks subsistence to two gangs workmen under *Richard Jones & William Hughes*	205 18 10
Feb–29 Mar	*Jones*: carriage of iron rails	15 15 0
	(*J. Simnel, Edward Jones, George Cunnah* also carry rails)	
3rd May	*George Cunnah*: carriage of stores (and more to 26 July)	8 11 5
22nd July–21st Aug	*James Arnold & Edward Jones:* carriage of rails	
		£3404 12 0*

25th Oct, 1800	*James Jay* for carriage of 111T 15C 2Qr 14 lbs.				
	Rails from Salop to Wrexham†				128 9 10
18th Oct	Cash paid *James Arnold* for 'Carriages'				5 5 0
18th Oct	*E. Jones* 4 Qrs Rent to Michaelmas				200 0 0
30th Sept	*John Harrison & Pearson*: rails				
	200 Rails 4T 3C 0Q 4 lbs. @ £11				48 1 1
	100 Rails 2T 2C 1Q 14 lbs. @ £11				24 16 4
	610 Rails 12 16 2 21 @ £13				166 16 11

'Rails delivered 29th October–18th December, 1800 – before mortgage and ordered before it.'‡

The accounts cover timber fencing of the Rail Road, together with 'Quays, Buoys, Whimsey at Greenfield Colliery (£21) and '3 Oil Cans'. On one site or the other, there was a Coking Oven and a Lime Pit. There is a footnote giving the cost of the Rail Road up to 30th June, 1802 as £5,910 14s. 7½d. and its repair to the end of that year (obviously for the half or full year only) as £15 17s. 10d.

Other brief single entries are tantalisingly insufficient to build up much information, but on 2nd January, 1802 the tonnage for coals shipped the previous month amounts to over 6,516 tons at a value of £1,687 10s. 5½d.,

*The itemised account is short by an entry of £1176 18s. 2d.

†Rails from Coalbrookdale Foundry? (Coal Brook Dale (sic))

‡There is no totalisation of this section of the accounts.

(i.e. selling at a little over 5/2d. per ton); it does not follow that such tonnage actually passed over the Rail Road in the previous month.

In another set of accounts the heading is:

REPAIRS OF RAIL ROAD

1801	To amount expended	£203	14	9	By amount received	£125	17	11
1802		329	18	6½		160	9	11
1803		221	6	1		73	16	0
1804		481	6	10	(no entry)	—	—	—
1805		179	16	4	By Coal Account	905	12	11½
					Balance	150	5	9
		£1416	2	6½		£1416	2	6½

1st July, 1803–5th September, 1805	Surplus on coal & trading	£8908	8	4

The last sheet of accounts reads:

RAIL ROAD No. 5

1800	To amount of sundries paid out this year	£3961	4	4½	Balance	£5760	8	10½
1801	(to 30th June)	1799	4	6	(being the cost thereof)			
		£5760	8	10½		£5760	8	10½

There is no clarification of 'Rail Road No. 5' as there are no maps accompanying surviving documents: there is reference to the source of materials and their cost, and presumably for 'Carriages', wagons are meant. The Company built colliers' houses for which accounts were kept separately, as was a 'Horse Keeping Account' – the animals would be used around the colliery and on the tramway – one item being 'mare killed by accident £23 3s. 0d.'. Bricks were made too, and shipped or sold locally.

Hewitt's solicitor complained that these figures, supplied by Bell, were 'a fictitious one as no payment has been made either for rent or other charges on the Road previous to the execution of the mortgage by Sir John McCartney'.

The local Irish place names which include 'Rennie's Row' and 'Dublin Row' may date from the time of the Irish Coal Company. The lower part of Northop Hall was called Pentremoch (The Place of Pigs). The Census Returns suggest most of the workforce was locally-born.

Northop Hall Colliery was working again in late 1839 – it is mentioned in a document of that date.[4] Coal was worked spasmodically after the failure of the ICC and therefore the Iron Road would not lie unused for long ... Among the pits worked by the ICC was that pit called 'The Slutch' (or Northop Hall), and when working the site for opencast coal after World War II, tubs, shovels and bodies were dug out. Intermediate work between 1810 and 1859 may have been carried on in a small way but William Hancock told the 1859 Enquiry 'Northop Hall Colliery comprises 2–300 acres ... it is undeveloped at present'. 'Norfolk [sic] Hall Colliery lies about 2 miles from Connah's Quay' and the work 'has been idle 8–10 years' but had begun again in a trifling manner . . . 'they have sunk 2 yards but they are not in working order yet'.

There is much more to this period concerning coal extraction but knowledge of the tramroad system is not extended by it. The Wepre Iron Road (of 1799) did not in fact serve Northop Hall Colliery; after passing south of Bryn Gwyn it fanned out into several branches (*see tip-in map at rear*). Later maps show a tramway (it is assumed this was of rails and not a plateway) from the roadside near Bryn Gwyn and crossing fields, reached The Slutch: it was of not more than 2 ft gauge and lightly laid over the ground; its earthworks and dimensions were not of the customary tramroad type. Robert Roberts (Engineer and Land Surveyor employed on behalf of Northop Hall Colliery) said in 1859:

> he had been surveying the tramway between Northop Hall and Connah's Quay.

When asked:

> Is there intention now to carry out repairs and bring the tramway into working order?

(The lessees were under covenant to do this), he replied:

> The tramway cannot be connected to Northop Hall Colliery without going through other people's land.

A light tramway may have been the answer to the problem – it seems to have had a roadside terminus and at one time, an exchange siding with the Buckley Railway at Northop Hall Siding.

The Buckley Railway Act protected the Wepre system ('the Buckley Railway shall not have the power, after the expiration of one year from and after the passing of the Act, to take by compulsion any portion of the Tramway known as the Wepre Tramway, now held on lease by 'The Northop Hall & Dublin Coal Co. Ltd.' or of the land in and upon which the same is situate.') Despite earlier assertions that the Buckley Railway took part of the course of the Wepre route, this was never the case: the route of the tramway is still very recognisable for much of the way. The ICC's 'large quay and pier' at Golftyn 'at the mouth of the New Dee Channel' would be an important shipping development.

The fate of the Wepre Iron Road was sealed when the Buckley Railway opened on 7th June, 1862. The local collieries, including those known to have had tramroad connections, continued to trade long after and it is not known when exactly the tramroad closed. The last colliery (Galchog or Pennyventure) shut down just after the commencement of the First World War. The official List of Mines gives:

Operating 1873/4

Galchog Colliery Co. Ltd., Northop	(2 pits each named Galchog)
Dublin Main Coal Co. Ltd., Northop	('Currently sinking 2 pits')
Plas Bellin Colliery (Malcolm Williamson), Northop	(1 pit)

Mines abandoned during the period 1873–79
Castle Hill Coal & Firebrick Co. Ltd., Northop
Plas Bellin Mine
Galchog Colliery Co. Ltd.

Fieldwork around Northop Hall

This area has been partially covered by extensions to the village and opencast coal working. The remains of Galchog Colliery with position of chimney and shafts, and weighbridge at roadside gate from whence products were carted to Northop Hall Siding (Buckley Railway) are visible: the tramroad site here and across Smithy Lane has been lost but around Bryn Gwyn there are earthworks, and stone blocks remain. A heavy embankment leads to a shaft beside St. Mary's Church; the name of this shaft may be Boar's Head but is unconfirmed. North of Bryn Gwyn the Wepre Iron Road lay in a fine and very deep cutting which survives near Broad Oak Farm up to where the line crossed the Northop–Connah's Quay road; beyond here the site is partly covered by recent housing but survives in places as a footpath. The steep fall into Connah's Quay was partially removed by a claypit but Dock Road is the course where the tramway fell to the quays – there is a suggestion this last section was worked as a steam-operated cable incline.*

Returning to Northop Hall: behind (south of) Bryn Gwyn the tramroad bifurcated and a southward extension crossed the village road on the level and led into a colliery on the site of what was later the Dublin Main Colliery (which had its own siding off the Buckley Railway). This branch tramroad would have had the Buckley Railway close by its east side at this point, but the two routes were still individual.

Trackwork

The stone blocks are very large, usually roughly cubiform @ 15 in. There is a channel on one face of some: all of this type have a hole for the plate pin (iron). Some blocks have a double parallel slot in them the purpose of which is not clear; they were probably used at joints and the slots may have accommodated materials which were punched at varying dimensions. Others have a single slot and a few have one slot and one hole. The slots appear to lie longitudinally with the plate. The blocks are set 4 ft 8 in. apart (approximately) giving a track gauge of approximately 4 ft 6 in. A tramplate found nearby (but not necessarily indigenous) was 3 ft long with strengthening rib cast below (*see diagram page 36*). Materials of this tramroad appear to be much heavier than used elsewhere in the district.

A close inspection of Boar's Head Farm walling etc. at the foot of Smithy Lane, and also in the barn of Bryn Gwyn, will reveal many stone blocks from the tramroad in their construction.

SANDYCROFT RAIL ROAD (II)

There is no doubt of the course of *this* line; it is shown on the 1815 Parish Map[5] and on Willett's Map of 1822 extending from near Lane End, Buckley down to the riverside at Sandycroft Wharf, length c.4½ miles. As usual with Flintshire tramways, there is confusion as to when it was built. A regular

---

*Dr G.I. Hawkes, an authority on Connah's Quay, writes of the steam winding engine system here, and the engine concerned:

> It was situated at the end of the tramway between the eastern side of the Quay House Inn, at the end of Dock Road. It was some distance from the quay, therefore there must be some doubt whether it was used as a crane to empty stone ballast from colliers, and then load them up with coal. It may have been used in a cable system to pull back empty wagons up the steep incline beyond, a system described in THE CHESTER CHRONICLE about this time.

(The actual relationship between an engine and a tramway winding system, remains in some doubt.)

statement gives a date around 1790, and the builder the landowner, Sir John Glynne. Rees Rawson gives Rigby (the Hawarden ironmaster) as builder (presumably through agreement with the Glynne Estate?) and as 'after 1800, and in iron'. From 1801 it was leased to Rigby & Hancock, who succeeded Botfield's lease to Little Mancot & Old Sandycroft (Buckley) Collieries; there was a tramway connection to the latter. There are also varying opinions as to its extent; some contend that the line terminated at its northern end with the existing 'Mancot New Railway' which linked Little Mancot Colliery with Sandycroft Wharf while others infer that the whole route was built as a fresh venture – perhaps there is truth in both i.e. the 'New Railway' site was utilised and perhaps its materials updated when linked to the incomer? In either event, the extent of the line was as given in Willett.*

Earlier writers have expressed doubts as to the existence of two separate tramways but a few yards apart between the Ewloe–Hawarden road and the Buckley district – as fieldwork confirms they were, and supporting early maps thereby – but as the Aston Tramroad led to Lower Ferry and Aston Wharf owned by the Dundas Estate, and the Sandycroft Rail Road (II) to Sandycroft Wharf there would be competition for business whilst some coalpits, brickworks and so on were linked to one line and not the other, so there was sufficient business for both . . . for a time.

This second Sandycroft line was fortunate in one way, passing as it did through Glynne property for virtually the whole of its route and having the ability to avoid the Dundas Estate but at the expense of having a wharf higher up the river with consequent tidal delays to its shipping.

After Rigby & Hancock built the Buckley–Aston Colliery tramway link (The Buckley Railway Co.) to connect with the Dundas Tramway beside the Ewloe–Hawarden road, this must (later) have hit the Sandycroft Rail Road business hard. Matters would become worse when Rigby & Hancock acquired absolute right to operate The Buckley Railway Co. together with its northern Dundas-built link down to a junction to connect it with the oldest section, the Leach & Co. line down to Lower Ferry, to the exclusion of other operators. Arrangements were then made to amalgamate the near-parallel tramway routes south of the Ewloe–Hawarden road and concentrate traffic from thence into Buckley, much of the course being that of the Sandycroft (II) which, being the earlier tramway along this length, possibly enjoyed the easier route. This exclusive right began about 1840 and is reputed to be the time from when the Sandycroft (II) line was abandoned as between Buckley and Little Mancot Colliery. The effect of this new arrangement was that former branches of the Sandycroft (II) line within Buckley were now connected to the re-vamped Aston system – not a difficult task in tramway construction. The rearrangement was curtly described, 'One Rail was taken up and the two trams were united'.

---

*Rees Rawson seems to confuse even further, saying:
> After 1800 the Rigbys made an iron tramway from Moor Mark to Mancot, and continued it to Sandycroft Colliery and the firebrick works of Buckley Mountain.
In fact Moor Mark to Little Mancot Colliery was the 'Mancot New Rail Way' built by Botfield in 1793.

Another account recalled the existence of

> the old Standish Railway . . . it is about twenty years [this would make it c.1839] that Messrs. Rigby & Hancock got it into their hands; as soon as they got the present one [The Aston Tramway] they stopped the other, so that their tramway became the only mode of access to the river.

SOUGHTON TRAMROAD

This tramroad (sometimes referred to as 'Railway') lay on the Wynne Banks Estate south of Northop. It was isolated from other systems and parts of it are just traceable today. The Estate surrounds Soughton Hall and the tramroad led from coal shafts southeast of Soughton (or Sychdyn) village, into that village where a walled coalyard stood at the village road junction. The line was about 5/8 of a mile long. The line is shown as 'Railway' on early plans but was certainly a tramroad: it appears on the Plan of Soughton Common 1823[6] and again on the 'Inclosure Map' of 1830. After leaving the coalpit it traversed meadows before joining the road and running along its southern edge to the coalyard; by 1830 the coalyard (shown as 'Coal Bank') had been moved to the north side of the village road junction where it was designated 'Coal Wharf'. It would be from here that the coal was distributed by carts.

Note: In 1820 the Estate was in the hands of Mrs Margaret Banks of Corfe Castle, a sister of William Wynne.

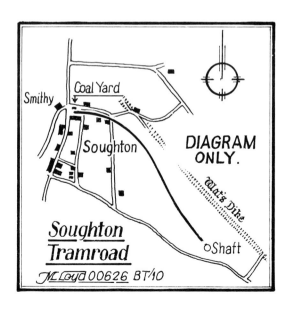

HANCOCK'S TRAMWAY, BUCKLEY

This short, industrial system was unique and deserves special mention among the tramroads of the district. Within the definitions set herein, it was strictly neither tramway nor tramroad, but rather a form of homespun yet efficient 'rail-way' for taking materials from Lane End Works to the exchange siding beside the WMCQR just south of (Old) Buckley station.

Its origins appear to stem from the time when the WMCQR was built. In the area immediately south of its (Old) Buckley station the incomer (the WMCQR) was obliged to cross the elderly Lane End–Lower Ferry Tramroad (*see page 32*) on the level. Hancock's Tramroad crossing is shown on all First Edition OS Maps. Hancocks, who had industrial and financial reasons for continuing to use the Tramroad, did not use the new Railway. However, in 1866 the WMCQR Act in that year, made it possible for the Tramroad to be abandoned and its personalities suitably compensated. Probably by 1870, the Tramroad fell into disuse in favour of the Railway, and though its stone (or) block 'sleepers' would fall prey to building etc. uses, its platerails could be utilised for fencing, roof trusses or scrap; these further usages were common.

Hancock consequently faced the necessity of making a connection with the WMCQR which he did in the most economical manner. A railway siding ('Hancock's Siding') with a wharf was constructed on the southwest side of (Old) Buckley station and a tramway led from the Works, through a tunnel and down onto the wharf where it split into a number of end-loading positions. 'Shipping Boxes' were drawn from the Works by horse and pushed onto a lateral-running flat truck which ran across the face of the wharf at a lower level, enabling the Shipping Box to be loaded onto the flat wagon which had its own guiding rails. The flat wagon was then pushed along its own tramway to a selected 'Shipping Wagon' (or 'Shipper'); here the Shipping Box was run off onto that Wagon. The most interesting feature of the trans-shipment area was its trackwork. The line from the Works (and most of the other tracks which did not involve curves) consisted of old standard-gauge double-headed rails laid on their sides, the Shipping Boxes' wheels running in the recess of the rail. At turnouts, former Tramroad material was salvaged and put to further use. Where the running line needed a curve (the double-headed rail system was unsuited to curves) curved plates off the former Tramroad were utilised. In consequence the wharf area was virtually a working museum of elderly equipment.

In this individual situation one hesitates to quote surviving dimensions as they may have no relation to what had gone before: however, the wagons used by Hancock within his precincts must have remained a constant. As described, the track was of mixed materials and the wagons were not the shipping type used elsewhere, being carried on four wheels, these being of light cast construction, narrow on tread; the wheels were solidly fixed to the axles which must have rotated in simple bearings. From breakages found on the site, it is clear the axles were weak at the bearing and fractured easily.

The wheels were set 48 in. apart and there was some variation in dimensions of the track plates (or rails on their sides, whichever) these giving a full 48 in. on curves and slightly less elsewhere. Beneath these plates or rails a stone 'causeway' ran under each – whether this was a simple support or evidence of an earlier track style, is conjectural.

The trolley which ran beside the wharf/platform travelled on 2 ft 6 in. gauge.

References

[1] (*See also Rees Rawson pp.130–1.* National Library Wales Deeds 1215, 1289, 1327, 1704, 1852).

[2] Clwyd Record Office: D/BC/602, D/BC/603, D/BC/614, D/BC/617.

[3] Clwyd Record Office: D/DM/225/1.

[4] Clwyd Record Office: D/P/38.

[5] Clwyd Record Office: D/DM/809/82.

[6] Clwyd Record Office: D/SH/843 & 846.

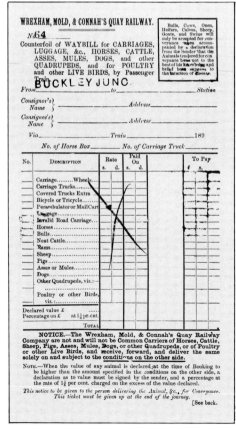

WM & COR waybill from Buckley Junction (not dated).   *Author's Collection*

Before the Wrexham, Mold & Connah's Quay Railway

The North Wales Mineral Railway

It was almost a century after the first wooden tramroads had been built to take Flintshire coal down to the ships on the Dee, that any sign of efforts to create a rail-way from the nearby Denbighshire coalfield to the Dee emerged. The most important commercial but rapidly decaying centre of the upper Dee was of course, Chester, which had been a port from the Roman occupation but was in serious decline even after the Dee had been canalised in the 1730s. From then onwards, it became more important for ships to load and unload as near the mouth of the Dee as possible, for the estuary did not enjoy stable conditions and its shipping ways, channels and sandbanks changed position constantly to the effect that to reach the upper portions of the river required several tides, helpful winds and adequate wharfage. By 1740 Saltney, about three miles down river from Chester, had become the most eastern reach for vessels of size, yet even this place might be closed for weeks in times of bad weather.

> Between 1835 and 1845 the iron trade showed signs of reviving . . . in September 1835 a brisk trade and a rise of 10/- a ton in the price of bar iron . . . the improvement in trade led the coal and iron masters of North Wales to seek transport improvements which would enable them to compete more effectively with the capitalists of Lancashire and elsewhere. The products of the Wrexham district . . . could only reach Chester by a circuitous route (of about 60 miles) along the Ellesmere Canal or by very expensive land carriage. It was realised that the two districts could be linked by a railway of considerably less than 30 miles in length, and this led to the formation of the Chester, Wrexham & Ruabon Railway Co.[1] . . . there was a proposal for a railway to link Chester, Flint, Greenfield, Mostyn etc. with the Great Orme from which coal and iron could be shipped. The Denbighshire, Flintshire & Chester Railway project similarly had its aim the development of coal and iron resources of the area. Coal and iron magnates like Mr Greenhow of Gardden Lodge, William Kenrick (Spelter Works) of Wynn Hall, George Kyrk of Bryn Mally, . . . John Wilkinson of Brymbo Hall were members of the provisional railway committees and addressed meetings in parts of the coalfield in support of the projects . . .

In short, the district might be smothered by railways, and the foregoing is but a sample of high hopes!

A little about the North Wales coal industry (having its origins centuries before a South Wales coalfield developed) has been said already (*page 12*). Chester was a useful market for its coal, not as a port of shipment but for local usage; thus in 1839 George Stephenson was engaged as Engineer for a railway linking Chester with the Wrexham and Ruabon coalfields of Denbighshire. Surveying was done and Plans deposited but times were bad and the idea was shelved, being revived again in 1842. Again, nothing tangible transpired; some of the big local landowners such as the Duke of Westminster were still dubious of the Railway Age, and the scheme was not taken up with energy.[2]

As with all new railway schemes, certain men of vision did not allow such trifles to staunch their enthusiasm; thus Robert Roy (1795–1873) of Brymbo Hall and J.B. Ross of Chester, William Betts and Alex. M. Ross promoted a new scheme, took the Bill to Parliament where it survived the opposition, and the North Wales Mineral Railway was born. It was to link Chester with a Wrexham terminus at Brynyffynnon. Henry Robertson was Engineer. In fact, at the northern end it did not enter Chester at all, but through the good offices of the Chester & Holyhead Railway with which it would make junction at Saltney, it would continue into the city on their metals (the C&HR had been authorised in the same Parliamentary session, namely 6th August, 1844). Chester already had a railway; the Birkenhead Railway (virtually a satellite of the LNWR) and this terminated about 2 miles from the proposed Saltney junction of the C&H and NWM Railways.

The emphasis was to be on mineral traffic but the Company was independent, and not the child of any one operator. As projected there was to be a branch to Brymbo district to serve coal and iron works but due to squabbling among competitive industrialists, it was not made . . . however, extensions were authorised from a junction about 10 miles south of Chester (to be dubbed Wheatsheaf Junction) to Brymbo and Minera. Further extension of the main line to Ruabon was sanctioned and authorisation of additional branches to Broughton and Gwersyllt followed.

Robert Roy had left Fort George in Inverness-shire and come south in 1841 to purchase John Wilkinson's Brymbo Works and Estate which were then in Chancery. Behind this purchase lay the continuation of the Brymbo business by Wilkinson's Trustees after his death in 1808; it was not until 1828 that the Trust was wound up, the intervening period being taken up by the many claimants to the Estate, Wilkinson not having left any legitimate male issue. Much of Wilkinson's fortune was spent after his death in the associated legal costs.

Henry Robertson (born in 1816 at Banff) was sent to Brymbo on the recommendation of a Mr. Mathieson, (a Glasgow contractor) to report on this mineral area of North Wales for which a Scottish bank had advanced money to develop. Robertson reported favourably, and money was advanced through him for the purpose. He reached Brymbo in April 1842 and soon he and Roy were working together to reorganise Brymbo Works and improve local industries which utilised the rich geological properties at hand. The Brymbo Co. was formed in 1846.[3] They considered the Flintshire tramroads and at first thought that a similar system would serve them to the Dee. The existing method was to cart to Chester, 16 miles away. (Some industries to the south of Brymbo and outside the brief of the present study, used a successor to the Ruabon Brook Tramroad – the Pontcysyllte Railway to the canal at Pontcysyllte where goods were put into boats and taken to Chester via Ellesmere and Nantwich, involving about 60 miles of waterway.)

The Brymbo Mineral & Railway Co. was formed on 10th September, 1842 in London and began business on 3rd October following; its objective was to expand Brymbo Ironworks and sink new coal shafts. The promoters and partners were Robert Roy, Henry Robertson, William Betts and Alexander Mackenzie Ross.[4]

Of the NWMR, having obtained its Act in 1844, it found itself in the position of a mineral railway with no access to the local coalfields! Its birth – as already noted – had not been easy. As planned, the southern terminus was to be Wrexham and the northern would include a branch which passed under the C & HR and led to the Dee bank at Saltney. However, when the good people of Wrexham learned that there were extensions afoot and the railway would proceed southwards to Ruabon, there was an outcry. The first meeting of the Company was held at 42, Moorgate Street, London when 'one of the proprietors enquired if it was proposed to extend the line from Wrexham to Brymbo Works?' The Chairman was guarded; there would probably be a branch. Some weeks later, news broke out of the projected extension to Ruabon; Robertson and Roy attended and were accused of breaking their undertaking not to extend the line beyond Wrexham. Robertson swayed a protest meeting and a week later the NWMR shareholders approved new lines to Cefnmawr, Christionydd (from Wrexham), and from Rhosrobin through Gwersyllt, Stansty, Broughton and Brymbo to Minera where great lime deposits lay. To avoid angry landowners on suggested routes, certain surveys had to be made after darkness, one squire hoping an aggrieved landowner would 'throw Robertson and his damned theodolite into the canal'.

The portion of the NWMR which lay at the heart of the creation of the WMCQR was the 6 m. 20 ch. mineral branch from Wheatsheaf Junction, built under the Act of 1846, to Brymbo and Minera, opened in July 1847.* The unhelpfulness of the terrain was such that it had to thrust westwards and upwards from the junction to traverse two ridges of high ground. The two miles from the Junction to the outskirts of the Brymbo Works were almost in a straight line; a short distance from the Junction began the Wheatsheaf or Summerhill Incline, variously described as rising at 1 in 15 (the steepness varying according to the purpose of the narrator!) It was worked on the balance method, the rope passing round a large horizontal wheel at the summit near where the line entered the Summerhill Tunnel (220 yards). The route swung north and west out of the Tunnel (which still carries a plaque bearing '1847') and passed by the Westminster Colliery. Now running northwestwards across the Moss Valley it reached the foot of the Moss or Cerni Incline, on which there was more unanimity in describing the gradient as 1 in 4: initially this was balanced too, but a stationary engine was installed instead at the summit by 1860. Both these inclines were known locally as 'brakes', the upper (western) end of the Moss Incline – when abandoned on 22nd May, 1862 – becoming part of the site of the Brake Weslyan Chapel, built in 1885.

Beyond the head of Moss Incline the line entered a second tunnel, Brymbo Tunnel (396 yards) and shortly reached the Works themselves on the far side of the Brymbo Valley. The branch then made a sinuous course to Minera Lime Works, but avoided further engineering extravaganza.

Lest it should be thought that the Wheatsheaf–Minera line was exceptional, this was far from being the case. Rope-worked balanced inclines were much in favour in those times, it being considered (correctly) that steam locomotives were more suited to the near-level sections, and the steeper pitches could be overcome by inclines. In northeast England whole mineral systems led from coalfields to rivers which flowed into the North Sea, in

---

*To mark the completion of the line an excursion was run to Birkenhead on 28th June, 1847 (BRYMBO WORKS MAGAZINE). [Did passengers travel down the inclines in wagons?]

some cases being little more than a series of inclines following one another. As on the NWMR, these routes carried no passengers.

To clear away main line NWMR matters, it is necessary to return to 1844: in the following years the NWMR, with Henry Robertson as Engineer and some powerful backing from two of its directors, Messrs Ross and Roy, resurrected a Shrewsbury, Oswestry & Chester Junction Railway plan for their own ends in order to counteract a threat from the C&HR (with some little-disguised support from the Birkenhead interests) who in the mania of 1845 were planning a rival direct railway of their own from Chester to Shrewsbury. This had the effect of annulling C&HR aspirations and without opposition, the SOCJR received its Act on 30th June, 1845 and the following year was amalgamated with the NWMR under the title of the Shrewsbury & Chester Railway. The whole NWMR line including the Ruabon Extension and the Saltney branch was opened on 4th November, 1846,* at the same time as the C&HR's line from their Chester terminus of the Birkenhead Railway was opened to Saltney. It was all very tidy. Thus there was a railway south from Birkenhead, into Chester and down to Saltney where the Holyhead and Wrexham lines divided, the south-seeking track passing Wrexham and Ruabon only to end up at Rhosymedre, one mile south of Ruabon. Here the nominal NWMR tracks ended and an end-on junction with the SOCJR-authorised line was made in due course. 'An Engine house and workshops were established on the Dee branch at Saltney.'

Affairs on the new S&CR system have only limited bearing on later WMCQR history from this time onwards, save in the matter of its Brymbo and Minera line which was critical to it. In early 1847 the 'Minera line was not yet finished. It went to the lime rocks at Minera with two tunnels respectively 220 and 400 yards long' in the course of two rope-worked inclines. Opening to mineral traffic right up into Minera occurred in July† 1847 (6 m. 20 ch. from Wheatsheaf Junction) and two small branches off it ran to Brynmally and Ffrwd, opening in the November: in due time Westminster, Southsea, Brymbo and Vron Collieries were also rail served off the Minera Branch.

To round off the NWMR main line saga, Chester General joint station came into use on 1st August, 1848, and the S&CR duly reached Shrewsbury, being the first railway to do so. At first a temporary station there was in use: opening took place on 16th October, 1848 whilst the permanent joint station opened on 1st June, 1849.

Return is now made to the operating problems of the NWMR's Wheatsheaf Junction – Minera Branch's inclines (the Achilles' heel of the system) as they figure prominently in the Committee Stage of the Bill to promote the WMCQR (*page 47*). (When NWMR and S&CR titles lost their individuality, and later the S&CR became part of the GWR on 1st September, 1854, Paddington became acutely aware that customer goodwill and that particular Branch did not go hand-in-hand).

A new railway, the Wrexham & Minera Railway, connecting to the Shrewsbury–Chester main line immediately south of Wrexham station on the west side, (where at Croes Newydd there was a triangular junction with

*Some say 6th.

†Some give November.

an engine shed in the centre) was authorised on 17th May, 1861 and opened on 22nd May, 1862. This enabled the Moss Incline (known locally as Brake Incline) with its tunnel to be abandoned from 1862, but even the climb on the new line from Croes Newydd to the outskirts of Brymbo, where the new line joined the old NWMR route, was steep and circuitous.

Some nice details of early days were published in WHEATSHEAF during October 1910:

> The Brymbo Tunnel was surveyed by William Taylor Jones . . . who was then Manager of the Brymbo Company's collieries (he also surveyed the Berwyn Tunnel on the Llangollen and Corwen Railway), and engaged two sets of men to work simultaneously from each end; although only a youth at the time, the two sets worked to an exactitude of a perpendicular line. The material from the cuttings near the Works were used to construct the 'Tai' embankment, but striking a good seam of coal in the process, every house in the area replenished its stocks. The navvies during daytime, threw coal, soil etc. in the contractors' wagons indiscriminately, but women and children hand-picked the slopes for coal before they could remove it. During the night when the navvies had gone, local colliers attacked the coal in the cutting.
>
> I well remember the first train of coal, iron etc. being run from the hot pool siding down to the gates crossing; there were only ordinary brakes to hold the wagons and a large number of the public availed themselves of the opportunity to have a ride on the first train . . . there was one wagon in the train having a load of flange pipes about 15 inches diameter and the writer remembers being ensconced in one of these pipes for the first ride. Many continued . . . while the train went through the tunnel to the top of the Moss brake.

The same account confirms that at first loaded wagons – at least between the inclines – ran loaded down the favourable gradients in rakes of six or eight vehicles, attended by men and horses. Two men were allotted to each brake to act as brakesmen; three horses were required for each rake and trains for Brymbo and Minera ran alternately, in charge of Charles Jones and John Harrison respectively. A part of their journey would be through the Brymbo Tunnel to the head of Moss Incline; there would have been another short horse-haul between the foot of Moss and the head of Wheatsheaf Incline. This arrangement continued for about two years when a steam locomotive ('a splendid machine . . . its name, I think, was CHARLOTTE; it was moderately short in structure and suitable for the many curves on the branch') arrived. Later, it was confined to the section between Moss Incline top and Minera/Brymbo and its origin or owner is not known. The BM&R Co. had built a network of lines around the Works and perhaps the engine was their property? (The Works began business under that Company in 1846.) Edmond Bond was its first driver, with Thomas Powell (Chirk) as fireman and Charles Dodd (Summerhill) cleaner. An incident occurred on 2nd July, 1852 when Bond was on holiday and Powell driving, having Robert Harrop as fireman and with John Mumford on the engine also. Mumford was employed as a 'runner' to convey the weights of coal and ironstone from the Summerhill weighing machine, to the Brymbo office, there being no weighing machine at Brymbo at the time – he would ride on the engine in the course of his duties. Hauling a train towards Brymbo with footplate (carrying the men) leading, they were struck by a runaway wagon which had broken loose from Minera sidings and loaded, hurtled down the branch to hit the engine; this impact was beside the boundary wall of Brymbo churchyard. The lime was shot from the wagon and buried the three men instantly. 'Powell escaped with a mangled and much fractured leg and was maimed for life. The other two had succumbed before they were extricated . . . as a result of lime suffocation and being burnt by the engine firebox.'

The Minera line and adjacent Works' system were the scene of several accidents, some caused by errant wagons: on 30th July, 1866 the CHARLOTTE was derailed and the wagons from behind 'jammed the engine tender' and injured the driver. This reminiscence might suggest the engine was a tender variety but probably the coal bunker of the engine was struck by the wagons and it was a tank type. The story does imply that as late as 1866 privately-owned locomotives might be found on Great Western metals . . . the site where the train of 21 wagons derailed was at the foot of the Penycoed bank.

More importantly for the end-product of this history is that the Wheatsheaf Branch was now truncated to one incline, the Summerhill Tunnel and a fan of industrial lines at the west end of the tunnel, the most important serving the Westminster Colliery. In due course the GWR would stable a steam locomotive on this section, and build an engine shed at the east end of Summerhill Tunnel, i.e. at the summit of Wheatsheaf Incline.

Though the Act enabled the W & MR to carry passengers, the GWR did not see fit to do so and for twenty years ignored the protestations of the locals, only succumbing to their cries on 24th May, 1882 when the threat of a WMCQR Branch had become a reality . . . but that is much ahead of the time under review.

As to the Wheatsheaf Incline and the land upon which it was built, and the House of Lords Enquiry (The Select Committee on Recommitment sitting from 15th June, 1882 re the WMCQR Bill of 1881): during the proceedings the Duke of Westminster revealed that it had been engineered by Henry Robertson. The then-Duke had insisted upon its construction as part of a bargain he had struck with the NWMR whereby the Duke would allow their main line to 'pass through Pulford under the Duke's Park' in exchange for which the Incline would evolve. By 1880, the Duke's Colliery (Westminster) was sending 200,000 tons of coal down that Incline annually.

A sequence can be noted, coming as it did – and it was certainly no coincidence – that the opening of the W & MR should take place in May 1862 when on 7th August the next year the usurper in the form of the WMCQR had obtained their Act for the main line, and a Branch to Ffrwd also; to follow were WMCQR Bills for an extension to Buckley, Brymbo, Minera etc.; these passed Standing Orders and were reported with great delight in THE CHESTER CHRONICLE for 3rd February and 10th March, 1866. Paddington could scarcely ignore the pressures building up; in February 1866 the GWR erected a small hut between the Works and what later became Brymbo station, to serve as a booking office; furnishings included a clock and suitable finger boards to denote times of arrival and departing trains, ticket racks and all the appurtenances required for the purpose. But when the WMCQR's threatened invasion did not materialise, Paddington sent orders that the contents of the building were to be returned to Headquarters: this being done, the hut remained – empty – for several years afterwards (*see also page 181*).

THE BRYMBO WORKS MAGAZINE adds a little more to this story; a month after
the hut arrived a gang of men came to

> prepare the foundations for a station and the necessary sidings, and a month
> afterwards the platform and approach signals and sidings were complete; on 15th
> May, 1866 the Board of Trade Inspector was expected. The Inspector (Captain
> Ritchie) however, turned up on 12th July, spent about five minutes at the station
> and returned to report to Headquarters. Expectation ran high for weeks, but
> gradually the barometer fell . . .

This was the end of rumour which was rife to the effect that passenger trains
would run (one train each day) between Wrexham and Minera on Tuesdays,
Thursdays and Saturdays only. After a fatal accident to a stage cart, the jury
considered the GWR might be amenable to providing limited public accommodation, but nothing transpired. It is recalled that by December 1866 the
mineral traffic had increased to such extent that two locomotives were
allocated to the Branch.

To complete the picture, the WMCQR, who in May 1882 had had their
Brymbo Branch Bill thrown out, had it passed in August, to the fright of the
GWR who (as just stated) started a Wrexham–Brymbo passenger service in
anticipation of competition. Three passenger trains ran daily on weekdays;
on 1st August 1889 the WMCQR began its own passenger service.

This account has now over-reached itself and is long past the time when
the NWMR had become a part of the GWR, but this has been necessary in
order to set the stage for the creation of the WMCQR and to demonstrate that
although the GWR took steps to mitigate some of the physical shortcomings
of the NWMR section by the building of the W&MR, this failed to suffocate
cries for an alternative railway. It is convenient now to examine how the
NWMR's customers felt about the shortcomings of the GWR monopoly.

An estimate of tonnages passing annually through Brymbo (upper) and
Summerhill (lower) tunnels had been made in 1858: these were 200,000 and
320,000 respectively.

No better summary of the existing situation could be found than the
contemporary article in THE MINING JOURNAL for 29th July, 1865 which (variations in spellings of place-names accepted) deserves quoting:

> The only railway accommodation in this district at the moment is that afforded
> by the Great Western Railway whose line from Chester to Shrewsbury skirts the
> end of the Coal Measures. As all the workings are or rather were from two to three
> miles to the west of this line a branch (The Wheatsheaf Branch) was made to the
> collieries turning off from the main line about 11 miles south of Chester and one
> mile north of Wrexham. This Branch has ordinary gradients for about a mile to the
> Wheatsheaf (an inn on the High Road from Wrexham to Mold) but west of this
> there is a steep incline (The Wheatsheaf Incline) averaging about 1 in 15 for about
> half a mile in length up which the empty trucks are drawn with a wire rope by the
> weight of the full trucks coming down. At the top of this incline there is a short
> tunnel which brings the line into the Moss Valley close by the Moss Pits of the
> Westminster Colliery. From this two branches go up the valley, one on the west
> side to Mr Clayton's Bryn Mally Pits and another on the east side to Mr Clayton's
> Pendwllyn Pits and to the Frood Pits and blast furnaces. From the Moss Valley to
> the Brymbo Valley the line was carried up the west side of the Moss Valley
> opposite the tunnel by a very steep incline (The Moss Valley Incline) of nearly 1 in

4 then through a tunnel about a quarter of a mile long which opened into the Brymbo Valley nearly opposite the Brymbo furnaces.

In the Brymbo Valley two branches were extended south, one on the east side of the Valley to the Nant Pits of the Westminster Company and to the pits of the Broughton Company and another on the west side of the Valley to the pits of the Vron Colliery. Northward the line is continued skirting the western side of the Brymbo Valley until it debouches into a branch valley of the Nantyffrith along which, skirting the outcrop of the measures, it continues its course for about three miles to the Minera lime quarries and lead mining district.

As far as the Moss Valley (comprising the Moss pits of the Westminster Company and the Bryn Malley and Frood Pits) was concerned this arrangement gave sufficient accommodation. No practical difficulty was found in working any reasonable traffic over the Wheatsheaf Incline. With regard to the Brymbo Valley (including the Brymbo, Vron and Broughton Pits) the case was very different. The Moss Valley Incline was a serious stumbling block over which it was practically found that no considerable traffic could be worked. When the pressure came it was found impossible to time the full trucks so as to bring up the empties so that it more than once happened that the collieries were brought to a standstill in a time of flourishing trade for want of trucks which were lying at the bottom of the incline almost within sight of the pits where they were required. This was to some extent met by the erection of a stationary steam engine at the top of the Moss Valley Incline for the purpose of drawing up the empty trucks, an arrangement which was found to palliate but not to remedy the evil. About four years ago this was effected by the making of a branch line going directly up the Brymbo Valley starting from the main line about half a mile south of Wrexham and joining the branch already made to the Broughton Colliery along the east side of the Valley.

All the traffic from Minera and from the works in the Brymbo Valley is now worked over this branch, the Moss Valley Incline and tunnel being entirely disused; indeed at present there is no railway communication between the two valleys any traffic between them having to go round by Wrexham. This branch has been an immense boon to the entire district for not only has it given facilities to the collieries in the Brymbo valley and enable them to do a trade which before would have been impossible but it has also helped those in the Moss Valley by relieving the Wheatsheaf Incline over which the present traffic of the valley can be worked with ease and comfort.

Up to the present time therefore the Great Western Railway has had a monopoly of this district and as is always the case where any great company has a monopoly it has made itself intensely unpopular and is accused on almost every side of retarding the progress of the district. However this may be it is obvious that in a district like that of Wrexham where local markets are insignificant and where consequently the collieries are so entirely dependent on getting their coal on easy terms into distant markets nothing but competition is likely to satisfy public opinion.

Some additional notes on Incline working and colliery openings were revealed when the Parliamentary Enquiry into the WWM & CQJR Bill (28th July, 1862) took place – not every colliery mentioned was dependent on the GWR:

Westminster Colliery	sending 120,000 tons a year
Hope Colliery	was about to open (no railway link)
Broughton Colliery	sending 60,000 tons a year
Vron Colliery	sending 90–100,000 tons a year
Brymbo Colliery	sending 60–70,000 tons a year but much of this used to make iron at the Works
Penycoed Colliery (Brymbo)	sending 18–20,000 tons a year

The Great Western Railway a few years ago installed a very large stationary engine at the top of the incline in the Moss Valley at a place called Kenw (Cerni?). The Great Western provide locomotives to work between the foot of the Moss incline through the tunnel to the top of the Wheatsheaf incline.

When the loaded wagons were few and not enough to draw the empty wagons up from the Wheatsheaf Incline the engine was attached to a rope and run down with the rope and drew up the empty wagons which went running up the incline empty.

And finally, an extract of four years previously (1861) sufficiently concludes the pre-WMCQR period.

NORTH WALES MINING DISTRICT

The coal trade is looking up both in the Wrexham and Ruabon Districts good orders having been received during the week but the iron trade shows no symptoms whatever of returning activity. A new pit has recently been opened at the Vron Colliery by Messrs. Maurice and Lowe the proprietors which it is understood will be the largest in the district. The complaints as to the management of the Wheatsheaf Brake are likely to lead to an alteration. A Director of the Great Western Railway has been appointed to investigate the matter with the view of remedying the evils complained of and the engineer has been instructed to send in a report as to the desirableness of erecting engines at the Wheatsheaf and Moss Inclines* with the estimated expense and also as to the expense of branch railways up the valleys. This is a proper step and it is to be hoped will lead to a practical and beneficial result – MANCHESTER GUARDIAN.[5]

The threat of local railway competition had at last alerted Paddington!

Throughout the early years of the foregoing period there was the constant threat – not overlooked by the far-sighted – that the GWR's Broad Gauge ended at Wolverhampton: that Company did not intend they should remain there; Birkenhead was to be the Broad Gauge terminus, an ambition not culled until Parliament rejected the proposals of 1853. The effect of the Broad Gauge passing through Chester, and the consequences to the existing standard gauge mineral line system, were perhaps too complex to be considered in their relations with the industrial ambitions of the Wrexham area, but such intentions gave little confidence to GWR-linked customers!

[The Summerhill Incline (Gwersyllt-Moss: 42 ch.) survived until October 1907: the last section, the Wheatsheaf Junction–Gwersyllt length, remained until 1951.]

---

*an engine at Moss was already in use.

References

[1] [DENBIGHSHIRE HISTORICAL SOCIETY (TRANSACTIONS), Vol. 15, 1966, p. 134. (this lists original sources, including biography. CHESTER CHRONICLE, etc.)

[2] THE RAILWAY COMPANION (Edward Parry) pub. 1849, quoted by G.G. Lerry HENRY ROBERTSON (PIONEER OF RAILWAYS) pub. 1949.

[3] BEYER, PEACOCK & CO. LTD. (Hills & Patrick)

[4] BRYMBO WORKS MAGAZINE (March 1930). (Works began operating 2nd October, 1842: first coal pits sunk under title in July 1843.)

[5] THE MINING JOURNAL 17th April, 1858, p. 253.

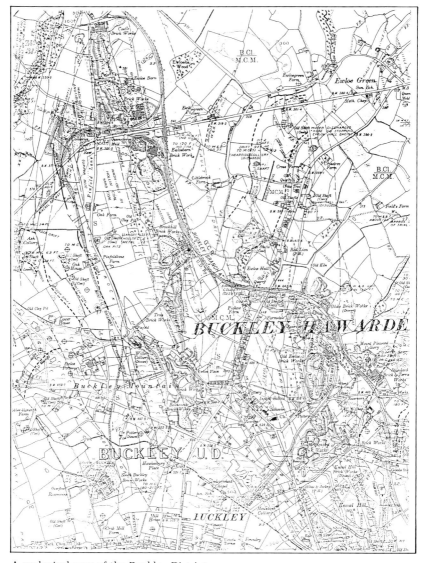

A geological map of the Buckley District.

Courtesy Second Edition 1914, 6" Ordnance Survey

Wanted – Another Railway

The Industrial Revolution had many cradles, one of which was this part of Denbighshire and Flintshire. Beneath the earth's surface were to be found coal, clay, ironstone and limestone in close proximity: so in earliest times coal was being extracted from open pits, and allied to these excavations businesses grew up which utilised the associated geological treasures . . . pottery, earthenware, iron foundries and of smaller importance, limestone products. In this intensive scene, one industry leant on another, coal being burnt in hundreds of tons to fuel the brick and pottery kilns, to supply furnaces and the like, so supporting a community which derived a living from employment as miners, colliers, foundrymen, quarrymen, brick and tile makers . . . and so on.

The origins of the idea for a railway from the Flint and Denbighshire coalfield to the sea lay in a Memorial from local coalowners to the Chairman of the Birkenhead Railway* (E.G. Salisbury, then MP for Chester) who wanted a line 'lower down across the Dee for the conveyance of minerals for shipment at Birkenhead and other ports . . .' but the line was then bought by the GW & LNW Companies (i.e. the Birkenhead Joint line) and the GWR did not favour any other scheme which took traffic away from it. 'The Birkenhead Railway was ready to propose a line direct to Wrexham over the Dee lower down but it was likely GW & LNW would oppose any such Bill'.†

The district most attractive to railway connection was that around Brymbo; for it relied entirely on road transport, was far from the river and had no canal or tramroad. The opening of a locomotive-worked line from Croes Newydd, Wrexham to the summit of the Brake Incline of the former NWMR at Brymbo, on 7th June, 1862 can now be considered in a wider context. Years of fruitless efforts to defeat the GWR in its indifferent attitude towards those who felt they were ill-served produced a ray of hope in that a Mr. Attree had designed a line from the towpath beside the canal north of the Pontcysyllte Aqueduct 'to join an unfinished railway at The Frith and carry it to the Mold & Chester Railway. But it met with little favour from the coal and iron masters of the district' so the WREXHAM & DENBIGH WEEKLY ADVERTISER of 25th October, 1862 reveals. However, there was no submerging enthusiasm for a new railway of local ownership which would serve the needs of everyone and make junction with the GWR at Wrexham. So, unfettered by the selfishness of the GWR which could only offer the poor facilities at Saltney (well up the Dee and near to Chester) or suffering the discouragement to the carriage of coal on the Joint Line between Chester and Birkenhead a new railway could drive northwards from the Wrexham district, and not hesitate at the Dee but to go over or under that river as most practical. The goal was Birkenhead where the demand for coal had already attracted new railway ventures such as the Newport, Abergavenny & Hereford, the Shrewsbury & Hereford, the Shropshire Union Canal and the Chester & Birkenhead lines into providing a through route for South Wales

---

*The subject of much manoeuvring on the part of the LNWR – finally becoming LNW & GW joint property in 1860.

†It is necessary to add that a well-tried method of transport was the initial development in this regard, being a branch of the Ellesmere Canal which would lead into geologically-promising reaches of the Windy Hill district northwest of Wrexham. It was begun half a century earlier but failed to be given a connection with the main canal, so lapsing into disuse (if ever in use) before 1809.

steam coal, delivered in huge quantities to bunker steamships on the River Mersey. The Wrexham & Minera Railway tied Denbighshire industrialists to the GWR.

By 1862 it was clear that the coal owners would have to restrict their ambitions to a line down to Connah's Quay. 'Connah's Quay' it is well known, is better suited for shipment of minerals than Saltney'. 'The GWR would not build a railway to Connah's Quay to get 10*d*. instead of 2/6*d*. for minerals (consigned to Saltney): they would not mind spending £200,000 if they could block up the country'.

The promoters of any competitive route to that of the GWR had to prove Want, and against a powerful opponent as the GWR would prove to be, Want meant Determination and overall, Finance. Attree's project had failed for lack of support from some of the larger local industrialists, whose co-operation especially in terms of finance was imperative. It did frighten the authorities at Paddington into taking action, for they were clearly aware that Moss and Summerhill Inclines were outdated and created delays which growing industry would not suffer . . . thus the Wrexham & Minera Railway, whilst serving many important industries, was of no use to those who were still served by the truncated end of the former Brymbo branch of the NWMR; its remaining users now had to compete with the competitors on the steam-worked W & M line . . . so for them the frustrations of Summerhill Incline remained. Neither did the W & MR do anything for industry in the Ffrwd region, an area once served by the failed canal and having great coal and iron potential. Owners of that area joined in dissent . . . they had proved that the W & MR was not the answer to their local industry.

Our remarks so far have concerned the Denbighshire interest for a new railway. Not more than seven miles further north another group of industrialists in Buckley, Flintshire was faced with a similar problem; and they too, wanted an outlet to the sea and to be rid of the monopoly of existing tramroads and the alternative of carting to the river.

The Flintshire men were to show the Denbighshire men by example – they were the first in the field with a railway. Around Buckley the horse and cart was improved-upon by the tramroad, firstly built with rails of wood and later with track of iron plates. So heavy was the demand of local industry that by 1820 most of the major coal pits were worked out, yet industrialists from outside the region were still searching for sources of coal and were ready to explore and exploit the untapped coal measures where deep-level mining (as opposed to pit and near-surface working) could be developed. The creation of the Buckley Railway demonstrated that industrialists of the district had thrown off the shackles of the Tramroad Period with its attendant methods of working in the manner of the old turnpikes, and were prepared to put money behind a thoroughbred railway which would take their products to the seaboard or a physical junction with another railway – in this case the Chester & Holyhead Division of the London & North Western Railway – and so, in theory, give their output access to any rail-connected community in the Kingdom.

Whilst the Buckley Railway went some way towards answering the transport problems of a small district enjoying an intensely close manufacturing community, that other district further south and at more distance from the Dee remained wholly dependent on the good graces of the Great Western Railway. So, whilst the Flintshire Buckley Railway would break the monopoly of the Aston Tramroad, plans were afoot in Denbighshire and Wrexham to break the monopoly of the Great Western . . . a formidable assignment!

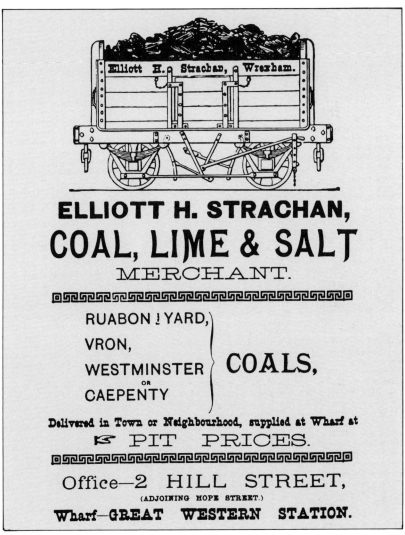

A local coal merchant's advertisement of 1886.

Buckley and Connah's Quay (Flintshire) Railway.

(Power to make Railways to Connah's Quay, and to join Chester and Holyhead Line; Working Arrangements with Chester and Holyhead and London and North Western Railway Companies; Amendment Acts.)

NOTICE is hereby given, that application is intended to be made to Parliament, in the ensuing session, for leave to bring in a Bill to incorporate a Company for making and maintaining the railways hereinafter mentioned, or some of them, together with all necessary and convenient stations, wharf-yards, approaches, bridges, roads, communications, and other works, and to confer upon the Company to be thereby incorporated (hereinafter called "The Company") all necessary and proper powers for effecting the objects hereinafter mentioned, or some of them (that is to say):

To make and maintain a railway, commencing in the parish of Hawarden, in the county of Flint, on the north side of the Know Lane, at or near the brickworks belonging to and in the occupation of Messrs. Richard Ashton and Company, and terminating in the parish of Northop, in the said county, at or near Connah's Quay, upon land adjoining the river Dee, belonging to, and in the occupation of, Messrs. William Dentith and Company.

Also a railway diverging from, and out of, the said intended railway, commencing in the said parish of Northop, on the north side of the turnpike road leading from Flint to Queen's Ferry, in a garden belonging to Messrs. Davison and Company, and in the occupation of Benjamin Bennett, and terminating in the parish of Northop aforesaid, by a junction with the Chester and Holyhead Line of the London and North Western Railway, 200 yards, or thereabouts, on the east side of the ninth mile-post from Chester, on the Chester and Holyhead Railway, which said intended railways and works will be made or pass in, from, through, or into, the several parishes, townships, and extra parochial and other places, following, or some of them (that is to say), Hawarden, Ewloe-town, Ewloe-wood, Northop, Soughton, Golftyn, and Wepre, and the bed or shore of the river Dee, all in the county of Flint.

To cross, divert, alter, or stop us, whether temporarily or permanently, all such turnpike roads, parish roads, and other highways, streams, pipes, sewers, canals, navigations, rivers, bridges, railways, and tramroads, within the parishes, townships, and extra-parochial and other places aforesaid, or any of them, as it may be necessary to cross, divert, or alter, for the purposes of the said railways and works, or any of them, or of the said intended Bill.

To purchase, and take by compulsion, lands, houses, tenements, and hereditaments, for the purposes of such railways and works, and of the said intended Bill; and to vary or extinguish all rights and privileges in any manner connected with the lands, houses, tenements, and hereditaments, so purchased or taken.

To levy tolls, rates, and duties upon, or in respect of the intended railways and works, and to confer exemptions from the payment of such tolls, rates, and duties.

To confer, vary, or extinguish other rights and privileges.

And it is also intended by the said Bill to empower the Chester and Holyhead Railway Company and the London and North Western Railway Company, or either of them, and the Company, to enter into and carry into effect contracts, agreements, and arrangements, for, or with reference to, the construction, maintenance, working, and using, by any, or either, of the contracting Companies, of the railways and works of the other or others of them, or any part thereof; and with reference to the regulation, management, and transmission of the traffic thereon, the supply and maintenance of engines, stock, and plant; the fixing, collection, payment, division, appropriation, and distribution of the tolls and other income and profits arising therefrom, and the employment of officers and servants. And also to empower the said Chester and Holyhead Railway Company and the London and North Western Railway Company, or either of them, to take and hold shares in, and subscribe towards the said intended undertaking of the Company, or any part thereof, and to guarantee to the Company such interest, dividend, annual or other payments as may be agreed upon between them, and to apply their existing funds, or to raise further capital for those purposes by the creation of new shares or stock in their undertakings, and to borrow further monies.

And it is intended so far as may be requisite or desirable for any of the purposes of the said Bill, to amend or repeal the provisions, or some of them, of the several Acts of Parliament following, that is to say, local and personal Acts, 7 and 8 Victoria, chapter 65; 8 and 9 Victoria, chapter 33; 10 and 11 Victoria, chapters 147, 162, and 238; 11 and 12 Victoria, chapter 60; 12 and 13 Victoria, chapter 41; 14 and 15 Victoria, chapters 21, 131, and 146; 17 and 18 Victoria, chapters 168 and 222; 21 and 22 Victoria, chapters 130 and 131; and the public general Acts 13 and 14 Victoria, chapter 111, and 22 and 23 Victoria, chapter 60, relating to the Chester and Holyhead Railway Company; and the local and personal Acts 8 and 9 Victoria, chapters 36, 37, 43, 105, 111, 112, 123, 156, and 198; 9 and 10 Victoria, chapters 67, 80, 82, 152, 182, 184, 192, 193, 204, 231, 232, 233, 244, 248, 259, 261, 262, 269, 300, 309, 322, 323, 324, 328, 331, 359, 368, 369, 380, and 396; 10 and 11 Victoria, chapters 73, 107, 114, 118, 120, 121, 131, 132, 139, 159, 161, 178, 188, 228, 236, 270, 278, and 294; 11 and 12 Victoria, chapters 58, 60, and 130; 12 and 13 Victoria, chapter 74; 13 and 14 Victoria, chapter 36; 14 and 15 Victoria, chapters 28 and 94; 15 and 16 Victoria, chapters, 98 and 105; 16 and 17 Victoria, chapters 97, 110, 157, 160, 161, 205, 216, and 222; 17 and 18 Victoria, chapters 201 and 204; 18 and 19 Victoria, chapters 172 and 194; 19 and 20 Victoria, chapters 52, 69, and 123; 20 and 21 Victoria, chapters 64, 98, and 108; 21 and 22 Victoria, chapter 131; and 22 and 23 Victoria, chapters 2, 88, 113, and 134 relating to the London and North Western Railway Company.

And notice is hereby also given, that plans and sections of the proposed railways and works, with a book of reference to such plans, and a published map, with the lines of the proposed railways delineated thereon, and a copy of this notice as published in the London Gazette, will on, or before, the 30th day of November, 1859, be deposited for public inspection with the Clerk of the Peace for the county of Flint, at his office at Mold, in the same county; and that on or before the said 30th day of November, a copy of so much of the said plans, sections, and book of reference as relates to each parish or extra-parochial place in or through which the said railways and works, or any part of them are or is intended to be made, together with a copy of this notice as published in the London Gazette, will be deposited for public inspection in the case of each parish with the parish clerk thereof, at his residence; and in the case of each extra-parochial place, with the parish clerk of some parish immediately adjoining thereto, at his residence, and printed copies of the said intended Bill will be deposited in the Private Bill Office of the House of Commons, on or before the 23rd day of December next.

Dated this 12th day of November, 1859.

A. T. Roberts, Mold.

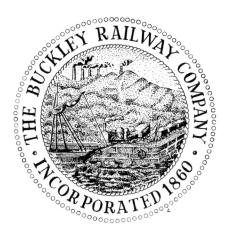

The Buckley Railway

In the beginning

The Buckley area was one of those pockets of industry to be found in the eighteenth century; it is often cited as being a child of the Staffordshire pottery industry, a contention which the Buckley people have contested vigorously maintaining that in fact the reverse was the case and that industry was well established in that part of Flintshire before it spread elsewhere, notably in matter of the pottery trade. The discovery of suitable clay led to a well-rounded business in the manufacture of bricks, firebricks, coarse pottery, roof and floor tiles. Such somewhat delicate wares needed careful carriage to the water's edge, and to that end tramways had served the Buckley district well since c.1750 but, with demand and increased productivity, something better was needed now that the Railway Age was established. So a number of Buckley businessmen banded together to consider the building of a railway down to Connah's Quay whose purpose would be solely to convey the output of the district; passenger traffic was not then considered. It would be a Buckley railway for the use of Buckley . . . and it came to be just that.

The subscribers were Philip Bryan Davies-Cooke of Gwysaney, George Moore Dixon*, William Reynolds, Charles Davison*, John Williams, Thomas Richard Popplewell Royle*, Charles Butler Clough*, Edward Thompson*, Robert Williams*, and Edward Parry* . . . a considerable list! Of these, the first directors are marked thus*, and underlined are land-owners through whose property the Buckley Railway ran; the number of directors being limited to seven, each of whom must hold 20 shares in his own name.

The importance of persons on the Board of railway companies cannot be overestimated; indeed it is possible to outline the progress and activities of railways, their amalgamations, take-overs, aspirations etc. by investigating the vested interests of such men. The Buckley is an excellent example of this.

59

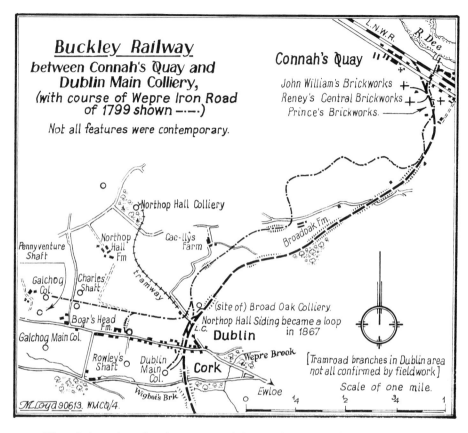

Buckley Railway
between Connah's Quay and
Dublin Main Colliery,
(with course of Wepre Iron Road
of 1799 shown ─·─·)

Not all features were contemporary.

Connah's Quay

John William's Brickworks ┼
Reney's Central Brickworks ┼
Prince's Brickworks. ────

L.N.W.R.   R. Dee

Northop Hall Colliery

Pennyventure Shaft

Northop Hall Fm

Cae-llys Farm

Broadoak Fm

Galchog Col.   Charles Shaft

tramway

Boar's Head Fm.

(site of) Broad Oak Colliery.
Northop Hall Siding became a loop in 1867
L.C.   Dublin

Galchog Main Col.

Rowley's Shaft   Dublin Main Col.   Cork   Wepre Brook

[Tramroad branches in Dublin area not all confirmed by fieldwork]

Scale of one mile.

M. Lloyd 90613. WMCQ/4.

Wigbais Brk   Ewloe   ¼   ½   ¾   1

Though jumping ahead to 1864 (whilst on the same subject) it is significant to see how in those short years the Board had changed – local representation was now limited to four men, these were:–

Dr William Reynolds of Mold   *Chairman*
C.B. Clough of Mold   *Deputy Chairman*
Charles Davison of Connah's Quay
G.M. Dixon of Wrexham

Thompson, Williams and Parry had gone, and wider interests had taken their place reflecting the launching of the nearby Wrexham, Mold & Connah's Quay Railway and the further implication of involving William Barker Buddicom of Penbedw nearby, (1816–71) locomotive and civil engineer and railway contractor. His two new colleagues were J.P. Wilding of Montgomery and Richard Kirke Penson of Kidwelly – the former had directorships on the Bishop's Castle, Drayton Junction and WMCQR lines, and the latter on the WMCQR.

By this date, Reynolds was a director of the North Union Railway in Lancashire, and the Jamaica Railway: Clough and Dixon were on the Board of the Mold & Denbigh Junction and only Davison had no other railway links. Buddicom, currently in Italy, brought worldwide expertise; he was on the Board of the Royal Portuguese and Central Argentine Railways. In other words, there was a balanced mix of local, territorial and experienced interests, so desirable to continue the ambitions of the Company which, to say the least, were not high-flying. Elsewhere it has been shown where Davison's loyalty lay in furthering the cause of the locality.

The story of the Railway has so far centred on people – and very properly, for the Buckley was a People's Railway.

The Bill was submitted in November 1859 as follows:

BUCKLEY & CONNAH'S QUAY RAILWAY. *Engineer*: George Bellis, Mold.*

The railway was to begin at the Knowl (Knowle) Lane Brickworks, Buckley, and pass around the various existing 'craters' formed by the clay pits of the district, also tapping collieries en route. The line would pass Northop Hall village, all the foregoing sites being on a course which was later to be largely adopted. Beyond Northop Hall it would have been laid near the site of the Wepre Iron Road as far as Oak Farm, from whence a more direct course would have taken the railway down steeply into Connah's Quay.[1] At the Quay the line would bifurcate – as was later done – with a 5 chain curve making junction with the Chester–Holyhead line towards Holyhead, and a second line passing under that main line and making a 3 chain curve in the other direction along the river bank between the Chester –Holyhead (LNWR) and the waterside.

In the reverse direction the climb from Connah's Quay would have been at 1 in 40/33/132/82, then level to Northop Hall; thereafter at 1 in 38/Level/45, i.e. not as steep as the adopted route which left Connah's Quay at 1 in 28.

The Buckley Railway duly received the Royal Assent on 14th June, 1860 for what BRADSHAW'S MANUAL described as the 'construction of a single line 5 miles long from the populous village of Buckley in Flintshire to Connah's Quay, a small port on the southeast coast of the Dee estuary where a junction was to be made with the Chester & Holyhead Railway': and basically, it became and remained, just that†. The shares were held by traders in the district, and capital was £30,000 in £10 shares, with loans permitted up to £10,000.

The Act permitted:

> Railway No. 1. 'To commence in the Parish of Hawarden . . . near to the village of Buckley and terminate in the Parish of Northop at or near Connah's Quay on the River Dee'

(which was less exact than some railway Acts!) Deposited Plans show the

---

*He assisted William Davies occasionally on the Vale of Clwyd construction, c.1859.

†The Buckley section of British Rail closed:
   Connah's Quay–Northop Hall – 1959
   Northop Hall–(Old) Buckley – 5th July, 1965
   (Old) Buckley–Buckley Junction – 3rd May, 1965

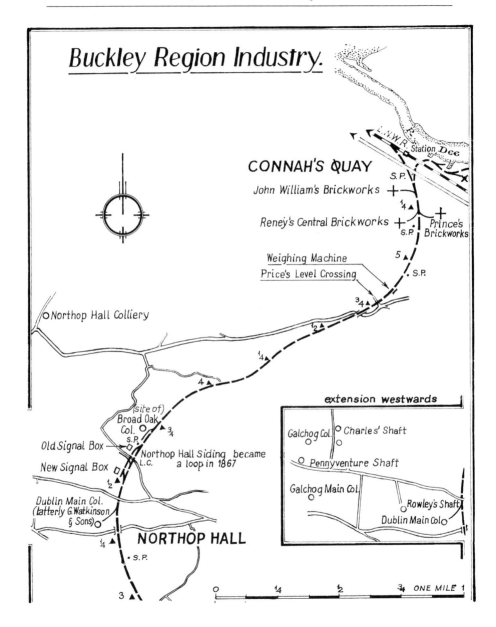

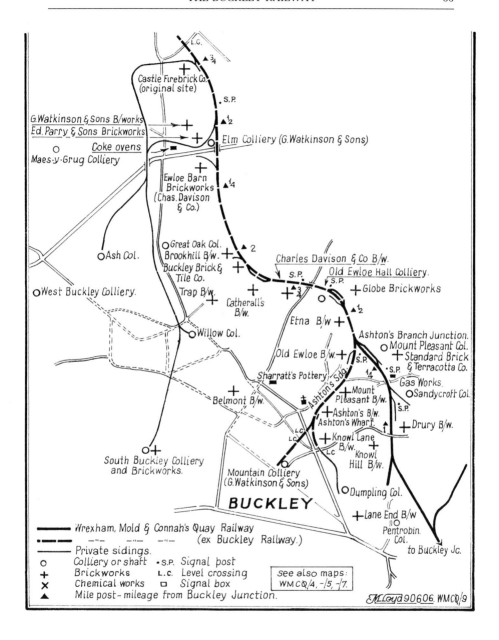

Castle Firebrick Co.
(original site)

S.P.

G.Watkinson & Sons B/works
Ed. Parry & Sons Brickworks

Coke ovens
Maes-y-Grug Colliery

Elm Colliery (G.Watkinson & Sons)

Ewloe Barn
Brickworks
(Chas.Davison
& Co.)

Ash Col.

Great Oak Col.
Brookhill B/w.
Buckley Brick &
Tile Co.

Charles Davison & Co B/w.
Old Ewloe Hall Colliery.
S.P.
S.P.

West Buckley Colliery.

Trap B/w.

Globe Brickworks

Catherall's
B/w.

Etna B/w

Willow Col.

Ashton's Branch Junction.
Mount Pleasant Col.
Standard Brick
& Terracotta Co.

Old Ewloe B/w.
S.P.
S.P.
Gas Works.
Sandycroft Col.

Sharratt's Pottery

Mount
Pleasant B/w.

Belmont B/w.

Ashton's B/w.
Ashton's Wharf.

Drury B/w.

South Buckley Colliery
and Brickworks.

Knowl Lane
B/w.
Knowl
Hill B/w.

Mountain Colliery
(G.Watkinson & Sons)

BUCKLEY

Dumpling Col.

Lane End B/w

Pentrobin.
Col.

to Buckley Jc.

Wrexham, Mold & Connah's Quay Railway
— " —   — " —   (ex Buckley Railway.)
Private sidings.
o   Colliery or shaft   • S.P. Signal post
+   Brickworks   L.C. Level crossing
×   Chemical works   □   Signal box
▲   Mile post - mileage from Buckley Junction.

see also maps:
WMCQ/4, -/5, -/7.

J.M.Lloyd 90606. WMCQ/9

southern terminus at the foot of Knowl Lane and at first the line ended about ¼ mile short of this point and was extended a year or two later.

> Railway No. 2. The link between No. 1 and the LNWR (C & HR section) at Connah's Quay.
>
> Stations or Lodges were to be erected at road level crossings and a person appointed to superintend them. The line was to be completed within three years.

There were powers to take over the Wepre Iron Road compulsorily for the first twelve months after the Act.

Joseph Howells (mining engineer of Bagillt, employed by Messrs. Rigby & Hancock), in giving evidence at the subsequent Parliamentary Enquiry, into the Bill for the Buckley Railway said 'the promotional map has been prepared by my son under my superintendence'. As opened, (he continued) 'the line was single track with no crossing place, but a short siding was put in at Northop Hall, roughly halfway down the line, which held about 10 wagons. The line was steeply graded, falling from Buckley with gradients of 1/30, 1/33 for ½ mile, 1/38 and 1/40. At a later date, about 1890, Northop Hall was made a crossing place with goods sidings* and a small signal box . . .'

The opening on 7th June, 1862 seems to have escaped the notice of the press which, in view of the many minutiae (from local incest to sermons) reported at length, ought to be explained; but is not! Indeed, the first reference to it appears in a timely advertisement by Charles Davison & Co. in THE CHESTER CHRONICLE for 28th June (repeated for the next two weeks). As Davison's business premises lay at the very foot of the Buckley Railway as well as in Buckley itself, he was going to find the new line exceptionally advantageous. The advertisement reads:

MESSRS. CHARLES DAVISON & CO.
Firebrick & Tile Manufacturers

Buckley Mountain

Have the pleasure to inform their friends that both their works at Buckley are now in direct communication with the LNWR by means of the Buckley & Connah's Quay Railway just opened. It enables goods to be delivered direct from the Works to various stations and sidings and renders loading and unloading from carts and tram-wagons un-necessary . . . Connah's Quay is three miles nearer Holyhead than Dundas' Sidings where the bulk of bricks sent by rail is usually loaded . . . In future Connah's Quay will be used as a shipping port instead of Queens Ferry – its superiority over other places on the Dee is well known and needs no comment.

Packing for Shipping. Bricks and tiles will be put into boxes on wheels at the Works, placed on the top of a railway truck and lowered by a crane into the hold of a vessel, thus entirely preventing the snipping and breakage unavoidably caused by four or five handlings.

These facilities cannot be offered by any other manufacturer as none of the other firms have availed themselves of the facilities of the new railway . . .

In consequence of the new railway, Davisons moved their chief office from the Lower Ferry Wharf to Connah's Quay.

---

*Crossing loop alleged to have been put in by 1867 according to one source: shown as a siding-cum-loop on GCR Survey of 1904.

Plate 1: Wepre Iron Road. A surviving cutting leads northwards near Bryn Gwyn.
(274683)   April 1987   (J.I.C. Boyd)

Plate 2: Plateway-acceptable wheels, axle and bearings from a typical shipping box.
Bentley Collection   June 1989   (J.I.C. Boyd)

Plate 3: Sandycroft Rail Road (II). The considerable embankment stretching south-wards from the site of Little Mancot Colliery, at Daniel's Ash.

(320664)   *April 1987*   *(J.I.C. Boyd)*

Plate 4: Tram Lane, Buckley (formerly Tram Road) with the course of the tramroad (*left*) leading to Ewloe Place. This section was the farthest extent of the Sandycroft Rail Road (II). *(2856440) February 1988 (J.I.C. Boyd)*

Plate 5: Horse drawing shipping boxes on Hancock's Wharf, c1925: Sam, with his driver Alex Hughes stands on a section where flat-bottomed rails are evident. *(290643) (Clwyd Record Office)*

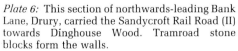

Plate 6: This section of northwards-leading Bank Lane, Drury, carried the Sandycroft Rail Road (II) towards Dinghouse Wood. Tramroad stone blocks form the walls.

(297646)   April 1987   (J.I.C. Boyd)

Plate 7: Brick insets and plate rails remain on Hancock's Wharf.

(290643)   April 1987   (J.I.C. Boyd)

Plate 8: On a different portion of the afore-mentioned Wharf, Tramroad turnouts (removed here) and standard gauge double-headed rails laid on their sides, have formed a very permanent way.

July 1969   (J.I.C. Boyd)

Plate 9: Knowl Lane Brickworks, the ori-ginal southern terminus of the Buckley Railway.

(287645)   December   1876

(M. Mollington)

Plate 10: Old Ewloe Brickworks Siding with its typical two-level loading wharf and the trolley which ran along the lower section. In the background is Ashton's Branch Junction: the newer line to join the WMCQR leads off to the right.

(286648)   December 1876   (M. Mollington)

Plate 11: Etna Brickworks Siding, with train of loaded Traders' Wagons standing thereon. The nearest vehicle is a coal wagon having the owner's name painted on the end. Note the wretched state of the track in the mainline.

(286653)   December 1876   (M. Mollington)

Plate 12: Old Ewloe Hall Colliery Siding (apparently out of use) looking northwards. Liverpool Road, Buckley, passed under the line just beyond the Colliery points.
(285654)   December 1876   (M. Mollington)

Plate 13: The Buckley Brick & Tile Company's Sidings incorporated an overhead tippler for narrow gauge wagons (*left*). Note the single wire telegraph line and the point lever with box.   *(278657)   December 1876   (M. Mollington)*

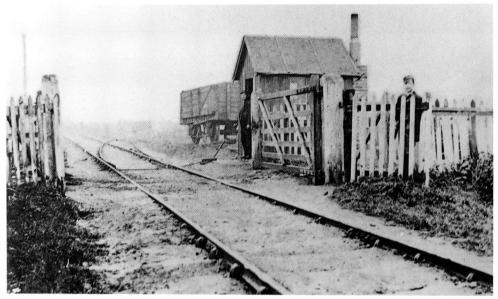

Plate 14: This gated crossing protected the road leading to the Castle Brickworks; this view looks southwards, with the original junction into the Brickworks beyond. The wooden hut was later replaced by a proper gate house; the gradient here was 1 in 38. *(276669) December 1876 (M. Mollington)*

Plate 15: The Dublin Main Colliery Siding turned off southwestwards just south of the overbridge carrying the Northop Hall village main road. The hired wagons are dumb-buffered and there is a hinged scotch block to prevent vehicles running onto the main line. *(273677) December 1876 (M. Mollington)*

Plate 16: The quayside, Connah's Quay in 1876. Wagons stand on the coal wharf in the background whilst ships dry their sails in the dock. The open wagons and closed vans appear to be among those hired by the WMCQR; extreme right are Buckley Traders' Wagons carrying Shipping Boxes. [The photographer was standing on the Chester & Holyhead Railway section.]

(M. Mollington)

Plate 17: A 1930s view of the junction between the former Knowl Lane Brickworks Siding (by this time used only for wagon storage) and the newer line (*right*) to Mountain Colliery, seen with gates closed across the rails. Today the whole of this area is now built over. *(G.H. Platt)*

Plate 18: A post-World War II scene: Ashton's Branch Junction looking towards Old Buckley with the main line curving away left – the Mount Pleasant Colliery is just in view. To the right, the original Buckley Railway course disappears towards the junction of the previous photograph. *(G.H. Platt)*

Plate 19: Entering Old Buckley from the north is a short pick-up goods train from Connah's Quay with ex-Great Eastern Railway (LNER Class J67 of 1899) No. 68585 at the head. *May 1957   (G.H. Platt)*

Plate 20: Time is running out for Old Buckley station and storage sidings, here seen from the adjacent road bridge. The main line falls to the left where the chimneys of Bannel Colliery indicate the position of Buckley Junction. Out of sight on the right, sidings serve Hancock's Wharf. The station buildings continue to be a useful shelter for local railwaymen. *(A. Brown)*

Plate 21: The skyline of chimneys may suggest that the cluster of works including Mount Pleasant Colliery, The Standard Brick & Terra Cotta Co. and Buckley Gas Co. have a future ahead of them, but within the next two decades all will have closed down. The railway here has just left Old Buckley a short distance behind: a turntable once occupied the site on the left. The track climbs northwards towards Ashton's Branch Junction.   *(290647)   (G.H. Platt)*

Plate 22: The timber overbridge at Northop Hall where the main Chester–North Wales road passed under the line, was a familiar landmark to thousands of motorists making for the Welsh coastal resorts. But few knew what the bridge carried.
                                                    (274675)   November 1961   (J.I.C. Boyd)

Plate 23: The yard at Northop Hall became more weed-entangled as usage of the Connah's Quay line diminished. The field-gated occupation crossing was left with gates open to the occupation road, as the passage of a train to the river was now a rarity. This scene looks south towards Old Buckley.

(275679)   February 1963   (J.I.C. Boyd)

Plate 24: With the site of the former Locomotive Shed in the foreground, the foot of the climb from Connah's Quay makes a depressing scene. The standpipe is still used for watering engines but access to the Inspection Pit is blocked by a pile of sleepers. The former Buckley Railway climbs towards Northop Hall and in the distance is the chimney of Prince's Brickworks. Hereabouts the former Wepre Iron Road crossed the later railway site from far right to near left.   *(294694)   (A. Brown)*

Plate 25: The chord to the rear of the then-LMSR station at Connah's Quay remains in use for loaded coal wagons awaiting transfer to the North Wales main line. The ex-LNWR stop signal, half hidden by boscage, was unworked: it had a LNWR arm on an ex-GCR lattice post. Note the butchered edges to the brick-work of the low arch of the road overbridge.

June 1946   (J.I.C. Boyd)

Plate 26: At one period the land owned by the WMCQR was marked by Boundary Posts such as this cast-iron specimen at Hope in an adjoining field. Formerly there were many such posts. In certain sites they were replaced by similar cast-iron pieces lettered "G C Ry": one survives today at Hope Village station. *January 1964   (J.I.C. Boyd)*

Plate 27: The approach to Connah's Quay; in the foreground the line divides. Directly ahead there is a connection with the North Wales main line at the rear of Connah's Quay station. Curving right the steep fall and restricted bridge-opening of the line to the quays saw many a runaway: extreme right is the trap siding intended to end the journeys of such runaways. The smoke-encrusted stonework on the right-hand road bridge reveals where the quay shunter stood to protect its crew from wind and rain.

(A. Brown)

Plate 28: The Buckley line fell to the riverside at the Old Dock, seen here before the First World War with a Fleetwood-registered ketch-rigged sailing trawler passing up river; she appears to be towing two shrimp boats. John Summers' wharf lies on the far bank. *(Clwyd Record Office)*

Plate 29: A late 1940s view of the point where the former Buckley Railway debouched onto the quays from under the coastline, taken from the latter railway. The crew of the ex-MS&LR Pollitt Class 5 of 1897 six-coupled saddle tank on duty here (now No. E8200, Class J62) shelter from the drizzle in the quayside hut. Being only 11 ft high to top of chimney, this class could pass under the adjacent bridges; E8200 was withdrawn in November 1951. *(H.F. Wheeller)*

ANNO VICESIMO TERTIO

VICTORIÆ REGINÆ.

****

Cap. lxxxix.

An Act for making a Railway from *Buckley* to *Connah's Quay* in the County of *Flint*, and for other Purposes. [14th *June* 1860.]

WHEREAS the making of Railways from *Buckley* to *Connah's Quay* adjoining the River *Dee* in the County of *Flint*, and also to connect with the *Chester and Holyhead* Railway in the Parish of *Northop*, would be of public and local Advantage: And whereas the Persons herein-after named, with others, are willing, at their own Expense, to carry such Undertaking into execution, but the same cannot be effected without the Authority of Parliament: May it therefore please Your Majesty that it may be enacted; and be it enacted by the Queen's most Excellent Majesty, by and with the Advice and Consent of the Lords Spiritual and Temporal, and Commons, in this present Parliament assembled, and by the Authority of the same, as follows:

I. "The Companies Clauses Consolidation Act, 1845," "The Lands Clauses Consolidation Act, 1845," and "The Railways Clauses Consolidation Act, 1845," (save so far as any of the Clauses and Provisions thereof respectively are expressly excepted or varied by this Act,) shall be incorporated with and form Part of this Act.

8 & 9 Vict. cc. 16. 18. and 20. incorporated.

[*Local*.]   13 Y   II. The

The title page of the Buckley Railway Act, 1860.

The advertisement contradicts the impression that the Buckley Railway was supported and built by the Buckley traders – if it is to be implicitly believed, only one trader had supported and was using it! True, other directors were landowners through whose properties the Railway passed and, other traders had declared their loyalty to, and continuing use of, the 'Aston Tramway Company'.

So the Buckley Railway was opened, and a strange line it was! Although local enterprise was responsible for similar lines (for example, the Brampton Railway, Cumberland) like all such fruits of local energy, the Buckley was an individual and in terms even of railways in the time up to the nationalisation (1948) was – apart from its use of the standard gauge – a most idiosyncratic institution. No better description of it could be made than a quotation from the General Manager of the Manchester, Sheffield & Lincolnshire Railway who paid it a private visit:

> I should think there is no line in the country where there is so lean a mileage as this and where the number of trains are so great unless it belongs to some private company . . . this might be a grand feeding ground if it belonged to a company which went further away . . .

a statement which could only be bettered by John Broughton, then the WMCQR General Manager, who had had 30 years experience in railways:

> The only line which was as difficult to work as the Buckley of which I had experience was the railway going up the Ghats on the Great Indian Peninsular Railway . . .

The ruling gradient of the Buckley line was 1 in 28 and the average grade 1 in 47.

It is now helpful to summarize all that has gone before. The Railway was promoted by those industrialists who were denied the use of the Aston Tramroad or found it indifferent to their needs. The Parliamentary Plans for its main line of 5 miles were drawn up by a local engineer, George Bellis, practising in Mold; he would know the local scene intimately. The initial cost was met by capital of £30,000 with borrowing powers of £10,000 and when the WMCQR made agreement with it on 30th June, 1863, that Company spent a further £66,942 as 'the works and conveniences were in a very incomplete state'. (The WMCQR maintained that even by 1876 they had received no remuneration by way of dividend or otherwise on that expenditure.)

The Buckley rolling stock consisted of but two locomotives and two brake vans – it owned no wagons, all such being provided by the traders who used the line; the stock position remained the same until the WMCQR leased the line from the time of the WMCQR Act of 5th August, 1873. The lease was stated to have been a 'back door' means of silencing WMCQR objections to the Buckley's Bill!

Promoted by local coalowners and traders, and one large landowner (Philip Bryan Davies Cooke of Gwysaney) when it reached Connah's Quay its immediate outlet was a connection to the Chester & Holyhead section of the LNWR. Powers to build shipping places there, though given under the Buckley Act, had not been followed up; it was the WMCQR which was to build them, under the Buckley Act. At the other end of its line, the Buckley Railway had no intention of reaching out further southward.

The gradients of its main line were of a nature to which other engineers might refer as an example of extremes which steam power could negotiate unassisted by cable, rack (or) such as was usually done at that time. Worse was to be found in the sidings and branches to the various traders' premises. These had been built under the inspection of Bellis, the Company's engineer, by the traders themselves (it seems without much knowledge or regard for efficiency) with the exception of two 'sidings' constructed by the Buckley Railway on behalf of traders.* One was to Buckley Colliery under an arrangement whereby the Colliery Co. would find the land and pay 10% of the cost of construction together with a guaranteed level of traffic, and the second 'at the Buckley end' (this is assumed to be Ashton's Branch Siding).

The Company had no buildings, warehouses, goods sheds, stations; there was a small office on the dockside at Connah's Quay.

The tolls were fixed by the directors, who were themselves among the promoters, and this would lead to problems with the incoming WMCQR when working the line in later years.

There was a signalman (not necessarily signals at that time) at the one gated road crossing, known as the Holly Lodge Crossing†; a railway house was provided (at this initial stage, the Brick Co. and its siding did not exist). The hand points were worked by the train crews 'sometimes the fireman'; the train crew consisted of driver, fireman and two guards, the guards acting as brakesmen who ran beside the wagons when the train was on the move if necessary, and operated the wagon hand brakes as required. This practice led to runaways, as will be seen.

Further finance became available under the Buckley Act of 1863, the amounts being the same as originally. The improved shipping arrangements duly provided by the WMCQR included another siding at Connah's Quay and a coaling staith which the Buckley collieries refused to use as there was a fall of 30 feet from wagon (suitably tipped) to the hold of a vessel and this broke the coal into small pieces, making it unsaleable. The staithes were erected to accommodate coal coming from collieries on the WMCQR, and incoming iron ore. Sometimes a whole Shipping Wagon, with load, would fall into a hold.

Had we lived and watched the Buckley system at this period, it would have been borne on us that, despite its rail connection to the LNWR at Connah's Quay, it was a sea-orientated railway; its business depended on sailing ships, tides, winds and the changing channel of the River Dee. Shipping required the Railway to be available when required, but shipping could not always foresee when it would need railway facilities. Storms would close Connah's Quay for days; contrary winds would hold up sailings for days; neap tides would prevent ships from reaching the wharf. The Buckley Railway was indeed an unusual undertaking; it carried goods to and from industries whose owners were also owners of the Railway, and to and from ships many of which were owned by the same people.

---

*A firebrick and tile manufacturer, William Shepherd contemplated a ¾ mile branch from the main line, but it was not built.

†Castle Brick Co. crossing.

(1)

Buckley Railway.

SECRETARY'S OFFICE,

WREXHAM.

_____ *Augt 23rd* 18*71*

Sir,

I beg to inform you that a _____

Meeting of the Board of Directors will be held at *the*

Black Lion Hotel, Mold

previous to the Half-yearly Meeting

on *Saturday* the *26th inst*

at *1. 0* o'clock *PM*

I am, Sir,

Your obedient Servant,

[signature]

J J Kelly Esq Secretary.

Solicitor

Mold

Notice of Board Meeting dated 1871.

From Beginning to End

We left the first section dealing with The Buckley Railway at the time when the WMCQR assumed responsibility for its operation. It is helpful to summarize events to this point, not overlooking that a railway was conceived as early as 1852, 'but we could not find the money in the locality to justify attempting to bring in a Bill'. When notice appeared in THE LONDON GAZETTE on 22nd November, 1859 and a subsequent Enquiry by a Lords' Committee took place, Lord Mostyn put the objective: 'to transport heavy goods to the riverside . . .' and to break the monopoly of the existing tramroad whose charges were unnecessarily high, it being 'perfectly insufficient' for what local industrialists sought.

A short history to 1873 would be: Act of Incorporation 1860: Opening 1862: Working by WMCQR 1866: Leasing by WMCQR for 999 years 1873. In

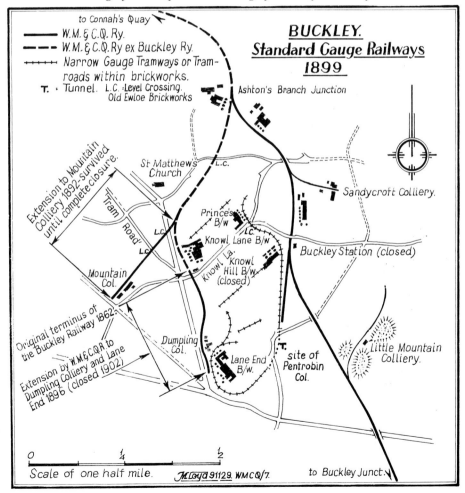

to Connah's Quay

— W.M. & C.Q. Ry.
- - - W.M. & C.Q. Ry ex Buckley Ry.
+++++ Narrow Gauge Tramways or Tram-
roads within brickworks.
T. - Tunnel. L.C. -Level Crossing.

BUCKLEY.
Standard Gauge Railways
1899

Old Ewloe Brickworks
Ashton's Branch Junction

St Matthew's Church   L.C.

Extension to Mountain Colliery 1892 Survived until complete closure.

Tram Road

Sandycroft Colliery.

Princes B/w
L.C.
Knowl Lane B/w
L.C.
Knowl La.
Knowl Hill B/w (closed)

Buckley Station (closed)

Mountain Col.

Original terminus of the Buckley Railway 1862.

Extension by W.M&C.Q.R. to Dumpling Colliery and Lane End 1896 (closed 1902)

Dumpling Col.

Lane End B/w.

T.
site of Pentrobin Col.

Little Mountain Colliery.

0   ¼   ½
Scale of one half mile.   M.Lloyd 91123. WMCQ/7.

to Buckley Junct.

July 1867, due to financial pressures on the WMCQR, Benjamin Piercy had offered to work both railways.

The financial arrangements were that the WMCQR would fund interest on mortgages, pay 4½% annually on Buckley Railway Ordinary and 5% on Preference shares until 1883, and an annual rent of £872.[1] Far from being an extinction of the Buckley concern, it continued in business until it too, was taken over by the GCR on 1st January, 1905 under the GCR Act of 22nd July, 1904. In the meanwhile, the mandatory half-yearly meetings were held – quorum permitting, business was done on the appointed day!

Since the line opened there had been a further Act, 29th June, 1863, to raise further capital: another Act for the same purpose was obtained on 18th May, 1866 and had the additional power to carry passengers, the tolls for whom make amusing reading:

2*d*. per mile in carriages not provided by the Company
3*d*. per mile in carriages provided by the Company

and if either of these categories of carriages was hauled by locomotive, an extra 1*d*. per mile might be charged. In this wise, the Act hinted at revenues which were more commonly raised by railways of the 1820s rather than one of the 1860s.

With an income of partially guaranteed nature, the remainder was linked to the tolls of its users, and from time to time the Company raised additional sums simply by reducing the dividend. Throughout its life it continued to show credit balances.

In the formative years, it makes diverting reading to note what other railway links its proposers/subscribers/directors had. Among the more curious bedfellows were: Aberystwyth & Welsh Coast Railway, Bishop's Castle Railway, Mold & Denbigh Junction Railway, Wrexham, Mold & Connah's Quay Railway, Beddgelert Railway: and that some represented Piercy's Trustees on the board of the WMCQR, another was the solicitor to the Bill for building the Buckley Railway[2] and naturally, many had direct or indirect interests in the land, clay or coal industries of the Buckley area. Another little curiosity was the situation of the Registered Office before 1873; for much of this time its address was The Library, Oswestry: latterly it was at Mold.

In 1870–72 the Reports are made more interesting by the inclusion of the Engineer's Report; this ceases thereafter. In 1871 he said, 'I have this day inspected your Railway and have to report that the rails, sleepers and fencing referred to in my former Reports require further attention.' In 1872 he continued, '. . . renewals are still required . . . are slowly being made . . . fencing in still a very ruinous state – no posts, their remains held up by the wires . . . there are even yet embankment slips at Wepre and Wigbai Brook.'[3]

The Engineer also mentioned locomotives in 1872: 'No. 1 engine which was undergoing repairs at Crewe Engine Works during my last report . . . now at work and in good order. Your No. 2 locomotive would require a considerable expenditure upon her to make her equal to No. 1.' (Clearly a sex-change, as both engines were named after men!)

The same year he refers to the new dock at Connah's Quay, and the extension of staging along the river bank towards Chester 'which will add considerably to the present limited accommodation at the Quay.' A second dock was ready by July 1875.

By 1893 Kyrke and Whitwham were the only Buckley directors on the board of the WMCQR also, and so long before the GCR takeover, the continuing existence of the Buckley Railway was simply a formality.

[A random survey of the outskirts of Southport shows the following Buckley products surviving mainly as footpath tiles, walling and roofing materials: (Titles as marked on the wares).

Birkdale –   'Catherall Ltd., Buckley, Flints.'
Hesketh Park –   'G. Davison & Son'.
Knowsley Road – 'G. Davison & Son'.

In most suburban roads in the Southport and Ainsdale district a wide variety of clay industry products exists; suppliers range from Buckley in the north to Ruabon in the south. These products still display but limited wear.]

Route of the former Buckley Railway (mileages from Buckley Junction signal box)

At Buckley Junction the WMCQR's original line to (Old) Buckley forged ahead whilst the newer Loop Line fell away at 1 in 74 on a righthand curve and down into the cutting: conversely the older railway climbed the bare hillside at 1 in 70, a small colliery to its right (Little Mountain, abandoned by 1886), and towards a forest of chimneys and winding gear on the skyline ahead. Buckley itself was approaching, unmistakeable for its clusters of brick ovens, open-sided buildings, stacks of finished bricks, pipes, and all manner of associated clayware; and many of these buildings, as the railway drew nearer them, could be seen hanging precariously on the cliffs above deep claypits.

From the bowels of such buildings emerged inclined tramways which fell, cable-operated, into the same pits to spew out in all directions on the floor of the excavation. Mixed in amongst this anthill of chimneys, ovens, kilns, waterlogged lagoons of former pits, domestic dwellings and chapels, the Buckley line found its way; branches and sidings made junction with it at a score of trans-shipment platforms, each having a separate identity. And as if variety thereby was insufficient, here and there a coalmine with its winding gear loomed tall among the chimneys of the clay-linked businesses.

So after Buckley Junction and crossing Chester Road on a girder bridge, a signal post with an arm for each direction of running and atop high embankment, came the dour surroundings of the Buckley stretch the WMCQR line reaching it on the hillside ¾ mile from the Junction. Up on slopes on the left came the first and largest concern, the brickworks' complex of William Hancock & Co. with its tramroad emerging from a tunnel to fall down beside a fan of trans-shipment sidings where Hancocks internal trolleys could be loaded onto traders' wagons for onward transport. In the fork between Hancock's Siding and the WMCQR stood a single road engine shed, which by the time of the take over by the GCR had become relegated to a goods

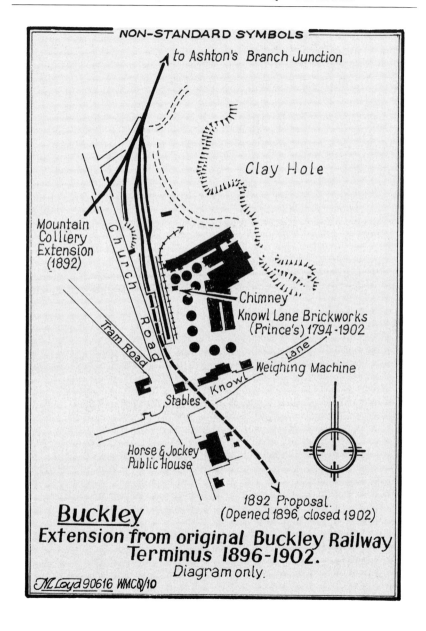

NON-STANDARD SYMBOLS

to Ashton's Branch Junction

Clay Hole

Mountain
Colliery
Extension
(1892)

Chimney

Church Road

Tram Road

Knowl Lane Brickworks
(Prince's) 1794-1902

Knowl Lane

Weighing Machine

Stables

Horse & Jockey
Public House

1892 Proposal.
(Opened 1896, closed 1902)

Buckley
Extension from original Buckley Railway
Terminus 1896-1902.
Diagram only.

N. Loyd 90616 WMCQ/10

shed. Here too, stood two sets of starting signals for Wrexham-bound trains: on the right was the short platform of (Old) Buckley station with its primitive building. Entering a cutting, the line passed under Knowl Lane by brick-arched bridge: on its further side stood a water tank and stand-pipe to supply the branch engine which was based on Connah's Quay to work this section. A stop signal for southbound trains stood here and behind it on the right, the considerable Drury's Brickworks (1 mile) with its loading platform and siding; beyond that platform a branch disappeared to the right to serve Sandycroft Colliery, down at 1 in 264 and 40. Immediately opposite the colliery junction there had been a turntable – this had gone before 1905. On the left, alongside it, was a stop signal to protect northbound trains which had limited sight of the level crossing here. At this crossing – and to the left – was a small claypit with the Methodist (New Connexion) Chapel beside it; a building said to have been built with bricks made from material out of that same pit whose owner was a member of the Chapel!

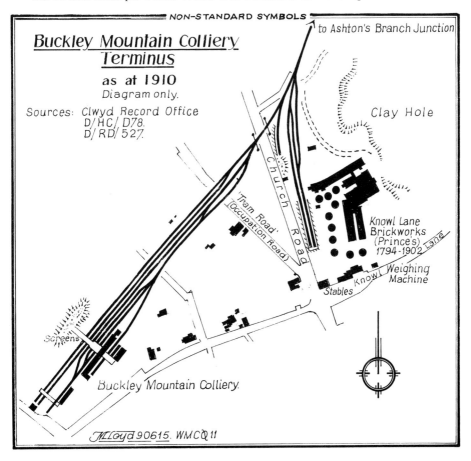

NON-STANDARD SYMBOLS

Buckley Mountain Colliery Terminus

as at 1910
Diagram only.

Sources: Clwyd Record Office
D/HC/ D78.
D/ RD/ 527.

to Ashton's Branch Junction

Clay Hole

Church Road

'Tram Road' (Occupation Road)

Knowl Lane Brickworks (Prince's) 1794-1902

Knowl Lane

Weighing Machine

Stables

Screens

Buckley Mountain Colliery.

J Lloyd 90615. WMCQ 11

Climbing at 1 in 90, to the right of the level crossing stood the Gas Works and siding, and following in quick succession on the same side, the Standard Brick & Terra Cotta Works' siding (1¼ mile), and the Mount Pleasant Colliery siding. Here also was the (level) summit loop*, crossed by a tramway carried by a wooden bridge supported on brick piers. A long fall at 1 in 38/40/38 ensued and cast-iron property boundary 'posts' marked 'WMCQR' were frequently seen.

At the north end of the summit loop the WMCQR proper came to an end where it met the Buckley: it made junction with Ashton's Siding coming in from the left at Ashton's Branch Junction. No evidence of such high-sounding name was visible on the ground – the points were simply controlled by the customary hand lever, often of a pattern also used by the Cambrian Rlys. but initialled 'WMCQR'. Similar evidence of simplicity and economy would be noted in the lack of ballast and paucity of fishplate bolts. A quick glance down Ashton's Siding as it passed by, would reveal the nearby Old Ewloe Brick & Tile Works with its ovens and tramway leading to the loading platform and its own private siding off Ashton's. This Works was one of Davison & Co.'s undertakings. Within a dozen yards another siding (facing our direction of travel) went off to the left into the Works of the Etna Brickworks, a comparatively small enterprise. Opposite it on the righthand side stood the Globe Brickworks (1½ mile) whose platform was helpfully served by a short loopline, making it among the few easy places to shunt! At the loop's north end stood a single signal lever to operate a signal for southbound trains standing near the ensuing Liverpool Road under-bridge; it protected a level crossing immediately ahead. (This crossing was more in the nature of an occupation crossing, and of minor remark.) Beyond it, on the left, with the Railway now up on embankment and curving left, had once stood the Old Ewloe Hall Colliery, closed before 1900, its siding then removed: then on embankment, the Liverpool Road (1¾ mile) was crossed by skewed girder bridge, and the track began a slow righthand curve. Here sidings and platform appeared on the left where Catherall & Co.'s tramway terminated from both the Ewloe Place and Trap Brickworks. Liter-ally feet beyond, there was a facing siding into the Brookhill Brickworks sidings (2 miles) and platform of the Buckley Brick & Tile Co. A tramway from this point led away westwards and south to serve their Belmont Works; these Works had no standard gauge railway connection – nor indeed one by tramroad in former times.

Next on the left hand side came Davison & Co.'s Ewloe Barn Brickworks pit (2¼ miles) followed at once by a facing junction curving sharply away on that side. The yard here was a considerable one, with a greater cluster of buildings etc. than most seen alongside. The Railway, up on embankment again, then crossed the main Ewloe–Mold road by girder bridge: if looking westward here towards Mold, the traveller might see a further railway/road overbridge where the Castle Brick Co.'s railway spanned the highway to gain the Ash Colliery.

Just on the other side of the road bridge, again on the left, another impor-tant feeder curved in to make junction: this was the exit of George

---

*Summit loop was 475 ft a.s.l. (Old Buckley station was actually a few feet higher.) Buckley Junction was approximately 400 ft a.s.l.

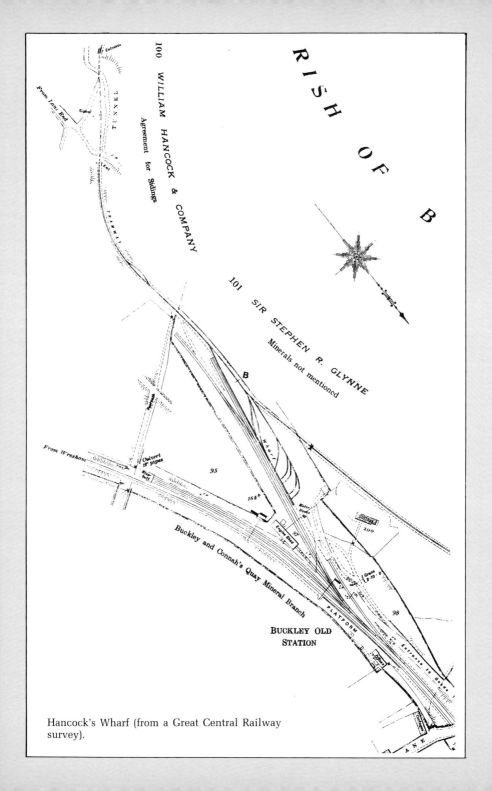

Hancock's Wharf (from a Great Central Railway survey).

Watkinson's mineral railway (*see page 88*) marked by a fan of sidings and evidence of brickworks' activities (2½ miles).

Although it remained to pass one more clay-linked concern, (the Castle Brickworks a few yards further on, also on the left) this bridge marked something of a 'watershed' in the route of the Buckley line. From Buckley Junction the Railway passed continuously through the clay belt with its associated businesses; once beyond the Castle Brick site, this crowded, smoke and smell-laden industrial conglomeration was left behind as quickly as it had been entered. Looking northwards down the still-falling line the Dee estuary can be seen spread out like an apron below: the fields now on either hand give way to towns and industry on the riverside; across the river was the multi-chimneyed steel works of John Summers and the Hawarden Railway Bridge could be seen beside them. Beyond Summers stretched the Wirral peninsula to the left, the Cheshire Plain to the right, with low escarpment at Helsby, then the Kelsall hills and finally to the east, Beeston Tor rising from the horizon. Ahead the eye would reach out over Liverpool to the low line of the Lancashire Pennines. Left again, and Blackpool Tower and seashore can be discerned on a clear day: in the best of weathers, the Lakeland Hills appear. It is a place to put behind one the signs, sounds, and smells of industry, and to plunge down towards the sea! The Railway was about to do just that.

Back on the train: first came a signal to protect the road leading through the Castle premises; a gatehouse was provided here, plus gates themselves, the only instance on the Buckley line. Just prior to the crossing, on the left, a trailing junction was made to the Castle Works; it involved an awkward double-shunt for that Company, using a ridiculously-short headshunt siding.

So over the road crossing, falling 1 in 38 down on embankment and cutting (3 miles) passing the gate signal for southbound trains on the way, the main Chester–North Wales road (avoiding Northop Hall village) was crossed by an interesting timber bridge on a short level length (3¼ miles). On the other side the Railway continued in cutting and very shortly a junction was made on the left hand with the branch from the Dublin Main Coal Co. Nothing could be seen of the Colliery from the Railway as that branch curved out of sight in its own cutting. Here at Dublin, the Railway passed under a brick arch carrying the old main road through Northop Village and, emerging from cutting, reached the Northop Hall Siding (3½ miles), once a depot for local pits where coal could be loaded into railway wagons. Latterly it was little more than a coal delivery yard for local fuel consumption. There was no goods shed, yet this was the nearest place with the slightest hint of being a 'station' on the former Buckley line. Beyond this yard, but still with the siding in the form of a loop alongside, the Railway passed over the road by ungated crossing and entered into a new 'scenic' phase for the remainder of the journey to Connah's Quay. A fall of 1 in 44/33 was now encountered.

Commencing through pastoral countryside, the site of the one-time Broad Oak Colliery on the left could be identified by a flooded area of sunken ground – returned to nature completely. The long siding ended here, joining the running line at a small 'signal box', more in fact an open ground frame with a hut beside it. Each track carried the protection of a trap point before they came together, thus safeguarding the steep fall to the river from runaways from any source. Just beyond the 'box' stood a stop signal which protected both an occupation crossing close by, and also the Northop Hall crossing; the siting of this signal gave upgrade trains in full cry to breast the bank, early warning of these features, especially for those which were *pushing* vehicles in front of the locomotive . . .!

The train now entered a cutting, curving to the right and becoming deeper (4 miles). A platelayers' hut and a cart-track level crossing follow, then the cutting opened out into a wide valley, heavily wooded with large trees and a small winding river alongside – a sudden sylvan setting indeed. Still falling at 1 in 33 the curve now swung leftwards following the wooded dell in Devon-like surroundings but the charms of this unexpected environment would hardly entice the trainmen as they struggled to keep the train in check from a downward hurtle, or urge their locomotives up the hill. Frost would linger on railheads, and leaves would cling to running surfaces in this sheltered place. The grade changed to 1 in 35/30/48 and a final 30 in quick succession: one mile from the Dee the surroundings opened out again and a straight length ensued, ending in a lefthand curve to cross the Mold–Connah's Quay road by skewed girder bridge, and Price's level crossing (4¾ miles).

Curving lefthand, a stop signal marking the approach to Connah's Quay was met and a complex of tracks ensued (5 miles). For many years traces of the former Wepre Iron Road could be identified hereabouts as it came in alongside and merged with its successor. Double track began here. There was a junction into Prince's Brickworks on the right and shortly after, another with T.J. Reney's Central Brickworks on the left – these Works were like a 'detached piece of Buckley!' Opposite the latter Works, and beside the large clayhole of the unconnected Williams' Brickworks, stood the single road engine shed (closed June 1919) which housed motive power for working the Docks and the Buckley mineral line. Beyond this came a small crossing for an occupation road, sited on the last length of straight track; this length ended with a sharp curve to the right. A spur into Charles Davison's Connah's Quay Brickworks bore off to a wharf on the left (5¼ miles); a trap siding then ended the northern side of the double line. Here, the double track ended and, becoming one, the single line divided at once, the line ahead passing a stop signal and then fanning into several sidings as it passed down 1 in 30 under the main Chester–North Wales road, and so into the interchange yard at the rear of Connah's Quay LNWR station (5 m. 17 ch. 50 links) and Connah's Quay West Junction (LNWR). [Closed 28th December, 1954.]

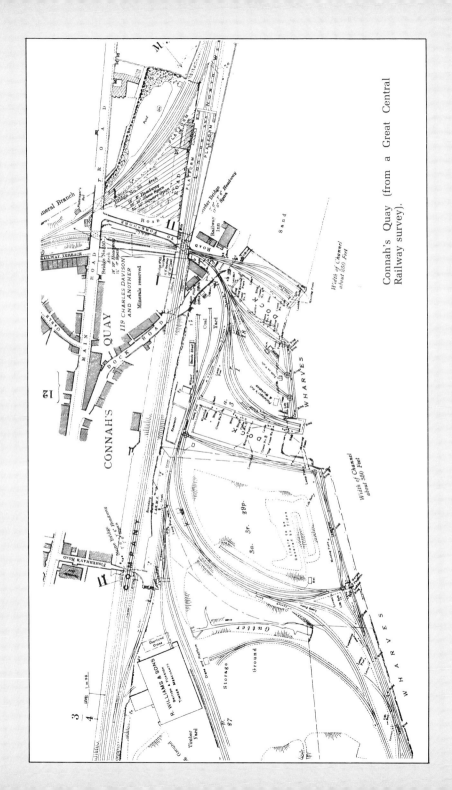

Connah's Quay (from a Great Central Railway survey).

Whilst the bifurcation of the single line gave good access to the LNWR, the righthand track, now running in front of a terrace of houses, ran into problems immediately. But first it threw off a sharply-curved righthand spur to end in a catchpit: thus both tracks were fitted with the means whereby, on whichever line runaway vehicles might approach, they could be turned into trap sidings to prevent them entering a) the LNWR yard or b) running out onto the Quay into the river. In practice, relations with the LNWR were often put to the test in protection of human life; wagons were usually directed into the LNWR yard where they created mayhem but without human fatalities.

Returning to the dockside feeder line with its physical difficulties: it was obliged to fall at 1 in 45/97 by sharp curve of 20 chain radius and in a cutting, under the main road and then under the LNWR's North Wales main line.[4] The former was carried by a stone arch of limited railway dimensions (14 ft span and 12 ft 10 ins. centre height of arch) witnessed by its fractured surface: it had received many a nasty blow and even the occasional locomotive chimney or cab had been dislodged unexpectedly by this means.

Once safely through, the lines fanned out onto the wharves.* There were two docks and an extent of open ground; somewhat simple wharves led alongside the river bank, topped by the inevitable steam crane (at times there had been more than one). Here, the shippers' wagons were relieved of their trolleys (still carrying their claywares) and trolleys loaded into ships. These wharves were much at the mercy of tide and wind; delays were frequent and dredging and tugging were a part of their life. The various drab buildings behind the water's edge had had a miscellany of occupants including chemical, timber and wagon-repairing businesses. The open ground between the sidings, which up to the time when the WMCQR was taken over tended to mushroom in number, though nominally the property of the Railway Company, was like all such places, a dumping ground for those who are employed in deep waters . . . anchors, chains, baulks, skeletal boats which would never put to sea again, masts, spars, ropes, the occasional deckhouse, capstan and so on. Surrounding all, the tang of the open sea not far away, and the 'pong' of rubbish-covered mud as the tides receded. It was a fitting place to end a journey which, beginning in Buckley's dismal surroundings, terminated in that dowdy riverside location.

[Note: Datum for the Buckley section was 94 ft above High Water Mark.]

WORKING THE BUCKLEY SECTION

Something of the flavour of the line at the time of the Enquiry which followed the dispute between The Buckley Traders and the WMCQR, comes from the mouths of the men who spoke at the Enquiry and described their

---

*The Railway Clearing House JUNCTION DIAGRAMS (1915) show an end-on junction from a spur off the dockside tracks to a spur from a trailing connection with the Up – eastbound – LNWR main line. (Connah's Quay East Junction). Evidence suggests this was used but occasionally as between WMCQR and LNWR, being mainly for LNWR access to the Chemical Works.

daily work.* There is no account of working all the sidings, nor indeed of any between Connah's Quay and the Dublin Main siding at Northop Hall. Neither are the brickworks and collieries between Ashton's Siding Junction and Buckley station, mentioned in the evidence. A combination of their evidence and a description of the layouts at this time, follows; the Minutes describe the train operation as between Connah's Quay and Buckley, but the account has been reversed herein so as to pursue the course from source of origin to quayside.

Mountain Colliery (1897–1930)

This colliery was created by George Watkinson & Sons Ltd. and was complementary to their Elm Colliery (q.v.). The sidings formed a second terminal to Ashton's Branch, a junction being made off the Knowl Lane Brickworks line immediately before Church Road which the Mountain Colliery line crossed on the level to enter what were quite the most practical sidings on the Buckley Railway section: this is understandable as they were not laid in until 1897 and by the WMCQR. Between the junction and the Colliery sidings the approach to the Colliery crossed the route of an early tramroad (now known as Tram Road, a residential quarter).

This short branch survived until closure of the system by British Rail in 1964, the sidings having been used by the Elm Colliery as storage yards from 1932.

Note: There is no contemporary account of shunting this yard, it being a development made subsequent to the Buckley Traders' dispute.

Old Knowl Lane Brickworks (c.1794–1902)

This was the original southern terminal of the Buckley Railway. It became one of two termini on Ashton's Branch after the WMCQR made junction with the Buckley Railway at Ashton's Branch Junction.

The original terminus brought the BR to end alongside Church Road and up to the side of Knowl Lane. The considerable Brickworks' claypit lay behind (to the northeast) of the terminus and within that pit was a cluster of narrow gauge tramways with an incline leading out of it. The standard gauge layout was simple to the point of being a problem; hardly convenient to operate and with a short runround, wagons might be coupled to either end of the engine, as was most expedient.

The Brickworks opened in 1792 and had tramroad connections with William Hancock & Co.'s premises further south at Lane End Brickworks (opened 1792). Its original owners were William Leach (Leach & Co.); after other owners it was purchased by Richard Ashton of Liverpool (Ashton & Co.) in March 1841, and by Frederick and Richard Herbert Prince when Richard Ashton died in 1867. Owners in 1888 included John Bales Gregory and Thomas Kenyon, plus the Prince brothers. The works closed in 1902.[5]

The connection to the Buckley Railway was made early in 1863, Ashton providing 1½ acres for building the branch and sidings.[6] There was an

---

*The practice of railway shunting has virtually disappeared. The methods used herein became outmoded as regulations on safety were increased by law: some dangerous practices used on the Buckley line did not survive – officially – after World War I.

extension southward (existing 1896–1902) serving Lane End (or Dumpling) Colliery, leased by Prince from W.E. Gladstone for 21 years from 1st January, 1892 'to connect Prince's Colliery works with the railway siding in Buckley called Ashton's Siding . . . stone shed, men's cabin and stable, barn and cart shed to be removed and re-erected on adjoining land . . .' Annual rent £100.

Shunting at the Brickworks was described as 'difficult and we have to shift any LNWR wagons out of the way and go inside if there are any wagons for Connah's Quay. It takes us 5–20 minutes.'

The Brickworks had its own 8 ton wagons, with single chain and hook couplings and dumb buffers.

During the latter time of Ashton, they owned 'a ship, a flat cutter named OLD ENGLAND'. There was considerable crossing of interests here as in other local concerns; Richard Ashton was one of the principal investors in the Ewloe Hall Colliery Co.

In 1890 the Prince brothers took a 21 year lease of the Etna Brickworks from Thomas Richard Popplewell; but by 1902 Frederick Prince was unable to pay interest on the mortgage, and as the property was less in value than the mortgage, that and the Etna lease was conveyed to George Watkinson, the local colliery proprietor, who under an Agreement, did not re-open. In 1907 most of the property was sold to Wm. Hancock & Co. Ltd. The 'stop' on brickmaking was to continue.

Wm. Hancock & Co. (Ltd.)

The Company had brickworks at Lane End and Buckley Junction: the former had no direct standard gauge rail link but its own tramway to Hancock's Siding on the Buckley section of the WMCQR. In partnership with John Rigby ('ironmaster and chemical works proprietor of Hawarden'), Hancock founded Wm. Hancock & Co. in 1792 and constructed a tramroad to join Dundas' Aston Tramroad to give access to the river (see page 41). Owners of several ships.

For many years in the mid-19th century, this firm was the largest brick-making undertaking in the whole of Wales. The Company was purchased by the Castle Fire Brick Co. Ltd. in 1956.

Old Ewloe Brick & Tile Works (Charles Davison & Co.)

This brickworks had opened about 1862 and was owned by Charles Davison & Co. Its siding lay on the lefthand of Ashton's Branch at the approach to Ashton's Branch Junction.

Davisons had the customary tramway linking clay pit and kilns: it also brought internal narrow gauge wagons ('boxes') to a wharf where they could be run onto a flat-topped transporter which ran the length of the wharf on rails. Loaded with the small trucks, the transporter could move to the point where a Buckley Trader's wagon stood; the small trucks would then be run off onto the Trader's wagon.

Of working the siding it was said

> . . . We only call here if required, and then only for one truck or two. We often stop for one truck and have to wait while they finish loading it, it takes three minutes to

pick up a wagon if it is ready loaded. Sometimes we have to wait for a brake to be altered and that takes 10 minutes. By now the main line is on an incline. They may have 9–10 trucks when they draw out of the siding; we have to put them out with a stick or pole, the engine running on one set of rails, and the wagons on another; the propping is up an incline.

In a later examination the WMCQR Inspector said

We usually take the wagons out from this siding with the engine; they are generally loaded. If they want a shunt made we generally make it, in the case of the empties that are beyond a lot of empties with the diamonds* we have to shunt them out. If there are LNWR empties in front of full ones, we have to do it in case the vessel at Connah's Quay is waiting and they want the stuff to go down there for them.

One may hope the Enquiry understood what it was all about!†

Etna Brickworks

Immediately beyond Ashton's Branch Junction came the siding of Ashton's Etna Brickworks. Photographs of the siding in 1876 show it to have been roughly laid, with severely damaged rails and track much out of alignment – perhaps materials were secondhand when installed? At first there was nothing to prevent vehicles running out of the siding unattended and fouling the main line, but by 1905 a trap point had been fitted. There is little reference to the contemporary working of this siding other than it was noted that the points for it faced Buckley.

The brickworks was opened by John Royle & Son in the first half of the 19th century and then had tramroad links. The GCR Plans of the line show the Works as closed in 1905, and that 'Messrs. Davison pay £1 1s. 0d. for the use of its siding'.

Globe Brickworks

Within yards of the junction for the Etna Siding came the summit loop; alongside it was the loading platform of Davison's Globe Brickworks. Here the railway was 475 ft above sea level and in the immediate period before the line closed the loop was laid with WMCQR chairs.

Old Ewloe Hall Colliery

There were two (parallel) sidings here raised on an embankment on the left of the line just before it crossed Liverpool Road by a bridge. Working this place was straightforward: the wagons could be left standing on the main line whilst the engine, detached, ran forward over the points and set back into the Colliery sidings. 'We go back and catch hold of 10, 12, or 14 or whatever the number is and back them up the siding onto the train' – which though an actual quotation, is not exactly what the shunter meant!

The Census of 1861 shows Edward Parry as Manager: he had a financial interest in it (see also Parry's Brickworks).

---

*LNWR wagons had white diamonds painted on their sides for recognition.

†[The Davisons hailed from the Deeside area. Thomas (farmer and collier of Aston and Shotton) died in 1815. His eldest son Charles (1794–1848) had a son Charles (1822–1908) who created the family brickworks and was also a shipowner. Several other male members of the family were mariners and river pilots.][7]

It had closed before the GCR made its survey of the line in 1904. On the site of it the survey shows the shaft as 'ruin'; the only other feature is 'Chimbley', (the local vernacular exactly as spoken!)

Catherall's Brickworks

This was one of those typical Buckley Railway sidings which were laid out with little comprehension of the difficulties the trainmen would have in working it. The premises were to the left of the line and access was through a trailing point for Down trains, where there was a wharf line ending in two remarkably short stubs. At an angle to the wharf was a fan of tramroad (plateway) lines which gave high-level loading into the standard gauge wagons. These tramroad lines converged to make a cross-country connection built between 1871 and 1882 which led to the Ewloe Place and Trap Brickworks; at the standard gauge siding itself, the wharf was simply a stockyard for the finished products of that Brickworks.

By 1876 the siding appears to have been but one single road against the wharf. At that time it was the practice of the shunters to work the siding in conjunction with the Buckley Brick & Tile Co.'s siding which was entered by a facing junction a few yards below Catherall's connection. It was said: 'We pick up brick and tile wagons and prop out Buckley Brick & Tile Co. traffic into Catherall's Siding – it takes 5–7 minutes to work Catherall's Siding dependent on the number of wagons you have to bring out in the boxes and Traders. If you have a big load you have to prop them out upon the road and catch hold and have a run with them to get them up the incline.'

So there we have it!

The Trap and Ewloe Place Brickworks both lay some distance from the Buckley Railway; they were opened before 1800: original connection was by tramroad, and Lane End.

Buckley Brick & Tile Co.

The position of this siding relative to Catherall's Brickworks siding has been mentioned, and the junction points faced Buckley. There were two parallel sidings with a loading platform on one; the usual travelling trolley was used, onto which the loaded narrow gauge tramway trucks could be run, and then the trolley moved along to the particular Trader's wagon onto which the loaded trucks were pushed. There was a disused overhead loading gantry built with timber staging, but the siding which passed under this erection had been lifted before 1876; presumably the transfer platform took its place.

The account of shunting procedure said 'We have to sort loaded and labelled wagons from the empties. We have to stop on the incline and brake down the train at this point' i.e. apply a number of handbrakes to a portion of wagons in the train to restrict its speed down into Connah's Quay.

The BB & T Co was incorporated in February 1865 and was one of several enterprises set up on the Gwysaney Estate (P.B. Davies-Cooke) where the fireclay belt was near the newly-opened railway. In reality there were two works, the 'Upper Works' or Belmont, and the 'Lower Works', Brookhill.

Belmont was unprofitable, it was off the railway and needed coal carting to it and finished goods carting away. Unable to sell Belmont, a tramway was built to link it with the railway in 1871 during a time when trade was better. The Company was frequently at odds with the WMCQR over wagon shortages and at one time maintained the Railway was giving preference to Hancock's. Wagons were hired from 'The Birmingham Wagon Co.' and North of England Wagon Co.'. The Company owned a ship, PROBLEM, bought in 1869.

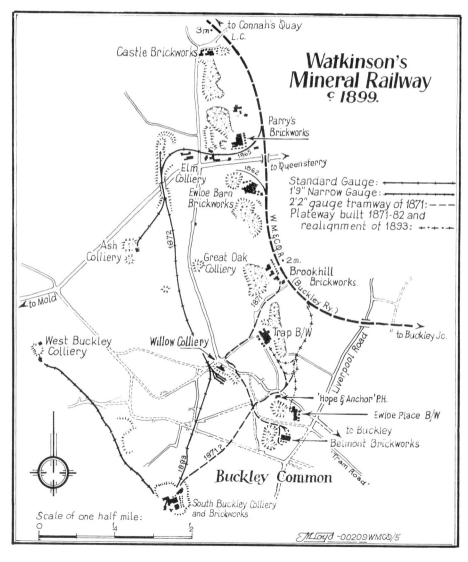

The tramway route was based on plans from G.A. Bell of Chester, dated 28th August, 1868.[8] It was to run via Willow Colliery to Brookhill with passing places and sidings, to a gauge of 2 ft 2 in. Horse traction (and 'a small locomotive' later) was envisaged. The idea was postponed in November 1868 and in October 1870 Catherall's were offered 2d. ton to use their tramway: Catherall's wanted 3d. or £40 p.a. rental.

In December 1870 John Meakin (called in to advise) recommended a tramway via Willow Colliery; the line to begin at a large kiln on the south side of Belmont, cross Buckley Common near Willow Colliery and terminate by the first kiln at Brookhill. The line was to be worked by a contractor for 3d. ton. In February 1871 the Meakin scheme was agreed upon and the tramway was at work by March 1871. It used 20 lb./yard rails on wooden sleepers and was inclined at 1 in 23.

Production was much affected by water shortages and in August 1884 Brookhill – always short of water in the summer – received it in casks carried by tramway from Belmont.

Shipments from Connah's Quay included Ireland, Bristol, Portsmouth and Workington.

Belmont was abandoned in 1913; the clay was exhausted.

The Company passed to the Castle Brick Co. in 1940 but Brookhill itself did not close until 1961.

Ewloe Barn Brickworks (Charles Davison & Co. Ltd.)

Though opened in 1847 this brickworks always suffered from an absence of tramroad or railway connections, having to cart down to Lower Ferry at great expense and inconvenience. It was therefore no surprise when the Davison family gave strong backing to the building of the Buckley Railway, and the siding was put in at the opening of the Buckley Railway. It curved westwards off that line, with junction points facing Buckley. The 1876-method of working was in effect that used for a very short branch line:

> We hook off the engine and go up on the siding and get loaded wagons out. It depends on the way they are loaded – some are loaded at one end and some at the other: I can only get out of the siding one way. If there are a good many wagons I cannot get out. If there are only two we can get out at the other end but if there are two at one end and two at the other we have to go round and prop the others out. And if there are any Wrexham wagons we have to pull the whole lot out and make two or three chumps of them on the main line, and prop them in again. Sometimes it takes more or less 15 minutes. I have been there 35−40 minutes with eight loaded wagons when it has been slippery. It is a difficult siding to work out of. Some traffic goes to Connah's Quay, some the other way occasionally.

Which all goes to demonstrate there was a lack of experience by those who laid out the line!

Davison's Works at Buckley were later owned by two brothers named Hurlbutt – they were the main local competitors of the Castle Fire Brick Co. Originally working for Davisons themselves, they had come from Staffordshire and married into the Davison family. They had clayholes at Ewloe and Buckley.*

Charles Davison & Co. Ltd. (Hurlbutt) was sold to General Refractories of Sheffield shortly after World War I. The site was closed in 1976.

*Notes supplied by Brian Lewis to J.S. Wilkinson.

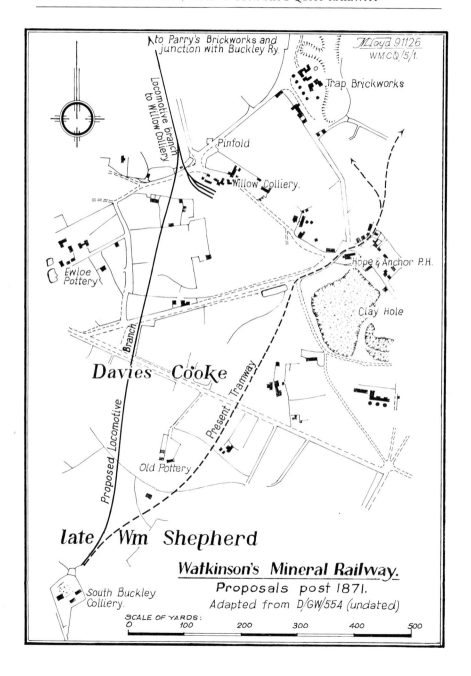

to Parry's Brickworks and junction with Buckley Ry.

J. Lloyd 91126
WMCQ/5/1.

Trap Brickworks

Locomotive branch to Willow Colliery

Pinfold

Willow Colliery.

Hope & Anchor P.H.

Ewloe Pottery

Clay Hole

Branch

Davies – Cooke

Present Tramway

Proposed Locomotive

Old Pottery

late Wm Shepherd

Watkinson's Mineral Railway.
Proposals post 1871.
Adapted from D/GW/554 (undated)

South Buckley Colliery.

SCALE OF YARDS:
0   100   200   300   400   500

Buckley Colliery, Main Coal Colliery and Parry's Brickworks
(or 'Watkinsons – Parry & Main & Cannel Co.')

In the journey from Buckley to Connah's Quay, and immediately after the junction to Ewloe Barn Brickworks, came a trailing junction from the above concerns, their individual track layouts coming into one set of pointwork.

There were numerous titles for the brickworks etc. at this place, but after 1873 the longest owners involved were Edward Parry & Sons Ltd. (Edward Parry himself died in 1873) and the Watkinson family. The Parry family had origins in Ireland. Other local names included 'The Main Coal & Cannel Co.' and 'Watkinson's'. The junction was first made for Parry's use when they opened for business after 1862; Parry signed a lease with the Buckley Railway in June 1862 giving him the right to build sidings to the new railway: the firm remained in business under the title Edward Parry & Sons Ltd.[9] until merged with the Castle Brickworks in 1957. Edward Parry himself had been Manager of Old Ewloe Hall Colliery immediately prior to setting up the Brickworks: trading here ceased about 1969. An extension of Parry's siding running past coke ovens, was built around 1872 by the Watkinsons, and ultimately extended southwards* to the South Buckley Colliery & Brickworks.[10] Watkinson's had their own steam locomotives for working this system; occasionally they worked over the Buckley Railway itself when they were short of engine power; most other local firms used horses where it was necessary to bring their wagons to and from their junction with the Buckley Railway.

It was said of working this siding (the Railway Company was obliged to enter it no further than to pick up and set down wagons) . . .

> We have some difficulty; they go as far to the very back end of the siding past the offices, often pushing LNWR wagons for them to drop in and load. Sometimes they cannot get in because Watkinson's wagons are upon the road, Watkinson's leaving empty wagons in the way.

Watkinson's Siding

> This siding provided the heaviest traffic on the line.

> There are often between 30–40 wagons here to sort; it needs 15–20 minutes. The main line here at the junction is 1 in 38 and 1 in 91; connections off the junction siding are made on Buckley Company's property.†

In the case between the Traders and the WMCQR, the latter maintained they had no legal obligation to shunt beyond the boundary of their property and this was upheld. Parry had no shunting horses, relying entirely on the WMCQR to do his internal work for him.‡

> Empty wagons have to be propelled up 1 in 52 for 500 yards before they can get onto Parry's Siding (1876).

---

*See page 84 for a map of this private mineral line.

†There was a gate across the rails dividing the railway properties.

‡According to Mr Peers, interviewed in his 90th year and a former employee, after World War I Parry employed a number of shunting horses – these may have been introduced to answer the Railway Company's limits of obligation demands.

Buckley Collieries – George Watkinson & Sons Ltd (Buckley Colliery Co. Ltd.)

George & Samuel Watkinson trading as George Watkinson & Sons Ltd. (founded 1836) possessed large wool-stapling interests in Halifax, Yorkshire, and went into the coalmining business in North and South Wales; the firm was registered in Cardiff.

Their coal interests came about when – in the case of the South Wales ventures – John Crossley of Halifax, who in conjunction with Messrs. John and Mark Oldroyd of Dewsbury, (trading as Crossley & Co. and The Fernhill Coal Co.) completed two shafts in the Rhondda Valley to be known as Fernhill Collieries. Their interests were sold to George Watkinson & Sons Ltd. in 1877: Watkinson was already operating at Buckley. In 1893, on the reversion of the lease of the nearby Dunraven Colliery, both properties came into Watkinson's control and they acquired a lease which would take them to 1926. THE SOUTH WALES COAL ANNUAL for 1911 describes this as a 'half-hearted enterprise' which had ended when Watkinson sold out to new owners in 1910, and the 'property entered one of enlightened development'! (The ANNUAL relied on the goodwill and support of the local collieries for its existence, needless to say!)

John Watkinson, youngest of four sons of George, came to the Buckley area in the late 1860s and built a residence for himself in 1872, Brook Park, at Northop Hall (this had formerly been a farm; and later became the Chequers Hotel). The first acquisition was the Willow Colliery (a drift mine?) followed by Maesygrug shortly afterwards. New work began at what was to be called Elm Colliery, where shafts were sunk (rather than the adits of the drift mines) in 1876, dubbed No. 1 and No. 2, a third, No. 3, was sunk in 1894; between them they were the largest coal mines and No. 3, at over 1,000 feet deep, was the deepest in the district.

Maesygrug had a chequered career, opening and closing more than once, and opening for the last time just after World War I but unsuccessfully, being heavily 'watered' and it was allowed to 'drown out' in 1921. Elm No. 1 closed in 1934.

Watkinson was an important supplier of steamer coal to the City of Dublin Steam Packet Co. at Holyhead, and the family business continued until March 1920 when John Summers & Co. Ltd. of Shotton acquired the remaining pits. Considering there to be good coal still available, and having spare generating capacity at their steelworks, Summers built an overhead transmission line sited alongside the Buckley Railway section, and electrified the surviving pits, Elm and Mountain, later also doing the same at Bannel which they acquired in 1923 but finding it loss-making owing to water difficulties, it was closed in 1923. Elm was converted to brickmaking by Summers. John Watkinson died in 1907.

Mountain Colliery was a shaft which led down into a long underground roadway extending southwards from Elm No. 1 with a horse-worked tramway. Much coal was taken up to the surface here for carriage by rail from the branch mineral line off Ashton's Siding laid in 1892. Mountain opened in 1897 and closed in 1930.

Watkinson built a private mineral railway from the end of the ex-Buckley Railway branch to the Elm pits, taking it across the Mold–Ewloe road to serve Ash and Willow Collieries (both drift mines) in 1872, and extending it southwards to South Buckley Colliery & Brickworks under wayleaves in 1883 and 1889.* (From the last-named a horse tramway on narrow gauge was laid across to the West Buckley Colliery in the early years of the 20th Century.)

At times of severe locomotive shortage, Watkinson's engine was permitted to work over the ex-Buckley Railway with his wagons: this would naturally be when a ship was held up at Connah's Quay and this emphasises the central factor running throughout the annals of the BR and WMCQ Railways and their tramroad predecessors – that all were operated with the end in view of loading ships which were at the mercy of tide and wind, no less the vagaries of the shifting channels of the Dee Estuary.

Watkinson obtained his wagons under the traditional methods of the times – by hire. He used The Western Wagon Co. Ltd. of Bristol for twenty 8 ton capacity wagons in June 1875 for a period of 7 years for an annual sum of £243 15s. 0d. (these being for the Fernhill Colliery, in fact). For Buckley he had 55 wagons built by Metropolitan Wagons Co., Cardiff, for 5 years from May 1880 @ 37/6d. per wagon per year. There is a note on the Agreement that the firm was working coal near Owen Jones, Soughton Hall, Northop Hall, and trading as Buckley Collieries 'near Chester'. A last example is an Agreement with Gloucester Wagon Co. Ltd. for twenty 8 ton wagons for 3 years from October 1881. At the end of the contract, the wagons were to be returned to Chester.

A typical contract between the firm and the City of Dublin Steam Packet Co. is dated 1st September, 1891 to deliver 150 tons of 'Main' coal daily at Holyhead, for two years (as previous contract). [Watkinson's seal on this contract shows a colliery and a 2–2–2 tender locomotive.][11]

Though after the WMCQR as such had disappeared, Watkinsons sought agreement to use certain Great Central Railway sidings at their old Knowl Lane Brickworks, and at their (Buckley) Mountain Colliery (*diagram page 73*) but the draft contract inspected has not been signed. In 1932 the sidings at Mountain Colliery (itself closed) were used by arrangement for Elm Colliery purposes, the wagons being brought from Elm itself. Agreement was made with the London & North Eastern Railway.

Again, a GCR-period matter, the short-lived Bannel Colliery was given sidings at the coal screens southwest of Bannel Bridge, just to the south of Buckley Junction station; the work was done by the Railway Co. under Agreement dated 2nd December, 1920.

Castle Brickworks

This was a trailing junction for trains descending to Connah's Quay, the points coming awkwardly just before the only gated level crossing on the line; this caused trains to block the crossing whilst shunting. It was made more difficult as, whilst the siding itself formed a loop of moderate length with a very short headshunt beyond it, the siding was little more than a

*Owing to a difference in levels, Great Oak Colliery could not be connected.

reversing neck to enter the Brickworks' yard proper; it was in fact necessary to do a double shunt to extract wagons from the yard onto the main line.

Photographs of the layout in 1876 show the railheads had worn down excessively; the track was laid in the S-shaped base chairs so widely used in the 1860s. The Brickworks did not open before 1865 so the single-gated crossing and the gatehouse on the Buckley Railway were both already in existence. The Brickyard was owned by The Castle Brick Co. who were ultimately bought out by John Summers & Son.

To work the siding, the engine was detached on the Down run; the siding had been laid by the Brick Co. at its own expense but with approval of the WMCQR Engineer. It was the practice to return from Connah's Quay with the wagons for this undertaking propelled in front of the engine, and 'fly shunt them'* into the siding. Loaded wagons were left standing 30–40 yards inside, the marshalling of wagons being done by the Brick Co. with its own horses. The point of junction was made where the mainline was 'dropping at 1 in 35' (given elsewhere as 1 in 39) but the siding was nearly level; it was approximately 180 yards long.

Castle Brick Co. wagons of the Traders' type 'were especially prone to heavy wear and tear due to continuous brake applications on the incline', so it was stated; though why they should suffer more than others is not clear.

Castle Fire Brick Co. was established as a private concern by G.H. Alletson in 1865 – became Limited within a decade and in that year (1875) the Company owned:

> Castle Brickworks
> Plas Bellin Colliery
> Northop Hall Colliery & Tramway

and of its seven directors, five came from Waterford, one from Kilkenny whilst Alletson of Northop was the seventh. The Irish connection and suggestion of new finance with distant control is interesting; perhaps their holding was only nominal and most were customers and shippers – the man from Kilkenny was the Accountant.[12]

Coal for its own use was obtained from its own Elm[13] and Buckley Collieries. Among its other (local) ownerships with date of acquisition in brackets, were:

> Catherall's Firebrick Works   (1936)
> Buckley Brick & Tile Co.   (1940)
> Edward Parry & Sons Ltd   (1944)
> William Hancock & Co. Ltd   (1956)

The Alletson family (many were Quakers) had strong Irish family links.

John Summers & Sons purchased the whole undertaking in 1916 in order to acquire the whole output of its silica bricks for their No. 2 Steelworks then being erected at Shotton.

---

*'Loose-shunt' was the correct term.

Dublin Main Colliery Co. Ltd. (etc).

This was another trailing junction for trains proceeding to Connah's Quay: the siding was not laid in until c.1874 when the Colliery Co. (which had been registered in 1873) began production. The coalyard layout consisted of workable loops to pass wagons around each other; the train crew had less trouble here than anywhere else. The siding split into two just after the junction (originally controlled by a simple boxed lever) and there were scotches on the splitting points' blades to derail runaways; it was 1 furlong 44 yards long.

The men 'never have much trouble here . . . a tolerably good siding and one of the best on the railway . . . the two roads are used alternately to handle full or empty wagons'. The Coal Company's wagons bore 'Empty to Connah's Quay WM&Chs Qy Rly'.

To facilitate return of empty wagons, it was the practice to propel them in front of the engine (and in front of any empties for Castle Brick Co. – just mentioned) so that they could be loose-shunted into the colliery premises without the locomotive entering the siding.

The coal seams at Galchog, Northop Hall, Dublin, Merllyn and around, had been worked in various places in the district before the coming of the Buckley Railway; [the earliest enterprise has received mention under the Wepre Iron Road (*page 35*).] From then until the Buckley line appeared, such workings were exploited by various owners, none with lasting success. Most of these had the use of the plated tramroad and at the time of the building of the Buckley Railway that tramroad was protected and possibly remained in operation during its first years, clearly an uneconomic position for both parties. However, whilst the tramroad clawed its way out to the various pits, the railway did not, and it was necessary to cart coal to Northop Hall Siding, involving double handling and coal breakages; in this respect the tramroad was preferable.

In February 1859 The Northop Hall & Dublin Coal Co. Ltd. was formed (Registered Office, Cooper Street, Manchester): a letter (25th January, 1860) from Jos. Rowley and R. Stephenson (solicitors of 29 Booth Street, Manchester) – the former an ex-shareholder in the 'Northop Hall Coly.' – to Wm. Southall of Lansdowne Place, Bath (presently a director of that concern) points out that the NH&DC Co. now has liabilities of £5,500 and that the National Provincial Bank, Manchester, is very impatient for its repayment. Rowley recommends not winding-up, but working the coal on the Dublin Estate and forming a new Company with £3,000 capital to buy the property; a further £15–20,000 would then be needed 'for re-opening out of the Dublin Colliery'. It appears that the Dublin workings at this juncture were drowned out but fresh borings had proved there were 50–60 acres of Hollin Coal which Cottingham (the surveyor) valued at £24,000, and 'it could be worked over two years'.

Such a letter is typical of the intermittent workings of these small ventures. So is the board of directors – Haigh, Mellor, Haworth and Forwood of Liverpool, Rowley of Hale Barns, two Dugdales of Manchester, Shipman of Lymm, Southall of Mold (who moved to Bath at this time) and Bailey of Blackburn, i.e. not one of them was locally resident. They relied on their local Manager Roper, 'a most difficult man to deal with who suggests they set up a brickyard; the local coal is so faulty, but they have hit upon a bed of clay never been found before in the district'. This discovery was not to be revealed to an outsider.

This correspondence[14] contains the only known reference to a narrow gauge tramway which is marked on later OS maps, connecting the coal pits near 'Northop Hall' (also known as Merllyn) and leading down to the roadside just northwest of Northop Hall Siding but not apparently entering the railway yard there. [This tramway formation can still be traced where the ground has not been disturbed by recent pipe works.] Southall received a letter from Shipman (also of Booth Street) dated 25th March, 1863 saying that the colliery at Merllyn Pits is now so very far advanced that 200 tons of coal can be raised each day, but that the local sale is not above 35 tons a day. 'It is therefore necessary to provide means of transport . . . by a railway from the colliery to the Buckley Railway – say a mile at £1,500 – or a tramway for small trucks might be made for about £750 but there are decided objections to this on the score of inconvenience, breaking of coal and constant expense . . . desirable immediately to make the Railway . . . The water in the Dublin pits is sinking, due to a new colliery at Buckley . . . all this would be a great advantage to us.' All these pits were part of an area already leased to Rigby and Hancock, with the right to extract coal etc.

On 15th November, 1865 a Galchog & Northop Hall Colliery Co. Ltd. was registered and featured in an advertisement on 24th November, 1868 as being on the market.[15] Which pits were to be worked and if the Company had been active, is not clear.

The Official List of Mines for 1873 includes 'Galchog Colliery Co. Ltd., Galchog, Northop (2 pits).'

In 1875 the Castle Brick Co. became owners of 'Plas Bellin Colliery' and the 'Northop Hall Colliery and tramway' (i.e. Wepre Iron Road): the former were isolated pits northwest of the Merllyn pits – perhaps they were purchased from The Northop Hall & Dublin Coal Co. Ltd?

It was January 1870 before a decision was made to work the Dublin site which was close by the Buckley line at Northop Hall Siding. A Share Certificate of this enterprise has the seal showing a miner wielding a pick. But the venture under this title was shortlived; The Dublin Main Colliery Co. was formed on 25th April, 1873 'to acquire the colliery held under lease from Wm. Hancock & Others'.[16] It liquidated on 23rd October, 1879 and was sold to Messrs. A.B. and Jos. Rowley for the bargain price of £1,500 – perhaps they hoped for a quick sale? The Final Meeting was 21st September, 1880. (Coal continued to be extracted from these local pits until at least the onset of World War I; much of the surface area was later worked for open-cast coal).

In considering the traffic of the Buckley section it is evident that the clay trade – with its differing products – relied on these local pits for their coal, but that the pits themselves were plagued with problems, and did not offer the Buckley Railway the continuity of tonnages which the clay-orientated businesses did: by 1900 there were a dozen such.[17]

Summing up the situation at Northop Hall Siding; it is apparent that for a period after opening, the 'Iron Road' deprived it of some coal business, but at irregular times it was visited by carts from the following local pits:

Plas Bellin
Galchog
Merllyn
Northop Hall

Connah's Quay

> We do not put the traffic down at the side of the steamer – we put them on the bank.

By leaving the wagons for both the LNWR interchange sidings and the Quay 'on the bank', they could gravitate wherever they were needed; a locomotive would only be required when empty wagons had to be taken Up. There would be a limited amount of Up loaded traffic. Shunting horses were employed by the Railway on the wharves.

References

[1] Clwyd Record Office: OS/DR/47.
[2] Clwyd Record Office: D/GW/B/107. Frequently given as 'The Buckley & Connah's Quay (Flints.) Railway'.
[3] Clwyd Record Office: D/KK/59.
[4] National Library of Wales: Piercy Papers (Fraser 576).
[5] Clwyd Record Office: BUCKLEY No. 7 (1982).
[6] Clwyd Record Office: D/NC/D78–81.
[7] Clwyd Record Office: BUCKLEY No. 7 (1982) page 15–19.
[8] Clwyd Record Office: D/GW/B/622.
   Clwyd Record Office: BUCKLEY No. 8 (1983) page 24; No. 9 (1984) page 34; No. 10 (1985) page 10.
[9] Clwyd Record Office: BUCKLEY No. 5 (1979) page 23.
[10] Clwyd Record Office: BUCKLEY No. 12 (1987) page 34.
[11] Clwyd Record Office: D/HC/D71–81.
[12] Clwyd Record Office: BUCKLEY No. 6 (1981) page 25; No. 9 (1984) page 32.
[13] Clwyd Record Office: D/DM/355/21.
   Formerly one of Watkinson's pits (which later became a brickworks in the ownership of Castle Brick Co. Ltd.). Sold to Castle Brick Co. Ltd. in March, 1920.
[14] Clwyd Record Office: Keen & Kelly, D/KK/1044.
[15] Clwyd Record Office: D/HA/1031.
[16] Information per Public Record Office, Kew.
[17] Clwyd Record Office: BUCKLEY No. 11 (1986) page 34 on deals with Trade Associations, rivalries, disputes, members, working conditions, discord with the Railway Company etc.

Note: There was some mining on the 1873 Dublin Main site which was connected more conveniently to the Wepre Iron Road. Possibly 'Merllyn', 'Plas Bellin' and 'Northop Hall' were in fact a collective name for the same group of pits: 'Galchog' had several pits, and 'Dublin' probably embraced Rowley's Shaft and others whose sites are still visible but enquiry has failed to determine their names.

29° & 30° VICTORIÆ, Cap. ccclix.

The Wrexham, Mold, and Connah's Quay Railway (Extensions) Act, 1866.

The SCHEDULE herein-before referred to.

HEADS for an ARRANGEMENT between the Wrexham, Mold, and Connah's Quay Railway Company (the Company) and the Partnership called the Buckley Railway Company, in respect of their Leasehold Interest in the Aston Tramway belonging to Mr. Dundas and Messieurs William Hancock and Company in respect of their Right of Use of that Tramway, and Mr. Dundas (an Infant and a Ward of the Court of Chancery) as Owner of that Tramway, and Mrs. Dundas and Mr. Houblon as his Guardians appointed by the Court.

1. These Heads to be subject to the Sanction of Parliament, and, if Parliament permit, to be scheduled to and confirmed by the intended Wrexham, Mold, and Connah's Quay Railway (Extensions) Act, 1866.

2. The Arrangement, so far as the Interests of the Infant are concerned, to be subject to the Approval of the Court.

3. The Company to accommodate and convey on their Railway the Traffic usually conveyed on the Tramway.

4. Until that Traffic be so accommodated and conveyed the Tramway to be maintained and used as at present.

5. When due Provision made by the Company for the Accommodation and Conveyance on the Railway of that Traffic, the Tramway on their Request to be closed and permanently disused.

6. The Compensation to be made by the Company to the Parties interested in the Tramway, whose Rights are prejudicially interfered with by the Company, and whether in Money or in Facilities for Traffic, or partly in Money and partly in Facilities for Traffic, or otherwise, to be, if not agreed on, determined by Arbitration.

7. The Compensation to be made by the Company in respect of the Lands of Mr. Dundas taken by them under the intended Act, and all Damage by Severance, Execution of Works, or otherwise, to the rest of his Estate, and whether in Money or in Works, or partly in Money and partly in Works, or otherwise, to be, if not agreed on, determined by Arbitration.

8. A formal Agreement for giving Effect to the Arrangement, with all such Details and incidental Provisions as he thinks consistent with the general Intent of these Heads, to be settled between all Parties by John Bullar Esquire, and to be executed by and binding on all, but, as regards the Interests of the Infant, to be previously approved by the Court.

Dated this Twenty-second Day of March One thousand eight hundred and sixty-six.

For Mr. DUNDAS and his Guardians.
    DOMVILLE, LAURENCE, & GRAHAM.
    J. DEVEREUX PUGH.

For WREXHAM, MOLD, AND CONNAH'S QUAY RAILWAY COMPANY.
    GEO. BOYDELL, for John Rigby, as representing the Buckley Railway Company.
    GEO. BOYDELL, for William Hancock, as representing Wm. Hancock & Co.

LONDON:
Printed by GEORGE EDWARD EYRE and WILLIAM SPOTTISWOODE, Printers to the Queen's most Excellent Majesty. 1866.

Schedule of the Arrangement between the WM & CQR, Buckley Railway and the Aston Tramway: 1866.

The Wrexham, Mold and Connah's Quay Railway

Historical Chronology 1861–1905

1861

In this year there was launched the genesis of the Wrexham, Mold & Connah's Quay Railway, a scheme for a railway linking Whitchurch, Wrexham, Mold and Connah's Quay, the Whitchurch link being by a junction with a projected line joining Oswestry and Whitchurch with Thomas Savin chosen to be the contractor. The latter was revealed on 24th October as the intended Oswestry, Ellesmere & Whitchurch Railway. It published notices for a branch to Brymbo and Ffrith, and when a Whitchurch, Wrexham, Mold & Connah's Quay Junction Railway scheme was produced as a Bill in November, a branch to Park Eyton would have made junction with this OE&W line.

There was a meeting on 11th November of the promotional committee in Wrexham, and the title 'Whitchurch, Wrexham, Mold & Connah's Quay Junction Railway' was formally adopted. A promotional map was issued and Deposited Plans[1] placed before the relevant bodies. The Engineer to the scheme was John Pilkington of Wrexham. It was an extensive plan stretching from Wrexham to the intended Oswestry, Ellesmere & Whitchurch Railway at a junction near Bettisfield, so giving the Wrexham line a desirable outlet over the LNWR at Whitchurch and included the southward branch at Park Eyton where it met the projected OE&W branch to Brymbo. A northward line from Wrexham would make end-on junction with the Buckley Railway near Buckley. There were to be other branches to Ffrwd, a junction with the Chester–Mold line at Hope, and a link with the Wrexham & Minera Railway immediately outside Wrexham. The connection to the Buckley Railway was to be made at a point where the later Ashton's Branch Junction was sited.

95

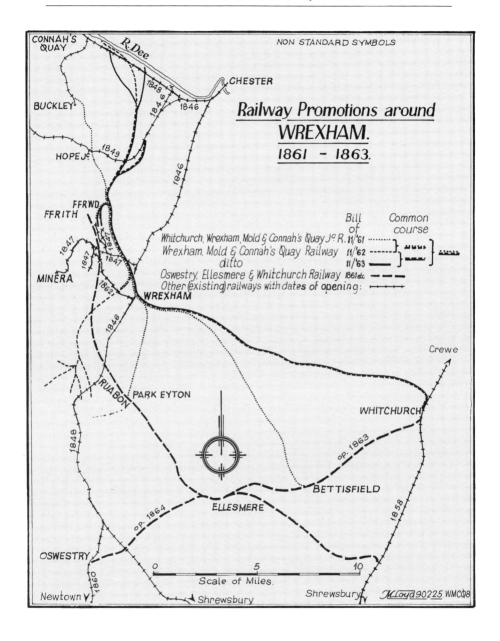

[The WMCQR Act of 7th August, 1862* authorised only a part of these ambitions viz:–

1) Wrexham–Hope
2) Hope to the junction with the Buckley Railway
3) a short line linking 1 & 2 at Hope Junction
4) a branch to Brynmally
5) a branch to Ffrwd
6) the link with the W & MR near Wrexham.]

1862

It will not pass unnoticed that there were several close links through personalities among the small Welsh railway companies in the late 1850s and early 1860s: Gasquoine refers to them and mentions that David Howell of Howell & Morgan at Machynlleth (involved later with the local Talyllyn Railway) kept his Secretaryship of the Newton & Machynlleth Railway at his offices there. This was typical of a temporary period but Machynlleth was too far-flung to be retained: for a time the small border lines – nominally independent – kept office in the ample building provided for them at Welshpool. It was to be in the persona of George Lewis† that there had been a wholesale move to 9a Cannon Row, Westminster by January 1862, where he held office as Secretary to the Oswestry & Newtown; Llanidloes & Newtown; Oswestry, Ellesmere & Whitchurch; Buckley; and Whitchurch, Wrexham, Mold & Connah's Quay Junction Railways (the last-named at promotional stage). Below them in the same building was the Registered Office of the Aberystwyth & Welsh Coast Railway. More conveniently, Benjamin Piercy – whose family will receive considerable mention in connection with the WMCQR – and Thomas Savin, the Welsh railways' contractor, were nearby. At the Lewis establishment were all the foregoing companies' meetings now held, for its convenience for planning and Parliamentary work was undoubted. The spin-off and fall-out between them, and the opportunity for brotherhood to defeat the big battalions, was obvious!

When Thomas Savin was bankrupted in 1866, what by then was the 'Cambrian Railways' group, moved to a Head Office in Oswestry station; the Buckley Railway and WMCQ Railway interests moved to Wrexham station under the Secretaryship of John Broughton at the same time.

There was considerable opposition to the WWM & CQJR proposal, much of it from the GWR in the person of local worthy and landowner Sir Watkin Williams Wynn of Wynnstay, Ruabon, who became one of the most unpopular figures in the district in consequence. Of course his position on the Board of the GWR had to be demonstrated, and no doubt he felt that a small local undertaking could easily be trampled underfoot by the long-established Great Western . . .

In January 1862 a circular was issued to call attention to the wider aspirations of the promoters at a meeting to be held in The Music Hall,

---

*In this and other Bills/Acts, care must be taken where Railway Numbers in the Bill do not coincide with the same Numbers in the Act.

†Made Secretary of the proposed Wrexham undertaking on 1st February @ £200 per annum.

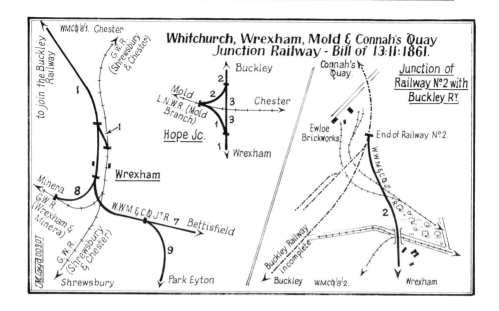

Wrexham. By April circumstances and feelings in Wrexham had reached a high point as the exasperated citizens were calling for a new railway. THE WREXHAM & DENBIGH ADVERTISER published letters and opinions throughout the April period:

> A Wrexham tradesman complained that GWR charges for local traders such as he 'were higher to send produce to Chester than to London'.

The character-assassination of Sir Watkin Williams Wynn continued . . .

> whose GWR proclivities are well known . . . he should be told the true feelings of the Wrexham people and change his opinion . . . Col. Biddulph has given it his warm support and will not be forgotten when the proper time comes.

Following upon this, 'Old Conservative' wrote:

> Wrexham is paying 50% more for carriage of goods to Chester than London, and for shorter distances even higher charges are made, and delays . . . Sir Watkin should forgo his GWR leanings and back Wrexham – The Good Old Town.

Other letters complained that the GWR had more provision for goods at Ruabon than Wrexham, which was still treated as a village. (This was of course, strictly a Shrewsbury & Chester Railway situation.)

> I would rather see stage waggons on the road again than to have to depend on the GWR for the delivery of goods. With the old stage waggons we did know when to expect our goods and we could calculate with a tolerable degree of certainty what hour of the day the goods would be sent . . . with the GWR four days' detention is not uncommon . . .

ANNO VICESIMO QUINTO & VICESIMO SEXTO

VICTORIÆ REGINÆ.

****

Cap. ccxxi.

An Act for incorporating a Company for making and maintaining the *Wrexham, Mold, and Connah's Quay Junction* Railway; and for other Purposes. [7th *August* 1862.]

WHEREAS the making and maintaining of a Railway from *Wrexham*, to join the *Buckley* Railway at *Buckley*, with Branches to *Frood* and *Moss* and *Gwersyllt* and Junctions with the *Shrewsbury and Chester* Branch of the *Great Western* Railway at or near the *Wrexham* Station, and with the *Chester and Mold* Branch of the *Chester and Holyhead* Railway near the *Hope* Station, would be of public and local Advantage: And whereas the several Persons in that Behalf in this Act named, with others, are willing at their own Expense, to execute the Undertaking: And whereas Plans and Sections showing the Lines and Levels of the Railways and Works by this Act authorized to be made and the Lands to be taken for the Purposes thereof, and Books of Reference to those Plans, containing the Names of the Owners or reputed Owners, Lessees or reputed Lessees, and Occupiers of those Lands, have been deposited with the respective Clerks of the Peace for the County of *Flint*, the County of *Denbigh*, and County of *Salop* respectively; and those Plans, Sections, and Books of Reference, are in this

[*Local.*]   42 *A*   Act

The title page of the WM&CQJR Act of 1862.

A word now about other railways which enter the scene. The LNWR had completed their line from Crewe to Whitchurch and opened it on 2nd September, 1858. Until now the smaller Welsh railways had their only outlet at Oswestry and were dependent on the GWR there for access to the GWR's Shrewsbury–Chester section. The experience of these small undertakings was exactly that of the nascent WWM & CQJR – they would be happy to be rid of GWR monopoly. 'A nigger in the woodpile' was the presence of four GWR-men on the board of the Oswestry & Newtown, Sir Watkin Wynn among them. The arrival of the LNWR at Whitchurch was a gleam of light in an otherwise dark sky and with LNWR-promised support, the OE & WR was launched despite GWR threats to build competing lines.

So where did the WWM & CQJR fit into this picture? Its curious short branch to Park Eyton would have made junction with the Ffrith branch of the OE & WR, conceived in answer to pleas from Wrexham-based industrialists to be rid of the GWR monopoly. However, the OE & WR resisted promotion of this branch until their main line was complete; on 24th October, 1861 they published Parliamentary notices for the Ffrith branch – a line from west of Ellesmere up to Ffrith with a branch to Wrexham . . . and other matters. So the Wrexham/Brymbo district, currently a province of the GWR, might have expected to see an OE & WR on its doorstep plus the further promise of another company with headquarters in Wrexham! However, that portion of the OE & WR Bill concerning the Ffrith branch was thrown out, and no more heard of it; this cannot have been but beneficial to the (now) WMCQR party who by then had more support from what had previously been divided opposition to the GWR.

The matter of the WWM & CQJR terminus in Wrexham and its situation was something of a hot potato. In January THE WREXHAM TELEGRAPH had had an editorial:

> RAILWAY STATION IN TOWN – could not they have had the new station in town instead of the proposed site which is neither in the town nor in Brymbo?

A meeting of promoters held on 9th January had been chaired by the Mayor who made no secret of where his affections as to railways, lay. The paper said they had only one railway system in Wrexham 'and it would be better if we had one more'. The promoters had meant to run into the GWR station but there were problems there (!), 'a station nearer the Beast Market would be better'. It appeared that the GWR had promised a station nearer the town but had not honoured that promise; they purchased a site for it and then sold it. 'The time was ripe for Wrexham to become a second Wolverhampton or Merthyr Tydfil'.* A Memorial was then passed praying the House of Commons to support the WWM & CQJR Bill.

Optimism was a feature of the day – the local papers had some new angle to present with each weekly edition: thus on 23rd January it was suggested that 3,000 tons of minerals daily would make their way to the sea for shipment from the district. On 6th February they announced the Standing Orders of the Bill had been complied with at a cost of £240,000.

---

*Until 1855 Merthyr Tydfil was the largest place in all of Wales, a cradle of heavy industry.

Thomas Minshall, solicitor to the Bill and of a leading firm of solicitors of Oswestry, was to the fore; he maintained the GWR's service was insufficient for the needs of local trade, and did not give enough consideration to the wants of the town and district; the new line would connect them with a much better port than Saltney. James Brunlees, acting as Consulting Engineer said the scheme had been laid out to avoid all expensive works.

One of several attempts to link Birkenhead with North Wales and avoid Chester was a plan for a Birkenhead, Flintshire & Holyhead Railway Co., an official notice for which appeared on 20th February. This intended to link Hooton and Queensferry to the Chester & Holyhead and Buckley Railways: the Dee would be bridged and its aim was to 'cross the Dee and give access to Birkenhead with the mineral districts of Flintshire'.

It was not only in London where momentous events were taking place – there was a double-act on 7th June when the Wrexham & Minera Railway opened to goods and mineral traffic (it was a satellite of the GWR), whilst on the same day the Buckley Railway opened for similar traffic; the latter issued a Rule Book on 17th October. There was a mishap at Connah's Quay before the opening day when 'engineer' James Williamson was thrown from a ballast wagon and injured; THE CHESTER CHRONICLE read:

> ACCIDENT ON THE RAILWAY – On Thursday last, as James Williamson Engineer was sitting in a ballast wagon at Connah's Quay, the speed of the train was suddenly increased which jerked him off and jammed him between the truck and the engine. His head came into contact with the truck and was slightly hurt, as also his hips. He was taken to the Chester Infirmary, and will soon be able to attend to his duties.

Opposition to the WWM&CQJR Bill from Sir Watkin resulted in an Enquiry by a Select Committee of the House of Lords during July: as something of its flavour should not be lost, portions of it follow: during it the Chancellor of the Exchequer (Mr Gladstone) was called, and a paraphrasing of his evidence (and others) demonstrates the rumour, allegiances and detail of the situation.

The Enquiry

The Chancellor of the Exchequer (W.E. Gladstone) is brother-in-law of Sir Stephen Glynne. The river Dee and Chester links are vital for the Buckley District. The Buckley Railway gradients are bad; it only touches one end of Buckley and does not connect with the most important part of it. He admits the gradient is 'a matter of being bad downwardly'. He implies that the traffic for the Dee could go round via Mold and Chester line and Counsel for the GWR politely ties him in knots on the subject. He states that the worst gradient on the Buckley Railway is 1 in 37 down to the river and the WMCQR's to the Mold line is 1 in 43: he refers to the Aston Tramroad to the LNWR and the River Dee. The Aston Tramroad still carries a good deal of traffic indeed the bulk of it from the district down to the Dee. He refers to Sir Stephen Glynne's Agreement. The Aston Tramroad is very old and imperfect and is worked by horses and not by locomotives at all, 'It is of a very rude construction indeed belonging to a former period'.

Benjamin Piercy is engineer of the proposed line and the evidence recites all the other lines in which he has been involved.

He states that Railway No. 1, Wrexham–Hope Junction (south) is 7 m. 2 fur. 4 ch. in length: its sharpest curve is 2 fur. 7 ch. and its steepest gradient is 1 in 80. Railway No. 2, Hope Junction (north)–(Old) Buckley is a continuation of Railway

No. 1 to the Buckley and Connah's Quay Railway 2 m. 3 fur. 2 ch., the sharpest curve having a 12 ch. radius and the steepest gradient being 1 in 80 for 2 miles. Railway No. 3, Hope Junction (south)–Hope Junction (north) connects Nos. 1 and 2 over the Mold Branch and is 3 fur. 8 ch. with a gradient of 1 in 80 for 18 chains. Railway No. 4 (not shown on map accompanying Bill) to the Moss Valley is (? miles, I think 1 mile) 1 fur. 8 ch. with a sharpest curve of 1 fur. and the steepest gradient of 1 in 40 for 25 chains. Railway No. 5, is 3 fur. 8 ch. long from Railway No. 4 to Mr Clayton's works with a curve of 1 fur. sharpest and a gradient of 1 in 26 for 38 chains which will probably be worked by a self-acting incline. Railway No. 6 is to join at Wrexham station to the GWR's new Minera branch for heavy traffic without actually going on to the GWR main line. The total estimated cost is £150,000 and Railways Nos. 1, 2 and 3 are to be double line and the remainder single line. The objective of the plans is to provide room to go round the back of Wrexham station.

The Buckley Railway objected to compulsory running powers over their line and stated they would object to the Bill so the clause was taken out. No through rates for the Buckley had been agreed. The Buckley is still objecting to the Bill.

He confirmed that no powers had been taken to make a junction with the GWR at the foot of the Wheatsheaf Incline. The only present working collieries to be served by the WMCQR are Sparrow's, Clayton's and 'Vuest' (? Gwersyllt). He agreed that the Wheatsheaf Incline needed a stationary engine to work it and embarked on an argument about the amount of room left for the GWR to extend Wrexham station.

The Subscription Contract was produced and it was shown that Mr Savin had subscribed £50,000, Mr Piercy £3,000 or £5,000 and Mr Ashbury £10,000. Mr Ashbury was from Manchester and was one of the largest builders of railway carriages in the world.

James Brunlees[2] is an engineer and says the line has been gone over by Mr Piercy and himself together last autumn and by Mr Harrison about the same time. The principal engineering point in the Commons was the damage done to the GWR at Wrexham station. In discussing inclines Brunlees cites the Oldham Branch of the Lancashire & Yorkshire Railway at 1 in 27 formerly worked by endless rope but for the last 8 or 10 years by locomotive.

Colin Napier is manager of Westminster Collieries: he said that if the GWR branch to Brynmally is joined to the WMCQR branch the Westminster Colliery would have to pay under the 6 mile clause to the GWR for the use of 500 or 600 yards of that Company's line to reach the WMCQR.

William Lowe is engineer, manager and part proprietor of Vron Colliery and is viewer for the proprietors of Brymbo and Westminster Collieries. He states that last year's production was as follows:

Colliery	Tons
Westminster	106,565
Vron	92,144
Brynmally	91,767
Broughton	74,077
Brymbo	71,538
The Ffrwd	30,000
Pen y Coed	11,481
Talwyrn	15,000

Also in the district are iron works at Brymbo, Broughton Forge, Minera Lead Mine, Minera Lime Works and the Berwick (? Berwig) Stone Quarries. He says that the Vron Colliery sent 3,000 tons of coal in the current month to the LNWR at Crewe. In his opinion the WMCQR would be madmen if they proposed to find wagons for their customers.

William Liston Newcombe said he was Traffic Manager to the GWR from 1854 to 1857 and now works for the Midland Railway. The GWR withdrew their trucks from the local collieries for Saltney and Birkenhead traffic because they were detained at Birkenhead. It did not take them a week to work the traffic only one or two days. He denies telling Mr Clayton that the GWR would take 10 days and he is not aware of any complaint from Mr Clayton. The trucks were generally made use of by the colliery owners as warehouses on the dockside at Birkenhead.

Henry Robertson is MP for Shrewsbury and engineer to the Shrewsbury & Chester, Shrewsbury & Birmingham, Shrewsbury & Hereford and was engineer to the GWR until the amalgamation of 1854. He is also interested in the 'Ruabon Coal Co., Westminster Colliery, the Brymbo Colliery and the Broughton Works'. He had probably spent £100,000 developing collieries and works in the district. In 1842 when he came to the district trade was on the point of collapse. Most iron works were stopped and not 40,000 tons of coal were sold out of the district.

The Wrexham & Minera line was a locomotive line opened this spring and the Wheatsheaf Incline was worked by a simple horizontal pulley (i.e. cable). 600,000 tons were formerly sent down the Wheatsheaf Incline and this is now reduced to 200,000 tons by the opening of the Wrexham & Minera branch. The line to Brynmally was laid alongside the road: it was the simplest to do so and a special Act was promoted by the Shrewsbury & Chester who paid for the branch. The Ffrwd branch was made by agreement with and under the supervision of the present proprietor (Sparrow). Robertson thinks it is unfair of the Brynmally and Ffrwd proprietors to encourage the GWR to lay out money on the branches and then to take the traffic away to a rival company.

The GWR has no access to a decent port, it only had Saltney and Birkenhead on equal terms with the LNWR but the LNWR has the whole of the Liverpool side of the river. There is 'one shipping stage at the end of the Mold line, the Aston shipping stage serving Sir Stephen Glynne's collieries, King's Ferry and Connah's Quay.' The GWR would have liked to have got to Connah's Quay. The Buckley Railway was five miles long and the upper part was level, it was single line with sharp curves prohibited from carrying passengers. It is admitted that the main part of the money paid out on the branches was laid out by the Shrewsbury & Chester before the GWR acquired it in 1854 although of course the GWR financed the construction of the Wrexham & Minera branch and it was noted in passing that the GWR spent £3,000,000 on buying the Shrewsbury & Chester.

It is stated that the Aston Tramroad is, as a 'tramway', a relatively good one and 16 years ago it was highly valued by its owner.

Philip Brian Davies-Cooke is the Lord of the Manor of Ewloe and owns large areas of fire clay and coal in the district and has 1,000 acres at lease. He and his family own about one third of the shares in the Buckley Railway. He has £8,000 out of a total of £30,000 in the Buckley Railway Co.'s capital and he wants the GWR to develop the Buckley Railway.

John Taylor is the largest mineral operator in the United Kingdom. The Llangollen Slate Works and Minera Lead Works (which latter are the richest lead mines in the world at present) are operated by him. He ships Bryn-yr-Owen coal to Seville and Alicante in two or three hundred ton ships from Connah's Quay and he could ship more coal. French vessels won't go up to Saltney on account of the treacherousness of the river. Taylor thinks the Buckley Company has an arrangement with the GWR.

Benjamin Piercy (recalled) stated that the junction had been put near to the Wrexham station with the GWR since it was considered that the GWR would object to running half a mile over their main line. On the 'Brynmally branch', he said that they would leave the 9 foot vertical difference between the two lines: the colliery has 'little trains' which would tip coal down into GWR or WMCQR wagons. There would be a platform out over the WMCQR to tip into the GWR wagons. There would be no locomotive, the trucks would be taken by horse a distance of some 100 yards.

Thomas Clayton is owner of three local collieries. He was obliged to use the existing incline system and Saltney wharf. The wagons in use were small, carrying only 6–8 tons [the usual for that time]. He was presently importing haematite ore from Barrow through Saltney but was concerned that weather closed the river there and interrupted his supplies. [He must have used GWR wagons (besides hiring his own?) for he explained repairs (such as new couplings) were carried out at the Wheatsheaf depôt, but that all major repairs had to go to Chester.] The GWR was selective about carriage rates; he averred that the Ruabon Coal Co. (a competitor) enjoyed a special rate which undercut him. He worked his traffic with horses for the first 100 yards from the Colliery.

Edward Jones (of Sparrow's Ffrwd complex) said the coal deposits at 'Frood' were owned by Mr Merrick of Leek. He recommended the installation of blast furnaces at Stansty for which haematite ore might be imported from Whitehaven through a new railway from Connah's Quay, supplemented by Staffordshire ore through Chester. Saltney was almost useless during the neap tide period.

James Sparrow (interviewed) was lessee of 'Frood and Windy Hill and of the Plas Madoc and Frood Ironworks', he said – also Secretary of the Denbighshire Coal Owners Association. The output at Ffrwd was 100 tons daily in coal (shortly to be increased to 300 tons) and they made 11,000 tons of iron annually; currently they sent their output down the GWR Ffrwd branch to Westminster Colliery, and so down Summerhill Tunnel and Incline to Wheatsheaf Junction. Of this journey, 91 chains had to be done by Sparrow himself at 4*d*. ton; and it was 1½ miles from Ffrwd to Wheatsheaf.

He was bringing in through Saltney annually, 1,000–2,000 tons of iron ore @ 3/6*d*. ton and 3,000–4,000 tons of hydrate of lime @ 6/- ton, carriage to Wheatsheaf. To bring this traffic from there to Ffrwd cost an extra 6*d*. ton for the 1½ miles (of which he himself worked 91 chains of it). Output sent down to Wheatsheaf over that same 1½ miles cost an initial 1/- ton; and these additional costs were known locally as The Branch Charge and paid for operation of the Incline. It was said that it was only the joint interest of the LNWR in Birkenhead traffic, and the competition of the canal, which kept rates from rising further.

He was a provisional director of the WMCQR he admitted [but he never became one].

So much for the Enquiry!

Wrexham sent a petition to the Lords on 17th July in support of the Railway and there was joy throughout the Wrexham district when the Bill passed the Lords on 31st July. Wrexham went 'en fête' and of such importance was this seen – an occasion which would arouse but limited notice in present times – that the townsfolk made great celebration of the event. Scarcely had the sound of the bells of Wrexham Church died away when arrangements for cutting the first sod were concluded. Wednesday 22nd October was to be the day, the Rt. Hon. W.E. Gladstone (Chancellor of the Exchequer)* would do the deed, and Thomas Savin (contractor for the

---

William Ewart Gladstone 1809–1898

Chancellor of the Exchequer in Lord Palmerston's Government	1859–1866
Leader of House of Commons on Palmerston's death	1865
MP for South Lancashire	1865–1868
Prime Minister	1868 (1st)
	1880 (2nd)
Founded St. Deiniol's Library, Hawarden for Theological Students	1895
Last public speech at Opening of Victoria Jubilee Bridge, Queensferry	2 June 1897
Died 19 May 1898. Buried in Westminster Abbey.	

Works) would present the barrow and spade to Mrs Gladstone. Afterwards, a dinner would be held in the White Lion Hotel, Hope Street.

There was a triumphal arch in High Street but even this could not cheer the gloom for the 'rain fell in torrents'. Gladstone had 'overnighted' at Hawarden Castle (his brother-in-law's residence) and after the Gladstones (husband, wife and daughter) arrived in Wrexham by train, they were escorted by the Denbighshire Yeomanry along Rhosddu in procession to the field where the job was to be done. The rain eased a little and apparently The White Lion was thwarted for the meal afterwards was taken at The Wynnstay Arms.

The affair did not go down well with the public who complained the tickets had found their way into the wrong hands and the whole business had been mishandled; the 'right people' had been snubbed. Clearly Gladstone had done the chivalrous thing and it was his wife who cut the sod, probably somewhat gently as the spade was of silver; she wheeled it in a 'handsome barrow along the platform put up at Mr Savin's expense'. From trains passing alongside on the GWR 'the cheering was immense'.

The day seems to have been marred by an aura of sour grapes; in the evening 'the pig roast was futile . . . the rolls and treacle farce was ridiculous . . . a number of boys amused themselves by discharging squibs and other fireworks much to the annoyance of the respectable community.' Thus ended the cutting of the first sod.

Sir Watkin Wynne came in for ' a lot of stick'; as Chairman of the 'rival railway' he had refused to allow the 1st Denbighshire Rifle Volunteers to attend (so it was reported) but the truth was they required permission of the Lord Lieutenant of the County and he was out of the country. Altogether, the day was not really as euphoric as had been hoped.

The newspapers wisely reported extracts (only) from Gladstone's speech, a portion of which was:

> The Speech of Right Hon. W.E. GLADSTONE, MP, Chancellor of the Exchequer at Wrexham, October 22nd, 1862.
>
> *On the occasion of cutting the First Sod of the Wrexham, Mold, and Connah's Quay Railway.*
>
> 'I have a very confident opinion that ten years hence your proportion of the total product of Coal in Great Britain will be very considerably larger. This is a district singularly rich . . . More or less the district of Flintshire may be said to labour under the disadvantage of broken mineral, which may be set off against other advantages . . .
>
> . . . The perfection of mineral arrangement appears to be, the combination of a very rich and strong Coal, like the coking Coal of Durham, with large quantities of ironstone and mineral, which it may be employed to smelt on the spot. We have not got that, but we have a splendid Steam Coal, with an immense demand for it – a demand greater than we can at present supply. This extraordinary treasure of the Cannel Coal, which is, as you know, far better fitted for the manufacture of Gas than any other Coal whatever . . . this treasure is really the material on which the Wrexham, Mold, and Connah's Quay Railway has to work.
>
> I do not presume to speak for Wrexham – it is for you to judge and speak of that; but I do speak of the other end of this Railway . . . the district of Buckley, through

which this Railway is to run. . . . the making of this railway will confer a great boon on that district. Besides its Coal, that district is possessed of large quantities of Firebrick Clay, which I believe to be of as fine quality, for its purpose, as any in the Country.'

Success came on 7th August when the Act received the Royal Assent, in spite of influential and costly opposition.

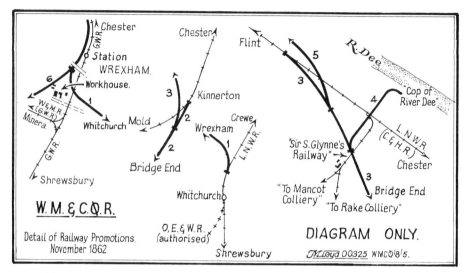

The section south of Wrexham was not approved and running powers into Mold were not given: however, two chord lines with the Chester–Mold railway were approved.

On 7th June, 1862 as already noted, two important events had taken place: the Buckley and Wrexham & Minera Railways each opened for goods and mineral traffic. In anticipation of the latter, the GWR had closed its Moss –Brymbo section on 22nd May; this included the notorous Brake Incline, all being part of the original NWMR access to Brymbo and Minera. The incidence of the two dates, near together, was due to the section from Croes Newydd (South Fork) to Broughton opening on 22nd May, and the remainder (Broughton–Brymbo) on 7th June.*

The heady success of the venture to date brought a further Bill[3] on 29th November with Piercy & Co. as engineers to it, and entitled 'WMCQR (Extensions)'. Second thoughts had now taken place; the object was to keep clear of the Buckley Railway with which they had not come to terms over running powers, and to avoid its curves and steep gradients with a scheme to by-pass it by a junction with the authorised main line at Bridge End and continuing northwards, cross the Chester–Holyhead line of the LNWR on the skew at Sandycroft (at the same time making a chord junction there) after crossing the Glynne Railway at the Chester–Flint road. Running westward,

*The Brymbo–Minera length was, of course, already in use, being part of the NWMR's Wheatsheaf–Minera Branch.

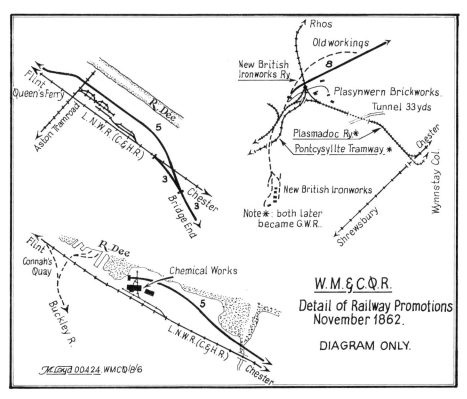

Rhos

Old workings

New British Ironworks Ry

8

Plasynwern Brickworks.

Tunnel 33yds

Plasmadoc Ry*

Pontcysyllte Tramway *

Chester

Wynnstay Col.

Flint

Queen's Ferry

R. Dee

Aston Tramroad

L.N.W.R.(C.&H.R.)

5

3

Chester 3

Bridge End

New British Ironworks

Note *: both later became G.W.R..

Shrewsbury

Flint

Connah's Quay

R. Dee

Buckley R.

Chemical Works

5

L.N.W.R.(C.&H.R.)

Chester

W.M.&C.Q.R.

Detail of Railway Promotions November 1862.

DIAGRAM ONLY.

M.Lloyd 00424. WMCQ/8/6

trans-shipment facilities with the Aston Tramroad would be made and the line would end alongside the Buckley Railway at Connah's Quay. Thrown off this line would be a short branch to King's Ferry at 'Cop of Dee' and where the line crossed over the LNWR's Mold Railway at Kinnerton, another chord would give a linking spur towards Chester. The aggressive nature of these proposals is clear.

At the further end – geographically – the Bettisfield project was supplanted by a new route from Wrexham to Whitchurch on their LNWR's Crewe–Shrewsbury, the junction at the latter place being made just north of the station – here the WMCQR might enjoy endless possibilities for making southwards!

Not content with these dramas, a courageous plan to strike southwards from Wrexham into Great Western country is revealed by Railways Nos. 6–12 which would carry WMCQR metals into the growing industrial area at the mouth of the Vale of Llangollen – into which the Vale of Llangollen Railway had opened for business in the previous June and was intending to reach westwards in stages towards the coast of Cardigan Bay. Here, in the area containing Acrefair, Trevor, and Cefn there was a maturing complex

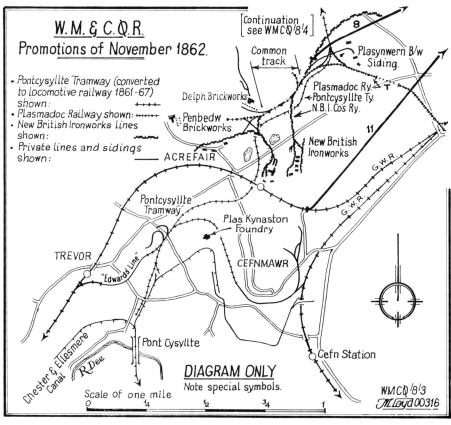

involving foundries, claypits, brickworks, tileworks and potteries; this area extended northwards almost to reach Wrexham, being about 7 miles north-south and 3 miles wide. All lay to the west of the GWR Ruabon–Wrexham railway. To the south the district was 'contained' by the Dee and coming up from even further south, the Ellesmere Canal crossed that river by the famous Pont Cysyllte Aqueduct, and came to a terminus on the north bank of the Dee where the basin contained a combined canal loading stage and locomotive shed! This marked the termination of the Pontcysyllte Railway, a conversion of the former Ruabon Brook Tramway of 1861–7 into a locomotive-worked railway; conversion at the time of this Bill was not complete, but it remained a desirable objective for WMCQR plans as the PR would reach the outskirts of Rhosllanerchrugog, a centre of brickmaking.

The WMCQR was not alone: other enterprises also saw the attractions of reaching this district; the GWR had a foot in the door already. The canal, part of the Shropshire Union system, was in fact, a subsidiary of the LNWR, to the effect that the PR was an isolated section of that Railway. It was

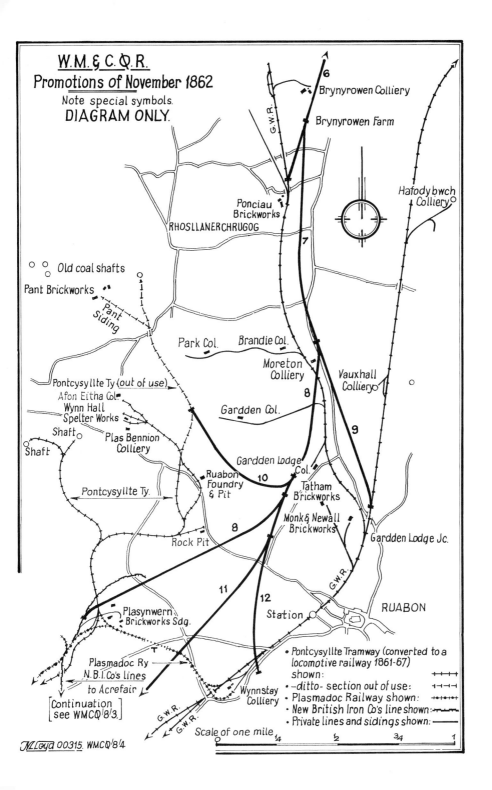

W.M. & C.Q.R.
Promotions of November 1862
Note special symbols.
DIAGRAM ONLY.

G.W.R.

6

Brynyrowen Colliery

Brynyrowen Farm

Hafody bwch Colliery

Ponciau Brickworks

RHOSLLANERCHRUGOG

7

Old coal shafts

Pant Brickworks

Pant Siding

Park Col.

Brandie Col.

Moreton Colliery

Vauxhall Colliery

Pontcysyllte Ty (out of use)

Afon Eitha Col.

Wynn Hall Spelter Works

8

Gardden Col.

9

Shaft

Plas Bennion Colliery

Shaft

Gardden Lodge Col.

Pontcysyllte Ty.

Ruabon Foundry & Pit

10

Tatham Brickworks

Monk & Newall Brickworks

Gardden Lodge Jc.

8

Rock Pit

G.W.R.

11

12

Plasynwern Brickworks Sdg.

Station

RUABON

Plasmadoc Ry N.B.I. Co's lines to Acrefair

[Continuation see WMCQ/8/3.]

T

Wynnstay Colliery

G.W.R.

G.W.R.

• Pontcysyllte Tramway (converted to a locomotive railway 1861-67) shown:
• -ditto- section out of use:
• Plasmadoc Railway shown:
• New British Iron Co's line shown:
• Private lines and sidings shown:

N.Lloyd 00315. WMCQ/8/4.

Scale of one mile   ¼   ½   ¾   1

ultimately purchased by the GWR in 1895 for £51,000. All this is but background to the WMCQR's assault!

The WMCQR aspirations hereabouts were for the following:

Railway No. 7 from a point south of Pentre Bychan at Brynyrowen Farm, southward and east of the GWR branch from Ruabon to Brynyrowen. Near Brandie Pit this line would have thrown off a junction (Railway No. 9) to make a trailing connection with the GWR en route to Ruabon, to the north of Ruabon station and the GWR Gardden Lodge Junction. Railway No. 7 would have continued to Gardden Lodge Pit and about this point spread out into four probing fingers viz: Railway No. 8 a continuation of No. 7 westward to make junction with the New British Ironworks'* private railway near the latter's junction with the Pontcysyllte Railway (then more accurately a tramway but under active conversion) near the Delph Brickworks.

Railway No. 9 (as above)

Railway No. 10 a northwestwards branch to join the Pontcysyllte Railway near Wynne Hall, a junction facing northwards.

Railway No. 11 a projection to reach the recently-opened Vale of Llangollen Railway (a satellite of the GWR) near Acrefair.

Railway No. 12 a branch off No. 11, southwards and across the GWR main line south of Ruabon, but on the north bank of the Dee, to give independent access to the important Wynnstay Colliery.

Patient examination of these designs will expose the empirical desires of the Wrexham promoters; here was no parochial enterprise and the gloves were off! However, opposition was strong and when the Act of 25th July, 1864 ultimately gave the green light, there was virtually nothing left south of Wrexham. Four lines were approved:

a) Wrexham–Whitchurch

b) a branch from the WMCQR main line to link with the GWR Wheatsheaf Junction–Minera line near the foot of the Wheatsheaf Incline . . . not much more than a chord which would allow through working from the south (i.e. Wrexham) onto the GWR Wrexham–Brymbo–Minera section. (Though later built as a fan of exchange sidings, a definite 'chord' never materialised).

c) the already-authorised Brynmally Branch was to link up with the existing GWR Brynmally Branch at Brynmally Colliery (this item replaced Railway No. 5 of the 1862 Act).

d) from c) a line to make junction with the Wrexham & Minera Railway near Brymbo.

Little can be added concerning the start of the Buckley Railway in June. As to Connah's Quay imports in the early days of the Buckley line, a typical notice in THE WREXHAM TELEGRAPH read: (22nd May, 1862)

W. Thomas begs to inform his friends, colliery proprietors, mine agents, builders and the general public that the ship FRONDERNE of Norway is now discharging at Connah's Quay, a cargo of Redwood . . .

(*Timber Yard & Wharf, Railway Station, Wrexham*)

---

*Robert Piercy was Chief Engineer there.

In that same month of June, other railways were attempting to reach Connah's Quay, and none was destined to be successful; so we read: (THE CHESTER CHRONICLE, 7th June)

> THE WELSH RAILWAYS   The rival lines of LNW and GW to get to Connah's Quay from the Wrexham and Mold mineral districts, have been for more than a fortnight before Lord Stanley's Committee and at the adjournment last Thursday the evidence was not concluded . . . will resume next Thursday.

1863

The House of Commons Select Committee on Private Bills sat on 30th April and 1st May to consider the WMCQR Bill of the previous 29th November. Lord Kenyon expanded on the desirability to extend the line from Wrexham to Whitchurch and referred to the powers they had been given last year for the line to Buckley: in the latter case they now sought a line parallel to that proposed but two miles away from it, with the object of avoiding the Buckley line altogether; to run over it the Buckley required 2 d. per ton mile on loads over 50 tons, 2½ d. ton on loads 50–20 tons and 3 d. ton on less than 20 tons.

Benjamin Piercy said that both the LNWR and GWR had opposed the WMCQR: the LNWR wanted its own line to move coal from the Buckley district, but to mollify the WMCQR intended to make connections with both the Mold Railway (LNWR) and Buckley Railway. In the 1862 session of Parliament, both GWR and WWM & CQJR had intimated end-on junctions with the Buckley: the Buckley had sided with the GWR to ward off the WWM & CQJR. They had opposed WMCQR Running Powers as the 'gradients were so hard that the line requires working with our having running powers over it would interfere with' (if that is clear !!)

The promoters had some difficulty in persuading the Committee that the change of mind to serve Sandycroft instead of Connah's Quay was advantageous; 'The Buckley Railway does not serve the flat of the Dee' and 'Buckley clay needs a good outlet to the south', do not seem very convincing arguments.

It did seem however, that coal sent to London via LNWR was subjected to delays between Crewe and Stafford; John Thompson said vessels preferred to use the Aston Quay at Queen's Ferry in preference to Connah's Quay but as he owned Queensferry Colliery (as well as the Nerquis Colliery near Mold) which had a branch of the Aston Tramroad running down to Aston Quay, he could hardly have been expected to support Connah's Quay.

Of the other lines proposed by the Bill, the Whitchurch Extension was just over 15 m. long and would cost £144,076; the steepest gradient was 1 in 80. The line from Hope Junction to the Mold line of the LNWR near Kinnerton was over 3 m. long and would cost £36,172; the steepest part would be 1 in 60. The remaining three lines of the Bill (all linking lines in the neighbourhood of Sandycroft) would aggregate £288,000. The Committee had some hard things to say about gradients – it was felt that those on the Whitchurch line would limit goods trains to 20 wagons. Lastly, Hugh Fenton, a wire rope and telegraph cable manufacturer with works only 200 yards from the Chester–Holyhead section showed that he had not been wooed away from

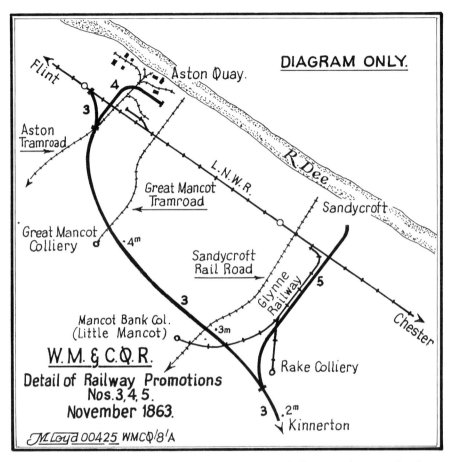

using the 'Dundas Tramway' (i.e. Aston Tramroad) down to the Quay by the incoming standard gauge main line. He preferred the Tramroad.

Some patching-up of relations between the Buckley and the Wrexham faction was achieved and a draft Agreement was drawn up: this did not have legal effect until 23rd July, 1866.

In September Richard Ashton sold land enabling the Buckley Railway to build a branch line and siding to the Knowl Lane Brickworks. This became known as Ashton's (Branch) Siding.

Popplewell suggests that during the year Thomas Savin had begun construction work on the WMCQR and this is confirmed by contemporary newspaper accounts. However, the Minutes clearly state 'Edward Humphreys was contractor' (August 1864). On 29th December Benjamin Piercy asked the Board for £5,000 on account of his engineering services during 1862–3.

A portion of Railway No. 1 on which under half a mile of earthwork was begun and then abandoned, survived until comparatively recent times. It comprised (from west to east) an unfinished cutting beginning at a lane known as Brynycabanau (in those days), which led into the open fields south of Hightown off the Wrexham–Overton road. This cutting led eastwards to the Overton road passing north of and alongside the Barracks. It was intended to pass under that road; to east of it the earthworks were more advanced and the cutting was dug to almost full extent. At King's Mills the land falls away sharply into the valley of the River Clywedog so requiring embankment work on the upper slopes of the valley; this curved eastsoutheast to a point above where the corn mill stood beside the road bridge over the river. Here the earthworks ended abruptly.

This earthwork is even shown on OS Maps printed since 1946; the portion of ground immediately north of the Barracks has been levelled off but remains a narrow grassy site at present (1990). On the east side of the Overton road a council housing estate runs along the edge of the cutting which has been filled in; the estate was built about 1946 and a resident

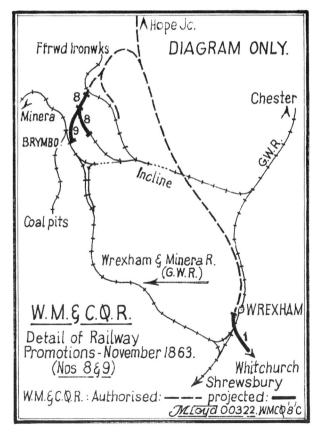

recalls rails being pulled out of the earth along the edge of the property – if true, these must have been light rails used during construction. On the embankment beyond, all trace has been lost again by recent domestic building.

On completion of the main line in 1866, did Piercy's men move to begin this work upon acquisition of the necessary land, and then leave the site when he resigned on 19th October, 1868?

In the matter of the Buckley Railway, an Act to raise new capital was passed on 29th June allowing it to issue £30,000 on terms and £10,000 on mortgage.

This year was yet another one which was not allowed to pass without further Bill[4] on 30th November attempting to widen the boundaries of the promoters' dreams! A portion of it referred to lines given previous authority but for which time had run out before building commenced.

Railway No. 1   Wrexham–Whitchurch
Railway No. 2   Bridge End–Kinnerton
Railway No. 3   From off No. 2 south of Kinnerton to another junction at Moor Lane, Hawarden (by Harding's Farm)
Railway No. 4   From Harding's Farm to Aston Quay (terminus of the Aston Tramroad) with sidings to either side of that Quay
Railway No. 5   A line from Harding's Farm to Sandycroft Quay
Railway No. 6   (not allotted)
Railway No. 7   A spur from off the main line at Wheatsheaf
Railways No. 8 & 9   Southwesterly projecting branches off the authorised Ffrwd branch towards Brynmally Colliery (8) and the GWR Brymbo Branch (9)

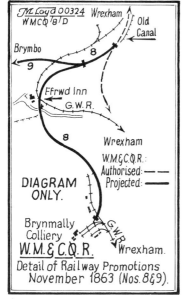

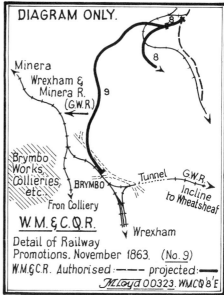

The 1864 Act authorised Railways Nos. 1, 7, 8 & 9 but of these only part of Nos. 1 and 8 were built: it involved an up-gradient of 1 in 26 but did not make the intended end-on junction at Brynmally Colliery with the GWR branch there.

1864

Up to now there had been no station on the Chester–Holyhead section of the LNWR at Connah's Quay but in June plans were published for it; two years were to pass before the necessary land was purchased.

On 21st June the shareholders approved a Bill for the Drayton Junction Railway.

According to information given to J.M. Dunn not all the work being done on the Buckley Railway was being executed by its locomotives WHEATLEY (delivered April 1861) and KENYON (delivered Spring 1862) – being the first locomotives built by Hudswell, Clarke & Rodgers of Leeds – for he notes that by 30th June this year 'locomotives had replaced horses, but not at Connah's Quay where they continued to be employed down on the wharf'. Whether this is accurate cannot be tested, for much of Dunn's information came from the work of E.L. Ahrons which was researched at the turn of the century. It is difficult to see how mixed locomotive/horse workings could be combined, and possibly this was meant to infer that the private sidings could now dispense with horse haulage as locomotives were able to shunt them. Even this hypothesis is not watertight, as it was one of the complaints of the Buckley traders that locomotives (at least a few years later) were not entering private sidings to shunt their wagons. The note must remain obscure.

On 25th July an Act gave authority for extensions to Whitchurch and Brymbo, and these have already been described in 1862 (*see page 110*). Five years were allowed for completion.

The Company's geographical situation made it imperative to reach the Dee and in October the Solicitor was authorised to seek Parliamentary powers to lease or amalgamate with the Buckley Railway.

The Board was still fired with ambition; a Bill of November proposed extensive docks and new railways at Connah's Quay, with a diversion of the river to accommodate the scheme; the engineers to the Bill were Robert and Benjamin Piercy. This first of three Bills this year became law as the Extension Act of 1865 (5th July). Even though the main line was not yet ready, nonetheless this demonstrated the Board was putting pencil to paper and resurrecting some of its old ideas with little alteration so that here again was another version of the plan to avoid using the Buckley Railway and sweep in an easterly half circle from a point south of Buckley town, past Hawarden and down to Connah's Quay from the southeast. A branch would leave this to serve the Mancot Colliery (did the promoters know how little life was left in this pit?) and another would serve the enlarged docks at Connah's Quay ... these are only outlined in the Plans and look very like those on the Buckley Railway Bill of November 1865 ... which indeed, they turn out to be. There is a significant dotted line on the Plan leading off the dock branch in a northerly direction across the river towards Birkenhead, always the Company's ultimate goal.[5]

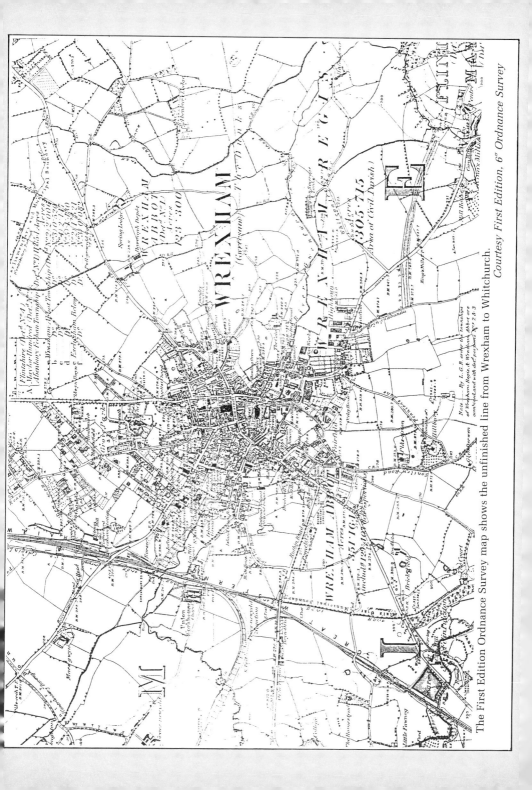

The First Edition Ordnance Survey map shows the unfinished line from Wrexham to Whitchurch.

Courtesy First Edition, 6" Ordnance Survey

On 28th December the Buckley directors – it can only be imagined as a result of the verbal agreement of the previous 30th June (q.v.) – requested the WMCQR to 'attend to the Buckley Railway permanent way and buildings'. This is a strange entry even accepting that the arrangements had come into force immediately (they were realised by the Act of 23rd July, 1866). The WMCQR had no locomotives of its own before 1865, and the track of the Buckley which had been poor from the outset, must have been flimsy for but two locomotives to have wreaked such havoc on it in so short a time. Probably its directors saw a panacea for their troubles in collaborating with the WMCQR, and were acting without delay. As to the 'buildings', it is certain the only one the Buckley Company possessed was a small office on the dockside at Connah's Quay.

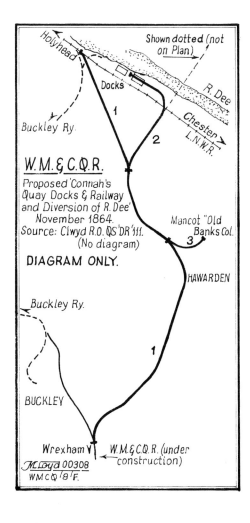

Also on 28th December the WMCQR agreed to complete the bridge over the Saltney–Mold line at Hope Junction to specifications supplied by the LNWR: obviously the latter was taking no chances.

That hardy annual event so beloved of the Board was repeated again a second time in November; 'Let's have Another Railway' took the form this time of an extension from the Whitchurch line – as yet but just started – to Farndon, dubbed The Dee Valley Extension. Parliament liked it, and on 29th June the following year, the scheme was enacted. And there the matter lapsed.

Not content for having submitted two Bills in November, a third was presented entitled 'WM & CQR (New Lines)', and was shown to be a ragbag of bits and pieces built up on the disappointments of earlier promotions. Whilst the preamble was not proved and the Bill[6] did not progress very far, the seven projects have a certain curiosity.

No. 1 from near Cefnybedd on the main line then building, to the Chester –Mold line near Kinnerton.

No. 2 from near Cross Lanes on the authorised Whitchurch line, westwards to the GWR to make junction north of Ruabon. A branch of this would serve a coal pit then sinking near Erbistock. (No. 3)

No. 4 from off the Whitchurch line in Wrexham, and following nearly the Wrexham & Minera course, push on past Brymbo to make end-on junction with the LNWR where its Ffrith branch terminated.

No. 5 a branch from No. 4 to Westminster Colliery.

No. 6 a branch off No. 4, south and west of Brymbo Works towards Vron.

No. 7 a linking railway in Brymbo (see diagram p.119)

As if this was not sufficient, aspirations to reach Mold were renewed by a cunning idea to lay a second line beside the LNWR from Hope Junction to Mold via Padeswood: Mold would either become a joint station or the WMCQR would build an independent one. Furthermore, running powers over various lines were also sought.

The Whitchurch line was begun but never completed – there was an acute shortage of cash anyway, and when the above-mentioned Act was obtained, the Company had to all intents and purposes, over-reached itself; Farndon never had a railway at any time. With enthusiasm no less than ever, and as if 'Tomorrow' was to be the 'first day' in the remainder of the Company's life the Bill of 30th November, 1865 for alterations in the Whitchurch route and a proposal to reach out beyond Chester and to the OE & WR from the Dee Valley coincided with the building of the already-authorised lines north of Wrexham, and which were opened to goods and mineral traffic on 1st January, 1866. And that was that. Although Brymbo would be served by a new railway in due course, and small attachments would be made to each end of the main line, for many years the WMCQR was and remained a railway from beside the GWR station in Wrexham and leading northwards to make junction with the Buckley Railway – hardly a grandiose development on the railway map. Yet its main line survives today whilst so much has been lost, albeit for quite different reasons. The industries which secured its creation have quite disappeared but the district through which it passes is

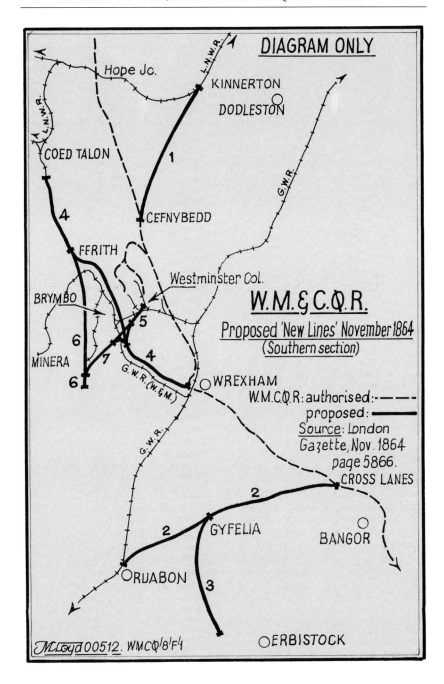

now populated to a degree which could never have been envisaged in the 1860s: it may be said to be almost a dormitory suburb of Merseyside.

Though there were to be further developments and Acts of Parliament from midsummer 1866, and ambitions were still firing the Board, the additions to what had already been accomplished would be minimal.

1865

At the start of the year the Company had continued to occupy 5, Manchester Buildings, Westminster, London for their office but in September this year a more rational locale was opened at 56 Hope Street, Wrexham which was far more convenient for Board members who lived locally. Later, administration was moved again to an office block on Wrexham station.

Board Meetings thus moved from London to Wrexham and were often held on Saturdays, a point which seems to underline the pressure of other pursuits upon the directors. Early in the year the Board considered 'the question of stations and the Chairman (R.K. Penson) was authorised to select a design after consultation with the Engineer'. It is suggested that portable type wood and corrugated iron structures were chosen, probably as much for economy than anything else.

Throughout the year the WMCQR was under construction but due to the impending bankruptcy of Thomas Savin, the intended contractor, in January agreement was reached with Benjamin Piercy to take up the work.* In consequence of the resultant delay, when the Railway opened there were many features unfinished, but they were permitted in that state subject to completion by a date, by the Board of Trade.†

John Cunnah had been killed in an accident on the Buckley line – the claim was settled at £25 . . . even in those days, a paltry sum for a man's life.

Later in the year the obvious omission of any means to embody the word 'Mold' in the Company's title in the activities of the concern, was an embarrassment to the directors who then discussed how this might be done: for the time being the answer eluded them.‡ As yet the rail link between WMCQR and the Chester–Mold line was incomplete (and was still thus when Col. Yolland inspected on 25th January, 1866).

No rules had yet been drafted, and Piercy, Lewis (Secretary) and Mr Braithwaite Poole (Secretary of the Hoylake Railway) were empowered to draft them. Also agreed was that 'superior officers' were to have blue uniforms with red facings, and porters drab corduroy with red letters [sic]. However, orders were not placed.

During May the Resident Engineer, T.E. Minshall, anticipated that the 'Original Line' [sic] would be ready for inspection during August, and in that month Piercy said he had ordered the rolling stock for the opening day and the working thereafter. Problems had arisen with the acquisition of land near Wrexham and the delayed opening date of 15th September was put back to October when it was hoped difficulties would have been overcome.

---

*Popplewell gives as contractors: (1) Thomas Savin (1863+), (2) Richard Samuel France, Monkland Hall, Shrewsbury (1865+), (3) Abraham Pilling. It seems that Benjamin Piercy arranged for France to take up the work in January 1865. A GAZETTEER OF THE RAILWAY CONTRACTORS & ENGINEERS OF WALES AND THE BORDERS. 1830–1914 (Lawrence Popplewell) 1984

†Actually inspected 25th January, 1866 and 26th April, 1866.

‡Mold became the County Town in 1836.

They were not. Piercy then came back with the news that he had paid for the rolling stock and wanted payment for same in paid-up shares to the value of £20,000 – this was done. By the year's end it was clear that the line would only be finished sufficiently for it to carry goods and minerals; the Board of Trade would not permit passenger working until signals had been erected and Stevens & Co., the suppliers, had not yet provided them.

The desire to expand was constantly in the mind of the Company. The inhabitants of Malpas had noted the Royal Assent of June 1865 for a line from Wrexham to Whitchurch (which was one of the promotions then in abeyance), and asked that the course be altered from using the Wych Valley so as to serve their town (October). Two months later Benjamin Piercy, anxious to press on, said the Wrexham–Buckley section was nearly complete and he wished to transfer his staff and plant to the Whitchurch section. He also wanted £30,000 on account. An Agreement was prepared between Piercy and the Company to build the Whitchurch Extension.

On 29th June an Act was obtained for the extension to Farndon referred to in 1864 and an 'extension to Connah's Quay' was acquired by an Act of 5th July, the Bill for which had had shareholders' approval as recently as 20th May!

On 26th August the Secretary notified the Board of Trade that the line as between Wrexham and Buckley was complete, but it was 25th January, 1866 before Col. Yolland came to inspect it. It is helpful to anticipate that visit. His report was written from Shrewsbury on 1st February and reveals at last the reality of the original dream. He had been taken from Wrexham to the junction with 'the Buckley & Connah's Quay Railway near Buckley (9 m 40 ch.)' of single track, though provision had been made in the works for doubling the line, each track having a formation level of 10 ft. The rails were of double-headed section 75 lbs/yd. in 18 ft and 24 ft lengths, carried in cast-iron chairs weighing 27 lbs each. Chairs carried wooden keys, placed outside the rail; the foreign timber sleepers were 9 ft × 10 in. × 5 in. of half-round 'scantlings' to which the chairs were held by iron spikes: the sleeper intervals were 3 ft with 2 ft at joints and the gravel ballast would have been from a local source, and was laid to a depth of 2 ft below the surface of the rails. In other words, the track was of intermediary type, better than some predecessors but still using double-headed rails which were then out of favour, and half-round sleepers instead of rectangular section.

Engine turntables were to be found at Wrexham and Buckley stations, perhaps an unusual feature as the line would be best suited to tank locomotives which did not necessarily require turning at journey's end.

There were 13 under and 10 over bridges, and 2 viaducts: that over the River Alyn had five openings but was not made of good quality stone; it tended to split and crack '. . . the remainder are fair structures'. The sharpest curve was 17 ch. radius and steepest gradient 1 in 70.

'Temporary stations are put up at Wrexham, Gwersyllt, Cefn, Caergwrle, Hope Junction and Buckley . . . it is intended to build a joint bridge with the Great Western at Rhosddu to avoid a level crossing'. There was to be a junction with the GWR at Wrexham but it was not yet built.*

*It appears therefore, that the only link initially with any railway giving outlets from the combined Buckley/WMCQR system, was the chord with the LNWR at Connah's Quay.

The Inspector did not like parts of a lean-to shed on the arrival platform at Wrexham and the corner of the goods shed there – they were too close to the running line and fouled carriage doors when such were inadvertently left open. Neither did he favour the layout at Wrexham which included too many facing points, and he ordered that the arrival and departure platforms must be altered to avoid them.

Displeasure at finding the palings 'on platform ends too close to the edges' produced some situation names, and he made complaint 'there are either no signals at all or in an unfinished state or are not locked as they should be so that it will be impossible to lower them except when the points are set for the right line . . . some points are not visible from the signal box . . . Sidings are in fact loops at stations giving a facing point in each direction – if used for passenger trains these must be given a second platform . . . the branch with the Chester & Mold Railway is incomplete . . . some bridges have bridge-railed track and should not be secured to longitudinal sleepers by coach screws . . . some rail joints are too wide . . .' A list of situations followed:

Stansty Forge Sidings
Wheatsheaf Junction
Frood Junction – the junction with the GW branch at Wheatsheaf
Hope Colliery Siding
Long siding near Hope Colliery and Lakell Siding
Hope Junction
Buckley Junction

Note: the above are all spelt as given: the second and third-named probably arise from a misunderstanding – there was no junction at Wheatsheaf (this was on the GWR) and Ffrwd Junction led to the Ffrwd Branch not the GWR. 'Lakell Siding' would be Lascelles' Siding, indicating that the brewery at Caergwrle was given connection from the beginning.

It worried Col. Yolland that he could not find sufficient people with an idea of how the railway was to be worked, and he refused to sanction opening – in this he referred to safety on the single line sections i.e. the whole railway at this juncture. To anticipate the Colonel's next visit on 26th April following, by then the methods of working the single line had been agreed; the main line would be divided into two sections, with one single line staff on each a) Wrexham–Caergwrle and b) Caergwrle–Buckley; this was acceptable to the Board of Trade. On that same day Robert Piercy undertook to build the Rhosddu bridge within six months, and was gathering material so to do.

In the autumn the bye-laws were now ready and contained certain of special interest:

If there should not be accommodation for all the passengers to whom tickets had been issued, those holding tickets for the longest distance would have preference according to the order in which tickets had been issued i.e. as shown by the consecutive numbers printed on them.

Any person smoking tobacco in a carriage or station is hereby subjected to a penalty not exceeding 40/-.

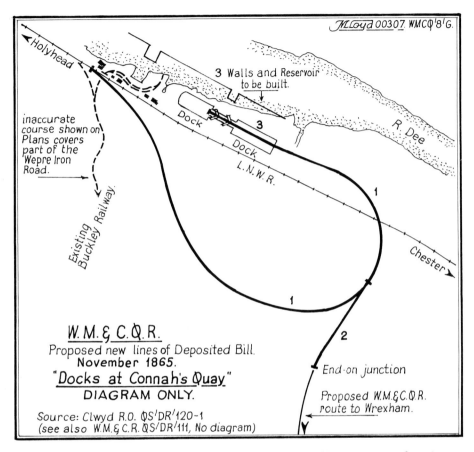

Holyhead

ℋLloyd 00307 WMCQ'8'G.

3 Walls and Reservoir to be built.

inaccurate course shown on Plans covers part of the Wepre Iron Road.

Dock

Dock

3

L.N.W.R.

R. Dee

1

Chester

Existing Buckley Railway

1

W.M.& C.Q.R.
Proposed new lines of Deposited Bill.
November 1865.
"Docks at Connah's Quay"
DIAGRAM ONLY.

Source: Clwyd R.O. QS'DR'120-1
(see also W.M.&C.R. QS'DR'111, No diagram)

2

End-on junction

Proposed W.M.&C.Q.R. route to Wrexham.

Anyone damaging windows, upholstery etc. shall pay a sum of £5 in addition to the amount of damage for which he may be liable.

Also in the autumn the station master at Wrexham was permitted to occupy a house known as 'The Crispins', but at 2–3 months' notice: and towards the close of the year allocation of employees was arranged: there would be:

Wrexham	5
Gwersyllt	3
Frood Junction*	2
Cefnybedd	2
Caergwrle	2

N.B. Allocations for Hope Junction and Buckley do not appear. (Spellings are as given in the Minutes.)

---

*Shown at this time as a 'station', and for some years given as Frood (later Ffrwd).

Other than the 'top management' which is not listed, there would also be:

Assistant Manager; Manager's Clerk; Accountant & Auditor; Passenger & Goods Drivers; Passenger & Goods Guards; Stokers.

In November the Buckley Railway Company was requested to present a Bill for the raising of additional capital, the construction of docks at Connah's Quay and the power to carry passengers – it was, 'All Go'.

The postscripts to the year now followed – a 'Hardy Annual' as it had become – in November two Buckley and three WMCQR Bills were submitted to Parliament:

BUCKLEY RAILWAY *Engineers:* J.F. Bateman & Benjamin Piercy, London.
[This Bill must be considered alongside the WMCQR Bill of November 1864: the WMCQR was still under construction and its Bill was designed to avoid using the steeply-graded section of the existing Buckley Railway.]

A short branch from the foot of the Buckley Railway at Connah's Quay, to the southeast and then north, under the LNWR and so westwards to reach two docks with protective river walling, the docks to be built between the LNWR and the river. A second branch off this would give direct junction with the proposed WMCQR route from off its main line at Hope – there would be an end-on junction just outside Connah's Quay. A reservoir would be built to serve the dock basins.
Ref: Clwyd Record Office: QS/DR/120* QS/DR/111 (WMCQR Bill of 11/1864)

BUCKLEY RAILWAY *Engineers:* J.F. Bateman & Benjamin Piercy.
These Plans were exactly as the previous Bill, but herein the docks were outlined in full. There were to be two in line, joined by a short channel having two sets of lock gates. Access from the river is not shown, but presumably would have been a westerly one.
Ref: Clwyd Record Office: QS/DR/121

WMCQR DEVIATIONS & EXTENSIONS November 1865.
Firstly: an alteration in the course permitted under the 1865 Act to allow it to take a more northerly course on the Whitchurch extension.
Secondly: to form the 'loop line' to Connah's Quay as on the previous Bill of November 1864 but to terminate it at that place and omit the Docks' Scheme. There would have been a branch to Aston Hall Colliery and Brickworks from Hawarden in addition to that serving Mancot which appeared in the November 1864 Bill.
Note: this Bill covered proposals for Railways 1–3; a second Bill concerned Railways 4–9 (q.v.)
Ref: Shropshire Record Office: DP/457 and Clwyd Record Office: QS/DR/136 QS/DR/138

Henry Robertson gave evidence for The Loop Line (June 1882) before the Lords Committee of Enquiry: he averred that

the Buckley Railway was not well laid out. It is a very defective mode of getting to the Docks . . . the WMCQR's proposed new route would have a 12 chain curve onto

*The 1 inch/mile OS map which accompanies the Bill, shows the projected course of the Railway, wrongly.

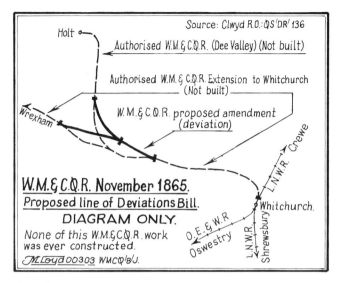

the Docks and would cross the existing Buckley Railway on the dockside by level crossing. It was the intention that this line would supersede the existing Buckley route which would then be closed . . .

in short, the WMCQR was looking for a safer descent to the riverside.[7]

WMCQR (EXTENSIONS IN SHROPSHIRE & CHESHIRE) *Engineer:* Robert Piercy.

This scheme would have given northward extension to the Dee Valley branch at Farndon, giving a chord to the Chester–Crewe line and making a triangular junction with the authorised Chester & West Cheshire Junction Railway east of Chester (Railways 1–4).

Railways 5 & 6 gave southward extension to the Dee Valley line, crossed the authorised Wrexham–Whitchurch Extension and made a) junction with the Oswestry, Ellesmere & Whitchurch Railway east of Bettisfield and b) junction with the proposed Market Drayton Railway, deviated for that purpose.

(No Act followed which permitted these schemes, being lost in the Lords in favour of an LNWR plan).*

Ref: Clwyd Record Office: QS/DR/140

---

*[Dow suggests this was part of a MSLR attempt to make assault on the Wirral; Chester was to be the gateway for this and further incursions into Central Wales. To this end, Watkin went into alliance with Benjamin Piercy, then not only Engineer to the WMCQR but also the Mid-Wales which featured in his thrusts; with Piercy acting in similar capacity for Hoylake and WMCQ Railways the Bill was revived again in 1866. By this plan, the MSLR would have reached Birkenhead by means of the extension from West Cheshire Junction and by an independent line into Chester. The WMCQR would have enjoyed such Cheshire links by its extension of the Dee Valley line.

According to the dating of the Parliamentary Plans (1865 & 1866) – both years saw defeat in the teeth of LNWR competing lines.]

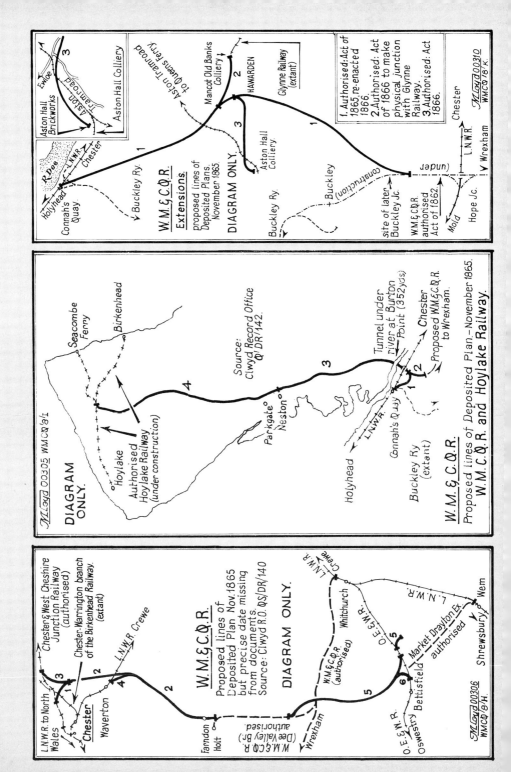

WMCQR (WMCQ & HOYLAKE RAILWAYS) *Engineers:* J.F. Bateman and Benjamin Piercy.

A further Bill of November 1865 gave substance to the intention to reach Birkenhead; an extension from Connah's Quay would have tunnelled under the Dee at Burton Point and, following almost exactly the route of the later Liverpool & North Wales Railway, made junction with the Hoylake Railway (then building) near Seacombe. The Dee Tunnel was to be 352 yards long and the line would have fallen to it at 1 in 55 on the south bank, and climbed out on the north at 1 in 80.

Again, it will be noted that the WMCQR was as yet incomplete! No Act followed this Bill.

Ref: Clwyd Record Office: QS/DR/142

A little needs to be added about the Hoylake Railway for Edgeworth and Penson, two of its directors, were on the board of the WMCQR in 1865, and at times Messrs. Barnes, Everitt and Fynney of the WMCQR were on the Hoylake board. Benjamin Piercy was Engineer to both. In 1864 there had been talk of extending the incomplete Hoylake Railway from its western terminus (Hoylake) with an embankment and two viaducts across the mouth of the Dee to reach the Welsh shore at Mostyn.[8] A Bill had been submitted for the 1863/4 Parliamentary session but no Act ensued. The Plans show a westwards facing junction with the Chester & Holyhead line at Mostyn; such a railway would have given Merseyside – in the ultimate – a direct link with North Wales avoiding the necessity to go round via Chester. Affecting the promotions of the WMCQR would have been its extensions to Connah's Quay, and links with the existing tramroads at Mancot and Aston Hall Colliery: this is only the fringe of what would have been further inroads into Flintshire.[9]

[To continue with a limited reference to the Hoylake Railway. In 1881 it was renamed the Seacombe, Hoylake & Deeside Railway, its board now headed by Henry Robertson whose ties with the Brymbo Company, Beyer, Peacock & Co. Ltd. and the WMCQR receive frequent mention herein – but the Railway Company did not prosper.]

When the Wirral Railway was incorporated under the Railways Construction Facilities Act of 1864 in March 1883, to build a line from the then-building Mersey Railway to Bidston and thence to Hawarden Bridge down the Wirral under powers of 1885, it failed to carry out those powers and the name 'Wirral Railway' was given to the original Hoylake Railway. A Wirral Railway Co. Ltd was incorporated to acquire shares in the SH&DR and Wirral Railway under an Act of 11th June, 1891; then the two concerns amalgamated as the Wirral Railway. It was this second Wirral Railway which acquired powers (and failed) for the Hawarden Bridge connection, these then being given to a combined WMCQR/MSLR venture.

Complex? And is it necessary to be informed about these many unfulfilled schemes in order to understand the WMCQR? Strictly no: but in the days when railways had no transport competition, when lines once built were envisaged as standing unchallenged for centuries ahead and earning good money for their owners, a plethora of connections was the natural outcome of any management seeking expansion. WMCQR expansions followed human links – success or failure depended on personal ties, with neighbouring promotions or existing companies. Like other railways of the period, the WMCQR had its enemies and friends. It sought friends to obviate infiltration by the LNWR or GWR, friends whose enemies were likely to be those two same companies. It found friends in boards of directors, landowners, industrialists and statesmen with common bonds; in this way some unusual alliances came about: it tried to make junctions with railways who shared directors, engineers, ambitions, with it. Puffed up with its own efforts at expansion, the WMCQR inevitably burst itself; Parliamentary business was an expensive affair and only a portion of the Bills put forward obtained a satisfactory result. Powers which were obtained but not prosecuted were the subject of a statutory funeral in 1873 when the ambitions of the past were given an embarrassing burial.

Birkenhead, that shipping place which always evaded the WMCQR's ambitions, is again in the picture next year, and may as well be the first subject.

Note: Certain Bills and Acts covered both 1865 and 1866 and the latter should be read to obtain full coverage of this aspect: the following Bill is dated 1865–66.

WMCQR (ADDITIONAL POWERS/DEVIATIONS & EXTENSIONS)[10] 1865–66 *Engineer:* (not stated).

Another ambitious project though the main line was still incomplete! The Railways' numbering followed on from the previous Bill:

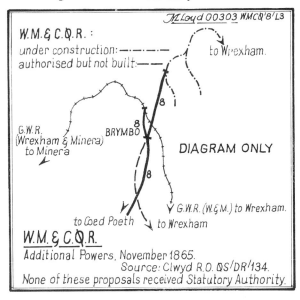

W.M.& C.Q.R. :
under construction:—·—·—·—
authorised but not built:——

𝒥.L.Loyd 00303 WMCQ'8'L3

to Wrexham.

G.W.R.
(Wrexham & Minera)
to Minera

BRYMBO

8

DIAGRAM ONLY

8

G.W.R. (W.&M.) to Wrexham.

to Coed Poeth   to Wrexham

W.M.& C.Q.R.
Additional Powers, November 1865.
        Source: Clwyd R.O. QS/DR/134.
None of these proposals received Statutory Authority.

Plate 30: In about 1895 the scene on the river bank looking upstream was one of pockets of industry surrounded by flat meadowland. One such pocket was Connah's Quay, the prominent feature here being the coaling stage with a line of emptied coal wagons, their side doors dropped open. The chimney of the Chemical Works belches out black smoke. *(Clwyd Record Office)*

Plate 31: A loaded topsail schooner (possibly the ELLEN HARRISON, built at Ulverston in 1878 and owned by local shipowners, the Vickers family) has already cast off at the stern and the steam tug stands by to tow her to the river mouth and beyond if necessary. Note the steam cranes, and the line of Traders' Wagons carrying their boxes. *(Clwyd Record Office)*

Plate 32: Another topsail schooner sits on the mud at low water, with two small hand-cranes on the adjacent wharf. These were used to sling the loaded shipping boxes straight off the Traders' Wagons into the hold of the ship. One box has been dropped onto the quay; at each corner was an eye to which the chains (hung from the spreaders of the crane) could be attached.   *c.1900   (J. Thomas Collection)*

Plate 33: Wrexham Central during construction, looking west towards Exchange. St. Mark's Church now stands upon a promontory which will become the goods yard. There seems to be an official visit taking place on the site of the platforms; the contractor's engine and wagons appear in the background.

c.1887   (J.M. Dunn Collection)

Plate 34: Wrexham Central in the early years of the present century. On the left the GCR train of assorted six-wheeled carriages lines up behind a 0−6−2 tank engine. On the right a Cambrian Railways train awaits departure for Ellesmere. Yet the whole station is almost devoid of people. St. Giles Church figures prominently, then as now.

(F. Fox-Davies)

Plate 35: By 1966 the evidence of recession in railway affairs was all around Wrexham Central; the goods yard and subsidiary tracks have been stripped under a policy known by British Rail as 'Recovery'. Even then, the present-day car park covering much of this area, would hardly have been contemplated.   *(H.B. Priestley)*

Plate 36: The somewhat drab appearance of Wrexham Exchange (the former GWR station is out of sight on the left) looking towards Central, persists to this day: here, in early British Railways days, the air of LNER ownership remains. *(C.L. Mowat)*

Plate 37: Photographs of Rhosddu Engine Shed are rare: this is clearly posed and consists of Cambrian Railways No. 79, a MS&LR type 0–6–2 tank (a WMCQR specimen?) with three of the WMCQR Beyer, Peacock 0–6–2 saddle tanks, that in the background being No. 13 with the short tank. This is a GCR-period scene.

(*J.I.C. Boyd Collection*)

Plate 38: Brymbo North Junction, looking towards Buckley Junction in the mid-1930s with Clayton's Brickworks on the left. The locomotive is an ex-Lancashire, Derbyshire & East Coast 0−6−0 tank engine, a number of which were drafted to this remote arm of the then-LNER. *(R.E. Thomas)*

Plate 39: Gwersyllt; the Down WMCQR-period platform in GCR days. One of a number of stations having quite individual buildings. *(Oakwood Collection)*

Plate 40: Gwersyllt again but post-World War II; pedestrian bridge access has been changed, electric lights have replaced oil lamps and the Nestlé Chocolate vending machine has disappeared (along with like others) during the War. The bridge carrying the Wheatsheaf Incline over the line appears in the distance. *(Oakwood Collection)*

Plate 41: River Cegidog Viaduct, seen from the northwest.
(J.I.C. Boyd)

Plate 42: In April 1956, the 2.29 pm from Seacombe drifts into Cefnybedd, a typical train formation of this period. The station is still lit by oil lamps and passengers cross the tracks on the level. *(H.B. Priestley)*

Plate 43: Caergwrle Castle station, looking south, was still very much in WMCQR condition in 1959: the overall roof had been added some years after the main building was rebuilt. Beyond the platforms is the junction for the Llay Hall Branch. *(C.L. Mowat)*

Plate 44: In January 1964 Hope Village still retained its early 1900s buildings but the signal box was an exception. On the former Up side the shelter and stone-faced platform, together with the wooden goods shed, were exactly as they were when the railway was first doubled. *(J.I.C. Boyd)*

Plate 45: Hope Junction, with its bracket signal, signal box and platform oil lamps had changed little by August 1952. It was 6.30 am and the only other living creature in view was a mole scuttling along the platform. *(J.I.C. Boyd)*

Plate 46: Another typical train formation draws up at Hope Exchange in the late 1940s. The engine of LNER Class C13 was one of a number of the class which worked the ex-LNER and Cheshire Lines Committee systems for several decades. Passengers alighting from this Wrexham-bound train here would have to pass down a footpath to the ex-LNWR station below; the station was simply an exchange point.

(W.A. Camwell)

Plate 47: Buckley Junction, seen from Bannel Bridge, was a favourite viewpoint for watching trains. The track to the left led to the former Buckley Railway at Old Buckley and the double line on the right formed the commencement of the Hawarden Loop. The signal box was of note for the melodious sounds of its block bells and gongs; its height enabled the signalman to see south over the Bridge.

1968   (C.L. Mowat)

Plate 48: A trainload of pit props has arrived from the north side of the river at Buckley Junction headed by LNER Class N5, 0–6–2 tank No. 5922 and is standing on the wrong line at Buckley Junction to allow a passenger train to pass before putting its train onto the Buckley line loop. In due course the Buckley Branch engine will collect the wagons and deliver them and their loads to the colliery customer on the Branch. Note the trap point.   *1934   (R.E. Thomas)*

Plate 49: Northbound side of Buckley Junction in October 1964; apart from some substitutions in concrete, virtually the station as it was when built . . .
                                                                        (M.E. Morton-Lloyd)

Plate 50: . . . whilst at the same date the Wrexham platform had this unique shelter, also in local brick. *(M.E. Morton-Lloyd)*

Plate 51: Hawarden, looking northwards and as opened about a decade previously. The seats have just been repainted and are reversed to prevent accident; beyond the platforms the line falls sharply towards the river. *(M.E. Morton-Lloyd Collection)*

Hawarden Railway, Station

Plate 52: Another view of Hawarden showing the curious Down side wooden shelter. The line re-assumes its climb towards Buckley Junction once the station precincts are left. The polished rails of the crossover confirm that certain passenger workings terminated here. *(F. Fox-Davies)*

Plate 53: The foot of the climb on The Hawarden Loop began at Shotton, here seen in Edwardian days. Note the ballasting over the sleepers, wooden platforms, wooden Down side building and the rural nature of the surroundings. *(F. Fox-Davies)*

Plate 54: Seen from the north bank of the Dee, the Hawarden Bridge in the week of its centenary, is still an impressive piece of engineering. However, though the driving mechanism of the nearest span, once capable of being swung, remains in place, all other machinery has been removed and the span has been fixed.

August 1989   (J.I.C. Boyd)

Plate 55: Up on the railway, above the last view, Hawarden Bridge Halt remains open. The operating tower for the Bridge has since been demolished, so even this near-recent record is now historic.   *(M.E. Morton-Lloyd)*

Plate 56: The north side of the Brymbo North Junction remained intact to the last. Here it curves sharply onto the main Wrexham–Shotton line at Stansty. Note the trap points to prevent runaways fouling the main line.   *January 1966   (J.I.C. Boyd)*

Plate 57: It is hard to believe that once this was the site of a complex junction at Plas Power between GWR, WMCQR and local collieries. The ex-WMCQR line to Brymbo remains intact, rounding the curve to the left: the ex-GWR Mineral line from Croes Newydd to Minera remains a double-track and both are in use. The useful connecting spur between the two has yet to see much traffic but its pointwork is hand-operated, there are no junction signals and the sites of the two former WMCQR signal boxes here have been lost to view.   *January 1966   (J.I.C. Boyd)*

Plate 58: Ochnall's Bridge still carries the Brymbo Branch embankment over the Brymbo Toll Road. It is a tunnel-like structure with ingenious brickwork.

October 1989 (J.I.C. Boyd)

Plate 59: The Brymbo terminus remained in use so long as traffic to and from Vron was offered; it was the only non-GWR access to Vron and though out of use for passengers since 1917, was essential as a headshunt to reverse up the steep Vron Branch. By 1934 as seen here, the passenger buildings had decayed but little, but a Second World War bomb, intended for the steelworks, made a direct hit. As if expectant of restoration of passenger traffic, the station nameboard stands intact; the firebuckets are complete and two railwaymen sit on the platform.   *(R.E. Thomas)*

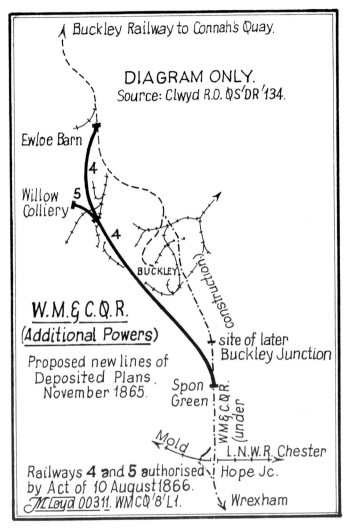

Railway No. 4 to leave the main authorised line between Hope Junction and Ashton's Branch Junction, and move northwestwards; at Spon Green to join the existing Buckley Railway near Ewloe Barn Brickworks.
Railway No. 5: a branch from No. 4 would lead westwards to serve Willow Colliery.*

The diagram (*page 130*) shows Railways 7–9, all in the Brymbo district and being extensions of line already authorised. The two-pronged westward thrust to reach Coed Poeth, Talwrn Colliery and Grosvenor Colliery, together

---

*To make any sense of this project it must be assumed that construction of the authorised Spon Green to Old Buckley length of the WMCQR was not yet begun – there would have been no advantage to construct both routes.

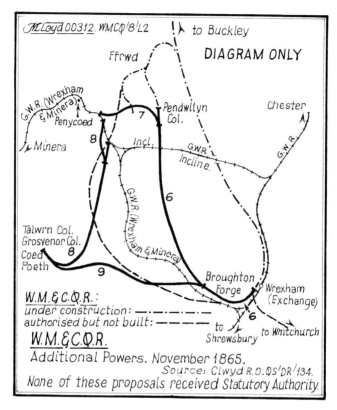

with the authorised route for a Wrexham–Brymbo line (never actually built on this site) and the Wrexham–Pendwllyn Colliery and Penycoed Junction lunge underwrite the determination of the Company to tap all possible sources of business.

There were to be two Acts in 1866: Railways Nos. 4 and 5 were given sanction but Nos. 5–9 were not approved.

The second Act of 1866 allowed deviation of the Wrexham–Whitchurch Extension permitted under the 1864 Act and abandoned the construction of railways allowed under the 1865 Act, and to build substitutions. The Act allowed a) a 'loop line' course so as to avoid using the Buckley Railway – a line thus re-enacted from the 1865 Act, b) a branch to Aston Hall Colliery, c) a branch to Sir Stephen Glynne's Railway at Little Mancot Colliery (here dubbed Mancot Old Banks Colliery). Keen readers will find evidence of repetition!

Not one of the lines envisaged in the foregoing Bill was ever made yet despite the frustrations which the Company must have felt, the board continued to adopt a far-seeing policy.

1866

The WMCQR and Hoylake Bills contained the vital issue of finding some way of crossing the river so that Birkenhead and North Wales might be rail-linked independent of going through Chester. The proposal was the brainchild of John Frederick Bateman, in conjunction with Benjamin Piercy . . . the line would pass under the Chester & Holyhead route almost at right angles, with a headway of about 14 feet; and it might be necessary to pump out drain water here which fed off the C&H but this could go into the nearby Wepre Brook. The new railway would then enter a 352 yd tunnel, falling into the bore at 1 in 55 and climbing from it on the north side at 1 in 80; the tunnel would be level under the water for some distance: here the Dee is about 250 yds wide at high spring tides, and the crown of the tunnel would be a minimum of 8 ft below low water level. Construction would be by coffer dam and details were fully explained in THE CHESTER CHRONICLE for 17th March, 1866. Bateman would arrange that navigation could circumvent such obstructions and dredge a deep channel round them for the purpose, also widening the river at that point. It was clear that the promoters had gone to great lengths to meet objections from Chester and the Dee authorities.

The plan met with criticism from engineers cross-examined on behalf of opponents to the scheme. It was apparently the practice for all ships proceeding up river to wait for the tide at Connah's Quay in order to have sufficient water to carry them further east: with bridge works there, they would have insufficient room to moor, and it was thought the sand disturbed by the works would be borne down river by the usual current of 4–4½ mph and settle in the mouth to impede navigation.

The GWR wharf at Saltney had received as many as 1,041 vessels in 1865; these came up river three abreast and required 100 ft clearance of water to do so: Captain James Knox was the Wharf Manager there. John Evans, Supervisor of the River Dee confirmed what Knox had said and Henry Robertson, Civil Engineer and supporter of the GWR, agreed works would endanger shipping and two river pilots concurred. However, this had little effect as Bateman was in fact, Consulting Engineer to the River Dee Company at the time, and they were bound to keep the river in a state of efficiency he said. The opponents' worry was that a 50 ft coffer dam would stand in the middle of the river until the tunnel was finished. To support the promoters, James Brunlees was brought in and said objections could be dismissed – he saw no difficulty in carrying out the job, which could be finished within 18 months. Overall, the gravity and effect, more of the consequences to other interested parties should a railway tunnel be completed, rather than the temporary difficulties of navigation during construction, were underlined by the 'Big Guns' which each party had brought to support their case.

The effect of a tunnel would be to break the monopoly of routing through Chester, would reduce the importance of Saltney still further; through the enterprise of two small companies, the Hoylake and the WMCQR, the mighty Great Western and LNW Railways' dominance would be ended. (In the end, however, events took a different turn. It would be August 1889 before WMCQR trains crossed the Dee, and by bridge not tunnel, and not on their own metals.)

The WMCQR and Hoylake (Extensions) Bill was submitted in June 1866 and revealed that Birkonians found the existing LNWR/GWR line gave them links to places to which they would have preferred a more direct route than through Chester, (a South Wales line being oft-quoted). James Taylor, for instance, owned a large ironworks which sent 2,000–3,000 tons of machinery annually and the Joint Line did not despatch with alacrity. He preferred a line which would, by the present-proposed Cheshire extension, cross the Wirral marshes and connect with the Great Northern and Midland railways: it would seem these latter companies would treat Birkenhead with more enthusiasm. The proprietor of Brynmally, Pendwll and Gwersyllt was Thomas Clayton; he employed 3,000 to 5,000 men and raised up to 180,000 tons of coal annually, and Birkenhead was his chief market for shipment but presently his output had to go down the GWR Wheatsheaf Incline, causing 'great inconvenience and delay', obliging him to use horses above the Incline. The WMCQR's existing line to Wrexham was of comparatively little use without the proposed extensions. Lord Grosvenor waxed enthusiastically at the scheme; Charles Turner of the Mersey Docks & Harbour Board said they needed further railway access; James Sparrow, owner of Ffrwd and Pont Plasmain Collieries, B.G.D. Cooke of Colomendy, landowner, and others all looked to Birkenhead – heady figures of 100,000 tons of fireclay per annum were envisaged for the Birkenhead market. The existing 3 ft gauge Aston Tramroad traffic required re-loading into main line wagons @ 1/2d. per ton, with an additional allowance for breakages, resulting in the coal being too 'spoiled' for Birkenhead interests.

THE CHESTER CHRONICLE (14th April, 1866) was enthusiastic over the merits of new schemes compared with existing GWR arrangement (Wheatsheaf Incline etc.) and said it was a pity the Hoylake Railway was so named as it had nothing to do with Hoylake! It was Birkenhead where they all wished to go to enable coal, bricks etc. to go by the new route instead of the GWR who charged 3/0½d. per ton transit of coal to Birkenhead and no security that GWR would not increase that charge; proposed new arrangements would be not more than 1/1¼d. per ton.

'Accidents are continually happening on the first portion of GWR line*' says Mr Thomas Clayton of Brynmally Colliery . . . branch from GWR to his works was very steep and he was losing local traffic as people dare not come up with horses and carts.'†

On 21st April, 1866 THE CHESTER CHRONICLE summarised:

a) Buckley Railway Docks Bill had no opposition as the monetary clauses were withdrawn.
b) Hoylake Bill – the Preamble had passed Committee stage.
c) WMCQR – the Preamble proved so far as Parkgate.

New Year's Day marked the opening of the WMCQR to goods and mineral traffic. It was a system starting from a terminus adjacent to the GWR station at Wrexham, on its west side, and reaching northward by single line, threw off a westwards branch to Ffrwd at Ffrwd Junction and continuing, passed over the Mold branch of the LNWR (originally part of the Chester & Holyhead Railway) at what shortly would be Hope Junction but at that time

---

*i.e. Wheatsheaf Incline.
†The meaning of this statement was that the railway ran in the roadway itself.

would only be a footpath connection. It continued to a point east of Buckley where it remained until after an Act of 10th August which permitted it to join the existing Buckley Railway: this place became Ashton's Branch Junction* and the remaining length of Buckley Railway down into town became known as Ashton's Siding. The Wrexham–Ashton's Branch Junction section, and the Ffrwd branch were opened simultaneously.†

The opening passed without formalities or demonstrations; on 6th January, 1866 THE ADVERTISER noted:

> . . . marked by nothing but the running of trains that have already traversed the line for the last month without any notice of the fact having been given to the general public. The line is not yet in a complete state for passenger traffic; the signals have to be erected . . . at the opening . . . (in a few weeks) the Chancellor of the Exchequer is expected to be present and take a prominent part in the proceedings.

Of course, everyone knew who HE was!

The same paper added more on 20th January:

> The line is all ready for the Board of Trade inspection but this is delayed due to the non-arrival of signals. Ballasting was completed some weeks ago and stations are built. Stationmasters have been appointed and a magnificent set of passenger carriages have been ready for the rails at any moment . . . last Thursday an engine and two composite carriages left Wrexham station after half past two and performed the journey to Connah's Quay, a distance of 14 miles, in 20 minutes.

THE CHESTER CHRONICLE for 6th January, 1866 reported under two headings: OPENING TO GOODS AND MINERAL TRAFFIC and WMCQ, both versions being virtually the same, viz:

> This railway was opened for through goods and mineral traffic on Monday last. There was no formality or demonstration on the occasion which was marked by nothing but the running of the trains that have already traversed the line for the last month without any notice of the fact having been given to the general public. The line is not yet in a complete state for passenger traffic, the signals have to be erected and other minor matters have to be performed. At the opening of the line (in a few weeks) the Chancellor of the Exchequer is expected to be present and take a prominent part in the proceedings. Due notice of the ceremony will be given.

As to the opening, a typical notice in THE WREXHAM WEEKLY ADVERTISER read:

> ### Notice to the Public
>
> This Railway has now opened for through goods and mineral traffic. Application for rate to be made to Mr H. Davies, Traffic Manager's Office, Hope Street Chambers, 13, Hope Street, Wrexham.
>
> *February 1866*

THE CHESTER CHRONICLE for 3rd and 17th February, 1866 had not failed to note the changes which would affect the city of Chester by railway proposals in hand. The Hoylake Railway (Extensions) and Buckley Railway (Docks at Connah's Quay) Bills had passed Standing Orders, and were each likely to take business away. Indeed, Chester Council meeting on 13th December,

---

*On some early Railway Clearing House maps shown as Buckley Junction.
†In 1990 the section Wrexham–Buckley [Junction] is part of a line which remains open. The Ffrwd Branch was closed in 1930 and lifted in 1935. (The first ½ mile was retained initially as a shunting neck for sidings beside the main line but in 1937 'no traffic but kept in repair and working order'): RAILWAY MAGAZINE, November 1937, p.364.

1865 had instructed the Town Clerk to prepare a petition against these Bills, and also that of the WMCQR, such petition not to be presented if suitable protective clauses were inserted, including the preservation of public interests whilst the work was in hand. The Council objected to interference with the river at Connah's Quay by the contractor for the WMCQR, and they sought the 'assistance and co-operation of the Board of Trade' in this respect.

When Col. Yolland returned to re-inspect on 26th April he made a point of reference to the proposal for a line linking the GWR Wheatsheaf Incline with the WMCQR main line 'with reference to the inclined GW sidings which fall at Wheatsheaf Junction towards the WMCQ – all barred by stop blocks – no traffic likely to be interchanged with the GWR at this point for some time to come.' How right he was! 'Land for a double line is already in hand here and a suitable Blind Siding will then be made at the Wheatsheaf Junction . . . (for safety reasons).'

With the 'go-ahead' for a passenger service, there was a special train on 30th April to celebrate the occasion; passengers – in borrowed vehicles, there being insufficient for the occasion – were taken on an outing to Buckley and Connah's Quay, an event which the physical features of the Buckley Railway must have made doubly exciting. A representative of THE CHESTER CHRONICLE was on the trip and said:

> On Monday last directors and friends of this undertaking had a trip to Buckley and Connah's Quay previous to the formal opening of the line for passenger traffic. On the following day between 600–700 persons availed themselves of the opportunity of having a trip gratis and soon after 10 am the train started, calling at the different stations on the line which were decorated with flags and banners etc. After enjoying themselves the train returned soon after 2 pm bringing a great number of people from Connah's Quay, Buckley and neighbourhood. The last return trip took a number of persons from Wrexham to Bridge End, Hope, where a concert was held. The day's proceedings closed without an accident. On Thursday passenger trains commenced running* and the opening of the WMCQR is now an accomplished fact. The line is likely to be most beneficial to the district through which it passes.

The following day, 1st May, the line was formally opened to passengers. The service was limited to Wrexham–Buckley only, a station at the latter place being provided at a point where Knowl Lane crossed the line, a few yards short of Ashton's Branch Junction. North of this, and over the Buckley Railway, passenger trains did not run – save occasionally. The Ffrwd branch never had a passenger service, either. There is a tradition that for a few days, trains ran only as far as Gwersyllt.

Throughout the spring the newspapers carried various speculative reports as a possible opening day for the WMCQR to carry passengers, most of them the product of optimistic imagination, but at last THE WREXHAM ADVERTISER of 28th April carried the news, long awaited:

---

*(but not on the old Buckley section – JICB!)

WMCQR

Notice – the Public are respectfully informed that this Railway will be opened for passenger traffic on

Tuesday 1st May, 1866

upon which date and until further notice, trains will run as under

Wrexham to Mold & Buckley

	Weekdays			Fares from Wrexham				
				Single			Return	
				1st	2nd	3rd	1st	2nd
Leave				s. d.	s. d.	s. d.	s. d.	s. d.
Wrexham	9.40	2.00	7.00					
Gwersyllt	9.45	2.05	7.05	6	3	2	9	5
Cefnybedd	9.53	2.13	7.13	10	6	4	1. 3	9
Caergwrle	10.00	2.20	7.20	1. 2	9	5	1. 9	1. 2
Hope Junction	10.07	2.27	7.27	1. 8	1. 0	7	2. 6	1. 6
Mold (bus)	10.40	3.00	8.00	2. 6	1. 9	1. 4	4. 0	3. 0
Buckley arr.	10.15	2.35	7.35	2. 0	1. 4	9	3. 0	2. 0

Buckley & Mold to Wrexham

	Weekdays			Fares from Buckley				
				Single			Return	
				1st	2nd	3rd	1st	2nd
Leave				s. d.	s. d.	s. d.	s. d.	s. d.
Buckley	8.25	12.00	5.15					
Mold (bus)	7.50	11.25	4.40	1. 3	1. 0	9	2. 2	1. 11
Hope Junction	8.33	12.05	5.23	5	3	2	8	5
Caergwrle	8.40	12.10	5.30	10	6	4	1. 3	11
Cefnybedd	8.45	12.15	5.35	1. 2	9½	5½	1. 9	1. 2
Gwersyllt	8.52	12.22	5.42	1. 7	1. 1	7	2. 5	1. 8
Wrexham	9.00	12.30	5.50	2. 0	1. 4	9	3. 0	2. 0

Third Class tickets were issued on a limited basis, but Market Tickets at 3rd Class fares were issued for Mold Market on Wednesdays and Saturdays, and on Fair Days; and to Wrexham Market on Thursdays and Saturdays.

At this time the traffic manager's office was still in Hope Chambers at Wrexham.

Even in this first month (May) the popularity of the Railway was such that extra trains had to be run on Saturdays: these left Buckley at 2.45 pm and Wrexham at 9 pm; and here again, only 1st and 2nd Class tickets were issued, 3rd Class tickets being restricted to Market Days and dubbed 'Market Tickets'.

Exciting though the new railway must have been, 1866 was to be overshadowed by events of national nature which affected everyone. There was financial instability throughout the country and on 10th May the bankers, Overend, Gurney & Co. suspended all payments: the crisis ensuing had great effect on the railways, large and small, and especially on contractors who were in the process of construction. The matter is too broad for detail herein but it affected Benjamin Piercy to the degree that his assets were handed over to Trustees.

No sooner had the WMCQR been opened, than there were numerous petitions to Parliament to bring about the removal of the Turnpike Trusts' toll gates: within half a mile of Wrexham centre, there were still five Trusts and a Toll Bar as late as 1869. George H. Whalley (MP for Peterborough) successor to the Lloyds at Plas Madoc and Sheriff for Denbighshire, led the cry to have the roads opened, and of his activities some wags had written:

> In a bar wig and sword he walks, the Laird of Plas Maggot.*

In the summer months not all the excursionists were from the town to the riverside, and in July a newspaper reported:

> On Monday last the people of Wrexham were surprised to see some hundreds of well-dressed strangers crowding our streets . . . an excursion from Connah's Quay rather a novelty in Wrexham although we have had a railway passing by our town for nearly twenty years . . . happy to state church and steeple were open to them which proved a nice hour's wile away [sic] . . . about 7 o'clock they all took their departure in safety from the station . . .

This implied that there were doubts on the latter score!

A week later the Ragged School took the train to Cefnybedd:

> . . . and spent a delightful day rolling and romping . . . about the hill . . .

Simple pleasures indeed. By now the WMCQR had been dubbed 'The Connah's Quay'.

Penyffordd (where presumably the chord line was now ready) was taking a more important role as the link line into the LNWR for excursions: during August the handbills were headed:

WMCQR & CHESTER & HOLYHEAD RLYS

Cheap excursion to Rhyl, Abergele, Llandudno Junction, Conway and Bangor via Hope Junction & LNWR without change of carriages on Tuesday 28th August . . .

There was an opportunity for passengers to extend their journey from Bangor to Carnarvon [sic] and a connecting train left and returned to Buckley for Hope Junction and vice versa; the 2nd Class fare was 3/6d., double for 1st. The world had indeed become a smaller place in less than three months.

A cheap trip using WMCQR train into Wrexham Exchange and continuing by GWR took excursionists to Llangollen for the first time; over 500 people took part.

Safety came to the fore again in August:

> . . . A few days ago a flock of geese – an old bird and a score of young – strayed onto the WMCQR near Stansty Forge when a luggage train came upon them and killed the old bird and more than half the young ones.

A horse omnibus linked the WMCQR station in Wrexham (probably the GWR also) with the Wynnstay Arms; but on 6th October:

> . . . the axle broke and the bus fell on its side with great force: a guard of the WMCQR who was with the driver, was thrown violently to the ground . . .

---

*'Plas Maggot' – a play on his residence's name!

The novelty of the railway stirred the pens of the local correspondents. For example:

WREXHAM & DENBIGH WEEKLY ADVERTISER 26th May, 1866.
    WMCQ. The Saturday evening train advertised in the last issue brought 400 passengers, a result highly gratifying to the Company and to the tradesmen of Wrexham . . . 'grist to the mills of both'. The number of passengers in a week far exceeds what the Company were warranted in expecting.

and again the next week, 2nd June:

    WMCQ. Cheap trip along WMCQ line to River Dee, thence by packet to New Brighton is likely to be afforded to the inhabitants of Wrexham and district on Monday week. Considering the beauty of the scenery on the river from here to Connah's Quay, we think it will afford an excellent treat for all who wish to profitably spend a day's holiday.

The passenger carriages were in fact, secondhand, four-wheeled vehicles purchased from the LNWR. They impressed sufficiently for it to be written:

    . . . they are roomy, lofty and nicely furnished, the panel of the door of the 1st Class compartments having the arms of Shropshire and Flintshire painted thereon, with a plume of feathers. The plume of feathers is to be erased, and the borough arms of Wrexham painted in its place.

The appearance of the Shropshire emblem was due to the intended incursion to Whitchurch, but clearly Denbighshire was slighted.
    Of the locomotive SIR STEPHEN ('named after the baronet of Hawarden Castle')

    . . . it was one of those which carries its load of water on its own back, dispensing with a tender . . . this does not add to the beauties of the locomotive.

It appears that the building of the railway had robbed the GW station-master of his entire garden, and the line had had to make a detour round Crispin Cottage as the Company had failed to take possession of it.

    The cottage stands, napped all round its foundations, as isolated a pillar as 'Lott's wife', forming, we should imagine, a delightful residence to an occupant or small family particularly if they should be of nervous temperament and prone to dream of earthquakes.

The GWR had stipulated that enough space must be left between the WMCQR station and Rhosddu to allow the GWR to double their line at some future date.
    Throughout this time the Company was plagued by 'malicious trespassers', the worst cases being in the neighbourhood of Stansty Iron Works, and Buckley: extra police were put on by the Board, and a reward of £25 offered if conviction was made.
    An immediate effect noted by local traders was:

    . . . the greater disposition to meet the wants of tradesmen by the GWR since the WMCQ line opening, with goods delivered earlier since competition; we have heard that a bet was placed on a cask of oil being delivered to High Street, Wrexham by 9 am after leaving Liverpool by GWR at 1 pm the previous day. The GWR succeeded in meeting the delivery time. A new hat depended on this punctual arrival and the winning party has since displayed a white hat, whilst the loser has shown a white feather.

Such humour is seldom found in local papers today!

Wrexham Town Council voiced loudly that the new Railway's Works etc. should be built in the town – when the Council had asked the GWR to do the same

> . . . they took no notice of the matter: the Saltney people petitioned for the GWR works and got the benefit . . .

and the Council said the town had done so much to promote the WMCQR that it thought at least this much was due to it.

Excursions down to Connah's Quay and thence by steamer were a popular feature of this first year; in June the flavour of the newspaper advertisements varied somewhat and there was:

> . . . an agreeable hour in a saunter on the shore, or a sail on the water and inhale the refreshing breezes that will reach them from the Irish Sea. The trip there and back, a distance of nearly 30 miles, can be accomplished in comfortable carriages for 1/6d.

(Not for those early excursionists the rubbish and black mud of the Dee shore which it would ultimately become, nor the inhalation of fumes from Connah's Quay Power Station or John Summers' steel establishment across the river!)

Not only did the riverside entice, but later that month

> . . . a WMCQ train left Wrexham for Manchester last Monday. The weather was as unfavourable as it could be. 700 took tickets for the 'cotton metropolis'. It rained during the whole journey and of course it rained in Manchester all day.

But for the folk of Wrexham, this must have been as exciting as anything they had experienced before in their lives. Which route did the train take? via Hope Junction with reversal?

The following month a 'Delightful Sea Voyage from Connah's Quay' was announced '. . . embarking in a steam boat at Connah's Quay by sea to Llandudno.' The train left Wrexham at 7 am and was allowed 5 hours at Llandudno, returning from there at 5 pm. The 1st Class fare was 5/6d. with slight reductions for 'covered cars' (the nature of these is not known but there would hardly be sufficient passenger stock for a full booking). Interest is centred on the availability of tickets: stations are not mentioned, but rather they were obtainable from Mr W. Edwards, Cannon Inn and Mr W. Bayley, bookseller of Wrexham, Mr H. Seddon of Brynmally, Mrs Edwards, Holly Bush, Mr John Jones, Cymmau, Thomas Cotterill, Frood (a common spelling), and Mr W. Venables, Moss. Wrexham apart, those in the outlying places had no rail transport to carry them to the excursion. The enterprise of the Company was considerable.

THE WREXHAM ADVERTISER regularly gave mention of the 'Four-horse Omnibus' which ran from there to Mold via Wheatsheaf, Cefnybedd, Caergwrle, Pontblyddyn to Mold (Black Lion Hotel). It commenced in Wrexham at the Talbot Inn and left there at 6 pm calling at the GWR station and leaving on the arrival of the train from the south; arrival at Mold was 7.30 pm.

The single fare was 4/- (inside) and 3/- (outside), return tickets being available from Wrexham and Mold only. It was stressed that 'No fees to be paid to Coachman or Guard'. The edition of 21st April, 1866 said:

> On and after the opening of the WMCQ Rly for passenger traffic, the omnibus will run between Mold and Hope Junction station in connection with all trains to Wrexham, of which due notice will be given.

Later advertisements gave the inward run as leaving Mold at 10 am to arrive Wrexham 11.30 am.

Leaving the WMCQR proper for a moment: passenger trains on the Buckley section appeared to come a stage nearer when the Buckley Railway (Additional Powers) Act came into being on 18th May permitting passengers under Section 4. But there the matter ended!

A look at the Parliamentary scene shows the Acts affecting the WMCQR during the year:

> 1) 18th May. Allowing the Company to raise additional capital viz. £180,000 in preferred and deferred shares, and £60,000 in loans.
> 2) 23rd July. 'The Buckley & WMCQR Co.'s Act' allowed the WMCQR to work the Buckley Railway in return for a guarantee of 5% on Buckley Ordinary and Preference Shares, and interest on the Debentures. This confirmed the original Agreement of 30th June, 1863, thereafter the Buckley Railway became a first charge on the WMCQR. A rent of the Buckley Railway was fixed at £436 per half year. The effect of this Act was to allow the two railways to be worked as one system.
> 3) The Act of 10th August was one with two chapters; the former was The WMCQR (Additional Powers) Act, and the latter The WMCQR (Extensions) Act. These concerned the aforementioned northward extension of the WMCQR to join the Buckley Railway; Railway No. 1 (5 m. 1 fur.) to extend to Connah's Quay (a forerunner of the later Hawarden Loop); Railway No. 2 (5 fur.) a branch off No. 1 to Little Mancot Colliery to join Sir Stephen Glynne's Railway; Railway No. 3 (1 m. 4 fur.) a branch off No. 1 to Aston Hall Colliery; there was to be a deviation of Railway No. 4 of the unbuilt Whitchurch Extension.

None of these powers was ever exercised.

Although the fruits of the Extensions Act of 1866 were to prove a disappointing harvest, the Act had the effect of a reconciliation between the owners of the 'private Tramway called the Aston Tramway' and the WMCQR. Under Section 35, the owners 'of the Tramway (Charles Amesbury Whitley Deans Dundas, an infant, and in the partnership called 'The Buckley Railway Company and Messieurs William Hancock & Co.') are interested, and the Heads for an Arrangement relating thereto which are set forth in the Schedule to this Act annexed ... by this Act confirmed and binding ... and shall be carried into full effect', would receive financial compensation.

The Schedule states that the WMCQR agreed to take over the traffic formerly carried by the Tramway (there were in fact, two Tramways by title making end-on junction with each other so that in practice they formed a continuous route: the Buckley Railway Co. was the southern portion, the Aston Tramroad the northern).

Back to the line, no steps had been taken to replace Rhosddu Level Crossing with the promised bridge and angry letters appeared in the papers. Money was short and this was stated to be the cause of lack of progress; it was confirmed when Thomas Barnes (a former Chairman) had to lend cash to the Company to buy essential rails from 'The Ebbw Vale Co.' in mid-December. The new dock at Connah's Quay received its first vessel on 13th October.

T.E. Minshall, up to now the Resident Engineer, was replaced by Benjamin Piercy's elder brother Robert in early July; his salary was to be £340 p.a.

A curious note in THE WREXHAM ADVERTISER appeared on 24th November under the WMCQ heading:

> The inhabitants of Frood are querying why Frood station is kept closed when users would total any three stations together. The inhabitants of Moss are equally inquisitive.

This is a strange comment; such stations would have been on the Ffrwd mineral line – had stations been built thereon initially in the expectancy of a passenger service in due course? This year the WMCQR was among other railways to be part of a proposed amalgamated Welsh Railway system under a later arrangement, others would be: Denbigh, Ruthin & Corwen; Mold & Denbigh Junction; Buckley; Bishop's Castle and Manchester & Milford.[11]

The Secretary's office, previously at Wrexham station, was moved to Oswald Chambers, Oswestry in August and all future Board Meetings were to be held there. This followed Savin's bankruptcy in April and was to accommodate the Secretary, George Lewis who acted for the Cambrian Railways there (1864–1882).

The year again closed with the submission of yet another Bill.

Whilst no doubt the Secretary's desk was groaning under the weight of paperwork associated with various Parliamentary promotions, the little local bother came to the fore again: it was the matter of the promised bridge in lieu of the road crossing at Rhosddu. The Wrexham District Highways Board had found that writing to the Railway's Secretary was a waste of time; they addressed the Board of Trade direct saying that 'goods trains run over this crossing without first having erected a bridge' (by then, the WMCQR had been open for a month) 'as provided for in the Deposited Plans'.

The Board of Trade gave reply by return, saying the Act permitted the Company to cross the road on the level and they cannot stop goods trains. When on 23rd March the Company undertook to build a bridge, the Highways Board was mollified. Then came trouble. It was pointed out that the GWR and WMCQR crossings are virtually one crossing though the GWR is double track and the WMCQR single,* as the two systems are only 7–8 ft apart and separated by gates; the crossing therefore suffers from three sets of gates. The GWR now insists that the WMCQR agreed to build the bridge . . .

We must now pass on to 1871 – in the meanwhile nothing had been done. In August the GWR repeat – direct to the Board of Trade – that the WMCQR agreed etc. . . . and that no action had been taken by that Company since April 1866. The WMCQR made excuse for this by pointing out that prior to August 1869 the Company was under the control of the Court of Chancery and that its present Board was only constituted at that date. 'The directors are now trying to meet their legal obligations including the erection of this bridge'.

---

*Ironically, in 1990 the 'WMCQR' is double and the 'GWR' is single – so to speak!

1867

The year began with a favourable termination to competition with the Aston Tramroad, the last of the local plateways still in operation. In January Mr Pugh submitted an Agreement with Messrs. Hancock & Dundas 'as to the Aston Tramway'. But the Buckley Railway and Tramroad were in the lime-light again in September: owing to chronic locomotive condition only 168 tons passed down the Railway for shipment in six days instead of the customary 500 tons and therefore competing brickmaking firms resorted to the old tramroad and shipped from Queensferry. Complaints were legion.

Financial problems still dogged the Company, and were to last way beyond the year in question. The Sheriff had seized the rolling stock in the matter of a solicitor's debt for £500 right at the start of the year; but fortunate-ly it was almost as quickly released on payment and the Inspectors of the Estate of Benjamin Piercy advanced £1,554 3s. 8d. with which to pay the Railway Clearing House which threatened legal proceedings. Nonetheless, the Company found itself in Receivership by January 1868, George Lewis, the Secretary being made Receiver at the suit of Mr Fynney, a Debenture holder.

The year was also notable for the Company's entry into marine matters; early in the year a tug HERO had been hired @ £26 a month from Charles Hughes of Mowl & Co. following instructions to the Traffic Committee in February to secure the services of a steam driven tug for Connah's Quay. (The GWR had tugs based on Saltney, named MANXMAN and ANN POOLE). Presumably HERO's duties were confined to Connah's Quay interests but it was not a successful steamer, and it was replaced by another hired steamship in November 1868. This was the SECRETARY; details of it are unknown, but in June 1870 it was involved in the retrieval of the PROGRESS which had been abandoned in a sinking condition in the river, loaded with Patent Manure from the chemical works. The matter went to Mold County Court where the PROGRESS owners sued the WMCQR 'for illegal detention and damages for £50' – the verdict went in favour of the Railway Company, with costs; SECRETARY was then purchased for £1,500 but was out of use by August 1874; it was sold that month for £430.

Rule Books had been compiled by November 1865 but were still not available and in an effort to meet a crisis with the Board of Trade, copies were borrowed from the Hoylake Railway with which there were strong links.

Richard Samuel France of Shrewsbury* the WMCQR contractor for part of 1865 had become bankrupt in 1868: he was replaced during 1867 by Abraham Pilling, the latter coming to notice in connection with work at Connah's Quay, for which the Board had allocated £5,500.

Robert Piercy reported a continuing trespass by Mr Clayton of Brynmally Colliery – whose character was well known to the Board – who was pump-ing water from his new coal pits and turning it down alongside and damag-ing the Railway. Clayton was not the only man in trouble for on the recom-mendation of the Traffic Committee, Mr R. Hughes Davies the Traffic Manager was suspended on 30th March, all stationmasters and traders being informed to that effect.

---

*also Mold & Denbigh Junction Railway contractor since June 1865 and Potteries, Shrewsbury & North Wales Railway prior to this.

Thomas Barnes was made Chairman on 7th May for a second time and a little confidence appeared. At the same time Benjamin Piercy demonstrated his interest in the business in tangible form – it must be recalled that he and Robertson were largely instrumental in founding the business and he may now have considered that its management and conduct, so leading to its bankruptcy, could have been avoided. He then offered to work the WMCQ and Buckley Railways, in conjunction 'with others' for a term of years @ 50% of gross receipts. The Railways would find the rolling stock out of capital, and the offer was on the assumption that the Buckley Railway would be made into a passenger line. Faced with this proposition, the Board was willing to entertain further negotiations so long as his associates were persons of responsibility in the opinion of the Chairman (Barnes), Deputy Chairman (R.K. Penson) and Mr Fynney. This condition suggests that the Board was dubious of some of Piercy's connections and it was clear that Piercy and friends were equally dissatisfied with WMCQR management.

Turning now to the locomotives: CHANCELLOR, the original WMCQR engine (0–6–0 tender arrangement) had had to receive heavy repairs at the Cambrian Railways Oswestry Works. The Company having no funds, the engine was held at Oswestry until payment was made: in the end (in July) the Chairman James Barnes personally advanced the cost of £450 on a two-month loan basis. Nevertheless, the engine was out of traffic again in the next year, and repaired at Wrexham. On the short branch at Caergwrle (to serve Lascelles' (or Lassell's) Brewery) Robert Piercy complained of the 'injury sustained by locomotives working Mr Lascelles' branch': the cause or effect is not clear; the site of the branch can still be traced and gives no evidence of operational problems.

The LORD RICHARD was now out of service awaiting repair (was this the engine 'injured' on the Brewery branch?) – it had only been in service for eighteen months and required £300 spending on it; this work was to be done by a Mr Durgan who would be paid in monthly instalments of £26 each.

Any lineside observer at this time might be excused for his bewilderment at the variety of locomotives seen at work or under evaluation; a flavour of this situation – arising entirely from the antique condition of what the Company owned to date – continues throughout 1867 and can be conveniently summarized:

1) August; Robert Piercy instructed to 'accept the engine of Henry Hughes, Loughborough, on trial for one clear week'.

2) The above engine returned to Loughborough as being found too light for the traffic (9th September).

3) In September, Manager reported arrival at 'Hope Junction' of an engine which might replace that returned to Loughborough. This new arrival (sent by Messrs B. Piercy and F. Mackenzie) 'for the Company's use'; another would follow in the course of a week and a third would follow – the source of these is not known and the above circumstance created a recommendation directing these gentlemen to the priority of regaining possession of wheels at Hudswell's, rather than new engines.

4) In the same month, WHEATLEY taken out of traffic as quite unfit to work.

5) In the next month F. Mackenzie recommended that HERCULES, on hire from Isaac W. Boulton of Ashton-under-Lyne should be returned there, as it had broken down.

6) Messrs. J. Taylor & Co. (of Sandycroft?) had been repairing locomotives and remained unpaid for the work: they were offered Buckley Railway Stock in lieu when they threatened to enforce payment. The Secretary was told to see them and emphasise the value of the security offered!

7) On 20th November the hire of the engine sent by Mr Mackenzie was terminated (HERCULES?)

8) Clearly the Secretary had had partial success with Taylor whom it would seem had been repairing LORD RICHARD. According to the earlier Minute that engine was being repaired by Mr Durgan – or was Mr Durgan of Messrs. J. Taylor & Co.? Whatever, Taylor agreed to take £350 in cash and various amounts at intervals to follow: Buckley Stock @ £250 was lodged as collateral security for the deferred payments.

9) In December Mr Mackenzie asked for £110 for engine hire, and wanted 'the large engine sent by him to be returned immediately' but he was told the large engine had been returned 'some time since' and that the charge for hire had been referred to Mr Piercy. (Clearly the Board was not going to finance any measure which Piercy may have done without their consent.)

All in all, there is a savour that the right hand did not know what the left was doing, and that the Board was being embarrassed by the Piercy brothers' activities, urgent though they may have been in Piercy eyes.

Though the Company may have appeared to own the vehicles which ran upon it, it was clearly stated that all the rolling stock was now hired from The Midland Wagon Co. (this was in practice, all goods and mineral waggonage). A somewhat cumbersome arrangement had taken place on 1st July; up to that time the stock had been owned by Mr William Blackmore as trustee on behalf of Messrs. Brown, Shipley & Co. With the Railway Company's consent, this was now sold to The Midland Wagon Co. for £6,500, payable in three instalments at six, twelve and eighteen months; and the Wagon Co. gave three Promissory Notes bearing interest @ 5% from date until payment.

Consequent upon the foregoing, the stock was to be vested in Mr Blackmore on behalf of the vendors and Mr Short on behalf of the MW Co.; the MW Co. would release the stock to the WMCQR on due payment of Promissory Notes. It would then be hired from The Wagon Co. by the Railway Co.; there was to be a financial arrangement on a bond of £10,000 due to Brown, Shipley & Co. from the Railway Company. In July three vans on hire from MW Co. were sent back as being too light for the traffic.

On 15th August an Act was obtained which allowed an extension of time for the Whitchurch Extension – for which only a few spades had entered the ground. It was now the turn of Benjamin Piercy's elder brother Robert to centre the stage; he became (in addition to his £300 a year position as Resident Engineer from 10th July, 1866) controller of the locomotive department 'until the details of management are finally arranged' on 17th August, and the following week 'Manager of the Line in all Departments' in place of R. Hughes Davies. He told the Board that by spending £2,000 at Connah's Quay, traffic would increase by upwards of £150 per week. The Traffic Committee, keeping a close eye on things, was now meeting every Saturday in the Company's office.

An incident which might have had serious consequences took place on 4th September when the Down 7.20 pm train left Wrexham without the

Train Staff and a collision between trains 'was narrowly averted'. The Manager, Robert Piercy, had discharged the driver immediately, but maintained the stationmaster was partly to blame; the latter excused himself by saying he had too much to do in the goods warehouse, and had left the Staff in the custody of the porter, who was severely censured for neglect of duty.

On 9th September George Lewis (Secretary) resigned – clearly on good terms as he was back again later – and F.G. Whitwham,* the friend of Benjamin Piercy, took his place. On the same day, payment regarding release of the locomotive wheels which were being held at Hudswell, was sanctioned.

In October the Buckley Board received complaints that the WMCQR was not working traders' traffic expeditiously; bricks were shipped in irregular manner at Connah's Quay; berths where vessels loaded were not kept in good order; Connah's Quay crane men were not at work as they had not been paid.

During November a provisional arrangement was confirmed with the Bishop's Castle Railway (another Company with mutual personnel i.e. through the Piercys) for John Craston, Manager (1865–1893) of that line, to work for the WMCQR on the basis of £175 pa salary, for four days each week, giving two days to the Bishop's Castle Railway, as Assistant Manager and Accountant. The GWR refused to grant him a Pass over their system! Out on the line during the year, work had begun with exchange arrangements at Hope Junction on 18th November; and an unconfirmed source states that the passing loop was now installed at Northop Hall on the Buckley section; certainly there was already a siding here, and a loop extended north of the siding itself, over the level crossing and towards the site of Broad Oak Colliery siding, before 1895. (There appears to have been no *proper* provision to exchange passengers at Hope Junction until the end of 1867, when the Engineer was told to put such in hand and an exchange platform Hope Junction opened in February 1868.)

1868

During January THE CHESTER CHRONICLE reported that the Mold & Denbigh Junction Railway was seeking running powers over parts of the WMCQR; and the next month an idea was considered for reducing the Company's debt, including an arrangement for working by the LNWR, put forward by Mr Cawkwell who suggested that, subject to satisfactory arrangements being made with the GWR regarding Wrexham traffic, the LNWR would be prepared to work the WMCQR for 50% gross traffic receipts. The Board agreed that these negotiations might continue on such a basis . . . but the matter then fades from the Minutes. The interlinking station with the LNWR at Hope (Hope Junction) was opened. 'Station' it was not; like its complementary on the low level LNWR beneath, it was simply a platform in open countryside, linked by a footpath to the other: it was ¼ mile north of the LNWR.

A few days later (15th February) Thomas Edgeworth the Secretary died; and his place was filled by the former Secretary, George Lewis who had joined the Board on 8th February; he had become its first Receiver.

---

*Piercy's executor and chairman of his Estate affairs after his death.

On 4th February the two Buckley engines came into collision at Connah's Quay, No. 1 being overpowered when descending with a train. THE CHESTER CHRONICLE for 8th February reported:

> WMCQ. On Tuesday an accident occurred to a goods train on the Buckley branch of the above line. About noon the train broke loose and owing to the slippery state of the metals the driver and guard lost control over it. The train ran down the incline into a throw-off line provided for that purpose. A number of trucks were damaged, but fortunately all the men in charge escaped with a few bruises.

Word for word, the same story appeared in THE WREXHAM ADVERTISER. Another account mentions 'engines collided' . . . they did.

The newspaper accounts of the runaway did not please everyone; one reader wrote to THE WREXHAM ADVERTISER on 15th February suggesting that the Oswestry papers should not have 'such an imaginative reporter on the staff', and 'what absurd and sensational reports some of the newspapers have published recently of this accident'.

THE OSWESTRY ADVERTISER was accurate in this wise:

> A goods train on the Buckley line, rushing down the incline with the velocity which the efforts of the driver and all the breaks [sic] on the waggons (there was no brake van) were unable to lessen, rushing into the siding which was constructed a short time ago to prevent a runaway waggon from going onto the LNWR . . . the train became a complete wreck . . . the engine was overturned . . . waggons piled one upon the other . . . happily all the men had jumped off except one who was badly hurt about the head . . .

The article continued on a 'might-have-been' basis, had the recent catch points not been installed to forego a collision in the LNWR station; went on to paint a lurid picture of wagons hurtling down onto the decks of ships at the quay . . . an event which fortunately, did not occur.

This accident contributed in some measure to the financial crisis of the Company; for on 8th February Mr Fynney (appointed a director in 1867) wrote to the Secretary 'the Company's property seems to be injured and smashed in a most extraordinary manner. I hope you have been able to obtain the temporary hire of an engine to do the work'. Fynney would have had good cause to worry, for both the Buckley engines were now out of service. The Locomotive Superintendent of the Cambrian Railways (Walker) was called in to report on the amount of damage to locomotives and wagons, and later in the month Mr Clarke of Hudswell, Clarke & Rodgers, makers of the engines, attended the Board Meeting and was asked to furnish an estimate for the repair of WHEATLEY and KENYON. Walker also attended that meeting; his estimate of damages must have proved well wide of the actual; it was:

One engine	say	£30
12 wagons		£64 16s. 0d.
1 wagon (Mr Jones)		£22
1 wagon (WMCQR)		£20
4 wagons (Messrs. Davison's)		£75
18 small lorrys [sic]*		£12
		£223 16s. 0d.

*Small trolleys used by Buckley traders and transported on flat wagons.

By March Hudswell's estimate was to hand; it 'exceeded that of other parties and could not be entertained'. with influence from the Chairman (Thomas Barnes) it had been arranged that WHEATLEY be repaired by the Lancashire & Yorkshire Railway at their Miles Platting Works; meanwhile Mr Craston had received an offer from the Metropolitan Carriage & Wagon Co. to repair the nine wagons, property of the Ewloe Hall Coal Co. for £140, and the four belonging to Davison & Co. for £116.

The work on WHEATLEY's repair was soon done and by the beginning of April the engine was in service again. Not so KENYON; so arrangements were made to hire an engine from Parry & Co. of London (probably HERCULES) for three months at £12 10s. 0d. a week. Further expense in the locomotive department was necessary: SIR STEPHEN's tyres were worn out and new ones were ordered from Sharp, Stewart & Co. Ltd. of Manchester for £69, whilst James Durgan offered to 'do certain repairs to the same engine for £68'. This offer was taken up, but Durgan exceeded his estimate and claimed an additional £29 19s. 8d. . . . he may have had to whistle for that amount.

KENYON still lay around in that same useless condition as resulted from the accident and it was clear that begging and borrowing could not put off the evil day when a fundamental restoration must be done. So, with payment guaranteed by the Chairman on behalf of the Company, the engine was sent to Hudswell, Clarke & Rodgers* whose price had earlier been rejected; meanwhile the Receiver was authorised to pay the L & YR for work done on WHEATLEY, and by the late autumn the engine was back in traffic.

A report from the Traffic Department on the imperfect performance of CHANCELLOR and HERCULES (the latter on hire) resulted in an edict that 'they were not to be worked unless safe', and in consequence both Mr Lewis and Mr Hughes were empowered to hire additional engines as necessary – in general, 1868 was not a happy year for locomotives.

More expense was foreshadowed in a Minute 'The Inland Revenue claimed Passenger Duty of £104 2s. 8½d. for duty in respect of cheaper train traffic from the opening of the line than had been approved by the Board of Trade'.

More personnel problems followed – Robert Piercy the Resident Engineer had his engagement ended when he asked for his salary due to him on account. The offices of Secretary, Manager and Accountant were now to be combined and with the wages of a clerk, the combined salaries were not to exceed £350 pa and then Craston, by now Traffic Manager also, resigned; all the foregoing on 6th April. Walker of the Cambrian Railways was called in to keep a watching brief on things until William Holker (at an unknown date) was appointed as Locomotive Foreman, John Broughton† became Manager

---

*Hudswell, Clarke & Rodgers repaired KENYON by November at a cost of £825 (it had cost £1,956 only six years before).

†John Broughton became the Belfast & County Down Railway's first General Manager in April 1861, coming from the West Midland Railway. He may have been a brother of the then-Manager of the Ulster Railway. His twelve-month probationary stay with the B & CD did not result in a permanent post: he had caused most of the other chief officers to be sacked and lost much of the goods traffic. In August 1862 he was Manager of the Dublin & Meath Railway when it opened at that date. From then his movements are not known; in due course the working of the D & MR was taken over by the Midland & Great Western Railway. It seems as if Broughton survived this period.

in April, General Manager and Accountant on 6th August, and Secretary also on 1st October after Whitwham resigned: as if all these changes in personnel were not enough, Benjamin Piercy conveniently resigned† on 19th October and in his place, George Owen, Engineer of the Cambrian Railways agreed to act as consultant engineer for twelve months from December, when any remaining goodwill towards Piercy was discontinued after Piercy asked for payment due to him.

Most of all these troubles can be traced to lack of finance and prospects. In October too, the Registered Office at 56 Hope Street, Wrexham was closed, and moved to the Wrexham station [but wasn't it already in Oswestry, having moved *from* Wrexham station?! Perhaps so many changes of Secretary were confusing the entries in the Minute Book!]

The Mold horse bus only survived until about the end of July 1867; it appeared not to pay its way rather than shortage of custom. So the word 'Mold' in the Company's title remained forever but an ambition. (The Board was under the misapprehension that the 'bus was operated by the Company and was astonished when, having given notice for it to be discontinued, it remained at work!) Of this service, R.S. France (the contractor) wrote to Lord Redesdale:

> The obstructions you have named compel the WMCQR to put their passengers down in the middle of a field into which a temporary coach road has been made . . . the passengers then have to go on on the outside of a four-horse coach . . . five miles to the town of Mold, and that not withstanding there is a railway communication actually constructed the entire distance from Wrexham to Mold.

But of course, no through passenger carriages!

During the summer the stationmaster at Gwersyllt asked to have another room built as the accommodation was insufficient for him. (The latterday house was of brick, and is likely to be that existing until recently).

The Company was alerted to the risks of the Buckley line; if accidents were to involve trespassers, the Company would be held responsible – trespass on that line was increasing (it had always been a convenient route for pedestrians) and the Chief Constable was asked to appoint a Police Constable for the line at the Company's expense; so Isaac Jones was duly sworn in and he wore the uniform of the Flintshire Constabulary. In September decision was made to run passenger trains over the Buckley line and the Secretary was instructed to advise the Board of Trade of the matter; although correspondence on this subject has not been traced, by the following May this intention had been reversed.

On 12th September Edward Jones alighted from a moving train at Cefnybedd station, and was killed in the attempt.[12] THE WREXHAM ADVERTISER reported on this fatality:

> On a Saturday evening in September there occurred one of those accidents which take place when a passenger leaves the train before it is stationary at a platform. There was an inquest to investigate how the death of Edward Jones, a stonemason, who was travelling with his wife and child from Wrexham to Cefnybedd came about.

---

†Seemingly, a 'put up job' to be rid of him after a stormy interview with the Chairman.

With typical frankness in those times papers did not spare their readers, and THE WREXHAM ADVERTISER reported that the jury viewed the body

> . . . a frightful spectacle, skull being completely smashed to pieces, brain scattered about and one hand nearly severed from the arm.

Apparently the train had overshot Cefnybedd:

> Jones had said 'they have overshot and are taking us up to Gwern-Alyn' (about 200 yards beyond the station). The train stopped and reversed; before it stopped again, Jones had opened the door and was standing on the step, but the station was unlit save for one small lamp. The train gave a jerk, started again, and Jones fell down onto the track: it seems the train was in fact now at the platform; he lay under the carriages and the Station Master (who was not on the station but was travelling from Wrexham on the train) called for more lights. Some witnesses said the train went backwards and forwards twice after Jones fell; others said the train jerked several times so someone ran to the driver to tell him to 'put the break [*sic*] on'.
>
> The Station Master had left the porter in charge (which he was permitted to do) and maintained there were two lights on the platform; they had more lights but were not using them that night. After leaving the train, he had called out 'Keep your seats' and then instructed the driver to back the train. John Broughton (Manager) said 'the station had more lights than many about the country, the rails were greasy and even an experienced driver might have overshot the platform'.
>
> The jury found that Jones had 'violated the law and brought about his own death'; the Coroner said the stations should be better illuminated and drivers instructed not to overshoot platforms. Jones' widow, 'Sophie Jones, a respectable-looking young woman' was left in no doubt; the jury had made her husband the scapegoat for the accident, whilst we readers are left with the impression that Jones might have lived, had a combination of fateful circumstances not taken place.

Although finance plays a vital part in the running of a railway, it makes dull reading. THE WREXHAM ADVERTISER went to some lengths to simplify the WMCQR's position in September 1868, explaining that the directors had filed a scheme in Chancery to relieve the Company of its financial difficulties. There would be additional Debenture Stock to take priority over existing Debentures, the conversion of existing debts into Debenture Stock at a reduced rate of interest for 3 years, and the creation of 1st Preference Shares for payment of all other debts of the Company. To overcome the Company's embarrassment, greater profits would be needed; and before such profits could be made, further outlay would be essential; so to pay for the latter money would have to be raised which would rank as a first charge on the undertaking. Existing Debenture holders were being asked to convert their Stock to that bearing interest not exceeding 4% per annum, which the Board felt it could earn. Everything was dependent on shareholders and creditors pulling together to extricate the Railway from its problem. And the paper was wise to warn that sacrifices were essential.

The year had shown that the Railway had not fulfilled the expectations of its promoters, and the hasty changes of faces in high places was symptomatic of attempts to patch up the cracks in the plaster. 'Make do and mend' at such an early stage in the Company's life was to stamp it as ill-equipped; with a lack of continuity 'at the top', it was the victim of disorderly administration. Reading between the lines of the Minutes, it is clear that the various characters who were called in on a temporary basis to act for a limited period and who in certain cases, were overdue for payment, had taken on the work in the clear understanding of the Company's parlous position and were willing to submit their resignations when it was obvious there would be no benefit in remaining.

To conclude 1868, one Bill was deposited in November.

WMCQR. *Engineer:* George Owen, Oswestry.

The documents accompanying this Bill are incomplete, but the proposed dock arrangements at Connah's Quay are partly shown in detail.

Such arrangements would have been obsolete by the proposals in the next Bill, intended to transform the Connah's Quay dock site completely.

No Act followed this Bill.

Ref: Clwyd Record Office: QS/DR/156

1869

Earlier in the year the Board was proud to record that 'the engine CHANCELLOR had been thoroughly repaired at the Company's shed at Wrexham at a cost of £54 17s. 9d.; the trade cost would have been about £105'. The term 'shed' was probably a very exact description of the existing pile.

The uniforms 'for superior officers', and those 'for porters', which had been chosen and agreed in 1865, were at last placed on order with Mr Lewis (tailor) of Oswestry, 'at the same price as charged to the Cambrian Railways'.

Revised arrangements for the supply of locomotive coal were now made, half the tonnage coming from Mr Clayton's Brynmally Colliery (connected by branch to the Ffrwd line) and half from Little Mountain Colliery (south of Buckley proper) each @ 6/2d. per ton. This was for twelve months. Still with locomotive matters, Dixon of the Buckley Railway Company complained about the state of the two Buckley engines; but his accusation was contradicted when Bellis, the Buckley Railway engineer, inspected them and pronounced them to be in efficient condition. Even more surprisingly came the news that F.G. Whitwham had offered to buy a turntable 'at present lying on the line, not erected, for the sum of £40. The offer was declined'. Why such a piece of equipment was acquired is not known, for the Railway only owned one tender engine (CHANCELLOR) at this time.

Down at Connah's Quay dock Mr Kitchen of Warrington had, within six months, put up two cranes for £102; also at the same place, on 1st February the LNWR placed a contract with Thomas & Sons of Bangor for a station to be built at Connah's Quay: the land was purchased from the WMCQR.

There was evidence of shortage of cash in March when the Birmingham Wagon Co.'s bill for repairing the wagons damaged in the accident on the Buckley Line on 4th February, 1868 for £206, was met by paying £50 on account – another £50 was paid in October.

In May wet weather caused an embankment on the Ffrwd Branch to slip and fall onto the GWR below; the cost of clearance was £65. An important decision, prompted by unknown reasons, was made the same month when it was resolved that passenger trains should not run again over the Buckley Railway; but on receiving this information Mr Mason of the LNWR – who had many interests both current and contemplated in the WMCQR – wrote to the Board suggesting that the line should be made suitable for passenger traffic; the Board was moved sufficiently to agree on considering their decision again at a later date. Events were to prove the decision was never reversed.

At this period attempts were made to reduce the financial crisis by having the line worked by the LNWR (who had offered so to do for 50% of the gross receipts), or by that Company jointly with the Great Western, in return for a fixed rent . . . this ploy failed.

A complex arrangement was made with the Company's creditors under an Act of 9th August,* whereby Debentures A, B, C, D in descending order of priority were created: the Board would be made up of six persons, three representing shareholders and three mortgagees: an arbitrator was appointed each year to iron out differences, and the appointment of the Receiver was ended. Separate meetings of each division of the Board were held in February and August.

During August the Board of Trade enquired why the Company was not using the Block System to protect their passenger trains: the reply was that it did not own one and was too impoverished to install a telegraph system.

In respect of the Act of 9th August, a summary of the position as at 31st December, 1868 was listed therein;

a) The outstanding interest on the mortgage debt was £18,672.
b) A Receiver had been appointed by the Court in Chancery in the cause of Fynney v. WMCQR.
c) About £3,000 was due to the Railway Clearing House in respect of carriage over the GWR.
d) All rolling stock was owned by The Midland Wagon Co., and hired from them. It was insufficient for current needs and required to be purchased. Agreements for hire had been made with the Midland concern in 1866 and 1867.

The Act laid down the names of the six directors:

To represent shareholders: Thomas Barnes, Richard Champion Rawlins, Charles Hughes.
To represent mortgagees: Frederick Adolphus Fynney, Charles Tricks Bowring, James Richardson Barnes.

During December George Owen of the Cambrian Railways, who had acted as Consulting Engineer since December 1868 applied for payment for services rendered; but the Board was obliged to inform him the Agreement could not be renewed, not due to dissatisfaction but for reasons of economy. (The amount was £25 p.a.)

Also in December an application from the WMCQR to abandon certain lines was heard by Colonel Yolland, one of the Board of Trade inspectors (*see 30th June 1870*). Still in December, the needs of patient passengers awaiting connection at the elements-exposed Hope Junction station were considered, and Mr T. Williams of Buckley was permitted to lease the Waiting Room for use as a Refreshment Room.

*WMCQR 'Arrangement Act'. The Act also covered an Arrangement between the Companies (Buckley and WMCQR) in respect of the 'Aston Tramway belonging to Mr Dundas and Messieurs Wm. Hancock & Co. in respect of their right of user of that tramway, and Mr Dundas (an infant . . .) as owner of that tramway . . . etc. providing for the discontinuance of that tramway . . . heads of agreement dated 31st December, 1866 for payment to Mr Dundas by a mortgage . . .'

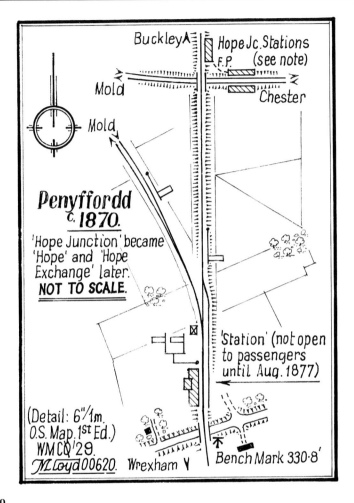

1870

In passing it could be noticed that the entry in BRADSHAW'S RAILWAY MANUAL still continued to be entitled The Whitchurch, Wrexham, Mold & Connah's Quay Junction Railway.

In May it came to the notice of the authorities that the Company was building an embankment below the High Water Mark at Connah's Quay, for the purpose of erecting a pier. Complaints took the form of Board of Trade submission that the Railway had not submitted plans for their approval, though it was admitted that in 1852 Messrs. Rigby & Boydell had had sanction to build an embankment there, and the Buckley Railway Act of 1860 authorised a pier and embankment. The WMCQR countered by complaining they had received no earlier request from the Board of Trade and that no work had been done at Connah's Quay save for some levelling and filling of land bought from the Connah's Quay Chemical Company, which did not affect navigation on the Dee. The local fishermen claimed that their rights to anchor boats and dry nets were under threat, and their anchorage had deteriorated due to irregular and loose stones being used in embankment construction. The moorings and those of the Pilot Boat had been interfered with, and a deep-water reservoir near the new dock under construction, had not been fenced off.

The River Dee Authority (115, Northgate Street, Chester) for once took the side of the Railway, from whom they were clearly going to benefit; they said the fishermen 'had every necessary facility' but after inspection the Authority agreed with the Railway to have mooring rings and chains set up to replace former mooring posts. This was done by February 1872 and was a typical example of the friction between WMCQR and navigation interests throughout; those with fear of losing their livelihood due to the coming of the Railway naturally shouted before they were dispossessed.

The Buckley Railway Minutes of 30th June record the reduction in the dividend in anticipation of an application by the WMCQR to the Board of Trade concerning the abandonment of certain lines; this followed the hearing by Colonel Yolland in the previous December.*

On 1st September the LNWR opened its new Connah's Quay station: this had been intended since the first days but was deferred owing to shortage of money. Although there was an interchange passenger platform on the Down side there is no hint it was ever used as such. The LNWR gave notice that this would decrease the siding accommodation there, to the consternation of Buckley and WMCQ Companies.

---

*Parliamentary Papers 1873 (419) LVII (12.1 to 3): Abandonment Order under s.37 Abandonment of Railways Act 1850.

Under this Act the shareholders of the company had first to pass a resolution to abandon and then apply to the Board of Trade. The application was then advertised in *The London Gazette* and the BoT under s.14 could appoint an Inspector to visit the railway and make enquiries. After he had reported the BoT could then by warrant authorise abandonment. The warrant then had to be advertised in *The London Gazette* and claims for compensation submitted by any parties affected.

Accordingly Colonel Yolland was appointed to inspect and report to the BoT. He stated that 'Railway Nos 1, 2, 3 and 4 of the year 1862 and either No. 5 of 1862 or No. 3 of 1864 and also No. 2 of 1864 have been constructed but the rails on the latter line have since been taken up and it is no longer used.'

Of Railway No. 1 of 1864 about 20 chains near Wrexham Station were made and used for traffic and also about 30 chains in length of the same line were partially made about one mile from Wrexham.

Nothing had been done to construct railways authorised in 1864, 1865 and 1866 save as above. Although Railway No. 6 of 1862 'has not and is not intended to be constructed it is not included in the notice for abandonment'.

Application for abandonment was made in 1870 and was opposed by Sir S.R. Glynne Bart, and Mr Robert Howard and the Buckley Railway Company (who subsequently withdrew their opposition.)

The BoT authorised abandonment of so much as had not been constructed of railways authorised by Acts of (Extension) 1864, (Dee Valley) 1865, (Extension) 1866 and (Additional Powers) 1866 and capital was reduced by £410,000 (unissued) and borrowing powers reduced to the extent of £171,600 unborrowed.

The Warrant was granted on 28th August, 1873.

The Warrant was advertised in *The London Gazette* on 9th September, 1873 at pp. 4144–4145 and the notice was signed by John Broughton as Secretary.

The lines advertised as abandoned were Nos. 1 and 4 of 1864, the Dee Valley branch of 1865, all four lines in the 1866 Extension Act and both lines in the 1866 Additional Powers Act.

In October there were some underhand goings-on at Mr Clayton's Brynmally Colliery where his wagon No. 37 had run away on the 20th, being smashed to pieces [*sic*] after colliding with a WMCQR wagon. There was sufficient of No. 37 to be loaded up onto another wagon, and put into a siding as 'surety for £1 damages which Mr Clayton refused to pay'. A few days later it was discovered the wagons had been shunted from the WMCQR and secreted in Mr Clayton's sidings by his horse shunters. Mr Clayton denied all knowledge.

1871

On 25th February a stock summary was drawn up which revealed that the Company actually owned only two locomotives and two brake vans '. . . the remainder are on hire but will eventually become the property of the Company'.

```
 5 locomotives
 1 tender
 6 3rd Class carriages
 2 1st-2nd Class carriages
 2 luggage vans
71 open goods wagons
 5 covered goods vans
25 coal or coke trucks
 6 cattle wagons
 2 goods brake vans
```

At the end of the following month it was decided to rename Gwersyllt, Wheatsheaf, but it appears that this was never carried out.

An Engineer's Report on the state of the Buckley Railway on 30th June revealed the wretched state of its rails, sleepers and lineside fencing.

In the Halfyearly Report of 19th August it was said that the halfyearly 'payments to The Midland Wagon Co. were very heavy' and there was insufficient rolling stock to meet the traffic needs.

On 2nd October matters concerning the dangerous Rhosddu crossing came up again. The Company wrote to the Board of Trade explaining that since they had been under the control of the Court of Chancery and although the directors appointed under the new arrangements of 1869 were trying to meet all their legal obligations including the provision of a substitute bridge, this has not been done. In late October the London papers advertised rolling stock for sale: the Secretary was authorised to buy one 1st Class coach and one 2nd Class brake @ £110 and £65 respectively, 'if suitable'. These were in fact, LNWR vehicles, and were bought.

By the Act of 1871 the Wrexham & Minera Joint system was divided as between the GWR/LNWR jointly and the GWR alone; an end-on junction was determined at a point south of Coed Talon and north of Llanfynydd where mileposts were set up showing the distance to Paddington (to the south) and to Euston (to the north); the operational results seem to have not been altered, but the immediate mileage north of Brymbo (GW) became the responsibility of the GWR. At the divergence of the line from the W & M track proper, a large sandstone boundary stone was embedded; this read 'GWR' on the one side and 'L & NW & GW Joint Railway' on the other. Although the Act of 1871 made this stone inaccurate, it remains to this day (1990).

1872

In the darkness of Tuesday 2nd January (a bad month for accidents on the WMCQR), Richard Higginson fell off the footboard of the carriage of a moving train, which ran over his legs; he died a few days later. The lad, (he was 16) was employed by the WMCQR in charge of the delivery cart. The train concerned, driven by Driver Tomlinson (who was to feature in the 1891 Connah's Quay runaway) left Wrexham at 8.10 pm and the boy along with two others had jumped onto the moving train; two jumped off again, but Higginson remained until the train was going past Rhosddu engine sheds when he too jumped and fell under the vehicles. Broughton, the Manager, and William Holker, Loco. Foreman, gave evidence at the inquest.

A short account of a runaway on 4th January on the Connah's Quay incline appeared in THE WREXHAM ADVERTISER for 6th January. It explained that the train had only 14 trucks instead of the usual 20, together with 'guards and brake vans'. Driver Cross had driven on without stopping at Northop Hall and the guards had clambered along the speeding train to put down brakes. Guard Newall had been thrown off the brake without injury; 'the other guard and driver stuck to their posts', and the fireman had jumped. Ultimately the train ran into brick-loaded wagons at Connah's Quay, but the line was cleared during the following night. However, a fuller account of the inquest etc. following the death of the driver as a result of his injuries, can be paraphrased from THE CHESTER CHRONICLE of 13th January:

Death of Frank Cross, engine driver on the WMCQR. Witness Henry Newall of Rhosddu, guard of goods train driven by deceased, left Frood Junction 5.25 pm. Proceeded to Hope Junction and left 6.55 pm, went on to Buckley, the train then a tank engine, seven waggons of coal and a break [sic]van. At Ewloe Hall picked up seven more waggons of coal and witness signalled fireman to go on slowly as it was dark and raining heavily. They started, witness thought, rather more quickly than usual down the incline and he commenced to pin down breaks. He got five down and then had to jump on as they were going too quickly. He could not get sixth down and so went over to the other side and put down two more. They were then going from 20–25 mph. He re-crossed to the other side and again tried to pin down the sixth break and stuck to it as long as he could with the lever and then fell off. At that time the train had been pulled up a great deal and was not going more than 10 mph. He got up and ran down the bank and when he was within ¼ mile of Connah's Quay he met too [sic] men who were coming to look for him and the deceased. He said the rules permitted 20 waggons down the incline, but this could be reduced at his discretion; he did not think that 14 were too many at night. He did not put more on because the rails were slippery. They (he and his assistant) did not begin to pin down breaks until the train began to descend the incline, if he were to do so (earlier) the engine could not draw the waggons onto the incline. The reason he did not pin down the sixth was because he could not see, having left his lamp on the buffer.

Thomas Cartwright, manager of the Denbigh, Ruthin & Corwen Railway since 1865, had been requested by Mr John Broughton, Manager and Secretary of the Company, to attend the Enquiry: he said that in addition to the Rules, there was a board at Northop Hall as to the pace they were to go. They were supposed to stop there and pin down and it did not occur to him that the driver had too much steam on when the engine pulled the train off the level at Ewloe Hall, but the train 'might have gone over rather quick because it was shorter than usual'. The train had passed Buckley Junction* (i.e. the top of the incline) where the Rule states that the breaks of every waggon must be carefully examined by the guard and all breaks pinned down in addition to the break of the guard's van being on.

Henry Newall had been in employ of the Company for 4 years and frequently had charge of this particular train . . . if rails are slippery the breaks will not hold until the train has gone some distance and they have become dry and hot. The break in the van was screw type and he had never known it to fly back. The driver had three sandboxes available.

The line's first incline was 1½ miles long, then there was half a mile of level followed by another incline at 1 in 30. At the bottom of the last-named the train ran against some waggons in a siding.

Robert Humphries was assistant guard; he was from Brymbo. When they began to descend the incline he pinned down four 'breaks' but the train was then going too quickly for him to do more until they reached the level. He was trying to pin down the last and was pressing on it when he fell off so he did not see the train go into the other waggons. He was 20 and had been on the line about four years, and he stuck longer on the train than Newall. He could not use his lamp when pinning down as it would be hung on the buffer.

George Whittingham of Rhosddu was the stoker and had been so employed for three months; he did not think 14 waggons was too many to take. They put on steam when starting from Ewloe Hall . . . he was not certain 'breaks' were down as he did not look. Guard gave signal to start and go on slowly, and deceased put steam on. The engine would not move until he had sanded the rails; then they started as usual, or a little faster. They went on for ¼ mile but found the waggons were pushing heavily. Deceased blew for breaksmen to attend to breaks. Deceased reversed engine and witness continued to put sand on. Engine break was on tight all the way down the first incline and along the level. They had passed the notice board and deceased asked if they had passed it yet? Deceased then put steam on against the train and kept it on. Asked witness to get down and see if he could find a break to put down. They were not going above 7–8 mph. He went as requested and put down two breaks on one side and one down on the other side, and found another down but the pin not in. By that time they had got near the bottom of the second incline. Seeing that there was no chance of saving the train and it was close on some waggons, he jumped, and what became of deceased he did not know, but 200 yards further on the train came into collision with some waggons in a siding. In jumping he fell but afterwards got up and went down one side of the train where he picked up deceased's cap and a shovel. He went back and down the other side of the train and about 5–6 yards further than the engine he saw the deceased lying in the fourfoot. There was a piece of sheet-iron (part of tender†) which witness picked up and saw that the leg was cut, also a cut on deceased's thigh. When an attempt was made to move him he cried out for them to take care of his leg. He was removed to a public house, placed on a mattress and then conveyed by LNWR to Chester.

In reply to Cartwright's question, witness said he thought that if steam had been put on against the train sooner it might have brought it to a standstill before the second incline was reached. Also thought deceased must have been mistaken as to distance they had gone.

(It was explained that the points were set for the siding but if they had not gone there they would have run on towards the Holyhead line and perhaps blocked that.)

---

*Ashton's Branch Junction.

†The bunker would be meant.

Thomas Lloyd, labourer of Connah's Quay, had only begun duty with the Company the previous week: he suggested deceased's thigh might have been cut by two wheels which were between his legs. Alfred Lewis a pointsman at Connah's Quay, said his duty was to be at points and shunt the engine to the main line for coal and water, and assist guards in lowering the train into the siding: on the night in question he heard the train coming; the driver whistled for 'breaks' and he said to an engine cleaner that he was 'coming a bit fast'. The whistle blew again so he went out and began to sand and while sanding, driver blew two or three times and after putting on all the sand he could he went back to the points and stood with the handle in his hand. The points were open for the main line but he thought they were going too fast so he loosed the handle and the train went into the siding; as the train passed he saw someone on the engine in a stooping position as if he were sanding, and he also saw the extra breaksman and shouted for him to get off, and he rolled off. The distance from the points to the Holyhead line would be 500–600 yards and from the points to where the collision took place about 160 yards. It would have been dangerous to let the train go onto the Holyhead line as the siding was full of waggons.

Cartwright suggested that deceased might have jumped off the engine, but Lloyd did not think he did so. The jury was told the siding and not the main line was the 'proper place for the train'. Cartwright added that if he had gone onto the siding of the Holyhead line (which was full of wagons) the result might have been to interfere with passenger traffic on the LNWR.*

Manager and Secretary John Broughton had had 27 years experience of railways in this country, Ireland and India, and said this was the first casualty since he became connected with the WMCQR. Part of the line spoken of was not used for passengers; he had travelled over it many times, the last 3 days before the accident when it was raining; deceased was the driver and had no difficulty in stopping the train. The object of the Rule was to enable guards to go round the train to see if pins were in the 'breaks' – the notice board at Northop Hall was an additional precaution because from that point the gradient became heavier.

What they knew as 'Buckley Junction' was that point where Ashton's Branch Siding joined it, and the top of the incline began opposite the Ewloe Hall Sidings. It was not the duty of the guards to see that the breaks were pinned down before reaching Ewloe Hall Incline as the engine could not then pull the train onto the incline; and so far as he could gather the guards acted in accordance with the spirit of the Rule which must be liberally construed as meaning when the train began the descent of the incline. He thought deceased resisted putting on steam against the train as he was fearful of breaking a crank axle, which did sometimes occur when this was done; he would certainly know the danger he was in – he had driven that line for 4–5 years and other lines before that. He was a respectable and sober man, a smart young fellow occasionally given to driving fast . . . that was, he knew how to make up time if required. His judgement was generally correct. There was no Rule to prevent a fireman jumping off if in danger 'and in not jumping the judgement of the deceased was against himself'. He looked at the effects of the collision and thought the train could not have been going more than 8–10 mph at the time because if they had been, waggons would inevitably have mounted on top of the engine, and they had not done so; two waggons had their fore wheels taken off but none were damaged; from what he heard he thought that after falling, deceased must have been struck by a piece of the coal bunker; and he fully approved of the judgement of the Pointsman Lewis in turning the train into the siding.

The deceased was brought to Chester Infirmary at 10.40 pm on Thursday evening suffering from shock resulting from the severe smash of the left leg; also he had

---

*There is clearly a desire not to involve the LNWR in any way, even to the extent of putting the WMCQR's train in danger.

a cut on the right thigh and bruises on head and arms. He never rallied but gradually sank and died on Saturday at 9 am. He said he could not tell how he met with his injuries or how the accident happened.

In summing up the Coroner said that the Rule alluded to might be put in clearer terms, and that it should be explained. Neither breaksman nor anyone else was to blame.

Verdict – Accidental Death.

Cross's widow was paid 10/- a week for ten weeks.

The shortage of wagon stock did not improve: Buckley traders' complaints were on the increase and the Company was not assured when it was learned in February that wagon hire was costing them £2,106 12*s*. 0*d*. annually. That month it was arranged that five wagons should be purchased from the Lancashire & Yorkshire Railway – who did many of the Company's repairs – to a design by Fay: and payment would be made personally by Thomas Barnes, the Chairman, for which he would receive £1,300 in Debentures. Five were ordered ('as samples') from Whittle, Rush Mill & Co. @ £70 each [29th March]. Such wagons only suited the general traffic; Buckley traders provided their own wagons but only for their own products; they relied on general purpose wagons for their coal, timber etc. and in due course this problem would come to crisis point.

It was a common practice to use the railway as a footpath and a typical instance appeared in THE CHESTER CHRONICLE on 10th February:

> A man named George Lloyd banksman at the Rhosddu Colliery, Wrexham, was walking from the pit to the town on Wednesday night, along the GWR when he saw a train approaching. He then stepped upon the WMCQ line when a train, coming in the opposite direction, knocked him down the wheels passing over his leg and neck, and causing almost instantaneous death.

On 27th February: the Secretary was instructed to apply to different engine builders with a view to obtaining two new locomotives on the best terms he could by payment in A Stock either whole or in part. He was also to ask the LNWR for a temporary loan of an engine; also to repair the engine damaged at Connah's Quay in January and apply to I.W. Boulton of Ashton-under-Lyne for the hire of a suitable engine.

By 24th May replies had been received from the following re the applications for locomotives:

1) Mr Fenton, Gen. Man. Metropolitan Rly.   Sale of an engine.
2) Black, Hawthorn & Co., Leeds
3) Mr Henry Robertson   An engine being capable of being hired or purchased.
4) Mr George Stanley, Liverpool
5) Mr Hancock
6) Mr John Waddington, London
7) Hunslet Engine Co., Leeds

Further enquiries had revealed that the engine mentioned by Mr Robertson was not for sale or hire, and those offered by Messrs. Stanley and Hancock were unsuitable. No firm could supply locomotives in under four to six months. The Metropolitan engine appeared to be the most suitable and negotiations were continued: Mr Walker (Loco. Supt. of the Cambrian Railways) had been to London with the Secretary to see 'the Metropolitan engine but as it weighed about 43 tons it was too heavy for the Buckley line'.[13]

At this time there was complaint about a shortage of wagons and 3rd Class coaches; it seems business was too brisk for the quantity of equipment.

In early June the Company had corresponded with F.W. Webb concerning the LNWR locomotive No. 1829 which was for sale at Liverpool for £900; and in November the LNWR sent an account for hire of a locomotive:

Hire of engine	£465	0	0
Repairs	341	6	8
	£806	6	8
Paid on account	150	0	0
Balance	£656	6	8

In June this secondhand LNWR engine was bought and in the next month, an Ashbury-built brake van from the Hoylake Railway (with whom there were still strong personal links at Board level) was acquired. The locomotive position could not be improved by taking an extra machine; the weakness of the system lay in the absence of any proper repair facilities at Rhosddu. On 1st April, Mr Walker recommended the provision of a small fitting shop at a cost of £1,050 but nothing was done and in June William Adams (Loco. Supt. of the North London Railway) was approached 'on what terms would he design a suitable engine for the Company?' Adams' reply cannot be traced but nothing further was done in this matter either.

The shortage of repair facilities must have 'come home' to the Board for in November they 'resolved that all tools required for the Fitting Shop be purchased at a forthcoming sale to be held in Wrexham'. A drilling machine had been bought for £55.[14] The workforce was small, the blacksmith being the epicentre of the place, supported by men who worked mainly on passenger and goods stock. They were virtually without facilities, and anything beyond a simple nature went to the L & YR's 'Newton Heath Works', or to the Cambrian at Oswestry.

Labour problems were bad at Rhosddu, the Minutes of 1st April state that the men employed in the Engine Shed, i.e. boilersmith, carpenter and wagon repairer, had asked for their working hours to be reduced to 54 weekly, failing which they said they would leave the Company's service on 27th March; the Secretary said he had found it policy to agree. The enginemen had requested a reduction of hours to 10 per day with overtime based on 8 hours a day; after seeing the men the Secretary had agreed that their hours should not exceed 12½ hours a day with overtime based on 12 hours a day.

In May the Secretary urged the Board to install a telegraph system which he stressed as a necessity.

We must look beyond the locomotive situation and Rhosddu: during February harbour works at Connah's Quay were completed, but clearly these were only an initial stage as there was to be another phase which ended in July 1875. It seemed that the Railway would soon become a vital link in projected railways linking the northwest and central Wales, a grand design conceived by Edward Watkin of the MSL and in late 1872 Watkin, together with William Philip Price (Chairman of the Midland Railway) had discussions with Thomas Barnes to consider an extension of the Cheshire Lines Committee's system from Chester to Wrexham.* At this time the WMCQR was having parley with a potential Birkenhead, Chester & North Wales Railway which would build a line from Birkenhead to Wrexham (in effect making use of WMCQR metals as between Buckley and Wrexham), and the Dee was to be bridged. The outcome was an offer by the Birkenhead faction to work (and etc.) the WMCQR but this was not accepted. Although the BC&NWR received Royal Assent on 5th August, 1873, it was a dead duck in another five years time.

A good example of sloppy working methods and the 'happy-go-lucky' attitude of the operators is found (*see page 160*).

In June work was begun on a small station between Cefnybedd and Caergwrle, to be named Bridge End; the cost was only £50 – it was aimed at Wrexham Market Day business.

THE CHESTER CHRONICLE for 31st August said the downward trend of traffic on the WMCQR was not surprising, for the brickmakers of Buckley had been on strike for six weeks, and railway business on that line in particular had worsened due to want of wagons 'and a lack of accommodation for goods traffic at stations'. The paper made reference to the increased shipping facilities which would be available in future when the works then being carried out by Abraham Pilling (and later by Thomas Barnes) at Connah's Quay were complete.

1873

The background to this year was a boom in the Flintshire coalfield with the WMCQR virtually working 24 hours a day, seven days a week, with the coal going to the LNWR at Hope Junction and ships at Connah's Quay; but the most important event was the lease of the Buckley Railway for 999 years as from 30th June.

The consequence of the foregoing was to worsen the ability of the Company to carry the traffic – wagons became shorter in supply. John Broughton was the butt of all complaints and did not mince his words when he warned the Board that basically the trouble lay in the inability to keep locos and stock in repair as follows:

> . . . we are having to work some of the engines night and day, and now have three in for repairs and two for heavy repairs, which will take us about six months. I am constantly having to borrow tools and get work done and materials supplied by other companies as a personal favour and I now have a number of tools lent by Mr Walker of Oswestry. I am afraid however, that I have nearly exhausted the patience of the Locomotive Superintendents . . .

But the Board was not swayed by his problems and resisted any inclination to install a workshop. Does this suggest the purchase agreed upon last November had fallen through? From a Company which was admittedly low in funds but was alleged to possess directors with commercial imagination, one wonders why this obvious step was not taken? Under the terms of the Act 36/7 v.c. 232 (5th August, 1873) the Buckley line was to be adapted for

---

*A joint undertaking between MS&L, Midland and Great Northern Railways.

WREXHAM, MOLD, AND CONNAH'S QUAY RAILWAY.

Board of Trade,
Sir,
23rd January 1872.

In compliance with the instructions contained in your minute of the 9th instant, I have the honour to report, for the information of the Board of Trade, the result of my inquiry into the circumstances connected with the collision that occurred on the 4th instant at Connah's Quay station, on the Wrexham, Mold, and Connah's Quay Railway.

The railway in question is only opened for passenger traffic between the stations of Wrexham and Buckley. From Buckley to Connah's Quay it is used for mineral traffic only.

The railway falls considerably from Buckley junction to Connah's Quay.

There is a level piece, which is about a quarter of a mile long, at the north side of the junction. The line then falls on gradients of 1 in 40 and 1 in 38 as far as Northop Hall level, which is about a mile and a half from Buckley junction. Euloe Hall coal sidings are situated about half-way between Buckley junction and Northop Hall level.

The level portion, called Northop Hall level, is about half a mile long. There is a notice board about the centre of this level portion, which directs all engine-drivers to bring their trains to a stand at the notice board. The object of this regulation is to ensure the engine-drivers having full control over their trains before getting on the next incline, which descends on gradients of 1 in 44, 1 in 83, and 1 in 30, as far as the sidings at Connah's Quay.

The Wrexham, Mold, and Connah's Quay Railway terminates on the quays at Connah's Quay, and there is a short branch to connect it with a siding of the London and North-western Railway at Connah's Quay station.

On the day in question, a mineral train, consisting of a tank-engine, which was running with its coalbunk in front, seven waggons loaded with coals, and a break-van with two guards, arrived at Euloe Hall sidings about 7.10 p.m., and stopped there.

The engine was detached and went into the sidings to fetch seven more waggons of coals, which it pushed back on to the other seven waggons, and the whole were coupled together.

The guard of the train then told the driver to proceed steadily, as the night was dark, and it was wet.

The engine-driver put on steam, and the head guard pinned down the breaks on five waggons as they passed him. He tried to pin down the sixth, but he could not do so, as the train was going too fast.

The assistant guard, who was standing at the opposite side of the train, succeeded in pinning down the breaks on four waggons as they passed him. The break of the break-van had been put on before the train stopped at Euloe Hall colliery sidings.

The head guard jumped on to the eighth and the second guard on to the twelfth waggon of the train as it proceeded down the incline, and they put on two more breaks while the train was proceeding.

They stated that the train was running about 20 to 25 miles an hour as it reached Northop Hall level, and that the speed was checked to about five to seven miles an hour while on the level, but that the train was not stopped.

In descending the incline between Northop Hall and Connah's Quay, the train appears to have gained a speed of about ten miles an hour.

The fireman stated that the engine break was on, and that the engine-driver had reversed his engine before he reached Northop Hall level, and that when he found that he passed the stop notice board without being able to stop his train, he put steam on while the engine was reversed, and asked him (the fireman) whether his break was hard on, which it was.

The fireman then managed to get down off the engine and put on two of the waggon breaks, which were the only breaks at that side of the train that were not on. He then jumped on to the break-van and got out at the other side and pinned down one more waggon break, which was the only one at that side that was not already on. As the train approached Connah's Quay, and gained a speed of about ten miles an hour, the fireman jumped off.

The two guards stated that they fell off as the train approached Connah's Quay, while they were trying to press down the waggon breaks, but I suspect that their falls must have been partly intentional.

The train ran into nine waggons loaded with bricks, that were standing on the line at the bottom of the incline, close to Connah's Quay.

The practice has been to stop the trains before they reach the place where the waggons of bricks were standing.

The engine-driver of the coal train was found on the ground after the collision. His left leg was broken, his right thigh was injured, and his head was cut. He died two days after the accident. Four wheels of the engine were thrown off the rails; the coal bunk, framing, buffers, and motions were damaged. Two of the coal waggons were thrown off the rails; one of them was damaged.

Three of the waggons that were loaded with bricks were thrown off the rails, and two of them are reported to have been damaged.

The accident appears to have been caused by the engine-driver of the coal train starting from Euloe Hall at so great a speed that he was unable to control his train.

The incline in question requires to be worked with powerful engines, powerful breaks, and with very great care.

I would recommend that the points of the blind siding at the east side of the railway, near Connah's Quay overbridge, be weighted so as to stand open for the blind siding, and that this blind siding, as well as the one at the west side of the railway, be raised, so as to check the speed of anything that may run into them; and further, that the ends of the sidings be filled up with loose shingle, so that waggons that run wild may bury their wheels in the shingle.

I have, &c.

F. H. Rich,
Lieut.-Col., R.E.

The Secretary,
Railway Department,
Board of Trade.

passenger traffic ... this was a perpetual cry, but was never done. The Company was authorised to raise a further £6,000 in Debentures.

On 7th November the Board of Trade gave the Company a Warrant which declared the unbuilt extensions to be abandoned.[15]

Detail of the locomotive position is all too prevalent at this time: and on 29th November Broughton clarified his needs – he could manage the traffic with six engines properly maintained: No. 6 (the LNWR purchase the previous year) had been satisfactory but had been off the road for five weeks awaiting material from Crewe Works. CHANCELLOR (which had had repairs at Wrexham in 1868) needed firebox repairs; one cylinder was already patched. Obviously proper consideration had not been given to the engine when it was acquired, as its wheelbase was too long for the Ffrwd branch's curves and the Buckley section overbridges were too low. A new firebox was needed on KENYON, for which tenders were being sought, and to spread the cost over 12 months. WHEATLEY and LORD RICHARD were running at reduced pressures with weak fireboxes: SIR STEPHEN was stripped down for repairs but no work was being done on it as the other engines required constant attention. Broughton added that the heavy gradients of the Buckley line took their toll of the ageing engines and made for heavy coal consumption: traffic movements fell behind and there were penalties to pay on wagons held up, but his Parthian Shot was 'I respectfully submit that it is almost unparalleled that a railway should continue to work as long as this company has, without stock or the means of repairing locomotives ...'

In September there was a change of attitude; three engines were sent away for heavy repairs and on the 27th the Secretary reported he had hired:

One LNWR engine from 13th September @ £3 3s. 0d. a day.
One L&YR engine from 16th September @ £1 5s. 0d. a day.

Nothing else was done to meet the growing complaints of the Buckley Traders Society who now threatened to make complaint to the Railway Commissioners.

A slight mishap occurred on 27th December:

> On the arrival of a goods train at Frood Junction in the morning the engine upon reaching the points at the junction box left the line with all six wheels. It was afterwards found that some person had broken open the signal box, also the staff ticket box, and had placed the point lever in such a position as to leave the points leading to a mineral branch half open. No one hurt and the damage done was very slight.[16]

1874

At the end of 1873 the engine which had been hired from the LNWR since the previous autumn, was returned but on 4th January the Minutes record that two others had taken its place, being 'one ex-Crewe and one ex-Manchester @ £9 9s. 0d. per week each'. (These were possibly LNWR and L&YR machines).

On 4th April, only three locomotives were workable (two of them being hired) 'and there were no spares'. The directors decided to face reality on 28th February by accepting a tender for £510 from one Hughes of Liverpool for which sum he would supply a Fitting Shop; to raise the money for this, land at Wrexham had to be sold. Another interested party named Crowther who was currently hiring an engine to the Company, proved willing to install tools etc. and receive rent in lieu of immediate payment. Even this seemed pedestrian enough, for another fifteen months would pass before the premises came into use and formed part of the existing engine and carriage depot at Rhosddu, just outside the Company's Wrexham terminus. KENYON had gone to the Worcester Locomotive Works for repair; they were completed by July for nearly £600. LORD RICHARD 'had been nearly rebuilt' at Nasmyth, Wilson & Co. at a cost of £1,120.

In the same month we learn of properties and their insurance cover:

The Carriage, and the Carriage Shed	£1,500
Goods Shed	500
Hay Stack	100
Engine Shed	1,000
Engines' insurance	4,000

All of which goes to show what was considered to be valuable!

The railway line continued to be a place where pedestrians might walk their last –

14th February. A man while trespassing on the line between Gwersyllt and Cefnybedd stations was run over by a train and killed.

30th April. A man while trespassing on the line near the Stansty Iron Works about a mile from Wrexham station was knocked down by a passenger train and so badly injured that he shortly afterwards died.[18]

In late August the tender of J.B. Saunders & Co. of Taunton, well-known in these matters, was accepted for the installation of a telegraph system at a cost of £617 10s. 0d. and part of it came into use the following December; Saunders' also maintained it, being paid for the work in Debentures.

The brief flirtation with ships ended this year when it was decided to sell SECRETARY which by this time was laid up out of use; it was sold in August for £430. (A summary of the ship saga was given under 1867.)

Abraham Pilling, who had first begun work on new docks at Connah's Quay way back in 1872 under the supervision of George Caulfield (Engineer to the Neath & Brecon Railway) was now in trouble . . . his workmanship did not meet Caulfield's demands and the rate of progress was irksome; Pilling was dismissed and in this year Thomas Barnes took over – it is said reluctantly.

Cash was clearly an embarrassment – mainly the shortage of same, for in mid-December Nasmyth's solicitor had demanded payment of the full amount due for the repair of LORD RICHARD. The Secretary was instructed to pay £500 on account and haggle with Nasmyth, Wilson & Co. as best he could over the balance.

1875

The manner in which the Buckley section was worked involved men jumping on and off moving trains to pin down wagon brakes: and on 25th January William Dodd, a goods guard, fell off the train en route to Connah's Quay and fractured his thigh.[19]

What might have been a quiet year was notable for the growing restiveness of the Buckley Traders' Society whose complaints were not receiving the attention they felt they deserved, and who were clearly unlikely to get it! More obviously the works at Connah's Quay were brought to an end in July at a cost of £15,665 – this was quite a feat for Barnes as Chairman, whose efforts as a contractor (not his normal role) deserved much praise.

In October more sidings were laid down at Penyffordd to cater for inter-change traffic with the LNWR. There was a current plan to build a joint exchange station there instead of 'the present objectionable stations of the LNWR and this Company', said Broughton. The LNWR apparently thought otherwise and nothing was done; the two stations, each known latterly as Hope Exchange, remained dismal places to the end. (Members of Denbigh Ladies' Hockey team, for instance, returning home after a January away match at Wrexham, were obliged to descend a somewhat uncertain path in darkness from the upper to lower level, and shelter in a small dank building without lights where no member of the female sex would feel confident on her own.) This idea for a joint station was finally dropped in early 1876.

1876

This was another year of consolidation; the new sidings at Connah's Quay in connection with the dock works and the LNWR interchange there were completed in February.

Although the Fitting Shop construction arrangements of spring 1874 appear to have been conclusive, (and some accounts suggest that Hughes of Liverpool would complete the building) there must have been some hic-cough – possibly linked to payment – for in January an arrangement was made with Mr Crowther (see April 1874) 'for the erection of the Fitting Shop for £864 15s. 11d. and the supply of the necessary machine tools for £969 10s. 8d.'

On 4th February a trespasser, when lying between the rails near Gwersyllt station, intoxicated, had his arm run over by a train.[20]

On 23rd July, and perhaps caused by a spark from a locomotive, the wooden bridge and signal box at Ffrwd Junction (the spelling Frood is used in the Minutes) were set alight. Damage caused was estimated at £30.

On 22nd November the LNWR gave Parliamentary notice for powers to take over the Buckley Railway.

On 4th December, two accidents occurred:

As an engine was propelling five waggons from Northop Hall siding to Watkinson's siding they came into collision with the gates at Castle Brick level crossing and the waggons were thrown off the rails damaging the signal and telegraph wires. The head guard who had been riding on the leading waggon was killed. The distant signal of the crossing was down and the gateman was absent from his duty.

Two waggons ran out of a private siding and came into collision with an engine on the main line between Etna siding and Old Ewloe siding. No person was injured but the engine was damaged. The slip point had been blocked over by some person in the employ of the owner of the private siding.

It was on 12th December that the impending storm clouds broke and the Traders brought their threatened Appeal before the Railway Commissioners: the case was heard on 12th–13th and 15th–16th December and 20th January 1877 under the chairmanship of Sir Frederick Peel, entitled 'Watkinson and Others v. WMCQR'. R.G. Underdown General Manager of the MS & LR, Alfred Henshaw of the Neath & Brecon Railway, and George Owen of the Cambrian Railways had advised the defendants.

The Traders' case bore on the obligation of the WMCQR to collect and deliver wagons to the private sidings alongside the Buckley section, especially if the wagons were brought to or taken from, the point of junction on the main line. Also concerning charges and the supply of wagons (the latter bearing upon the fact that Traders' business so far as their own products was concerned (bricks, tiles, etc.) were carried in Traders' wagons) and the WMCQR (the Company operating the Buckley line) maintained it was not obliged to provide more than motive power and brake wagons – which it did.

The case is fortunate for the historian: firstly, the Company had a record in camera made of the Buckley section; secondly, the methods of operating the section were given to the Commissioners (*see page 79*) and from the various persona appearing, the pecking-order for traffic and the competing interests of members of the Society made a lively debate.

Published facts surrounding the case may conveniently be recorded here as they show the position in 1876: a contemporary WREXHAM ADVERTISER said the line had 16 collieries or brickworks, and the average length of a Traders' siding was 100 yards. There were 11 sidings, only one of which belonged to the Company. There were three working collieries on the section: Ashton's brickworks was the farthest from Connah's Quay; Castle the nearest. The Buckley Colliery Co. was producing c.150,000 tons a year. The Collieries' requirements varied – some sent almost all their output by the interchange sidings with the LNWR and others by sea from Connah's Quay.

At the time the WMCQR lease of the Buckley Railway was drawn up, many of the Traders' sidings were in an incomplete state and the WMCQR was involved in considerable expense to bring them to completion: this expense was not passed on to the Traders.*

> The wagons used are of peculiar construction adapted only to the traffic of the district and used exclusively . . . from the applicants' works by means of sidings **constructed by and belonging to the applicants** . . . when wagons are empty they are returned to the owners' sidings.

The Traders maintained there was a perpetual state of strain between the respective solicitors of the Buckley and WMCQ Railways in that the WMCQR 'always seem to take up a hostile position towards the Buckley Railway, especially in the matter of inspection by the WMCQ solicitor, of the BR Minute Book currently in the hands of the Buckley solicitor who refuses to surrender it.'

During the judgement following the Case, the ruling that the WMCQR must supply wagons meant it had to do so only for its own system (NOT the Buckley section) – which was hardly favourable to the applicants! In com-

---

*This statement would seem to negative the suggestion that the sidings were Traders' property!

ment the Railway said that 300–400 would be needed, and they had no money.

When the dust had settled, observers passed judgement on the outcome. Typical were the comments of THE COLLIERY GUARDIAN and THE NORTH WALES GUARDIAN, the editorial of the latter for 12th April, 1879 – rather late in the day? – being 'The Buckley Traders' Society is not an inch better off than when litigation commenced'.

1877

The Buckley Traders' Society had succeeded in convincing the Railway Commissioners who issued an Order on 20th January requiring the WMCQR to supply requisite wagons for the convenience of Traders. Whilst the Traders were storming about the inadequacies of the Railway Company, the latter was actually hit by one of special severity at Connah's Quay on 30th January – it was of such nature as to be remembered for many years afterwards; the tide rose to a level which inundated the docks but the new work survived though the tracks were flooded and left without ballast, which was washed into the river.

With the conclusion of the Railway Commissioners' hearing in January, the Company acquired 25 more wagons by hire purchase.

John Broughton (Secretary and Manager) had been in office since 1868 but on 28th April he resigned: he must have had a trying time of it. Edward Fraser was appointed Secretary pro tem: he was not seen as a suitable candidate for final adoption but on 3rd May he personally recommended that Thomas Cartwright, should be given a post with the new title of 'Consulting Manager': he had previously come over and given assistance frequently, and he discovered there were no Working Timetables, without which the Company had, up to now, operated for over a decade! Presumably the trains ran – happily now with the aid of the new telegraph – on an ad hoc basis, the movements being comparatively few and to a regular pattern which everyone knew. It is well-remembered that every employee was aware of the whereabouts of every train at any time, and who would be the crew employed. And the WMCQR was not alone in this type of 'family business' atmosphere. Cartwright immediately produced a working draft to improve efficiency.

It was a timely opportunity for Cartwright, who accepted the position when the Board made the offer; he was currently passing through an unhappy phase concerning some missing goods on the DR & CR and had sent an insolent reply to influential Cornwallis-West of Ruthin Castle when he was questioned about the matter.

Looking ahead, Cartwright (fired from the DR & CR on 31st July) was appointed General Manager on 1st August at £350 a year on release, and James Fraser (son of Edward) became Secretary at £200 a year on 1st September, so separating the responsibilities of Secretary and Manager. From the previous May, Cartwright had swept in with a new broom; on 19th May the Board received a Report condemning much of what he found. The track was in a bad way, sidings had no buffer stops, there were no notices of any kind to warn of trespass on Company ground; nor mile nor gradient boards. Jackson, the WMCQR Permanent Way Inspector, was instructed 'to give matters immediate attention' and promptly resigned. Twenty wagons were under repair: there were few wagons sheets and roping materials, and in little over a decade from construction, buildings needed repair and repainting. On 9th June a longer Report came from George Owen, Engineer of the Cambrian Railways, supporting Cartwright's view of things.

Within weeks action was taken – public and working timetables appeared. The Midland Wagon Co. received order for twenty five 8 ton open wagons @ £12 9s. 0d. per wagon per annum for five years so lessening dependence on other railway's equipment. Cartwright, living at 5 Grove Park, Wrexham, brought his reputation on the DR&CR with him and at once began to earn his £350 salary: he is on record as being a 'thoroughly competent railway officer, trained on the LNWR under Sir George Finlay': 'he was a smug, self-satisfied character lacking in popularity. He had a somewhat exalted opinion of himself, but had first-rate ability'.

Before a month was out, William Holker the Locomotive Superintendent had resigned (perhaps being unable to work alongside Cartwright?) and Frederick Willans, who moved to 2 Witton Terrace, Wrexham, was appointed on 29th September; the initial appointment was dubbed 'working locomotive foreman' at a salary of 60/- a week subject to one month's notice.

Willans seems to have been the right innovative and resourceful personality for the economic strait-jacket of his employers. His 'somewhat inferior designation would not necessarily detract from the responsibility of the post, and Willans was both a lucky and a very brave man. He not only received his salary without having to ask for it but had the temerity from time to time to express dissatisfaction with it; he received advances now and again and succeeded in holding office until the GCR finally took over in 1905, when he retired. In 1896 he had been designated 'Locomotive Superintendent' subject to the supervision by the MS&LR Locomotive Superintendent for the time being. The latter received £100 for his pains, Willans' salary being £250'.

Dunn writes:

> ... had two sons, the elder of whom John Frederick, was his father's right-hand man at Rhosddu Works and eventually became a District Locomotive Superintendent ... He was followed at Rhosddu by his younger brother George who is reputed to have been the leading light in the metamorphosis of the engine No. 3. Not long before the end of the WMCQR's independent existence he was appointed Locomotive Superintendent of the Smyrna Railways in Asia Minor. It has been said that Willans Senior had difficulties with his staff but one who knew him personally and paid many visits to him at Rhosddu said there seemed to be no foundation for this statement as although he was a strict disciplinarian his staff invariably appeared to be a loyal and contented body of men.

Willans' department sent the Secretary a note on 9th June saying LORD RICHARD had broken a crank and would cost about £80 to repair.

In August the existing unused platform at the junction for the Mold –Chester line was named 'Penyffordd' and opened.* This month was not all plain sailing for the Company – The Midland Wagon Co., no doubt with bad memories of long-winded payment and having an adequate Order Book,

*and Hope Junction became 'Hope'. (WM&CQR)

declined to proceed with Wrexham's order for 25 wagons. [Confusingly, the Minutes of 29th November record 'The 25 wagons had been received' (!)] Neither did the course of events please all concerned.

The branch to Llay Hall Colliery was opened in September and was 1¼ miles long and worked by the Colliery's own locomotives as far as the exchange yard at the junction at Caergwrle. [The Colliery possessed a number of Manning, Wardle & Co. engines and the largest, THE WELSHMAN, was named by Mrs E. Stanley Clark, wife of the proprietor in January 1891. After the naming, the Clark family climbed onto the footplate to drive to Llay Hall Junction and back. The engine was then attached to twelve loaded wagons and 'despite steep gradients, hauled them with ease'. The engine was 'a six-coupled saddle tank, with 15 in. × 20 in. cylinders and Holker's Patent Slide Valves', so a reporter from the paper was informed.]

This Colliery supplied considerable quantities of slack coal to Connah's Quay chemical works, but this traffic was lost to Lancashire pits who were more competitive.

Later the same year 50 tons of steel rails @ £6 10s. 0d. per ton were received from the Dowlais Iron Co., South Wales, and a November storm blew off the roof of Wrexham Engine Shed.

In December George Owen was asked on what terms would he act as Engineer to the Company and in the same month the Secretary had been to the Sandycroft Foundry which had a small engine suitable for Connah's Quay Docks, for sale @ £665; 'it was five years old, and considered to be worn out'. No purchase was made.

In RECOLLECTIONS OF WREXHAM, MOLD & CONNAH'S QUAY RAILWAY, the author recalls:

> . . . only one loco available to haul the mixture of goods and passenger traffic . . . when traffic was heaviest on market days and Saturdays, people would travel on top of the coal in the tender and it was not unusual for women with their market baskets to crowd the footplate of the engine.
>
> At the time there were no facilities for repairs, no telegraph, no timetable, no rule books or uniforms for the staff. There were upheavals between directors and officials of the Railway and after a year it was in debt.[21]

A Report on the line in 1877 said:

> . . . deplorable conditions, and rails needed renewing, buildings and rolling stock in need of repair, no gate notices, trespass or gradient boards, mileposts. But only 15 people were ever injured.

At least the engine WHEATLEY was back in service by February 1877 – repair had all been done at Rhosddu for a sum of £613 9s. 0d.

1878

This year dawned as a quiet one. Perhaps with the changes in personnel in the twelve months previously, it was a time for settling in. However, our old friend George Owen of the Cambrian Railways was appointed Consulting Engineer in January at fifty guineas per annum and with indication of changing times, a locomotive replaced the first horses on the Connah's Quay shunting duty. This second event resulted from an offer by Hudswell, Clarke

& Co. Ltd, The Railway Foundry, Leeds to provide a suitable engine for Connah's Quay Docks at a cost of £1,200 payable in twelve quarterly instalments: this engine had been new to Samuel Allsop & Sons, Burton-on-Trent and had left Leeds for Burton 25th May, 1876.

A decision to purchase was made in February but en route for Connah's Quay one of the eccentric straps broke and it was renewed at Hudswell, Clarke's expense. In April the Minutes had, 'the new small engine at Connah's Quay is working well' – two displaced horses were sold for £22 5s. 0d.

In the spring the Board decided to 'let their hair down' and agreeing that the coaches were now shabby [sic], they had them re-painted; the colour is not stated.

1879

During March a connection with the Wrexham & Acton Colliery was opened – this pit had started business in 1868.

On 20th March the now familiar trouble, 'Watkinson & Others' resumed again when complaints were made against the continued shortage of wagons and working of private sidings.

Chancery proceedings against the Company began in the summer and on 12th July James Fraser, the Secretary, was made Receiver by an Order of that date.

What lay behind the July decision to terminate a facility on the Buckley Railway section as from 31st March in the following year, is not explained. At this time travel in the brake vans of goods trains on this line was granted to representatives of traders against Permits issued from Wrexham: this would naturally be at their own risk, and maybe the Company saw some folly of allowing this to continue.

1880

During the year the continuing problems of Watkinson and the Buckley Traders disturbed the otherwise unremarkable continuance of life along the line.

The Minutes of 20th February record a decision, 'a new engine was to be ordered from Sharp, Stewart & Co. to the Railway's specification for the sum of £2,136 0s. 0d. payment to be £336 0s. 0d. on completion and balance in half-yearly instalments of £225 0s. 0d.' (This was Works No. 2932 of 1880 PREMIER (WMCQR's No. 8) 0–6–0 Tank.)

At this stage it is helpful to say more about Connah's Quay – so much the bull's-eye of railway promotions hereabouts – as it would become in the early 1880s. The advantage of this site against Saltney (then dying rapidly) was that a vessel could reach it on one tide whereas Saltney required two: the competitors for Connah's Quay were Birkenhead and Liverpool: Connah's Quay could compete with neither. That is not to say the Mersey ports were perfect for traders; those who sent goods via GWR and Birkenhead for shipment from Liverpool (for instance, Wrexham's Cobden Flour Mills*) faced a trans-shipment at Birkenhead into a 'flat' for ferrying over the

---

*built 1864. 'Dominated East Denbighshire milling scene for 52 years.' Closed c.1916.

river to Liverpool. Flour in sacks would burst under this extra handling: Cobden's preferred to send flour to Liverpool for shipment via WMCQR and Hope Junction, and thence by LNWR to Chester, which went straight to the quayside. Connah's Quay was short of sidings, storage area and undercover facilities. A cargo of wheat for Cobden's from America shipped into Connah's Quay for delivery by WMCQR to Wrexham was ruined when it was unloaded in the wet at Connah's Quay; though Cobden's would continue to send 18,000 tons of flour a year down the WMCQR to Penyffordd they did not use Connah's Quay again!

The capacity of the Quay was limited to vessels of about 600 tons; in 1881, 135 ships called there and discharged 25,000 tons, or about 185 tons per ship. In railway terms, had all that tonnage passed inland via the WMCQR, it would have involved over three thousand 8-ton wagon movements a year or 100 wagon movements southward per working day of six days per week. Clearly not all imports were carried away by rail, but if half the daily tonnage involved approximately fifty wagon movements a day, and (as is known) there was a loading limit of 6−8 wagons (according to the locomotive involved) between Connah's Quay and Northop Hall, then the two locomotives allocated to the Buckley section were fully engaged on the basis of fifty southward-bound wagons per day. [From Northop Hall to Buckley Junction an additional 5 wagons could be taken.] The above disregards any empty coal wagons returning to the Buckley pits.

Connah's Quay received large tonnages of pit props from Scandinavia; the ships would arrive in convoy, about fifteen at a time, and this fleet of vessels tried the capacity of the WMCQR very sorely.

Of outward iron ore shipments from Connah's Quay, the biggest tonnages came from James Sparrow & Sons' Ffrwd Ironworks on the Ffrwd Branch; the 1881 figures were:

James Sparrow & Sons	8,940 tons	
Lilleshall Coal Co., Oakengates	690 tons	
Thomas & Co., Bloxwich	870 tons	
	10,500 tons	Iron Ore

Coal shipments were mainly to Dublin, Barrow and the Isle of Man: of those arising on the Buckley section were:

Dublin Main Coal Co.*	8,433 tons	
George Watkinson & Sons	4,011 tons	
North & South Buckley Coal Co. Ltd	78 tons	
Sandycroft Coal Co.	1,105 tons	
Hawarden Collieries Co.	1,312 tons	
	14,939 tons	Coal
Off the Llay Hall Colliery Branch (the Colliery had been out of action for some time)	21 tons	
Off the Ffrwd Branch James Sparrow & Sons	1,690 tons	
	16,650 tons	Coal

*The titles listed above are those given by the Manager (Cartwright) to the Lords Select Committee (June 1882) and are not necessarily the correct commercial titles of the firms in question.

Rates were a bone of contention: it was possible to send a ton of coal from Ffrwd Colliery per WMCQR to Connah's Quay for 1/3d. Westminster Colliery could only send to the decaying Saltney for a cost of 2/4d. a ton, a charge magnified by the use of the Wheatsheaf Incline, and although Westminster was only half a mile away from WMCQ metals, to reach them meant either (a) sending via Brynmally Colliery along the adverse 1 in 30 of the GWR branch there which ran along the street in Moss so that house-holders were obliged to cross the tracks to enter their doors: even when Brynmally was gained, WMCQ rails could only be entered through the colliery yard, a private area of land; and worse, the wagons would have to pass under the Brynmally Colliery screens. Or, (b) 800 yards of the GWR Ffrwd line could be used as far as Pendwll Colliery where the WMCQR was adjacent but not on the same level; to make a link line there which could only cater for 6–8 wagons at a time and would involve an adverse gradient and the use (again) of private land. Until now neither of these northward-leading WMCQR-connecting proposals could be prosecuted due to the intransigence of Thomas Clayton who owned both Brynmally and Pendwll Collieries, and who would discourage rail links through his property which would benefit a competitor! So, in regard to one of the largest collieries in the district, Connah's Quay (though ultimately benefitted when Westminster was at last served by a WMCQR branch) was denied this traffic for almost two decades.

More about rates: figures proved that the GWR was carrying South Wales coal more cheaply per ton/mile than North Wales coal; this infuriated the North Wales colliery owners whose pits were frequently on short time, whose coal contained at least 25% slack and who found customers with great difficulty. In consequence their labour-force was working less hours than their South Wales colleagues, and was much the poorer.[22] North Wales miners struck regularly for better wages, rarely received them and went back to work the worse off for their actions; their employers looked for any panacea to create new markets, to overcome the costs of geological difficul-ties and flooding and above all, to convey their coal for overseas markets by the cheapest route to the seaboard. Their bitterness over a disinterested GWR and their support for the WMCQR can well be understood.

That is not to say the district had no good customers for its coal: The Great Indian Peninsular Railway, The Pacific & Oriental Steam Navigation Co. and San Francisco all bought Denbighshire coal; it could be taken by 'steam flat' from Connah's Quay to the Mersey for 5d. per ton* (considerably cheaper than the existing system) and there loaded into ocean-going vessels.

Connah's Quay was also to share in the newly-formed alliance between Robertson and Piercy: Robertson had by 1882, bought 58 acres of land there from the Wenlock Estate, whose title to that land was then in dispute!

Of the shipment of bricks, Charles Davison & Co. owned 15 sailing vessels and sent products from the Quay to Bristol, the English Channel, and some ports abroad: further destinations were reached by shipping the bricks to Liverpool and transferring them there to larger vessels. Davison himself thought Connah's Quay should be five times larger to cope with the poten-tial business; some incoming ships had to wait two or three weeks to be unloaded because there were berths for only six at a time; and problems

*H.E. Taylor thought 16d. per ton was a more realistic figure.

were magnified when timber vessels arrived and there was not enough trackage to marshall the loaded wagons. The WMCQR excused these failings by admitting the gradient of 1 in 27 [sic] was too steep for their engines; if the WMCQR Act of 18th August, 1882 had had the effect of creating a new route, then the gradient would be reduced to 1 in 200 . . . but that line was never built.

1881

The year began with further evidence of future expansion when a second-hand passenger brake van and a second-hand 3rd Class coach were purchased from the LNWR for £50 and £70 respectively.

The outstanding feature of the year was the return of Benjamin Piercy to Wrexham, and his renewal of WMCQR connections; he had left the Company in 1868 and after working overseas for much of that time (latterly on the Royal Sardinian Railways which had a link with the Company through the mutual directorship of both by Thomas Barnes) was soon a force with which to reckon. Teaming up with Henry Robertson, heady plans were in the air and on 28th October a scheme was revealed to bring the Railway closer into the centre of Wrexham and to make links with all the collieries of the district, to double the main line in places, provide more sidings and build a new line to Brymbo; additionally there would be better connection with the LNWR at Connah's Quay. The scheme was the subject of a Bill in November 1881. As will be seen as the tale unfolds, Robertson and Piercy were not to be delayed by waiting for the outcome of that Bill. October's revelations made public their aims for a Brymbo link and on Robertson's initiative work began on the section which, under the eventual Act, was dubbed 'Railway No. 2'. But at this stage, it was a private venture known by its supporters as The Gatewen Branch. Messrs. Meakin & Deane, connected (but not related) to Robertson's family, were building[23] it and progress was rapid for the ground required little heavy civil engineering, and shortly a search was being made for rails. Before December 1881 ended The Ebbw Vale Company had offered 200 tons of steel flatbottomed rails, rolled for the New South Wales Government. They would sell for £5 a ton on site at the Works, 'payment at six months notice to Piercy and yourself' (i.e. Robertson): Ebbw Vale pointed out that if rolled specially, the price would be £6–£6 10s. 0d. per ton. The offer was taken up and the Branch – as far as the Gatewen Colliery – was laid in these rails. (Whitwham was the intermediary between the Steel Works and the entrepreneurs.)[24]

The Branch made a northward facing junction at Stansty: shortly, rails were laid on a southward spur but not connected to the main line. The north spur ended at 'Gatewen Junction' (later Brymbo North Junction) and a siding led off this spur in Clayton's brickworks. (The Deposited Plans show that the southern spur was at first intended but this would have made an operating nonsense for northbound coal trains.)

The financing of this venture had begun in the previous February (1881) when Robertson had exchanged shares with Piercy, the former obtaining an interest in the WMCQR and the latter in the Broughton & Plas Power Coal Co. Ltd.: between July and September 1881 Piercy bought more B & PPCCL shares for cash at par.

A month prior to Meakin & Deane starting work (September 1881), Piercy wrote to Robertson saying he 'would not put down a sou for the WMCQR branch without assurance it will obtain a share of the Westminster Colliery traffic'.* Piercy must have been satisfied in some way, for in October he agreed to 'go halves' with Robertson in funding the Gatewen Branch; in November they each sent £1,000 on account for this purpose, and Meakin & Deane were sent £700 for work done: they had another £800 in December and as just noted, arrangements for the rails were concluded at the month's end.

We must continue into 1882: fishbolts and dogspikes were delivered from Ebbw Vale, and it was arranged that sleepering should be at yard intervals. Robertson and Piercy had hoped to delay delivery of this material as their cash flow was becoming faster than they anticipated. Meakin & Deane were sent a further £500 in February and, the Ebbw Vale materials being laid, Robertson had second thoughts and asked Ebbw Vale to submit a drawing for a chair in order to stiffen the flatbottomed rail.

There was never any doubt that Robertson was building the Gatewen Branch for the benefit of the B&PPCCL rather than the WMCQR, though in public he had said it was for the benefit of his other trading colleagues in the coal industry. No one could have been convinced by that! All the same, it was obvious that the Gatewen Branch would not stop short at Gatewen. When in February 1882 Robertson suggested to Piercy that the Branch (already the proposed Railway No. 2 of the WMCQR Bill) be leased to the B&PPCCL, Piercy replied 'It would be difficult to raise capital for the Brymbo and Coed Poeth branches if leased land lies between them and the main line'. So we know that besides Brymbo (a goal which *would* be achieved), the Grosvenor and Talwrn pits near Coed Poeth were also to be connected.

At the end of February, more rails were delivered. By April 1882 the new Gatewen Colliery was under approach by rail on two flanks; the GWR's Moss Valley Branch reached it first by a short head – the Branch had started in business on Monday 8th May: and on that day too, the Wheatsheaf Incline was stopped – but must have reopened until October 1907; its current working methods had been to work six loaded wagons down against six empties up the Incline, but when conditions were unfavourable, six empties could be pulled up by the locomotive.† As to the opening of the Gatewen Branch, there are conflicting accounts: one said 'The Gatewen private line opened on 8th June' and another '17th June; it is without Parliamentary powers and it is reckoned that passengers can be carried without them'. This brings the Gatewen Saga up until June 1882, and it will be necessary to return to 1881 and other affairs. Nonetheless, the fact that Robertson and Piercy were deliberating if they should now build Railway No. 3 in the following December (authorised under the WMCQR Act of 18th August, 1882) has high significance.

---

*Piercy could not mean Westminster traffic over the then-building Gatewen Branch, but rather that his commitment hinged on the successful outcome of Railway No. 6 which would lead from the WMCQR's Brynmally terminus (Ffrwd Branch) and extend into the Westminster Colliery.

†*See page 53* re locomotive stabled on Incline.

The track arrangements at 'Gatewen Junction' show the single line spur joining an incomplete WMCQR doubled main line with a proposal to give Clayton's brickyard a connection: at that time his premises were served by a spur off the GWR Wheatsheaf Incline.[25]

On 23rd July THE NORTH WALES GUARDIAN made reference to the feud between the Company and the Buckley Traders, saying that the WMCQR had applied to the Master of the Rolls for a prohibition against the Railway Commissioners who had issued an Order compelling the WMCQR to supply wagons to the Traders for use on their own private sidings and branches. The Traders wanted wagons (as far as pit's mouth) and the Railway Company maintained that this was not within their terms. A second Order said the WMCQR was bound to take Traders' wagons 'from the end of the sidings'. The Master accepted the Commissioners' first Order but restrained them on the second.

The horses which worked the wharf at Connah's Quay were finally displaced when a second locomotive (secondhand) was obtained in October for this work from Hudswell, Clarke & Co. Ltd. at a cost of £750 0s. 0d. payable in instalments. (This was works No. 119 of 1872, DEE (WMCQR No. 9) 0−4−0 saddle tank.)

WMCQR EXTENSIONS & DOCK BILL   November 1881

This must be considered along with another less glamorous 'Grand Design' of the following year. In this Bill docks were to be built on the **north** shore of the Dee opposite Connah's Quay and the serving railway was to make junctions with the Chester & Holyhead section in either direction; the whole plan was to be connected with the Buckley Railway section near Northop Hall . . . an entirely new concept. The fall to the riverside would have been at 1 in 40 and the water crossed by a swing bridge with two opening spans of 70 ft each; there would have been twelve fixed spans of 30 ft each[26] and the dock was to have a water surface area of 1,500 × 35 ft.

From previous Bills which failed, several 'old friends' were resurrected, especially for lines in the Brymbo district: most of these enjoyed horrendous gradients.

No Act ensued, but the Act of 18th August, 1882 was a modified outcome of it.

Ref: Clwyd Record Office: QS/DR/186

WMCQR PROPOSES TO CROSS THE RIVER 1881/2

A GWR scheme to reach Buckley which was rejected in 1862 would have covered more or less the same ground as that sanctioned for the WMCQR from Wrexham, so Henry Robertson revealed in June 1882. The GWR and LNWR were always fearful of WMCQR ambitions to cross the Dee and gain Birkenhead, he said, and together they were successful − on the basis that the intended Dee Bridge was not high enough above water level − in convincing the Lords' Committee. Consequent Parliamentary costs were so high that the WMCQR could not have pursued the matter. In 1881 the WMCQR Bill just mentioned proposed yet another bridge but once more opposition was successful and in consequence the WMCQR abandoned that part of the Bill concerning the bridge and docks on the north shore of the river. Robertson's version of this event was that such a river crossing was 'not essential to the WMCQR who preferred, should they ever contemplate Birkenhead, to meet opposition there' rather than on the river bank.

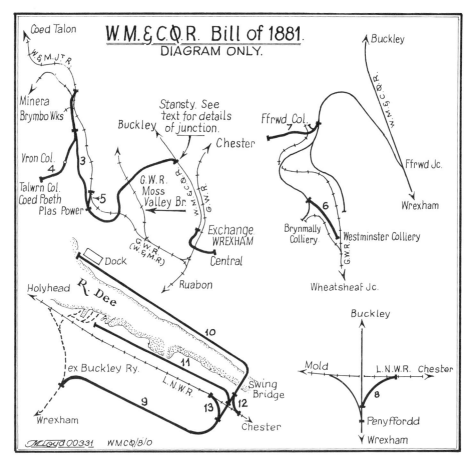

This WMCQR scheme to reach Connah's Quay provided the usual sarcasm from Counsel. 'Does any living creature ever want to go to Connah's Quay? Are you serious?' he quipped. His opponent's reply included that venerable reference to the GWR as being 'The Great Way Round' . . . Henry Robertson drew attention to the two bridges on the Buckley section at Connah's Quay which gave a vertical clearance of only 11 ft; under the 1881 Bill it was intended to 'reconstruct the tops of these two bridges' and make an exchange platform with the Chester & Holyhead there.* The Act gave the WMCQR powers to carry passengers, 'but Board of Trade approval and signals are required'. Another witness said the WMCQR shunting engine constantly blocked the C&HR section 'they let wagons down by gravity and their little engine'.

*A platform was incorporated into the south face of the LNWR station. The bridges are referred to in S.4 of the WMCQR Act 1882.

WREXHAM & MINERA JOINT LINE (The LNWR/GWR Joint Line)

It was inevitable that this single line which linked Brymbo with Coed Talon should be mentioned at the recommittal by the House of Lords concerning the WMCQR 1881 Bill. Questions were asked as to why traders did not use it to send their products northwards and so reach the LNWR that way? Or in other words, was a WMCQR line to Brymbo which would route traffic bound for the LNWR only via Brymbo North Junction and Penyffordd, really necessary?

There was general agreement about this Brymbo–Coed Talon link; 'it is practically a blocked line – it is of no use whatever, any more than if it did not exist'. Whilst it was the route which lay closest to the LNWR North Wales system, yet it was retorted, 'Physically it is, but commercially, and as to our traders, it is not worth a rap'.

Counsel for the WMCQR said it was a line straight out of PUNCH. It was worked on alternate days by the GWR and LNWR: Tuesdays and Fridays were LNWR days and Mondays and Thursdays GWR days; 'the GWR engine starts from Brymbo and the LNWR one from Coed Talon or Mold, only one engine in steam being allowed on the line at a time. What becomes of the other two days I do not know . . . and when they get to a level crossing the driver gets down and opens it . . . there was lately a case before the bench of magistrates following an altercation between the engine driver and a car driver as to who should take precedence'.

Nathaniel Robert Griffith (a local mining engineer) maintained that the line was simply a footpath: 'I know that Mr Osborne Morgan* uses it as a footpath to go to Church'.

Cartwright said the LNWR had a line to Hazlewood Colliery from the north and the line had been extended south to Brymbo jointly with the GWR to meet the GWR at Brymbo – traffic was only carried from Trimley Hall lime works.

In the Board of Trade Report on Bills for the 1882 Session comes the surprising news that it was proposed to change the title of the Company to NORTH WALES RAILWAYS & DOCK COMPANY.

1882

In January and September a financial arrangement with a Mr E.D. Till covered – in the first instance – the purchase of 50 new goods wagons – and in the second – for the hire and purchase of locomotive EMILY, a six-coupled saddle tank locomotive bought by the Broughton & Plas Power Coal Co. Ltd. to whom it was supplied by Beyer, Peacock & Co. Ltd. of Manchester as a new engine as recently as the previous May. This humble machine was a few years later to find itself decorated, and principal actor, in the opening of the Railway Company's Wrexham extension.

The strength of the Robertson/Piercy team, with Piercy newly returned from successful exploits abroad and Robertson expanding his Brymbo empire had been encapsulated in the extravagant Bill of 1881. A useful map showing industries and ambitions of that Bill headed 'Wrexham, Mold & Connah's Quay Railway (Extensions & Dock Session 1882)' showed the intended railways superimposed on the separate Flintshire and

*MP for Denbigh; residence Brymbo Hall.

Denbighshire coalfields. It might be noted that the touchy issue of a Dee bridge and docks on the north shore of the river had now been dropped – most of the former ambitions remained as before. 1882 was to see disappointment and success in turn with regards to these matters, yet it is ironic that the Deeside lines accepted by the Methuen Committee would never be built, but the lines (in the Wrexham area) turned down by that Committee were brought into existence.

Events of 1881 were to spill over into 1882, as already described. The Gatewen Branch was under construction without statutory authority and there was some hesitation about extending that line, probably it was thought better to await the outcome of Lord Methuen's House of Lords' Committee of Enquiry before making a decision. By April the Gatewen line was almost ready.

The blow came on 11th May when much of the 1881 Bill was thrown out, the Lords Journal stating on 15th May '. . . and the Committee are of the opinion that it is not expedient to proceed further with the said Bill'. Despite this rebuff to the Company's ambitions, the Gatewen Branch opened the next month and Robertson and Piercy began earnest deliberations concerning its extension. There followed some strange events. As could be expected, the inhabitants of Wrexham sent a Memorial praying that the Bill 'may be recommitted to another Select Committee' on 2nd June; the Duke of Westminster proposed the very unusual motion that the 'WMCQR (Extensions and Dock) Bill be recommitted to another Select Committee'. Objections were raised but the matter was resolved in the affirmative with all speed and on 13th June a new Select Committee was formed chaired by Lord Cottesloe. The matter of the displacement of many persons who would lose their dwellings in a poor part of Wrexham when Railway No. 1 was built, was met by the explanation that they 'would easily find accommodation in the immediate neighbourhood'. There were other amendments including one of title. Such was the pace of events that on 11th August the Commons was able to send the amended Bill back to the Lords and it was approved; on 18th August the Bill became law! It is possible that the WMCQR was perhaps the only railway company to achieve a reversal in this way. The 'private' Gatewen Branch was now part of the authorised Railway No. 2.

Of the 1881 Bill the principal objector had been, naturally, the GWR. The Duke was anxious to see that Railway No. 6 which would take his Westminster Colliery output to the LNWR via Ffrwd Junction, was built; he maintained the Methuen Committee had only examined 10 of the witnesses out of 40 whom the promoters wished to bring forward and only three hours were given to the matter when the Chairman announced they would only pass those lines which related to the Dee, a decision quite unfavourable to the WMCQR for those lines were quite useless unless the others were also built. Lord Methuen complained that in considering the Bill in the first place, they had not been given a map of the proposals 'so that they might have been able to see those lines projected all over a particular tract of land like an octopus, and they would be able to see that one limb of the octopus was not sound . . .' The Earl of Dartmouth refuted the suggestion that the Committee had been 'corrupted by Great Western influence': he had the 'misfortune of living on a northern branch of the Great Western and could confidently affirm that a more unsatisfactory line to dwell upon there could not be'. He simply wanted 'to prevent the creation of unnecessary branches by an impecunious and almost insolvent company'. Making matters worse, Lord Aberdare said he lived at Glamorgan and had never heard of the WMCQR, and when he did 'he found it doing very little business'. He felt that the WMCQR was like a tree deprived of branches; no wonder the line was impecunious, and he would support the Duke in his motion. By and large, the Lords were not against the recommitment of the Bill but strenuously defended the actions of the Methuen Committee in a whitewashing exercise to uphold the honesty and good intent of their brother Lords.

There are several issues of the foregoing affair which would repay further study, no less an entry in the Commons Journal for 25th July, 1882 to the effect 'Parties promoting the Bill had stated that the evidence of Robert Thubron of Newcastle-on-Tyne was essential to their case'. This could not be procured without the intervention of the House, and he was ordered to attend the following day.

So success – as mentioned – was achieved by Act of 18th August, 1882:

Railway No. 1 (7 furs.) An extension from Wrexham Exchange to a new Central station.

Railway No. 2 (2 m. 1 fur.) From a junction with the main line at Stansty (later called Brymbo South Junction) terminating in a field reputed to be the property of the Broughton Colliery Co. and in the occupation of the Broughton & Plas Power Colliery Co. Ltd. As built, this would be the section of the Brymbo Branch from Brymbo South Junction to Southsea, where the Plas Power Colliery was situated (and was just opening).

Railway No. 3 (1 m. 2 furs.) Was from No. 2 to a junction with the Wrexham & Minera Joint line of the GWR/LNWR (i.e. by title the Wrexham & Minera Extension Railway which led from Brymbo to Ffridd and beyond where it joined the LNWR near Coed Talon). For reasons unknown, this line was never built. Instead Railway No. 2 was extended north and west to the outskirts of the Brymbo Works and, according to the Minutes of the Broughton & Plas Power Coal Co. Ltd., was constructed by Robertson (its Chairman) and handed over to the WMCQR – which had no statutory authority for this precise route. As the intervening land was all the property of Robertson and his associates, no problems were incurred in providing a route for this line.

Railway No. 4 (1 m. 5 furs.) This was the branch involving reversal from Brymbo terminus and leading up to the Vron Colliery.[27]

Railway No. 5 (1+ fur.) A linking crossover between WMCQR and W&MR at Southsea.

Railway No. 6 (4+ furs.) An extension of the existing Ffrwd Branch at Brynmally, southwards to serve the Westminster Colliery.

The foregoing comprise the first block of authorisations in the Act, and all save No. 3 (as above) were constructed.

There were a further four Railways:

Railway No. 7. A chord line to Hope Junction to link the WMCQR with the LNWR and give direct running to and from Chester without reversal (see 'Hope Dashed' page 244). This work was begun then abandoned after Piercy's death.

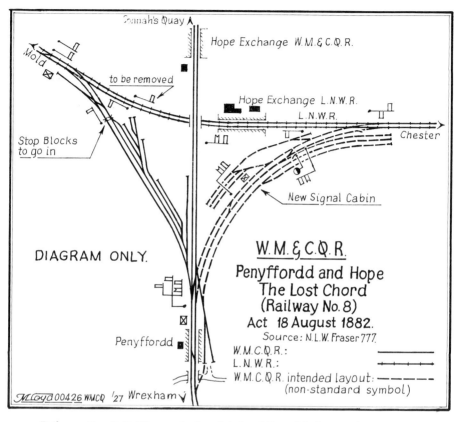

Railways Nos. 8, 9, 10, were in the vicinity of Connah's Quay to improve access thereto in lieu of the steep lower part of the Buckley Railway, and to make further junctions with the Chester–Holyhead line, and the Dee shore. None was made.

Even whilst these matters were passing between Commons and Lords, there seems to have been indecision about the Brymbo line (Railway No. 2) – an uncompleted lease for that railway as between Brymbo Junction and Moss & Pentre is dated to begin on 1st August, the parties being Piercy and Robertson and the Railway Company. That lease would run for 20 years at an annual rent of £500 plus ½d. per ton paid on all coal, ironstone etc. passing over the line, when the tonnage was over 120,000 per annum. By this scheme (which must have predated the building of the branch as a private venture), the WMCQR was to build, and to hand over on 1st August: thereafter maintenance would be the responsibility of the lessees.[28] As to the responsibility of what was originally called The Gatewen Branch (i.e. the private undertaking of the Broughton & Plas Power Coal Co. Ltd.) Colliery Minutes of August 1881 confirm their arrangements with Robertson and Piercy to construct such a line 'in the shortest possible time' for which work they were to be paid by wayleave: 20 years later Piercy's Trustees were still not fully paid for his work at that period.

The disappointments to the WMCQR at having their Bill thrown out in May cannot have been lessened when the overdue opening of the GWR's Moss Valley line took place (minerals only) on 11th May, and the importance of this to the Westminster Colliery was limited by the fact it would only carry their coal southwards and not seawards. Passenger traffic on this Branch began on 1st May, 1905 as between Wrexham and Moss Halt; it was withdrawn on 1st January, 1931. When Brynmally Colliery closed in 1935, the Branch was closed entirely.

There followed a nail-biting period for the WMCQR as the Duke of Westminster's efforts to have the 1881 Bill accepted by the second Lords' Committee were awaited: THE WREXHAM ADVERTISER's man was a key figure in communications, and at last the paper proclaimed:

> The Lords Committee sat on 15 June in Westminster Hall . . . at length the tedium ended, the doors opened and the throng rushed in . . . 'The preamble of the Bill is proved!' Off rushed the more anxious to wire the delightful intelligence to Wrexham, one enthusiastic Town Counsellor making his voice re-echo through the sacred precincts of the Palace of Westminster . . . afterwards all adjourn to the Westminster Palace hotel where success to the WMCQR Bill is drunk . . .

The year not yet over, the raising of separate capital to pay for the Wrexham Extension (Railway No. 1) was agreed upon in October, after which a Bill for further work was lodged in November[29] with Robertson as Engineer and Piercy's brother-in-law William Davies as his assistant. All this capped an exciting twelve months. This additional work was for a new line (later to be named 'The Hawarden Loop') with what would become Buckley Junction as its starting point from the existing line: it would fall in sweeping curves through Hawarden to Queensferry and from thence satellite companies of the MS&LR would carry the tracks across the Dee on a high level swing bridge to make a triangular junction on the north shore. From here, westwards, the objectives would be Birkenhead and Liverpool: eastwards they would be Chester and, via the Cheshire Lines Committee, Manchester: there would be an interchange siding with the Aston Hall Colliery Railway. (Powers for this scheme to proceed were obtained under an Act of 29th June, 1883 – and the railway remains open for traffic to this day.)

Robertson's image was not all that favourable – in June 1882 he had admitted before the Lords' Committee that he and Piercy had bought the land for Wrexham Central station, and intended to sell it to the WMCQR which was then in Receivership and could not make the purchase itself. It was little wonder that a section of local opinion believed that as soon as Robertson had brought the WMCQR to a fit condition, he would sell his interests to the LNWR (or) but his death in 1888 prevented this being proven, and Piercy's death at the same time did in fact, lead the WMCQR to the MS&LR's door.

Rumours about Robertson's motives were strengthened when he admitted at the 1882 Enquiry that 'they' had endeavoured to sell the Buckley line to both the GWR and LNWR: the two companies had then made a pact that

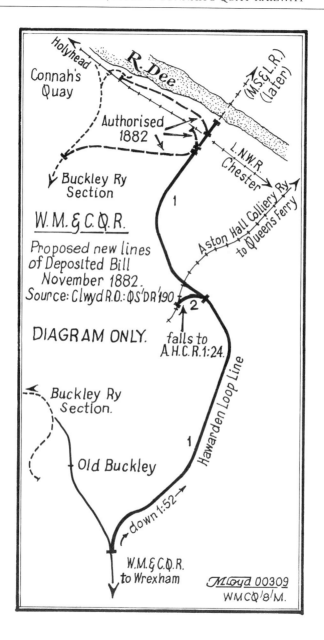

neither would purchase the line 'so there is no market for it'. Counsel for the GWR said this was another example of Robertson's investment in the WMCQR with a view to re-selling it.

Railways in which Piercy had an interest were not noted for their profitability; as to his joint venture with Piercy, Robertson was once asked 'Have you ever heard of a shareholder who ever got a dividend out of one of Mr Piercy's lines?' His opposition to the WMCQR given at earlier Parliamentary hearings were oft-quoted to embarrass him.

Throughout the Enquiry, there was all-round ill-feeling towards the GWR – William Lester, proprietor of Lester's Lime Works at Minera hoped to connect his firm with the proposed WMCQR line at Plas Power and when asked why he was not satisfied with the GWR which literally passed his door he said:

> The GWR certainly starts from my door; but it is a door which takes a great deal of opening and shutting. The accommodation is very indifferent.

He did not want to remain at the mercy of the GWR.

The local people had in 1868 and 1871 asked the GWR to provide a passenger service between Wrexham and Brymbo but the GWR maintained that to make the line up to Board of Trade requirements would be too expensive; however, when the WMCQR 1881 Bill was threatened, they began a service on 24th May, 1882 – 'The line had had to be doubled'. A station at Moss & Pentre was opened on 1st August.

Rev. William Jones (Vicar of Brymbo) said the GW station was not very convenient:

> the line was doubled less than a year ago – it was not necessary to double more than the last few yards to the station, but the bridge at Plas Power had to be renewed to take the double line.

Counsel for WMCQR said:

> Hitherto GWR have never attempted to carry passenger traffic as we know?

Jones replied:

> Never, except that in 1865 I saw a lot of workmen putting up a very rough kind of shed and on making enquiries they said they were going to carry passengers immediately . . . and they put a train on . . . and then when the pressure was taken away the tickets were taken away: there were tickets and stamps and everything and they were all packed up one fine morning and taken back to the storeroom at Paddington. The station was closed and the end of that station was that it burned down.

(There never had in fact, been a passenger train.)

In defence of their inaction, the GWR had costed the Board of Trade requirements at £12,000: although they carried heavy mineral traffic the Board of Trade said the bridges were not strong enough. Unaware of WMCQR proposals, the GWR was innocent for it had given instructions to commence work to meet Board of Trade wishes, nine months before they had heard of WMCQR intentions. It was an error that Plas Power station was not built and opened when Brymbo was so benefitted. Passenger traffic was disappointing; April–June 1882 figures were averaging 128 per day; on one day they had only 33 Up and 16 Down passengers and takings were but 15/5 *d.*

The GWR obviously believed that the WMCQR intended to run a passenger service on Railway No. 4. Counsel for the GWR said 'The public benefit of a passenger service from Wrexham to Vron via Railway No. 4 was illusory'; the service would be 'circumbendibus'.

It was not until the House of Lords Select Committee Enquiry of June 1882 concerning the WMCQR 1881 Bill that Cartwright disclosed the surprising news that 'both the Ffrwd and Brynmally Branches were out of use, the latter since 1877.* Brynmally Colliery was shut but may be opening soon: some of the rails to Brynmally had been taken out'. He said 'Ffrwd and Brynmally lines are out of repair; we have no traffic for them. However, the Brynmally Branch could be put back into working order for the expenditure of £400 –£500, and two or three weeks work'. He added that the Llay Hall line was also disused due to the after-effects of an explosion at the Colliery in 1880/1 which closed it for three months. The business was now in liquidation.

Cartwright's news must be taken with reserve, for he later said that Sparrow's had sent 8,940 tons of iron ore and 1,690 tons of coal to Connah's Quay for shipment in 1881. What he probably meant was that the line beyond Ffrwd to Brynmally had been closed.†

1883

Wrexham was now agog with the preparations for the new railway literally in its midst, for a line from Exchange station – as it would now be called – to a new centrally-located station was going to alter the face of the town towards the south, and give the place the status and convenience of being fully served by two railway companies . . . for Wrexham a railway which extended northwards was of far more importance than one making for London by GWR!

Ere long, 'considerable surprise and disappointment was being felt and expressed in Wrexham and district at the long delay in commencing the work . . . sanctioned by Parliament in the last session . . . and for providing increased railway and dock accommodation in North Wales. The supporters of the scheme, promoted by the WMCQR, gave the public to understand that the present railway would be extended into the heart of Wrexham . . . cutting of a line to Brymbo . . . doubling of existing line from Wrexham to Hope with steel rails . . . construction of large docks at Connah's Quay . . . would be commenced immediately the Bill received the Royal Assent'. Stirring up the mud, THE RAILWAY TIMES of 27th January succeeded in eliciting a reply; it was the GWR which was holding back the scheme, as their Chief Engineer had not approved the plans for the bridge which carried the GWR over the WMCQ extension south of Wrexham station. Evan Morris, the

*It may have been disused before that: Cartwright could only speak from the time of his appointment as Manager.

†There is always some doubt that the transcripts of such proceedings are precisely accurate. (The ability of shorthand writers to cope with Welsh place-names and other inaccuracies have been shown to be commonplace.)

WMCQR solicitor, had been instructed to make immediate remonstration to the Board of Trade. THE LIVERPOOL MERCURY waxed long on the same subject.

At the June half-yearly meeting of the Company the Chairman was able to say that a half of one of the branches was now complete and operating; this was an exaggerated, linear description of that short section of the Brymbo Branch which had now reached Gatewen Colliery, but it sufficed for the gathering. Arrangements with contractors to build the new extension in Wrexham had not been concluded. Between the lines of the Chairman's statement one may read that the GWR had not yet agreed, and that the necessary land had not all been bought. Promises were made of a large and handsome station [sic] in the centre of town, the building of 'a dozen branch lines in populous parts of Denbighshire and Flintshire (etc. etc.)'. 'Jam tomorrow' swayed the meeting and satisfied the local press for the time being.

Throughout the year steel rails were replacing iron in the main line which was still single, of course: there was also some new rolling stock, it was said. Evidence of new financial arrangements backed by Robertson and Piercy could be seen in the Act of 16th July when fresh capital was to be provided for all these ambitious plans. The Receiver, appointed on 12th July, 1879, was discharged on that same day.

The Hawarden Loop was given authority by an Act of 29th June for a double line of 4½ miles of railway branching off the existing system about one mile south of Old Buckley station – 98% of its route was on Gladstone land.[30] There would also be a new link between the foot of that Loop on the Dee shore, which would follow the south river bank westwards, leading to Connah's Quay and make connection with the former Buckley section there: and there was to be separate capital for this work.

The year ended with another 'news-splash'; the main line would be doubled and a contract had been placed with Piercy's Trustees. Bridges on Ffosygo and Brynmally branches had been renewed; beyond Gatewen Colliery the Brymbo earthworks were being prosecuted and at last, the Company had no rolling stock on hire: also the Westminster Colliery line link was in hand.

This was the High Point in the Company's existence, with so much under way and so much promised: and now without leased rolling stock commitments, a list of vehicles owned was prepared:

8 locomotives (1 hired on deferred purchase)
1 tender
6 – 3rd Class carriages
2 – 1st/2nd carriages
2 – luggage & break [sic] vans

Of the goods stock, there were:

5 covered wagons
25 timber wagons (hired on deferred purchase)
25 coal & coke wagons
6 cattle trucks
5 break vans [sic]
2 horse boxes

Of the second list, what better description of the type and volume of traffic which the Railway carried?

For the last time the Accounts read:

Hire of Rolling Stock (six months)	£234 0s. 0d.
Hire of Locomotives (ditto)	£506 5s. 0d.

And most important for morale 'the Receiver of the last four years has been discharged'.

1884

January began with an important appointment when William Davies* (brother-in-law of Benjamin Piercy) was made Resident Engineer @ £200 a year to oversee the work authorised by the Act of 29th June, 1883, i.e. The Hawarden Loop and Deeside line. This was a very useful arrangement indeed, for Davies had previously been with: Vale of Clwyd Railway; Denbigh, Ruthin & Corwen Railway (begun 5th September, 1859) (the above were supervised from his Welshpool office); Oswestry & Newtown Railway (Pool Quay–Buttington); Nantlle Branch in 1862; Carnarvonshire Railway in 1863; Sardinian railways.

By 26th January F.G. Whitwham had begun work on doubling the main line; his had been the only offer to do so; his estimates were:

Wrexham station – Junction of Gatewen Branch	£6,010 10s. 6d.
Gatewen Junction – Hope Exchange	£35,596 5s. 6d.
Hope Exchange – Junction Hawarden Loop	£4,203 10s. 9d.
Station accommodation and appliances	£1,460 0s. 0d.
	£47,270 6s. 9d.

(the titles are those used by Whitwham)

On 27th April the extension to Westminster Colliery was opened to mineral traffic – it never carried passengers: this was Railway No. 6 on the Deposited Plans of 1881 and on 27th June Railway No. 2 of the same plans was opened to Plas Power from Brymbo South Junction, again for minerals (the north chord was already open). These dates are taken from the Minutes, and are at variance with those given elsewhere.

Developments were taking place quickly. Even the passenger business was to thrive for when on 10th August, 1889 the WMCQR introduced a passenger service to Brymbo it had the effect of enhancing business on the GWR also instead of killing it. As Brymbo branch construction came nearer to that place, several stone overbridges to carry the track were required. A mason from Mold became contractor for these (his father had worked for Robertson on the Shrewsbury–Chester Railway). Bridges at Old Broughton, Plas Power and Gatewen on the WMCQR were his: from humble beginnings he became Alderman Rev. Edward Roberts JP, a notable local worthy.

The pattern of railways around Brymbo was fast taking its ultimate form, yet the course the WMCQR was taking was one which was forced upon it

---

*an Alderman of Flintshire County Council from 1888, a JP from 1893. Died 1915.

rather than that intended. Deposited Plans confirm that the WMCQR wanted access to Brymbo by an extension of its Ffrwd branch: had this taken place, a branch off it would have served the Moss Valley while Brymbo itself would have been gained via Holland Cottage and The Green. A public meeting at Brymbo Schools chaired by G.H. Whalley MP and supported by the Darbys of the Brymbo Company had attempted to get this scheme off the ground. It was always said that the W&M Joint line to Ffrith and beyond to Coed Talon, was the fruit of combined LNWR/GWR tactics to block this sortie by the WMCQR.*

In consequence of the Manchester, Sheffield & Lincoln Railway's Bill for Chester–Connah's Quay railway (via a proposed Hawarden Bridge), a House of Lords Enquiry was held during the summer months of 1884. Connah's Quay docks might even threaten Birkenhead and would certainly give the MS&LR great advantage over the GWR wharves at Saltney and permission was sought to allow the MS&LR to subscribe up to £50,000 towards the construction of quays, sidings etc. there, a portion of the WMCQR Act of 1882 which had not been taken up. A junction line was intended off the foot of The Hawarden Loop to run westwards along the south river bank to meet the Buckley section at Connah's Quay. At the time ships lying there could not load coal adequately – a wet dock was needed. The WMCQR was conveying 640,000 tons of coal annually; 100,000 tons of this was shipped from Connah's Quay and the rest was consumed locally. Cartwright (the WMCQR Manager) wanted Connah's Quay to compete with Birkenhead and Liverpool. Opponents of the MS&LR (the GWR in particular) said that the Chester–Connah's Quay line would prove to be the first instalment of a Chester–Birkenhead route . . . which of course was denied. But it was. Watkin of the MS&LR in aggressive mood said, 'I will not bind myself that at some future date I might not extend in that direction'! A Wirral line would be a piece of that plan.

John Watkinson, Managing Director of George Watkinson & Sons, owners of Buckley and Fernhill collieries – (*see page 87*) who came to the district in 1871, said his firm would benefit immensely from connection over the river to the north: at present they were sending locomotive coal to the LNWR at Chester but he could find no market for his slack coal (about 30% output) which some years ago he could send to the Northwich salt district; the delays and high rates charged by the LNWR by the route it was sent, via Mold Junction, Crewe and Winsford, made this unprofitable. Lancashire collieries could compete so effectively that Watkinson ceased this trade in 1875. It cost them 2/4*d.* per ton from Buckley to Northwich, whereas Lancashire pits could send for 1/- per ton less. The GWR did not delay his wagons, but the LNWR always did. In general he had no complaints against any railway company save in the matter of the salt district traffic; the salt owners used to send their own empty wagons to Watkinsons and after loading, it was sometimes six weeks between leaving those loaded wagons at Connah's Quay and their arrival at Winsford or Northwich.

The area around Winsford, Northwich and Middlewich was responsible for over 75% of British salt production in the last quarter of the 19th century. The traditional open pan process employed was for brine, pumped from

---

*WHEATSHEAF October 1910.

underground sources, to be evaporated in shallow rectangular iron pans up to 24 ft wide and 30–80 ft or more, long, resting on brick supports that formed flues for coal fires along one end. As the salt crystallised out, it was raked off, to be drained and then dried by the flue gases leaving the far end of the pans. Rock salt was also mined and this required dissolving in water, allowing insoluble matter to settle and then evaporating the clarified brine in the same way. The higher the temperature the faster the evaporation and the finer the grain of the salt produced and, of course, the greater the consumption of coal; typically, a ton of coal would yield 1½ to 2 tons of finer grained salt.

The Cheshire output was some 1¾ million tons of salt in 1887, 1 million tons of which was exported; apart from meeting domestic dietary and food preservation requirements, most of the remainder fed the rapidly growing alkali industry of South Lancashire, producing soda which in turn was used in the manufacture of soap and glass.

At that time Watkinson was exporting 25% of their output via Birkenhead – he would welcome the MS&LR plan, and financial support for Connah's Quay docks would be most beneficial.

When Cartwright gave evidence, he confirmed the Railway Company as yet owned but two small docks and considerable wharfage at Connah's Quay. He was made the butt of some humorous banter on the subject of Connah's Quay, such as:

> Do you mean that anybody beside two or three people who wish to go there to shoot wild ducks, or two or three wild ducks who want to go there, would ever go as passengers to Connah's Quay? It is the most miserable place that I was ever in.

To which Cartwright was equal:

> I have not had the pleasure of meeting you there. (*Laughter*)

It was explained that until more money was spent on Connah's Quay, ships would continue to use Birkenhead: there was a shortage of return cargoes at Connah's Quay and this, in addition to the limited facilities, made Birkenhead preferable to ship owners.

Cartwright was able to break down the 1887 coal traffic figures over the WMCQR; coal and like traffic totalled 475,000 tons. Of this, 435,000 tons passed off the WMCQR at Hope Junction and Connah's Quay onto the LNWR and 80,000 tons was used as locomotive coal by the LNWR itself. Another 34,000 tons went onto GWR metals at Wrexham Exchange.*

There was much talk about the uncompetitive attitude of the North Wales mines; whilst South Wales pits could work all week, three- or four-day working was common in the North, the cost of transport and the lack of customers for the 25+% slack coal extracted militating against such suppliers. Some slack could be used by the chemical works at Connah's Quay but collieries on the WMCQR produced 1,500,000 tons annually; of this some was used locally and certain pits burnt the slack themselves ... perhaps no more than 1/5th of the slack they mined. Slack used in the evaporation process in the Cheshire salt trade no longer came from North Wales. Chester took 150,000 tons of non-slack coal annually.

Author's note: Assuming the contemporary loading of coal wagons at 8 tons each, and a six-day week, such tonnages would involve 90 outgoing loaded wagons per day, and an equal number of empties returning.

The special interest of Messrs. Beyer, Peacock & Co. Ltd., of Gorton, Manchester (geographically alongside the MS&LR Works etc. there) was highlighted: there were personal links of this firm with iron, steel and colliery undertakings in the Brymbo district; until Autumn 1879 they had bought coal from Derbyshire but were now investigating the potential of coal from Southsea where the Company had common directorships in the Broughton & Plas Power Colliery Co. This colliery was controlled by its principal owner, Henry Robertson, at the time enjoying the same position with the Brymbo Company, and a partner in Beyer, Peacock & Co. Ltd. (The Manager there had recently been Nathaniel Griffiths, now acting on his own as a Civil Engineering Consultant in Wrexham.) But Beyers found that coal from Shireoaks Colliery to Gorton (52 miles) cost 3/2d. ton for carriage whilst that from Plas Power (Southsea) to Gorton (56½ miles) cost 5/- ton. The depression in the North Wales coalfield was the direct result of such transport drawbacks; local pits now working only 3 days a week had suffered a long strike in 1882 when 7,000 men came out, and this had hit customer confidence in North Wales' suppliers and thus made matters worse. Though Plas Power sent coal to Wolverhampton by GWR in tune to 35,000 tons a year, this was a 'one company transport method' – where coal was sent elsewhere involving (for instance) GWR + LNWR etc. 'every transporter wanted his share of the cake'. It was hoped the WMCQR Brymbo Branch would, on reaching Plas Power, reduce costs, but the earthworks were only just being completed at the time of the Enquiry (June 1884) 'and they have not sent any traffic over it yet'. Output at the time went solely over the GWR via Croes Newydd.

Griffiths, under examination, informed that the Buckley firebrick trade was an extensive one and much went to export; Connah's Quay only shipped the firebricks to Liverpool where they were trans-shipped and sent to America. He confirmed that the intended chord line at Hope Junction – from south to east – was made at the instigation of Robertson and Piercy under pressure from the Plas Power coal interests, who were sending great quantities by LNWR. Since 1882 it had suited the LNWR to send empty wagons to Hope Junction and thus onto WMCQR tracks; they collected locomotive and steamship coal in this way, all of which went via Chester. The Westminster Colliery, formerly a user of the GWR's Saltney Wharf had now abandoned that place in favour of Birkenhead; trade was so bad however, that the pit was only working two days a week. Similarly short of work, and having its own independent standard gauge railway with a transfer yard to the LNWR coast line, but mainly serving the wharves at Queensferry, was the Aston Hall Colliery 'owned by Gladstone'. Its business now relied on local customers and very little coal was going down to the river.

Griffiths divulged more about Connah's Quay than had Cartwright: its inward traffic was mainly in timber, being pit props from the Baltic and its outwards traffic was in bricks and coal. A table of inwards goods showed that compared with timber, other commodities coming off the river were small – they included creosote for mines, iron ore for the chemical works, gravel, pitch, whitening, sulphur and salt. Concerning towage on the river, a tug would take up to six sailing vessels at a time: in a crosswind it needed care to keep the towed vessels off the shore. He had no adverse comment about the width of the channel under the proposed Hawarden Bridge on this issue – as had other witnesses – and he recalled that before the river was straightened, the towpath for horses was on the north bank in a position where the canalised channel now flowed.

James Abernethy, a past President of the Institute of Civil Engineers, who had long worked with Piercy and had 40 years experience in marine work, thought the position for a bridge was the best one. He acted in a consultative role, took his instructions not from Piercy, but from Evan Morris, the WMCQR's solicitor in Wrexham. He said Morris had a two-fold interest in these affairs, for he also acted as agent for Messrs. Lingard, Monk, who were agents in turn for the MS & LR and solicitors to the Bill now being considered.

When Henry Enfield Taylor[31] was examined, he revealed some local and personal feuds: he described himself as a coal owner and Civil Engineer in Chester and had lived for 12 years locally, was a Dee Pilots' Trustee and a Hawarden Embankment Trustee. He refuted the slackness of business at Aston Hall Colliery, 'the railway runs past the front of my house and the engines and trucks are running up and down all day long so it is not shut. Four to five years ago Queensferry shipped bricks and coal to Ireland but not now due to the bad state of trade. Aston Hall Colliery would send out 30–40,000 tons annually. All the locals and I oppose the Bridge; it would close the upper river'. He was convinced that most of the work at Connah's Quay was of sidings for the benefit of Robertson's coal traffic. In his opinion the WMCQR Bill of 1882 (abandoned prior to going before Parliament) was a scheme to build docks on the north side of the river and connect them to the south bank with a swing bridge; he denied he was involved in any way and said he objected to the construction of the bridge then proposed. An inquisition then began and he was obliged to admit he chaired a meeting at Connah's Quay in March 1882 in support of the 1882 Bill. He agreed he was engaged by Evan Morris in a professional capacity, taking his instructions from him – though he denied the railway and bridge were part of his task. As he understood it, the 1884 scheme was simply for docks on the north side of the river and he was unaware of any plan to extend the railway northwards beyond those docks ... the issue on which both GWR and LNWR had always fought. He averred that the Robertson/Piercy 1882 Bill, though nominally a WMCQR proposal, was backed by the MS & LR: it would be of advantage to both WMCQR and MS & LR: it was understood that Robertson would finance the 1882 scheme which Parliament passed on the basis of his good faith; Piercy had personally bought the land at Connah's Quay for building the docks. Taylor did not come out of the cross-examination very well.

Throughout the Enquiry, the underlying issue was the mining of coal: local problems were clearly exposed, differentiating between the Buckley (Flintshire) mining district served by the Buckley Railway section, and the Brymbo (Denbighshire) mining district served by the WMCQR branch. The latter coalfield had less mines of greater size than the former; coal was more easily worked than in Flintshire and in that year (1884) Denbighshire output would be double that of Flintshire. This makes comparison of heavy coal traffic passing down the WMCQR main line between the Wrexham coalfield and Hope Junction or Connah's Quay, more easily compared with smaller output from the Buckley mines passing down to Connah's Quay only a small portion of whose output went south to Hope Junction. It was hoped that the current conversion of the Brymbo Works from iron to steel making would improve that situation, but throughout the Brymbo district it was admitted that until the WMCQR had direct access to Birkenhead, coalmines would never work full-time.

Aston Hall Colliery in the Buckley area coalfield (which had its own private railway not linked to the WMCQR) worked its lower seams more productively than any other pit. Around Brymbo, the pits of Plas Power, Gatewen, Brymbo and Grosvenor were the largest. Yet Aston Hall, though heavily capitalised by John Crossley of Halifax and other Yorkshire industrialists, went into liquidation.

> Their money was wasted; I am afraid that when we get Englishmen into our country we waste their money for them . . . Mr Robertson was linked with Mancot for a time, but then he abandoned it . . . The Dublin Main is a working Colliery, worked by Mr Dixon (the National Provincial Bank, Manchester) who managed it for the liquidator, he is a sort of mortgagee in possession . . . (in the Buckley district), Lexham Green (owned by Hancock), Ewloe Hall and Pentrobin are not working.

Coal traffic on the Buckley section was estimated to source:

Watkinson's	150,000 tons per annum
Dublin Main	40,000 ('but water broke in recently')
Hawarden Collieries	80,000
North Buckley	10,000 ('but this place is more a brickworks')

(say) a total of about 250,000 tons. All this goes down to Connah's Quay but the lack of accommodation there reduces the chances of shipment: rather, much is transferred onto the C&HR section of the LNWR.

It was emphasised *ex cathedra*, that Gatewen, Llay Hall and Gwersyllt Collieries had all opened as a result of the building of the WMCQR main line. Llay Hall, having a branch railway to serve it, raised 150,000 tons but its 35% slack content (40,000 tons) was left to burn week in, week out, on their tip. 'It would be cheaper to leave it down the pit'.

To improve their coal traffic, the WMCQR link to the Westminster Colliery opened in May and was 800 yards long. Owners were now the Westminster Brymbo Coal & Coke Co. Ltd.; Gwersyllt was currently closed but would reopen shortly under the ownership of this company. It was hoped to prosecute a stone quarry near Westminster Colliery: stone from there had been used to build part of the Walker Art Gallery at Liverpool, and more orders would be obtained.

As a consequence of cattle trains being diverted by the LNWR between Chester and Rhyl by sending them over the Mold–Denbigh route to overcome congestion on the coast line, traffic off the WMCQR at Hope Junction was held up by LNWR business there. Livestock was virtually non-existent on the WMCQR and had brought in but £40 in 1883; 1st Class passengers accounted for even less, £32! 2nd Class passengers showed £63 and 3rd

THE RAILWAY TIMES.

£175,000 FOUR PER CENT. "A" DEBENTURE STOCK OF THE

WREXHAM, MOLD, and CONNAH'S QUAY RAILWAY COMPANY.

Ranking as a first charge, with priority over £175,000 "B" Debenture Stock, and over £387,750 Consolidated Stock.

Price—Par, or £100 per £100 Stock.

Actual clear net revenue avavailable for the "A" Debenture Stock, after payment of Rent of Leased Line, for the half-year ending 30th June, 1884 .... £5,503 13 11

Amount required for half-year's Interest on the whole of the "A" Debenture Stock... 3,500 0 0

Surplus clear half-yearly net revenue 2,003 13 11

The Interest accrues from 1st July, and is payable by warrants half-yearly on the 1st February and 1st August, at the North and South Wales Bank, Limited, Wrexham, and at their London Agents, the London and Westminster Bank, Limited, Lothbury, London.

The Directors of the Wrexham, Mold, and Connah's Quay Railway Company are authorised to receive applications for £90,000, being the balance of the above £175,000 Four per cent. "A" Debenture Stock, created, by virtue of special Act of Parliament, 46 and 47 Vict., cap. 108, in substitution for Debenture Stocks bearing higher rates of Interest, and for the purpose of doubling the Line, and providing additional Rolling Stock, &c., rendered necessary by the great increase of traffic.

Price £100 per £100 Debenture Stock, payable £10 per £100 Stock on application, and the balance on the 1st of October.

The traffic actually carried by the Railway during the six months ending 30th June last was as follows:—

Minerals .... 323,068 Tons.
General merchandise .... 27,823 ,,
Passengers 82,140

The traffic receipts of the Company for the year ending 30th June last amounted to £33,117 13s., equal to £45 10s. per mile per week; a return greater, it is believed, than that of any other single line of railway (except one) in the United Kingdom.

Without reckoning the great increase of traffic which must come upon the Railway when additional Collieries are connected with it by means of the new branches, and taking into account only the receipts from the working of the Railway as it is, the clear net Annual Revenue of the Company now available for payment of Interest on the "A" Debenture Stock, after deducting working expenses, rent of leased line, and all charges, is considerably in excess of the sum required to meet such Interest, which is a first charge thereon.

The Wrexham "A" Debenture Stock is therefore as amply secured as that of Railway Companies generally, the market price of whose 4 per cent. Debenture Stocks average at least 110, or 10 per cent. above the price of the "A" Debenture Stock now offered at 100. It is intended to apply to the London Stock Exchange for an Official Quotation for the Stock.

The Acts of Parliament and last Report and Statements of Account of the Company can be seen at the Offices of Messrs. James Fraser and Sons, 2, Tokenhouse-buildings, King's Arms-yard, E.C.

Applications for Debenture Stock (which can be for any sum being a multiple of £10) must be forwarded to the North and South Wales Bank, Limited, Wrexham; the London and Westminster Bank, Limited, Lothbury, London, E.C.; or to the Secretary at the London Offices of the Company, 2, Tokenhouse-buildings, King's Arms-yard, London, E.C.; from all of whom detailed Prospectuses and Forms of Application can be obtained.

Applications will be received up to Saturday, the 27th inst.

Class £1,290 – there was no mistaking that the WMCQR was not a railway whose income depended on passenger travel.

On 8th August the new (Up) line of the double track between Penyffordd and Caergwrle, now complete, was thereafter used for goods traffic under train staff regulations. An unusual state of affairs was so created between these two places, with two parallel lines each reserved for one class of traffic. The telegraph system was still incomplete.

In November a drawing was approved by Messrs. Cartwright, Davies and Willans for a locomotive; two were to be supplied by Beyer, Peacock & Co. Ltd. for £2,325 each. Mr Fraser (the Secretary) was to be paid £150 for 'special services' and the General Manager's salary was to be increased to £500 per year; the Locomotive Superintendent's (Willans) was also increased to £182, a move which brought a letter from him expressing his dissatisfaction with the amount.

A Bill was being promoted for a Denbighshire & Shropshire Railway to link Wrexham with Welshampton and this would have WMCQR support.

1885

Throughout 1885 there was a sombre mood about: a prolonged and severe depression in trade had affected the traffic receipts of this and many another railway company, but the Chairman expressed the hope that when the line from Plas Power to Brymbo was finished, figures would improve.

A new wharf at Connah's Quay had been extended 136 yards from the old quay there, and was almost completed. There was anticipation about the connection with the Cambrian Railways which would stem from a new link in Wrexham; the Bill for the Wrexham–Ellesmere line had received the Royal Assent.

The Chairman's Report for March stressed that the MS&LR's Act had resulted in plans for crossing the Dee[32] to make end-on junction with The Hawarden Loop at Shotton on the south bank. In consequence the WMCQR would become 'a link in a string of sausages', with the MS&LR and LNWR at its north end, the GWR and Cambrian at the southern; it was an exciting prospect for those involved.

Major General Hutchinson had passed the additional line of rails for passenger traffic subject to the Block Telegraph being installed between Wrexham Colliery Junction (Rhosddu) and 'Hawarden Junction', within three months of 13th April that year, and in July such a Telegraph was completed at a cost of £393 14s. 9d.[33]

Hutchinson's Report confirms the farsightedness of the promoters: land had been taken for double line and bridges could accommodate it. Opportunity had now been taken to re-lay part of the existing single track and all the new one in double-headed steel rails 72 lbs. per yard weight; the track was therefore similar to that already in use save that iron rails were now steel and half-round sleepers were now of rectangular section. Ten over-bridges had stone abutments carrying wrought iron girders, and ten under-bridges had masonry or brick abutments carrying timber or wrought iron girders; their floors were decked in timber.

The continued existence of Rhosddu level crossing is excused by 'it will shortly go'. Second platforms had been built at Gwersyllt, Cefnybedd, Bridge End, Caergwrle, Penyffordd, and Hope Junction. Signal Cabins were listed (*page 323*). Of the stations, detailed comment was:

Gwersyllt	A new building was in progress
Bridge End	Old signal box impedes the view from the new one: it must be removed
Penyffordd }	Catch points to be provided, together with notice
Hawarden Junction	boards
Ffrwd Junction	Notice board to be provided at catch points

At occupation crossings, gates must open away from the track, not inwards.

1886

It was a case of keeping a low profile during the continuation of the trade slump and the year was notable for reduced activity both in traffic and, to counteract the fall in income, reduced expenses; construction authorised in 1882 was continued but only at a pace which would enable the Board to tell the shareholders work had not stopped, and certainly not fast enough to please the local people who had expected some 'fireworks' in the progress: of course, the links at both ends of the line were much to the fore in the 'jam tomorrow' stakes. A slight improvement was noted in business during August/September, and the Connah's Quay wharfage accommodation had been further increased by a modest new length. Perhaps and secretly to the satisfaction of the directors who were anxious to reduce expenditure where they could, the new line through Wrexham had not advanced as was hoped as the Court of Quarter Sessions had refused certain road diversions, even though they had been approved by the Corporation of Wrexham.

At the end of November a secretive ring concerns the Minute Book when it was recorded that the Secretary had a 'friend' who was willing to take over the Hiring Agreement for the two recently-built Beyer Peacock engines at a lower rate of interest. Not surprisingly the matter was intimate enough not to appear in the Minutes again.

1887

The complex background to the origins of the Brymbo Branch, its partially private construction and then the authorisation as a statutory undertaking, made it necessary for the Railway and Colliery Companies to cover themselves for the future. Two draft Agreements were drawn up in 1887 and although neither surviving specimen has been signed, their contents are unusual.*

The First Draft:

The Railway will cross the Colliery's private railway on the level at a point between its junction of the private railway and the GWR. This Agreement gives power to the Colliery Co. (who have made lands available to the Railway):

1) To cross and recross Railways 2, 3, 4, 5 for the purpose of carrying their traffic . . . to and from the GWR or from other works of the Coal Coy. free of charge.

---

*The Railway means the WMCQR. The Colliery means the Broughton & Plas Power Coal Co. Ltd.

THE NEW RAILWAY EXTENSION INTO WREXHAM — JUBILEE STATION.

Supplement to the "*Wrexham Advertiser*," June 25th, 1887.

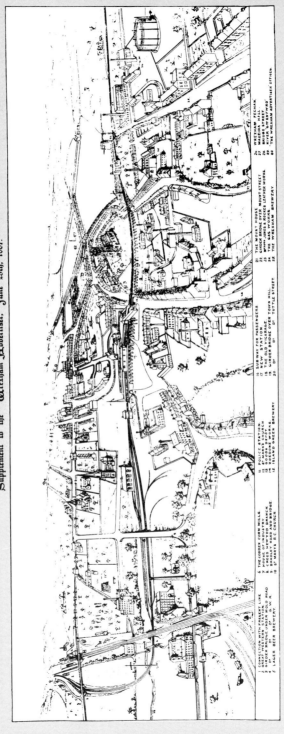

2) (This clause binds the Colliery Coy. to send down certain minimum tonnages per week etc. etc.).

3) The Colliery Coy. may use the Railway at charges based on actual distance to work traffic between any one of their several collieries, erected now and in the future, and Brymbo Steelworks, in their own wagons with their own locomotives and workmen.

4) Colliery servants working under clause 3) must observe Railway byelaws and will be responsible for accidents, and must keep the Railway indemnified.

The Second Draft adds a clause preventing the Railway giving more favourable tolls to anyone else, and another stated that if either Robertson or the Broughton Coal Co. required it, the Railway would make and maintain at their own expense 'the bridge now existing on Railway No. 3 over the GWR near the Broughton Colly.' Finally, should the Railway make alterations to Robertson's railways during its building, laying and construction, it must fund such alterations; and should the Colliery Co. add further railways to its system, they must be laid to the satisfaction of the Railway's Engineer.[34]

On 6th August THE CHESTER CHRONICLE said:

> Gladstone will drive the first pile of the MS&L Rly bridge

(hitherto the paper had referred to it as the Cheshire Lines Committee Bridge)

> across the Dee on 16th inst. The ceremony will be performed in the middle of the river about half a mile below Queensferry, and will be reached by a temporary pier or gallery at the end of which Gladstone will stand.

In fact the first cylinder was laid after Gladstone had waved a flag at which it was lowered into position; he then declared the cylinder was well and truly laid. The CHRONICLE (13th August) listed nine earlier attempts to build a bridge hereabouts.

The bridge caused a considerable addition to the signalling not only on the railway but also to the river 'the necessary buoys, dolphins and lights enable river traffic unimpeded day or night'. Although outside the geographical system of the WMCQR, the bridge was to become such an integral part of that Railway's existence, that more may be said of it. The log of the control tower has in part survived and records how trains were delayed by the openings, and the method of ship towage. They cover part of 1901–2. The control tower was open day and night seven days a week at this period. The Log Book is in analysis form with headings:

Time advised from Signal Box	Vessels Up
Time rung for Bridge	Vessels Down
Released from Shotton Box	Time at which passed
Released from Wrexham Junction	Time Bridge in Normal Position
Time Signal Boxes released	

Ships' names were only recorded in hours of daylight: most passed through at High Water and if this was at noon the Bridge would swing about three times each day for tugs and flotillas of towed vessels behind. The tug would return alone about three hours later and the vessels taken up river

SWING BRIDGE OVER THE DEE, MANCHESTER, SHEFFIELD, AND LINCOLNSHIRE RAILWAY.

MR. F. FOX, M. INST. C.E. ENGINEER.

(For description see page 452.)

VIEW LOOKING DOWN THE RIVER

MOVEABLE GIRDER

FIXED GIRDER

LAND END OF MOVEABLE GIRDER

would on average return behind a tug three days later. Towed vessels included sailing ships without power, 'flats' and barges. Trains were severely delayed at times, 15–20 minutes being frequently recorded, as the vessels were given priority over trains. The control tower locking mechanism, once actuated, locked all the appropriate levers in the railway signal cabins. The 'Remarks' column of the Log has some choice specimens:

Delayed Launch & Yacth* and passenger train 5 mins at Shotton
Delayed CLC Express 4 mins at Chester Junction
Delayed tug 4 mins & pass train 3 mins at Birkenhead Junc
Not for got (ship)
SS Viking showing know light signal for Bridge
Blocks out for fitters
Ship only whistels

[In about 1912 the GCR (by then the owner of the Bridge) asked that the opening of the span be discontinued between certain night hours and on Sundays. Today, the span is fixed, the control tower had been demolished; and yet, it is only within recent years that the double-armed semaphore signals controlling river traffic, disappeared from the river banks.]

At the end of August the Board was alerted by the news 'It was reported that the Llay Hall Co.'s workings were approaching Cefn-y-Bedd Viaduct', an arresting announcement which might have heralded that the enemy was at the gates of Wrexham. However, subsequent enquiries showed that the aggressor was actually quite friendly and there were to be no encroachments on the WMCQR's mineral rights either in the vicinity of, or under the Viaduct.

Things were looking better in the spring of the year – traffic had indeed held up and a pact had been made with the Wrexham Corporation so that work was now advancing, and the Chairman hoped his next Report would announce completion . . . which it did. As to the official Board of Trade Inspection this was a very satisfactory affair: the track had to be moved nearer Exchange platform, signals and a clock were missing from Central and the method of working the single line had to be arranged. The last-named was settled on the basis of One Engine in Steam and the line opened on 1st November. The linking track was single but bridges etc. provided for doubling when desirable; the ruling gradient was 1 in 100 on a 10 chain radius curve. There were three overbridges, one carried the GWR and the others, roads: also a covered bridge was provided at the outset between the Central and Exchange stations.

At the half-yearly meeting in September the Chairman made his customary twice-yearly oration on the glories of things yet to come and proudly announced that interest in full had been paid on the Debenture Stocks and such was the increase in traffic that there might even be the possibility of a dividend for Ordinary Shareholders . . . but not yet.

The contractors began work on the new Hawarden Loop on 6th September.

*actual spelling.

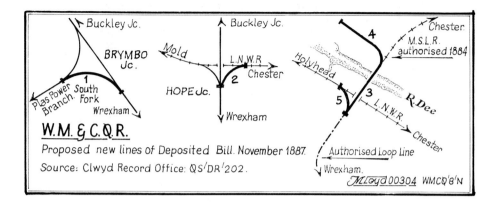

Proposed new lines of Deposited Bill. November 1887.

Source: Clwyd Record Office: QS/DR/202.

WMCQ AND W&E RAILWAYS Bill. November 1887
(This was the last Bill.)
     A small chord from the south would give the 'Plas Power Branch'
(actually the Brymbo branch) access to the main line from the south – The
South Fork (Railway No. 1): a second chord would result from revised
powers for the main line to have junction with the Mold–Chester LNWR
line at Hope Junction to allow Wrexham–Chester through trains (Railway No. 2) – powers had been obtained originally as Railway No. 8 in
1882, but had lapsed.
     There was to be a chord onto the Chester–Holyhead line at Shotton and
a bold attempt to cross the river on its own authority and make junction
with railways heading to meet it, but then at the planning stage (Railways
Nos. 3, 4 and 5).
Ref: Clwyd Record Office: QS/DR/202

1888

     On 7th February Piercy sent a letter to Cartwright concerning his liaison
with the LNWR, the Penyffordd–Hope chord then under construction and
the intended through working of LNWR coaches. It was planned that LNWR
stock would work out from Chester and after stopping at their Hope station,
a WMCQR engine would take the place of LNWR haulage there and draw the
carriages along the new chord and so to Wrexham: however, the LNWR
found that the layout at Hope was unsuitable and maintained that the
WMCQR layout at Penyffordd would have to be modified 'as to junction and
sidings' to allow engines to be changed there.
     THE CHESTER CHRONICLE told its readers that the WMCQR was about to build
hotels and refreshment rooms at Wrexham and Connah's Quay.
     Willans sent several letters to the Board during February asking for an
increase in salary: he was ultimately successful, and it was increased to £220
per annum – his letters survive.

(COPY)

Chairman & Directors of the Wrexham Mold & Connah's Quay R'y Company.

Application for an advance of Salary.

Gentlemen,
    I trust you will pardon my liberty in appealing to you for an advance of salary, but I do so from a feeling of confidence, that my application will be met with a Cordial & Substantial recognition for the services I have rendered the Company during the past seven years.
    I hardly think it is necessary for me to state the uphill work I have had to contend with, during that time, to get the rolling stock etc, into it's present efficient condition, but I do think I should remind you, that I have had no advance during those seven years, whilst almost all the Company's Officials have had one or more advances.
    I think I should also remind you that my responsibilities are about triple, to what they were at the commencement of my service. Therefore Gentlemen, I beg to leave my case in your hands, to deal with as you think it deserves.

Remaining
Your most respectfully
(Signed) F. Willans.
Loco Superintendent.

Aug' 4th, 1884.

(COPY)

WREXHAM MOLD AND CONNAH'S QUAY RAILWAY.

August 4th, 1884.

Memorandum from Loco' Dep' to Benj'm Piercy Esq, Marchwiel Hall, Wrexham.

Dear Sir,
    You will see from enclosed that I am making a formal application for an advance of Salary, a copy of which I enclose.
    May I ask if you will kindly support me in the matter and you will ever receive the thanks of your

Humble Servant,
F. Willans.
Loco Superintendent.

Copy of two letters from F. Willans to the WM&CQR requesting a salary advance, dated 1884.

March brought a double death-blow to the Company – Henry Robertson died on the 22nd, and Benjamin Piercy in London (age 61) two days later; it was a bitter event from which the organisation never recovered.

THE CHESTER CHRONICLE carried an obituary of Robertson (died 22nd March) on 24th March, and this summarized not only his interests, but gave explanation to the various alliances which assisted the WMCQR in its early years and, after an interregnum, in the last years of his life. From being a fervent supporter of the GWR in the 1850s, he joined the opposition and became one of the pillars of the WMCQR. His connections could be traced south and westwards from Chester to the North Wales Mineral, the Shrewsbury & Hereford and thence into South Wales; he was associated with the Wirral Railway Co., Birkenhead 'and the projected lines across the Hundred of Wirral to the bridge now being thrown across the Dee!*

He was an originator of railways down the Dee Valley from Llangollen to Dolgelley and up to Ffestiniog, and was with Messrs. Beyer and Peacock in the founding of the Gorton firm of locomotive builders in 1854. In earlier times he had recognised the value of the Dee for shipping and investigated its navigational improvements: in this, his links with Brymbo Ironworks and Broughton & Plas Power Collieries had at first directed his mind towards using the Dee as the obvious outlet for local industry. After residence at Broughton, Chester, he moved to Shrewsbury when his railways reached towards South Wales, and later built Pale, near Bala about 1873. He became Liberal Member for Shrewsbury but retired from Parliamentary life in 1886; he died aged 74. Though the WMCQR lost a champion, the whole of north-east Wales had also been under his leadership.

The Broughton & Plas Power Coal Co. Minutes disclose that those parts of the Brymbo Branch which had been built by the Robertson/Piercy consortium, were to pass into Company ownership on 1st July. Though throughout the two had claimed they were responsible for backing the scheme from their own pockets, payment was made through the Broughton & Plas Power Coal Co.'s accounts insofar as the length from Brymbo North Junction to Gatewen was concerned. It was to be 1902 before the Coal Co.'s Minutes state: 'paid to the representatives of Robertson & Piercy £2,160 5s. 6d. for making the branch from the Connah's Quay Railway to our Gatewen Colliery'. Interest had been added for the intervening period viz. June 1888–June 1902.

Of Piercy, the third son of Robert Piercy, valuer and surveyor in Montgomeryshire, Denbighshire and Flintshire: he was born in 1828 at Trefelglwys and trained in his father's office. Robertson employed him in 1851 to prepare plans for a Shropshire & Cheshire Railway (Shrewsbury –Minsterley) and he established himself as a witness in the Parliamentary Committee stage affecting that Bill. Thereafter he was involved in many railway projects in Wales, afterwards working in Sardinia, Italy and Assam. He acquired Marchwiel Hall in 1881 and contested Peterborough in 1883; he is buried in Kensal Green Cemetery.[35]

---

*The Hawarden Bridge proposed by the MS&LR.

His links with the WMCQR were in the earlier and later years of his life, the middle of that 'sandwich' occurring when he was appointed Engineer by the Concessionaires of Railways in Sardinia* in 1862.

At the time of Piercy's death there was a great depression in the coal trade in North Wales and this was hitting Buckley especially: Hawarden Colliery was obliged to close down and threw hundreds out of work. Piercy's ability to put money into the WMCQR was said to have come when he realised his investments in Sardinia – the construction of the Hawarden Loop not only benefitted the WMCQR's widening interests, but gave employment to many miners; his death therefore, was of the greatest concern. He left a family of ten and a fortune of £330,000 which his Trustees were roundly condemned for handling, together with their collaboration with the MS&LR and Sir Edward Watkin. It is significant that his eldest daughter married E.B. Bernard (Chairman of WMCQR), his second daughter married an Italian prince and, coming from a family of Welsh Nonconformists, became a Roman Catholic; one of his sons also married an Italian.

In 1883 he and Robertson served on a Committee 'to advance and promote the claims of Wrexham' as a site for a North Wales college; they showed anxiety to promote both Wrexham and the goodwill of its inhabitants towards them. Both were prominent speakers at the Public Hall promotional meeting on 10th February and together they had purchased six acres of land opposite Grove Park to be transferred as a free site in the event of Wrexham's success in securing the college. But it was not to be.

There were considerable wrangles between his Trustees (Frederick George Whitwham, E.B. Bernard, Sarah (his widow) and H.E. Piercy (his son) after his death. Evan Morris solicitor both to the Railway and Piercy himself, handled matters on behalf of the Trustees who struggled to settle financial affairs with the Railway Company: these dragged on for a decade and involved the MS&LR, and proceedings between the Trustees and the WMCQR took place in December 1897 – January 1898, Sir Benjamin Baker ultimately making an Award to the Trustees, dated 19th January, 1898. Even then the work of the Trustees was not over; they were involved until 1921.

By Act of 5th July, 1888 the Company was empowered to abandon certain lines authorised by the Act of 1882:

1) Railway No. 3: from a point 1 m. 3 ch. from its commencement, to its end.
2) Railway No. 4.
3) Railway No. 9: from its beginning to a point 1 m. 2 fur. 7 ch. from that starting place.

New work was enacted thus:

Railway No. 1 was the South Fork at Brymbo Junction. From documentary evidence it seems it was already built and carried rails, but the junction with the main line had not been made. This work was completed.

Railway No. 2 was Railway No. 8 of the 1882 Act, being the chord connecting Penyffordd and Hope. The work had begun but was never finished.

*He was given plenary powers to complete railways when in 1873 financial and other causes delayed his work; by 1881 all projected systems, amounting to over 300 miles in all, were complete. Piercy was decorated by the King of Italy: one of his pupils was a son of Garibaldi, a close friend of his.

Railways Nos. 3, 4, 5 being
a) part of Railway No. 9 of the 1882 Act,
b) being the whole of Railway No. 11 of the 1882 Act,
c) being Railway No. 13 of the 1882 Act respectively.
In practice these became the double-line junction on the north side of Connah's Quay & Shotton station which forked westwards along the south shore of the Dee, ultimately to join the dock lines which tentacled from the foot of the former Buckley Railway. It will be noted that the proposed line over the river of the November 1887 Bill was among the casualties of this Bill.

The November 1887 Bill was the last WMCQR enterprise; the deaths of Robertson and Piercy ensured this. The consequent Act of July 1888 gave the Company the last opportunities to complete their line, and the circumstances in which Railway No. 2 (ex Railway No. 8) was never finished must lie in the demise of these gentlemen, for it would not have been in the interests of the approaching MS & LR to encourage that particular work. On the other hand, Railways Nos. 1, 3, 4, 5 (above) were of vital interest to that concern, which had powers to subscribe to work at Connah's Quay. This exactly explains the situation as it came to pass.

None other than Gladstone was due to open the Eisteddfod at Wrexham in September, and this was a marvellous opportunity for Watkin to stamp his personality on the occasion. Though The Hawarden Loop was incomplete, the contractor's line leading down from Hawarden Junction (as it was then) was fettled up as far as Hawarden itself where a temporary station made in timber had been built; its roughness was disguised by a jungle of shrubs and evergreens. It had been widely publicised that the MS & LR locomotive and train of saloon and two composite coaches, so recently shown at the Manchester Exhibition, would carry Gladstone from Hawarden to Wrexham.[36] However, the truth was that a more humble mode of travel conveyed the Great Man from Hawarden to Hawarden Junction in the form of contractor Woolley's engine PIERCY hauling vehicles which THE WREXHAM ADVERTISER for 8th September (perhaps wisely) did not describe

> . . . so the journey was a slow one, the MS & LR engine JUBILEE being too heavy.

The MS & LR exhibits at The Royal Jubilee Exhibition, Old Trafford, Manchester were:

Stand 641   Bogie Locomotive for Express Service
Stand 643   Six-wheeled composite lavatory Carriage

in Section III (Machinery), so the Official Catalogue lists. However, no engine ever carried the name JUBILEE when in MS & LR traffic, so the name was possibly bestowed for the period of the Exhibition only, and may have been retained for this one special occasion.

A change of train at Hawarden Junction found Gladstone in the more appropriate setting of the Exhibition Train, travelling with Watkin in one of two saloons. William Pollitt (who had become MS & LR General Manager in succession to R.G. Underdown) was in charge. The newspaper implies that Watkin's position would usually have been on the footplate . . .! Gladstone's speech at the Opening did not overlook this experience: 'I have come this morning by . . . The Hawarden Loop line to Hawarden Junction, and from

Hawarden Junction to Wrexham and I hope I may come many times'. Praise for Sir Edward Watkin followed in respect of all he was doing for the railways in Wales etc.

It may be wondered by what route the MS & LR train reached Hawarden Junction? And how many people that day foresaw that all too soon MS & LR/ GCR stock would become commonplace over WMCQR metals?

THE CHESTER CHRONICLE was full of accounts of the new railway lines which would link that city with North Wales via the new Hawarden Bridge. In September it reported that the works of the WMCQR authorised in 1882 were being proceeded with rapidly: the single line in Wrexham had been doubled (i.e. between the two stations) and new warehouses and sidings built at Central; and such was the progress with The Hawarden Loop that from the second week in that month trains would run from Wrexham to Hawarden in connection with the National Eisteddfod at Wrexham . . . one wonders if the Company obtained authority from the Board of Trade – there is no reference to this in surviving documentation? In this instance it seems the newspaper was over-optimistic.

Still in September, a reporter from THE WREXHAM ADVERTISER went along to see the Brymbo terminus in the last stages of its completion:

> . . . situated at the bottom of steelworks' bank and conveniently placed to suit both The Lodge and Brymbo . . . a very neat structure of brick, with coloured facings and stone dressings . . . three rooms with booking office, and general and ladies' waiting rooms . . .
>
> . . . A third station between Wrexham and Brymbo will be built on the Rock Field near Gatewen Colliery to meet the requirements of the inhabitants of Poolmouth, Pentre and the Nant, Moss. The erection of this station is now proceeding . . .
>
> . . . anticipated the line will be ready in 2–3 months when signals and points will be completed . . .

Next month, he was back in the district and the newspaper (6th October) had 'The Vron branch of the WMCQR is practically completed' whilst on another page we learn the 'metals are laid . . . fully expected to be ready for opening next week'. Obviously there would be mineral traffic from Vron Colliery before the whole Branch was passed for passenger traffic (but never on the Vron Extension with its spectacular gradients).

The following week the reporter was there again, and the line was:

> . . . expected to open in a few days . . . the new branch is the cause of considerable dispute between WMCQR and GWR.* . . . it ascends one of the steepest inclines in the district and assumes gigantic proportions as regards height with other lines in close proximity to it . . . the line will require very careful working to prevent accidents. It is rumoured that the men at the Vron are to be favoured with a free trip by the Vron Company on the WMCQR, to inaugurate the completion of the new branch.

The geological problem of slack coal of such quantity in local pits is mentioned elsewhere (*page 186*); one solution was to burn the slack on

---

*To the GWR the WMCQR must have seemed too audacious for belief. To construct such a line to an important colliery which the GWR had had all to itself for years, and to nudge against it for much of the GWR colliery trackage, was no doubt all that the GWR feared and the fulfilment of all that the WMCQR had intended from the day of its birth.

tips at the pithead; but in September this practice endangered the Brymbo Branch at Southsea which in this area, was composed of slack to build up embankments. A tip near the Plas Power Colliery had been burning for two months and the site 'had undergone considerable change' – water being poured onto the tip to extinguish the fire had completely severed the embankment leading onto it which was used by wagons emptying the slack there; this embankment had been so washed away it was divorced from the main line. An animated scene took place during daylight as women and children from Plas Power picked the tip for coal before the flames could reach it. It was confidently expected the fire could be put out within days, but months later it flared up again and the train service was suspended for a time.

The Secretary James Fraser, retired on 30th September and though not in the best of health, agreed to accept a seat on the Board. His son (also James) was appointed on the same day.

During October the Rhosddu fitting shop was rebuilt and extended at a cost of £150.

On the 8th of that month, all the Brymbo line and its Vron Branch was opened for mineral traffic: the latter, of course, never had a passenger service: J. Woolley was its contractor, with William Davies as Engineer and signalling by McKenzie & Holland of Worcester; the signal cabins were of timber.

On the 13th, THE WREXHAM ADVERTISER reported a sad accident to George Whittingham, one of the oldest drivers on the WMCQR.

> It appears he was in charge of engine No. 13 which was standing in Hope Junction attached to a luggage train. He was examining the bearings of the engine and placed his arm through one of the wheels. Whilst in this position, the brake appears to have been taken off, the engine moving, crushing Whittingham's forearm between wheel and frame. The injured man bore the shock with wonderful fortitude and walked by himself into the train which brought him to Wrexham.

Though his arm had to be amputated at the Infirmary, his progress thereafter was favourable.

1889

At the half-yearly meeting in February it was recorded that double track now extended from the new terminus at Central, out to Rhosddu; the pathetic station at Exchange had been rebuilt; all had been open since 1st September last. At Rhosddu new connections were made with the GWR; members were reminded that the Brymbo line (opened for minerals on 8th October, 1888) should open for passengers on 1st August. During January of the current year, the Vron Branch carried 5,000 tons. On The Loop Line, the new works carried north from Buckley Junction had almost reached Hawarden and the remainder was expected to be ready by the summer. In that very month Piercy Trustees had been given the contract to build the Shotton –Connah's Quay link.

It was hoped to promote a Welsh Railways Union Bill in company with other geographically-placed lines and so to connect Merseyside and

Manchester with South Wales in competition with the existing Crewe–Shrewsbury–Hereford–Newport route: this project would use the then-building Hawarden Bridge, and the WMCQR would form an integral part of the artery. Trouble now arose when the GWR and LNWR brought in a Bill to acquire both Wirral Railway and Seacombe, Hoylake & Deeside Railway, on whose co-operation the Union scheme would rely, and it became essential for the WMCQR to block it. Accordingly the WMCQR threw in its lot with the MS&LR so that together they might complete the Hawarden Bridge –Birkenhead (Wirral Railway) line and deny it to Paddington and Euston. These were deep waters for the little WMCQR and to make things worse, commitment had to be made with the Dee Conservancy Board.[37]

However, times were more propitious: the February meeting endorsed these steps as the Chairman had emphasised that Trading Returns were now the best ever in the history of the Company; there was a touch of euphoria when he said 'traffic was nearly £50 per ton mile . . . scarcely any other line in the United Kingdom could show such a mileage receipt . . . the WMCQR was really in the neck of the bottle on the Union plan . . .' Waxing further, F.G. Whitwham compared the shrine of Gladstone at Hawarden to the shrine of Mahomet, but fortunately stopped before he overreached himself. The meeting was further gladdened when reminded that Benjamin Piercy himself had conceived the Union dream at the opening of the Oswestry & Newtown Railway in February 1864.

How had the Union idea been reborn? It was due to the Bridge, and in an effort to bring more traffic over it, other companies had to be wooed to use it. The directors of the MS&LR became apprehensive when it was now apparent the Wirral railway* interests now favoured the GWR and LNWR. Watkin was the very man for this challenge; of him it was written:

> a very forceful and astute young man . . . he never strikes one as a railwayman in the truest sense of the word, yet he was one who saw in the construction and working of railways a way of making money, manoeuvring with established concerns and pulling off favourable deals for his shareholders, perhaps without laying a yard of permanent way, let alone running trains . . .

Watkin, together with two other MS&LR directors, had made an 1888 tour of a chain of lines southward from the Dee and included the important little Mid-Wales system of which Piercy was Engineer: they travelled over Taff Vale, Neath & Brecon, Brecon & Merthyr and Cambrian lines. Watkin became Chairman of the Neath & Brecon. On 12th August, 1889 a Welsh Railways Through Traffic Act involving 18 companies both in and out of Wales, was born and attempts by the GWR and LNWR to purchase lines in the Wirral were thrown out by Parliament.

But to return to the February meeting – Evan Morris, solicitor to the Railway, made a significant statement which underlined the movement of the WMCQR into the orbit of the MS&LR:

> . . . when Benjamin Piercy died, we lost our great strength, and when that sad event took place I placed the whole matter before Sir Edward Watkin whom I believe to be the greatest railwayman in the world.[38] Sir Edward very kindly took up the matter and to him must be accorded the credit for introducing the Welsh Union measure into Parliament. (*Cheers.*)

---

*Not Wirral Railway, be it noted.

And so, unsuspectingly, the WMCQR had put its head into the lion's mouth.

Back on the line itself, on 23rd February a passenger train had been involved in an accident outside Rhosddu, and the Board of Trade Report of 6th April read:

WREXHAM, MOLD, AND CONNAH'S QUAY RAILWAY

Board of Trade, (Railway Department,)
6th April 1889.

Sir,

In compliance with the instructions contained in the Order of the 26th February, I have the honour to report, for the information of the Board of Trade, the result of my inquiry into the circumstances which attended the accident that occurred on the 23rd of February, at the north side of Wrexham Exchange station, on the Wrexham, Mold, and Connah's Quay Railway.

The engine and passenger train left the rails.

Eleven passengers, as well as the driver, fireman, and guard of the train are reported to have been injured, but not seriously.

The train consisted of a tank-engine, which was running funnel in front, a London and North-Western empty horse-box, a third-class coach with a brake compartment in which the guard in charge was travelling, a composite carriage, and four third-class coaches.

The vehicles were coupled together in the order in which they are given. The engine was fitted with a screw and a steam brake, which worked iron blocks on the six wheels, and the coach in which the guard rode and the three coaches next to it were fitted with Clark and Webb's chain-brake, which could be applied by the guard. The train, which was due to leave Buckley at 2.53 pm, left seven minutes late, and after stopping at the several stations on the way, was approaching Wrexham at a speed of about 24 or 25 miles an hour, when the horse-box mounted the outside rail of the curve, about 60 feet north of the Wrexham Exchange station up home-signal, which, as well as the up distant-signal, had been lowered to 'All right' for the passenger train to pass. The train was still about six minutes late when it left the rails.

The near side wheel of the horse-box appears to have mounted the near side rail at the joint, and to have run along the top of the rail until it dropped on to the outside jaw of the chair and broke it, as well as a second chair a little further on. The wheels then appear then to have crossed the rails to the off side. One of them left its marks close outside the off side rail. It chipped and broke eight chairs at this side, until it reached the V, where a siding rail crosses the off side rail of the passenger line. The siding rail that formed the V was forced out of its place and bent. The sudden jerk, caused by the bending of the V rail, appears to have pulled the engine off the rails. It was then passing over the points and crossings of the siding and cross-over road junctions. The permanent way was considerably damaged from the V to where the train came to a stand. The engine became unhooked from the horse-box, ran across, towards the Great Western Railway, and came to rest foul of the down line of that railway, and about 125 yards from where the horse-box first mounted. The rest of the train remained coupled together and came to rest with the horse-box on the near side of the Wrexham, Mold, and Connah's Quay up line, the guard's carriage across the line on which it had been running, and the rest of the train remained close to but off the rails at the near side of the up line on which it had been running.

The engine, horse-box, guard's coach, composite carriage, and one third-class coach were damaged.

Description

The railway approaches the Exchange station at Wrexham on the Wrexham, Mold, and Connah's Quay Railway on a falling gradient of 1 in 173 and on a curve which varies from a mile to five chains radius.

The Great Western Railway runs close alongside. The down line of the Great Western Railway is about 45 feet from the up line of the Wrexham, Mold, and Connah's Quay Railway at the place where the engine came to rest. Before it came to rest it ran across a junction line and a Great Western siding, which are used for exchanging traffic between the two railways.

The Exchange station, where the passenger train was timed to stop, is a little over a quarter of a mile from the place where the accident occurred.

The evidence is as follows:

George Williams, who was the driver of a shunting engine in Wrexham yard on the 23rd February, stated: I was on my engine, which was standing on the down road attached to three waggons of coal, when the 2.53 pm passenger train from Buckley to Wrexham approached the home-signal. I was about 30 yards north of the home-signal. I was working towards the passenger train. After the passenger train had passed me about 30 yards, I saw that the horse-box, which was next to the engine, was off the rails. I cannot say at which side. I think the horse-box was about 20 yards north of the home-signal when I first saw it off the rails. When the engine reached the crossing to the transfer sidings it got off the rails. I think that all the other coaches in the train got off when they reached the same crossing. I think the passenger train was running about 25 miles an hour at the time. Steam was shut off. I cannot say whether any brakes were applied to the train. I saw the driver as he passed me. He was leaning out towards my side. He was looking forward. The engine of the passenger train was running funnel foremost. It was a side tank-engine with a cab. I did not see it break loose from the train. I saw it fall over on its left side and right itself again. When it came to a stand it was upright on its wheels. I think it came to a stand between our railway and the Great Western Railway. I have been 12 years in the Company's service, and about two years a driver. Fireman Charles Jones and shunter George Jones were on the engine with me at the time. I did not see either the fireman or driver leave the passenger engine.

George Jones stated: I am a shunter in Wrexham yard. On the 23rd February I came with the shunting engine and three waggons of coal from Wrexham and Acton Colliery to Wrexham yard on the up line, and I had put my train across on to the down line about 12 minutes before the passenger train arrived. I had put back the levers in the ground frame which is interlocked from the cabin, and the signalman in the cabin had lowered the up signals before I saw the passenger train. These signals cannot be lowered until the levers in the ground frame are placed right for the passenger line. The driver of the passenger train had his head outside the cab as he passed. I noticed him draw it in quickly, and then I saw the horse-box jumping up and down. It was off the rails. The horse-box was then just south of the home-signal. I next saw the leading wheels of the engine strike the crossing and the engine run forward crosswise, till it turned and ran towards the Great Western Railway. The engine appeared to me to turn over on its left side and to right itself. It came to a stand on its wheels across the Great Western Railway with the front buffers foul of the Great Western down main line. I saw the engine break loose from the train as it turned towards the Great Western Railway. I think the rest of the coaches left the rails at the crossing. As soon as the engine separated from the train the coaches came to a stand. They were all off the rails. I have been ten years in the Company's service, eight years shunter at Wrexham.

George Owen, Esq., engineer of the Cambrian Railways, stated: I was at Wrexham on the 16th February. I have lately been engaged by the Wrexham, Mold, and Connah's Quay Railway Company in measuring up the works on the Company's new lines, and on the 16th I was inspecting the crossing and measuring the work near to where the accident occurred. I never saw a crossing better put in, in fact it was so well done that I called my assistant's attention to it. I said to him, 'These Wrexham people know how to put a crossing in.' I also particularly noticed the up and down lines at both sides, and observed that they were in excellent order and well ballasted up with cinder ballast. The top of the rails was good, and the keys were all tight in the crossings and check rails. I have been 37 years employed on railways. I think the accident was caused by a vehicle, not the engine, mounting the outside rail about 160 feet north of the point of the crossing.

Joseph Rhodon, engine driver of passenger train from Buckley to Wrexham on the 23rd February, stated: I left Buckley late with the passenger train; I cannot say how late. I think the train approached the Exchange station, Wrexham, at about the proper time. I was running at a speed of about 24 miles an hour when I felt a jerk at the rear part of the engine. I was about an engine's length from the home-signal at the time. I heard something behind me off the road. I was leaning out at the right side of my engine and looking forward, and on hearing the noise I jumped to my whistle, but missed it owing to another severe jerk, which broke the gauge-glass at the right side of my engine, and the leading wheels of my engine ran towards the Great Western Railway. The engine gave a sharp jerk with her trailing and driving wheels and crossed the up main line and then went joggelling along a little further, when the other gauge-glass broke and the engine turned over on her right side. I recollect nothing further. I believe I was stunned for a time and buried in the earth. When I recovered I found myself in a big hole in the ground, and the engine was on her wheels about an engine length from where I lay. I got a severe blow on my back, on my collar bone and two wrists. I walked straight home, and was off work about three weeks. I am still a little sore, but have been at work about three weeks. I have been 10 years in the Company's service, and about five years a driver. I went on duty at 6 am on the 23rd February; the accident happened about 3.36 pm. Fireman Hayes Bellis was the only person on the engine with me. The horse-box was attached to my engine at Hope junction. After attaching it to my engine I backed it on to my train. My guard coupled it up. The horse-box coupling was hooked on to my engine hook. We do not always do this; sometimes the engine coupling is used. I think there was about two inches between the engine buffers and the horse-box buffers. I cannot say why the coupling was not screwed up tight. I cannot say whether the coupling was simply put over the hook or somewhat screwed up. I did not notice the height of the horse-box buffers compared with the engine buffers. I had a screw coupling on my engine; it has always been on. There is no safety catch on the engine drawbar. I noticed the horse-box wobble when I shut off steam at the engine shed as if it had short brasses. I was then about 350 yards from where the accident happened. I had a screw-brake with iron blocks on the six wheels of my engine. I had Clark and Webb's chain-brake, which was worked by the guard, on four of the coaches of my train. It was a slight falling gradient when I noticed the horse-box wobbling. I had not noticed it oscillate before that, though I had come down steeper gradients with it at about the same speed. I did not think the oscillation dangerous or I should have whistled for the guard's brakes.

Benjamin Jones, guard of the 2.53 pm train from Buckley on the 23rd February, stated: The passenger train consisted of a tank-engine running funnel in front, a London and North-Western horse-box, a third-class coach with brake compartment in which I rode, a composite carriage, and four third-class coaches, coupled in the order given. The coach in which I rode and the three coaches next to it were fitted with Clark and Webb's chain-brake, which was worked from my brake compartment. The train left Buckley seven minutes late. The train is due at Exchange station, Wrexham, at 3.32 pm. I believe the accident occurred about 3.38 pm. I was standing at my brake when I heard a crushing noise and observed dust flying. I applied the chain-brake. My coach was on the rails at this time, and I think the train was running at a speed of about 25 miles an hour, which is about the ordinary rate of speed. I think my coach was not many yards from the home-signal at the time. The home-signal was off and the distant-signal was also off as the train approached Wrexham. A crash came and I was thrown out of my brake compartment when I was putting the brake on. I do not think I had got it full on before I was thrown out. I was hurt in the side and right shoulder, but I got up and went to open the carriage doors and assist some passengers, but they jumped on me and I got stunned. I was off work about 14 days. I am a little sore still. I have been nearly nine years in railway service, and over five years a guard. I coupled the horse-box to the engine at Hope junction. I used the coupling which was on the horse-box, because I was with the horse-box in the siding, and the engine coupling, might be too short. I screwed up the coupling, but there was a little distance between the buffers of the engine and the buffers of the horse-box. I screwed the coupling as tight as it would go. I cannot say how much the engine and horse-box buffers were apart. I also hooked the horse-box on to my train. The coupling between the horse-box and the train was tight, and the side chains were hooked up. I did not see anything wrong with the horse-box when it formed part of the train. I observed it oscillating on the journey, but nothing unusual. I used my brake to stop at the station. I observed that the engine buffers were smaller than the horse-box buffers, but I did not observe any difference in their levels. The horse-box was brought to Wrexham to take a horse to Ruthin.

Hayes Bellis, a fireman of the 2.53 pm train from Buckley on the 23rd February, stated: My driver shut off steam on passing the Wrexham engine-shed. The train was running 20 to 24 miles an hour at the time, and it passed the home-signal all right at about the same speed. This signal was at 'all right'. I saw the driver looking back. He mostly does so, after passing the shed. I felt a pull from behind and saw the driver jump towards the whistle, but he did not reach it, as another pull fetched him back. He then shouted 'Whoa' to me, and I commenced to put the brake on. The engine was on the rails at this time; I cannot say whether it had reached the crossings. I recollect observing the engine running towards the Great Western Railway, but I cannot recollect whether she was on the crossing or where she was. I do not recollect anything except that I found myself on the ground and saw the engine on the Great Western line. I cannot say how far she was from me. I do not think I got my brake full on. I have been four years in the Company's service, and about two years a fireman. I was a little hurt in the arm and off work for a week. I am all right now.

Wm. Davis, engineer of the Wrexham, Mold, and Connah's Quay Railway, stated: I got to the scene of the accident about three hours after it occurred, and I found the first marks of a vehicle having mounted the eastern rail of the up road about 60 feet north of the home-signal. This mark extended along the rail for about 20 feet, when it ran on to the chair and broke the outside jaw. There was another broken chair about 25 feet further on at the same side. About 20 feet further on I found the chairs chipped on the outer side of the western rail of the up line, as if the vehicle that was off had crossed. Seven chairs from this forward were slightly chipped, and one broken close to the V, where the siding crosses the up line. The western rail of the V was pushed out and bent and the chair was broken. The damage was slight up to the V, but from that forward the road was much broken up. Two 24-ft rails, 118 ordinary, nine crossing chairs, six ordinary sleepers, and four long timbers under the crossings were renewed. I had seen the road on the morning before the accident, it was in perfect order. I have been seven years engineer on the Wrexham, Mold, and Connah's Quay Railway. After the accident I gauged the line a long distance back from the V and forward towards Wrexham, and it was in perfect order, except where broken by the accident. The superelevation on the curve, which had a radius varying from a mile to five furlongs, would be about 2½ in. where it was greatest. No men had been working on that day where the accident occurred. I do not know of any vehicle having left the rails previously at that place.

Frederick Willans, locomotive superintendent, Wrexham, Mold, and Connah's Quay Railway, stated: I was at the scene of the accident a few minutes after it occurred. I found the whole of the train from Buckley off the rails as shown in the sketch. I went to seek for the place where the first vehicle left the rails and caused the accident. I found that one vehicle had mounted the eastern rail of the up line at a joint about 57 feet north of the home-signal. It ran along the top of the rail and then dropped on to the outside of the chair, which was the 13th chair north of the home-signal. Two chairs were broken at the east side, and then the vehicle crossed to the west side of the up line. I understood from all the people who were about the line that it was the vehicle next to the engine that first got off, and I arrived at the same conclusion from the marks I saw. This was a London and North-Western horse-box. This horse-box had become detached from the engine by the accident, but the coupling was not broken. I think the coupling is the same length as the Wrexham, Mold, and Connah's Quay carriage couplings. The engine coupling is 1½ inches shorter than the horse-box coupling. I think the engine coupling could be screwed up about 6 inches, and the horse-box coupling about 8 inches. I examined the brasses of the horse-box. They were worn. Those of the leading wheels, which I think first got off, one was ¾ inch short, and the other about ⅝ths of an inch. The flanges of the tyres were sharp and worn thin about ⅜ths of an inch off their original thickness. I found that the buffers of the horse-box were about 3 ft 5 in. above the rails, and that those of the engine were 3 ft 4 in., the same as the buffers of the rest of the train. I think three feet is the greatest length the coupling can be extended, measuring from the inside of the links, and it can be shortened eight inches. The engine that drew the train was re-constructed about five years since, and was as good as new. It left the shops on the 30th August last, having had new tyres, new crank-axle, new crank pins, and after having been thoroughly overhauled.

John B. Williams, assistant carriage superintendent, London and North-Western Railway, stated: The horse-box that was attached to the train from Bucknel was built at Wolverton in 1874. It left Wolverton workshops after being thoroughly overhauled on the 19th January 1886. It was last repaired at Earlstown works, and left there on the 28th November 1887. It was lifted and new brasses were put on at Earlstown. The company have 265 of the same type of horse-box, which are running on the London and North-Western main line indiscriminately with the Company's present standard boxes. The body of the box is 14 ft 6 ins. on 8 ft wheelbase, as against 19 ft 6 ins. and 10 feet wheel-base, which is the size of the new boxes. The buffers were gauged when the box arrived at Wolverston after the accident. They were 3 ft 6 ins. from rail level to centre of buffer, which is the London and North-Western's standard gauge. The gearing springs were tested and found in good condition. After pressing them quite straight 12 times they resumed their original camber. The length of the springs is 3 ft 10 in., and there are 10 plates at one end of the box and eight at the other; the new horse-boxes have springs 5 ft 6 in. long. They are made up of ten ⅜-in. plates and one ½-in. plate. Although one of the brasses on the leading axle of the horse-box is ½ in. and the other ⁹⁄₁₆ short, I do not consider they would prevent the safe running of the vehicle. The tyres are very little worn in the tread.

Conclusion

This accident appears to have been caused by the unsteady running of the horse-box, which was next to the engine, and was not tightly coupled up to it, as it should have been, when the guard attached it to the train at Hope junction.

The horse-box, which was empty, was a light vehicle compared to the engine and to the other vehicles which were behind it, and which could be actuated by a powerful chain-brake. It is possible that some slight jerk, by the application of the brake to the train or by shutting off steam, may have contributed to the accident and to the horse-box leaving the rails, especially as the lightest end was nearest to the engine and the buffer centres of the horse-box were at least one inch higher than the buffers of the engine, which was in front, and of the third-class carriage which was behind the horse-box. The fact of this vehicle having run off first to the near side and then to the off side, of the rails would tend to show that the coupling between it and the engine was not strained when the horse-box mounted the near side rail. The coupling between the engine and the horse-box became unhooked when the engine left the rails and was rolling about amongst the points and crossings of the siding junction.

The horse-box should have been placed behind instead of in front of the passenger coaches.

I have, &c.,
F.H. Rich,
Colonel, R.E.

The Assistant Secretary,
Railway Department, Board of Trade

Printed copies of the above report were sent to the Company on the 27th April.

Carriages – WMCQR

It may be considered that the purchase of outdated carriages from the LNWR for use on the WMCQR to be a mean step to the disadvantage of passengers, but in fact such stock was no worse than was used elsewhere in the district by the mighty LNWR itself. Thus there appeared currently, angry letters in THE CHESTER CHRONICLE concerning accommodation on the Mold line with its 'dirty, forbidding boxes'.

Cargoes – Connah's Quay

THE CHESTER CHRONICLE for 23rd March, 1889 said:

Large quantities of straw from Ireland for paper are being shipped into Connah's Quay, together with iron ore from Cumberland. This has taxed the officials of the WMCQR to full extent to get the vessels discharged and loaded to clear the port before the neap tides. Relays of men were working both hand and steam cranes night and day; being loaded were several thousand tons of Buckley pipes, bricks etc. for ports in the United Kingdom. Edwards of Ruabon have bought a steamship for their terra cotta goods, based on Connah's Quay . . . the only drawback is the wretched condition of the river.

If only those so engaged could contemplate the scene of abandonment here in 1990, a century later!

MS&LR – Hawarden Bridge–Chester (Northgate)

As the WMCQR awaited connection with the outer world by rail – so to speak – the reporter from THE CHESTER CHRONICLE waxed journalistically on the building of the line from the north Dee shore to Chester Northgate. So on 30th March, 1889:

The sound of snorting and puffing of railway engines has replaced the sound of birds on the line between Chester and Connah's Quay . . . mighty steam navvy makes relentless headway through land where hitherto only the humble plough was driven . . .

Logan & Hemingway were the contractors and 'Mr Woolley is the contractor for the WMCQR; the work was begun in August 1888'. There had been trouble over acquisition of land from Lord Wenlock. There had been a grave shortage of materials for civil engineering work, cuttings having to be dug either side of the formation near Sealand to form the embankments elsewhere. Two steam navvies, eleven contractors' steam locomotives and 500 men and further steam cranes were at work; construction continued after dark by the help of 'Wells Lights'. Presiding over all was Cottrell, the MS & LR Engineer.

The paper kept close watch over such events, for they were important to Chester; unfortunately, so close a watch was not always given to accuracy, so we had (27th April):

> NEW RAILWAY AT CHESTER. On Easter Monday a meat tea was given to about 570 men employed on the WMCQ Rly, at Christ Church Schools, Newtown. (Chester). The men do not know how to spend a holiday.*

In the summer each year it was the occasion for collieries to indulge in an annual outing: destinations varied; Vron men, with wives, often chose Liverpool, each man paying 2*d*. every fortnight to pay for the trip. Before the WMCQR opened to Brymbo, the GWR faced the transport of 700 employees with followers extra; the train would leave Brymbo before 6.30 am. It was the operating practice to divide the train at Plas Power and re-unite it at Wrexham; ten carriages in each part making twenty carriages in all – probably all four-wheeled? After the full day, the return would leave Liverpool at 10 pm.

On the WMCQR main line, Gwersyllt station would be inundated by 600+ passengers for Liverpool on a June Saturday, leaving at 6.15 am. They would change into the LNWR at Hope Junction and travel via Chester and Runcorn. The more ambitious in the 1889 excursion made an inspection of the incomplete Manchester Ship Canal works at Eastham. Thus the men of Llay Hall Colliery chose to spend their day.

Such works' outings, using the only transport system then available for passengers on this scale of numbers, had been a feature of the railways since Thomas Cook's time (*regular* excursions began in 1842). Until the recent days of Dr Beeching, rakes of redundant carriages might be stored for ten months of the year, to appear on such Saturday or week-day excursions when vast crowds, indifferent to the damp, run-down condition of the stock, would travel enormous distances for perhaps 5% of their weekly wage, and so come to know places which to their fathers would have been almost inaccessible. Small companies, like the WMCQR, could offer these opportunities only with difficulty – the Company had no spare carriage stock and clearly the conveyance of 600 souls from Gwersyllt only as far as Hope Junction would be done before a time of day when the stock would be needed for regular services. Failing that availability, stock from the LNWR would be used.

The success of the Wirral Railway Bill was essential to the WMCQR interests and when in June the House of Lords Enquiry took place,

---

*The object was to keep the men out of the public houses.

Cartwright clearly intended to advance his employer's cause. On being asked as to the financial standing of the Company, he asserted that the

> Debenture Stock of the WMCQR was regarded as a property quite as good as LNWR or GWR Stock ... in fact, he thought the WMCQR was in a better position financially than the London, Chatham & Dover Railway.

(*which brought forth laughter from the gathering*). Undeterred, Cartwright continued:

> It is a fact that the WMCQR is not in the hands of a Receiver; owing to the exertions of the late Mr Piercy and the late Mr Robertson, we are now free from all financial embarrassments.

The Report for the half-year ending 30th June contained the good news that financial gains were continuing: the bad news was that poor weather in the spring had retarded progress on the Loop and now it might be September before a link was made with the MS&LR from Chester; this meant the Shotton–Connah's Quay line was also unready and losses would follow: but further good news from Parliament was that the Union Bill had been accepted.

On 12th August two Acts of the same date were passed – by the first (The Wirral Railway Transfer Act) certain portions of that line were passed to the MS&LR and WMCQR: by the second, the Union Act (before-mentioned) came into being. The former ended a time of great anxiety; since 1885 the powers to reach northwestwards from the Dee Bridge towards Birkenhead had not been exercised and for too long it had seemed they would be wrested from the WMCQR. This was not only a Railway matter, it affected most traders in Wrexham: the mayor, aldermen and burgesses of that town had sent a petition to the House of Commons:

> that the Wirral Railway should not be permitted to sell any portion of their undertaking to the LNWR or GWR who have hitherto held the monopoly of this traffic.

On 17th July it was known that the WMCQR Bill had been approved by the Lords; Wrexham was agog with excitement such as had only been experienced when the WMCQR was first authorised. Many peals were rung on the Parish Church bells and a Subscription List was opened to benefit the bellringers. The Town Clerk headed the List with 2/-: £2 12s. 6d. was collected. Fog signals 'were laid in front of the 5.15 pm train which went out in a rattle of explosions which startled the bystanders'.

Queen Victoria visited Wrexham on 24th August, being a part of a Welsh visit which included a stay at Pale, the new home of Henry Robertson who had invited the Queen to use the Hall; but due to his death, his son Henry Beyer Robertson, 'a charming self-effacing young man, and very rich',[39] did the domestic honours.

The WMCQR was not directly involved in this visit (the GWR was deeply so) but carried 19,261 passengers on that day – a record. Major Evan Morris, now Mayor of Wrexham, 'the leading railway lawyer of the day' was the hero of the hour and he did not overlook the debt that was due to Piercy.

The opening of the Brymbo line *for passengers* occurred on a Thursday – an awkward day for the newspaper which only gave two lines to the event.

However, it was not caught unawares for space the following week and so:

A NEW ROUTE TO BRYMBO

THE LONG EXPECTED opening of the WMCQ branch to Brymbo . . . judging by patronage bestowed upon it, the directors have 'struck ile' which we hope will continue to flow in an increasing and profitable stream . . .

The first train left Brymbo at 8 am . . . a smart engine drew the train of some five carriages on which the trace of the painter was freshly left. Brymbo station is more convenient for the centre of population than is the GWR one . . . it is of brick. Plas Power is alongside the GWR station of the same name . . . the line passes under the GWR in the direction of the Poolmouth Valley which it crosses by means of a substantial bridge; close by is Moss & Pentre station (this is in brick and the bricklayers are still at work). For the present Moss & Pentre residents must use stage carts, those miracles of discomfort. The line then passes along a steep embankment to the main line . . . on Saturday nights, two extra trains are needed.

In anticipation of passenger traffic, the initial length of flat-bottomed rails on the Branch was replaced by bull-head.

The year would be a harbinger of heavy expense, both now and in the immediate future: the Regulation of Railways Act of 30th August, 1889 could not be ignored and though along with many another impoverished company the WMCQR would plead poverty, provision would clearly have to be made to fit the stock with suitable brakes, and the signalling system with safeguards.

In the same month the Board agreed to fit the stock with vacuum brakes (engines and carriages, but not goods vehicles) at a cost of £55 for a locomotive, £18 for a coach and £24 for a passenger guard's van. This prudent anticipation did not prevent the Secretary writing a pleading letter to the Board of Trade in December, asking them to bear in mind 'the exceptional position of this line of Railway'. The points were set out as follows:

1) That the Buckley Railway was a leased line 'a mineral railway on which trains travel at a slow rate of speed, and should, as it is not used for passenger traffic, be exempt from requiring the Block System'.

2) The carriages are already fitted with Clark & Webb Patent chain brake and this is capable of being worked from the engine. Trains stop at all stations, the greatest distance between them being less than 2 miles . . . it is submitted that the brake currently in use is sufficient.

3) Mixed Trains. Our ordinary passenger trains are made up of 4–6 carriages and the proposed one/sixth limit would amount to total prohibition preventing cattle, perishable and urgent traffic from getting rapid transit . . .

4) The WMCQR is a local line, 'practically a branch of the LNWR having a junction with that Company at Hope Junction, and with the GWR at Wrexham. If urgent traffic off these lines arrives after the last goods train, and if prevented from being attached to slow passenger trains, serious delay, cruelty to cattle (etc.) will ensue . . . suggest the WMCQR be permitted to run mixed trains to the extent of at least six unbraked vehicles in front of the train.

The Company also reminded the Board of Trade that between the two Wrexham stations, it was exempted from Block Working. The Board of Trade was not the least moved; it could make no exception in the matter of brakes as the Clark & Webb system 'does not comply with the conditions specified in the Act, and cannot be accepted as sufficient'. The work had to be done within two years.

Events have run on a little and we must retrace steps: on 1st July Fraser had advised the Board of Trade that the Brymbo Branch (Railways Nos. 2, 3, 5 forming a consecutive line) was ready for inspection as to its suitability for passenger traffic. Colonel Rich inspected on 17th July; certain shortcomings would have to be amended, and trains must stop at all stations. Intermediate stations were at Moss & Pentre, and Plas Power. The track was said to be of 'WMCQR standard pattern', substantial, well-ballasted and well-fenced. The steepest section was at 1 in 38, and the sharpest curve 10½ chain radius. There was one brick overbridge; three bridges had cast-iron girders, two were of stone and one was of timber on brick piers, all these were overbridges. There were several underbridges; one with cast-iron girders, one of brick and timber, one of brick and another had cast-iron girders supported on stone abutments. The brick bridge mentioned by Rich had a distorted arch 'owing to tipping upon it'. The line had already been worked by mineral trains for about seven years, and the Colonel did not think the arch would move further but that it must be carefully watched. (It was pointed out that the use of cast-iron in underbridges was now forbidden, but this bridge had been built before any restriction).

At Moss & Pentre signal alterations were necessary and trees cut down to ensure better sighting: there must be an outside clock, and a shelter on the Down platform. At New Broughton (there was a ground frame here but no stopping place) an Up Home signal was needed, whilst at Plas Power the same features as Moss & Pentre needed attention: Brymbo required an outdoor clock, a screen in front of the urinal and W.C. doors. Starting and Advanced Starting signal must be interlocked with the points. 'As there is no turntable at Brymbo, passenger trains should be stopped at each station, and as the railway has steep gradients, good automatic continuous brakes should be worked on all passenger trains'. On 31st July all this work was finished, and services began the next day. Single line working was controlled by Block Telegraph and the Staff & Ticket System. Colonel Rich was accompanied by Messrs. Cartwright, Davies and Woolley and McKenzie & Holland were represented by Mr Deakin.

On Sunday 14th July THE WREXHAM ADVERTISER had:

> . . . an informal inspection of Hawarden Bridge by a party from Manchester and a test of the hydraulic machinery . . . party included Sir Edward Watkin, Sir Alexander Malet, Woolley of Wrexham (contractor) and Cochrane (Junior) for the Bridge. Two Robey engines are employed at the Bridge which is yet to be painted and the rails laid. Buckley station is constructed of Buckley bricks and copings, and the cutting below it to Hawarden passes through fireclay and rock. A crop of hay has already been gathered from its seeded sides. Hawarden station platforms are under construction, 425 ft long. The rails are laid from Buckley Junction to Hawarden but beyond the men are still digging the cutting north of Hawarden, to be 32 ft deep and through sand . . . the cutting near Shotton is through quicksand and its contents are used for the embankment right up to the LNWR overbridge. [The latter had required 300,000 Buckley bricks and 'its girders were put in place a few days ago'.]

At the end of July, due to the unreadiness of the WMCQR, the Gladstones drove from Hawarden to Chester by road. Mrs Gladstone declared the Bridge open on 3rd August; it required 50 seconds to swing the span. 'A large number of navvies was working on the Flintshire section . . .' readers were assured. The bridge was to be the saviour of industry hereabouts; 'it is to carry us over all our difficulties' announced Mayor Evan Morris, which was just what people wanted to hear, for short-time working in the local pits was widespread, only Vron – sending coal down the WMCQR connection – was working full time. Coupled with the euphoria for the new MS&LR link, anything that Sir Edward Watkin did was – so THE WREXHAM ADVERTISER would have us think – for the good of Wales. A current headline read, 'Watkin Buys Snowdon' – which was a little misleading when one knew the facts.

The MS&LR had a strong publicity department and the Hawarden Bridge was the brightest jewel currently in its crown; Wrexham was not allowed to fall behind with information of the Bridge opening. A special train was arranged and a feature adorned THE ADVERTISER headed by an engraving of Woolley, the contractor, together with a large map. The Bridge plans had been prepared by Francis Fox and the builders were John Cochrane & Sons, Westminster.

The party travelled:

> in some fine (borrowed) MS&LR carriages as far as Hope Junction complete with the band of the 1st Volunteer Brigade of the Royal Welch Fusiliers and four ladies . . . changed into four open wagons provided by Mr Woolley – not upholstered but provided with seats – a great novelty . . . The Line between Hawarden and Shotton is not finished and needs ballasting and lifting. The train with Mr Woolley, stopped for one hour at Hawarden and the band marched through the streets. Another engine was provided and a 'rough and jolty ride ensued', the train ending its journey on embankment 300 yards from the Bridge. The party descended, walked over the LNWR bridge . . . thence, a considerable gap remains! Wombersley & Co, decorators of Leeds, had tastefully adorned the Bridge with pennants and flags of large size.

A marquee had been erected on the Welsh bank where the top brass would take lunch provided by the Grosvenor Hotel, Chester.

The party was informed of safety arrangements; ten minutes were allowed for the Bridge to swing into the line of the railway after the passage of shipping; the mechanism was so arranged that the swing span rose 5–6 inches before it turned. In this party there were members of the 'south bank faction': R.V. Kyrke, H.E. Piercy, W. Davies, T. Cartwright and H.E. Taylor.

Looking ahead; by 17th February, 1894 the Company could report that:

1) there was a Block System on all passenger lines
2) all points and signals were interlocked
3) all passenger trains carried the vacuum brake
4) all tank engines were fitted with vacuum brake (there were no tender engines)

By that date all mixed train running had had to be discontinued; an exception was the attachment 'of vacuum fitted horse boxes and carriage trucks'.

So ended what was probably the Company's most significant year, one of great hopes, considerable expense supported by current activity and the promise of better things to come within a very short time. It was probably the last year when those involved were still unaware that the Company's independence had been sacrificed and that Gorton would interfere increasingly in its affairs. The Board Meeting of 19th December brought a rude reminder that Sir Edward Watkin and his subordinates would come to be seen as the 'Bullyboys' of the WMCQR. The affair arose when a MS & LR special train carrying Mr Gladstone and party on 2nd December from Hawarden to Manchester via the new Loop and Bridge (albeit incomplete for Board of Trade satisfaction) had passed under the Ewloe–Queensferry road bridge north of Hawarden only moments before the bridge collapsed onto the line. The consequence was that when the party returned a few days later it could not proceed by rail beyond Chester (Northgate). Watkin was incensed; his self-esteem had been blunted and worse, the MS & LR had not been notified of the event until two days after it had occurred.

> Inspection of the bridge reveals inferior workmanship and defective material; the bridge may have actually been collapsing as the train passed underneath;

so wrote Sir Edward. Continuing in the same vein . . .

> Our fine bridge is ready and your line is in a disgracefully backward state. The Piercy interest predominates on your Board so that friends of mine who are shareholders are unable to interfere with work not over-well designed, and engineered in a most ridiculous manner.

Against this diatribe, Bernard (the WMCQR Chairman) had replied that the line was still in the hands of the contractor and permission to run the train was done without the Board's consent by Mr Woolley as an act of courtesy, though in doing so he had clearly made a serious error of judgement.

> The Company wishes to maintain friendly relations . . . but the Hawarden Loop was in no more backward state than some of the MS & LR lines now under construction.

The year was to prove a dark one and the beginning of the undoing of the WMCQR as an independent Company. When, together with the MS & LR it took over the unfinished railways and powers of the Wirral Railway* (Hawarden Bridge–Bidston (Dee Junction)) it entered into a half share of the financial commitment which later it could not meet: the amount was £59,129.

It will be helpful to look ahead to complete this affair; the North Wales & Liverpool Railway opened March 1896, but the MS & LR could not take up their share of the working as they had no running powers over the Wirral Railway between Bidston Junction and Seacombe: therefore, the WMCQR worked the line on its own, using MS & LR engines hired to them, but with their numbers painted out and WMCQR numbers added. The MS & LR numbers were restored in 1898 (*see page 293 for locomotives*). Powers for the MS & LR to operate were obtained in 1898.

It was the intention of the MS & LR to connect with the Mersey Railway at Birkenhead Park with a view to working its carriages into Liverpool by the line under the river i.e. the Mersey Railway; but objections by the Mersey Railway were upheld and the MS & LR had to be content with terminating at Seacombe on the Wirral shore.

---

*Often referred to as 'The Old Wirral Line': officially renamed Dee & Birkenhead Railway (1895) and North Wales & Liverpool Railway (1896).

In February 1901 the GCR (formerly MS&LR) took over working the NW&LR section completely with the effect that only occasionally did WMCQR locomotives appear north of Shotton: it was rarely that No. 6 (which became GCR No. 400) found its way to Bidston (Dee Junction).

1890

This year dawned and became a good one; the Brymbo Branch passenger traffic (which had carried 67,000 in 6 months) continued to grow despite the competition from the near-parallel GWR route: all over, passenger receipts were 50% higher than the same period in 1888. The early year marked the completion of a new engine shed at Buckley (Old)* and a goods warehouse and wagon building and repair shop at Rhosddu, Wrexham. The existing engine shed there was under reconstruction and extension. Hope Exchange, still the first small timber building and brief platform, was being upgraded with a brick erection on the Up side and longer platforms; a timber building continued to do duty on the Down side and the platforms were rebuilt and extended.

The Board of Trade was given notice that The Hawarden Loop was nearing completion in February, but the connecting link to Connah's Quay wharves was still under weigh . . . this was an exaggeration: H. Croom Johnson was not given the contract to build it until the following August. The Chairman was careful to point out the continuing co-operation with the MS&LR over the promoted Wirral Railways Bill to seek extension of time for completion of the authorised lines under the Wirral Railways Act of 1889. In his address at the March meeting he emphasised:

> it is of the utmost importance to this Company that the independent route to Birkenhead and Liverpool should be carried out . . .

The Company was benefitting from a countrywide expansion of trade, and the new Loop, with its recently-named Buckley Junction and Hawarden stations, would fulfil important but different roles, the latter expecting heavy passenger excursion traffic with its Gladstone connections.

> Both were substantial with permanent brick buildings.

said the Report; which was only 75% true!

> The Company could look forward to through trains between Chester and Wrexham . . . our General Manager has received already applications for huge trains of carriages to accommodate excursionists to Hawarden and is making preparations to receive them from all parts of Great Britain . . .

no doubt this pleased the faithful, but the ordinary shareholders were still getting nothing of the cake.

Negotiations were going on with the LNWR for a more convenient inter-change station 'between Queensferry and Connah's Quay' than the one sanctioned by Parliament: the objective was the line of resorts along the North Wales coast, a mecca for those involved in the heavy industries of the Wrexham district. The ultimate station (Connah's Quay and Shotton) was to enable passengers to walk down from the WMCQR at High Level, to the

*closed, dismantled and moved to Wrexham June 1919.

LNWR station below, but the rail link from the junction south of the Hawarden Bridge, westwards through the dock area and onto the Buckley section at Connah's Quay remained a mineral connection.

On 29th March Colonel Rich inspected the doubled line between Penyffordd and Buckley Junction and this Report was favourable subject to the installation of a set of catch points a train length from Buckley Junction Home Signal (in the Down direction). Davies complained that their effect, so close to another set, would be to have less than a train length between them: however, the WMCQR complied. At this time the address of the Engineer's Office was still 'The Old Vicarage', Wrexham.

In consequence of control by the MS&LR from August, William Davies was given three months' notice; Alexander Ross of the MS&LR was appointed Engineer @ £105 per annum at the December Board Meeting.

Important as it was to the WMCQR, The Loop was but a link in the chain to the MS&LR, whose Sir Edward Watkin's vision did not end with the continuation of the course as between Wrexham and Ellesmere (a line at that time, not yet under construction), so southwards by Cambrian and other lines to Mid and South Wales; his empire would take to the seas at Aberystwyth and Aberdovey – at least – and steamers would ply to Rosslare and Waterford. New Irish-based railway routes which served these ports would receive backing from the MS&LR; among them were to be a Cork & Fermoy line and the Waterford & Wexford Railway of 1864. Neither came into being. At some date in March, anticipating the opening of The Loop, Old Buckley station was closed to passengers (but after months of complaint, it was restored to service on 1st June, 1893). The double line Penyffordd to Buckley Junction saw its first passenger trains on 29th March and two days later the Wrexham–Chester through line was opened, its four-daily each-way trains being worked by MS&LR locomotives. A new station on The Loop, the best answer to the interchange with the Chester–Holyhead line, was built cheaply by William Williams for a little over £800 – and it looked it: was named Connah's Quay & Shotton and was in business from October 1891.

Connah's Quay docks were further expanded (this expression occurs frequently but the degree of expansion each time must have been very moderate) and had been graced by the inauguration of a Harbour Master since 1888. The unfinished goods link through to Connah's Quay docks started at Hawarden Bridge Junction, whilst 3 chains ahead of it the WMCQR made end-on junction with the Chester & Connah's Quay Railway (alias MS&LR). Branching west, the goods line carried on for almost a mile before reaching the foot of the old Buckley Railway tracks; a junction was made en route with the Buckley section, as previously noted.*

On 1st August No. 6 QUEEN was reputed to be in an accident at Connah's Quay, a notorious black spot for engine damage, but this has not been confirmed.

By this date, the holding of the Piercy Trustees' Ordinary Stock was all in the hands of the MS&LR. At the year end, other personalities (apart from Davies) were squeezed out.

---

*This link line closed 4th September, 1967 – all traffic had ceased 1st April, 1967.

Perhaps, dull as it may seem, it is appropriate to look a little more deeply into financial matters which in the end, would bring about the demise of this plucky little Company; negotiations between Pollitt (now Chairman of the WMCQR [and having interests wherever it might benefit the MS & LR – see THE RAILWAY NEWS for evidence of his presence at meetings of most peripheral railway companies)] and Piercy's Trustees were now coming to an end, the MS & LR having gained possession of £339,807 WMCQR Ordinary Stock. Effectively the WMCQR was therefore controlled by the MS & LR. E.B. Bernard had meanwhile resigned and H.E. Piercy (Benjamin Piercy's son who had become a director only in 1889) had also resigned. Pollitt and Edward Ross (the MS & LR Secretary) took their places on 15th August – fifteen days later Pollitt as just mentioned, became Chairman. T.H. Jones, who had been on the Board since 1875, gave in in October and Herbert Gladstone MP took his place. Willans survived a little longer, even acquiring a rise in salary without having to ask for it, whilst Cartwright became Receiver and Manager of the Bishop's Castle Railway from 1893–1922, initially with MS & LR blessing, subject to his heretofore attention being given to WMCQR matters.

Shortly, after the death of Edward Ross, J.W. Maclure was put on the Board on 19th April, 1892 – but this is looking ahead.

George Bellis, still officially Engineer to the Buckley Railway, appeared in the papers again, his sewerage scheme for Buckley was recommended for immediate attention '. . . the place is now very thickly populated – it is impossible to keep ditches etc. clear.'

The only legislation for the year was on 4th July allowing a further five years for the MS & LR and WMCQR to complete the undertaking of the Wirral Railway, known as the Wirral Railway Act, 1890.

1891

Severe weather was affecting the whole country and as the winter months were always a tricky time for operating the Buckley section, January proved to be another occasion for débâcle. On Friday 9th January driver James Tomlinson and fireman Thomas Dougherty found themselves being unable to control their engine which was being pushed down the incline below Northop Hall. As is usual on this line, the train waiting to ascend was standing in the loop at Connah's Quay. The train engine crew jumped from the footplate and though spared death, they were injured seriously and carried to Chester Infirmary: the brakesman and guard also jumped, but were only slightly hurt. THE WREXHAM ADVERTISER made much of the occasion:

On Friday a heavy coal train, called 'Watkinson's short trip', was the first train of the day. Due to frost and the slippery nature of the rails the train went out of control . . . the men leapt from the train near the level crossing at Broad Oak Wood. Joseph Cunnah (brakesman) of Buckley, and Edward Jones (guard) of Wrexham were severely shaken.

The unattended train dashed on at a furious rate. Near the engine shed at the top of the hill, the engine and some wagons crossed onto the loop line. About 50 yards from this is a water column, to the right of which an engine which had previously brought a number of wagons containing slack, tiles and large baulks for pile driving in the Dee near the new bridge, was taking water. Its wagons were stationary on the line where the runaway wagons were approaching. On the middle line stood the guard's van. Some rear wagons of the runaway left the rails, struck the van and smashed it completely, a portion landing in an adjoining field. The rest of the wagons were driven along the line, uprooting the water column, which was driven against the engine standing stationary; it stove in the side and top and considerably damaged it. The guard in his van was having breakfast but seeing the danger, jumped clear. The driver was oiling his engine and escaped but his fireman Joseph Lloyd was struck on the head by the cab.

The runaway continued unchecked. It passed trucks with tiles and dashed into the baulks, crashed through a wagon of slack and landed on another wagon. The wagons, locked together, continued down the line with the locomotive, the engine striking the bridge carrying the main road at Connah's Quay, the boiler bursting. The brickwork of the bridge is greatly damaged.

There is 300 yards of debris, axles, springs and bits of two engines; at the top of the hill where the collision took place, debris was piled up several yards above the high bank, all mixed up in tons and tons of slack. Fire from one of the engines ignited the scattered timbers, but a good bucket service prevailed.

The enginemen were found seriously injured and taken to Connah's Quay on stretchers. The Bangor Express was stopped specially at Connah's Quay and Tomlinson was taken to Chester Infirmary, Dougherty, feared to be dead was taken later to Chester by the 11 am train. Both patients are now progressing satisfactorily.

Both lines were cleared by Saturday and the damaged engines towed to Wrexham sheds on Sunday. The damaged bridge may have to be pulled down. There will be no Board of Trade Enquiry. Tomlinson is a steady driver and has been on the line since it opened.

THE CHESTER CHRONICLE had a similar version but added some opinions of its own. The frost was blamed for the 'breaks' failing to act. The driver of the stationary engine at Connah's Quay was in fact, oiling around and did not hear the oncoming train as his safety valves were blowing off steam; he fortunately saw it and called out to the guard who was breakfasting in his van. The last wagon of the runaway on leaving the track, struck the water tank and it was the tank which damaged the engine. The runaway –

being turned by the points onto the main line ran straight into a train of standing trucks . . . with tremendous crash, the engine, leaping over the baulks of timber crashed through one wagon of timber onto the top of another, this bringing it to a standstill. A brick-burner, who was standing in an adjacent field, said the trains struck with a deafening crash, a cloud of steam and slack coal arose in the air, and when it settled the timber baulks and wagons of coal were seen piled up to 50 ft high in greatest confusion. Of the runaway's engine, the firebox end of the engine was demolished and the truck on which it rested was broken into fragments . . . altogether 42 wagons were demolished in the collision.

The paper concluded by adding that the WMCQR was expected to exonerate the driver, and that the cost of the accident would be £3–400.

Whichever account is accurate, it must have been a most spectacular event; the engines concerned were No. 6 QUEEN on the runaway, and No. 8 PREMIER at Connah's Quay.

On 31st January the MS & LR announced that as from 1st April all 2nd class stock would be withdrawn save for Manchester suburban trains and the Wrexham–Chester service: the WMCQR was still offering 2nd class on its own trains.

Evidence of the bitterness, so well-known in the present age of 'take-overs' by incoming owners, between the old regime of the WMCQR and the new bosses at Gorton, came almost immediately. William Davies, ousted at the end of 1890, wrote applying for Engineer's Office expenses, and a testimonial. He was seen by the incomers as a 'Piercy man' (perhaps with mistaken idea that he was a blood relation rather than through marriage,) and they intended to show their muscle; he was refused any further payments and told it was not customary to give testimonials except for special purposes.

Gorton, on the other hand, could see that it might not be so easy to write off the Piercy party; there was an outstanding matter of the costs for building The Hawarden Loop and various colliery branches which had been done by the Piercy contractors. Other growlings could be heard rumbling in the distance, and these would shortly come to the fore: meanwhile the case went to arbitration.

A 'Railways & General Co. Ltd.' was formed to acquire and develop properties in Wrexham from the Piercy Trustees: such properties were associated with Railway No. 1 (Exchange–Central stations).

Not surprisingly, traffic figures showed much upward growth as the line over the Dee began to play its part, but so did working expenses; it was the time when coal prices would continue to rise and workmen press for a greater share of profits.

Even now, the branch from the main line into the Connah's Quay wharves was not quite ready, and the Wrexham–Ellesmere line's building had not even begun; negotiations with the Wirral Railway were proving to be sisyphean and to simplify what would otherwise become tedious, it had become necessary to align with the MS & LR once more to overcome obstacles: and there was a threat from the LNWR to obtain running powers over the whole WMCQR* system, and this was being opposed in Parliament. Thomas Henry Jones (mentioned under 1890 events) died; he must have been an unhappy man in these affairs.

The failure to start the Wrexham–Ellesmere section was partially due to inability to acquire certain land, no less the capital required (£180,000) had yet to be raised. Its operation by the Cambrian however, was backed by the MS & LR which had put £25,000 into it.

In the spring of the year F.G. Saunders (Chairman of the GWR) and Watkin had conspired, and in May, Watkin revealed his proposition:

1) that the GWR give the MS & LR running powers between Wrexham and Oswestry

2) that the GWR join the MS & LR and Cambrian to build the Wrexham–Ellesmere

3) GWR and MS & LR to join together to lease the WMCQR, assuming fair terms could be agreed

4) MS & LR to give GWR access to Hawarden Bridge on commercial terms

5) GWR and MS & LR to build Hawarden Bridge–Bidston line together

---

*as the WMCQR Chairman phrased it: 'that they shall fetch from the collieries the traffic which we now hand over to them at Hope Exchange . . . their traffic would be impeded by another Company running duplicate trains . . .

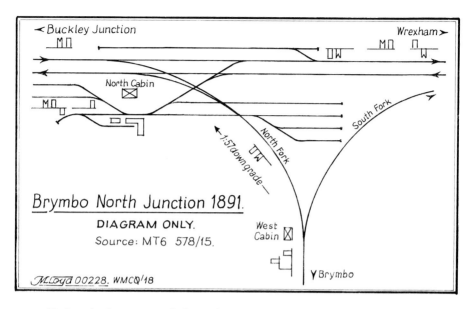

Brymbo North Junction 1891.

DIAGRAM ONLY.
Source: MT6 578/15.

Had such plans succeeded, Watkin's main opponent, the LNWR would be kept at bay, and his own Company's financial resources, now with sights firmly on building its London Extension, would be less taken-up with lines in the Wirral area. The missing link between Wrexham and Ellesmere was a key section in Watkin's Welsh Union scheme.

In consequence of Watkin's approach to Saunders, and the unavoidable necessity of keeping the LNWR informed, the General Managers of the three companies met, but agreement eluded them, and in September 1892 (twelve months later) the MS&LR started the Hawarden–Bidston line alone. Its instigation only concerns the WMCQR insofar as it brought the hammer to put the final nail into its coffin. The Hawarden–Bidston line, dubbed officially as the Wirral Railway Committee, was – as stated – a responsibility shared between MS&LR and WMCQR; the MS&LR financed the deal and £52,000 was now due from its partner. In the previous year the MS&LR had acquired £339,807 of Ordinary Stock held by Piercy Trustees – it cost the new owner £64,458 including all transfer charges. It was anticipated that the Bidston–Hawarden line would cost £300,000, and Watkin told the WMCQR it would be required to find 10% interest on its half share of the construction cost – an impossible situation for that little Company. But enough of clouds on the horizon, and so back to the WMCQR line itself.

There was a great falling off of traffic in iron ore for the various ironworks served by the Company; in part this was due to trade depression, but coal and other materials had risen greatly in price. In the autumn, the Company began to press the Dee Conservators to deepen the river not only at Connah's Quay but above it; the Company depended on improvements in navigation of the river.

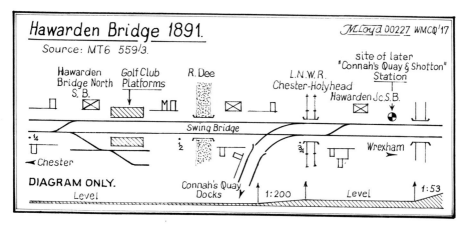

Hawarden Bridge 1891.

Source: MT6 559/3.

DIAGRAM ONLY.

Major General Hutchinson inspected new platforms and altered signalling at Hawarden Bridge[40] on 1st August, and returned to inspect Connah's Quay & Shotton station on 4th September. [The former were not the platforms of the later Hawarden Bridge station but 'solely for the members of the Golf Club'; they were not of course actually on WMCQR metals as they lay on the north side of the bridge.]

On 21st December the Company advised the Board of Trade concerning track and signalling alterations at Brymbo North Junction[41] – between Wrexham and Gwersyllt, whereby a new loop had been formed on the single line from Brymbo so as to make a proper double junction with the main line. A new frame in the North Cabin now contained 6 working levers; the sharp curve from main to branch did not please the inspector, Major Marindin, who required a check rail; we are left in doubt as to whether the intention was, in due course, to run passenger trains over this chord, but the work was completed to Board of Trade satisfaction by 19th May, 1892.

1892

At the February half-yearly meeting the dwindling of mineral traffic and the threat of a prolonged miners' strike was noted, and in due course the strike would severely reduce business. Negotiations over the Wirral Railway affair were concluded, their powers now being held jointly by the MS & LR and WMCQR. Work on the Wrexham–Ellesmere line had still to begin, though a contract had been made. By August, the striking miners had cut mineral traffic on a railway so intimately bound up with the coal trade: a branch was under construction to make exchange sidings with the Aston Hall Colliery Railway at Aston Hall Junction signal box on The Loop Line. Nonetheless, by the summer the Company was congratulating itself on weathering the serious trade depression which had hit the district, largely due to strikes in the collieries; down on the Wrexham–Ellesmere construction, 600 men were at work.

On 21st October Gladstone, by now Prime Minister, cut the first sod of the Bidston–Hawarden line ('The Wirral Railway') near the site of the present Dee Marsh Junction. Dow[42] gives full description of what was then 'one of the biggest sod-cutting ceremonies . . .'

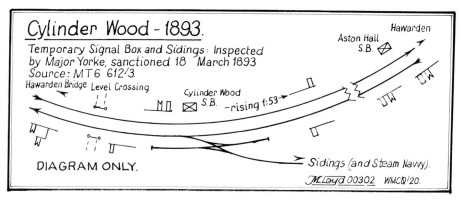

Cylinder Wood - 1893.

Temporary Signal Box and Sidings: Inspected by Major Yorke, sanctioned 18 March 1893
Source: MT6 612/3.

DIAGRAM ONLY.

1893

As before-mentioned, Cartwright was made Receiver/Manager of the Bishop's Castle Railway in this year; the line was in fact managed from Wrexham and Cartwright continued in this rôle until 1922.

The years of independence remaining to the WMCQR now quickly lose their lustre, for expansion would no longer stem from Wrexham but from the empirical ideas of Watkin. The WMCQR would continue for another twelve years, but it was little better than a 'paper existence': however, out on the line events were far from stagnant – H. Croom Johnson, contractor for 'The Wirral Railway', built a short connection to Lane End Colliery, Buckley, during the year. On 18th March Major Yorke inspected signals etc. at Cylinder Wood[43] where a temporary junction (for 12 months) and loop line were installed in connection with construction trains serving the new route out into the Wirral. Precautions against an accident should the jib of the steam navvy there threaten the running line, were taken.

In May alterations were made to the signalling at 'Old' Buckley[44] to make it acceptable to Major Marindin's inspection prior to the restoration of passenger trains, which coming up from the south, would terminate there. The restored services began on 1st June but the Company could not report the completion of the signalling to suit the Board of Trade until 20th October. The service was short-lived, and disappeared in February 1895, never to be reinstated.

An amusing correspondence took place with the Board of Trade over the accommodation for ladies at Old Buckley station, which even by that same October, was incomplete.

Marindin had written on 8th July '. . . the accommodation needs improvement . . . some waiting accommodation for ladies, an outside clock . . .' (He then recommended the station be opened subject to completion within three months; the line would be worked by Staff & Ticket system.)

Plate 60: Headed by No. 15 (a 0−6−2 saddle tank built in 1888) a train of ex-LNWR stock has arrived at the Brymbo terminus. Some carriages remain in LNWR livery.

(F. Fox-Davies)

Plate 61: Viewed from above the GWR Minera Branch in the foreground, the Brymbo Steelworks stands on a huge pile of its own excrement. To its left a horizontal area of ground marks the position of the then-new Brymbo terminus, at this early juncture hardly threatened by the Works above. The countryside behind, with its row of trees on the skyline, would soon be swallowed up in the Works complex.

(302533) June 1890 (Clwyd Record Office)

Plate 62: A recent aerial view of Wrexham looking west, shows Central station (*above centre*) with the ex-GWR main line running left to right in the upper half. In the left-hand upper corner is Croes Newydd triangular junction with the ex-GWR engine shed contained therein. The former Cambrian Railways line to Ellesmere disappears in the bottom left corner.

(Welsh Industrial & Maritime Museum)

Plate 63: Seen from the south, the sprawl of Brymbo Steelworks with its newer extensions demonstrates the growth of the plant. To the left is the railway complex to the west of the Works, the ex-WMCQR terminus and reversing neck to Vron, but the track within the old station is partially lifted though the platform remains. On the right-hand edge the Croes Newydd–Minera line proceeds northwards, past the junction with the Coed Talon line (its formation is clear at the top edge of the picture) and out of sight. During 1990 the Steelworks itself closed down.

(Welsh Industrial & Maritime Museum)

Plate 64: Ewloe Barn Brickworks Siding at the height of its importance. The trolley running along the lower level of the two-tier wharf may be seen on the right, where also stands a rake of Traders' Wagons.　　*(277663)*　*(J. Bentley Collection)*

Plate 65: The Buckley Brick & Tile Co. Ltd. Brickworks seen from the north side in June 1908: this is typical country through which the former Buckley Railway passed; that line makes its way to the left and passes off the picture where the chimneys of Etna Brickworks can be seen.　　*(278657)*　*(J. Bentley Collection)*

Plate 66: This is the "business side" of the Belmont Brickworks with narrow gauge tramways in the foot of the claypit linked to an incline at the back of the "Brikil".
(278657)   1894   (Clwyd Record Office)

Plate 67: Mount Pleasant Colliery (owned by J.B. Gregory) a scene taken in the 1890s with engine No. 6 in the siding built for the Colliery by the WMCQR. This is clearly a formal occasion; a horse and trap stand beside the far engine house and men are posed on every vantage point.   *(289650)   (J. Bentley Collection)*

Plate 68: This unexplained scene took place at Aston Hall Colliery where seven official-looking gentlemen stand alongside a bust on a plinth. Was the bust of a Dundas or a Glynne? Other men stand under the pithead gear. The dumb-buffered coal wagons in the yard include a privately owned wagon "J.P. Davies Chester" and another "BNC-". In the foreground is the Aston Hall Colliery Railway. Curiously too, the Engine House boiler is sited outside a building and must be a temporary installation as the tall chimney for the Boiler House can be seen to the left of the outdoor boiler. *(294659)   (Clwyd Record Office)*

Plate 69: This fascinating view of Westminster Colliery shows the line which formerly connected Wheatsheaf and Moss Inclines across the head of the Moss Valley. By this date the latter Incline had closed. The GWR four-coupled saddle tank with cut-down mountings, allocated to this pitch, may be discerned as may also (small though they are) three horses on a train of wagons from Brynmally Colliery; these stand in front of the building on the extreme right. Landscaped as this place is today, it is hard to credit the sprawl of a century ago. *(307534)   (Clwyd Record Office)*

Plate 70: Gatewen Colliery was connected on its southwest side to the GWR Moss Valley Branch only weeks before the new privately-built branch off the WMCQR at Stansty was opened. In due course it became one of the Broughton & Plas Power collieries. This view shows the screens with the Moss Valley line in the foreground; the (by then) Brymbo Branch of the WMCQR comes in from behind the screens. The illustration is taken from one of the Coal Company's Annual Reports.

(313518)   (Clwyd Record Office)

Plate 71: Also from the foregoing report, is this picture of New Broughton Colliery at Southsea. There are several permutations of dumb-buffered side and end-doored privately-owned wagons.   *(306514)   (Clwyd Record Office)*

Plate 72: The Lane End (or Dumpling) Colliery at Buckley was given a short-lived rail connection by an extension of the Ashton's Branch across Knowl Lane. Among its interesting locomotives was a four-coupled saddle tank by Walker Bros. of Wigan, seen here. (The Author saw a similar machine at work at Walker Bros. in 1935.) The privately-owned wagons were brick-red in colour, with white lettering and a large "M" on the centre door. The pit closed down in 1903.

(286641)   (Clwyd Record Office)

Plate 73: Vron Colliery, set high up on the hillside and south of Brymbo Steelworks, had Offa's Dyke on its western boundary and the escarpment above Tanyfron to the east. It was served by both GWR and WMCQR. The photograph looks north with the village behind the Colliery; to the left the tops of the Lancashire boilers are exposed and there is a run of loaded pit tubs coming from the shaft-top in front of the building on the right.   (292521)   (Clwyd Record Office)

Plates 74, 75 and 76: Early track materials surviving on the ex-Buckley Railway section in the early 1950s.

Plate 74: S-base chairs and double-headed rail at junction with Castle Brickworks Siding.

Plate 75: Nail and screw fastenings on WMCQR-period chair at Old Buckley station. (Rail here was bull-head.)

Plate 76: "WM & CQRy" four-screw crossing chairs on the summit loop. *(J.I.C. Boyd)*

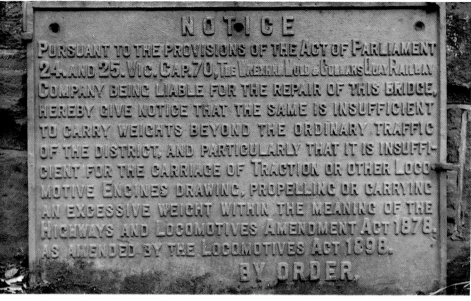

Plate 77: Standard form of bridge Warning Plate, suitably inscribed for the WMCQR; there was clearly but little space to insert the Company's title in full.

January 1966   (J.I.C. Boyd)

Plate 78: The water storage tank at Hope Village, part of the installation described in the text; the tank is dated 1900.

January 1966   (J.I.C. Boyd)

Plate 79: The Buckley Railway's first locomotive, taken at the builder's premises, 1861. *(J.I.C. Boyd Collection)*

Plate 80: The same engine as above, but in later guise at Old Buckley. Buckley Railway section engines worked chimney-first out of Connah's Quay where possible, in order to keep the firebox covered by water on the steepest sections.

(J.I.C. Boyd Collection)

Plate 81: The Buckley Railway's second engine as in later days; there were differences compared with No. 1. (Numbers were not carried in Buckley Railway times.) Seen here at Rhosddu Shed. *(J.I.C. Boyd Collection)*

Plate 82: The pride of Rhosddu Works; No. 3 as it appeared new from there in 1901. *(J.I.C. Boyd Collection)*

Plate 83: No. 4 as rebuilt in 1889 with side tanks considerably wider than the cab sheets. To perform the passenger train duties which were to be its next duty, a vacuum brake had to be fitted. Note this engine carries on the tanks the Company's Garter above the leading wheels. *(J.I.C. Boyd Collection)*

Plate 84: No. 5 was rebuilt from saddle to side tank in 1884 and ran thus for nine years; this view is said to have been taken on the Ffrwd Branch.

(W.H. Whitworth Collection)

Plate 85: No. 5 reportedly "the prettiest engine on the line" as rebuilt in 1893; it was used at this time for Wrexham–Chester (Northgate) passenger workings via the new Hawarden Bridge. *(J.I.C. Boyd Collection)*

Plate 86: No. 6 began life as a six-coupled tender engine for the Manchester & Birmingham Railway and was rebuilt at Crewe to this form in 1870; the WMCQR bought it in June 1872, the beginning of a long, eventful career.

(J.I.C. Boyd Collection)

Plate 87: Metamorphosis: No. 6 in its 1890 form, with a pair of trailing wheels off CHANCELLOR's tender. An ex-Buckley Railway brake van is attached. The picture is the only one showing the completed building on Old Buckley station and the signal box on the platform. The photograph must have been taken before 1903 and is possibly the "new" engine of 1897 after the Connah's Quay smash.

(R.E. Thomas Collection)

Plate 88: In its final form as transformed to 0−8−0 with extended smokebox, No. 6 (now GCR 400B) stands at Rhosddu; "Great Central" is almost invisible on the saddle tank beneath a coating of sooty water shot from the chimney when priming. The date must be after 1907 when this venerable machine still had 16 years of life before it. *(W.H. Whitworth Collection)*

Plate 89: Bought second-hand for Connah's Quay Docks and the Buckley Railway section, No. 7 spent its working life on menial duties. *(R.E. Thomas Collection)*

Plate 90: Specifically purchased for working the Buckley Railway section, No. 8 did duty alongside No. 6 for many, many years. Here the engine stands at Rhosddu. The boiler mountings and cab were reduced to clear the overbridges at Connah's Quay.
(J.I.C. Boyd Collection)

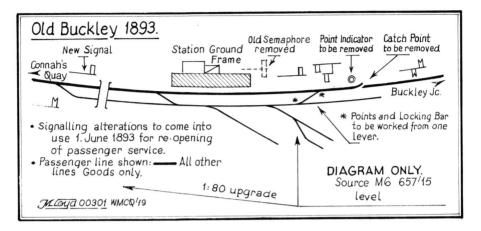

On 20th October Cartwright advised the Board of Trade that the signalling had been done but

> traffic has been disappointing, the number of passengers during the last month being 392, an average of fifteen 3rd Class passengers per day, with no 1st or 2nd Class ... the population is a very rough one, mainly mining and manufacturing, and we think we should hardly be called upon to provide special accommodation for ladies for which there cannot be any real necessity ... there was no such accommodation when the station was first passed for traffic in 1866 ...

To which the Board of Trade replied:

> I do not think that the use of any station should be considered unless there is some accommodation for females ...

(Clearly 'the opposite sex' was thus moved downwards in the social scale thereby!) Matters dragged on into the following year when on 12th April Cartwright told the Board of Trade

> The contractor to whom the job was let has failed us. We are bringing all possible pressure to bear upon him ... unless he carries out his contract we shall be compelled to take other measures.

These must have been successful, for on 30th April he could write

> The Waiting Room is now erected.

1893 was not a good year for the Company; the 'gigantic strike of colliery workers' cut nearly 80,000 tons of coal traffic; additional traffic by the building of the line to Bidston was notable but non-repeating, and once more the Chairman warned that the Company would be liable for its share of expenses of the new Railway, and he suggested the WMCQR might attempt to raise its share capital to meet the problems. He continued by describing the WMCQR as a 'One Horse Line', dependent on coal traffic which had been severely hit – relief would only come when the links to the Mersey and Ellesmere were complete: they would shortly become part of a 'Trunk Line'.

Outstanding matters with the Piercy Trustees concerning contracting done by him, and his Trustees after his death, were intended to go before an arbitrator, but the Trustees had withdrawn and a formal claim was anticipated.

On a purely domestic footing, the tenant of Rhosddu Lodge complained about smoke nuisance from the WMCQR engine shed: 'it was agreed to heighten the chimney' – if the Minute is correctly phrased, it must have been an unusual design of smoke outlet! However, the man in question (a Mr Kenrick) had more to add; he was annoyed by the noise from work being carried out in the Company's workshops.

The Company (together with others) was affected by an Act of 29th June, 1893 in being given extensions of time: the WMCQR's portions were concerned with 'The Wirral Railway' and the Deeside link from The Loop Line to Connah's Quay and a junction with the LNWR nearby. Powers were also given to obtain land on the south side of the approach to Wrexham Central station: two further years were allowed for completion.

1894

This was to be a black year – the coal mines had closed for four months whilst 'a great struggle, unparalleled in railway history, took place between capital and labour'. This affected passenger traffic too, with 70,165 less people using the Railway during the previous six months; it was pointed out that working classes spent their money on train travel, and as such were the backbone of the passenger business. The workless were not using the Railway. Over £6,000 was lost due to colliery stoppage. That was how the year began; as the months passed there was a little improvement. Anticipating the completion of railways to north and south, expenditure on heavy locomotive repairs, and renewal of track in more substantial materials from 72 lbs. to 86 lbs. per yard steel rails, took place; the Wrexham–Ellesmere line had been delayed again due to failure of the delivery of girders for the Dee bridge.

Litigation against what were considered to be exorbitant claims by the Piercy Trustees was being resisted – 'they give us great anxiety'. The Company had also incurred additional legal expenses in petitioning against a GWR-backed railway to connect Wrexham with Rhosllanerchrugog which contained an application for running powers over part of the WMCQR. The Chairman alluded to the GWR 'which had declined to accommodate this district ever since it was made . . . and only thought it expedient to do so when local parties were preparing to make their own railway' (shades of the creation of the WMCQR!)

In April inevitable events were foreseen when the MS&LR was asked by the WMCQR to meet its calls on the capital of the Wirral Railways Committee. In the following month the hours of locomotive men were reduced to 11 per day and a 66 hour week.

Matters on the MS&LR had a vital effect on the WMCQR – Sir Edward Watkin, though still remaining on the Board, quit the chair this year and was given a special annual fee of £1,000 in recognition of his services. It was a small financial relief to the Company when in January 1900 he waived the arrangement and in the following December he resigned altogether: he had been with the MS&LR since 1854. He died on 13th April, 1901, age 81 and so passed another rightly dubbed as a 'Railway King'.

1895

In February the shortlived passenger service between Buckley Junction and Old Buckley was withdrawn, though oddly, a few months later authority was given to spend a further £750 on improving the engine shed at Buckley. Croom Johnson's tender to do it for £309 15s. 0d. was approved. The Company purchased for £660 the Manning, Wardle-built 0–6–0ST engine from Croom Johnson, whose work with it on the Hawarden Bridge –Bidston contract was coming to an end (October) and it became No. 14 in the Company's books.

In the autumn the East Denbighshire Railway project for a line from Wrexham to Rhosllanerchrugog came to the fore again, rivalled by a GWR scheme to serve much the same area: the former was essentially a local project and there was a possibility that if successful, the WMCQR would be called upon to work it.

The commencement and growth of John Summers & Sons Ltd. Works at Shotton was quite as noteworthy as any of the new railways which were appended to the original WMCQR route; the steelworks would have enormous impact on the mineral and passenger traffic of the district, and increase the shipping on the river – their own vessels made use of a wharf almost opposite those at Connah's Quay.

Traffic became much better; the coal strike had been settled and a great backlog of tonnage needed to be moved. Not so on the passenger side where numbers were reduced by over 20,000 for the half year, it being suggested that the prolonged strike had affected the purse of the whole district. Heavier rails were still being laid in the main line.

Later in the year, when the build-up of mineral traffic had been carried away, tonnages fell away again. The hours of shunters, drivers and firemen were further reduced by Board of Trade decree, so that higher wages and more men had been involved. During the summer the East Denbighshire Bill was thrown out by the Lords and the competing GWR scheme was passed. However, the Commons threw out the latter so it was back to Square One with the WMCQR Chairman emphasising that a railway to Rhosllanerchrugog would be to everyone's benefit and his Company would (naturally) be ready to work it.

On 2nd November the Wrexham–Ellesmere was at last opened to traffic, the ultimate link in the Welsh Union chain under the enactment a decade earlier. It had been a long time coming. The Cambrian had running powers for freight only as far as Brymbo South Junction, and exercised them.

It was found necessary to extend the time to complete the junction with the LNWR at Connah's Quay. The 'Wirral Railways Committee' (acting in pursuance of the Wirral Railway Transfer Act, 1889) was renamed the 'Dee & Birkenhead Committee' by Act of 6th July, 1895 being the 'Manchester, Sheffield & Lincolnshire Railway Act, 1895'.

1896

As each year passed, events on the WMCQR came more and more to be dull and lifeless. True, new railways were opening up but the grip on the Company by the MS & LR was such by now as to make it but a small piece of the MS & LR jigsaw, useful only for the access it afforded to further destinations. There was no missing this trend – for in January the MS & LR continued to increase its hold on locomotive, carriage and wagon matters which henceforward were all subject to Gorton surveillance, and in future all heavy repairs were to be done there. Willans, nonetheless, was made Locomotive Superintendent @ £250 per annum, probably because he had a closer knowledge of local affairs than anyone up in Manchester. A new locomotive shed was opened at Bidston, where later the occasional WMCQR engine might be found, probably concealing its proper identity as a Gorton product.

On 28th March a special working wended its way from Hawarden to Liverpool Central (Low Level) by using Mersey Railway track under the river and negotiating the 1 in 27 gradient of that underground system and headed by a Mersey Railway engine (fitted with condensing gear) from Birkenhead Park into Liverpool Central: it had always been the intention that GCR trains would be permitted through working between Wrexham and Liverpool Central.* However, between 1898 and 1902 at least, special and excursion trains did traverse this route, engine changing as above, but even this facility ceased from April 1903 when the Mersey Railway was electrified.[45]

During the summer, Prince's Brickworks at Connah's Quay, was given a connection. Although there was a telegraph system between signal boxes, connected to the Block Instruments installed after the 1889 Act, it was only in January this year that boxes between Wrexham and Buckley Junction were connected by telephone – J.B. Saunders of Taunton did the work. The need for new locomotives was anticipated and Gorton prepared drawings for two new engines; Beyer, Peacock was invited to tender for them.

The Half-yearly Reports had now become a stylised affair and meetings were held at the MS & LR offices, London Road station, Manchester on the same day and in the same venue as those for the Wrexham & Ellesmere Railway – needless to add, virtually the same persons attended both, for each had become as it were, underlings of the MS & LR empire.

Throughout the year traffic fell away, due it was thought, to aftereffects of the long coal strike of some time back. Wages mounted savagely as railwaymen were given shorter working hours. The Company had had considerable sympathy with many employees with whom they agreed their hours were overlong. Offsetting benefit from the Wirral section was only just beginning but Hawarden was suddenly invaded by 15,000 passengers who arrived on August Bank Holiday Monday and completely overwhelmed the resources of the line. Many were left behind and the Board agreed that liaison with other railways would be necessary in future, and carriages would have to be borrowed for such occasions. The Chairman's remarks on the acquisition of more stock of its own, were without much confidence. He also pointed out that trains up into the Wirral had had to terminate at Seacombe

*opened only to Seacombe as the Mersey Railway would not permit trains over its line to Bold Street, Liverpool. WMCQR passengers were not allowed to book to Liverpool even if they changed trains at Park station, Birkenhead.

we have no facilities for running trains through the Mersey Railway to Bold Street, Liverpool . . . that Company is in a curious condition at the present time and although the directors are anxious for arrangements to be made, the undertaking is in the hands of Receivers and Managers . . .[46]

In consequence the matter was at a standstill, the Mersey Railway refusing to allow passengers to book through; as to through trains, these were unthinkable. So the long-hoped-for through service between Wrexham and Liverpool remained a dream . . . as it does today!

More trouble loomed. The Piercy Trustees 'took hostile action' when the Company backed down on increasing the capital proportion of its contribution to the North Wales & Liverpool Railway; they felt the money should and ought to be found. In consequence they raised two petitions in the House against other proposals by the MS&LR which were in due course, overruled. The Chairman said they had several outstanding matters to finalise with the Trustees and warned shareholders that if this was the spirit which prevailed, they were not likely to resolve them amicably. There had been a volte-face when a witness for the Trustees in the matter of compensation over The Hawarden Loop claim, then expressed the strongest opinions against the bona fides of that claim. In consequence, the Arbitrator found for the Company and gave costs against the Trustees. It was to be their coup de grace. Throughout, the Chairman (William Pollitt) wore a mask of hurt pride, and smug Christian indulgence, addressing the shareholders in the tone of a parent whose child had strayed from the flock but was more to be pitied than scolded. It was an appallingly transparent display.* Certainly the Trustees went on to claim for sums which they maintained were due to them for contracting continued after Benjamin's death.

1897

On 1st August the MS&LR adopted the title Great Central Railway.

Judgement against the WMCQR was obtained on 8th September for its failure to pay. For the third time a Receiver and Manager was appointed to 'protect its own interests', this time in the person of Frank Williams, (the GCR Accountant) who assumed the mantle on 31st October. There was but little to recognise of the old WMCQR of 1866: the GCR was owed £59,129 for its half-share in the as-then (1895–6) incomplete line Hawarden–Bidston, and £290,920 as its half-share in calls made by the North Wales & Liverpool Railway Committee during construction. Worse, the second sum was to be enlarged by 10% for late payment. The Piercy Trustees were owed £36,595, jointly with the late Henry Robertson's estate and together with the executors of Robertson, the Company owed £50,000. The North & South Wales Bank had permitted an overdraft, now £7,601. Later, most of these parties were satisfied by one scheme and another, but even excluding the debt to the GCR the Company still owed £37,320 so that on 30th July, 1903, Herbert Gladstone, Edwin A. Beazley and Henry Beyer Robertson, directors of the WMCQR testified on behalf of the Board that it could not meet its creditors.

---

*And what of the Piercy interests? The writer has had the opportunity of reading Piercy's papers and not unexpectedly, the descendants' view was that the Trustees had been negligent (perhaps, deliberately?) in disposing of Piercy interests at a derisory figure under heavy pressure from the MS&LR and certain of its officials.

It was estimated that £110,000 would be needed by the GCR to modernise the works and rolling stock.

During this year the Company had joined the Railway Clearing House (additional expense) and had had to pay more to its clerks whom the directors found were being paid less than those in any other railway company. There was a temporary increase of income in the locomotive department due to the WMCQR engines working the trains over the Connah's Quay–Chester section, and the NW & L line; the MS & LR was also paying for the facility of working some trains over WMCQR metals. The NW & LR had, by August, incurred a loss of £801, attributed to severe competition between North Wales coal and sources elsewhere. This had been worsened by the opening of a coal handling depot at Herculaneum Dock, Liverpool which seriously hit Birkenhead coal trade; 39,519 tons of coal traffic had been lost to the WMCQR in six months – approximately 4,000 wagon loads – much of this tonnage would have gone to Birkenhead, and the remainder by LNWR at Hope Junction, to Chester and beyond.

King's Ferry became Queen's Ferry at the request of Her Majesty when The Royal Victoria Jubilee Bridge was opened there.

The Mersey Railway was still refusing to book passengers onto the North Wales railways; the matter had gone before the Railway Commissioners but the wheels of law grind slowly and though the Mersey Railway was bound to bend, the effect of the judgement had yet to take substance. Carriage of ballast for the Hawarden–Bidston line had now ceased, and so therefore, had the income from it.

1898

Although these closing years may seem that the Company almost galloped to its undoing, there were of course, events and developments which affected it in other ways. On 19th May, 1898, Gladstone had died at Hawarden Castle and again, one of the supportive pillars of the creation of the little Company, passed away. In November there were alterations to two stations; Bridge End became Caergwrle Castle; and Caergwrle became Hope Village.

1899–1900

There had been an accident at Connah's Quay in consequence of which J. Farwell summoned the Company and Receiver for £30 damages and £33 17s. 2d. costs for damage to a ship loading at the WMCQR wharf, due it was claimed, to the defective state of the berth. The action was based on the implied contract to keep the wharf and berth in proper repair. This amount had not been paid, and Farwell issued a summons on 19th March, 1900, claiming priority over all the other creditors of the Company. His claim was not upheld. This was probably the occasion when a loaded 'shipper' fell from a crane and punctured the hull of a ship below.

1901

Sir Edward Watkin died on 13th April and with his close friend Gladstone also dead, the 'power-base' at Hawarden shut down.

Two small additional branches were put in during August and both lay a short distance south of Connah's Quay & Shotton station. To the northwest was established a siding to Mr Rowley's brickworks, and, separated from its junction by Wright's Bridge, there was another siding to the southwest to Messrs. Darbishire's brickworks. Both junctions were made into the main (double) line, here rising at 1 in 55 from the coast: and a new signal box (Wright's Bridge) was set up just to the north of the road bridge. Major Druitt inspected and reported to the Board of Trade on 6th September – he found the box had 17 levers and 4 spares, required the traps moving further from the junctions, and a clock was needed for the box which became a Block Post. The former works were owned by Harry Butler Rowley who advertised himself as Shotton Brickworks 'for firebricks, Dinas Silica Bricks, Anthracite Coals, Oxide Paints, Oils etc.' and so demonstrated that the basic trades of the Railway boundaries were exactly the same when the Railway Company failed in 1905 as they were when it was established in 1862.

In the immediate years before GCR takeover however, business along the line was troubled; strikes in collieries and general depression in the coal and iron trades continued to dampen the optimism of railway shareholders. Resources of minerals of all kinds were being worked out: coal seams became shallower; iron ore pockets emptied and only the industries dependent on clay survived . . . yet there was to be another half century before brickmaking and associate industries closed down, and the basis of existence of the former WMCQR mineral business disappeared.

The Great Central Railway Act, 1901 affected the sale of the WMCQR's surplus lands (26th July, 1901) not now required for the construction of its line.

1902–1903

A few items of domestic nature must not be overlooked – by this date the offices of the Company were in Westminster Building, Wrexham. A violent storm blew off the roof of the Rhosddu engine shed. Trespassers on the line, drunk or sober, suffered the ultimate penalty; George Roberts of Vernon Street, Rhosddu was killed on 9th April and Eli Breeze was run down and died at Cefnybedd on 18th December. The line was a tempting footpath for the unwary.

The Great Central Railway Act, 1903 affected the WMCQR peripherally in regard to a connection at Bidston.

1904–1905 on

In such a situation a Company might desire to cease to trade (i.e. to suspend its train service etc.) and wind up its affairs; a Statutory Company however, cannot complete such intent without a further Act of Parliament. The MS&LR's ambitions would certainly not permit all traffic to cease, so the natural course of events was for transfer of the WMCQR to its principal creditor, now the GCR. On 22nd July, 1904, by Act of Parliament, the WMCQ, Buckley and North Wales & Liverpool Railways were vested in the GCR. The provisions of the Act came into force on 1st January, 1905. By Act of 1904 the GCR had raised additional capital by means of 2nd Debenture Stock to complete the conversion of WMCQ and Buckley Railways (shares and debts) together with £600,000 of similar Stock for improvements to these Companies etc.[47]

As the last decade of the WMCQR's separate existence comes to an end, it is noticeable how that loss of independence affects the activities of its closing years. Control and ambition had passed out of its hands, so that ultimately its existence was simply a formality. The last years of the Chronology are tinged with the inevitable. The Chronology is indeed a mirror of hopes and fears.

References

[1] Shropshire Record Office: DP/405.
[2] NARROW GAUGE RAILWAYS IN SOUTH CAERNARVONSHIRE Vol. 1 (J.I.C. Boyd) [Oakwood Press 1988]
[3] Shropshire Record Office: DP/417.
[4] Shropshire Record Office: DP/435 – this appears to show more authorised lines than were the case!
[5] Clwyd Record Office: QS/DR/120–1, QS/DR/111.
[6] Clwyd Record Office: QSD/DR/127 (Ruthin).
[7] National Library of Wales: Robertson Collection (*not yet catalogued*).
[8] Clwyd Record Office: D/HA/1235.
[9] Clwyd Record Office: D/HA/1236.
[10] Clwyd Record Office: QS/DR/134.
[11] THE WREXHAM ADVERTISER 24th November, 1866.
[12] Parliamentary Paper 1868–69 LIV (291).
[13] Minute Book.
[14] Minute Book.
[15] Parliamentary Papers 1873. (12.1. to 3) (419) LVII pp. 59–71.
[16] Parliamentary Paper 1874 [c.1036] p. 178.
[17] BRADSHAW'S RAILWAY MANUAL 1876 p. 22.
[18] Parliamentary Paper 1875 [c.1224] p. 204.
[19] Return of Accidents [c.1225] (Jan.–Mar.) p. 80.
[20] Parliamentary Returns Oct.–Dec. 1876 [c.1689].
[21] Wrexham Reference Library: Cuttings file 084038.
[22] Broughton & Plas Power Coal Co. Ltd. v GWR (June, July, November, December 1882 and February 1883).
[23] National Library of Wales: Robertson Collection (Industrial Records) *[Not catalogued.]*
[24] National Library of Wales: Ms 9794E.
[25] National Library of Wales: Piercy Papers (Fraser Group) 308 & 309 (undated).
[26] National Library of Wales: Robertson Collection (Industrial Records) *[Not catalogued.]* Drawing.
[27] National Library of Wales: Piercy Papers (Fraser Group) 331.
[28] Clwyd Record Office: DD/LH/237.
[29] Clwyd Record Office: QS/DR/190.
[30] Clwyd Record Office: D/HA/1221. Plan of Loop Line on Gladstone Estate.
[31] NARROW GAUGE RAILWAYS IN NORTH CAERNARVONSHIRE Vol. 3, p. 134 etc. (J.I.C. Boyd) [Oakwood Press 1986].

[32] Public Record Office: MT 10 490H/6628/87.

[33] Public Record Office: MT 6 394/1.

[34] National Library of Wales: Robertson Collection (Industrial Records). *[Not catalogued.]*

[35] see also: Minutes of Proceedings of Civil Engineers XCVI 1889 pp. 333–9. MONTGOMERY WORTHIES (Williams) (2nd Edition) pp. 237–41. DICTIONARY OF WELSH BIOGRAPHY (Blackwell 1959) p. 767.

[36] ROYAL VISITS TO WALES (Wrexham 1889).

[37] Wrexham Public Library: Cuttings File item 084038. Copy of Plan by H. Whalley showing wharf frontage of River Dee as agreed with the Dee River Co. on 28th March, 1889 re land to be sold to the WMCQR.

[38] LNWR (O.S. Nock), [Ian Allan 1960] p. 12.

[39] THE WREXHAM TELEGRAPH (26th August, 1889) has a journalistic account of the whole trip.

[40] Public Record Office: MT6 559/3.

[41] Public Record Office: MT6 578/15.

[42] GREAT CENTRAL Vol. 2 (G. Dow) p. 226.

[43] Public Record Office: MT6 612/3.

[44] Public Record Office: MT6 657/15.

[45] WIRRAL RAILWAY (Campbell Highet) [Oakwood Press.]

[46] THE RAILWAY NEWS September 1896 gives further detail.

[47] BRADSHAW'S RAILWAY MANUAL 1906: pp. 92–3 gives detail.

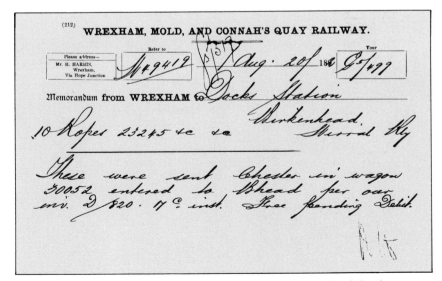

Memorandum note from Wrexham to Docks Station, Birkenhead dated 1892.

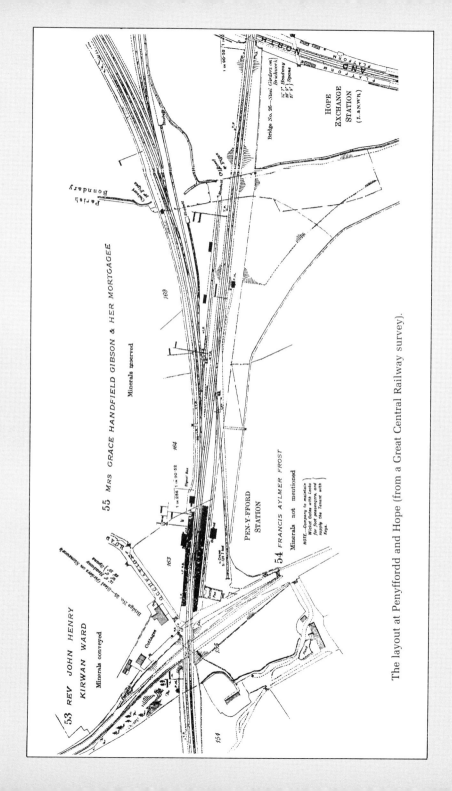

The layout at Penyffordd and Hope (from a Great Central Railway survey).

The Route

Notes on the route descriptions:

1. *The basic description is based on fieldwork and the GCR survey of 1904.*
2. *The gradients and mileages are taken from the GCR survey but do not agree with the profile published by J.M. Dunn in* WREXHAM, MOLD & CONNAH'S QUAY RAILWAY *(Oakwood Press) 1957. Some reconciliation has had to be practised in consequence.*
3. *Direction: trains proceeding towards Wrexham were Up; in the reverse direction were Down.*
4. *Caution is needed as certain station names have been altered over the years.*
5. *The railway as between Wrexham and Hawarden Bridge (the old WMCQ main line) remains open for passenger and mineral traffic (1990). However, all route descriptions are made in the past tense, describing as they do features surrounding the railway at the close of its separate existence. On the main line, most of the civil engineering survives, but modernisation has simplified the layouts, removed some signalling and ended the active life of almost all station buildings.*

The Main Line (Wrexham Central–Hawarden Bridge)

Since 1895 Wrexham Central had been both a terminal and through station, with five platform faces; optimistically, the southernmost three were nominally used by the Wrexham & Ellesmere section of the Cambrian Railways. The WMCQ portion was the northern part, retaining its dismal corrugated iron buildings well into British Railway times. Wrexham itself lay – as regards the town centre – close by on the northern side whilst the southern side spread downwards out of town over falling ground. The town, in the past the metropolis of North Wales, was not one of beauty though it possessed certain fine features; it was far from being picturesque or a typically Welsh town in fact, quite the opposite. Its glory lies in St. Giles Church, one of the 'Seven Wonders of Wales'.

In 1886 it was described as a 'Parliamentary and Municipal Borough, the largest and most prosperous town in North Wales, 177 miles from London, 30 from Denbigh and 12 from Chester: the Municipal Borough was constituted in 1857 . . . the principal streets are clean and spacious and the footways are flagged . . . coal, iron and lead mines are worked in the vicinity but brewing forms the staple trade of the town. Tanning, currying and leather manufacturing, paper making etc. is also carried on . . .' [The account omitted to say there were over fifty establishments where intoxicating liquor might be obtained.]

In building the railway extension from Exchange to Central stations much poor property, some of it ancient origin, had had to be demolished '. . . a detached fragment of Esclusham with the vicarage, the Town Well, and several gentlemen's houses long since obliterated by the ramshackle station knocked together by the old WM&CQR . . . most houses in old Wrexham succumbed to the railway . . . some of the most noisome slums removed by the railway extension at the end of the last century . . .'[1]

On this edge of the town too, there was a notable prevalence of Malt Houses, Breweries, a Mineral Water Works, the Town Well, a large pig farm

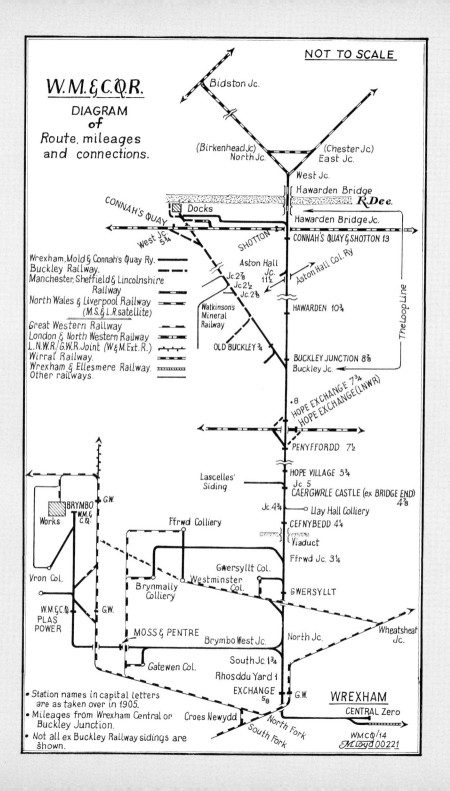

NOT TO SCALE

W.M.&C.Q.R.

DIAGRAM
of
Route, mileages
and connections.

Bidston Jc.

(Birkenhead Jc)
North Jc.

(Chester Jc)
East Jc.

West Jc.

Hawarden Bridge
R.Dee.

Docks

CONNAH'S QUAY

Hawarden Bridge Jc.

West Jc.
5¾

SHOTTON

CONNAH'S QUAY & SHOTTON 13

Aston Hall
Jc.
Jc.2⅞
Jc.2½
Jc.2¾
Jc. 11½

Aston Hall Col. Ry

The Loop Line

Wrexham, Mold & Connah's Quay Ry.
Buckley Railway.
Manchester, Sheffield & Lincolnshire
Railway
North Wales & Liverpool Railway
(M.S.& L.R. satellite)

Great Western Railway
London & North Western Railway
L.N.W.R./G.W.R. Joint (W.& M.Ext.R.)
Wirral Railway.
Wrexham & Ellesmere Railway.
Other railways.

Watkinson's
Mineral
Railway

HAWARDEN 10¾

OLD BUCKLEY ¾

BUCKLEY JUNCTION 8⅜
Buckley Jc.

•8

HOPE EXCHANGE 7¾
HOPE EXCHANGE (LNWR)

PENYFFORDD 7½

Lascelles'
Siding

HOPE VILLAGE 5¾
Jc. 5
CAERGWRLE CASTLE (ex BRIDGE END)
4⅞

BRYMBO
W.M.&
C.Q.
Works

G.W.

Ffrwd Colliery

Jc. 4¾   Llay Hall Colliery

CEFNYBEDD 4¼
Viaduct

Ffrwd Jc. 3¼

Vron Col.

Gwersyllt Col.
Westminster
Col.

GWERSYLLT

Brynmally
Colliery

W.M.&C.Q.
PLAS
POWER

G.W.

MOSS & PENTRE

Brymbo West Jc.

North Jc.

Wheatsheaf
Jc.

Gatewen Col.

South Jc. 1¾
Rhosddu Yard 1
EXCHANGE
⅝

G.W.

WREXHAM

CENTRAL Zero

• Station names in capital letters
  are as taken over in 1905.
• Mileages from Wrexham Central or
  Buckley Junction.
• Not all ex Buckley Railway sidings are
  shown.

Croes Newydd

North Fork

South Fork

WMCQ/14
M. Lloyd 00221

with attendant manure compound, all in juxtaposition and all contributed to its varied aromas. Thoroughfares on the south side included Brook Street and Watery Road to add to the sense of 'liquidity' on that flank. Passing under the east end of the station was Vicarage Hill leading up into the town; this thoroughfare carried a double-tracked electric tramway.

On the southwest corner of the Wrexham & Ellesmere side of the business, the Cambrian Railways (operators of the W & E) put in a small turntable; their engine shed alongside came before 1912 but meanwhile they borrowed the Rhosddu Shed of the WMCQR for stabling.*

On the north side the WMCQR had a large goods yard, with the wall of the prominent St. Mark's Church limiting extent by protruding well into it. Travelling westward, the tracks went under Bradley Road bridge and began a considerable curve towards the north. To the left were the Cobden Flour Mills and on the opposite side of the line, the Wrexham Lager Beer Works; the former had rail connections with the WMCQR, and both were linked to the Great Western Railway which lay on their higher level.

There was a speed limit of 8 mph on this curve which passed down at 1 in 232 under the GWR by a steel girder bridge to continue on its tight radius up-grade at 1 in 100 within a cutting. The curve ended at the ½ milepost and the line levelled out to run under the girder bridge supporting Regent Street (also with its trams) and so alongside the GWR station on the right hand. WMCQR metals were now directed northwards. (These Exchange Stations were far less conveniently situated for the town than Central.) Of interest is that WMCQR property between the two WMCQR stations here was largely upon land owned by promoter Benjamin Piercy (and later, his Trustees). The question may be asked, 'Did he buy the land when he knew the Railway would be extended over it, or was he astute enough to anticipate'?

At Exchange there was a footbridge connection between WMCQR and GWR passenger platforms but a gate upon it was often kept locked to the frustration of the many who were making tightly-timed connections between trains. On the WMCQR Down platform was the first-encountered of the yellow brick double-fronted station buildings erected in the latter years of the Company: the Up platform had no building at all. This was the site of the initial WMCQR Wrexham terminus, the land for which was bought from the GWR in September 1865, and also for Rhosddu beyond.

The two companies then ran side by side and there were single line facing and trailing connections between them. Squeezed between the older GWR and the parallel Crispin Lane, there was a long goods platform on the left and then Cudworth & Johnson's Yard beyond it. Next, rising at 1 in 149, Stansty Road passed under both companies' lines by a skewed girder bridge; it was the replacement of the unpopular level crossing which irritated the natives and displeased the Board of Trade (*see page 139–40*).

Conveniently, Crispin Lane swung westwards here, and between it and the GWR the WMCQR fanned out to site its Rhosddu Engine Shed and Workshops (1 mile) the extent of which is shown clearly on the survey plan. Drivers of engines leaving the south end of the Shed were forbidden to stand over Stansty Road bridge – the most convenient stopping place nonetheless – for fear of hot water and live coals falling down onto the road below.

*Cambrian Shed closed 1922 and moved to Aberayron 1926. (The WMCQR had refused the Cambrian a warehouse here.)

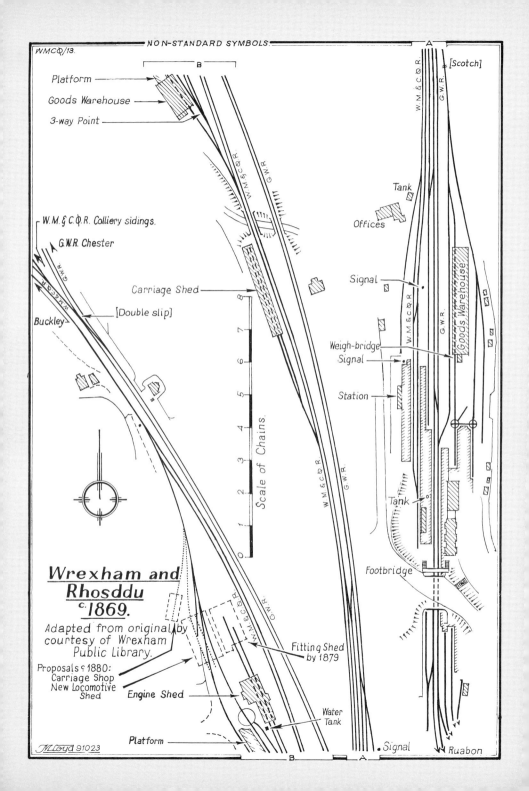

NON-STANDARD SYMBOLS

WMCQ/13.

Platform

Goods Warehouse

3-way Point

B

A

[Scotch]

W.M.&C.Q.R.

G.W.R.

Tank

Offices

W.M.&C.Q.R. Colliery sidings.

G.W.R. Chester

W.M.&C.Q.R.

G.W.R.

Signal

Carriage Shed

Buckley

G.W.R.

W.M.&C.Q.R.

[Double slip]

Goods Warehouse

W.M.&C.Q.R.

G.W.R.

Weigh-bridge

Signal

Station

Scale of Chains.

0 1 2 3 4 5 6 7 8

W.M.&C.Q.R.

G.W.R.

Tank

Wrexham and Rhosddu
c. 1869.

Adapted from original by courtesy of Wrexham Public Library.

Footbridge

Proposals c. 1880:
Carriage Shop
New Locomotive Shed

W.M.&C.Q.R.

G.W.R.

Engine Shed

Fitting Shed by 1879

Water Tank

M.Lloyd 91023

Platform

B

A

Signal

Ruabon

At 1¾ miles the GWR and WMCQR bore away from each other: almost at once a skewed wrought-iron girder bridge of 40 ft length and supplied by the Worcester Engine Works in 1871, carried Colliery Road (originally a level crossing) over the latter into the Wrexham & Acton Colliery, situated in the 'V' of the two companies' tracks; that colliery had rail connections with both the GWR and WMCQR. With staggered platforms either side of this road bridge, Rhosddu Halt* stood: beneath the bridge the line was double, but was triple to either side with attendant pointwork, all controlled from Brymbo South Junction signal box which stood under the lea of the bridge. The line fell for a little at 1 in 1571.

The triple track continued, straight, past the 1½ milepost and so into open flat countryside, the line now rising slowly at 1 in 153. At 2¾ miles, and after passing the ruined Stansty Ironworks on the right, the Brymbo South Junction swung sharply away to the west on an embankment, rising at 1 in 46 to begin the upward slog towards the concentrated hub of industry around Brymbo itself. Speed on the Brymbo Junctions' curves was limited to 10 mph; however, there was no speed restriction on the main line which, straight as a die, forged ahead. In the area of land formed by the triangle of junctions there were numerous interchange and storage sidings. Then came the incoming North Junction from the left, some complicated trackwork and Brymbo Junction North signal box. Opposite stood Clayton's brickworks, and there was a short gradient down at 1 in 100 in order to pass under the old North Wales Mineral Railway's Wheatsheaf Incline, carried above on girders supported by stone walling. On the left, between the end of the brickworks and the embankment carrying the Incline, a fan of sidings with a tangential connection allowed a single line junction between the two railways, the pointwork on the Incline being made into the most westerly of the ex-NWMR tracks. (Below this junction the Incline enjoyed no less than seven parallel lines for a short distance!) There was a short climb from under the Incline at 1 in 70.

A shallow cutting now preceded a girder bridge carrying the Gresford Road, and so into Gwersyllt station, one of the original brick erections with a later GCR extension, and serving a considerable centre of population. There was a signal box and small goods yard on the left. The railway now rose sharply at 1 in 80 as a more hilly district is now encountered and there is much housing and industry around. A wooden footbridge passed over the line then the main road from Wrexham to Mold crossed skew-wise over on girderwork. On higher ground to the left was the rail-connected Gwersyllt Colliery, its trailing junction for sidings coming in beside an iron footbridge behind Claremont Terrace on the main road, now lying below the railway on the right.

After a short distance – there being triple tracks for the whole of this length – and the passage of a level crossing with an Occupation Road, the railway is in pleasant countryside on the east flank of Summer Hill. This is typical of the district, collieries and brickyards appearing suddenly in rural conditions, and disappearing again to allow open country to resume.

Now, on the left, the embankment carrying the line widened and there were six parallel tracks from the 3 milepost. The line next reached a minor

*It was only used by Brymbo Branch trains and existed 1906–1917, strictly outside the WMCQR's time: did not formally close until 1926.

summit level and at 3¼ miles passed Ffrwd Junction signal box, marking the divergence of the Ffrwd Branch, sometimes spelled Frood as pronounced. This opened on the same day as did the original system (1st January, 1866), though it was never worked for passengers. Further complicated trackwork was necessitated for storage of Branch wagons, a long passing loop at the foot of the Branch itself, (and a curious bottleneck in the main line also where it was reduced to four tracks) where it passed over the very narrow Windy Hill road. A water column for Up trains stood alongside the bridge and diagonally opposite was an 'engine house' (hardly a shed proper) on a stub siding where the Branch engine could stand, coal, and take water from a tank carried on piers there.

Still on the sylvan hillside and with the main line descending at 1 in 87 (while the Branch climbed at 1 in 75) the two lines veered away from each other in slow divorce. Just beyond 3½ miles the main line was crossed by the Sydallt road (girder bridge) at Oak Alyn marking the northernmost corner of Gwersyllt Park, (residence of Col. Wheatley) an estate which has extended along the east side of the railway almost from Rhosddu. From the right at lower level, the valley of the River Alyn is reached where the confluence of the River Cegidog with the Alyn occurs: in the gorge below the line to the right, habitation, river, rail and road enter a narrow valley. The WMCQR was forced to bridge the Cegidog by a 5-arched stone viaduct, the most impressive piece of civil engineering on the system.

A railway would have been noticed below and down on the right in the bottom of this valley: it too crosses that same river on its own much-less-imposing bridge and at ground level; this was the long siding which paralleled the main line here leading to the Hope and Llay Hall collieries.

Ahead the line is carried over an awkward junction of roads at Cefnybedd, so out of Denbighshire and into Flintshire, in which it remains for the remainder of the journey to the south bank of the River Dee. Cefnybedd station (4¼ miles) followed immediately and marked the end of the 1 in 87 fall and was well situated for the considerably built-up district which threads this now narrow valley. There was a small goods yard on the west side, and signal box. In the latter days of the independent WMCQ the Down station building had been rebuilt in the 'Wirral' style, namely a pseudo-half-timbered and roughcast effect with slate roofing, an attractive improvement over its predecessor. On the Up platform a small yellow brick shelter with pent roof, slated, did duty. Passengers crossed the line between platforms on the level. Here the line was carried on an embankment above the valley floor, the Alyn continuing beside it below and on the right: the road to the abandoned Hope Colliery was crossed.

Continuing northward, the fall continues at 1 in 166 and just prior to 4½ miles, increases to 1 in 90. The land on the right was the property of the Lilleshall Coal & Iron Co. who were by this date, owners of the Llay Hall Colliery, whose original operators had failed. Here the long storage sidings of that colliery came alongside on the right; the main line fall eases to 1 in 160 and junction was made with Llay Hall tracks at 4¾ miles, a point where the Alyn obliges such junction by virtue of its closeness to the main line embankment.

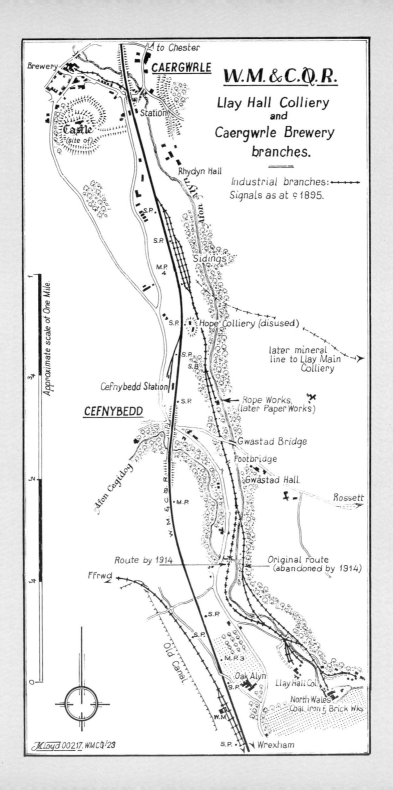

W.M. & C.Q.R.

Llay Hall Colliery
and
Caergwrle Brewery
branches.

Industrial branches: •—•—•—•
Signals as at c.1895.

to Chester
Brewery
CAERGWRLE
Castle (site of)
Station
Rhydyn Hall
Afon Alyn
S.P.
S.P.
M.P. 4
Sidings
S.P.
Hope Colliery (disused)
later mineral line to Llay Main Colliery
S.P.
S.B.
Cefnybedd Station
Rope Works (later Paper Works)
CEFNYBEDD
S.P.
Gwastad Bridge
Afon Cegidog
Footbridge
Gwastad Hall.
Rossett
W.M. & C.Q.R.
M.P.
Route by 1914
Original route (abandoned by 1914)
Ffrwd
S.P.
S.P.
M.P. 3
Old Canal
Oak Alyn
S.P.
Llay Hall Col.
North Wales Coal, Iron & Brick Wks
W.M.
S.P. Wrexham

Approximate scale of One Mile.
1
3/4
1/2
1/4
0

J. M. Lloyd 00217. WMCQ'23

The narrowness of the valley, and the appearance of more open country beyond is heralded by further easing of the now-downward gradient to 1 in 527, but for the moment, a narrow 'doorway' in the valley marks its northern portal so that the railway, Caergwrle Castle station*, road and river are tightly hemmed together, and the road falls steeply behind the station to join a nasty complex of roads under the railway bridge just to the north of it. There is positively no space for a goods yard. On the Down side the buildings were of yellow Buckley brick with timber awning, and on the Up, that same type of small shelter as at Cefnybedd; the signal box was alongside it, on the platform. The platforms here were alleged to be longer to accommodate excursion traffic for the Castle and Well. Still northwards, and over the above-mentioned road bridge (girders on stonework) (5 miles) there was an unfenced branch leading off a connection in the Up line (trailing) north-westward along the south bank of the Alyn to Lascelles & Sharman's Caergwrle Brewery, known as 'Sharman's Siding'; this extended for 250 yds. and beside its junction with the main line there was a short storage siding for empty vehicles. [The GCR thought it wise to erect a boundary fence and gate across this siding in 1909.] Little is known about the branch save that a WMCQR locomotive suffered damage on it (*see page 142*); it was shunted by the Railway Company: the Brewery's internal shunting was carried out by horse. This place lay at the foot of a dip in the system between the 'summits' at Ffrwd Junction and Buckley Junction.

Only yards beyond the Brewery junction, the main line crossed the Alyn on the almost-mandatory steel bridge and began to climb at 1 in 288 emerging from the valley onto a straight embanked section, passing under Fellows Lane bridge on the outskirts of what was then called Caergwrle Bridge End.

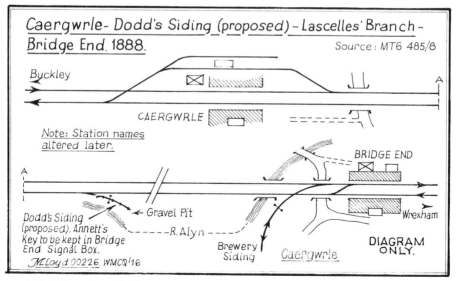

*Originally Bridge End and sometimes Caergwrle Castle & Wells: 'a one-time Spa with a decaying Pump Room in a leafy dell'.

Caergwrle itself, rising upon steep slopes with its ruined Castle at the 400 ft summit, could now be seen disappearing on the left hand as the train left the restricted viewpoint of the Alyn gorge. (Iron rails were given steel replacements of 75 lbs. per yard on this length in March 1892.)

The Alyn came up beside the embankment on the west side, but now in open meadows and flowing contrary to the direction of the journey: this was a diverted section to avoid two river bridges having to be built. At 5½ miles Hope Village station* was sited after crossing a small bridle road: this had a 'Wirral' style building on the Down side and the by-now familiar brick shelter on the Up. As with Caergwrle Castle and Cefnybedd there was no footbridge to connect the platforms. There was an interesting water tank on the Down side, embellished 'WMCQ Ry 1900' on a plaque, and a short siding opposite with a cattle bank – as if to confirm the Railway had passed from an industrial to a pastoral district – plus a small yard with a wooden goods shed on the right hand; this also served a timber sawmill.

Ownership of land hereabouts now contains some names familiar to the railway history of the district: Richard Henry Venables Kirk and Sir Stephen Richard Glynne, respectively a director and a resident of Hawarden Castle of whom more is written elsewhere.

Following the threading of another road overbridge (girders on stonework) there comes a longish length of open country; pleasant hilly slopes occur to the left, with the fascinating Plas Teg (built for Sir John Trevor about 1610) away at the foot of them. To the right, field and woodland slip slowly away onto the Cheshire Plain, with Beeston Tor making a noticeable hump on the skyline. The climb steepened to 1 in 83 for a considerable distance and several roads were crossed. Hanmer-owned lands were now traversed, another name linked with early railway development here. At 7½ miles came the summit at the important Penyffordd station, spelled in various ways by the railways hereabouts. Approach of this place was marked by the passage of the Penyffordd–Pontblyddyn road running below a girder structure; the platforms followed, the Down side having the 'Wirral' building and the Up the familiar brick shelter with a goods shed in corrugated iron behind. At the north end Down platform was a signal box controlling the tangential connection with the Mold Railway, which fell at 1 in 110/66 along a curve to the west and so down to the level of the Mold Junction, Mold and Denbigh line as it made its way westwards.

The Mold Railway was incorporated on 9th July, 1847 for a railway from near Saltney on the Chester & Holyhead Railway, to Mold via Kinnerton, Penyffordd and Padeswood, together with a branch to Ffrith limeworks via Pontblyddyn. The enterprise was short-funded and its board of directors, half of whom were also on the board of the Chester & Holyhead Railway, finding no other solution agreed to allow the C&HR to purchase the line.

It was worked by the LNWR (as was the C&HR) from opening on 14th August, 1849; its first 7¼ miles were of double track, the remainder was single. Initially, all trains ran mixed until the opening of the Ffrith Branch in 1851, a new station at Padeswood being sited at the junction.

[Padeswood might have been the northern terminal of a GWR-inspired line, the Mold & Wrexham Railway which proposed to link those places in

*Originally Caergwrle.

1862. By then the Buckley Railway was 'under way' and the LNWR and GWR were in Parliamentary dog-fight to keep each other off this territory; there was some curious lining-up among those who later would sit on the board of the WMCQR, some favouring the LNWR camp and others thought Paddington would be a better bet. As yet in the background, the Wrexham, Whitchurch, Mold & Connah's Quay Junction scheme was, here and there, recommended as a way out of all difficulties but Piercy, under examination at the contemporary Parliamentary Enquiry, did not fare well. Counsel maintained that four of Piercy's nominally independent railways were in the ultimate, financed by the LNWR, and that the WWM & CQJR proposals would not last long; he was wrong. The WWM & CQJR was given the freedom to build north of Wrexham and LNWR (and successors) and GWR were ever thereafter kept at arms' length from the district.]

At Penyffordd behind the Up platform were cattle pens, and another siding was served by a crane to lift 1 ton. It was not so much a passenger station, but an important centre of traffic for WMCQR purposes, much of whose mineral business descended onto LNWR metals (Chester & Mold line) here, to reverse and make its way to Chester and so into England. The WMCQR still northward leading, started a steep climb at 1 in 90 to cross the LNWR at right angles by girder bridge.

It is helpful to interrupt the progress of the route here and digress under what might be an appropriate heading of 'Hope dashed'. Such are the intrigues of the past that the area surrounding Penyffordd station conceals features of former ambitions which existing documentary evidence and evidence on the ground fail to explain completely.

The mysteries begin with the Act of 1862 wherein Railway No. 2 was to commence on the Mold Branch of the Chester & Holyhead Railway and form a chord to connect trains coming from Mold with the WMCQR, allowing them continuance along the latter's metals to the north. In view of the heavy coal traffic coming from the Mold area it would have been advantageous to be able to ship any destined for overseas from Connah's Quay; the chord was therefore a logical step, having in mind the warm relations between LNWR and WMCQR. A reasonable curve of 1 fur. 2 ch. radius is shown on the Deposited Plans, the line rising northeastwards from the Mold line at 1 in 80 and being obliged to enter a somewhat deep cutting before making junction with the WMCQR 'on the level' (as the Deposited Plans state). However, for reasons unexplained, this chord was never completed even though the earthworks are sufficient; in fact, the existing deep cutting would have brought that chord somewhat below the height of the present WMCQR section and the only possible explanation could be that when the chord scheme was set aside, the main WMCQR line, (falling off the bridge which carried it over the LNWR Mold Branch as the WMCQR went northwards) was not carried to such depth as the chord's earthworks would demand for a junction; instead the fall from the LNWR bridge was somewhat reduced in consequence. (Dunn's suggestion that the junction site is today masked by the more recent building of the Cement Works' sidings would only be acceptable if the radius of the chord line had been excessively sharpened, which in fact it was not.)

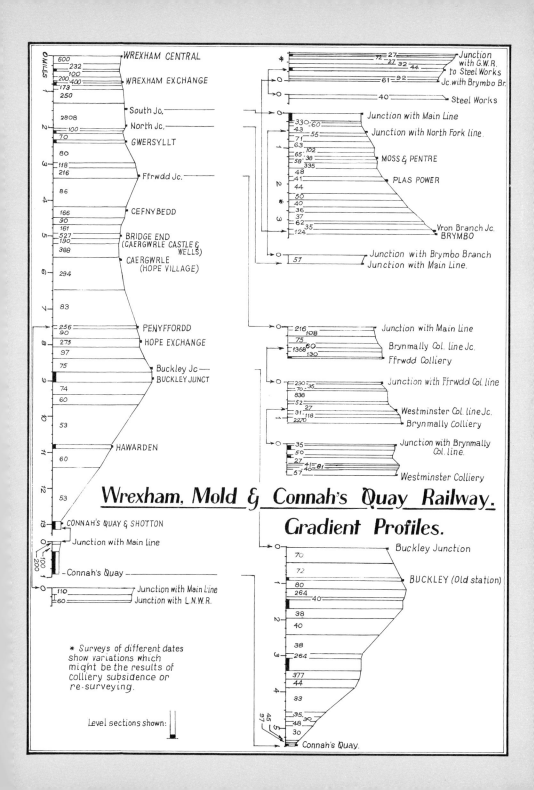

Wrexham, Mold & Connah's Quay Railway.

Gradient Profiles.

* Surveys of different dates show variations which might be the results of colliery subsidence or re-surveying.

Level sections shown:

This is not the only strange feature of the area. Twenty years later the Act of 1882 authorised Railway No. 8, a chord on the southeast corner to give direct running from the Wrexham direction, onto the Mold Branch so allowing WMCQR trains to run direct into Chester General. In the following year the LNWR planned a considerable enlargement of their Hope station (and its movement to west of the level crossing – which would be replaced by a bridge) to prepare it for the increased interchange of traffic but this was abandoned in favour of through carriages between Wrexham and Chester General, the LNWR to provide motive power between Chester and Hope. Second thoughts had prevailed in the LNWR camp when it was realised that Hope station was unsuitable for enlargement and that instead the WMCQR would have to be modified to provide the accommodation: presumably the through carriage answered both Company's objections to spending money!

The Engineer in charge of the scheme – which of course was in direct consequence of the new thrust shown by Piercy and Robertson – was William Davies, and according to his diary, 7th February, 1888, this new chord was completed sufficiently to carry a single track by March 1888, other permanent way materials being on site ready for laying. The full 38 chains of this chord were to be doubled in 1889, and there were to be 2,464 yards of exchange sidings. The existing (1990) spur in the southwest corner of the site (giving direct link between Wrexham and what is today the erstwhile Mold Branch in the Mold direction) was to be abandoned when No. 8 was complete. The LNWR's Hope signal cabin was duly enlarged in readiness for extra levers.

On 16th March, James Fraser (WMCQ Secretary) informed the Board of Trade that Railways Nos. 2, 3 and 8 of the 1882 Act were complete, but in August of the same year corrected this by writing to the effect that Nos. 2, 3 and 8 were *not* complete, but that doubling of the line along Railway No. 1 was done. [We shall return to the doubling later, but as to Railway No. 8, nothing more is written.]

The additional 'marriage' between LNWR and WMCQR per No. 8 being ready for another consummation, the unexpected deaths of Robertson and Piercy on 22nd and 24th March respectively halted further ceremony at the chancel steps; Piercy, the driving force of the WMCQR since 1881, the owner of half its shares and resident controller of its policy, was no more. The tragedy marked 'finis' to the venture and as will be seen elsewhere, his Trustees were lured from the corridors of Euston by influences from the MS & LR, the WMCQR dropping both this venture and that of Railway No. 5 under the 1882 Act (the proposed chord onto the LNWR coast line at Shotton).

Of this then-lonely rural spot W. Noel Davies wrote:

> Benjamin Piercy clearly intended closer working with the LNWR and interchange of traffic . . . had he lived a few days longer. The completion of the connection being established was prevented by the action of his Trustees, in collusion with Watkin & Co. and deprived . . . the local public . . . of through facilities to Chester and beyond . . . of greater utility than by Hawarden Bridge and Chester Northgate . . .
>
> The North Junction is shown distinctly on the OS 1887 and the local historian Harold Gregory of Buckley said that the north link was not only in existence, but

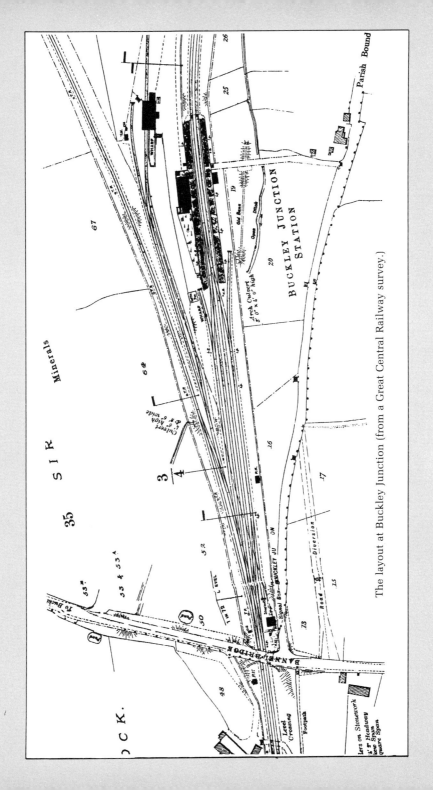

The layout at Buckley Junction (from a Great Central Railway survey.)

LNWR locos actually traversed it into Buckley and brought traffic from there occasionally.*

The present link was in existence before the Sheffield People (The Manchester, Sheffield & Lincolnshire Railway) 'boshed' it, together with the partly-made Railway No. 8. At the time of the 1881 idea it was possibly only an earthwork with no rails.† (The Wrexham–Mold link, that is.) Railway No. 8 was in existence by 1884 and Piercy intended to double it in 1887.

Of train working hereabouts, W. Noel Davies added:

> . . . even up to 1957 (time of writing) Wrexham–Rhyl excursions used this chord and reversed at Denbigh. The most noteworthy of trains over this line in June 55 years ago when the funeral train of Mrs. W.E. Gladstone from Hawarden to London used it. LNWR 'Precedent' Class ALBION with Driver Davies (later Loco. Inspector Davies) and Fireman Edwards, both of Crewe North, standing in the LNWR siding in dead silence, no steam or smoke showing until the engine moved to hook onto her train . . . might have been as lifeless as the late distinguished lady. ALBION was the Crewe Bank Engine. At 8 pm the Special from Hawarden arrived, 7 vehicles with MSL 0–6–2T 755 hired to the WMCQ and until recently bearing 'WMCQ' and 'No. 20' with Driver Rodney and Supt. F. Willans on the footplate. They propelled the train from Penyffordd station very gently through the junction until the whole of it including 755 was on LNWR metals, and stopped. 755 hooked off and departed for Wrexham. ALBION attached and left for 'Town'. All this was done with great decorum, no shouts, no whistle, no smoke or noise from the safety valves.

The earthworks of the abortive 'Piercy/Robertson' chord which would have formed a south to west link from the WMCQR to the Chester–Mold line and so given opportunity for through traffic between Wrexham (etc.) and Chester General without the need for reversal on the existing south to west chord, are now being lost to sight (1990). A long-standing survivor of the past is that the south-west interchange chord, now long deprived of the existence of the Chester–Mold railway and serving only as a set of storage sidings and reversal point for certain trains in connection with the Padeswood cement factory nearby; it is still dubbed by railwaymen as 'The Mold Line'.

Now high up on embankment, the WMCQR crossed the LNWR on a bridge to the LNWR's design: conveniently and just above on the high level, was the wooden-platformed (later brick) interchange of the WMCQ, Hope Exchange. The windswept platforms were crowned by a yellow brick building on the Up side and an original timber one on the Down. On this narrow earthwork, the Up platform was of reduced width, but obviously it satisfied the Board of Trade Inspector. Access to the outer world was denied, but there was a narrow footpath down the embankment side leading to the all-timber LNWR station below, also named Hope Exchange. In winter this was a lonely, dark and ill-lit place to be unaccompanied and waiting for the connecting train.

Here the WMCQR placed one of those imposing station name boards so familiar at junctions in former times; it proclaimed the station's name in bold large characters and added 'Change for L&NW line; Mold, Denbigh, Ruthin, St. Asaph, Rhyl, Bangor & Llandudno etc.' Happy days . . . and many

---

*This news must be treated with reserve. (JICB)

†He is wrong here.

residents of the Wrexham area took those LNWR trains to the seacoast of North Wales and with more adventure before them, the steamer from Llandudno Pier and sailed to the Menai Straits, the Isle of Man or Liverpool. Most of them had hardly been 'beyond the end of their own streets' before the coming of the WMCQR.

Pressing on, one reaches the 8th milepost and small signs of the unfinished chord line coming in from the left which would have made through running between Mold and the northward-reaching WMCQR in cutting here. The abandonment of this project might be due to the insolvency of the WMCQR in its early days, or second thoughts by the LNWR who might not have seen much advantage in it whilst losing some mileage over its own Mold–Chester line in consequence. The earthworks remain (1990).

Now off the 'hump' necessitated by crossing the LNWR, the main line falls at 1 in 304 into the cutting which would have marked this north junction. Here was a substantial wooden overbridge (8 miles) and a climb began at 1 in 93 which steepened shortly to 1 in 76/70/72; throughout this length the line is straight, pastoral and wholly in the Hawarden Estate of Sir S.M. Glynne. At 8½ miles comes a change; the industrial belt is reached once more as the clay district on the edge of Buckley supports the line. The Mold–Penymynydd road is crossed on steel girders, the line on embankment here which quickly becomes a cutting at Bannel Bridge where Bannel Lane straddles the cutting. The climb, now at 1 in 72, eased here to level. Beyond the bridge the tall Buckley Junction signal box gave the signalman adequate views of approaching northward-bound trains, seen over the bridge parapets. This was a good viewpoint for the railway lover; the junction of the Buckley section immediately to the north, the main line in full view either way, and the constant information of the track occupation resulting from the warm 'grandfather-clock' tones of the bell instruments in that signal box.

Buckley Junction station, on a slight curve, lay between 8¾ and 9 mileposts: it was preceded by relief loops on both lines and was a double-platformed structure in the 'V' of the junction. The ugly station building in the widely used Buckley yellow brick stood on the Down side, with a more substantial brick shelter – peculiar to this place – on the Up. The main line fell away along The Hawarden Loop at the platform ends, descending at 1 in 74.

On the west side, there was a small goods yard, with brick-built goods shed, wharf and cattle pen. Hereabouts the landowners were Piercy and William Henry Gladstone on the east, and Sir S.M. Glynne on the west. The WMCQR-built section of the Buckley line (making end-on junction with the former Buckley Railway construction at (Old) Buckley) led off to the north-west as single track. As a junction for passengers the station title was quite misleading – there had been no passenger trains to (Old) Buckley since February 1895 when the service was withdrawn for a second time.

Continuing to fall, and curving ever eastwards, the Loop followed through the Hawarden Estate, under Dirty Mile bridge (girders again) near the Old Cross Keys public house and straightened at 9¼ miles: the fall down towards Connah's Well Farm remained at 1 in 74 and 1 in 60 (9½ miles), becoming 1 in 53 as the route curved slightly westwards again and threaded under Drury Lane. Here the Engineer had decided upon a change, for the

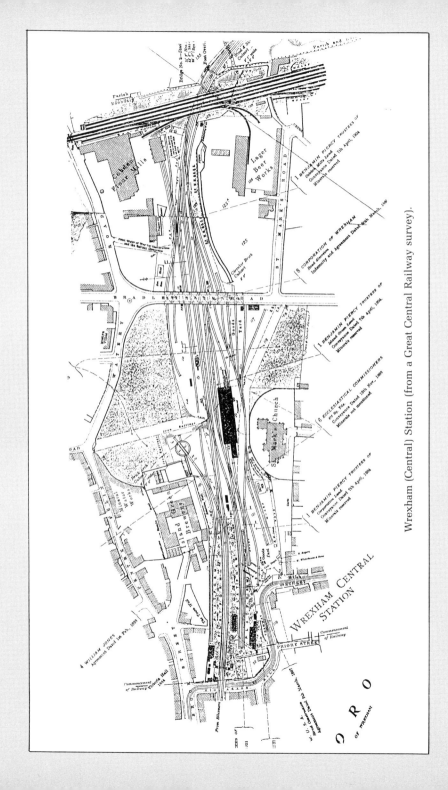

Wrexham (Central) Station (from a Great Central Railway survey).

bridge was of brick arch set in stonework. And so straight on, past 9¾ miles, back to a girder bridge construction again under the skewed Slack Lane and so down the sylvan dell of the Broughton Brook, falling through the heavily-timbered estate lands of Hawarden Castle to emerge on a tall embankment which crossed Tinkersdale after the 10th milepost, a brick arched bridge piercing its earthwork for an Occupation Road in the bottom of the Dale. Then, passing 10½ miles, yet still on embankment and over another brick arch, Groomsdale was gained with Hawarden Hayes Farm below on the right. Ahead, on the lip of the Dale, the housing of Hawarden village was to be seen: once off the embankment onto open ground and then, suddenly into cutting, Hawarden station was sited. It had refuge sidings on the Down side and a small goods yard and coal depot on the Up before the platforms were encountered. There was a brick built goods shed, iron lattice footbridge and signal box. Hawarden buildings reflected the proximity of the Gladstones, and the importance of the Estate and as a place of pilgrimage to excursionists bound for the seat of the Prime Minister. Having in mind the thirsty 30 mile run between Seacombe and Wrexham, water columns were set up at each end of the platform.

The buildings were an ill-assorted pair. That on the Up platform befitted the nearness to the Castle, and enjoyed the status of those yellow bricked double-fronted structures found previously – for instance – at Wrexham Exchange; on the other side a most curious flat-roofed erection in timber did duty; it was certainly no beauty, and had the appearance of an amalgam of croquet pavilion, a row of loose boxes or an upgraded garden shed . . . had it come from the Bishop's Castle Railway, one could have understood it. Sandwiched between the platform and tucked into the angle formed between it and the girder bridge carrying the Hawarden–Ewloe road above, was a Station Master's house in brick.

Down through the cutting, curving ever north and west, the tracks dropped at 1 in 60, making it heavy going for Up trains. About this point the contractors would have had to cut through the summit tunnel of the old Sandycroft II Tramroad, but there is now no evidence of it. Following the curve a narrow lane is crossed at Pantile Cottage for the track has now run out onto embankment: the bridge is a brick arch and formed quite a hazard for road traffic as the highway came into more frequent use (11¼ miles). Shortly after this, whilst still on embankment, the single tracked Aston Hall Colliery Railway* was crossed on its way down to Queensferry; this bridge, and a road underbridge which follows within yards, were both of steel girders. There followed a physical junction with interchange sidings of the Colliery line, controlled by Aston Hall Junction signal box.

The WMCQR is now running northwest and a wide panorama of industry, habitation and the long line of the River Dee, its flat monotonous fields on the north bank loom into view. The vast John Summers & Sons Ltd. steel works occupies that north bank immediately opposite the rail crossing of the river at the Hawarden Bridge, a feature easily discerned. However, the train would descend quickly along this length, and opportunity for absorbing this vista would be cut short as cutting engulfed it again: the long curve reversed direction to carry the line due northeast to the riverbank. A brick arch bridge

---

*note the surviving AHCR bridge in yellow brick which can be seen in the distance.

carried the Queensferry–Ewloe road over the railway at 11¾ miles; hereabouts the land was the property of the Enfield Taylor family whose links with this district were then at a zenith. It was this bridge which collapsed after the special train conveying Gladstone and party had just passed by en route for Manchester and was the subject of Watkin's wrath (*page 216*). Of this incident W. Noel Davies wrote of his father's involvement:

> The Loop was built by Benjamin Piercy's men under William Davies' supervision. John Woolley was in charge of the people on the ground. In order to accommodate certain parties, Woolley struck the centres of the Mold Road bridge before the brickwork had set, and it collapsed soon after the Gladstone/Watkin special train had passed under it. This was done against Davies' expressed orders given the previous day before he left for London for a meeting of the WMCQR. I think Woolley must have been bribed by the Watkin faction to take the risk. Woolley died not long after – he had been with B. Piercy for several years and had been in trouble before for heavy drinking. Piercy had made him sign the pledge before Canon Howell, Vicar of Wrexham. Of course, Piercy had died a short time before this incident.

The run down to the river continues at 1 in 53, where the railway emerges from cutting the fields above Queensferry, its flanks now dotted with factories, small coal mines and humble dwellings. Like a modern aircraft descending onto a flat runway, so the train ran out from the heights above onto the plain marking the river's edge.

Fair Road was crossed on a girder bridge and there were spurs leading to Darbyshire's Aston Hall brickworks (*on the left*) and to H.B. Rowley's wharf (*on the right*) and between the two spurs the interval of trackage was crossed by the wooden Wright's Bridge, on the north side of which was a signal box. Here the railway is just over 11½ miles from Wrexham Central.

Suddenly, a grubby township forms alongside: the rails cross Shotton High Street by girder bridge and on its north side came Connah's Quay & Shotton station, conveniently placed for access to the central part of the

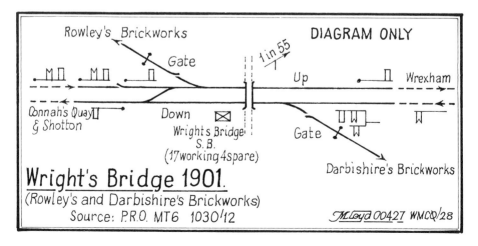

Wright's Bridge 1901.
(Rowley's and Darbishire's Brickworks)
Source: P.R.O. MT6 1030/12

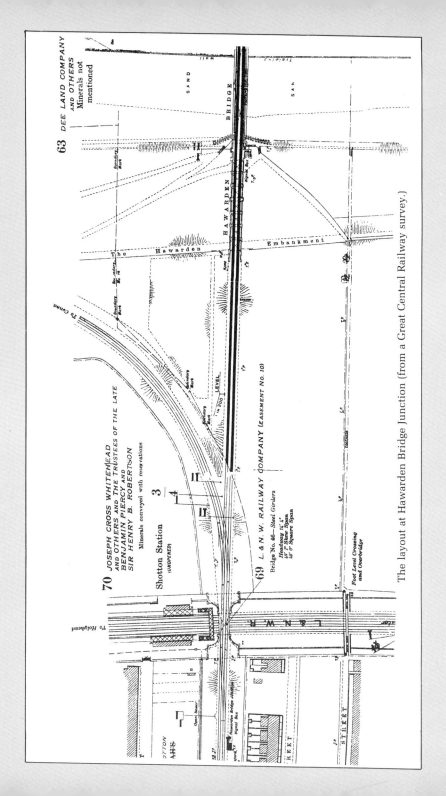

The layout at Hawarden Bridge Junction (from a Great Central Railway survey.)

town. Being on embankment, the platforms were of wood, thus avoiding the need for more substantial foundations had heavier materials been used: the Down building was also in timber but the Up shelter was small, of open-fronted style in red brick. Hawarden Bridge Junction signal box stood at the north end of the Up platform. [The WMCQR may also have hoped to fulfil its ambition for Railway No. 5 (a chord to link from south to west onto the Chester–Holyhead line) and used this station as a temporary measure, before building a permanent one on the south side of the main street.] This being the last station on WMCQR metals, the station name board (beside carrying the ample station name) added: 'Change for Saughall, Blacon, Chester, Northwich, Knutsford, Manchester Central and Cheshire Lines stations' and so underlined the fact that through services from Wrexham to this point favoured Cheshire as their ultimate destination. This was exactly 13 miles from the start.

Just beyond the platforms the LNWR Chester–Holyhead main line (four-tracked) passed beneath by girder bridge. Immediately on the west side was its own Shotton station (still unopened at the time of the WMCQR take-over by the GCR), linked by footpath. Next came the double-line junction with a double track leading westward along the dock and riverside to make connection with the lines at the foot of the WMCQR's Buckley section where it passed onto the river bank at Connah's Quay. Passenger trains did not traverse this portion. Back on the main line, the foot of the long fall which has continued unbroken (save a short level length in Hawarden station) from Buckley Junction (400 ft a.s.l.) onwards, ends here with a final, more gentle fall of 1 in 200. Now on the level and without visible sign, the railway here became the property of the GCR (built however, under MS & LR auspices) and ran across the Hawarden Bridge.

Therefrom our journey would be continued 'on foreign metals'; the railway north of this bridge bifurcated on the north bank of the Dee, the westerly route following the Wirral peninsula to the junction at Bidston. The railway diverging to the right continued east and south to make junction with the Cheshire Lines system outside Chester Northgate station.

The Brymbo Branch (All gradients are uphill)
The south (and original) junction for Brymbo diverged from the main line opposite the Stansty Iron Works (these became disused before the turn of the century) and curved west-south-west on an embankment in flat meadow surroundings. The West Junction marked the point where the original connection and north tangent was later made, to unite with the main line at North Junction, with Clayton's large brickworks alongside on the west side. The considerable siding and junction arrangements here were evidence of the importance of this interchange; most traffic passed off the Branch and made its way to the north, to be given over to the LNWR at Hope Junction. Once there, most of the traffic had to reverse to gain Mold Junction and Chester. Such a cumbersome arrangement led to uncompetitive rates for traffic off WMCQR metals.

All sides of the Brymbo junctions were carried above the surrounding ground on embankments and the Branch continued west-south-west under

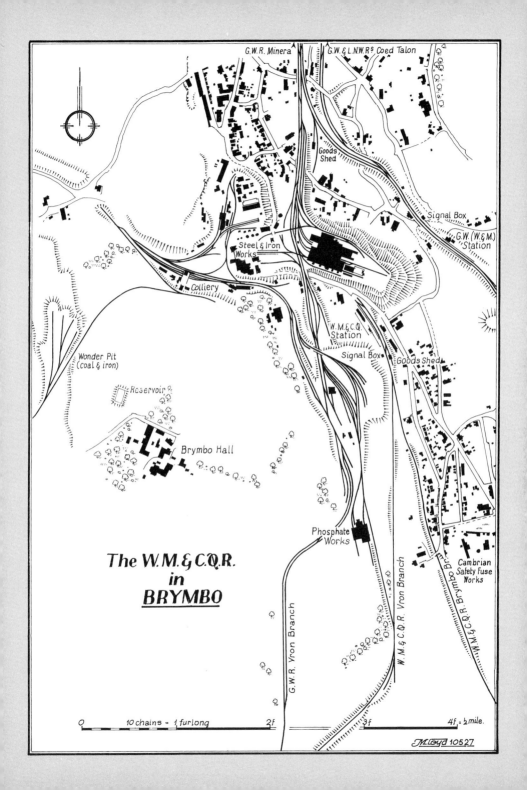

G.W.R. Minera

G.W. & L.N.W.R§ Coed Talon

Goods Shed

Signal Box

G.W. (W.&M.) Station

Steel & Iron Works

Colliery

W.M.&C.Q. Station

Signal Box

Goods Shed

Wonder Pit (coal & iron)

Reservoir

Brymbo Hall

Phosphate Works

Cambrian Safety fuse Works

The W.M.&C.Q.R. in BRYMBO

G.W.R. Vron Branch

W.M.&C.Q.R. Vron Branch

W.M.&C.Q.R. Brymbo Br.

0   10 chains = 1 furlong   2f   3f   4f = ½ mile.

M.Loyd 10527

the Wrexham–Cefnybedd road by girder bridge at Stansty Chain (1 in 71/63). Beginning a curve southwards to avoid the range of low hills in its path, it entered a cutting and within it, passed under a girder bridge carrying Summerhill Road at Henblas and the edge of Stansty Park; still continuing within the cutting, it reached a wooden platform on the south side – this was the curiously spelled Highfield Road Halte of GCR days, situated beside the equally curiously-named Pump House Road which crossed the railway here, again by girder bridge.

At a foot crossing beyond, a straight section of track and the cutting ended together; the Broughton Brook issuing from the Moss Valley was crossed by high embankment and a curve to the left (southwest) began, 1 in 102/65. A station called Poolmouth was intended here, but not built.[2] Here the line doubled and the Gatewen Colliery* Branch was thrown off (*see page 259*) to the left whilst the Brymbo Branch passed a signal box, and under the GWR Moss Valley Branch which was carried above on a stone arched bridge.[3]

Mileages were taken from Wrexham Central, and 2¾ miles exactly marked the start of a cutting which ensued, 1 in 38/58. Then came Moss & Pentre station (opened to passengers, 1st August, 1889), with a platform on each side; just to the west of it, the line singled again. A feature of this station was the footbridge which spanned the cutting. There were simple brick buildings on the Up (to Wrexham) platform, and a small shelter on the Down.

A gentle curve towards the south continued, all in cutting, 1 in 338; the Gatewen road passed over here on a stone arch, and shortly the curve ended and the track went under a girder bridge and the Wrexham–Moss road. At the 3rd milepost the start of an almost half-circle curve to the right began, taking the line northwest and north – here the long climb to Brymbo started, now at 1 in 48/41/44. On the left hand was the small GCR-period New Broughton station without buildings, and by arched bridge the Southsea road crossed the line (there were numerous road overbridges on this short section, but this is the last).

Out into the open ground now and curving ever to the right, the Branch passed under the GWR Brymbo Branch which was carried above by girder spans; it consisted of three tracks here, one being the branch to Thomas Clayton's New Broughton Colliery. The WMCQR continued its long rising route, there being no respite from the considerable gradients. To the right (on the inside of the curve) a spur was thrown off to that same New Broughton Colliery, 3¼ miles, and the River Gwenro appeared on the outer side of the embankment. To the left, Plas Power signal box was passed.

Here open country, which existed around Brymbo Junction, was resumed again as Broughton was left behind and for a short distance the surroundings were quite rural, with promising views of hillsides rising to the west. But ahead, and coming into view now so as to dominate it, the ultimate hilltop is crowned by the satanic Brymbo Steelworks and its satellite collieries, tips and servile dwellings: yet for the immediate moment, the traveller might look around at fields and foothills.

As the long curve straightened at 3½ miles, a complex array of tracks ensued. The GWR Branch came in alongside from the right but just before

---

*The spoil bank here buried Ffynnon Deuro, an arched building with a well noted for its healing properties.

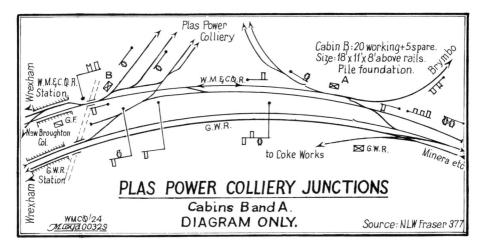

reaching it was the WMCQR Plas Power station (opened for minerals Autumn 1887: for passengers 1st August, 1889) situated immediately beyond a doubling of the line so that there was a platform on each side. The main buildings were of brick on the Up side. There was also a junction for Down trains into New Broughton Colliery, (also known as Clayton's Pit) and was controlled by a ground frame and gong on the Up platform. With GWR and WMCQR side by side each line crossed Southsea Road here at Southsea Inn. Beyond this bridge, the WMCQR had one of two signal boxes and there was a locomotive watering tank on the Up line. Both companies threw off connections to the left to give them access to Plas Power Colliery, the access branch crossing the Gwenro by its own girder bridge here; thus little Southsea village had three dominating bridges overlooking it. The Southsea Colliery (closed 1853) was buried by railways here. The GWR spur to Plas Power Colliery crossed the WMCQR lines on the level, but between the two sets of tracks the spur was gated; by means of a crossover it was possible to make interchange between the two companies. Semaphore signalling here was on a considerable scale in consequence of layout complication.

The Broughton Solvay coke ovens were also alongside the GWR here, as was Broughton Forge and Old Broughton Colliery: these had rail links with the GWR but not the WMCQR. Ernest Solvay conceived a plant to produce much-needed supplies of ammonia, then only available in limited quantity from gas works and public urinals. By 1882, in collaboration with his cousin Louis Semet, a gas works' owner in Belgium and France, the latter had designed an oven to make ammonia by heating coal by gas in a closed vessel. A secondary discovery emerged in that the coke so produced proved to be satisfactory 'metallurgical coke' for the iron and steel making industry. The erection of such a plant at Broughton was a logical step hereabouts. (Duly patented, the Semet–Solvay Coke Oven burgeoned: by the turn of the century there were over 450 installations in the British Isles, and four times as many on the Continent.)

The WMCQR branch now entered its final section; there was no mistaking its goal as the western hillside beyond – for which it is aiming – was (and is!) clothed with chimneys, works, housing, spoil banks from steel works and coal pits and all the paraphernalia of heavy industry. "A thick brown smoke pall is likely to hang overall, and the ground shakes visibly as the thud of foundry-work within the complex, takes place." With a fan of sidings between GWR and WMCQR (the former making its own way along the east flank of the valley, and thus avoiding a direct approach to the Brymbo Works), the WMCQR crossed a high embankment made entirely of colliery burnt slack, to reach the other side of the valley. Beneath, in a long skew bridge (Ochnall's Bridge) reminiscent of a tunnel, it passed over the Brymbo toll road in the bottom of the vale. [The 'tunnel' is notable for its skewed brickwork lining – the Toll House beside it also survives.] (4 miles)

Over the foregoing junctions the gradient stiffened to 1 in 50/40/36. One WMCQR siding ran up alongside the GWR for a short distance past its Broughton Forge signal box and its junction with the Broughton Solvay Coke Works, to give the WMCQR a spur into No. 3 Bank tip: the WMCQR was not allowed any further.

Returning to the Branch; the point of divergence between GWR and WMCQR Brymbo-bound lines was also marked by the second small signal cabin controlling a second junction with Plas Power Colliery which gave an outlet over the WMCQR to the north. The existence of this triangular junction (with two railway companies involved) together with a complex track layout on the steep hillside, plus considerable civil engineering works, created one of a most fascinating web of railways competing for the same traffic!

So the WMCQR moved across the valley to rural pastures and a shelf-like situation high above the valley bottom. On gaining the west flank, the line turned north again and passing 4¼ miles, a brief flirtation with countryside ended at 4½ miles with the outskirts of The Lodge, Brymbo.[4] Hill Street passed over the line, climbing steeply – 1 in 37/35/124[5] – up to the left; the line now ran along the hill flanks in such restricted circumstances that a retaining wall supported the slope on the upper side.

The valley now narrowing, the steelworks, still above the level of the railway, loomed ahead in brooding manner. Immense tips crowd above the line on the left and descending upon them came the steep, single line of the Vron Branch to join the Brymbo Branch at 4¾ miles: its headshunt was all too short, for immediately beyond the junction the line formed a terminal run-round loop, with siding and goods shed adjoining, and ended abruptly at Brymbo station (which was opened for minerals December 1887 and for passengers 1st August, 1889) with its signal box and platform on the left hand. The building was in yellow Brymbo brick with red brick quoins. The site was narrow and lay at the foot of those frowning tips, atop of which the steelworks commanded over all. Below, the road climbed up alongside, skirted by grimy housing in awesomely close proximity. The threat of a runaway down the Vron Branch into the passenger platform was ever-present. Neither was there relief from the engulfing odours, smoke and noise of Henry Robertson's empire surrounding it. (The effects of a German bomb

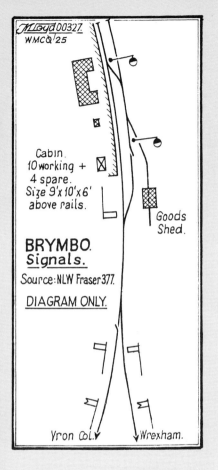

JMLoyd 00327.
WMCQ/25

Cabin.
10 working +
4 spare.
Size 9'x10'x6'
above rails.

Goods
Shed.

BRYMBO.
Signals.

Source: NLW Fraser 377.

DIAGRAM ONLY.

Yron Col. ↓   ↓ Wrexham.

(345 / 83999)

Wrexham, Mold & Connah's Quay Railway.

From *Brymbo*
To *Llynclys Cam* Railway.
Route via *Wrexham & Ellesmere*
Date *Aug 12th 1902* Wagon No. *497*
Consignee *Wm Parry*

URGENT
WESTMINSTER COLLIERY,
TO
Llynclys
Mr S Williams

No. *19*   Date *16/10/* 190

WHEN EMPTY REVERSE LABEL.

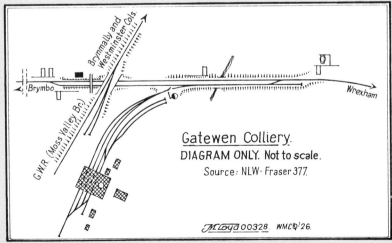

Brynmally and
Westminster Cols.

Brymbo

G.W.R. (Moss Valley Br.)

Wrexham

Gatewen Colliery.
DIAGRAM ONLY. Not to scale.
Source: NLW· Fraser 377.

JMLoyd 00328. WMCQ/26.

landing close by during World War II could hardly have defaced the by-then-abandoned station any further!)

Industries served by the Brymbo Branch

In considering the industries served by the Branch, the interwoven interests and miscellanea come to light in unexpected sources. Take for instance the Broughton & Plas Power Coal Co. Ltd., by 1889 a part of the Brymbo Steel Co. Ltd. (formerly Brymbo Iron Co.), and owning this and the Gatewen Colliery, and shortly to be owners of Gwersyllt too. Their customers, all of whom received their coal by railway wagon, included The Peninsular & Oriental Steam Navigation Co., The Cunard Steamship Co., Great Western Railway, Great Indian Peninsular Railway (by ship), London North Western Railway, Seacombe & Hoylake Railway, Birmingham Gas Co., Wolverhampton Gas Co., Bidston Gas Co., Cork Steamship Co. and Hereford Gas Co. Their coal was most suited for steam raising and gas works' use – it was large, hard and bituminous.

The Company was founded in January 1881 and its directors speak for themselves:

> Henry Robertson, Pale (virtual owner of the Brymbo undertaking)
> W.H. Darby, Brymbo Steel Works
> Richard Peacock, Gorton Hall (Beyer, Peacock & Co. Ltd.)
> Hermann Lange, Gorton Foundry (Beyer, Peacock & Co. Ltd.)
> Edwin Webb, Gorton Foundry (Beyer, Peacock & Co. Ltd.)
> W.D. Haswell, Accountant of Chester
> Evan Morris, Solicitor of Wrexham

(In July 1881 Benjamin Piercy took up £10,000 in shares but he was not a director.)

By 1889 F.G. Whitwham, a director of the WMCQR, and 1885 contractor for doubling its main line, was also a director; he was manager of the estate of the late Benjamin Piercy. The links with Beyer Peacock Co. Ltd. through Robertson, Peacock, Lange and Webb were prominent; was this to be the source of coal for the Gorton Foundry?

The Colliery sent its products by both WMCQR and GWR which ran past its very door at Southsea. In December 1888 (for instance) the Colliery paid these amounts for taking its output away, for a fortnight in each case:

> WMCQR   £1,844 17*s.* 7*d.*
> GWR   £1,292 16*s.* 10*d.*

The practice of burning coal slack on the pit banks (*see page 203*) led to the long-lived fire at Southsea; the railway companies attempted to charge the colliery with the cost of extinguishing it, but ultimately the colliery and WMCQR paid half each.

Some wagons were hired – 'The Birmingham Railway Carriage & Wagon Co.' and 'The Midland Wagon Co.' were the suppliers. In 1881, 50 were purchased and in 1894 10 ton wagons were in use; 30 on hire from 'Midland' and 20 on hire from 'Birmingham'. In late 1881, 100 wagons were bought from Midland on deferred 7 year terms together with a 37/6d. per annum per wagon Repair Arrangement; and in 1884 20 wagons came from The

Metropolitan Carriage & Wagon Co. Ltd @ £9 per wagon per annum for 7 years.

There had been problems with farmers when the Brymbo Branch was under construction, for the last mile (approximately) beyond the Southsea district interfered with harvesting and various parties involved were obliged to compensate farmers for loss of crops. The Colliery Branch railway was controlled by the Plas Power signalman, half of whose wages were paid by the Colliery Co.

Of vital importance to this colliery's owners was the cost of transport: first and foremost came the issue of supplying coal to Gorton Foundry. The LNWR, anxious to better the GWR in every way, made attempts to obtain running powers over the WMCQR (but did not succeed) and made sufficient overtures to the Robertson party that the Colliery backed the LNWR in that skirmish. Not that the Colliery had any special leanings towards the WMCQR who frequently used the Colliery's private sidings for the convenience of shunting its own trains; this practice brought the Colliery to a stop in January 1892 when it found its sidings were thus blocked.

At one of the Company's collieries a locomotive named COLLIER was worked.

The cost of the line from Brymbo South Junction to Gatewen Colliery was defrayed by the Colliery Company, together with expenses for an engine shed and laying track at Plas Power Colliery [years 1882 and 1884]). An outlet onto the GWR from Gatewen Colliery was built in early 1882 at a cost to the Colliery of £100, and sidings there were put in by J.P. Edwards but problems arose due to the protracted completion of the GWR branch. The GWR charged for their part in building the Plas Power Colliery signals and sidings, a figure which was contested; the GWR also tried unsuccessfully to charge half the signalman's wages at the Colliery junction: the GWR insisted that sum should be included in the charge for freight.

In November 1881 reference was made to Gatewen arrangements for a branch to the WMCQR 'to open new markets for the sale of coal'. (The Minutes of twelve months later disclose that the line opened in August 1882 and the GWR immediately dropped its rates to compete with the incomer.) The Gatewen Colliery had already made contract with the Brymbo Co. @ 2/4d. per ton albeit it had no rail connection as yet!

The costing of wagons was a sensitive factor in coal sales: for instance – for reasons unclear – the Midland Wagon Co. was approached for an estimate for repairs to 50 Oldbury constructed wagons in July 1882. (The Flintshire Wagon Co. was also contacted.) These cannot have been BPPCCL-owned and run-down within so short a time?! Perhaps they were available secondhand? They were wagons Nos 251–300 and presumably purchased, and certainly sent to Midland to form the initial fleet. It is likely these came from the Brymbo Co. as forty more 10 ton wagons were bought from them in February 1883 @ £41 each, to include repainting. Transfer took place on 1st April.

Some indication of the size of BPPCCL business and the improvements to traffic working since the bad old days of GWR monopoly and the mischievous Brake and Wheatsheaf Inclines came in 1887: by then the Colliery was working 758 wagons and in the June quarter only 11 of these had been away from the Colliery for more than 11 days.

Brymbo Branch and Broughton & Plas Power Colliery Co. Ltd

Origins of this Branch have been disclosed in 1882 and 1884, together with the original scheme of 1881. It is known that the line from the junction on the WMCQR at Stansty was in use by August 1882; it had been built by Piercy's men and Piercy received a wayleave on all traffic carried thereon. Payment for the construction was not made to Piercy's estate until 1902. In September 1884 the Colliery resolved that no change in the present working arrangements should be required pending the taking-over of the Branch by the WMCQR, but on 26th June of that year the track had already reached Plas Power Colliery. Who did this work? It has been assumed that between Gatewen and Plas Power, the WMCQR was responsible, but this seems unlikely in view of a letter from the WMCQR to the BPPCCL on 11th June, 1888 stating they were taking over the Branch line, Stansty–Brymbo on 1st July that year. This implies that the whole Branch to the Brymbo terminus had been laid out under an Arrangement (not surviving?) whereby Robertson's party would connect his Brymbo etc. undertakings to the WMCQR at Stansty, and build the whole Branch between these places. Certainly, the BPPCCL was the principal debtor in the matter of recompense paid to farmers for loss of crops when the line was extended Plas Power–Brymbo.

The Branch became WMCQR outright at the above date and the BPPCCL lost no time in sending a reminder to that Company (on 31st October) that they must complete the sidings at Plas Power Colliery.

The importance of linking Gatewen and Plas Power pits to Brymbo itself cannot be overestimated; in September 1888, 100 tons per week of steam coal was contracted to the steel works there for nine months @ 5/8d. per ton with 3d. per ton wagon hire.

Ffrwd Branch

Leaving the main line north of Gwersyllt station this Branch diverged gradually in a northwesterly direction, climbing at 1 in 108 up the eastern face of Windy Hill and through Sydallt to reach the bed of the erstwhile Ellesmere Canal branch as this climbed and curved anticlockwise round the head of the Hill. There was a catch point set to derail runaways before they reached the junction, a quarter mile before it. After passing under Windy Hill road the canal bed was crossed twice within yards – where that water-way had made a sharply-angled turn – and now becoming double track, the Branch completed a half circle from its original junction. Now on the west flank of Windy Hill and using the east side of the wooded Cegidog valley, it entered and followed the canal bed. Junction was made with the parallel GWR branch coming up from Wheatsheaf Junction to serve this same area. Both companies had spurs into Sparrow's Ffrwd iron and coal works situated to the west of them and sandwiched between the railways and the Cegidog. Railways and tramways within this elderly working were carried across that river to the other side of the valley to tap mineral workings in the

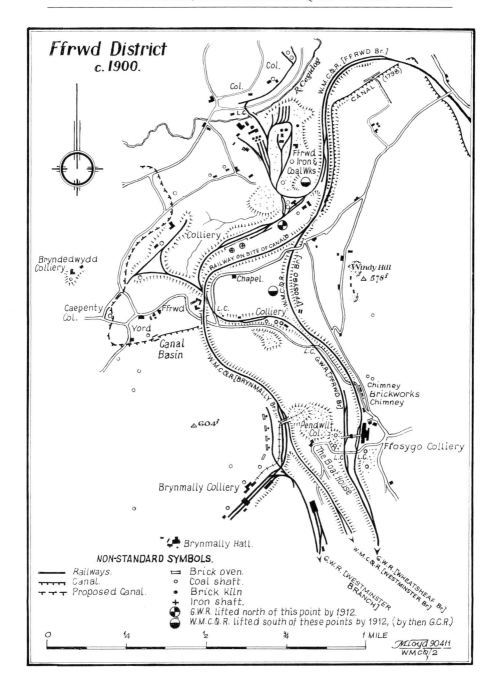

Ffrwd District
c. 1900.

Col.

Col.

R Cegidog

W.M.C.Q.R. [FFRWD Br.]

CANAL (1798)

L.C.

Ffrwd
Iron &
Coal Wks

Colliery

RAILWAY ON SITE OF CANAL

Windy Hill
△ 578'

Bryndedwydd
Colliery

Chapel.

W.M.C.Q.R. [FFOSYGO Br.]

Caepenty
Col.

Ffrwd

L.C.   Colliery

Yard

Canal
Basin

W.M.C.Q.R. [BRYNMALLY Br.]

L.C. G.W.R. [FFRWD Br.]

Chimney
Brickworks
Chimney

△604'

Pendwll.
Col.

Ffosygo Colliery

Brynmally Colliery

The Boat House

L.C.

Brynmally Hall.

G.W.R. [WHEATSHEAF Br.]

W.M.C.Q.R. [WESTMINSTER Br.]

G.W.R. [WESTMINSTER
BRANCH]

NON-STANDARD SYMBOLS.

Railways.
Canal.
Proposed Canal.

⊟ Brick oven.
○ Coal shaft.
● Brick kiln
+ Iron shaft.
🌐 G.W.R. lifted north of this point by 1912.
🌐 W.M.C.Q.R. lifted south of these points by 1912, (by then G.C.R.)

0   ¼   ½   ¾   1 MILE

M.Lloyd 90411
WMCQ/2

hillside. All adjoining land was the property of 'Henry Robertson & Others' (i.e. the Brymbo Co.).

Proceeding southwesterly, the WMCQR (single line again) lay alongside but above the GWR, each line working its traffic out of the area in opposite directions . . . the WMCQR northward and the GWR to the south. There now came an interesting piece of construction where the WMCQR still on the canal site but on embankment, formed a short siding to a wharf and crossed over the GWR on a skewed girder bridge at what is locally said to be a haunted site. Once across the GWR line the WMCQR continued its south-ward trend and immediately crossed the road by girder viaduct of three 24 ft spans* and entered further woodland on the other side of it. Down below the embankment here is the hamlet of Ffrwd with its former coaching inn and stables. Some yards south of this place, it may still be determined where the WMCQR abandoned the canal site and climbed up the wooded hillside: the canal turned sharply westwards just south of the road viaduct, and after a very short distance where it continued along the north face of the hillside here, ended in the Yord canal basin, a flooded area still to be seen. From here it was planned to extend towards Llanfynydd, but like the whole project, this was abandoned.

The WMCQR (crossing Robertson and Piercy lands) and GWR now fol-lowed the same depression in the hills, looking across at each other from their respective sides, the GWR being to the east of the other. With a final curve southwards and westwards, the WMCQR formed a triple trackage and ended in Thomas Clayton's Brynmally Colliery and Brickworks high up on the slope. From here an extension southwards was made later to reach Westminster Colliery (opened 27th April, 1884: also served by the GWR). At Westminster the WMCQR was now 1¾ miles from Ffrwd Junction, having traversed a variety of landscape and twisted in various directions en route. Gradients, entirely uphill, rose at 1 in 75 and 60 to the junction of the Ffrwd Ironworks' spur (and then fell slightly into that complex), but south of here into Brynmally the climb was horrendous and from the parting from the canal site, there was a nasty section of 1 in 27 and 31 amid trees which would make the rails greasy in season. Of course, upgrade traffic would be with empty wagons: nevertheless . . . !

On the Brynmally–Westminster section was a steep 1 in 57 and 1 in 40 fall to Westminster which would severely tax loaded trains; this length was one of few portions of the WMCQR which did not favour the working of trains. (There were unhelpful parts of the main line, but not of this severity: the Buckley Railway could not, of course, be included in such generalisa-tion!)

We must now retrace our way almost to the place where, near a disused brickworks, the spur to Ffrwd Ironworks was thrown off: about this place (where the line entered the canal bed) a later spur was laid in to serve the Ffosygo Colliery. This spur began southwards, under the Windy Hill road by girder bridge to emerge from woodland and find itself above but alongside the GWR Branch on its way northward to the Ffrwd Ironworks. Soon the

*The story goes that a collier was taking an unofficial ride in the brake van and mistaking the position of the train as it travelled behind Windy Hill, jumped from the van as it was crossing the road bridge here. His ghost is reputed to haunt the place to this day, and that there is a patch of red moss nearby, stained with his blood.

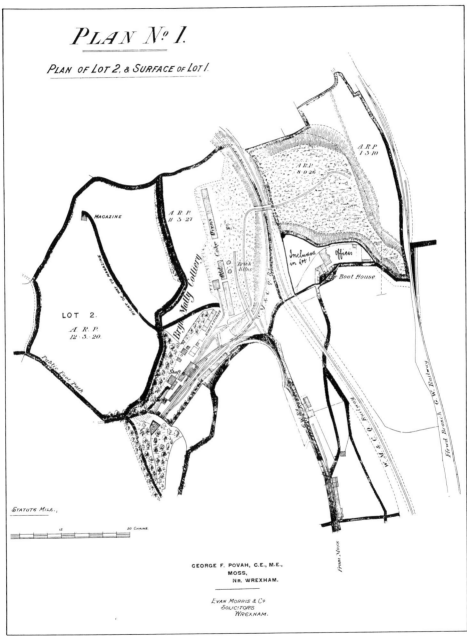

Brynmally Colliery – Face Plan.

Ffosygo Colliery was reached; the GWR being below, could not serve it here, but had a long more easily graded connection coming in from the south. There was, between the WMCQR and GWR alongside each other here (and with the same companies almost directly opposite where they served Brynmally Colliery), a lower area of land. In this depression was the little Pendwllt Colliery together with a small sheet of water known as The Boat House. The latter was intended to be the reservoir for the abortive canal scheme. This spur actually fell at 1 in 50 to come alongside the GWR, but climbed again to reach Ffosygo at 1 in 27.

From their junctions with the Ffrwd Branch, the Brynmally/Westminster and the Ffosygo spurs were respectively a little over 1 mile and about ½ mile long.

Vron Branch

This line was laid in during early 1888 and opened for mineral traffic (only) on 8th October that year. The trailing junction for the Branch was

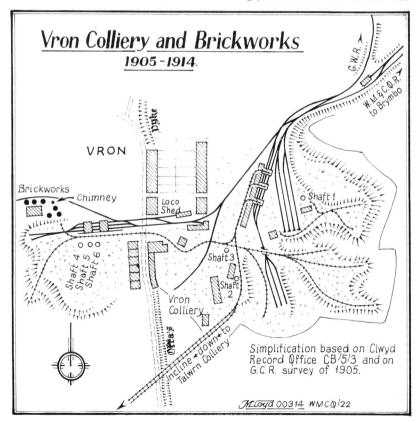

Vron Colliery and Brickworks
1905-1914.

G.W.R.
W.M & C.Q.R. to Brymbo

VRON

Dyke

Brickworks
Chimney
Loco Shed

Shaft 1

Shaft 4
Shaft 5
Shaft 6

Shaft 3

Shaft 2

Vron Colliery

Incline down to Talwrn Colliery

Simplification based on Clwyd Record Office CB/5/3 and on G.C.R. survey of 1905.

MLloyd 00314 WMCQ/22

made immediately south of the passenger platform at Brymbo station, and its course was a single line right up the side of the Brymbo Works' spoil tips, much of it at a gradient of 1 in 27/32. This placed the existence of passenger stock standing in Brymbo platform in considerable danger had there been a runaway, and measures were taken to prevent such a collision. It is believed that carriages were only permitted to stand there for the shortest operative time, and not when any movement was taking place above.

After rising to about 600 ft a.s.l. and about 500 yards from the Brymbo turnout, the Branch threw off a northward reversing spur which rose at 1 in 37 into the steelworks complex.

The Branch itself continued to climb at 1 in 38/62/99/33/63 and met the GWR Branch to Vron which came in alongside and which had approached this point from the GWR Brymbo connection around the Works on their north and west sides. Originally a junction was made between the two systems: the older GWR line served the Vron Colliery on the south and east, whilst the WMCQR made an angled crossing with it on the level, and served the north edge of the Colliery. There was a small engine shed here. This last section was extended after WMCQR days, across the site of Offa's Dyke into Offa Colliery and to the Vron Brickworks, and brought the Branch to an end a little over 1 mile from Brymbo station.

Dropping down southwestwards from Vron Colliery a narrow gauge coal tub line (possibly worked by cable) descended the hillside to the coal pits at Talwrn. The rails were of light 10 lbs. flat bottomed rail, or light bridge rail. The contents of loaded wagons from this tramway were tipped from overhead platforms into wagons of the standard gauge companies within the Vron complex.

Vron was 700 ft above sea level; by looking due east one could see the Plas Power Colliery immediately below; there the WMCQR was about 300 ft lower than at its terminus here in Vron; the ability to reach this point within the distance of approximately one mile was created by the Brymbo reversing junction.

Llay Hall Branch

Making junction with the Down main line by means of a trailing connection about ¼ mile south of Caergwrle station, was a 1¼ mile Branch opened in September 1877 and leading southwards. This followed a parallel course to the main line on its westward side, and down the valley of the Alyn towards Llay Hall. Whilst the main line on its southward journey, rose alongside quite steeply, the Branch, hugging the river, fell for all its length: though official gradients are not recorded, in places the descent was approximately 1 in 40, making the line hard to work for loaded coal trains working northwards.

At its southernmost end the Branch divided into two: the westward line served the Llay Hall Colliery and the eastern the Llay Hall Firebrick Works, each of these concerns having several titles/owners/lessees in their lifetime. The Colliery was commenced in 1873 and the Branch was closed when the Llay Main Colliery was shut down in 1966. The course of the Branch, as it descends to the banks of the Alyn, is sylvan throughout and before the days of industry this must have been an attractively wooded gorge, for the sides of the valley are steep, especially so on the east side.

Near the main line junction (controlled from the signal box on Caergwrle Up platform) were the Mineral Springs from which 'Caergwrle Wells' took its title. Excursionists from Birkenhead would 'take the waters' at small wooden booths set up in season, and the Ordnance Survey map actually shows 'Cafe' in the village, an unusual instance. But the Branch was concerned with coal, and water – a curse when flooding the local coal pits as it was prone to do hereabouts – was a thing to avoid. Immediately south of the junction the Branch became a number of parallel sidings for wagon storage, all enclosed by woodland. The course then fell between the main line and the river (yet far below), down through woodland to the Abermorddu Colliery which had access from the adjacent main road by means of a girder bridge passing under the main line which is on embankment here. Alongside the Branch, there was a series of waste tips on the east side.

By now, the main line had passed out of sight, being above and leading away from the Branch which here threw off a siding to the east to serve the Hope Rope Works (later a Paper Mill). Shortly, the road from Cefnybedd to Llay crossed over the Branch, now in deep cutting, by cast-iron-beamed bridge. High up to the west – out of sight – is Cefnybedd station, whilst below to the east, the Llay road falls to cross the river at Gwastad Bridge.

Before emerging from this cutting, the Branch was crossed by a footbridge of curious metal construction, having sheet iron sides; it is supported on piers of 'Llay Hall' bricks, and survives today: the related footpath appears disused. The line continued in a straight course and fell to the meadowside on the river bank; here the main road had come in alongside so that road, rail and river were confined to a bottleneck close by the New Inn. Now the railway crossed the Alyn by a somewhat lightly-constructed open girder-work span, to which the Colliery Company had added a stout rolled steel joist on the upper sides to increase strength and reduce hazard in case of derailment . . . an event which had in fact taken place. Beside this and other bridges, was carried a 6 inch cast-iron pipe to bring water from a reservoir at Caergwrle to the Colliery; it followed the Branch throughout.

From hereon the valley is very narrow: and the railway – now on the east side of the river – passes the confluence of the Cegidog which comes into the Alyn from the west. There have been several railway alterations hereabouts, but all have involved the siting of a junction; the western fork of it led to Llay Hall Colliery, the eastern to the Llay Hall Brickworks. (Below Rock Cottage may still be seen the remains of bridges by which the Colliery branch railway re-crossed the river.) Before the turn of the century the junction was made a little south of the point where the Cegidog and Alyn combined, the Brickworks' branch running below the ancient Wat's Dyke atop the steep valley face. Before 1914 this junction was moved southwards towards the Colliery entrance and the layout simplified. The rail crossings of the river here were made on the same pattern of open girderwork as the first river bridge mentioned; they too had had joists added to their upper sides. The original layout allowed Colliery trains to work over either of the two bridges, giving flexibility in times when the tonnages were heavy; the

Colliery owned three steam locomotives during its life (*see page 336*): and the engine shed was just inside its premises. Beyond the Colliery was a narrow gauge tramway leading to a brickworks for, as in many another instance in this district, brickmaking was also carried on by the Colliery owners.

The branch on the east side of the river was rather longer than that to the Colliery, and the Firebrick Works which it served was concerned with no other product and the premises had closed before World War I.

The permanent way of the Branch was laid latterly in redundant WMCQR materials, some being of double-headed rails held in S-shaped-base chairs, a typical form of the 1860s.

Finally, two coal adits remain visible below Rock Cottage; these were once served by a siding: they emerge in the steep bank on the west side of the river and each adit had its own tramway which was carried over the waters by bridge.

An imaginative, vast road scheme is now proposed which will sweep away many features of the valley between Cefnybedd and Llay Hall.

References

[1] HISTORY OF WREXHAM (A.H. Dodd) (Hughes and Son 1957).
[2] National Library of Wales: Piercy Papers (Fraser Group) 399.
[3] National Library of Wales: Robertson Collection. (Industrial Records) (*Not catalogued*).
[4] The Lodge, (A Village Community needlessly killed off by Industry). (Broughton & District Local History Group.)
[5] National Library of Wales: Piercy Papers (Fraser Group). 586–7. Gradient profiles taken from the GCR Survey.

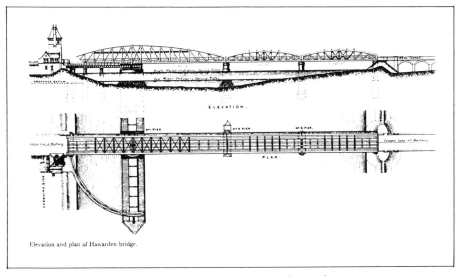

Elevation and plan of Hawarden bridge.

Elevation and plan of the Hawarden Bridge.

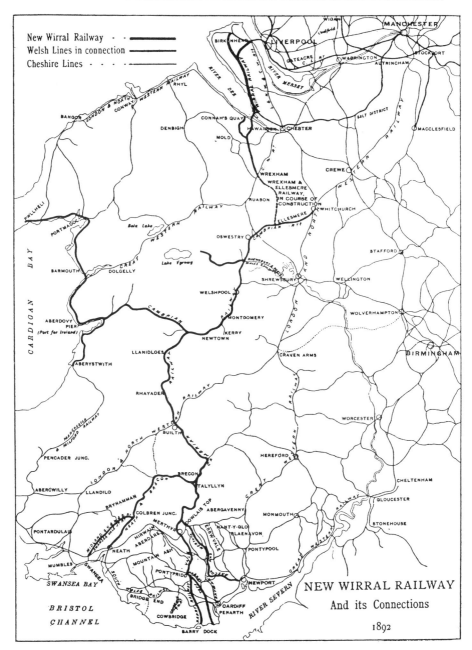

Watkin's Welsh invasion plan. Reproduction of an official map of 1892 showing the yet-to-be-built Wirral line (Bidston–Hawarden) and the connecting lines in the Welsh Railways Union.

Train Services and Timetables

It is hard to imagine that any would-be tourist would select this area of North Wales (which today is much nearer its original pastoral state than it was a century ago) as a place of resort: and diligent searching through contemporary Guide Books finds that they are careful to ignore the existence of it. However, the GOSSIPING GUIDE TO WALES for 1894 was braver than the rest and contains the following recommendation:

> ... there is another line of railway communication running via Mold to Wrexham and Chester. We will bring passengers to the other end of the line. Starting from Wrexham, first by the Wrexham, Mold & Connah's Quay Railway (which is converted into a link of a great chain of communication between Lancashire and North Wales by the Dee bridge), though there is no very remarkable scenery in this journey, they will find the route a pleasant one. At Cefnybedd they will get a charming peep down the valley of the Alyn. At Bridge End they can leave the train, if so disposed, for a visit to the ruins of Caergwrle Castle, which are seen on a mound to the left. Caer Estyn, an ancient British Camp, is on the right. Still better, it would repay the pedestrian tourist to explore the Hope Mountain and the valley of the Nantyffrith, about three miles to the southwest. Stations are thick about here, for the two we have just mentioned and Caergwrle are crowded within very little over a mile, the last being five miles from Wrexham: and the names are somewhat mixed, for Bridge End is close to Caergwrle village, and Caergwrle to the village of Hope. The villages seem to be mixed too, if we judge by an old saying in the district, 'I'll live in Hope if I die in Caergwrle': but the explanation may be in that Caergwrle is in the parish of Hope.
>
> The next station is Penyffordd, where towered Moel Fammau, the highest summit of the Clwydian range, comes into sight. The line runs on to the Dee, past Buckley, which is only 2 m. from Hawarden, but we change at Hope Junction to the Chester, Mold and Denbigh line ...

Which was just about all one could say for the Guide (perhaps it may be forgiven for overlooking the existence of the Dee bridge on one page, having acknowledged its existence on another) next recommends Hawarden to the visitor, adding that Sandycroft on the Chester–Holyhead line was the nearest station; Broughton station on the Mold–Denbigh line was considered a good alternative. One wonders if these Victorian excursionists ever followed such advice?!

In fact, Caergwrle and Hawarden were almost the only places likely to attract an outsider; the latter's popularity was based solely on its fame as the home of the Gladstones: the former was well liked for school and temperance trips. But the basic business of the WMCQR was its mineral traffic, the carriage of the output of mines, quarries, factories and iron works, of brick-yards, tileworks and potteries for overland customers in this island, or for shipment abroad. From the Dee the most distant overseas markets were reached by a short shipment to Birkenhead or Runcorn, and trans-shipment thereafter into a larger vessel.

Local passenger traffic hinged on Wrexham, then and now a centre for market and retail trades. Brymbo district being the one main centre of population on the Railway, created, and added, a heavy passenger traffic in workmen. Local people used Wrexham with its market, and domestic needs were satisfied by the largest number of shops in any town in North Wales. At one time the passenger service between Brymbo and Wrexham was half-hourly, and this over a line which was heavily graded and limited to single track. Considering the heavy mineral traffic passing down it and then northwards up the main line to Hope Junction for transfer to the LNWR, it is not difficult to imagine the intensity of single line occupation which this must have brought about.

From the first the local weekly newspapers were used to publicise the passenger timetable: at the opening it only offered transport between Wrexham and Buckley – but Buckley, like Brymbo, was a centre of concentrated population. Most of its products, based on the clay and colliery industry, went northwards over the Buckley Railway section to Connah's Quay, and there was no 'official' passenger service over this length. Mineral workings off the WMCQR were handed over to Buckley men for that section. The distance between Buckley and Wrexham was only nine miles; the line passed through a well-populated district and Wrexham was as attractive to Buckley people as it became to those living around Brymbo at a later date. Stations, though primitive, were close together and if the passenger service proved inadequate for all the business offering, it was due to the inadequacies of the locomotive department and the lack of carriage accommodation. The crowding of locomotive footplates by women with large shopping baskets on the way to Wrexham market, to the partial inability of the enginemen to operate their charge, is still the local recollection. The hired carriage stock was already overfull and no one, it seems was to be turned away. So to the timetable; the initial service was of three trains each

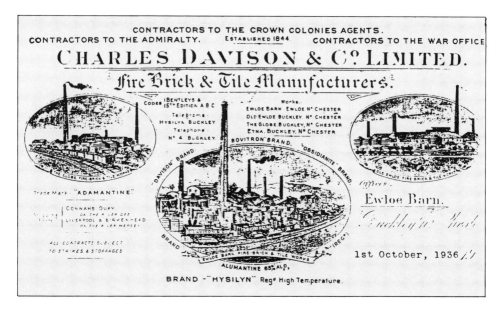

way per day (Wrexham – Old Buckley): none on Sundays. By 1868 this had become (as shown in THE WREXHAM ADVERTISER for 1st February):

	am	am	am	pm	pm
Wrexham	—	8.40	11.10	2.10	6.50*
Gwersyllt	—	8.47	11.17	2.17	6.57
Cefnybedd	—	8.54	11.24	2.24	7.04
Caergwrle	—	9.05	11.40	2.35	7.15
Hope Junction	—	9.12	11.50	2.42	7.22
[2]Hope (LNWR) arr	—	9.47	12.42	3.02	8.42
[3]Mold (bus) arr	—	10.05	1.00	3.20	8.00
Buckley	—	9.20	12.00	2.50	7.30

	am	am	pm	pm	pm
Buckley	7.30	10.00	1.00	5.30	—
[3]Mold (bus) arr	8.23	11.37	1.53	6.23	—
[2]Hope (LNWR) arr	8.10	11.13	—	6.10	—
Hope Junction	7.37	10.07	1.07	5.37	—
Caergwrle	7.44	10.14	1.14	5.44	—
Cefnybedd	7.54	10.25	1.25	5.55	—
Gwersyllt	8.02	10.32	1.32	6.02	—
Wrexham	8.10	10.40	1.40	6.10	—

*'This train on Saturdays will leave Wrexham at 8.30 pm.'
[2]Presumably horse-bus connection to Hope Village – timetable does not clarify.
[3]Bus connection – timetable clarifies.
All trains 1, 2, 3 classes.

It will be evident that even with only one locomotive and rake of carriages, it was possible to run such a timetable. The engine began and ended the day at Buckley, so driver, fireman and guard must have been based there rather than Wrexham. It is assumed the engines working Buckley – Connah's Quay were stabled overnight at Connah's Quay.

Ten years later (February 1878) it was still possible to economise with locomotives and carriages: the timings were often a little smarter: Bridge End (later Caergwrle), Caergwrle (as in 1868, later to become Hope Village), Penyffordd (opened August 1877) and Hope (earlier Hope Junction and still later, Hope Exchange) now follow on after Cefnybedd, not only making for some careful thought for anyone revisiting the line after a decade, but adding two extra stops for the enginemen. The engine roster now begins in Wrexham and BRADSHAW states:

M	DOWN	Gov	Morn	Aft	Aft	Aft	Aft*
—	Wrexham *dep*	7.00	9.40	12.05	2.25	5.35	8.40
1¾	Gwersyllt	7.05	9.45	12.10	2.30	5.40	8.45
3¾	Cefnybedd	7.12	9.52	12.17	2.37	5.48	8.50
4¼	Bridge End	7.15	9.55	12.20	2.40	5.51	8.53
5	Caergwrle	7.18	9.58	12.23	2.43	5.55	8.57
7	Penyffordd	7.24	10.05	12.28	2.50	6.05	9.03
7¼	Hope[2]	7.26	10.07	12.29	2.55	6.10	9.05
9	Buckley	7.35	10.18	12.35	3.05	6.20	9.15

M	UP	Gov	Morn	Aft	Aft	Aft
—	Buckley	7.50	10.45	12.40	4.15	6.30
1¾	Hope[2]	8.13	11.00	12.45	4.25	6.40
2	Penyffordd	8.15	11.02	12.47	4.27	6.42
4	Caergwrle	8.22	11.09	12.53	4.33	6.47
4¾	Bridge End	8.25	11.12	12.55	4.35	6.50
5¼	Cefnybedd	8.28	11.18	12.58	4.37	6.54
7¼	Gwersyllt	8.35	11.23	1.05	4.45	7.00
9	Wrexham	8.40	11.30	1.10	4.50	7.05

*Thursdays and Saturdays only. (*Wrexham Market Days*)
[2]Exchange Platform.

From the above, the fastest run was tabled for 30 minutes, and there is a curious delay to the first Up train from Buckley which might have left Buckley a little later without losing its 'Government' or 'Parliamentary' status.

At this period, Cartwright was Manager of this line and the Denbigh, Ruthin & Corwen Railway.

Going ahead to August 1887, there had not been much change except two Down and two Up trains ceased and began, respectively, at Hope Junction: and there were some strange differences in running times between stations.

DOWN	morn	morn	noon	aft	aft	aft	SO aft
Wrexham	7.10	9.55	12.00	2.20	5.45	7.25	9.20
Gwersyllt	7.15	10.00	12.05	2.25	5.50	7.30	9.25
Cefnybedd	7.21	10.07	12.12	2.32	5.57	7.37	9.32
Bridge End	7.24	10.10	12.15	2.35	6.00	7.40	9.33
Caergwrle	7.27	10.13	12.17	2.38	6.03	7.42	9.35
Penyffordd	7.34	10.20	12.23	2.45	6.10	7.48	9.42
Hope Junction	7.35	10.22	12.25	2.47	6.12	7.50	—
Buckley	7.50	10.37	—	3.00	6.20	—	9.50

UP	morn	morn	noon	aft	SO aft	aft	aft
Buckley	7.53	10.45	—	3.05	5.25	6.25	—
Hope Junction	8.05	11.00	12.45	3.12	—	6.40	8.00
Penyffordd	8.07	11.02	12.47	3.14	5.35	6.42	8.02
Caergwrle	8.15	11.09	12.54	3.21	5.43	6.47	8.07
Bridge End	8.18	11.12	12.57	3.24	5.47	6.49	8.10
Cefnybedd	8.21	11.15	1.00	3.27	5.50	6.52	8.12
Gwersyllt	8.30	11.23	1.05	3.35	5.55	6.57	8.18
Wrexham	8.37	11.30	1.12	3.42	6.03	7.05	8.25

SO = Saturdays only.

Note: Hope Junction: the meticulous will note this appears in the *Passenger Timetables* of 1868, only subsequently to be renamed Hope. Now in 1887 it appears along with Penyffordd as the name has been applied to the high level interchange station for the LNWR. In due course it became Hope Exchange. Caution is necessary. For the *Working Timetables* and the vernacular, Hope Junction was the divergence onto the LNWR at Penyffordd.

This table might involve some smart engine run-round times at Buckley, light engine or empty stock movements, and apparently two engines and carriage sets on a Saturday when the trains would pass each other between Cefnybedd and Gwersyllt.

For the opening of the Brymbo Branch to passengers THE WREXHAM ADVERTISER for 27th July, 1889 carried this advertisement:

WREXHAM MOLD & CONNAH'S QUAY RAILWAY

Moss & Pentre, Plas Power
and
Brymbo Branch

The above branch will be OPENED for PASSENGER TRAFFIC
on
THURSDAY AUGUST 1st 1889

Trains will run as under all 1st and 3rd Classes
3rd Class tickets issued to Wrexham Central by every train. From Brymbo
6*d.*, from Plas Power, Moss & Pentre 3½*d.*

	morn	morn	aft	aft	SATS. ONLY aft	aft
Wrexham Central	8.35	11.40	4.00	8.00	6.00	10.00
Wrexham Exchange	8.38	11.43	4.03	8.03	6.03	—
Moss & Pentre	8.46	11.51	4.11	8.11	6.13	10.14
Plas Power	8.51	11.56	4.16	8.16	6.18	10.20
Brymbo	8.58	12.03	4.23	8.23	6.25	10.28

Brymbo	8.00	10.40	3.25	6.35	5.00	8.35
Plas Power	8.07	10.47	3.32	6.42	5.07	8.42
Moss & Pentre	8.12	10.52	3.37	6.47	5.14	8.47
Wrexham Exchange	8.20	11.00	3.45	6.55	5.22	—
Wrexham Central	8.23	11.03	3.48	6.58	5.25	8.57

Westminster Buildings
July 1889

T. Cartwright
Manager

Note: the loco began and ended the day at Brymbo.

By September 1891 the table had expanded to:

	morn	morn	MON aft	SAT aft	SX aft	SAT aft	SAT aft	SAT aft	aft	SAT aft	SAT aft	SAT aft	SAT aft	MON aft
Wrexham Central	8.30	11.40	2.00	4.00	4.40	5.05	6.05	7.35	8.05	8.35	9.05	9.35	10.05	10.30
Wrexham Exchange	8.33	11.43	2.03	4.03	4.43	—	6.08	—	—	—	—	—	—	—
Moss & Pentre	8.41	11.51	2.11	4.11	4.51	5.16	6.16	7.46	8.16	8.46	9.16	9.46	10.16	10.41
Plas Power	8.46	11.56	2.16	4.16	4.56	5.21	6.21	7.51	8.21	8.51	9.21	9.51	10.21	10.46
Brymbo	8.53	12.03	2.23	4.23	5.03	5.28	6.28	7.58	8.28	8.58	9.28	9.58	10.28	10.53

	morn	morn	MON aft	aft	SAT aft	aft	aft	SAT aft	SAT aft	SAT aft	SAT aft
Brymbo	8.00	10.40	1.00	3.20	4.35	5.35	6.35	8.05	8.35	9.05	9.35
Plas Power	8.07	10.47	1.07	3.27	4.42	5.42	6.42	8.11	8.41	9.11	9.42
Moss & Pentre	8.12	10.52	1.12	3.32	4.47	5.47	6.47	8.16	8.46	9.16	9.46
Wrexham Exchange	8.20	11.00	1.20	3.40	4.55	5.55	6.55	—	—	—	—
Wrexham Central	8.23	11.03	1.23	3.43	4.58	5.58	6.58	8.28	8.57	9.28	9.57

WREXHAM, MOLD, & CONNAH'S QUAY
RAILWAY.

From 1st OCTOBER, 1900,
AND UNTIL FURTHER NOTICE.

Which includes all the alterations and additions which have appeared in previous weekly or monthly alteration notices since the issue of the Working Book. dated last July.

Working Time Table
OF
PASSENGER, GOODS, and MINERAL TRAINS.

This Table is printed for the guidance of the Company's Servants only, who are required to use their best exertions to enable the Trains to keep the times stated therein, but are not to guarantee the Arrival or Departure of Passenger or Goods Trains at those times or at any particular time.

When the times of Arrival and Departure are not stated, the times specified in the Time Tables are the Departures from the Stations. and in all cases the Trains should arrive in sufficient time to enable the work to be done, in order to leave the Station at the appointed hour. Italic Figures thus (*12 3*) denote passing times.

The time of arrival and departure of Goods Trains at Stations and Sidings is only approximate, and whenever practicable the Trains must be got away earlier. When short of a load, the Trains must run between point and point in less than the booked running time.

If before new Working Bills are issued, any man's Bill should be worn out, application must at once be made to the Head of the department for a New Book.

Stations printed in large type are Staff or Crossing Stations, and lines thus (‾‾) across the columns denote that trains are appointed to meet and pass each other on the Single Line Sections at those Stations.

Each Station Master is requested to examine and compare the Sheet Time Bills issued every month (so far as his own Station is concerned) and must correct any inaccuracies before issuing the Bills to the Public. All Inaccuracies must be immediately reported to this Office.

Figures in bold type thus—1, 2, 3, 4, &c., at the head of Columns are for the guidance of Breaksmen as to their working after leaving starting point, On Saturdays, the working somewhat differs owing to the passenger trains, particulars of which will be found in the foot notes.

Explanation of References.

R R Runs when required.	**W R** Will Stop when required to put off or pick up.
M O Mondays only.	
S O Saturdays only.	
M E Mondays excepted.	**M S** Mondays and Saturdays excepted.
A Stops to attach only.	**S E** Saturdays excepted.
M S O Mondays & Saturdays only.	**D** Stops to detach only.

NOTICE.—For General Information and Special Instructions, see issue of Appendix to this Table, dated October 1895.

T. CARTWRIGHT,
General Manager.

GATEWEN, PLAS POWER, BRYMBO, VRON, BRANCHES.

SINGLE LINE worked under the Train Staff and Permit and Block Telegraph Regulations.
STAFF STATIONS Brymbo (Main Line), South Junction, Brymbo West Junction, Brymbo (Main Line) North Junction, Moss and Pentre, Plas Power A Cabin, Plas Power B Cabin, Brymbo Station, Vron Colliery and Steel Works.

M—Mineral Trains.

WEEK DAYS.

UP TRAINS.	1	2	3	4	5	6	7	8	9	10	11	12	13	14	15	16	17
	M 3	M 2	M 4	pass 2	M 3	M 2	M 3	M 2	pass 3	M 4	M 2	M 3	M 2	M 3	M 2	M 3	pass 2
VRON COLLIERY dep.	a.m	a.m	a.m		a.m	a.m	a.m	a.m	a.m	a.m	p.m	p.m	p.m	p.m	p.m	p.m	p.m
Brymbo Steel Works		7 10				8 45 9 55				10 50			1 30 3 0				3 10
Station arr.														3 0			
Station dep.		7 20											1 40				3 5
PLASPOWER B Cabin	7 5			7 30		8 28	9 17 10 29	10 35		10 40 11 0 12 15		1 35	1 45		3 25		3 10
A Cabin										11 15 12 25							
Station						8 32											3 17
New Broughton Coll. Sid.						8 36		10 51				12 15		1 55			
MOSS & PENTRE						9 45	9 45		11 15			12 25 2 5			3 50		
Gatewen Junction								11 0									
BRYMBO West Jc. pass								11 3									
North Jc. arr.				7 50		8 45											3 30
South Jc. dp.						8 48											3 33
Wrexham (Exchange) arr.																	
(Central) arr.																	

UP TRAINS.	18	19	20	21	22	23	24	25	26	27	28	29	30	31	32	33	34
	M SO 2	M SO 3	M 4	M SESO 2	pass SESO 2	pass 2				pass SO MS 3	pass SO 3	M 3	SO MS 3	SO 3		Sun. night SO SO 3	SO SO 3
VRON COLLIERY dep.																	
Brymbo Steel Works	3 25		3 35 4 30		4 40	5 25 5 30 6 30				8 30 8 30 9	0 9 35			9 46		10 20 11 10	
Station arr.																	10 5 10 55
Station dep.				4 0	4 55 5 40					8 37 9 7		9 42				10 20 11 10	
PLASPOWER B Cabin			4 37		5 37 6 37						9 11			9 31		10 25 11 13	
A Cabin																	
Station																	
New Broughton Coll. Sid.				4 11 4 41		5 41 6 41				8 41							
MOSS & PENTRE						5 0 6 0				8 53		9 28					
Gatewen Junction																	
BRYMBO West Jc. pass				4 17		5 30 6 15				8 36		9 31					
North Jc. arr.																	
South Jc. dp.			4 50		4 53	5 06 6 0				8 52		9 22 9 37					
Wrexham (Exchange) arr.						5 36 6 3											
(Central) arr.																	

Tickets of Up Passenger Trains to be collected at Wrexham Exchange with the exception of Nos. 27, 29, and 31, Second ... which must be collected at Moss and Pentre.

No. 1 Up ... Traffic, including Loco. Coal for sheds, from Brymbo North Junction to be worked by Engine available on No. 1 Up. Engine working to Wrexham. Clayton's Brick Yard to be shunted by Engine and Guard of No. 2 Down.

Engine of No. 8 Down Mineral ...

Nos. 9 and 17—Engine to return to Brymbo Station attached to No. 3 down when practicable.

No. 10 on arrival at Brymbo North Junction to work to instructions from Brymbo North Junction

Engine and men of Nos. 28 and 30 Up to make trips as required.

Coaches of Nos. 33 on Saturdays to be put off at Cobden Mill Siding.

☞ The Mineral Trains and Times on these Branches vary according to state of Traffic, and the Trains will at times work as required, Station Masters, Signalmen, and Guards will therefore be responsible for so arranging the Train Staff that no detention will take place to Passenger Trains.

GATEWEN, PLAS POWER, BRYMBO, & VRON BRANCHES.

SINGLE LINE worked under the Train Staff and Permit and Block Telegraph Regulations.
STAFF STATIONS Brymbo (Main Line), South Junction, Brymbo West Junction, Brymbo (Main Line), North Junction, Moss and Pentre, Plas Power A Cabin, Plas Power B Cabin, Brymbo Station, Vron Colliery and Steel Works.

M—Mineral Trains.

☞ See Note bottom Page 3.

WEEK DAYS.

Distance from Wrexham (Cent.) M C	DOWN TRAINS.	1	2	3	4	5	6	7	8	9	10	11	12	13	14	15	16
		M 2	M 4	M 3		M 3	M 2	M 2	M 3	M 3	M 2	M 3	M 2	M 4	M 3	M 2	M 3
.49	Wrexham (Central) dep.	a.m	a.m	a.m	a.m	a.m	a.m	a.m	a.m	a.m	a.m	p.m	p.m	p.m	p.m	p.m	p.m
1.35	(Exchange)						9 0					11 45		1 0	1 45		2 45
1.76	BRYMBO South Jc.			WR			9 3					11 48			WR		WR
2.5	West Jc.																
2.51	North Jc.	6 15 6 40	7 25	WR		7 50			10 10		11 40 11 50		1 0 1 45				3 0
2.61	Gatewen Junction			WR			9 11		11 56			12 1			WR	1 55	
3.17	MOSS & PENTRE			WR 7 0													
3.48	New Broughton Coll. Sdg.	6 35			7 30		9 16			12 1			1 2	2 15 2 35			
4.69	Plas Power Station				8 0		9 23	9 30	10 25	12 8		12 45 1 9		1 5	2 20		2 45
5.8	A Cabin																
	B Cabin						9 40		10 36			1 5				2 25	
5.49	BRYMBO Station arr/dep																
	Steel Works arr																
	VRON COLLIERY arr																

Distance M C	DOWN TRAINS.	17	18	19	20	21	22	23	24	25	26	27	28	29	30	31	32
		pass SOSE 2	pass M SOSE 2	pass M SE 2	M 2	pass M SESO 2	pass M SOSE 2	M 2	ME				pass SOSO 3	pass SOSO 3	pass SOSO 3	pass SOSO 3	pass SOSO 3
.49	Wrexham (Central) dep.																
1.35	(Exchange)		4 0 10		4 40	4 50	5 0 6 0		8 0	8 30 8 39		9 0 9 35	10 25				
1.76	BRYMBO South Jc.		4 34 13			5 36 3	5 0 6 0		8 3				10 30				
2.5	West Jc.	4 13				4 50		5 50		8 48							
2.51	North Jc.	WR 7 0		6 45			6 11		8 11			9 18 8 46 9 18 9 46 10 36					
2.61	Gatewen Junction						6 11										
3.17	MOSS & PENTRE					4 14 21		6 16 6 6	8 11			8 46 5 19 16 9 5 10 41					
3.48	New Broughton Coll. Sdg.			7 30		4 16 4 26		6 16 6 0	8 16			8 46 5 19 16 9 5 10 41					
4.69	Plas Power Station				4 33	4 23 4 33		6 10	8 23			8 52 8 59 9 23 9 58 10 48					
5.8	A Cabin		8 0			4 40		5 0									
	B Cabin					5 0											
5.49	BRYMBO Station arr/dep																
	Steel Works arr																
	VRON COLLIERY arr																

No. 3 if not fully loaded for Vron Colliery, to make up Train with traffic for Brymbo Steel Works, detaching same at Vron Junction. This train must leave Brymbo Junction to time.

No. 6 on arrival at Brymbo to make trip from Vron Junc. or Plas Power to Brymbo Steel Works when required.

No. 14 Down to work to No. 23 Up and must not be delayed.

No. 21 Down to work No. 23 Up ... Saturday ...

No. 23 Down to be extended to Brymbo Steel Works when necessary.

Tickets of Down Passenger Trains to be collected at the respective Branch Stations with the exception of Brymbo Tickets of Nos. 17, 21, and 22, on Saturdays, which must be collected at Plas Power, and forwarded under cover to Brymbo.

No. 24, 30, and 33 Down to be worked by Engine and men of No. 23 Up Branch Train (M E excepted)

Nos. 26, 30, and 33 Down and corresponding Up Trains (Saturdays only) to be worked by Engine and Guard of No. 23 Up Branch Train.

No. 28 and 31 Down and corresponding Up Trains to be worked by Engine, Coaches, and Guard of No. 42 Up Main Line train.

MAIN LINE.

WEEK DAYS.

DOWN TRAINS

Distances. M. c.	Station		1 Goods	2 Goods	3 Engine and Brake	4 Goods	5 Goods	6 Passenger	7 Passenger	8 Goods⁴	9 Goods⁶	10	11	12 Passenger	13 Passenger	14 Passenger
—	Wrexham (Central)	dep.	a m 5 15	a m	a m 5 45	a m 5 30	a m	a m	a m	a m	a m			a m 7 25	a m	a m
48	(Exchange)				6 50	6 35		6 55			WR			7 28		
1 35	Brymbo South Junction	{ arr. / dep.			3 50 6 25				7 2		A			7 32		
2 4	Brymbo North Junction	{ arr. / dep.				6 40										
2 29	Gwersyllt								7 7					7 37		
3 19	Ffrwd Junction								7 9					7 39		
4 26	Cefnybedd								7 12					7 42		
4 73	Caergwrle Castle, Llay	{ arr. / dep.												7 47		
5	Hall and Lassells							6 47 7 17						7 48		
5 44	Hope Village					5 35		7 29						7 49		
7 38	Penyffordd Junction	{ arr. / dep.						6 50 7 32			7 53			7 52		
7 64	Hope Exchange													7 56		
8 55	Buckley Junction	pass.												8 4		
8 68	Buckley Junct. Station	dep.												8 5		
10 64	Hawarden													8 12		8 49
11 38	Aston Hall Junction													8 14		8 54
12 79	Connah's Quay & Shotton Station													8 18		8 9
13 12	Hawarden Bridge Junc.	pass.												8 24		9 0
14 27	Connah's Quay Docks	arr.												8 34		9 10
18 69	Burton Point													8 39		9 15
—	Neston and Parkgate															9 21
22	Heswall Hills													8 45		
25 69	Storeton															
27 59	Upton															
27 39	Bidston															
28 37	Liscard and Poulton	arr.														
29 27	Seacombe	arr.														

Engine of this train works home as traffic permits.
8 30 a.m. ex Chester.

No. 1 to clear all traffic from Transfer Siding Wrexham, for Penyffordd, and places beyond.
Wagons for Connah's Quay direction to be marshalled together.
Engine to work No. 7, to leave shed 6 25 a.m., and run light to Central. Guard to book on at Ground Frame No. 2, 6 25 a.m.
No. 12 may attach Cattle Traffic at Hawarden when required for Birkenhead Docks.

MAIN LINE—Continued.

WEEK DAYS.

DOWN TRAINS.

Distances. M. c.	Station		15 Passenger	16 Passenger	17 Goods	18 Passenger	19 Minerals⁶ (Goods and)	20 G.C.⁹ (Goods &) Minerals	21 Minerals⁹	22 Passenger	23 Passenger	24 Passenger	25 Mineral (Goods and)	26 Minerals⁹	27 Passenger	28 Minerals⁹
—	Wrexham (Central)	dep.	a m 9 09	a m 9 09	a m	a m	a m	a m 1030	a m 1130	a m 1145	a m 1145	a m	noon	noon	p m 1248	p m 1 15
48	(Exchange)		9 39	9 39			WR	WR 1151	1148	1148				1251	
1 35	Brymbo South Junction	arr.		8 10	5 10		1020	1055			12 0		1240	1255	
2 4	Brymbo North Junction	dep.		5 3			1110					1250		
2 29	Gwersyllt		9 12	9 12		10 7	WR	A	For Brymbo.				5		
3 19	Ffrwd Junction													1 0	WR
4 26	Cefnybedd		9 17	9 17	WR 1012	WR	A					1 15			
4 73	Caergwrle Castle, Llay	dep.		D	014	WR	A					1 25	1 25	2 WR	
5	Hall and Lassells			1 49	016								1 35		
5 44	Hope Village		9 24	9 24	1021	WR	A							8 2	5 0
7 38	Penyffordd Junction	dep.	9 25 9 26	1022			1 5 1145 1240	1135				1 5	50	
7 64	Hope Exchange			1023								1 16		
8 55	Buckley Junction	pass.	9 29	9 29	1026		A						19 3	15
8 68	Buckley Junct. Station	dep.	9 35	9 35	1033		A						2 10	25 3 30
10 64	Hawarden		9 41	9 41	1039		A						WR	31
11 38	Aston Hall Junction		9 42	9 42	1040	1235							WR	
12 79	Connah's Quay & Shotton Station	pass.							2 30				WR 32 4	25
13 12	Hawarden Bridge Junc.	pass.	9 49	9 49	1047		1148				2 30 1	2 30	32 4 35
14 27	Connah's Quay Docks	arr.	9 54	9 54	1052		1153						39	
18 69	Burton Point		10 5	10 5	1058		1159					WR	44	
—	Neston and Parkgate		10 10	10 10	11 8		12 4					WR	50	
22	Heswall Hills		10 15	10 15	1112		1214					WR	55	
25 69	Storeton				1116							WR	0	
27 59	Upton		10 22	10 22	1120		1221					3 30	2	
27 39	Bidston												2	
28 37	Liscard and Poulton	arr.											2 10	
29 27	Seacombe	arr.												

No. 17 to clear wagons from Wrexham and Ellesmere Line (Neck Siding), also other wagons there may be at Central, for the stations train is marked to stop at, also from Wrexham Exchange as the wagons stand, the same to be marshalled at Brymbo North Junction. Will also stop at Gwersyllt, Cefnybedd, and Hope Village when required to put out transhipts, and shunt whenever necessary for No. 20 Down to pass.

No. 20 Down must leave to time, Yardsman and Guard will be responsible for seeing this carried out.

No. 20 to attach at Brymbo South Junction, North Junction, Ffrwd Junction, and Llay Hall, traffic for stations and sidings between Hawarden Bridge (Wrexham Junction), Chester (Northgate), inclusive.

No. 26 to shunt at Ffrwd Junction for No. 27 to pass, and stop at Hawarden Bridge (Wrexham Junction) when required to attach, if load permits.

It is important that Traffic for Storeton and Burton Point from Connah's Quay and Shotton, Buckley Junction and other W. M. and C. Quay stations be worked by No. 26 Down.

MAIN LINE—Continued.

WEEK DAYS.

Distance M. c.	DOWN TRAINS.	29 Mineral 8	30 Goods 5	31 Passenger	32 Passenger	33 Passenger	34	35	36	37	38	39	40	41	42
		p m	p m	p m	p m	p m									
	Wrexham (Central) .....dep.	2 30			3 5										
48	" (Exchange)	2 45	2 45		3 8										
1 33	Brymbo South Junction ...		3 0												
2 4	Brymbo North Junction { arr.		3 15												
	{ dep.	3 15			3 12										
2 29	Gwersyllt	3 30													
3 19	Ffrwd Junction { arr.	WR 3 33	WR 3 35												
	{ dep.														
4 26	Cefnybedd				3 17										
4 73	Caergwrle Castle, Llay { arr.	WR	WR												
4 73	Hall and Lassells .... dep.	WR	WR		3 19										
5 44	Hope Village				3 21										
5 38	Penyffordd Junction { arr.	3 40	3 4		3 26										
	{ dep.	4 30	4 30		3 27										
7 64	Hope Exchange { pass				3 28										
	{ dep.														
8 55	Buckley Junction				3 31										
8 68	Buckley Junction Station dep.				3 36										
10 64	Hawarden														
11 38	Aston Hall Junction														
12 79	Connah's Quay & Shot- { ton Station				3 42										
13 12	Hawarden Bridge Junct. pass				3 43										
14 27	Connah's Quay Docks.... arr.														
	Burton Point .... dep.			3 50	3 19										
18 69	Neston and Parkgate..			3 56	3 24										
	Heswall Hills														
25 69	Storeton			4 3	3 30										
25 39	Upton			4 13	3 40										
39	Bidston			4 18	3 45										
37	Liscard and Poulton			4 24	3 51										
29 27	Seacombe .... arr.			3 5 14 24											

No. 29 to return from Penyffordd on Saturdays in time to work out No. 81.

When train for No. 30 is not ready at Wrexham Central, Engine and Guard must run to Wrexham Exchange with any wagons for that point. Yardsmen must have the wagons ready.

MAIN LINE—Continued.

WEEK DAYS.

Distance M. c.	DOWN TRAINS.	43 44 Mineral 11	45 46 Passenger	47 Passenger	48 49 Mineral 4	50 51	52 Passenger	53 Passenger	54	55 Passenger	56 Mineral 8
		R R — p m	S O S E — p m p m	S O S E — p m p m	p m	S O — p m	S O — p m		p m	S E — p m
	Wrexham (Central) .....dep.		4 04 10				5 0			5 30	
48	" (Exchange)		4 04 13				5 3			5 33	
1 33	Brymbo South Junction ...	3 15	4 64 16				5 6				
2 4	Brymbo North Junction { arr.	3 40		4 20	4 20						5 43
	{ dep.									5 37	
2 29	Gwersyllt	3 50									
3 19	Ffrwd Junction { arr.	4 5			WR					5 42	WR
	{ dep.										
4 26	Cefnybedd										
4 73	Caergwrle Castle, Llay { arr.	WR			WR					5 44 WR	WR
4 73	Hall and Lassells .... dep.	WR								5 47	
5 44	Hope Village										
5 38	Penyffordd Junction { arr.	4 35			4 55					5 52	
	{ dep.	4 45			6 10					5 53	6 24
7 64	Hope Exchange { pass									5 54	
	{ dep.										
8 55	Buckley Junction	WR			6 15			5 58		5 57	
8 68	Buckley Junction Station							6 3		6 3	
10 64	Hawarden	WR						6 6		6 9	
11 38	Aston Hall Junction										
12 79	Connah's Quay & Shot- { ton Station							6 14		6 10	
13 12	Hawarden Bridge Junct. pass	5 35						6 19		6 17	
14 27	Connah's Quay Docks.... arr.							6 24		6 22	
	Burton Point .... dep.									6 28	
18 69	Neston and Parkgate..							6 30		6 33	
	Heswall Hills									6 40	
25 69	Storeton									6 45	
25 39	Upton									6 48	
39	Bidston									6 52	
37	Liscard and Poulton	6 10									
29 27	Seacombe .... arr.										

For Brymbo. 3 40 p.m. ex Chester. 3 25 p m ex Vron Colliery.

No. 44 to run when required, and to leave earlier or later, as ordered out by Traffic Inspector.
No. 49 to be extended to Buckley Junction on Saturdays only to work No. 43 Up.
No. 56 to be extended to Bidston when required.

MAIN LINE—Continued.

WEEK DAYS. — DOWN TRAINS.

(Trains 57–70)

Distance	DOWN TRAINS	57 3 Mineral	58 Passenger	59 Passenger	60 Passenger	61 3 Mineral	62 Goods	63 2 Mineral	64 G.L.C. Goods	65 Goods	66 9 Goods	67 Passenger	68 Passenger	69 Passenger	70 Passenger
M. C.		S O S O	S O							S E		S O			M E
	Wrexham (Central) ... dep.	p m	6 0	6 3	6 6	p m	7 15	7 25			6 55	7 30			8 0
48	(Exchange) "											7 33			8 3
1 35	Brymbo South Junction "	5 45					7 25	7 30							8 5
2 4	Brymbo North Junction { arr. / dep.														
2	Gwersyllt ... arr.					6 5		6 30				7 37			
3 19	Ffrwd Junction { arr. / dep.					6 15									
4	Cefnybedd "					6 25		WR				WR			
4 26	Caergwrle Castle, Llay arr.					6 35		WR				7 42			
5 73	Hall and Lassells ... dep.					6 43						7 44			
5 44	Hope Village ... { arr. / dep.					6 53		7 0		7 35					
7 38	Penyffordd Station and Junction { arr. / dep.				6 10	7 5	6 15	7 30	6 20						
7	Hope Exchange { arr. / dep.											8 10			
8 55	Buckley Junction														
8 68	Buckley Junction Station				6 10										
10 64	Hawarden														
11 38	Aston Hall Junction				6 16										
12 79	Connah's Quay & Shotton Station				6 17										
13 12	Hawarden Bridge Junct. pass.											8 30			
14 27	Connah's Quay Docks ... dep.														
18	Burton Point "														
18 69	Neston and Parkgate "														
22	Heswall Hills "														
22 69	Storeton "														
25 59	Upton "														
27	Bidston "														
28 87	Liscard and Poulton "														
29 27	Seacombe arr.														

No. 62 must shunt at Buckley Junction for No. 65 to pass, and stop at Hawarden Bridge (Wrexham Junction) when required to attach, if load permits.

No. 64 to be extended to Bidston when necessary, or make extra trip Brymbo North to Brymbo North Junction when required.

No. 65 to stop at places marked to pick up traffic for Chester and beyond. The trucks must be placed together ready for attaching, to avoid shunting and delay to train.

Loaded Traffic of Foreign Company's Empties for Chester direction, arriving Wrexham by Cambrian Goods at 6 30 p.m. must be worked forward by No. 65 or 79.

No. 68 to be worked by Engine, Coaches and Guard of the 6 30 p.m. Brymbo to Wrexham on Mondays, and by Engine, Coaches, and Guard of No. 43 Up ex Buckley Jct. on Saturdays.

MAIN LINE—Continued

WEEK DAYS. — DOWN TRAINS.

(Trains 71–84)

Distance	DOWN TRAINS	71 Passenger	72 Passenger	73 Passenger	74 Passenger	75 Passenger	76 Passenger	77 Passenger	78 8 Mineral	79 G.C. Goods	80 Passenger	81 Passenger	82 Passenger	83 Passenger	84 Passenger
M. C.			S O	M O				M S	M S		S O			S O	S O
	Wrexham (Central) ... dep.		8 30	8 35	8 40		8 45	8 48			9 0	9 30		9 35	10 25
48	(Exchange) "			8 35	8 40										10 30
1 35	Brymbo South Junction "														
2 4	Brymbo North Junction arr.										9 15				
2	Gwersyllt arr.						8 52		8 55	A	5	9 37			
3 19	Ffrwd Junction dep.														
4	Cefnybedd "						8 57		WR A			9 43			
4 26	Caergwrle Castle, Llay arr.						8 59	WR	WR	A		9 46			
5 73	Hall and Lassells ... dep.								8 59 WR	A		9 49			
5 44	Hope Village arr.														
7 38	Penyffordd Station and Junction { arr. / dep.						9 4		9 15	A		9 54			
7	Hope Exchange dep.						9 6					9 56			
8 55	Buckley Junction						9 15					9 59			
8 68	Buckley Junction Station														
10 64	Hawarden						9 21					10 6			
11 38	Aston Hall Junction														
12 79	Connah's Quay & Shotton Station						9 22					10 12			
13 12	Hawarden Bridge Junc. pass.						9 30			10 15		10 13			
14 27	Connah's Quay Docks ... dep.						9 34								
18	Burton Point "						9 41								
18 69	Neston and Parkgate "						9 47								
22	Heswall Hills "						9 52								
22 69	Storeton "						9 57								
25 59	Upton "						10 1								
27	Bidston "						10 5								
28 87	Liscard and Poulton "														
29 27	Seacombe arr.														

Inspector Lawrence must wire Mr. Davies, Bidston, as soon as possible each day the quantity of traffic on hand for that direction, and whether necessary for the 8 0 p.m. ex Bidston to run as far as Wrexham end of the Section is concerned.

No. 81 on Saturdays to be worked by Engine and Guard of No. 29 Down.

MAIN LINE.

UP TRAINS — WEEK DAYS.

Distances			1 Goods	2 Goods	3 Shunting Engine	4 Passenger	5 C.L.C. Express Goods	6 gP Passenger	7 gP Passenger	8 Passenger	9 Goods & Min. Empties	10 Goods & Min. Empties	11 G.C. Goods	12 Passenger	13 Passenger	14 Passenger
M. C.			a m	a m	a m	a m	a m	a m	a m	a m	a m	a m	a m	a m	a m	a m
	Seacombe	dep.				7 15						8 6			9 55	10 20
70	Liscard and Poulton					7 21						8 9			9 59	10 24
1 68	Bidston					7 25						8 13			10 2	10 27
3 48	Upton					7 31						8 19			10 6	10 31
6 38	Storeton					7 40						8 23			10 12	10 42
10 38	Neston and Parkgate					7 46						8 29			10 25	10 49
	Heswall Hills														10 27	10 54
	Burton Point															
	Connah's Quay Docks						7 20		8 39 55					10 34		
	Hawarden Bridge Junc.	pass														
	Connah's Quay & Shotton Station	dep.						8 41					10 36		
	Aston Hall Junction															
18 42	Hawarden							8 49					10 42		
20 39	Buckley Junction Station			6 10		D		8 55			D		10 48		
22 32	Buckley Junction	arr.						8 10					10 49		
21 42	Hope Exchange	dep.						8 10					10 50		
21 65	Penyffordd Junction	arr.	6 15					8 17					10 52		
23 60	Hope Village	dep.						8 11		8 40 9 0			10 56		
	Caergwrle Castle, Llay	arr.								9 4					
24 57	Hall and Lassells	dep.						8 20		9 6			10 58		
25	Cefnybedd							8 23		9 9			11 1		
26 11	Ffrwd Junction	arr.							WR	9 13	WR		11 5		
		dep.													
27 1	Gwersyllt		6 45					8 28			D				
27 26	Brymbo North Junction	dep.	6 40 6 50							9 20		1056			
27 75	Brymbo South Junction	dep.						8 33	8 41	9 17		10 5 11 3			
28 52	Wrexham (Exchange)	dep.						8 36	8 45		D	11 2			
29 27	Wrexham (Central)	arr.							8 48			11 12			

Buckley Branch. — For Chester. — 7 0 a.m. ex Chester. — From Brymbo.

No. 2 to work Wrexham Goods traffic only. London or other traffic arriving Hope Junction too late for this train to be picked up by No. 9, which must be extended to Wrexham when necessary.

Engine of No. 2 on arrival at Wrexham Central to return to Wrexham Exchange, pick up wagons from Transfer Siding, working same to Central, afterwards returning to Ground Frame to do what shunting is necessary at Crispin Lane and Rhosddu Sidings, Engine then to shed.

No. 3 to leave Shed 6 0 a.m., and pick up Goods Wagons at Rhosddu.

No. 5 stops at Hawarden and Buckley Junction to put off trainslips as well as detach wagons when required.

No. 9 when extended to Wrexham Central with Goods Traffic must not be delayed, but returned to Brymbo North Junction all speed.

MAIN LINE—Continued.

DOWN TRAINS — WEEK DAYS & SUNDAYS.

Distances			WEEK DAYS 85 / 86 / 87 / 88 Goods and Mineral		SUNDAYS 1 Passenger	2 Passenger	3 Passenger	4 Passenger	5 Passenger	6 Passenger	7 Passenger	8 Passenger	9 Passenger	10
M. C.			p m		a m	a m	a m	p m	p m	p m	p m	p m	p m	p m
	Wrexham (Central)	dep.			8 50						5 45			
48	(Exchange)													
1 35	Brymbo South Junction													
2 4	Brymbo North Junction	arr.	10 20										
		dep.	10 20		8 57						5 52			
2 29	Gwersyllt													
3 19	Ffrwd Junction	arr.	10 30										
		dep.	10 40		9 2						5 57			
4 26	Cefnybedd													
4 73	Caergwrle Castle, Llay	arr.	10 50		9 6						6 2			
	Hall and Lassells													
5 44	Hope Village		11 0		9 11						6 7			
7 38	Penyffordd Junction	arr.	11 20										
		dep.	11 30										
7 64	Hope Exchange	dep.			9 15						6 11			
8 55	Buckley Junction		11 55		9 21						6 17			
8 63	Buckley Junction Station													
10 41	Hawarden				9 27						6 23			
	Aston Hall Junction													
12 29	Connah's Quay & Shotton	pass	WR		9 28						6 24			
		arr.	12 25										
	Connah's Quay Docks													
13 12	Hawarden Bridge Junc.	pass					9 35 10 23			5 20	6 36	8 31		
	Burton Point						9 40 10 34			5 33	6 42	8 42		
18 60	Neston and Parkgate	dep.	WR		9 46 10 39			5 37	6 47	8 47		
	Heswall Hills		WR		9 51 10 44			5 42	6 57	8 57		
22 59	Storeton		WR		9 55 10 49			5 47	7 4	9 4		
25 39	Upton		WR		10 3							
27 39	Bidston		1 10		10 7 10 55		5 53					
37 37	Liscard and Poulton												
29 27	Seacombe	arr.											

8 13 p.m. ex Chester. — 8 0 p.m. ex Chester. — 10 5 a.m. ex Chester.

MAIN LINE—Continued

WEEK DAYS.

(Right-hand table, columns 29–42)

Col.	Type
29	Goods and Mineral Empties
30 / 31	Mineral Empties
32	Mineral Empties
33	Passenger
34	Passenger (S O)
35	Express Goods
36	Passenger
37	Goods
38	Passenger (S E)
39	Goods
40	Goods and Mineral Empties
41	Passenger (S O)
42	Passenger

UP TRAINS.

Distances	Station	
M. C.	Seacombe	dep.
	70 Liscard and Poulton	,,
1 68	Bidston	,,
3 48	Upton	,,
6 38	Storeton	,,
	Heswall Hills	,,
10 38	Neston and Parkgate	,,
	Burton Point	,,
	Connah's Quay Docks	,,
	Hawarden Bridge Junct.	pass.
	Connah's Quay & Shotton Station	dep.
	Aston Hall Junction	,,
18 42	Hawarden	,,
20 39	Buckley Junction Station	,,
20 52	Buckley Junction	,,
21 42	Hope Exchange	arr. / dep.
21 65	Penyffordd Junction	,,
23 60	Hope Village	,,
24 27	Caergwrle Castle, Llay	arr.
25 4	Hall and Lassells	dep.
	Cefnybedd	,,
26 11	Ffrwd Junction	arr. / dep.
	I Gwersyllt	,,
27 26	Brymbo North Junction	dep. / arr.
27 75	Brymbo South Junction	dep.
29 52	Wrexham (Exchange)	,,
29 27	,, ,, (Central)	arr.

No. 32 to stop at Hawarden Bridge (Wrexham Junction) when required to attach if load permits. Traffic from W. and Acton for Rhosddu and Wrexham Central to be picked up by first train working home.

No. 37 to work traffic for Cambrian system from Connah's Quay, Buckley Junction Firwd Junction, Brymbo North and South Junctions, and Wrexham Exchange.

The Traffic must be placed ready at Connah's Quay, and together at the different places, so as to be attached without delay to train.

MAIN LINE—Continued.

WEEK DAYS.

(Left-hand table, columns 15–28)

Col.	Type
15 / 16	Goods
17	Goods & Min. Empties
18	Passenger
19	Goods & Min. Empties
20	Goods & Min. Empties
21	Passenger
22	Mineral Empties
23	Passenger
24	Passenger
25	Passenger
26	Passenger
27	Passenger (For Chester)
28	Passenger (S O)

UP TRAINS.

Distances	Station	
M. C.	Seacombe	dep.
	70 Liscard and Poulton	,,
1 68	Bidston	,,
3 48	Upton	,,
6 38	Storeton	,,
	Heswall Hills	,,
10 38	Neston and Parkgate	,,
	Burton Point	,,
	Connah's Quay Docks	,,
	Hawarden Bridge Junct.	pass.
	Connah's Quay & Shotton Station	dep.
	Aston Hall Junction	,,
18 42	Hawarden	,,
20 39	Buckley Junction Station	,,
20 52	Buckley Junction	,,
21 42	Hope Exchange	arr. / dep.
21 65	Penyffordd Junction	,,
23 60	Hope Village	,,
24 27	Caergwrle Castle, Llay	arr.
25 4	Hall and Lassells	dep.
	Cefnybedd	,,
26 11	Ffrwd Junction	arr. / dep.
	I Gwersyllt	,,
27 26	Brymbo North Junction	dep. / arr.
27 75	Brymbo South Junction	dep.
28 52	Wrexham (Exchange)	arr.
29 27	,, ,, (Central)	arr.

No. 20 to attach at Brymbo North Junction when practicable, traffic for Cambrian System.

MAIN LINE—continued.

UP TRAINS — WEEK DAYS (columns 43–56)

Distance (M.C.)	UP TRAINS	43 Passenger SO p.m	44 G.C. Goods p.m	45 Mineral Empties (ex Chester) S E	46 Mineral Empties	47 Mineral Empties S O	48 Empties 3	49 Express Goods R S 2 11	50 Minerals Empties M SO	51 Passenger	52 Passenger p.m	53 Passenger p.m	54	55	56
	Seacombe .... dep.														
70	Liscard and Poulton											7 5			
68	Bidston											7 9			
3 48	Upton		3 45 p.m.				6 45					7 12			
6 38	Storeton											7 16			
	Heswall Hills											7 26			
10 38	Neston and Parkgate ...											7 37			
	Burton Point														
	Connah's Quay Docks ...		5 45									7 44			
	Hawarden Bridge Junct.											7 46			
	Connah's Quay & Shot-ton Station		D	D			D	D				7 53			
	Aston Hall Junction ...								WR 7 50	7 30		8 0			
18 42	Hawarden	6 25	D	D			D	D	7 53			8 3			
20 39	Buckley Junction Station arr. dep.	6 27 / 6 30	D	D		7 0	7 30			7 58		8 5 / 8 9			
20 52	Buckley Junction														
21 42	Hope Exchange arr. dep.		D	D		7 0		WR	8 0			8 12 / 8 15			
21 65	Penyffordd Junction dep.	6 32 / 6 37	D					WR							
23 60	Hope Village											8 19			
24 27	Caergwrle Castle, Llay / Hall and Lassells arr. dep.	6 40 / 6 43	D					WR							
25 4	Cefnybedd					7 45	8 15		8 5	8 8					
26 11	Ffrwd Junction arr. dep.	6 48	D WR			7 0			8 8			8 23			
27 1	Gwersyllt		7 30												
26 26	Brymbo North Junction arr. dep.		7 0												
27 75	Brymbo South Junction arr. dep.		7 10												
28 52	Wrexham (Exchange) dep.	6 55	D			7 35						8 26			
29 27	(Central) ... arr.	6 58	7 35												

No. 45 to work from Chester all traffic for Cambrian System. Wrexham to be advised by wire when the train is conveying such traffic. Liverpool Road, Saughall, and Wrexham Junction must advise Chester (Northgate) the number of wagons they have for this train which must be sent prepared to clear.

Coaches to form No. 43 Up to be worked from Wrexham Central to Penyffordd by No. 17 Down, thence by No. 49 to Buckley Junction.

MAIN LINE—continued.

UP TRAINS — WEEK DAYS (columns 58–71)

Distance (M.C.)	UP TRAINS	58 Passenger S O p.m	59 Goods 5 m p	60 Goods	61 Passenger	62 Goods	63 Mineral Empties 10	64 Passenger	65 Passenger	66 Empty Coaches S O	67 Empties Mineral 8	68 Empties Mineral 8	69 Passenger S S F S O	70 Engine and Brake	71 Passenger S O
	Seacombe .... dep.								9 0				1015		1130
70	Liscard and Poulton								9 4				1021		1136
1 68	Bidston								9 7				1025		1140
3 48	Upton						8 0		9 12				1031		1146
6 38	Storeton								9 18				1035		1150
	Heswall Hills								9 28				141		1156
10 38	Neston and Parkgate ...								9 33						
	Burton Point														
	Connah's Quay Docks ...						8 35		9 40						
	Hawarden Bridge Junct. pass								9 42						
	Connah's Quay & Shot-ton Station dep.														
	Aston Hall Junction ...														
18 42	Hawarden	8 30					D		9 49		9 30				
20 39	Buckley Junction Station								9 55						
20 52	Buckley Junction						D		9 57						
21 42	Hope Exchange arr.								9 58						
21 65	Penyffordd Junction arr.						D		10 0						
23 60	Hope Village								10 5						
24 27	Caergwrle Castle, Llay / Hall and Lassells arr. dep.						D		10 7						
25 4	Cefnybedd														
26 11	Ffrwd Junction arr. dep.					9 45			1012		1010	11 0			
27 1	Gwersyllt														
26 26	Brymbo North Junction arr. dep.	WR		From Brymbo	16 / 9 28					From Brymbo	1020		From Brymbo	1110	
27 75	Brymbo South Junction arr. dep.	8 46 / 8 53	8 56 / 9 31	From Brymbo	9 22		9 51			1025	11 5			1113	
28 52	Wrexham (Exchange) dep.	8 52	9 31	9 22			9 57	1018							
29 27	(Central) ... arr.														

No. 65 calls at Hope Exchange on Saturdays only.

CHESTER, NESTON, BIDSTON, SEACOMBE, AND LIVERPOOL.

STATIONS.	1 Passenger.	2 Passenger.	3 Goods.	4 Passenger.	5 Passenger.	6 Passenger.	7 Passenger.	8 Passenger.	9 Passenger.	10 Passenger.	11 Passenger.	12 Passenger.	13 Passenger.	14 Passenger.	15 Passenger.	16 Passenger.	17 Passenger.	18 Passenger.	S1 Passenger.	S2 Passenger.	S3 Passenger.	S4 Passenger.	S5 Passenger.
	2·5 a.m. ex Wrexham.				9 5 a.m. ex Wrexham.	10 0 a.m. ex Wrexham.			45 p.m. ex Wrexham.		5 p.m. ex Wrexham.		5 30 p.m. ex Wrexham.				8 45 p.m. ex Wrexham.		5 30 a.m. ex Wrexham.				4·5 p.m. ex Wrexham.
a.m.	a.m.	a.m.	a.m.	a.m.	a.m.	a.m.	p.m.	p.m.	p.m.	p.m.	p.m.	p.m.				p.m.	p.m.	a.m.	a.m.	p.m.	p.m.	p.m.
Chester (Northgate) .... dep.			8 30	10 5				1130	3 3			5 40					8 33			10 5			8 13
,, (Liverpool Road) ,,			8 32					1132	3 5								8 35			10 7			8 15
Blacon ,,			8 36					1135				5 45								10 10			8 18
Saughall ,,			8 41					1140	3 11			5 50					8 41			10 15			8 23
Hawarden Bridge, Chester Junction ..... } pass						1030																	
Burton Point .... dep.	8 12		8 49		9 49	10 47	11 48	1 39	3 19	3 50		5 58	6 17				8 49	9 30	9 35	10 23	5 20	6 31	8 31
Neston and Parkgate .... ,,	8 18		8 54 WR		9 54	10 52	11 53	1 44	3 24	3 55		6 3	6 22				8 54	9 35	9 40	10 28	5 26	6 36	8 36
Heswall Hills ,,	8 24		9 0 WR		10 0	10 58	11 59	1 50	3 30	4 3		6 9	6 28				9 0	9 41	9 46	10 34	5 32	6 42	8 42
Storeton ,,	8 29		9 5 WR		10 5	11 3	12 4	1 55	3 35	4 8		6 14	6 33				9 5	9 47	9 50	10 39	5 37	6 47	8 47
Upton ,,	8 34		9 10 WR		10 10	11 8	12 9	2 0	3 40	4 13		6 19	6 40				9 10	9 52	9 55	10 44	5 42	6 52	8 52
Bidston Station ,,	8 39		9 15		10 15	11 12	12 14	2 4	3 45	4 18		6 24	6 45				9 15	9 57	10 0	10 49	5 47	6 57	8 57
,, Sidings ,,							1145																
Liscard and Poulton ,,					10 18	11 16	12 17						6 48				9 19	10 0	10 3			7 0	9 0
Seacombe .... arr.	8 45		9 21		10 22	11 20	12 21	2 10	3 51	4 24		6 30	6 52				9 22	10 5	10 7	10 55	5 53	7 4	9 4
Liverpool (Landing Stage) ,,	8 56		9 36		10 36	11 36	12 36	2 21	4 6	4 36		6 51	7 6				9 36	10 21	10 36	11 6	6 7	7 21	9 16

No. 4 on arrival at Bidston to work as required.

MAIN LINE—Continued.

UP TRAINS

Distances M. C.	Station	72 Passenger (S O)	73	74	75	S1 a m	S4–5 a m	S6 p m	S8 p m	S9 p m
		11 0 p.m ex Chester								
	Seacombe .... dep.					9 12	1030	2 30	7 04	9 04
70	Liscard and Poulton ..					9 15	1034	2 34	7 11	9 09
6 S	Bidston ,,					9 19	1037	2 37	7 17	9 11
4 S	Upton ,,					9 25	1041	2 41	7 21	9 17
6 3	Storeton ,,					9 29	1047	2 47	7 27	9 21
	Heswall Hills ,,						1051	2 51		9 27
10 3 S	Neston and Parkgate ,,					9 35	1057	2 57	7 32	9 32
	Burton Point ,,					9 40	11 2	3 2		9 39
	Connah's Quay Docks									
	Hawarden Bridge Junct.									
	Connah's Quay & Shotton Station	1117				For Chester	11 9	For Chester	For Chester	9 41
	Aston Hall Junction	1119					1111			9 49
18 42	Hawarden ,,									
20 39	Buckley Junction Station	1127					1119			9 55
20 32	Buckley Junction ,,	1135					1125			
21 42	Hope Exchange ,,						1130			10 5
21 65	Penyffordd Junction ,,						1135			10 9
23 60	Hope Village ,,						1140			1014
24	Caergwrle Castle, Llay ,,									
25 4	Hall and Lassells ,,									
4	Cefn-y-bedd ,,						1145			
26 11	Ffrwd Junction ,,									
27 1	Gwersyllt ,,									
27 26	Brymbo North Junction ,,									
73	Brymbo South Junction ,,									
29 27	Wrexham (Exchange) ... arr.	1155					1151			1020
	(Central) ,, arr.									

Wrexham Tickets of No. 72 to be collected at Buckley Junction.

CHESTER TO CONNAH'S QUAY & SHOTTON.

WEEK DAYS.

	1	2	3	4	5	6	7	8	9	10	11	12	13	14	15
STATIONS	C.L.C. Express Goods.	G.C. Goods.	Passenger.	Fast Goods.	Passenger.	Passenger.	Passenger.	Passenger.	Passenger.	G.C. Goods.	Passenger.	Passenger.	Passenger.	Passenger.	C.B.S.O. Passenger.
	a m	a m	a m	a m	a m										
Chester (Northgate) .... dep.	7 07	7 40	B 8 12	10 10	B 10 5		B 11 55	B 10 30		3 45	W R	C	B	B	B
37½ (Liverpool Road) ,,	W R	8 15	8 15	10 15	10 7		11 57	10 32		W R 5	1 07	5 27	2 09	5 11	5 11
1 39 Blacon ,,		8 20	8 21	10 21	10 15		12 01	12 32		W R 5	1 12	5 22	2 29	2 01	7 11
3 46 Saughall ,,	D	8 26	8 27	10 26	10 23		12 51	2 40		W R 5	2 07	5 27	2 49	3 51	9 25
6 69 Hawarden Bridge Junct. pass			8 27		10 23		12 13	2 48		5	4 45	5 77	3 89	31 21	31 11
Connah's Quay & Shotton arr.							12 13								
Hawarden ,,														33	33

Passengers by the trains marked B for Wrexham and Seacombe change carriages at Connah's Quay and Shotton, and by train marked C at Hawarden.

CONNAH'S QUAY & SHOTTON TO CHESTER.

WEEK DAYS.

	1	2	3	4	5	6	7	8	9	10	11	12	13	14	15
STATIONS	Passenger.	Passenger.	Passenger.	G.C. Goods.	Passenger.	Passenger.	Passenger.	Passenger.	C.L.C. Express Goods.	Passenger.	Passenger.	S.O. Passenger.	S.O. Passenger.	Passenger.	G.C. Goods.
	a m	a m	a m		p m	p m	p m	p m	p m	p m	p m	p m	p m		p m
Hawarden .... dep.	8 42	10 42	10 27		1 37	3 46		6 10	7 35	7		7 50	10 6		
13 10 Connah's Quay & Shotn. pass	8 43	10 43	12 28	12 01	3 73	3 47		6 17		7	8	9 50	10 12	9 30 p.m ex Wrexham	10 15
13 33 Hawarden Bridge Junct. dep.	8 48	10 49	12 29	12 04		3 83		6 23		8	9	10 13	10 13		
16 33 Saughall ,,	8 49	10 49	1 34	W R	4 53	4 47		6 28	D	8 10	9 57	10 25	10 25		
20 Blacon ,,	8 54	10 54	1 39	W R	5 24	4 93		6 31		8 10	5 79	10 5	10 5		
19 4½ Chester (Liverpool Road) arr.	8 57	10 57	1 42	W R	5 54	5 54		6 34		8 10	8 10	10 28	10 28		10 35
19 7½ ,, (Northgate) ,,	9 01	11 02	1 45	2 35	4 4	5 4				9	9				11 10

LIVERPOOL, SEACOMBE, BIDSTON, NESTON, AND CHESTER.

STATIONS	WEEK DAYS																				SUNDAYS				
	1	2	3	4	5	6	7	8	9	10	11	12	13	14	15	16	17	18	19	20	1	2	3	4	5
	Passenger.	Passenger.		Passenger.	Passenger.	Passenger.	Passenger.			Passenger.	Passenger.	Passenger.	Passenger.	Passenger.	Fast Goods.	Passenger.	Passenger.		Passengsr.	Passenger.	Passenger.	Passenger.	Passenger.	Passenger.	Passenger.
	a m	a m		a m	a m	a m	m p			p m	p m	p m	p m	p m		p m	p m		p m	p m	p m	m p	m p	p m	p m
															S E S O					S E S O					
Liverpool (Landing Stage) dep.	7 07	7 45		9 40	10 0	11 30	1 20			2 04	15 4	4 55	4 0 6	6 0		6 50	8 40		10 0	11 15	8 45	10 15	2 15	6 45	8 40
Seacombe .... ,,	7 15	8		9 55	10 20	11 43	1 35			2 04	27 5	0 5	5 56	6 17		7 59	0		10 15	11 30	8 10	30 2	30 7	09	09 0
Liscard and Poulton .... ,,		8 6		9 59	10 24					2 24						7 9	9 4				8	10 3	34 2	34 7	49 4
Bidston Station .... ,,	7 21	8 9		10 2	10 27	11 49	1 41			2 28	4 3	5 6	6 6	1 6 23		7 12	9 7		10 21	11 36	15	10 37	2 37	7 7	7 9 7
,, Sidings ,,															6 35										
Upton .... ,,	7 25	8 13		10 6	10 31	11 53	1 45			2 32	4 37	5 0	5 6 27	W R	7 16	9 12		10 25	11 40	19	10 41	2 41	7 17	11 9 11
Storeton .... ,,	7 31	8 19		10 12	10 37	11 59	1 51			2 38	4 43	5 16	6 11	6 39 W R	7 22	9 18		10 31	11 46	25	10 47	2 47	7 17	17 9 17
Heswall Hills .... ,,	7 35	8 23		10 16	10 42	12 3	1 55			2 42	4 48	5 26	6 16 6	37 W R	7 26	9 22		10 35	11 50	29	10 51	2 51	7 19	21 9 21
Neston and Parkgate ... ,,	7 41	8 29		10 22	10 49	12 9	2 1			2 48	4 55	5 26	6 23	6 43 W R	7 32	9 28		10 41	11 56	35	10 57	2 57	7 27	9 27
Burton Point .... ,,	7 46			10 27	10 54	12 14	2 6			2 53	5 0	5 31	6 28	6 48		7 37	9 33				9	40 11 2 3	2 7	32 9 32
Hawarden Bridge, Chester Junction .... pass																									
Saughall .... arr.	7 54						2 14				5 8		6 36	6 56 A						9 48	3 10	7 40		
Blacon .... ,,											5 13		6 41	7 1						9 53	3 15	7 45		
Chester (Liverpool Road) ,,	8 2	For Wrexham.		For Wrexham.	For Chester.	For Wrexham.	2 21			For Wrexham.	5 17	For Wrexham.	6 45	7 4	A	For Wrexham.	For Wrexham.			9 57	3 18	7 48		For Wrexham.
,, (Northgate) ,,	8 5						2 23				5 20		6 48	7 8	8 0					9 59	3 21	7 51		

Alterations for October, 1900.

Passenger Trains.

Wrexham, Buckley, Hawarden, & Seacombe.

1 52 p.m. Express, Wrexham to Manchester	
10 a.m. " Manchester to Wrexham	Will be
10 p.m. (S.O.) Seacombe to Wrexham	Discontinued
6 0 p.m. (M.S.O) " "	
5 5 p.m. Wrexham to Seacombe will be slightly retimed.	
7 30 p.m. Wrexham to Seacombe (M.S.O) will run to Caergwrle Castle only.	

" 9 a.m. Wrexham to Seacombe (Sundays) will leave at 8 50 a.m.
" 20 a.m. Seacombe to Wrexham will leave at 9 55 a.m.
" 45 a.m. Seacombe to Wrexham (Sundays) will leave at 10 30 a.m.
Additional Train will leave Caergwrle Castle for Wrexham (M.S.O) at 7 50 p.m.

Chester and Seacombe.

" 53 a.m. Chester to Seacombe will leave 8 30 a.m.
" 45 a.m. " 11 30 a.m.
" (Sundays) will leave 10 5 a.m.
Additional Train will leave Seacombe for Neston at 10 0 p.m. Saturdays excepted.

Chester and Connah's Quay, and Shotton.

1 15 a.m. Chester to Shotton will leave 10 5 a.m.
1 5 a.m. Shotton to Chester will leave 10 42 a.m.
1 45 p.m. Shotton to Chester will leave at 3 46 p.m.

Brymbo Branch.

8 25 a.m. Brymbo to Wrexham (M.E.) will leave daily 8 25 a.m.

Goods Trains.

12 0 noon Wrexham Exchange to Penyffordd (No. 21) will leave at 11 30 a.m.

BUCKLEY AND CONNAH'S QUAY SECTION.

Single Line worked under the Train Staff and Permit Regulations.—See page 7 of the Appendix

Staff Stations.—Buckley Junction. Buckley, Northop Hall, and Connah's Quay.

All stops to be "when required" only, according to the state of traffic.

Time-booked at Connah's Quay includes putting off Down Train, Loco. purposes, and picking up train for Up direction, and this time must be strictly adhered to.

The letters A and B at the head of the columns denote the trains appointed to work after starting, which will be done alternate Fortnights.

WEEK DAYS.

DOWN.

STATIONS.	1	2	3	4	5	6	7	8	9	10	11	12	13	14	15
	a.m M A	a.m M B	a.m M	a.m M	a.m M			M A	M B		M A	M B			
PENYFFORDD .... dep.	6 35	6 45									6 20	6 25			
BUCKLEYJUNCTION .... dep.	6 45	6 50	7 40		8 40 9 55	1015	1215				6 20	6 25			
BUCKLEYSTATION { arr.	6 57	7 0	7 45		9 55 1010	1030	1225	1 01 30							
{ dep.	7 0	7 35			1010 1025	1050	1230	1 10 40							
Mount Pleasant Colliery		7 40						1 40							
Law End Colliery	8 0							WR							
Ashton's Top Siding	8 0							2 25							
Old Ewloe Siding	8 20														
Lane Sidings	8 25			9 5	1025			2 25							
Globe	8 30														
Catherall's	7 15						1 25	1 30							
Buckley Brick & Tile	7 25						1 30							
Ewloe Barn	7 35						1 40	2 35							
Buckley Collieries		7 30	WR	9 15			1 55	2 55	3 35						
North & South Buckley															
Parry's Siding				9 25				3 5							
Castle Brick			WR	9 35				WR							
Dublin Main		8 0 9 0	9 35				2 10 3 20 3 50								
NORTHOP HALL .... { arr.		8 15 9 25	9 55				2 30 3 40 4 10								
CONNAH'S QUAY .... arr.															

Nos. 1 and 7 to clear Shipping Traffic from all Sidings as required.
No. 1 to clear Sandycroft Coal and other Empties from Buckley Junction, working same to Colliery.

WEEK DAYS.

UP.

STATIONS.	1	2	3	4	5	6	7	8	9	10	11	12	13	14	15
	a.m M A	a.m M B	a.m M	a.m M	a.m M			M A	M B		p.m M A	p.m M B			
CONNAH'S QUAY .... dep.															
NORTHOP HALL .... { dep.	6 06	8 7	8 30		8 40 9 55 1015	1030	8 0	3 0	3 25		4 30				
Dublin Main	6 56	107	8 35		9 1010 1030	1050	3 30	3 50			4 24 4 45				
Castle Brick	6 10														
Parry's Siding			9 5 1025												
North and South Buckley															
Buckley Collieries							11 0								
Ewloe Barn					1035						4 45				
Buckley Brick & Tile					1040						4 50				
Catherall's					1030										
Globe					11 0				5 0						
Etna Siding							1115				WR				
Old Ewloe							1150				WR				
Knowle Lane Siding							1145				WR				
Ashton's Top Siding							1210			5 105 30					
Lane End Colliery										5 40					
Mount Pleasant Colliery										5 45					
BUCKLEY STATION { arr.					1110		1115			5 55					
{ dep.	6 06	8 7	8 30		1115 1135		1225								
BUCKLEYJUNCTION .... arr.	6 56	107	8 35		1135										
PENYFFORDD .... arr.	6 10				1140										

ALL UP TRAINS MUST COME TO A DEAD STAND AT BUCKLEY JUNCTION CLEAR OF FACING POINTS ON BUCKLEY BRANCH.

No. 5 Up to shunt Buckley Yard.
No. 10 Up to clear Hancock's siding. No. 11 Up if necessary to work extra trip to and from Watkinson's.
No. 10 Up to run via Mountain Colliery Lane to Birkenhead traffic from Mountain Colliery, putting some off at Buckley Junction if labelled by that route as working to Penyffordd.
No. 11 Up to work through to Ashton's Top Siding with Empty Shippers when required, to clear Sandycroft Colliery Siding, and form train ready for No. 1 Up the following morning.
Mr. Miller, Connah's Quay, to wire Mr. Hall, Buckley, previous night before 6 30 p.m., when an early trip is required, so as to enable No. 2 Up to run to Buckley Junction.
No. 11 Up to be watered at Buckley Junction whenever it has traffic for or C.L.C. system or beyond
Nos. 5 and 10 Up to attach at Buckley Junction when required.

There was intense competition with the GWR Branch even though its trains offered but one third of the frequency and did not take its passengers into the centre of Wrexham. Neither did that Company cater for the Saturday evening traffic – perhaps its carriages were deemed too vulnerable!

Looking forward to the turn of the century, a Working Timetable is available for 1st October, 1900 and this is reproduced in full (*pages 277–87*). For the first time the minutiae of traffic working can be examined and comment on this can be confined to the following:

BRYMBO BRANCH – DOWN

    1) Six mineral trains for Brymbo Steel Works* are tabled: starting from Brymbo station, Plas Power 'A' Cabin or Brymbo North Junction; viz:

        two daily from North Junction at 6.15 am and 7.50 am

        two daily from Brymbo station at 9.30 am and 4.40 pm (Sats excepted)

        two daily from Plas Power 'A' at 12.35 pm and 2.35 pm

    2) Three empty wagon trains returning to Vron Colliery tabled to leave North Junction at 7.25 am, 1.45 pm and Brymbo station 4.40 pm (Sats excepted).

    3) Seven passenger workings from Wrexham on Saturdays at 4 pm, 5 pm, 6 pm, 8.30 pm, 9 pm, 9.35 pm, 10 pm. Tickets for Brymbo off the 4 pm, 5 pm and 6 pm were collected at Plas Power and forwarded 'under cover' to Brymbo.

BRYMBO BRANCH – UP

    1) Five trains leaving Steel Works between 7.10 am and 3 pm but none thereafter.

    2) Three loaded coal trains leaving Vron Colliery, but last does not run on Saturdays.

    3) All Wrexham passenger tickets to be collected at Wrexham Exchange except the last three workings on Saturdays Only which were collected at Moss & Pentre (where crossing of Down train would take place at same time).

    4) Stabling of empty passenger stock in Cobden Mill Siding on Saturday nights.

FFRWD BRANCH

There is no separate Table for this line.

MAIN LINE – DOWN

    1) The pattern of working stock to Brymbo North Junction – such workings must reverse there to continue up Branch. Branch engine collects stock from there.

    2) Trips Wrexham–Penyffordd for traffic to and from LNWR Chester–Mold line.

    3) 6.30 am light engine departs from Wrexham Exchange to work Ffrwd Branch empties via Wrexham Central and arrangements for collecting guard at Rhosddu.

    4) Reference to cattle traffic for Birkenhead Docks for shipment.

    5) Brymbo South Junction – West Junction chord largely confined to Branch passenger workings.

    6) Brymbo Branch Down mineral trains worked northwards from North Junction to Penyffordd at 10.20 am, 2.45 pm and 5.45 pm (Sats only).

    7) Brymbo Branch Down mineral trains worked to Connah's Quay docks from North Junction at 1.15 pm (i.e. one daily working only, and via Hawarden Bridge Junction and *not* Old Buckley).

    8) Penyffordd to Buckley Junction (for Buckley Branch) Down goods and mineral leaves at 12.15 pm and 6.15 pm daily including Saturdays.

    9) Down loaded coal workings ex Vron Colliery terminating at Buckley Junction: leaving Vron daily 3.25 pm and 5.05 pm (Sats excepted).

    10) The extensive northward links for passenger and other trains created by building of Hawarden Bridge, and the new titles appearing in consequence e.g. 'GC Goods & Mineral' and 'CLC Goods' (etc.).

---

*Worked out of Brymbo passenger station onto Vron Branch and then reversed into Steel Works.

Plate 91: No. 8 remained at Rhosddu, to be renumbered 405C in 1912: Buckley line working days are clearly over, for the boiler mountings and cab have been raised.

(W.H. Whitworth Collection)

Plate 92: No. 9 was purchased second-hand in 1881 and spent all its working life on Connah's Quay Docks.

(R.E. Thomas Collection)

Plate 93: All dressed up on Rhosddu Shed, No. 10 is garlanded for Queen Victoria's Diamond Jubilee in 1897. The gentleman in the straw hat is Thomas Cartwright, (the General Manager) and on the ground (*third from right*) is Frederick Willans, Locomotive Superintendent. Would that we knew the names of the others . . .!

(J.M. Dunn Collection)

Plate 94: In later, more mundane days, the engine is still clean and lined out. The boiler mountings have been lowered to enable it to work the Buckley line; this modification was done in 1904. It became 402B in 1910. *(W.H. Whitworth Collection)*

Plate 95: Taken in the shadow of the Ffrith Ironworks, an immaculate No. 11 with men in attendance. *(R.E. Thomas Collection)*

Plate 96: With Penyffordd signal cabin behind, No. 12 is a tribute to the design draughtsmen of Gorton. The saddle tank gleams with faithful polishing.

(J.M. Dunn Collection)

Plate 97: No. 13, with its shorter saddle tank, ended its days at Cefn Coed Colliery, Crynant, near Neath in South Wales. By then it had acquired a GCR-type chimney and smokebox.   *(A. Brown Collection)*

Plate 98: No. 16, together with No. 15, ended the "individual" design of engines supplied by Beyer, Peacock to the WMCQR. Apart from additional coal rails on the bunker, little has changed at this turn-of-the-century picture. Note the socket-style lamp-irons.   *(Clwyd Record Office)*

Plate 99: Both Nos. 15 and 16 were given shorter boiler mountings by the GCR and by the early 1920s had been removed to Gorton (GCR) from their native heath for the first and last time. There they were given the mark of condemnation, a white cross on the bunker side. Here ex-No. 16 awaits its end, age 34 years.

(A. Brown Collection)

Plate 100: Lasting until December 1936, former WMCQR No. 18 had been owned by WMCQR, MS&LR, GCR and finally LNER systems. It was 46 years old when scrapped. It had a stovepipe chimney when new.   *(A. Brown Collection)*

Plate 101: Among engines drafted to the former WMCQR section after the Second World War were these two ex-North Eastern Railway six-coupled tank engines of 1898 (LNER Class J72) found here, out of use, behind Bidston Shed in September 1959. Chimneys had been cut down: they had been LNER Nos. 2320 and 2307.

(H.C. Casserley)

Plate 102: An enlarged view of Connah's Quay Docks in 1876 gives some detail of the earliest wagons hired by the WMCQR.   *(M. Mollington)*

Plate 103: A Traders' Wagon carrying four shipping boxes: the double-wheel brake is on the far side. The hinged bar to prevent the Boxes coming off has been raised on the near side; on the far side the bar is in place and a wooden baulk also prevents the boxes from sliding off. The wagon is lettered BUCKLEY TRADERS' SOCIETY. The brake is clearly untrustworthy for movement is prevented by a brick under the wheel.

(M. Mollington)

Plate 104: This special wagon was built for grain traffic in 1904; it was the only example. *(J.I.C. Boyd Collection)*

Plate 105: Single side-tipping iron ore wagon for the Ffrwd Ironworks supplied on deferred payment by Gloucester Wagon Co., who made their first iron-built wagons in 1862.   *(Gloucester Railway Carriage & Wagon Co. Ltd.)*

Plate 106: A 10 ton end-door coal wagon for Westminster Colliery, another Gloucester product. Dumb buffers and wooden brake blocks, plus additional side coupling chains, were commonplace at this time.

(Gloucester Railway Carriage & Wagon Co. Ltd.)

Plate 107: A 10 ton coal wagon for Vron Colliery, by Gloucester in May 1898: this vehicle was a reconstruction. Colours were: body, purple-brown; lettering, white, shaded black. Sprung buffers and iron brake shoes now feature on this end-door vehicle. *(Gloucester Railway Carriage & Wagon Co. Ltd.)*

Plate 108: A hand-operated point lever at Northop Hall Siding, lettered "WM & CQ RAILWAYS". *February 1965 (J.I.C. Boyd)*

Plate 109: Single-line Staff for use between Old Buckley and Connah's Quay. This was in use until closure of the line. *(J.M. Lloyd)*

Plate 110: Buckley line signals were few and of MS & LR pattern; this one stood at the north side of the Castle Brickworks level crossing. The poles carrying the Summers-installed electricity supply to Mountain Colliery, Buckley, were a feature of this section.
February 1965 (J.I.C. Boyd)

Plate 111: The water tank of 1890 at the south end of Hawarden station fed stand-pipes at both ends of the platforms. The signal box was a replacement of the original.
October 1966   (M.E. Morton-Lloyd)

Plate 112: Goods train bound for Buckley Junction at Old Buckley, headed by ex-LD & ECR six-coupled tank, LNER No. 6408.   *1934   (R.E. Thomas)*

Plate 113 (left), Plate 114 (right): Variety in signal boxes: Buckley Junction was a tall structure to give vision over the adjacent road bridge. Brymbo South Junction was a low box so as to see under the Acton Colliery road bridge. The low timber platform (*extreme left*) allowed the signalman to exchange the Staff with Brymbo Branch trains.

(*H.B. Priestley*)

Plate 115: Latterly, Old Buckley was used simply for wagon storage; this is its final form. The "Shock Hybar" wagons have probably made their last loaded journey with local clay products.   *February 1965   (J.I.C. Boyd)*

Plate 116: LNER Class C13, 4−4−2 tank heads a train of six-wheeled carriages bound for Wrexham, out of Buckley Junction.   *1934   (R.E. Thomas)*

Plate 117: Five years into the era of British Railways; the 3.55 pm for Seacombe awaits departure from Wrexham Central.   *August 1953   (H.C. Casserley)*

Plate 118: The full extent of WMCQR working took their trains to Seacombe on the Mersey. This was always a very basic station, originally with timber platforms and very little shelter. Here, the same engine as heads the Seacombe train at Wrexham Central in the previous picture, prepares to return there.

August 1953   (H.C. Casserley)

Plate 119: In August 1950 the former Down platform at Connah's Quay & Shotton was exactly as built. The building was very dilapidated. The appearance of no less than five platform barrows suggests parcel traffic etc. was brisk. The engine is former LNER Class N5, at first No. 5548; this type had worked the WMCQR section since before the GCR took over the Company in 1905. *Real Railway Photographs*

Plate 120: The ex-LD&ECR six-coupled tank, now LNER No. 6408, has stopped at "The Cutting" on the Ashton's Branch Siding, Buckley, en route to pick up stored wagons at Mountain Colliery. The chimneys in the background belong to Old Ewloe Brickworks. *1934 (R.E. Thomas)*

11) In the footnotes:
   a) The exchange of traffic from the Wrexham & Ellesmere extension.
   (Cambrian Railways goods yard some way east of Central station).
   b) Use of Brymbo North Junction as marshalling yard.
   c) Use of engine bringing mineral off North Junction at 4.30 pm on Saturdays
   (being the 3.25 pm loaded coal train from Vron Colliery) being required to
   work Up 6.25 pm ex Buckley Junction–Wrexham passenger, a good example
   of the multi-purpose aspect of the locomotive stock. (The engine off the
   2.45 pm Down mineral from North Junction–Penyffordd had to return to
   Wrexham on Saturdays to work the 9.30 pm Wrexham–Hawarden Bridge
   –Chester passenger (Sats only). A similar instance was the Hawarden–Chester
   passenger working depart 6.10 pm).

MAIN LINE – UP
   1) Provision for shunting engine from 6 am at Rhosddu shed, to work Wrexham
   Central yard.
   2) Buckley Junction–Wrexham Central passenger working departs 8 am.
   3) Hawarden Bridge Junction–Hawarden passenger working departs 5.25 pm
   (originates as 5.10 pm ex Chester).
   4) Buckley Junction–Wrexham passenger departs 6.25 pm (Sats only) for which
   carriages are worked to here attached to Down mineral/goods workings.
   5) Caergwrle Castle–Wrexham passenger departs 7.50 pm (Mon & Sat only).
   6) The last Saturday passenger train from Brymbo for Wrexham leaves 9.51 pm –
   empty passenger stock off next train from Wrexham leaves 10.05 pm whilst at
   10.55 pm a light engine and brake van depart. The Brymbo branch on Saturday
   nights must have been a rewarding spectacle of railway working and social habit!
   7) Buckley Branch goods trains run south to Penyffordd at 6.10 am, 11.50 am and
   6 pm daily from Buckley Junction.
   8) Connah's Quay Docks (via Hawarden Bridge Junction)–Wrexham Central
   goods leaves daily at 5 pm i.e. return working of 1.15 pm ex North Junction due
   Connah's Quay Docks 4.35 pm. Note provision for Cambrian Railways' traffic.
   9) In the footnotes:
   a) Collection of mineral traffic at Chester and North Junction of wagons for
   Wrexham & Ellesmere (Cambrian Railways) line.
   b) Provision for Wrexham & Acton Colliery traffic working to Wrexham Central.
   c) Tickets off the last Saturday passenger train (departs Chester 11 pm) collected at Buckley Junction.

BUCKLEY–CONNAH'S QUAY SECTION
   1) Note that not every train works all Sidings and that the work is divided as to
   north and south of Catherall's Siding.
   2) Note the short workings to work traffic to/from Old Buckley station to Buckley
   Junction.
   3) 'Watkinson's Short Workings' 9.15 am and 3.35 pm Buckley Collieries–
   Connah's Quay; return empties leave Connah's Quay 8.40 am and 3 pm i.e. the
   same engine and van works throughout.
   4) Daily workings originate at Buckley Junction and end at (Old) Buckley.
   5) Trains pass at (Old) Buckley at 12.55 pm.
   6) There is no provision for light engine working from (Old) Buckley engine shed
   to work the first Down train.

Of excursion traffic, there are references as elsewhere (*pages 134, 136*).
Early days saw excursionists heading for the north coast, Anglesey and
Liverpool. Liverpool was always a favourite with colliers enjoying their
annual outing: Wirral folk looked to Caergwrle Castle and the hills around

for many a pleasant country outing, but it is hard to find they had much enthusiasm for Caergwrle Wells! Once the initial experiences of travel by train, the novelty of the ride and the accessibility of the seaside, became commonplace, excursionists continued their travelling habits but for changed reasons. Once The Loop Line was ready, Hawarden had become a place of pilgrimage. Wrexham was always a centre of wholesale and retail activity and probably did more Saturday-shopping business with Welsh people up from the country than did Liverpool, another popular shopping resort. Wrexham's Thursday and Saturday markets were reached by trains that only ran on those days.

William Davies' diary has entries concerning the well-used Rhyl excursions from Wrexham which took place in the summer months; such was the shortage of WMCQR stock that Vale of Clwyd and Mold & Denbigh Junction Railways' carriages were pressed into service. The train left Wrexham behind CHANCELLOR on a Saturday at 7.30 am and ran down the chord line at Penyffordd; here the engine was exchanged for a LNWR 'Coal Tank' which ran the stock non-stop to Denbigh where it reversed, and the same engine ran round and brought the train to Rhyl. Departure from Rhyl was usually about 6 pm.

At that time the WMCQR second-hand LNWR coaches were still in the livery of the sellers; that they were quite up to the standards then prevailing was shown when the LNWR itself used them for specials to the Shrewsbury Flower Show. The GWR however, refused to allow them on their metals as they had been accident-prone in the past. On one occasion this ex-LNWR stock was on a WMCQR excursion over the GWR when one of the oil lamps in the ceiling fell on John Morris, a Caergwrle butcher and man of substance. The oil ruined his suit which the WMCQR was obliged to replace.

Stationmasters were under instruction to ensure that goods trains passing at times when excursions were likely to be running, were shunted clear of them. Guards were instructed to load carriages at the rear of excursions before using the front carriages; otherwise at several stations with short platforms it would necessitate the train having to draw up twice.

On Fridays and Saturdays stations on the GCR in the Manchester district could issue 10-day and 11-day excursion tickets to all main stations on the Cambrian Railways; this traffic would pass through Wrexham Central to Ellesmere. Similar (but half-day tickets) were issued from Liverpool and Wirral stations on Mondays, Fridays and Saturdays to WMCQR stations and Ellesmere. There were other schemes to entice passengers to travel from GCR stations on the East Coast (e.g. Goole, Grimsby) to stations on the Cambrian Railways and there was a general long weekend reduced fare policy for stations on the WMCQR to Wirral and Liverpool and vice versa. For those intending to visit Antwerp, Rotterdam and Brussels for 16 days, residents of Wrexham and Hawarden could buy cheap tickets every Wednesday and Saturday in 1896; every weekday those same chosen fortunates, could reach Hamburg by GCR steamer. And besides these, there was an attractive formula by which almost everywhere to anywhere – so long as GCR routes were used – was ready to entice the adventurous by concession or stealth.

On 20th June, 1896 the Mersey Railway Loco Depot staff (numbering about 50 – the Mersey being then steam operated) had reserved accommodation (3rd class) to sample the delights of Hawarden. On the following Monday Brymbo-ites could leave there at 8 am bound for coastal resorts and Llandudno. A WMCQR engine worked the Brymbo–Penyffordd section but it was denied any frolics at the seaside; 'On arrival at Penyffordd Engine to return light to Wrexham Exchange to complete shunting'. Hard luck! It was stipulated that WMCQR coaches were to work through to Llandudno, 'Mr Johnson to provide the necessary roof lamps'. On return, Brymbo would be reached at 9.58 pm; they would need those lamps. On the same day, there was a return excursion to New Brighton, all 3rd class. Leaving Wrexham at 8 am it reached Merseyside at 9.10 am and did not leave New Brighton until 8.35 pm . . . a long day. The train stopped at Caergwrle in each direction to accommodate a party of 90 from the Presbyterian Sunday School. Of such traffic were excursion trains composed. And just to complicate matters, a special ballast train was to operate on the day of these two special trains; it left Wrexham at 6.30 am and must have been an irritant to all as it worked all day between Brymbo, Buckley and Hawarden Bridge Junction. And to wrap up this busy Monday, Methodists from off the LNWR travelled by the 8.20 am from Hope Exchange to Bridge End, and left there again at 6.17 pm. They too must have prayed for fine weather. This style of traffic for small parties was catered for throughout each summer.

As to locomotive loadings; between Hawarden Bridge Junction, up The Loop Line to Buckley Junction heavy goods trains might be assisted in the rear. Descending goods trains from Buckley Junction to Hawarden Bridge Junction were required to stop at the Junction to have hand brakes pinned down.

On the Buckley section, load limits were 35 loaded wagons, (Buckley –Northop Hall) and 30 loaded wagons, (Northop Hall–Connah's Quay).

Depending on the power available, up to 50 loaded mineral wagons could be brought south from Buckley Junction to Caergwrle Castle, and from Ffrwd Junction into Wrexham. In winter, loaded mineral wagons from Wrexham to Buckley Junction were reduced in number per train.

Some miscellaneous notes on working in general are called to mind. Firstly, the track was often so bad that the trainmen became experts at rerailing without recourse to calling on help from Rhosddu: there was a casual air about things as witness the empty mineral train returning to Brymbo and stopping whilst the fireman set rabbit snares in the field along-side . . . or the fireman alone on the engine, carrying out the shunting at Connah's Quay whilst his driver enjoyed the long-established privilege of fishing the day away.

Driver R.W. Tyler was the senior man at Rhosddu for some years; he it was who worked the first passenger from Wrexham to Chester with No. 5. After a few months he had No. 4 on the same duty. He also worked the first Wrexham–Seacombe passenger train; the engine was a MSLR 2–4–0 with Willans on the footplate: Cartwright and others rode in the train. There was a complaint that the rails were too lightly laid on widely spaced sleepers – when speed had been worked up and they were doing about 60 mph, the engine gave a 'beautiful roll which nearly sent the fireman headlong off the footplate', (so Dunn was told). At this time there was a great deal of bad feeling between the MSLR(GCR) and the WMCQR as to which would work the trains.

Before the days of passenger trains north of the river, the ex-LNWR carriages frequently placed passengers with the urgent need to attend to bodily functions, 'in extremis'. Fortunately, the Board of Trade never permitted a station to be opened without the proper facilities for both sexes and it was the informal practice to give notice to the guard when a passenger intended to alight at the next station 'for personal reasons'. The train would be held up meanwhile. Guards collected a useful sideline in income in this regard: the tip was 6d. 1st Class and 3d. for 2nd . . . tradition has it that 3rd Class passengers were expected to do the best they could, where they could.

Another Board of Trade requirement at each station, was a clock: Mr A.W. Butt of Wrexham supplied all the timepieces for the line.

The foregoing courtesies were never in more demand than when the Saturday night trains left Wrexham for Brymbo. 'There was a policeman at Wrexham Central whose language was of the brightest order and whose job it was on Saturday nights to assist the inebriates over the station footbridge to the platform from whence the Brymbo train departed'.

Though the staff of the Railway complained as usual that they were overworked and underpaid, their loyalty was seldom in question. It is recalled how like a large, happy family they were; each knew each other, and his whereabouts on the system at any hour. Edward Edwards was a Goods Guard: he lived to be 101 and died within recent years. He spoke of the line as 'a poor little thing' so reflecting an attitude of fatherly responsibility to his occupation. 'We were like a band of brothers'.

The nickname given to the Railway was claimed to have been resurrected by Mr Langshaw Rowland (senr.) who wrote, '. . . it was the congenital poverty and ramshackle nature of the system which gave it the title, 'Wretchedly Managed and Confoundedly Queer'. Though by far from being an original description, it certainly fitted the definition of being a 'Line of Character'.

'The New Dee Railway Bridge opened on 3rd August, 1889.'

Locomotives

Gorton Records: January 1903 (Great Central Railway)

A review of the locomotive stock took place and was listed at this date. Dimensionally this account is reasonably accurate as regards the existing condition, but the historic notes preceding each locomotive entry are inaccurate: where makers' records are available, these have been used in preference to those of Gorton.

All locomotive examinations took place at Wrexham, not Gorton.

The valuation of 18 locomotives at the above date was £21,715 0s. 0d.

Paragraphs at the end of each locomotive description prefixed § are verbatim particulars taken from these Records.

Automatic vacuum brake was fitted to certain engines in consequence of The Regulation of Railways Act, 1889.

Unless stated otherwise, engine overhauls and rebuilds were carried out at Rhosddu, Wrexham.

Over a period, names were removed.

———— · ————

No. 1 WHEATLEY (*not numbered by Buckley Railway*)

This was the first locomotive built by Hudswell, Clarke & Rodgers of Leeds, ordered by the Buckley Railway on 19th February, 1861, and leaving the makers on 16th April following at a cost of £1,956 10s. 0d.[1] Like many early engines, the buffer beams were of timber, faced with steel plate. There was no cab, and the name was painted on, the origin of it being a local family of landowners and industrialists of both Wheatley and Randall-Wheatley. The order was actually placed by George Bellis, Engineer to the Buckley Railway, but signing himself as 'Secretary'. A new chimney and half cab were provided in 1876; in 1886 the motion was modified and the cab extended to close entirely the footplate. Vacuum brake was fitted and in 1895 a new boiler received, the cylinders enlarged to 15½ in. diameter[2] and the motion modified again: the bunker was now placed within the cab.

On 4th February, 1868 it collided with its sister engine KENYON in a runaway at Connah's Quay and both received damage beyond the Company's ability to repair. WHEATLEY was repaired at the Lancashire & Yorkshire Railway Works at Miles Platting, and is said to have had the lesser damage, working WMCQR passenger trains with only one cylinder for some days, a pinchbar being used to start the engine when on dead centre.

Numbered 1B by the GCR on takeover, it was scrapped in April 1906.

§Condition: boiler in fair working order, frames cracked but effectively patched. Motion wants overhauling. Tyres worn down to 2 in. thick. Estimated present value £850 0s. 0d.

No. 2 KENYON (*not numbered by Buckley Railway*)

This was a sister engine to WHEATLEY and was completed in March 1862, the date of leaving Leeds not being known. The Buckley Railway opened to goods and mineral traffic on 7th June, 1862, so two new engines would be available: and it is possible that they may have been used on construction trains. After the 1868 accident (*see* No. 1), tenders were sought from the makers for repairs to both engines but in March the prices were judged to be too high; nonetheless, in June KENYON was at Hudswell's, the tricky matter of costs being guaranteed by Thomas Barnes (Chairman of the WMCQR) on behalf of the Company and in November 1873 tenders were sought for a new firebox.

The engine was given a full cab in 1879 and in 1899 a new boiler, together with alterations to the cab, an extended bunker outside it, and the chimney lip was altered; the cylinder diameter was enlarged to 15½ in.

The engine took its name from the Kenyon family, a long-established landowning and business family in the neighbourhood, with legal and industrial connections.

Latterly Nos. 1 and 2 worked the Wrexham–Buckley passenger trains until the opening of The Hawarden Loop (31st March, 1890) when they returned to goods workings on the Buckley section, and moving coal trains off the Brymbo branch from Brymbo North Junction to Hope Junction. They did not usually work the Brymbo branch. When under repair, Nos 6 and 8 took their places.

---

§Condition: at present undergoing repairs in the shop, is waiting for a new crank axle ordered from Messrs. Beyer, Peacock & Co. Ltd. Boiler and firebox practically done. Frames cracked but effectively patched. Wheel centres cracked in places but give no trouble. Tyres about 2½ in. thick. Motion and rods etc. in fair working order. Cylinders good. Estimated present value including the new crank axle £680 0*s*. 0*d*.

No. 3 CHANCELLOR

The two previous engines were ordered by the Buckley Railway and were all it had. No. 3 did not receive a number in the WMCQR list for some time after delivery; it was in fact the only and original engine owned by the Company and used on the opening day and thereafter for passenger trains. It had been purchased by Benjamin Piercy as a Ballast Engine [*sic*] on behalf of the Company, from the LNWR in 1865 for £1,250, the engine being six-coupled with a four-wheeled tender:* its ornamental dome and green paint were long recalled. Its origins were with the LNWR when it carried No. 1377 as a 0–6–0 tender engine but it started life as St. Helen's Railway† No. 11

---

*Crewe records show Piercy also purchased a 2–4–0 by Jones & Potts of Newton-le-Willows for £850 on 13th June, 1865 (LNWR 185/785 of 1862/1190) which may have been used by him for construction work on WMCQR and perhaps passed to the Bishop's Castle Railway.

†Incorporated as St. Helen's Railway & Canal Co. 1845: by Act of 1864 those portions not already leased to or vested in LNWR passed to that Company.

TYNE did not appear in St.H.R. stock list of January 1855 so was acquired later: however, St.H.R. purchased two 'Bury coal engines' in December 1858 from LNWR (N.E.Div.) ex Manchester & Birmingham Railway Nos 28/9 and built by Bury, Curtis & Kennedy, Liverpool, in 1846 (they built no six-coupled engines before this date). These two were intended to work the Poynton branch. Possibly TYNE was one of this pair? (There is no confirmation). TYNE was rebuilt at St.Helen's March 1864.

[Note per D. Baxter from Bertram Baxter records. 10th November, 1989.]

TYNE. Its first duties were to haul the mixed rolling stock on hire from the Midland Wagon Co.‡ but it was taken off passenger work in poor condition. It was too high to work down to Connah's Quay due to the low bridges on that line, and it could not work the Ffrwd Branch as its wheelbase was too long for the sharp curves of the Branch. Certain repairs were done by the Cambrian at Oswestry (1867) and Wrexham (1868), the latter at no less than £450. Little is known about the engine before July 1868 when the Locomotive Department reported so adversely on it that it was taken out of service and HERCULES, an engine hired from Parry & Co., took its place. It went into the Works and returned to duty in January 1869; there was pride in the result and the money saved by having the job done by themselves.

In November 1873 when the Board's attention was drawn to the fact that other railway companies were doing all WMCQ engine repairs and that goodwill was wearing thin, CHANCELLOR was described as having one patched cylinder and a defective firebox. It is said that except 1874 – c.1880 when it was on passenger work Wrexham–Buckley, it worked on the Buckley section. It was scrapped soon afterwards; the tender stood on the wharf at Connah's Quay until at least 1904.

The name's origin is not known; it may have been given when Gladstone was Chancellor of the Exchequer 1859–1866 in Palmerston's government, in recognition of his support for the WMCQR.

From the foregoing it is clear that something had been done to reduce the height of the boiler mountings to enable it to work down to Connah's Quay. The difficulties of avoiding wheelslip, and the problems of the engine being pushed down-grade with its wheels locked by the brakes, created some generous 'flats' on the tyres. These were the bane of Davy Jones' (the ganger) life for when a particularly bad flat met the rail above a chair, the flange of that wheel would fracture the inside jaw of that chair: Davy would run after the engine, waving his arms and cursing, 'I'll break your legs from under you, you so-and-so'.

No. 3 (ex 7) (*no name*)

This number was used a second time in 1901 when a 'new' engine appeared from Rhosddu: using parts of No. 7 (*q.v.*). The work had taken from 1899 to January 1901 as a stock job, and was accepted as less than successful. The reason once given that this was due to friction between Willans and his men had no foundation in fact; Willans is recalled as a pleasant individual, a somewhat strict disciplinarian and his staff appeared to be a contented and loyal little body, many members of whom were proud of their railway 'as if it conferred the prestige of their great neighbours, the LNWR and GWR, upon them'.

No. 3's weakness was its penchant for bending valve spindles, which may have been due to the indirect layout of the valve gear. The drag links (or intermediate valve spindles of the latter) were inclined downwards from the motion plate in the forward direction, whilst the steam chests with their accompanying valve spindles, were also inclined downwards, in opposition and this arrangement was said to set up undue friction and stress between

‡Who had purchased it from Mr Blackmore (Minutes 6th June, 1867).

Locomotive 'Wheatley' Buckley & Connah's Quay Railway. The first locomotive built by Hudswell & Clarke Engineers, Leeds. September 1861.   *Authors Collection*

Rhosddu-built locomotive NO. 3 of 1901.

Reproduced from The Dunn Collection

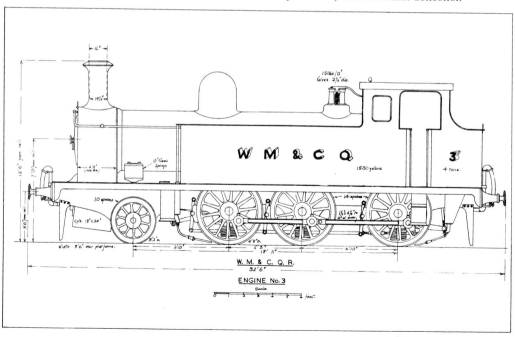

spindles and glands as there were no rocking arms to act as a medium. This caused overheating after a fast run; such an occasion occurred between Hawarden Bridge and Seacombe in 1902, after which the engine was disgraced and confined to local pick-up goods workings.[3] 'Nevertheless, it lasted until the 1923 amalgamation as a member of the GCR stock'.* (The foregoing incorporates notes verbatim from W. Noel Davies.)

All springing was of Timms coil type and the leading wheels had no radial axle.

§Described as 'Built at Wrexham by WM & CQR 1901'. Condition: all in very good working order. Tyres 2¼ in. thick. Estimated present value £1,950 0s. 0d.

No. 4 LORD RICHARD

The name was taken from Lord Richard Grosvenor (brother of the first Duke of Westminster) later Lord Stalbridge, Chairman of the LNWR.

The engine left the Leeds' works of Hudswell, Clarke & Rodgers on 30th November, 1865, to the order of 'B. Piercy, London, for the Buckley Railway' according to the maker's records. There is no reason to doubt it was intended for the WMCQR and not the Buckley, though the former was not yet opened. The design was similar to Nos 1 and 2 but the saddle tank was different.

One source states the engine was 'rebuilt' by Nasmyth, Wilson & Co. Ltd. of Patricroft in the summer of 1874 for £1,120 – a considerable amount – but the type of work is not stated.

During 1883 it featured in a runaway accident on the Buckley line which carried away the rear of the engine completely to the effect that in 1884 it was rebuilt as a four-coupled saddle tank with side coal pockets. In 1889 a pair of rear wheels was added and side tanks extending to the front edge of the smokebox took the place of the saddle tank.

Its maximum load on a northbound coal train was eighteen 10-ton wagons between Wrexham and Hope (whereas sister engine No. 5 could only take seventeen) and was considered a better engine than No. 5. 'It was extremely quiet and free from vibration little machine in motion, so looks apart, as compared with No. 5, it was another case of "Handsome is as Handsome does".'

Used on mineral trains on the Buckley section but on becoming four-coupled (1884) worked on Brymbo line as that branch was extended (i.e. 1884–1887). As 0–4–2T in 1889 worked Wrexham–Buckley passenger traffic – along with Nos 1 and 2 – until Hawarden Loop opened 31st May, 1890.

Along with No. 5 (as rebuilt) worked through to Chester on passenger duties after opening Chester–Connah's Quay line. When the Vron Branch opened 8th October, 1888 it headed a special train from there to Connah's Quay. (*L. Walker Records*) (A claim also made by Dunn for No. 6!)

It did not receive a GCR number, being scrapped in February 1905.

§Condition: cylinders want renewing, firebox wants patching; boiler old. Tyres good. Motion in fair working order: frames been renewed at hind end. Estimated present value £615 0s. 0d.

*In this regard, W.N. Davies was in error, for the engine was scrapped in June 1907 after carrying GCR 400B, which was then given to ex No. 6.

No. 5 SIR STEPHEN

Named after Sir Stephen Glynne of Hawarden Castle, Gladstone's brother-in-law. It was a sister engine to No. 4 and left Leeds on 30th December, 1865, again ordered by Piercy for the Buckley Railway, (this maker's entry may be due to the similarity of the engines to Nos. 1 and 2).

It was in Rhosddu for heavy repairs by 1873 when the fireboxes on both these engines had gone but repair work was repeatedly interrupted by urgent considerations and ten years elapsed whilst pieces of the locomotive were lying around. In 1883 it was decided to scrap it but second thoughts prevailed, and instructions to proceed immediately were given. The engine emerged in 1884 as a 0–6–0 side tank. To make it suitable for the new passenger service between Wrexham Central and Chester Northgate, via the new Hawarden Bridge, it was rebuilt again as a 2–4–0T in 1893 – this service had until then been worked by MSLR 2–4–2Ts 578 and 726, with WMCQR No. 4 occasionally. Both 4 and 5 were able to travel at 45 mph on the tight schedule on this working.

The rebuild included a copper-capped chimney. J.F. Willans (F. Willans' son) is credited with the design.

> She possessed a regulator handle shaped like a button hook, while the regulator itself wasn't exactly 'kind' in action and required a good deal of force to open it, with the result that it frequently opened too wide and the engine would leap forward like an antelope, rather than move away as a respectable engine should! If used on coal trains, the maximum load for the Down direction was seventeen 10 ton wagons . . .[4]

It was now said to be the prettiest engine on the line.

Utilised at first with No. 4 on Buckley section but from 1884 transferred to Brymbo line. As 2–4–0T worked inaugural Wrexham–Chester (Northgate) passenger train 1st April, 1890.

---

§Condition: boiler and firebox practically done; motion in very bad order. Tyres 2 in. thick. Frames cracked but effectively patched; wheels and axles good. Estimated present value £595 0s. 0d.

No. 6 QUEEN

This venerable machine was purchased from the LNWR at Liverpool on 22nd June, 1872 for £900 following the loan of an engine from the Metropolitan Railway which was found to be too heavy on the track.* By the end of the following year it had been out of service since October, awaiting materials from Crewe Works with which to effect repairs. A Report in November 1873 had said that the Company owned six engines; these were QUEEN, CHANCELLOR, KENYON, SIR STEPHEN, WHEATLEY, and LORD RICHARD. (The list is in the order as shown in the Minutes.) Not one was in good condition, but if they were kept in working order they would be sufficient; but this ideal was far from the case. They were suffering from lack of proper maintenance, age and the adverse gradients they worked. Their coal consumption was 'heavy'.

So, within months QUEEN had joined the half dozen demics which comprised the stud of the Company, even though F.W. Webb had maintained,

---

*Possibly one of their 0–6–0 side tanks built by The Worcester Engine Co. in 1868 and found to be too powerful, and offered for sale.

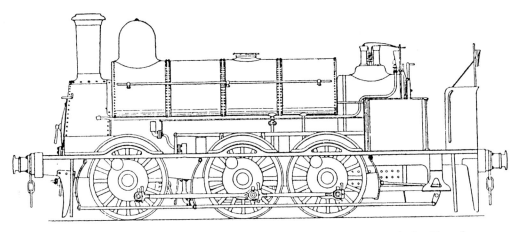

NO. 6, as purchased in 1874.   *Drawing by Ian Macnab*

before purchase was made, that the engine had had general repair at Crewe in June 1872.

The locomotive had begun life at Sharp Bros. of Manchester Works as a 0–6–0 tender engine in 1846 for the Manchester & Birmingham Railway (No. 30) and became LNWR No. 430 and 1222 in February 1866. It had been rebuilt at Crewe in 1870 as a 0–6–0 saddle tank and numbered 1029 in January 1872 and in this form came to the WMCQR. [A.C.W. Lowe, the locomotive historian, said that LNWR numbers 830 and 861 were stamped on the motion and E.K. Gregory added that before such engines were sold, they were given thorough overhaul and new boilers.]

In the guise as received, the engine worked the Wrexham–Buckley passenger service for eight years before being rebuilt at Wrexham in 1880 as a 0–8–0 saddle tank, when it was transferred to work coal trains from Brymbo North Junction to Hope Junction and then to the Buckley section where its coupled wheelbase pushed the section's curves out of line and the engine derailed frequently; it 'lacked boiler power' too. It is credited with working a special train to Connah's Quay to celebrate the opening of the Vron Branch. In 1890, Wrexham took the engine, together with a set of wheels off CHANCELLOR's tender, and converted it into a 0–6–2 saddle tank; in January 1891 it ran away down the Connah's Quay bank. The men jumped off and without a crew on board it was 'completely demolished' in the exchange yard there behind the LNWR station. It was averred that though neither driver nor fireman was hurt physically in any serious way, 'The driver lost his nerve and never drove again'.

After this most unregal event it was dragged from the gallimaufry and the remains dumped at Rhosddu whilst a decision might be made for, like other impecunious small railways, the WMCQR never disposed of anything which might be transferred into something useful. So it was with QUEEN. In 1897, matched to new frames, new water tank and bunker and containing very little of its 1846 birth, QUEEN emerged again as a 0−6−2 saddle tank (18⅛ ins. × 24 ins. cylinders: 4 ft 6 in. driving wheels:* weight in working order 47 tons 2 cwt.).

What circumstances dictated another change of policy is not known, but on the principle 'now you see me, now you don't' the engine disappeared into Rhosddu again to re-emerge in 1903 as a 0−8−0 saddle tank once more. Could one but see it, the engine now had a domeless boiler but one was added shortly afterwards − perhaps due to priming on the steep gradients? To obviate previous difficulties, the front and rear wheelsets were given axle boxes with much more play than before.

This remarkable survivor outlived the Queen after whom it was named. Receiving GCR No. 400, it became 400B in 1907 and was not cut up until the GCR had become part of the LNER: the end came at Wrexham in October 1923 and what better example could there be of the endless possibilities for extended use the steam locomotive of those times could be transformed and put?! The engine had continued to be shedded at Wrexham throughout its life under GCR auspices, but made occasional trips on goods trains to Bidston as well.

§Condition: boiler and firebox practically done: frames good: cylinders good. Motion good: crank axle nearly new. Coupled tyres good; trailing tyres want renewing. Estimated present value £1,220 0s. 0d.

No. 7 (1) (renumbered 3 in 1878) *No name but referred to as* OLD BET

Another fine old piece of engineering for which the WMCQR was well-known in those days. It had started life as a long-boilered 0−6−0 tender goods engine from Robert Stephenson & Co. of Newcastle-on-Tyne in 1851 and been purchased by one Crowther, a contractor, in March 1874: he offered it to the WMCQR who hired it, until purchased outright from the LNWR at Hereford shed in 1876. It cost £1,100. It was built for the South Staffordshire Railway as their No. 12, PELSALL, came into the LNWR on 5th May, 1852, and carried their No. 309 in 1861 and 909 in 1862; Crewe had rebuilt it as a six-coupled saddle tank in 1865, and renumberings were 1180 in February 1867 and 1806 in January 1872.

Rhosddu rebuilt it in 1882 using the second set of wheels from CHANCELLOR's tender, as a 0−6−2 saddle tank, the tank being extended backwards over the firebox, a cab was fitted with a longer bunker inside it, and the larger stovepipe chimney remained. The engine worked the Buckley Branch where it had the reputation for poor steaming. At times it took duty on coal trains from Brymbo Junction to Hope Junction (Penyffordd) alongside Nos. 1 and 2.

*4 ft 3 in. by January 1903.

No. 7 (2) THE DUKE

On 13th March, 1876 one of Hudswell, Clarke & Rodgers of Leeds standard four-coupled saddle tanks left their works, Works No. 178, a new engine for the WMCQR. Now, it is a coincidence that on 18th September Works No. 179 WATKINSON No. 2 (a similar engine) would also leave their premises. (*See page 87* for Watkinson). Two of the same design, destined for customers which were in rail link with each other cannot be unique, but must be unusual. Did Watkinson or the Railway Company influence one or the other, or did Hudswell's have a persuasive agent in North Wales? Did Watkinson require, as was frequently the case, a delayed delivery after the Works number was allocated in the books, or was it a case of payment in the matter of either customer? We do not know, suffice that the WMCQR paid £1,200 and the object was to replace the two horses at Connah's Quay, by steam locomotive.

The engine seems to have led an uneventful life for it passed into the ranks of the GCR, being numbered 401B, and scrapped in August 1909. It was distinguished by its stovepipe chimney, weatherboards and absence of cab. Although usually on the docks, it was purloined for ballast trains and when No. 14 (2) was off duty, shunted Wrexham (Central) yard.

§Condition: boiler and firebox require renewing. Tyres 2⅜ in. thick require turning up. Motion very slack; wheels good; frames good. Estimated present value £500 0s. 0d.

No. 8 PREMIER

Sharp, Stewart & Co. Ltd. of Manchester supplied this engine new to WMCQR specification in 1880 at a cost of £2,136. The full-length tanks and open-sided cab were suited to the Buckley section. It was contemporarily described as 'a powerful engine specially built for working the heavily-graded Buckley Branch, and capable of handling large loads up the bank'. One opinion is that the final closing of the tramroads around Buckley led to heavy increase in traffic.[5]

The side tanks were taken right up to the front of the smokebox, and were cut away for access to the inside motion. Together with No. 6, the two engines worked the Buckley line not only until the GCR took over but, as evidence of their satisfactory performance (and perhaps also as the lack of any GCR engine suited to the task) they continued on this duty until the early 1920s. Both engines were involved in the Connah's Quay smash of 9th January, 1891 when No. 6 hit No. 8 in the coal sidings there.*

Renumbering took place in 1905 as 401, 405 in 1910, and 405C in 1912: scrapping took place in September 1922.

§Condition: in good working order. Outside firebox patched; firebox has had new half sides. Estimated present value £1,375 0s. 0d.

*The version that pointsmen resisted turning the runaway No.8 and train into the LNWR exchange sidings for fear of retribution by that Company is not borne out by the newspaper account, for the accident appears to have taken place entirely on the 'inland side' of the LNWR!

No. 9 DEE

Thomas Butlin & Co., contractors of Wellingborough, bought this engine from Hudswell, Clarke & Rodgers in 1872; it was named DAVID initially and it left Leeds on 28th March of that year.

The WMCQR bought it on 28th October, 1881 not from Butlin, but from Hudswell who had the engine for sale; the price was £750 and the intention was that it should work alongside DUKE (the name had been abbreviated) on Connah's Quay Docks. As with the pair of engines working the Buckley line, so did Nos. 7 and 9 work together on Deeside for many years.

It was numbered 402B by the GCR and scrapped in August 1909.

(As with No. 7, it might be found on ballast trains or as Wrexham shunter.)

§Condition: this engine is in the shop being rebuilt with new boiler and firebox, new smokebox, cab fitted, coal bunker increased to 15 cwt. capacity. New slidebars, new crossheads, new rod ends and general overhauling. Nearly finished. Estimated present value £950 0s.0d.

No. 10 EMILY

This engine too, had interesting origins. At first, the Broughton & Plas Power Coal Co. (of which Robertson was an owner) had no WMCQR rail links: these pits were sunk in 1877 but not operative until 1882. In the early 80s, at the instigation of Robertson, R.A. Kyrke and others, a branch line was planned from Brymbo Junction on the WMCQR main line, but a change of policy resulted in the branch being extended up to Brymbo and the existing section of the branch between Brymbo Junction on the main line, together with the extension becoming the property of the WMCQR.

The original pit began as the Broughton Coal Co., the name being changed in January 1881. It already owned a Beyer, Peacock four-coupled engine of 1857 and another by Andrew Barclay, Sons & Co. Ltd. of 1876. It had a connection with the GWR Wrexham–Minera branch so was not rail-isolated: it closed in 1878.

The Beyer design was similar to an engine supplied to the Crewe Coal & Iron Co. named CREWE in 1867: the Crewe engine had no cab*, only a weatherboard, but the Broughton engine had a full cab. It was to be delivered by 26th February, 1882 but was late; a larger water tank of saddle type was extended over the smokebox to carry 1,000 gallons, and a larger 'coke box' fitted. The frames at the rear were extended 9 in. longer than the Crewe engine. It was named before leaving Gorton, and the drawing adds that boiler plates were to be supplied by Grillo Funke, and copper tubes by Pontifex & Wood. As built the smokebox door sloped, the Salter valves were in the dome and the working pressure 120 lb.

A financial arrangement with E.D. Till allowed the engine to pass to the WMCQR under a hire purchase scheme of September 1882. In 1904 the engine was rebuilt with new boiler and firebox and the boiler fittings reduced in height to enable it to work the Buckley line into Connah's Quay.

The GCR numbered it 402, and 402B in 1910; and it was scrapped in March 1913.

*Beyer, Peacock used the term 'house' instead of the widely used 'cab'.

Its most glorious day was to work, suitably garlanded for the event, the trains on the opening day of the new line between the Wrexham stations, 1st November, 1887: there was free travel for all on that occasion: however, most of its early life was on humble duty on the Brymbo branch.

Beyer, Peacock used the design once more in an engine for Leighswood Colliery, named LEIGH'S WOOD.

Another glorious day came when EMILY and five coaches worked the first passenger train on the Brymbo branch, stopping at Moss & Pentre and Plas Power stations – buildings at the former were unfinished (1st August, 1889). It worked the Wrexham–Buckley passenger trips whilst the large 0–6–2STs ran the Brymbo line. When Brymbo traffic fell away, No. 10 came back again, working all passenger turns except on Saturdays when the 0–6–2ST came on for the day. At the opening of the North Wales & Liverpool Railway it could be found at Bidston, Chester or Wrexham on passenger trains!

In April 1888 BPPCCL Minutes allow WMCQR to use the Plas Power Colliery's sidings and engine (COLLIER?) for 12 months 'after opening of their Plas Power goods shed', and on the basis of 2d. per ton.

---

§Condition: boiler in good order; firebox been recently patched inside and outside. Tyres 2 in. thick. The engine generally is in good running order. Estimated present value £1,030 0s. 0d.

No. 11

Hudswell, Clarke & Co. Ltd. (formerly Hudswell, Clarke & Rodgers) had built up a good relationship with the Company, and in earlier days the Board had often sought Mr Clarke's advice. So it was that the order for No. 11 also went to Leeds who supplied this four-coupled saddle tank in 1885, the engine leaving Leeds on 30th May. It was a special development for working the steep Ffrwd and Vron branches, though what engines had been allocated to this duty before is not known. With larger diameter cylinders but retaining the 20 in. stroke, it was a much stronger engine than other four-coupled tank engines on the line, weighing over 22 tons in working order. Short powerful bursts of duty were required. The engine was smart but simple though a copper-capped chimney gave it an air. W. Noel Davies wrote that 'a special daily train of 20–25 wagons (empties returning) to Vron Colliery, was hauled by WMCQR locomotive VRON'. The reference to a name has no official backing, and it may simply have been a nickname: it was the first WMCQR engine not to carry a name or nickname.

It received No. 403B from the GCR and was scrapped in February 1907, but had left WMCQR metals before this date to work at Grimsby docks.

---

§Condition: boiler and firebox in good order; motion rather slack. Tyres 2 in. thick and want turning up. Estimated present value £860 0s. 0d.

Nos. 12 and 13

The existing WMCQR stud was a motley collection with no standardisation whatsoever; it was a nightmare to keep such elderly machines in running order, and the individuality of each added to the time and cost of

Courtesy of Manchester Museum of Science & Industry

Maker's drawing of NO. 12, built 1885.

repairs. However, in the second Piercy Period from 1882 (if such may be dubbed) the finance was available to spend £2,325 on each of two 0–6–2 saddle tank engines from Beyer, Peacock; the order was placed in December 1884. Their task was to haul heavy coal trains from Brymbo, off the Branch onto the main line and thence to the LNWR exchange sidings at Hope Junction: also similar trains from Wrexham to that point. Another use for them was found on Saturdays when the half-hourly Brymbo Branch passenger workings were heavily loaded, not forgetting any passenger workings on Bank Holidays: but they were not permitted on the Buckley–Connah's Quay section.

These two machines must have seemed a miracle to the WMCQR enginemen. They were almost identical, but No. 12 was built with the saddle tank carried right up to the smokebox front whilst No. 13's was over the boiler and firebox only. The Minutes suggest that the original payment was by hire purchase (Beyer, Peacock records do not contain such information) but through whom is not known; however, on 27th November, 1886 the Secretary told the Board 'a friend was willing to take up the hire purchase Agreement at a lower rate of interest than at present'. We are not enlightened any further.

No. 12 ran away down the Brymbo line with a goods train from the terminus and through Moss & Pentre, during World War I.

It was intended to use these engines in connection with the export coal traffic from Connah's Quay, using the big dock then planned to be built there. Alas, that dock was never made.

No. 12 was given 403 by the GCR and 403B in 1910; it was sold to the Admiralty in July 1918 for use at Beachley Dock, Chepstow, but this work was never completed, and the engine found itself by 1920 in the hands of a dealer at Newport, one C.D. Philips. An unconfirmed report relates to it being sold and shipped out to Mauritius[6] – this cannot be.

After 1905 No. 13 was used as a banking engine between Hawarden Bridge and Buckley Junction.

No. 13 became GCR No. 404 and 404B in 1912. It too was sold to the Admiralty in July 1918 for the same work, and then passed to Llwynon Colliery Co., and later to Cefn Coed Colliery at Crynant, Neath, South Wales in 1922, per A.R. Adams & Sons Ltd. dealers of Newport.

The maximum load was twenty-four 10 ton loaded wagons, and both were still at Wrexham shed in 1919.

---

§[This report is most misleading. It was overlooked that No. 12 had been fitted with a larger saddle tank, and its dimensions are shown in the Records report as to water capacity and weight in working order, as identical with No. 13.]

No. 12 Condition: boiler has been recently tubed, and firebox repaired with new half side; motion in good running order. Tyres of coupled wheels nearly new, those of trailing wheels 2 in. thick. Estimated present value £1,500 0s. 0d.

No. 13 Condition: boiler and firebox in good order; motion in good running order. Tyres of coupled wheels nearly new, those of trailing wheels getting thin. Estimated present value £1,500 0s. 0d.

This engine was reboilered at Gorton in 1915, fitted with extended smokebox and given a GCR chimney before being sold in 1918.

No. 14 (1)

It would seem strange for the Company to acquire yet another elderly piece of machinery in 1887, but there were signs of growth on all sides; the new line right into Wrexham, the Brymbo Branch, the beginnings of The Hawarden Loop and – so it is said – the realisation that when The Loop was opened, there would be a short piece of line between the new junction on The Loop and the old route into Buckley which would require a passenger service as between that junction and what would later become 'Old Buckley'.

Tradition has it that No. 14 was purchased for this working.

The engine was once a four-coupled tender type by Isaac Dodds & Son of Rotherham, built in 1854, becoming No. 22 on the Newport, Abergavenny & Hereford Railway who rebuilt it as 0−4−2 side tank at Hereford (Barton) in 1860* and when that line was absorbed by the West Midland the latter Company gave it No. 92 in 1861. The WMR passed into the GWR who gave it No. 227 in 1863; in this guise it was purchased by the Bishop's Castle Railway in 1870, to become their PERSEVERANCE and due to links between BCR and WMCQR, the latter acquired it in 1887. Rhosddu rebuilt it (retaining the side tanks) in 1890 but following the cessation of Old Buckley passenger workings (finally) in February 1895 the engine was withdrawn and sold in September 1895 to W.Y. Craig & Sons, Brynkinallt Colliery, Chirk.

A driver said of it that it possessed the smallest firebox he had ever seen: it would only haul 7 wagons up the short rise from Llay Hall Colliery Branch onto the main line, and if put to work on passenger duties, as soon as approximately 30 mph was reached, the driving wheels would lose grip and slip violently.

Upon withdrawal, a new No. 14 took its place.

No. 14 (2)

A small six-coupled saddle tank (maker's Type Q) by Manning, Wardle & Co. Ltd. of Leeds, was acquired in 1895 for £660 from H. Croom Johnson, the contractor for the North Wales & Liverpool Railway on expiration of his work. It was new to J.D. Howell, contractor of Chorlton-cum-Hardy, Manchester, in 1889 for building the Chorlton-cum-Hardy to Manchester Ship Canal, Stretford link, before becoming the property of Johnson.

[Johnson was a local contractor based on premises in King Street, Wrexham. Among his railway construction was the Kerry Tramway (1887), the reconstruction of the Glyn Valley Tramway in 1887−9, together with Dee embanking in 1894. No. 14 was one of two engines he had for sale in 1895. The complex story of the brass and iron foundry of Cudworth & Johnson, The Eagle Foundry in Wrexham which had locomotive dealership interests which involved – unofficially – the use of equipment at Rhosddu, is inadmissible here, but Arthur Cudworth set up on his own from 1904, using his own name. Johnson appears to have continued in business under

---

*One of three of the same type purchased from Thomas Brassey (who had been working the line and supplying engines) in December 1854, being the last of the trio and the only one converted into a tank engine: the other two gave another decade of service as 0−4−0 tender engines on the GWR. [Apart from these three, all other NA&HR engines were supplied by E.B. Wilson & Co.]

the former partnership title. The ancestry of Johnson is not entirely clarified, and it may be asked if he was related to H. Croom Johnson?]

It was given No. 404B by the GCR whom it might be thought, would find little merit in such a small locomotive: however, it survived until 1910.[7]

It was used for shunting at Wrexham (Central) yard and relieved No. 11 on the Ffrwd Branch when that engine was in the Works.

§Condition: in good working order, except for a flaw in the crank axle. Tyres 2¼ in. thick. Estimated present value £1,000 0s. 0d.

Nos. 15 and 16

The 0–6–2 tank engine had proved itself a very suitable design for WMCQR work as Nos. 12 and 13 had demonstrated, so two further Beyer, Peacock-built machines were supplied in 1888 at a cost of £2,300 each. They were as the previous engines save that the saddle tanks were larger and vacuum brake – anticipating legislation – was fitted from the start to make them suitable for passenger working. They took up duties alongside Nos. 12 and 13 and at last the Company had a quartet of excellent progeny.

They were renumbered 405 and 405B (ex No. 15) and 406 and 406B (ex No. 16), the suffixes being added in 1910. Scrapping dates were 8th May, 1922 and July 1922 respectively. The maximum load was twenty-four 10 ton loaded wagons.

§No. 15 Condition: in good working order. Estimated present value £1,540 0s. 0d. No. 16 Condition: repairs wanted to firebox, but otherwise in good working order. Estimated present value £1,500 0s. 0d.

Nos. 17 and 18

It could be argued that Nos. 15 and 16 were the last true WMCQR engines as Nos. 17 and 18, being built to work the North Wales & Liverpool, and Wirral line to Seacombe (and although carrying WMCQR numbers) were virtually MSLR engines, designed by Harry Pollitt, to their Class 9F type. However, Beyer, Peacock again was the builder and they cost £2,300 each. Certainly they were the last engines to be added to the WMCQR locomotive list. Contemporary descriptions state that this was the standard MSLR goods engine of a type which had been running over the WMCQR for some time, according to the Running Powers given to the MSLR.

In due course they became GCR 409 and 410, the former existed as LNER 5409 and BR 69270 until October 1956 and the latter survived as LNER 5410 until December 1936. They were at first put on heavy coal train duty to Hope Junction, then on the Bidston goods. From c.1902 two double trips were worked by No. 17 until the end of 1904, being Wrexham–Seacombe and Seacombe–Chester daily, (the WMCQR timetable inferring at this period that the route – 29 m 27 ch. – over the whole distance Wrexham–Seacombe was the main line of the WMCQR!)

The maximum load was thirty 10 ton loaded wagons, though No. 17 was credited with hauling thirty-four 10 ton loaded wagons from Wrexham collieries to Birkenhead Docks.

§No. 17 Condition: excepting that the motion kicks a little and that the small ends of the connecting rods knock, the engine is in very good working order. Recently had new tyres, tubes and crank axle. Estimated present value £2,070 0s. 0d.

No. 18 Condition: recently had new tubes and a new crank axle. In very good working order except that the tyres are nearly done. Estimated present value £1,980 0s. 0d.

Locomotive epilogue (*The estimated cost of repairs follows in each case.*)

Having surveyed the locomotive situation in late 1902, Gorton set about a thorough examination during 1904 and sent a report to J.G. Robinson in December that year; not all was as well as before, and with the absorption of the WMCQR in view, the GCR was not anxious to load itself with a heap of old ironmongery. Hence:

No. 1 Frames patched. Cylinders new in 1903. Motion slack. Wheels good. Tyres will soon need turning up. Straight axles (no date) but probably old. Crank axle a secondhand one ex-LNWR put under in 1886. Brake work done. Spring link buckles much worn, with wheels rubbing. Boiler much patched. Tubes new in 1903. Firebox fair: new in 1895. Tank bad. Age of boiler 1861. Age of firebox 1896. (Not worth repairing.)

[Some dates are slightly odd, but with an original boiler shell and careful repairs executed in the simple surroundings at Rhosddu, this first Buckley Railway engine had become an excellent example of good workmanship on the part of its builders: Author.]

No. 2 Frames good. Cylinders good. Motion fair working order. Wheels good (two new ones recently put on). Tyres 2¾ in. thick. Straight axles no date, but probably old. Crank axle new in 1903, also cylinders and tyres. Boiler and firebox have just had some repairs done to them so may last a few months longer. They are done, however. Tank is very thin. This engine should have been scrapped before so much was put in during 1902–3. Age of boiler 1862. Age of firebox 1881. Age of front tubeplate 1881. Age of tubes 1894. (Not worth repairing.)

[No. 2 was clearly on borrowed time!: Author]

No. 3 This engine, built in 1901, can scarcely be said to have been new at that date as the cylinders and crank axle were taken from other engines. The boiler is patched all round casing, so it is very likely this was old loco. Excepting that the motion is very slack and that the slide valves blow, this engine is in good order generally. The tyres are 2 in. thick. Age of boiler 1885 (repaired in 1901): remainder 1901. (£45)

No. 4 Frames broken and mended with hornblocks. Tyres 2¼ in. thick and want turning. Motion slack. Axleboxes and slidebars knock. Spoke of l.h. trailing wheel broken. Cylinders want renewing. Boiler patched but in fair condition. Firebox done. Age of boiler 1864: ages of firebox and tubeplates 1884: of tubes 1898. (Not worth repairing.)

No. 5 This engine is done, nothing with the exception of the wheels and axles is fit for anything but scrap. Age of boiler 1865: firebox and tubeplate 1887: smokebox tubeplate 1883. Condemned – not in service. (Not worth repairing.)

No. 6 In good working order. Recommenced work August 1903 after having had new boiler complete, new trailing axle, new trailing coupling rods. Note: the boiler of this engine has a very short dome placed over the firebox end and is reported to make very wet steam. Tyres will soon want turning up. (£18)

No. 7 Motion rather slack. Tyres 2 in. thick and will need turning. Boiler patched leaks a little at bottom corners of firebox. Firebox in good condition. Top plate of one of leading springs broke. This engine was in shops for general repairs in 1903 when it had a new firebox and new smokebox tubeplate. Cylinders old. Engine may be said to be in fair working order generally. Age of boiler 1878: remainder 1903. (£75)

No. 8 Frames good. Wheels good. Crank axle new July 1903. Motion slack. Crossheads split and hooped. Tyres will soon want turning up. Cylinders new in 1897. Boiler much patched around bottom. Foundation ring leaks. Firebox done. Tubes new in 1893. Three burst. Age of boiler 1880: of firebox 1894. (£260)

No. 9 This engine was rebuilt in 1902–3 and commenced work January 1903 after the following repairs: new boiler complete: new cab, smokebox, coal bunker (capacity increased), slidebars, crossheads, connecting and coupling rod ends. Presently – wheels and frames good. Motion very slack. Tyres 2½ in. thick. Brakework very much worn. Boiler and firebox in good condition. This engine may be described as fairly good condition generally but the parts are too light and the bearing surfaces are too small for anything but very light work. (£30)

No. 10 This engine is now in the shop at Wrexham undergoing considerable repairs: new tyres: new pistons and rods, motion pins, crossheads, firebox tubeplate, door plate and half sides: new smokebox tubeplate and foundation ring. Wheels and axles are good. Cylinders in fair condition, but would be all the better for re-boring. Frames patched above driving horns. One hornblock broke across corner. The dome of the boiler has been reduced in height 7½ in.: wet steam may be the result of this.* Age of boiler 1882: remainder 1904 – boiler presently out of frames. (No figure.)

No. 11 Frames good. Wheels good. Motion rather slack. Tyres new. Boiler barrel repaired September 1904; appears to be good. Tubeplate want repairs; engine otherwise in good condition. Age of boiler and remainder 1885. (Say £60)

No. 12 Frames and wheels good. Motion fairly. Cylinders need renewing. Boiler needs 'cropping' round firebox casing. Big end journals of crank axle in *very* bad condition. Note: in order to clean out firebox water spaces, it is found necessary to have plugs *inside* copper firebox. Age of boiler and remainder 1885. (£800)

No. 13 Frames and wheels good. Tyres 2½ in. thick need turning up. Cylinders and motion good. Brakeblocks done. Axleboxes knock. Boiler and firebox fair condition. Tank thin. (Note: re plugs as for No. 12.) Age of boiler 1885. (£235)

No. 14 Frames and wheels good. Tyres 2⅛ in. thick and will soon need turning up. Motionwork very slack. Coupling rods need re-bushing. Flaw in crank axle. Boiler: smokebox tubeplate leaks at angleiron. Bottom corners firebox leak. Firebox nearly done. Age of boiler etc. 1889. (£255)

No. 15 Frames and wheels good. Tyres 2½ in. thick need turning up. Axleboxes knock. Motion in good order. Cylinders new. Boiler fair. Firebox needs overhaul. (Plug holes inside firebox.) New crank axle 1900. Age of boiler etc. 1888. (£30)

No. 16 Frames, wheels good. Tyres 2¾ in. thick need turning up. Crank axle new January 1904. Motion very slack: axleboxes knock. Smokebox side needs patching. Boiler and firebox in bad condition: tubes done. (Plug holes inside firebox.) Age of boiler etc. 1888. (£650)

---

*Had these domes been reduced in height to allow engines to work Buckley section?

Nos. 17 and 18 [Both these engines had had new crank axles and tyres. Boilers were good but fireboxes needed renewing. They were only eight years old.] (£240 each engine)

The 1904 report ended with a life-expectancy of each engine:

No. 1   May be useful for one year . . . too old to last in present condition.

No. 2   Not worth a new boiler considering age of engine.

No. 3   May last a number of years.

No. 4   Frames broke, cylinders done, firebox done, boiler very old, not worth overhauling.

No. 5   Ready for scrap heap. Nothing, with the exception of the wheels and axles, is fit for service.

No. 6   . . . may last a number of years, say 10 . . . some alteration of dome appears necessary.

No. 7   . . . may last a few years.

No. 8   . . . ditto.

No. 9   . . . but only fit for very light work . . . after overhauling may last for 10 years.

No. 10   After extensive repairs now in hand, should be good for about 10 years.

No. 11   . . . in good condition.

No. 12   . . . engine appears to be worth . . . repairs.

No. 13   . . . needs overhauling . . . otherwise in good condition.

No. 14   . . . engine appears to be worth (these) repairs.

No. 15   . . . in good condition.

No. 16   . . . needs (list of work follows).

No. 17   . . . in good condition.

No. 18   . . . in good condition.

Other Locomotives

HERCULES

Isaac Watt Boulton of Ashton-under-Lyne bought four 0–6–0 tender engines from Cardiff in 1866. They had slightly oval boilers and haycock fireboxes and HERCULES (a name bestowed by Boulton, it would seem) was possibly built by Thwaites & Carbutt of Bradford. Boulton sold the engine, as received including tender, to the WMCQR in August 1867 for £900.[8] With its 5 ft 6 in. diam. driving wheels it would have been at a serious disadvantage on the WMCQR and by 1868 it was back – having broken down – at Ashton: financial arrangements are not recorded. It was then converted to a saddle tank with 3 ft 6 in. wheels. Side sheets to the cab were cut from the redundant tender.

By August 1868 the engine was on hire to Parry & Co. of London,[9] but the WMCQR Minutes refer to arrangements made to hire an engine from Parry for 3 months @ £12 10s. 0d. In the following July the engine was stopped for repairs and instructions were given by the Board not to use it 'unless safe'.

The WMCQR's CHANCELLOR came out after repair in late 1868 and possibly by then (or sooner) HERCULES left the scene. Bennett states the engine remained on the WMCQR for 2½ years: there is no further reference in the Company's records, however, it was working at St. Helen's, Lancashire, by 1871.

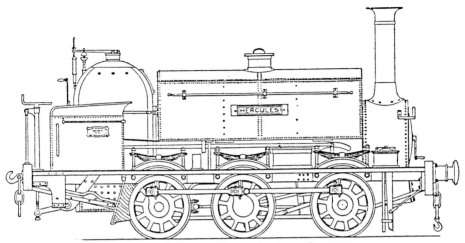

HERCULES, as rebuilt at Ashton-under-Lyne after 1868.

Engine Loads for Goods Trains

ex Buckley Railway section

WMCQR No.	Type	Down Wrexham to Hope Junc.	Brymbo Branch	Down Buckley to Northop Hall	Down Buckley Junc. to Connah's Quay
1 & 2	0−6−0ST	18	8	15	6 Up 30 Down
3	2−6−0T	26	—	—	—
4	0−4−2T ⎫				
5	2−4−0T ⎭	18	8	—	—
6	0−8−0ST	20	—	15	7 Up 25 Down
8	0−6−0T	24	—	18	8 Up 30 Down
10	0−6−0T	18	8	—	—
12, 13 15, 16	0−6−2ST	26	11	18	8 Up 23 Down
17, 18	0−6−2T	29	13	—	—

Increased load south of Northop Hall +5.

N.B. These are GCR figures – 'DOWN' was WMCQR 'UP'.

From time to time, as mentioned in the Chronology, it was necessary through emergencies to borrow/hire and consider other motive power. Among these are:

VOLUNTEER (similar to this drawing) was hired from the Cambrian Railways in the early 1870s.

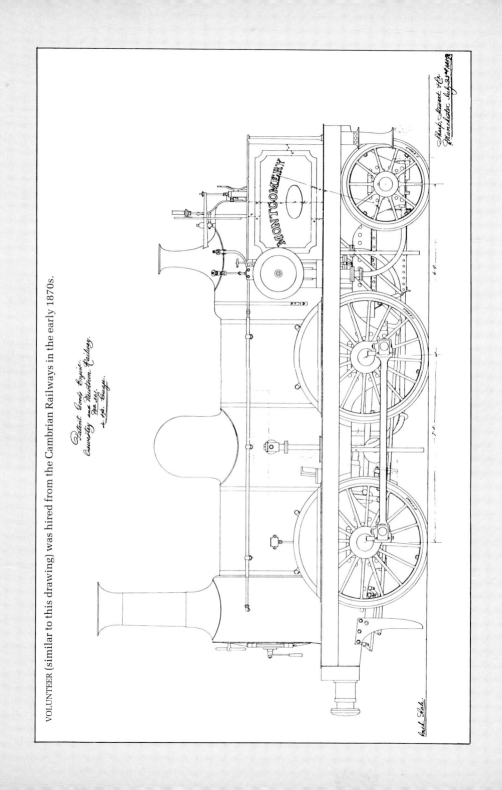

1) Cambrian Railways 0–4–2 tender engine VOLUNTEER,[10] (hired about 1872–3). Supplied to the Oswestry & Newtown Railway, No. 9 VOLUNTEER was built 12/1860 (SS 1226) – last of 6 of 'Volunteer' class 0–4–2 tender 5 ft driving wheels, 15½ in. × 22 in. cylinders. Sharp, Stewart & Co., Manchester, 1859–60. Named after Montgomeryshire Railway Volunteers.[11]

Original had name painted on footplate side sheets (no full cab, weatherboard only as bought and therefore as used on WMCQR). Ownership plate a narrow rectangle on valance above driving wheels. No engine brakes. [Oswestry & Newtown Railway became part of Cambrian Railways 25th July, 1864.] Maker's drawing MONTGOMERY 22nd July, 1859 states 'Patent Goods Engine'. Steam water pump l.h.s. firebox. Bell-mouth chimney, raised firebox casing – said to have Giffard injectors. Diameter rear wheels 3 ft 6 in. not 3 ft 1½ in. Weight in working order: 24 ton. 8 cwt. 120 lbs. Tractive effort: 9023 lbs. Wood block brakes, 4 wh. tender. After 1867 locomotive hired to Carnarvonshire Railway, but back by 1869.[12] Later fitted vacuum brake and steam brake. To surplus stock June 1893.

2) A locomotive from Henry Hughes & Co. of Loughborough in September 1867; returned as being too light for the work. If this is one of those advertised in the engineering press of those times, it would be a small four-coupled tank engine suited to industrial use.

3) The engine found to be too heavy for the Buckley line (*see page 158*) may have been a Metropolitan Railway six-coupled tank – these engines ultimately sold to Sirhowy, and Taff Vale Railways and known as the St. John's Wood 0–6–0 tanks.

4) Two engines from Lancashire & Yorkshire Railway, and one from LNWR in September 1873, plus a Cambrian Railways type in the mid-1870s.

Takeover by Great Central Railway (6th January, 1905)

At this date there were 18 engines on WMCQR books: the following action was taken:

    4 condemned
    6 placed in duplicate GCR stock list
    8 taken into GCR stock

Locomotives were taken off the passenger services on the Seacombe and Brymbo Branches and replaced by steam railcars built for the GCR in 1904–5.

Among locomotives allocated to the WMCQR section after takeover, there was a preponderance of mineral and shunting engines to replace the withdrawals of WMCQR-stock. Ex-GCR mixed traffic and passenger engines predominated for passenger work, but generally the latter were shedded off the WMCQR system.

The resident stock, based on Connah's Quay and Wrexham Sheds, did its work at Connah's Quay, on the Buckley section, on the dwindling business of the Brymbo Branch as collieries closed, and in the two Wrexham station yards. The Ffrwd Branch service was an early casualty after the 1923 grouping, as a reference to the closing dates of collieries thereon will show. The

Llay Hall Branch, with its own motive power, was independent and the mainline engine could run to the exchange yard at the Junction whilst its train stood, engineless, for as brief a time as possible, on the running lines.

Among six types of engine allocated for these duties were: (*with approximate dates*)

> Six 0–6–0ST ex-GCR of 1897. LNER Class J 62.
> One 0–6–0T ex-GCR of 1906. LNER Class J 63.
> Four ex-Lancashire, Derbyshire & East Coast Railway 0–6–0T of 1897.
>   LNER Class J 60 (between the Wars).
> Two ex-Great Eastern Railway 0–6–0T of 1899. LNER Class J 69 (1950s).
> One LNER Sentinel-built 2 speed four-wheeled of 1927.
>   LNER Class Y 3 (1930s).
> A small number of ex-North Eastern Railway 0–6–0T of 1898.
>   LNER Class J 72 (World War II).

Of the foregoing, Classes J 69 and J 72 were allocated to the Buckley –Connah's Quay section, and were permitted to shunt Connah's Quay Docks, a notice to this effect on the Docks drew attention to the restriction. The Class J 72 were later moved on to Bidston Shed from where they were withdrawn. Their place was taken by Drewry-built diesel shunting units for a time.

At this latter period three GWR type six-coupled pannier tanks Nos.1618, 1662 and 1669[13] were allocated to Rhosddu; the first was built in the 1949–50 period batch and the last two in the 1954–55 batch, 1669 being in the last to be built. These were essentially Swindon-style engines built to replace withdrawn 2021 Class machines, a light engine of which there became an acute shortage at that time. These three engines could be found anywhere on the former WMCQR system then extant, for instance, Llay Hall.

During this same time, Rhosddu remained an important centre for locomotive repairs and engines from other depots were sent there for that purpose. When Rhosddu closed, such engines as were stabled there for use on local duties, were transferred to the former GWR Shed at Croes Newydd, along with the men concerned. It was many months before Rhosddu and Croes Newydd men would deign to speak to each other, the establishment workforce alluding to the ex-Rhosddu employees as 'Those Eleneeah B.....*

Livery of Locomotives

Indian red, lined black/amber: tanks had initials in gold: some engine numbers on bunker in gold: saddle tanks had brass numberplates on red ground: beams, vermilion with white numbers: inside frames and motion, strawberry. Original WMCQR livery was green, but such old engines became red. From 1902, black, lined Indian red/amber: beams, black: cab interior, cream. (Original Buckley Railway livery was maroon).
Names – removed from 1880 on.
Note No. 6 rebuilt as 0–8–0, painted black and lined out. Indian red used after Nos. 9 and 16 had been repainted experimentally this way to see if it lasted better; it did! Thereafter became standard livery with black beams.

*I am indebted to David McIntosh, a Provincial Manager of British Rail, who started his railway career as a Cleaner at Rhosddu Shed.

Contractor's locomotive

The railways on which all the foregoing engines earned their keep were created by contractors who converted some unpromising terrain into a relatively near-level plateau on which these machines might do their work: the contractor would use a steam locomotive to prosecute the job; an un-authenticated story[14] concerns that used for the building of the Buckley Railway, (surely using Connah's Quay as his starting point as it would be a more convenient place to which materials could be despatched?). The engine is said to have been one of Manning, Wardle's six-coupled saddle tank engines, on hire. The suggestion that it was their Works No. 39 of 1861 and named ANNA MARIA has yet to be supported, for a copy of the Maker's Lists for this period does not reveal such an engine.

References

[1] THE RAILWAY FOUNDRY, LEEDS (R.N. Redman) has been consulted in connection with Hudswell, Clarke & Rodgers and Hudswell, Clarke & Co. products.

[2] Gorton Records.

[3] THE ENGINEER, 21st November, 1892. Shortcomings of the valvegear were a legacy of using parts off the old engine.

[4] Lawrence Walker Records show a reversion to 0–6–0T again in 1893 and a return to 2–4–0T in 1898!

[5] Lawrence Walker Records.

[6] RAILWAYS OF AFRICA. (A.E. Durrant.)

[7] Lawrence Walker Records.

[8] THE CHRONICLES OF BOULTON'S SIDING p. 80 (A. Rosling Bennett).

[9] THE CHRONICLES OF BOULTON'S SIDING p. 80 (A. Rosling Bennett).

[10] STEPHENSON LOCOMOTIVE SOCIETY JOURNAL 1943, p. 63. (R.E. Thomas).

[11] CAMBRIAN RAILWAYS; Vol. 1 page 148, plate 21. (Christiansen and Miller).

[12] LOCOMOTIVES OF THE GREAT WESTERN RAILWAY Part 10; p. K56 and fig. K82. (R.C.T.S.)

[13] LOCOMOTIVES OF THE GREAT WESTERN RAILWAY Part 5; pp. E85–6. (R.C.T.S.)

[14] Lawrence Walker Records.

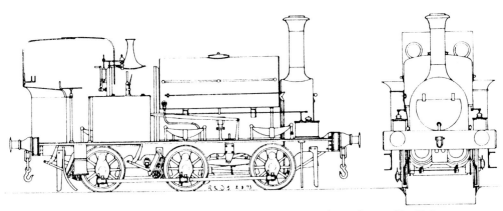

Manning Wardle & Co. Ltd. contractor's locomotive, similar to that used by H. Croom Johnson.   *Courtesy* RAILWAY MODELLER

WMCQR No.	Name	Type	Builder	Works No.	Date	Driving wheels diam. ft. in.	Cyls. in.	W.W.O. Tons Cwt	Gallons	(If secondhand, Seller)	Price £	Date	Great Central Nos. 1	2	3
1	WHEATLEY	0-6-0ST	HCR	1	1861	4 —	15 × 24	34 —	700	(new)	1,956 10s.	—	1B		
2	KENYON	0-6-0ST	HCR	2	1861	4 —	15 × 24	34 —	700	(new)	1,956 10s.	—			
3 (1)	CHANCELLOR	0-6-0 tender	BCK	?	c1845	4 6	14½ × 22	?	?	per B. Piercy exLNWR	1,250 0s.	1865			
3 (2) (ex 7)	—	2-6-0T	WMCQR	—	1899–1901	4 8	18 × 24	55 —	1,500	(rebuild from 7)			400B		
4	LORD RICHARD	0-6-0ST	HCR	63	1865	4 —	15½ × 24	c30 —	700	(new)	?				
5	SIR STEPHEN	0-6-0ST	HCR	64	1865	4 —	15½ × 24	c30 —	700	(new)	?				
6	QUEEN	0-6-0 tender	SB	349	1846	4 8	18 × 24	?	?	LNWR (at Liverpool)	900 0s.	6/1872	400	400B	
7 (1)	—	0-6-0 tender	RS	?	1851	5 —	18 × 24	?	?	Crowther (contractor)	1,100 0s.	1876*			
7 (2)	DUKE	0-4-0ST	HCR	178	1878	3 6	14 × 20	21 —	600	(new)	1,200 0s.	—	401B		
8	PREMIER	0-6-0T	SS	2932	1880	4 3	18 × 24	43 10	1,000	(new)	2,136 0s.	—	401	405	405C
9	DEE	0-4-0ST	HCR	119	1872	3 6	13 × 20	22 —	600	per HC, after Thos. Butlin (contractor)	750 0s.	1881	402B		
10	EMILY	0-6-0ST	BP	2157	1882	4 —	16 × 22	32 10	1,000	per E.D. Till, after Broughton & Plas Power Coal Co.	?	1882	402	402B	
11	—	0-4-0ST	HC	278	1885	3 6½	15 × 20	22 10	700	(new)	?		403B		
12	—	0-6-2ST	BP	2649	1885	4 3	18 × 24	50 7	1,300		2,325 0s.	—	403	403B	
13	—	0-6-2ST	BP	2650	1885	4 3	18 × 24	46 3	1,100		2,325 0s.	—	404	404B	
14 (1)	(PERSEVERANCE)	0-4-0T	ID	?	1854	4 6	14 × 20	?	?						
14 (2)	—	0-6-0ST	MW	1105	1889	3 6	14 × 20	27 —	650	H. Croom Johnson (contractor)		1895	404B		
15	—	0-6-2ST	BP	2962	1888	4 3	18 × 24	50 7	1,300		—		405	405B	
16	—	0-6-2ST	BP	2963	1888	4 3	18 × 24	50 7	1,300		—		406	406B	
17	—	0-6-2T	BP	3866	1896	5 1	18 × 26	61 1	1,400		—		409		
18	—	0-6-2T	BP	3867	1896	5 1	18 × 26	61 1	1,400		—		410		

*previously hired from Crowther

Abbreviations:
BCK – Bury, Curtis & Kennedy, Liverpool.
BP – Beyer, Peacock & Co. Ltd., Manchester.
HC – Hudswell, Clarke & Co. Ltd., Leeds.
HCR – Hudswell, Clarke & Rodgers, Leeds.
ID – Isaac Dodds & Son, Rotherham.
MW – Manning, Wardle & Co. Ltd., Leeds.
RS – Robert Stephenson & Co., Newcastle on Tyne.
SB – Sharp Bros., Manchester.
SS – Sharp, Stewart & Co. Ltd., Manchester.

Carriages and Wagons

Repeated reference has been made to rolling stock throughout the Chronology, and disappointingly there is little to add beyond what has already been stated. The earliest passenger carriages were hired, only to be replaced by second-hand vehicles from the LNWR.

When on 24th February the GCR prepared a review of all WMCQR stock there were '33 carriages and one carriage truck fit only for scrap' and valued at £5 each. Also, '66 wagons fit to add to capital stock and 84 as duplicates': this review confirmed that all existing carriages had come from LNWR sources in 1889* and that 'most already laid aside are unfit for work'. The January 1905 assessment states there were 219 goods vehicles but four of these could not be found: the next month correspondence suggests that not all the eighty-four 'duplicate wagons' had been discovered either.

There was some stock associated with Rhosddu; a Breakdown Train consisted of two vans (one containing inter alia 'twelve drinking mugs and one kettle') attached to a Mobile Crane (2½ tons capacity) with a match truck to carry its jib. The Train was completed by a Breakdown Brake Van and a Stores Van. The foregoing was allocated to the Locomotive Department.

The carriage stock details (made available per Messrs. A.M. Gunn, Mike Williams and Philip Millard) include an extract from the LNWR Locomotive Committee Minutes of May 1889 and record that 'one composite and three 3rd Class duplicate carriages have been sold to the WMCQR for £390' (i.e. a total of £390, or about the same price as one new six-wheeled carriage would have cost at that time). No running numbers are given. The oft-published photograph of these carriages standing in Brymbo station confirms they were 24 ft (composite) and 22 ft (Third) long, of typical LNWR construction and made at Saltley in 1860–2. The Saltley Register survives but without note as to those sold. Apparently the LNWR was not prone to sell its old vehicles, it being suggested that antique stock at high prices did not attract many buyers: however, the Bishop's Castle Railway (which had personal links with the WMCQR) owned carriages of this source and period, and a specimen measured about sixty years ago gave:

Length over body corners	24 ft
Length over headstocks	23 ft 11 in.
Width over body at top and waist	8 ft
Width over body at bottom rail	7 ft 7 in.
Wheelbase	14 ft
Solebars	10½ × 3½ in., set apart 6 ft 1 in.
Headstock	10½ × 3½ in.

When sold these vehicles may have had Clark & Webb's chain brake (as did those on the Bishop's Castle) to replace the original handbrakes. The BCR specimens had steps and grab rails on the ends to reach the roof and oil lamps: side chains and hooks were fitted in addition to screw couplings, and double footboards ran the full length. The carriages ran on Mansell wheels 3 ft 6 in. diameter: inside partitions were taken up to ceiling height. W.N.

---

*If there were other LNWR vehicles obtained at other dates, then presumably these had not survived to the time of the review.

Davies said that most of the stock was kept in LNWR livery until c.1901 and 'then painted chocolate all over'. The hired stock which preceded was painted yellow with red lining-out.

W.N. Davies's notes include ten 10 ton Brake Vans built by the Birmingham Carriage & Wagon Co. Ltd., and one 12 ton Brake Van, built at Rhosddu in 1903. A Ballast Train of ten wagons plus Brake Van was used in conjunction with a four-wheeled Passenger Brake Van (No. 10) [with open-spoked wheels] containing two passenger and one guard's compartment . . . the latter may have been an ex-LNWR vehicle.

Oblique references are made to goods stock in various places; the Act of 1869 said that it was inadequate for the existing traffic 'and is hired from The Midland Wagon Company under two separate Agreements'. In the Buckley Traders' evidence against the Company for failing to support them, it was said 'there are 60 wagons with the name of Wrexham Mold & Connah's Quay Company' marked on them, but they are all future wagons'. (The word 'future' is unclear – it may be a shorthand error during the hearing). Presumably the hired wagons carried a plate stating the owner?

The earliest open wagons were of 8 ton capacity with dumb buffers and painted dark grey. There were some low-sided ones of two planks; the brakes were on one side, each wheel having a large wooden block to retard it. The higher-sided wagons had round-topped ends and carried coal. In each case, lettering 'WMCQR' appeared in white though not every wagon was so designated . . . perhaps the exceptions were those on hire?

Covered wagons were very small and probably carried 8 tons also; their wheels appear to have been 3 ft 6 in. in diameter, larger than the opens.

Wagon sheets carried 'WM & CQR' on them, together with a large yellow-painted cross.

There was one long-wheelbase open wagon designed by Willans for Cobden Mills, Wrexham traffic. This firm imported grain through Connah's

Quay. The wagon was built at Rhosddu in 1904 with a capacity of 12 tons; the load was carried in sacks, about nine sacks to the ton. 'In order to avoid undue length a special construction of crib rails and side stanchions was adopted'. The length was 23 ft 1 in. over buffers, 20 ft inside the body, 2 ft inside body height, 12 ft wheelbase, width overall 8 ft 6 in. Wheels were 3 ft 2 in. diameter. To give added strength two truss rods were placed under the floor. As with earlier wagons, only the wheels on one side were braked but these could be operated from either side. The wagon was marked, 'Grain only. C. Quay & Wrexham'. Colours are not known but light grey is likely: ownership was shown by a rectangular cast plate on the solebar reading 'WM 24 CQRy'.

The original Buckley trade was carried on by 'Traders Wagons' or 'Shippers Wagons'; they had wooden ends but no sides and carried six 'Shipping Boxes' athwart on each. One iron drop-bar on each side was lifted up whilst the Boxes were being run on; when dropped they prevented the Boxes falling off sideways. A second security was to lay a long timber baulk behind the small, plain wheels of the Boxes once they had been placed: wooden battens on the wagon floor guided the Boxes into position. From the first these Traders Wagons were the property of the Buckley Traders' Society and carried that title on the solebar. Later, some were supplied by the Railway Company and had 'WMCQR' and a wagon number on the solebar in white; the woodwork was red oxide and the ironwork black. Certain reconstructed wagons carried a Rhosddu-affixed cast plate on the solebar (*see drawing page 318*).

An odd feature of these wagons was that they had dumb buffers at one end, and sprung ones at the other, a practice found on early South Wales coal wagons. These Traders Wagons did not leave Buckley section metals.

The Shipping Boxes were carried in twos on each of the three 'tracks' on the host wagon, six in all: if fully loaded with bricks, then each Traders Wagon would have 1512 bricks upon it. The Boxes were lifted from the Traders Wagons by steam cranes and dropped into the holds of waiting ships still bearing their loads of bricks; the 1512 bricks were calculated to be sufficient to build a single-brick wall 48 ft long and 6 ft high. The Boxes were 3 ft long, 3 ft 9 in. wide, 2 ft 3 in. high and with 2 ft wheelbase. The 8 in. diameter wheels were more like large castors – these had either a plain tread or carried a single groove in the centre of them, probably to run on simple bar rails on the loading wharf. Of these Boxes it was said, 'small tram carriages are taken to the wagons and loaded on them – the weight of these trams with bricks is not considered part of the load but as part of the wagons themselves, and they come back from Connah's Quay free of charge. The Boxes are 7–8 cwt each'.

Some of the brickworks' companies owned or hired their own wagons so as to make delivery nationwide. Charles Davison & Co. said, 'We own five wagons but hire twelve from a Wagon Company costing about £10* each to hire'.

---

*This would be the annual cost.

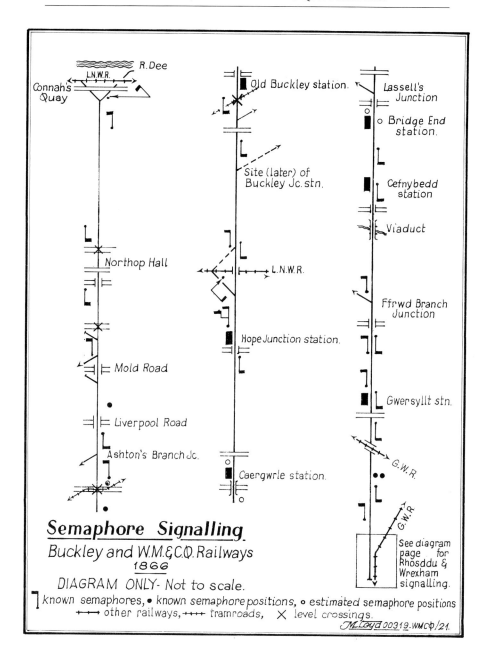

R.Dee

L.N.W.R.

Connah's Quay

Old Buckley station.

Lassell's Junction

Bridge End station.

Site (later) of Buckley Jc. stn.

Cefnybedd station

Viaduct

Northop Hall

L.N.W.R.

Ffrwd Branch Junction

Mold Road

Hope Junction station.

Liverpool Road

Gwersyllt stn.

Ashton's Branch Jc.

G.W.R.

Caergwrle station.

G.W.R.

See diagram page for Rhosddu & Wrexham signalling.

Semaphore Signalling.

Buckley and W.M.&C.Q. Railways

1866

DIAGRAM ONLY - Not to scale.

⌐ known semaphores, • known semaphore positions, ○ estimated semaphore positions
↦ other railways, ⊦⊦⊦ tramroads, ✕ level crossings.

M.Lloyd 00319-WMCQ/21.

Signalling

Signalling (1866)

When Colonel Yolland inspected the Wrexham–Old Buckley section on 1st February, 1866 he commented that there

> were either no signals at all or they are in an unfinished state or are not locked as they should be so that it would be impossible to lower them except when the points are set for the right line ... some points are not visible from the signal box ...

We know that there was a delay in obtaining the initial signals from Stevens & Co. and Yolland made a second visit when they were ready. At a later date this length of line was additionally signalled by The Railway Signal Co. of Fazakerley and the semaphore arms had the usual contemporary single red spectacle, a white light from the lamp giving the 'all clear' aspect. The diagram (*page 320*) shows the position of Stevens signals on the Buckley and WMCQR sections at the time of the 1869–75 map survey. The considerable signalling on the former line is only partly explained by the number of level crossings.

On the WMCQR line proper (which was then single – as was the Buckley) passenger station platforms (Hope Junction excepted) were all on the west side of the line. Opposite the single platform which served for each station, there was a passing loop: no doubt the Company intended these loops would ensure the smooth flow of trains but the Colonel was frightened lest a passenger train be held up in the east side of a loop where there was no platform ... perhaps the Company only intended these loops for mineral train use? However, one may see the Colonel's viewpoint, and he duly required a second platform to be provided if such loops were to be used for passenger trains.

The main line was divided into two Train Staff sections: Wrexham–Caergwrle and Caergwrle–Old Buckley.* There was no Block Telegraph working as would become mandatory under the 1889 Act and it is assumed trains proceeded by verbal instruction or time interval.

Doubling of the main line – 1885

The Board of Trade inspection report of 15th April, 1885 stated that the line was now double between Wrexham Colliery Junction (i.e. the point north of Rhosddu where the GWR and WMCQR diverged) and Hawarden Junction (to be renamed shortly, Buckley Junction). The Inspector required certain work doing; this was ready by 18th August following but on 3rd September the Company reverted to Up and Down single line working between Penyffordd and Hawarden Junction until The Hawarden Loop was ready. This was 'to avoid us the expense of keeping a signalman at Hawarden Junction' but expense *was* necessary as the Inspector then required alterations to the layout in consequence.

Doubling of the line apart, Block Working was introduced on the main line on 1st August.

---

*The later title is used; the correct name was then Buckley but by using 'Old Buckley' no confusion with the subsequent 'Buckley Junction' will arise.

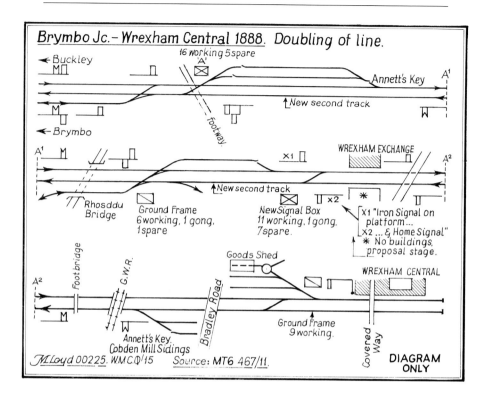

Doubling of the main line – 1888

On 21st August the Secretary, Fraser, advised the Board of Trade that the double line was ready for inspection; this also included the section between the two Wrexham stations and some new work at Brymbo South Junction. This was the second occasion he had written to the Board this year, for on 16th March he wrote to say Railways 2, 3 and 8 of the 1882 Act were ready for inspection; a statement he was obliged to withdraw when writing on 21st August – as just noted – admitting he had been mis-informed. However, 'Railway No. 1 was ready' and the portion which was worrying poor old Fraser was the length between Brymbo South Junction and Wrexham Central for he was under pressure to have everything finished for the Royal Eisteddfod on 3rd September. Could they send down Colonel Rich at once as 'Gladstone, accompanied by Sir Edward Watkin, had made up their minds to visit the Eisteddfod on the opening day'? The WMCQR was a past master in these matters, and a precis of the exchange of letters between Fraser and the Board of Trade went along these lines:

> B.o.T. to Fraser: 'Col. Rich cannot make Inspection before opening date of Eisteddfod.'

Cartwright to Fraser: 'Can we be allowed provisionally to use the double line? Can you say if such would be authorised?' (22nd August)

Rich to B.o.T.: 'I cannot recommend provisional sanction as the second lines are frequently not in a fit state to be opened.' (23rd August)

Cartwright to Fraser: 'Line will not after all be ready for inspection before 29th August.' (25th August) [*This was a telegram*]

The Colonel must have wilted somewhat under the pressures of statesmen for he agreed to inspect Rhosddu Bridge, a new structure replacing the old level crossing. The date of inspection is not given, but Cartwright was obliged to send a written undertaking to the Board of Trade on 31st August that within two months he would erect a permanent booking office and waiting rooms with conveniences at Exchange station's Down platform. The Board of Trade acted with speed and in the nick of time for the great men's visit, sanction to open on the double line Brymbo South Junction to Wrexham Central was given on 1st September. The Board seldom acted with such alacrity!

On this date the WMCQR was at pains to point out to the Board that Railways 2, 3 and 8 were still unfinished.

The Board of Trade Report is worth quoting, as it describes the new track situation exactly:

the old double line from the north ended at the south side of Brymbo South Junction. A new line thence to Central station, about a mile long, has been built. The effect is that the old single line junction cabin at Brymbo Junction becomes obsolete and a new cabin with 127 levers and 4 spares is now at a short distance north of the old cabin. The new cabin is called Brymbo Junction South Cabin.

Rhosddu level crossing is now a bridge.

There is now a second cabin at Wrexham Exchange with 12 working and 5 spare levers and a ground frame with 6 levers and 2 spares is interlocked from it; there is a third cabin at Central station.

The old line is now the Up line to Wrexham, and the new line of rails the Down line to Mold.

The Colonel wanted a shelter, clock and nameboard for the new Exchange station platform.

Signalling (by 1905)

Main Line * 13 Signal Boxes between Wrexham Central and Connah's Quay & Shotton. Wrexham–Buckley Junction (excl.) Railway Signal Co. Hawarden Loop, Dutton & Co. Worked by Block Telegraph and Sykes 2-position Instruments.

Brymbo Line (single) Brymbo North & South Junctions, to Brymbo. 5 Signal Boxes worked by Block Telegraph and Sykes 2-position Instruments with Train Staff & Permit. Train Staff & Permit by McKenzie & Holland, Worcester.

Brymbo Steel Works and Vron Colliery Line (single) No semaphore signalling, no Signal Boxes. Worked by Train Staff (wooden) and Ticket, which was kept in Brymbo station Signal Box.

*Details of 'Wright's Bridge Box' (1901) at Shotton are not known.

Ffrwd Line (single) Worked without Train Staff on permissive system: one or more engines coupled together at the same time between Ffrwd Junction to Westminster Collieries, and intermediate works.

Buckley Junction to Connah's Quay Docks (single) No Signal Boxes. Semaphore signals at Castle Brick Co. Crossing. Worked by Train Staff & Permit. Train Staff & Permit by McKenzie & Holland, Worcester.

Shotton to Connah's Quay Docks (single) As for Ffrwd Line.

The WMCQR installed a special frame by Dutton & Co. of Worcester in Hawarden Signal Box in 1890 (this was not that same one taken out for replacement in 1946, and now at York Railway Museum.)

Up to the takeover by GCR the WMCQR Signal Box at Wrexham Exchange controlled a Ground Frame about 250 yards to the north of it: this frame was linked to the Box so as to allow bell signals to be exchanged between them; the frame controlled the movement of engines to and from Rhosddu, and also trains attaching or detaching at the GWR's transfer sidings. A new GCR Box replaced the Exchange Signal Box at the north end of the Down platform, in 1906.

Certain relevant samples of Board of Trade Returns follow; these show how the Railway doubled its main line, added branches, increased the workings of its passenger services and improved its safety methods by more up to date single line working equipment.

Board of Trade Interlocking & Signalling Returns – 31st December, 1873

Mileages of Passenger Lines: single	
(Wrexham Central–Buckley)	9 m. 20 ch.
Worked on Train Staff system	
Mileages of Mineral Lines: single	7 m.*

Board of Trade Interlocking & Signalling Returns – 31st December, 1887

Main Line	11 sidings	
	10 Crossover roads	
	11 sidings have safety points	
Branch	1 crossing of another goods line on the level	
	8 sidings	
	3 concentrated and interlocked point levers	
	6 unconcentrated and unlocked point levers	
	9 sidings and goods lines without safety points	

Mileages of Passenger Lines: double (Rhosddu S.B.–Penyffordd)	6 m. 10 ch.
single	3 m. 38 ch.
Section worked on the *Absolute Block System:*	
Rhosddu S.B.–Penyffordd	6 m. 10 ch.
Section worked on the *Permissive Block:*	
None	

---

*Presumably made up of Buckley–Connah's Quay	4 m. 52 ch.
and the existing section of the Ffrwd Branch (say)	2 m. 28 ch.

Single Line:	1) Wrexham Central–Wrexham Exchange	52 ch.
	Worked by One Engine in Steam	
	2) Wrexham Exchange–Rhosddu S.B.*	60 ch.
	Worked on Train Staff system	
	3) Penyffordd–Buckley	2 m. 6 ch.
	Worked on Train Staff system	

Mileages of Goods Lines: all single line

	1) Buckley–Connah's Quay	4 m. 52 ch.
	Worked on Train Staff system	
	2) Brymbo Junction–Brymbo	4 m. 20 ch.
	Worked by One Engine in Steam	
	3) Frood Junction†–Brynmally & Moss	2 m. 75 ch.
	Worked by One Engine in Steam	

Board of Trade Interlocking & Signalling Returns – 31st December, 1888

Mileages of Passenger Lines: double (Wrexham Central–
                                            Penyffordd)   7 m. 42 ch.
Worked on *Absolute Block system:*
                          single (Penyffordd–Buckley)   2 m. 6 ch.
                          Worked on Train Staff system

Mileages of Goods Lines:

	1) Buckley–Connah's Quay	4 m. 52 ch.
	Worked on Train Staff system	
	2) Brymbo Junction–Plas Power	2 m. 19 ch.
	Worked on Train Staff system	
	3) Plas Power–Brymbo & Vron	2 m. 26 ch.
	Worked by One Engine in Steam	
	4) Frood Junction–Brynmally & Moss	2 m. 75 ch.
	Worked by One Engine in Steam	

Note: By this date the line had been doubled between Brymbo Junction and Wrexham Central.

Board of Trade Interlocking & Signalling Returns – 31st December, 1889

Mileages of Passenger Lines: Add to 31st December, 1888 Returns –

Single Line	1) Brymbo South Junction–Brymbo	3 m. 30 ch.
	Worked on Train Staff system	
	2) Penyffordd–Buckley	2 m. 6 ch.
	Worked on Train Staff & Ticket system	

Mileages of Goods Lines: Add to 31st December, 1888 Returns –

| Single Line | Brymbo (Works) Junction–Steel Works & Vron | 1 m. 50 ch. |
| | Worked by One Engine in Steam | |

Note: Brymbo South Junction–Brymbo is now a Passenger Line and is no longer listed under Goods.

Note: In considering the above, it must be recalled that only Brymbo South Junction to Penyffordd had been doubled by this date: 'Rhosddu S.B.' is an error.

†Note spelling in lieu of Ffrwd.

Board of Trade Interlocking & Signalling Returns – 31st December, 1890

Mileages of Passenger Lines: double: (Wrexham Central–

Hawarden Bridge) 13 m. 10 ch.

Worked on *Absolute Block system*

single: (Brymbo South Junction–

Worked on *Absolute Block* system   Brymbo) 3 m. 30 ch.

Mileages of Goods Lines:

1) Buckley Junction–Connah's Quay	5 m. 41 ch.	
Worked on Train Staff system		
2) Brymbo Works Junction–Steel Works & Vron	1 m. 50 ch.	
Worked by One Engine in Steam		
3) Frood Junction–Brynmally & Moss	2 m. 75 ch.	
Worked by One Engine in Steam		

Note: Alterations due to opening Hawarden Loop.

Additional signalling was supplied by The Railway Signal Co. Ltd.[1] of Fazakerley, Liverpool, in the early mid-1880s. Nine new Signal Cabins (the RS Co. term for 'Boxes') were listed (ref. Public Record Office MT/6 394/1) in 1885:

Title	Working Levers	Spare Levers
Wrexham Colliery Junc. (temp.frame)	8	0
Gatewen Junc. (later Brymbo North Junc.)	8	4
Gwersyllt Station	10	4
Ffrwd Junction	11	4
Cefnybedd Station	10	4
Bridge End Station	14	6
Caergwrle Station	13	4
Penyffordd Junction	15	9
Hawarden Junc. (later Buckley Junc.)	14	6

Note: The titles are those contemporarily in use.

On the Brymbo Branch the McKenzie & Holland boxes were of timber: that at the West Junction was very small. Those at Moss & Pentre and Plas Power were of medium size, the latter surviving at least until the early 1950s. The Brymbo box was little bigger than that at West Junction.

Though strictly off the WMCQR metals, the old-fashioned double-armed semaphores projecting either side at the top of a single post which controlled movement over the swing section of the Hawarden Bridge, were more typical of marine practice than railway equipment.

[Before their (comparatively) recent removal, the frames at Caergwrle and Wrexham Exchange were similar and probably by Dutton & Co. Each was a GCR replacement.]

References

[1] Ref. BRITISH RAILWAY JOURNAL No. 7 Spring 1985 p. 244.

Permanent Way

The Inspector's Report of 1st February, 1866 reveals the type of track in use between Wrexham and Buckley (but not The Buckley Railway). This is tabulated below against that in use about 1893 when, anticipating the completion of the Wirral Railway and the Wrexham & Ellesmere Railway, together with through traffic from South Wales to the north, the 75 lbs rails were replaced by 86 lbs.[1] In the early years some bridge rail was to be found on overbridges, coachscrewed to longitudinal sleepers: the Inspector disapproved of it.

	1866	c.1893
Rails (iron) double-headed	75 lbs/yd	
Rails (steel) bull-headed		86 lbs/yd
Rail lengths	18 & 24 ft	30 ft
Chairs weight	27 lbs each	50 lbs each
Fastenings	Two spikes + iron nuts/bolts	Two spikes + two treenails
Fishplates (pair) weight	22 lbs (iron)	28 lbs (steel)
Keys (outside of rail)	Oak	Compressed Elm
Sleepers 9 ft × 10 in. × 5 in.	uncreosoted	creosoted

Ballast was river gravel 2 ft deep, measured from the upper surface of the rails. The first sleepers were half-round scantlings laid at 2 ft and 3 ft intervals, the chairs then being S-base type 25 lbs weight each. At this early period the steepest gradient was 1 in 70 and the minimum curve 17 chains radius.

Reference

[1] RAILWAY NEWS; report 11th August, 1894.

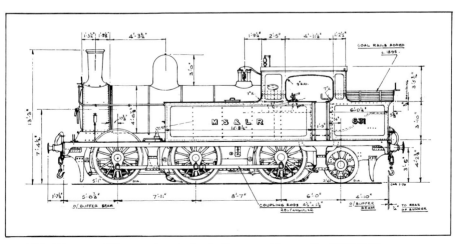

MS & LR, 0–6–2T locomotive similar to those working on the WM & CQR.

Courtesy RAILWAY MODELLER

A pocket timetable for July 1900.

Stations

The earliest description of the buildings came towards the end of the Company's independent life when the Great Central Railway was preparing a Scheme of Arrangement . . .

> the buildings consist of temporary iron and wooden stuctures and the accommo-dation for the travelling public and the merchandise traffic is of a very meagre description . . . more commodious buildings are required . . . at eight of the passenger stations footbridges or subways connecting the platforms are required . . . and at various points along the railway further sidings are necessary than exist at present . . .

Of course, it suited the GCR to paint a run-down picture in order to demon-strate their own worthiness when all would be rectified under their management. In fact, not all the buildings were as described, and a table of their construction follows dated 1905.

Of the buildings nearest to the foregoing, the longest survivor was the erection at Wrexham Central which lasted well into British Rail days; it cannot be proved that this once did duty at Wrexham Exchange, as some suggest.

There were fourteen places where trains stopped at the end of the Company's life; Old Buckley had closed. There were single buildings at Wrexham Central and Brymbo: Connah's Quay & Shotton had one building of timber, claimed to reduce the weight up on the embankment. Hawarden's Down side wooden building would have looked at home as a cricket pavilion; Hope Exchange was also wooden on the Down side, the Up side building being in brick and the original position of the station there . . . presumably the brick structure superseded a wooden one? So, the GCR was deliberately spreading falsehoods; but who would bother? In about twenty locations, perhaps but three were in timber – the rest were brick.

By 1905 there was little consistency of architecture. At Wrexham Exchange, Caergwrle Castle, Buckley Junction and Hawarden the local yellow and ruby bricks were prominent and Hope Exchange had a more bijou version of the style. Gwersyllt (Down) and Connah's Quay & Shotton (Up) had dismal brick structures of the late Victorian style. Cefnybedd, Hope Village and Penyffordd sported brick and pebbledash with a shot of 'Tudor' half-timbering: such buildings were also found on the line up to Bidston and dated from the opening of the North Wales & Liverpool Railway section.

Small shelters with pent-roofs were favoured for the Up side platforms on the main line: these also were in yellow brick.

Nothing is known of the intermediate stations on the Brymbo line; Old Buckley building was a primitive-looking brick 'box' of which more is said elsewhere.

In the Fraser Collection are three sets of drawings (undated) showing station buildings, stationmasters' houses, and simple platform shelters in timber obviously submitted for the WMCQR. Attractive or otherwise, they do not appear to have found favour. A proposed building for the contem-plated Poolmouth station is shown.

	Down side	Up side
Wrexham Central	Timber (joint with W & ER)	Corrugated-iron
Wrexham Exchange	Brick	None
Gwersyllt	Brick (orig. timber)	Brick
Cefnybedd	Brick/pebbledash	Brick
Caergwrle Castle	Brick	Brick
Hope Village	Brick/pebbledash	Brick
Penyffordd	Brick/pebbledash	Brick
Hope Exchange	Timber	Brick
Buckley Junction	Brick	Brick
Hawarden	Timber	Brick
Connah's Quay & Shotton	Timber (wooden platforms)	Brick
Moss & Pentre	?	—
Plas Power	?	?
Brymbo	Brick	—
Old Buckley (out of use)	—	Brick

Though many of the brick-built stations used the Flintshire-manufactured yellow and ruby bricks, with slate tile roofs, architecturally there were considerable differences in style and detail. It is thought that the brick/pebbledash style stations on the WMCQR main line were rebuilt when the line to Bidston was constructed, it having buildings of similar appearance.

Of the buildings at Wrexham, that at the former Exchange was excused by its owners as being 'not very extensive, nor are its architectural pretentions [*sic*] very great' . . . the GWR always referred to it as a 'shed' to which the WMCQR replied that it was merely a wooden hut because the GWR had threatened them with eviction and served them with a writ: under the circumstances there was no point in providing anything better. The issue stemmed from the GWR's vexation at the building of the underbridge at Rhosddu which was still a level crossing at the time (*see page 139*).

Platform edges were formed by a specially-made local tile having a non-slip serrated surface.

Sir S.M. Glynne's Railway ('The Hawarden Castle Colliery Co.')

The coal pits on the Hawarden Estate were leased out to operatives, but in the late 1850s Sir Stephen decided he would form a Company and work the coal himself. He used the services of J.A. Darlington, an Engineer from Chorley, Lancashire, to estimate the prospects of winning coal on the Estate, with special reference to a shaft to be sunk at Rake Farm. At some earlier date (the relevant Hawarden Estate Paper D/HA/1238 is undated) John Pilkington of Chester had surveyed for a railway to replace the Sandycroft Rail Road between the river at Sandycroft and the Great Mancot Colliery, together with a spur to a second, new shaft at the existing Little (or Old) Mancot Colliery, the line to make junction with the Chester & Holyhead section of the LNWR.

In the event, and linked to the Rake Farm scheme, a standard gauge line was built from the LNWR, across the coast road on the level and so south-west to Scotland Farm. Thence the line ran southward to the intended shaft

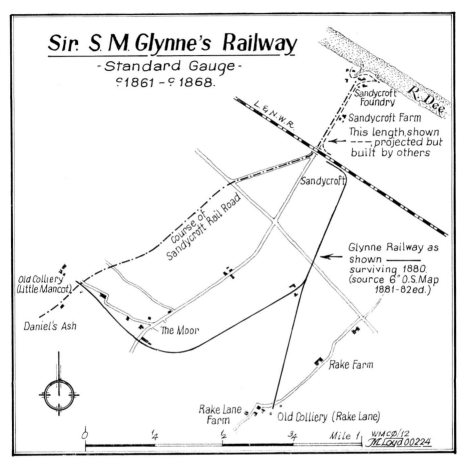

at Rake (or Harding's) Farm: this length was dubbed 'The Rake Railway'. At a later date a branch from Scotland Farm ('Railway No. 2') was built towards the intended new shaft at Little Mancot Colliery: an extension to the river was also contemplated. Railway No. 2 made a continuous clockwise curve to the new shaft and crossed Moor Lane on the level. This second length was termed 'The Mancot Banks Railway' and some of its course is still visible.

Negotiations with the LNWR for the making of transfer sidings began in October 1861, and LNWR records suggest the Rake line was in business by early 1862.

The Mancot line was duly built but LNWR sources show in 1873 'work stopped about five years ago' and Estate papers say Rake Lane pit was worked out by August 1864; the Exchange Sidings were out of use c.1868 so presumably the Mancot line was abandoned by then also. Accounts at the closing-down of Rake (or Hawarden Castle Colliery) are dated 14th May, 1866. Glynne himself, together with his brother-in-law William Gladstone, was foremost in the venture but the latter withdrew before the project was complete. Business affairs were conducted locally by Glynne's agent Gregory Burnett of Dee Cottage, Queensferry.

National Coal Board papers show that Great Mancot closed down by August 1879, reopened and closed finally in February 1885. As a pit which had been worked intermittently since c.1750, it had had a long life.

Sleepers for the Railway came from William Thomas at his premises on Wrexham (GWR) station. He apologised that 'sleepers of 9″ × 4½″ section were very difficult to find' but sent 200 9 in. × 5 in. to the transfer siding @ 3/6d. each: 'Mr Taylor had 600 for his branch at Sandycroft'. Thomas imported his timber through Connah's Quay. The laying of Railway No. 2 was done in Spring 1862, the New British Iron Co. of Acrefair (per J. Kenyon Blackwell) supplying 1787 yards of 60 lbs/yd. iron flat-bottomed rails in early February. Additional materials followed in July, including chairs for the 'Box Crossing' . . . was this a rail/road or a rail/tramroad crossing?

Altogether, the exercise was a disaster, the estimates of coal reserves underground being well wide of the mark. Rumour has it that a standard gauge steam locomotive was used on the line: some such power is likely but has not been confirmed.

[*See also* Clwyd Record Office: Hawarden Coalfield Plan D/HA/1113: Hawarden Estate Collieries D/HA/1128: re New British Iron Co. D/HA/1216: Prospects of Hawarden Castle Colliery D/HA/957: Junction with LNWR D/HA/1215.]

Aston Hall Colliery Railway

To understand something of the background to this line, the origin of the colliery should be noted. In 1837, Admiral Sir James Dundas, on whose estate the colliery was situated, leased the coal thereunder to Richard Hancock; in 1856 a new lease was assigned to William Thompson. These lessees used the existing tramroad to the river at Lower Ferry (The Aston Tramroad) which in its final form had been cut back to terminate at the Aston Hall Colliery and adjacent brick-making premises.

The Dundas family was in financial low water: Dundas was bankrupted in May 1872, but before this event, W.E. Gladstone had bought part of the estate for £57,000 in July 1861. In May 1865 Messrs. Fenton & Others took a 29-year lease of the estate's mines and minerals.

An Aston Hall Colliery Co. Ltd. was registered on 3rd May, 1866 which worked Aston Hall (and Pentrobin) Colliery, only to go into liquidation in March 1877. It is likely that the new Company worked coal from a new site to the south of that used by Fenton. It will be noted that its rail connection remained the truncated tramroad of what had become a continuous line of tramroad stretching from Hancock's Lane End Works in Buckley, and embracing the existing Aston Tramroad, to the Dee; due to the building of the Buckley and WMCQR lines, this full-length tramroad had been abandoned south of Aston Hall Colliery, which was left with virtually that same

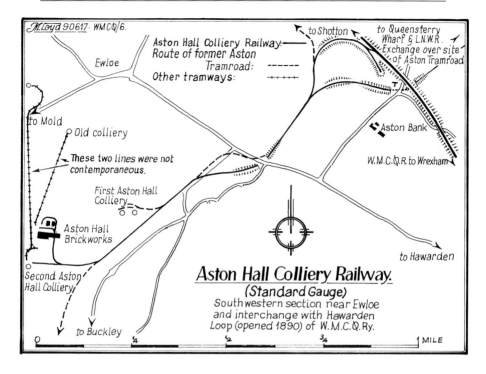

Aston Hall Colliery Railway:———
Route of former Aston
     Tramroad: ------
Other tramways: +-+-+-+

to Shotton   to Queensferry
      Wharf & L.N.W.R.
      Exchange over site
      of Aston Tramroad

J. Lloyd 90617· WMCQ/6.

Ewloe

to Mold

Old colliery

These two lines were not
contemporaneous.

First Aston Hall
Colliery

Aston Hall
Brickworks

Second Aston
Hall Colliery

to Buckley

Aston Bank

W.M.C.Q.R. to Wrexham

to Hawarden

Aston Hall Colliery Railway.
(Standard Gauge)
South western section near Ewloe
and interchange with Hawarden
Loop (opened 1890) of W.M.C.Q.Ry.

MILE

rail outlet to the river as it had had when it began in business . . . and it had it all to itself as no track occupation had to be shared with traffic from user-parties further south.

On 15th May, 1878 an Aston Hall Coal & Brick Co. Ltd. was formed out of the foregoing and shortly a lease was taken also of Lane End (or Dumpling Colliery) the property of Hancock.* Traffic from this passed onto the WMCQR via tramroad to Hancock's Siding; not a very convenient arrangement. In 1896 Ashton's Branch Siding was extended to give direct rail access to Lane End Colliery (*see page 112*). Beside the existing Aston Hall Colliery a new brickworks was set up.

At some date during the nine-year lifetime of the Aston Hall Colliery Co. Ltd. the limitations of its tramroad to the river must have been manifest; there is no record of the conversion date of the tramroad into a standard gauge railway but the LNWR SIDINGS DIAGRAMS show an interchange with a branch off the Aston Hall – Lower Ferry system at Dundas' Siding. This spur existed by March 1876 and therefore conversion to railway must have occurred before or during 1875.[1]

The business was put up for sale in 1883, and the Sale Catalogue reveals that Queensferry Colliery (connected by short branch to the Aston Hall Colliery Railway), Aston Hall Brickworks and Pentrobin Colliery were in-

*The Queen's Ferry Colliery Co. Ltd.: The Pentrobin Colliery Co.: were also acquired from Mrs Alex. Ward of Hawarden.

cluded; as to the railway system, the Catalogue has:

> The use of Railway about 3 miles in length connecting the collieries and brickworks with a junction on the LNWR near Queensferry Station and also with the Shipping Wharves and Coal Tips on the River Dee at the same place . . . the use of the Wharf with 3 landing stages about ¼ mile frontage to the river with exclusive right for shipping and landing thereat . . .
> Three locomotives (2 by Fox, Walker & Co., Bristol, and 1 by Walker Bros., Wigan) . . . Railway Wagons . . . some of them on hire . . .

In 1889 H.H. Gladstone leased the undertaking for 10 years; the brick-making side of the business now turned out a type of buff ware and terracotta akin to that of the Standard Brick & Tile Co.'s products, a local competitor: it probably produced these before similar work began at the South Buckley Brickworks.

When the Colliery was almost at the end of its life, an Aston Hall Colliery & Brick Co. Ltd., owned by Horace Mayhew, was in being. Over 1,000 men and boys were yet in employment. Continuing to use the railway also, was the Queensferry Colliery Co. Ltd., (under the same manager) employing 45 souls. All this was in 1907.[2] (This was clearly a revival of the title as the Aston Hall Coal & Brick Co. Ltd. was dissolved on 29th July, 1902.[3])

A plan of the Colliery 'belonging to Hugh Fenton & Co. 1865' shows two main shafts, dubbed the Main Coal Pit and the Rough Coal Pit; in the latter area are many small pits of former times named 'Goaf' workings. All such lay to the west of the Aston Tramroad: along its adjacent length an accident to 'Thomas Peters, 52 years, labourer from Hawarden, killed by the waggon wheels in March 1811' has been recorded in the Buckley Parish Registers.

The Colliery had an excellent safety record; when Davey lamps were introduced, it was one of the first to obtain them . . . but the men objected . . . The workings had been lit by electricity since 1894.

Shafts 1 and 2, (by then '4 ft & Yard Seam' and 'Wall & Bench Seam' respectively), were abandoned in 1906, and in 1908. Thereafter it was the Brickworks which occupied the Company's railway but not for long. Disused, the track was left in situ until World War I demands conscripted it for scrap; the rails on 'The Dry Bridge' where they crossed the Chester–Flint road were still in place in the mid-1930s.

The line was almost exactly four miles long: from the Colliery and Brickworks it ran parallel and to the west of Wood Lane to pass under the Hawarden–Ewloe road by brick-arched bridge, much of it in that peculiar yellow variety produced in quantity by the railway's owners. The line's route to this point was virtually along that same path as was occupied by the earlier tramroad, so much so that approaching the Hawarden–Ewloe road it appeared to continue on that same tramroad course as the tramroad had taken along the roadside itself for a short distance. But no! With a sudden change of direction, there was a facing junction and the railway swerved to right and left in quick succession to pass under the road at 'The Yellow Bridge' (its local name) situated at 250 ft a.s.l.

Returning to the place of divergence one might have noted the railway *did* continue as a short siding on the tramroad course, to end up in a coal merchant's yard behind Thomas's Buildings near the back of the old Methodist Chapel and almost opposite the Crown & Liver Inn.

Now onward. Passing under The Yellow Bridge there was beyond a length of considerable cutting, carrying the railway at a much deeper level than the tramroad would have been . . . the course of the latter, after its brief tryst with the roadway, would have been united with that of the railway until the railway took another parting with the older site and careered off to the right (due east) and then back northeastward again – this was to lessen the gradients and wanderings of the tramroad's route. The cost of this in the railway construction included a long cutting which carried the track under a road bridge and, after 1899, also under The Hawarden Loop. About here opportunity was taken to make interchange sidings between the two systems.

For this purpose a junction on the AHCR was made at the end of the cutting leading from The Yellow Bridge. Whilst the 'main line' went off to the right (see above) the interchange sidings made off left along the former tramroad site which itself veered off to the north after a few yards. All railway curves hereabouts were far from easy! The colliery railway layout was brought out on embankment to bring it up to the WMCQR height, and the interchange line made junctions with the Loop in both directions beside Aston Hall Junction signal box (*see Diagram WMCQ/6*).

[In passing; this arrangement was not the first considered, for 'Scheme No. 1' was 'submitted by the Colliery Co. to Mr Cartwright* on 27th August, 1890', the estimated cost being £1,900. This would have been for a smaller layout with less capacity and even more severe curves. The interchange sidings beside the Loop would have met the Colliery Railway on a fall of 1 in 40, probably no problem to Colliery Railway drivers whose own 'main line', where it passed under the Loop, was falling at 1 in 24!][4]

From these sidings the Colliery Railway ran straight as an arrow downhill, the panorama of Deeside spreading out like a cloth below it, due northeast in a straight line to the Queensferry Colliery. There, taking up a short link line, it turned to a northerly direction for a short distance to gain the elderly embankment earthworks of the Aston Tramroad which it used – suitably widened for the purpose – as it made a bee-line for Lower Ferry. The former tramroad spur to the LNWR was also converted to a railway.

The precipitous descent of the railway from Colliery to riverside put it firmly into Mineral Railway category! Beginning with a fall from the pit at 1 in 107, it then became 1 in 27 to the interchange sidings, and worsened to 1 in 24 for the remainder.[5] The function of the locomotive would be simply to act as a brake to restrain the loaded wagons as they came down the hill. Returning empty, the load limit was about six wagons. Remembered is the woebegone state of the track (carried throughout on brickbats, colliery waste etc.) and the careworn condition of the engines . . . the Company must have been an excellent customer to some foundry which cast renewable brake blocks.

---

*General Manager, WMCQR.

Engine power included:[6]

DOCTOR	0−6−0ST Fox, Walker & Co., Bristol. Works No. 167 of 1872.
STALYBRIDGE	0−6−0T Sharp Stewart & Co. Ltd., Manchester. Works No. 3475 of 1888. (ex T.A. Walker, contractor for Manchester Ship Canal).†
PROGRESS (ex BRINSOP HALL)	0−4−0T Crewe?† Walker Bros., Wigan.

†Worked at Lane End Colliery c.1900.

According to the Ordnance Survey 25″ Plans, the junction for the inter-change sidings at The Hawarden Loop, was semaphore signalled.

References

[1] Clwyd Record Office: D/RD/517. This date would agree roughly with other DIAGRAMS published at this time.
[2] MINING REGISTER & DIRECTORY FOR THE COAL & IRONSTONE TRADES 1907. (Potts.) [Published in North Shields.]
[3] Public Record Office: BT31/1257/3049.
[4] National Library Wales: Piercy Papers (Fraser Group) 362.
[5] Clwyd Record Office: QS/DR/190.
[6] DEESIDE ADVERTISER July 1969. (Article by George Lloyd).
  POCKET BOOK F. p. F80, (The Birmingham Locomotive Club.)

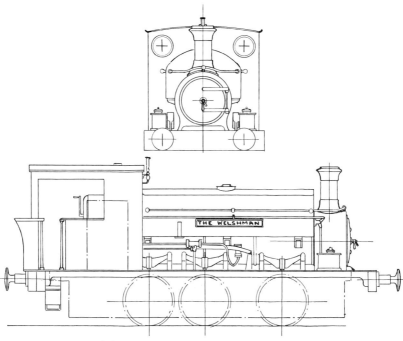

THE WELSHMAN, one of three locomotives at Llay Hall Colliery. (Manning, Wardle & Co. Ltd., Works No. 1207) of 1890. *Drawing courtesy* RAILWAY MODELLER

Appendix One

Route Distance Between Stations

Distance from Wrexham Central	Distance between stations	[Great Central titles at takeover – 1905]
m. ch.	m. ch.	
– –	– –	Wrexham Central
'0 48	0 48	Wrexham Exchange
1 34	0 66	Brymbo South Junction
2 4	0 50	Brymbo North Junction
2 29	0 25	Gwersyllt
3 19	0 70	Ffrwd Junction
4 21	1 02	Cefnybedd
4 73	0 52	Caergwrle Castle
5 45	0 52	Hope Village
7 39	1 74	Penyffordd
7 64	0 25	Hope Exchange
8 69	1 05	Buckley Junction
10 65	1 76	Hawarden
13 0	2 15	Connah's Quay & Shotton
14 18	1 18	Connah's Quay Docks
13 10	0 10	Hawarden Bridge Junction

Distance from Connah's Quay	Distance between stations	[Great Central titles at takeover – 1905]
m. ch.	m. ch.	
– –	– –	Connah's Quay Docks
1 61	1 61	Northop Hall
2 45	0 64	Castle Brick Siding
2 72	0 27	⎧ Parry's Siding ⎨ North & South Buckley ⎩ Buckley Quarries
3 12	0 20	Ewloe Barn Siding
3 40	0 28	Buckley Brick & Tile Siding
3 41	0 01	Catherall's Siding
4 08	0 47	Old Ewloe Siding
4 35	0 27	Knowl Lane Siding
4 57	0 22	Mountain Colliery
4 46	1 05	Buckley Station
5 36	0 70	Buckley Junction
–	– –	Wrexham Central
0 49	0 49	Wrexham Exchange
1 35	0 66	Brymbo South Junction
1 76	0 41	Brymbo West Junction
– –	0 20	Brymbo North Junction
2 36	0 40	Highfield Road
2 51	0 15	Gatewen Colliery Junction

Distance from Connah's Quay	Distance between stations	[Great Central titles at takeover – 1905]
m. ch.	m. ch.	
2 61	0 10	Moss & Pentre Station
3 03	0 22	New Broughton Road
		⎧ New Broughton Colliery Siding
3 48	0 45	⎪ Plas Power Station
		⎨ Plas Power A Cabin
		⎩ Plas Power B Cabin
4 69	1 21	Brymbo Station
5 08	0 27	Brymbo Steel Works
5 49	0 41	Vron Colliery & Brickworks

Appendix Two

Railway-linked Industries

[All these industries had closed by 1990 except Hancock's site.]

Establishment	Position	Map Ref.	Opened	Closed
UP (EAST) SIDE: CONNAH'S QUAY–BUCKLEY JUNCTION				
Connah's Quay Chemical Works	Docks	296697	1850	1887
R. Williams & Sons (Timber Yd)	Docks	295698		
Prince's (Connah's Quay) B'works	Wepre	293693		
Old Ewloe Hall Brickworks (Davison's Lower)	Wepre	293692	by 1840s	
Globe Brickworks	Ewloe Hall	287654		1912
Mount Pleasant Colly. & B'works (Wood Pits)	East Buckley	289650	c.1768	
Standard Brick & Tile Co.	East Buckley	289649	1886	1914
Buckley Gas Works	East Buckley	290648	1889	
Sandycroft Colly.	Burntwood Pentre	292647	1753	1901
Drury Brickworks (Ward's)	Burntwood Pentre	291646	1874	1976
Little Mountain Colly. (with Hawarden Colly.)	Drury	294639	c.1865	1886
Thos. John Shone (Boiler Mkr)	Buckley Junc.	295634	c.1900	c.1920
Carted to Buckley Railway:				
Cheapside Colly.	Ewloe Green	287658	c.1849	1876
Ewloe Hall Colly.	Ewloe Hall	290663		1879
Smally's Colly.	Liverpool Rd	283653		by 1914
Drury Colly. (orig. tramroad link)	Drury	298646		

DOWN (WEST) SIDE: BUCKLEY JUNCTION–CONNAH'S QUAY

Hancock's Siding (serving):

Pentrobin Colly.	Buckley	291640		
Lane End Brickworks	Buckley	287639	by 1792	
Knowl Hill Brickworks*	Buckley	287645		
Mount Pleasant Brickworks*	Buckley	287647		

(the four above linked to Hancock's Siding by private tramroad)

Ashton's Branch Siding (serving):

Old Knowl Lane B'works (Prince's)	Buckley	286645	1794	1902
Knowl Hill Brickworks*	Buckley	287645		
Lane End (Dumpling) Colly.	Buckley	286641		1903
Mountain Colly.	Buckley	284644	1897	1930
Ashton's Brickworks	Buckley	276647		
Mount Pleasant Brickworks*	Buckley	287647		
Old Ewloe Brick & Tile Works	Buckley	286648	1862	1979

(The seven above linked to Ashton's Branch Siding by own siding)

*Connected to both Hancock's Siding per tramroad and Ashton's Branch Siding by own siding.

Etna Brickworks	North Buckley	286653		c.1912
Old Ewloe Hall Colly.	North Buckley	285654	by 1873	1879
Old Ewloe Hall Colly. (Deep Engine Shaft)	North Buckley	284654		
Catherall & Co. (Siding) *(serving):*				
Trap and Ewloe Place B'works	North Buckley	282654	1793	
Buckley Brick & Tile Co. Ltd. (Brookhill & Belmont B'works)	North Buckley	278657	1865	1913 & 1961 resp.
Ewloe Barn Brickworks	North Buckley	277663	1847	1976
Edward Parry & Sons B'works	North Buckley	277664	1862	1969

George Watkinson & Sons Ltd. Railway (serving):

West Buckley Colly.	Aberllanerch	266652		
South Buckley Colly. & B'works (alias Buckley Colly.)	Buckley	274644	pre 1844	
Willow Colly.	Buckley Mountn.	277651		
Ash Colly.	Alltami	273656		
Elm Colly. Watkinson's B'works	Mold Road	274663	1876 & 1894	1934

The foregoing were frequently titled collectively, 'Buckley & Main Coal Co.'
((Great) Oak Colly. used Watkinson's Railway but carted to it.)

Castle Firebrick Co.	Ewloe Barn	275667	pre 1859	
Dublin Main Colly.*	Northop Hall	273676		
Northop Hall Colly.*	Nr. Merllyn	268688		
Galchog Colly.*	Galchog	263680		
Broad Oak Colly.	Nr. Bryngwyn	277683		
T.J. Reney's Central B'works†	Wepre	293695		by 1916
John Williams' B'works†	Wepre	293697		by 1916
Connah's Quay docks (various)	Docks	296698		

*see text for opening/closing details.
†amalgamated with Prince's B'works as one premises.

Spon Green Colly., Lexham Green Colly. (both Buckley) connected to Hancock's Siding by private tramroad.

UP (EAST) SIDE: WREXHAM–SHOTTON

Wrexham & Acton Colly.	Rhosddu	328523	1868	1924

Llay Hall Junction serving:

Llay Hall Colly.	Llay Hall	315551	1873	1949
Llay Hall Firebrickworks	Llay Hall	317552	pre 1866	1974
Hope Rope Works				
(later, Paper Mill)	Cefnybedd	313556	c.1885	
Hope Colly. (alias Glyn Alyn)	Cefnybedd	313556	1863	
Rowley's Brickworks	Shotton			c.1881

DOWN (WEST) SIDE: WREXHAM–SHOTTON

Cudworth & Johnson				
(St Mark's Engine Works)	Rhosddu	329512	c.1885	
Stansty B'works (alias Gwersyllt				
B'works or 'Clayton's')	Stansty	321527		1972
Gwersyllt Colly.	Gwersyllt	315537	1862	1887*
Lascelle & Sharman's Brewery	Caergwrle	306576		

Aston Hall Junction (serving):

Aston Hall Colliery [per AHCR]		294659		1912–3
Aston Hall B'works [per AHCR]		293658		c.1916

Either side of line: Ffrwd Junc.–Brynmally–Ffosygo

Ffrwd Colly., Brick & Ironworks	Ffrwd	303552	pre 1796	1904
Brynmally Colly. & Brickworks	Moss	306542	1770	1935
Westminster Colly.	Moss	308536	1846	1925
Ffosygo Colly.	Windy Hill	308543	post 1849	1917
Pendwllt Colly. (alias Pendwll)	Moss	306542		

UP SIDE: VRON–BRYMBO–BRYMBO JUNCS

(Old) Broughton Colly.	Broughton	303542	1850 and	1868
(New) Broughton Colly.			1869	1878
(Clayton's Pit)	Southsea	306514	1883	1910
Broughton Solvay Coke Ovens*	Southsea	303519		
Broughton Hall Ironworks	Southsea	305517	re-open 1883	

DOWN SIDE: BRYMBO JUNCS–BRYMBO–VRON

Gatewen Colly.	New Broughton	313518	1877	1932
Plas Power Colly.†	Southsea	299518	1877	1938
Brymbo Works	Brymbo	298535	various	1990
Vron Colly.	Vron	292521	1806 (not continuously)	1930
Vron Brickworks	Vron	288524	1873	1925
Offa's Dyke Colly. & Brickworks	Vron	290522		1943
Talwrn Colly.‡	Coedpoeth	288516	by 1845	c.1914

*per GWR connection

†incorporating former Southsea Colly.

‡per narrow gauge tramway/incline of 1845 to connect with Vron Colly.

Note: Opening and Closing Dates do not imply a site was in continuous production over that whole period.

There were considerable links between concerns as to lessees, management and personnel: also varying titles of lessees.

Appendix Three

Industrially-owned locomotives in the area served by the WMCQR up to 1905

Sites listed below where steam engines operated. (The number following each entry refers to the relevant page in INDUSTRIAL & INDEPENDENT LOCOMOTIVES & RAILWAYS OF NORTH WALES: pub. Birmingham Locomotive Club, 1968, which should be consulted for detail.)

Narrow Gauge
Castle Firebrick Co. Ltd.	F81/2
West Buckley Colliery	F96

Standard Gauge
Aston Hall Colliery	F80
Brymbo Works	F58
Buckley Collieries (Watkinson's)	F81
Cudworth & Johnson Ltd.*	F59/62
Ffrwd Colliery	F74
Hawarden Colliery†	F87
Lane End Colliery	F80
Llay Hall Colliery	F66
New Broughton Colliery	F57
Plas Power Colliery	F57
Vron Colliery	F57

*Locomotive dealers etc. Eagle Foundry, Wrexham. [Later also at Rhosddu, Llay Hall Siding and Gresford.] Partnership dissolved August 1904.

†or Little Mountain Colliery.

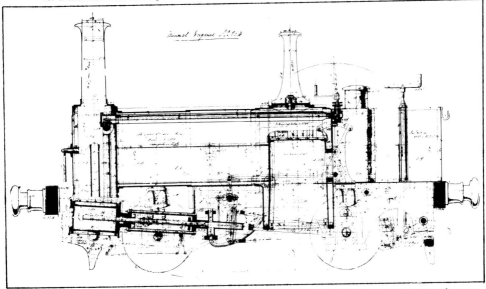

Drawing of locomotives by the Beyer, Peacock & Co. Ltd. for the Broughton Coal Company and Brymbo Iron Company respectively, 1858.

Manchester Museum of Science & Industry

Appendix Four

Post WMCQR Chronology

1st May, 1905 – GWR Moss Valley opened to passengers.

25th May, 1906 – LNWR Connah's Quay station rebuilt and opened.

October 1908 – GWR Summerhill Incline closed (Gwersyllt–Westminster Colly. section. GWR locomotive brought down from Loco Shed at east mouth of tunnel.[1])

1st March, 1917 – ex-WMCQR Brymbo Branch closed to passengers.

1925 – Brymbo Juncs. South Fork closed.

1926 – Brymbo Juncs. South Fork lifted.

1930 – Ffrwd Branch closed.

1st January, 1931 – GWR Ffrwd Branch closed: Moss Valley closed to passengers.

1935 – ex-WMCQR Ffrwd Branch lifted.

1935 – GWR Moss Valley closed to freight.[2]

1940 – GWR Brymbo–Vron closed and lifted.

30th November, 1954 – Iron ore for Brymbo now taken over GWR between Croes Newydd and Plas Power 'A' Box, thence over ex-WMCQR (double reversal required into Steelworks). At same time, ex-WMCQR Brymbo Juncs North Fork–Plas Power 'A' Box closed.

1958 – Brymbo Juncs North Fork–Plas Power 'A' Box lifted.

4th January, 1960 – Rhosddu Shed closed – locomotives to Croes Newydd with employees.

March 1965 – Gatewen Coal Depot outward traffic routed over truncated Moss Valley line, Croes Newydd, Penyffordd and thence via Mold–Chester line. Workings taken by Croes Newydd and Mold Junction-based engines. (This working became a diesel locomotive turn but derailment took place between Moss Valley Junction and Depot with heavy damage to the track. Workings ceased but track and damaged section still extant in 1989.)

1965–66 – Traffic arrangements continue as November 1954, and heavily used. Motive power mainly Stanier-type 2–8–0 train engines and ex-GWR 0–6–2T banking engines, the latter working in and out of Brymbo Steelworks on arrival from Wrexham. From 19th June, 1958 traffic switched back to ex-GWR route and suspended over ex-WMCQR route as between Plas Power 'A' Box and Brymbo Steelworks. On 1st March, 1965 position again reversed: motive power continues as before. Whole situation however, under review.   .

March 1966 – Llay Hall Branch. Llay Main traffic worked by GWR type 0–6–0PT based on Croes Newydd but whole Branch to Llay Hall due for closure. All coal traffic hereabouts now dependent on life expectancy of remaining open-cast coal workings.

1st April, 1967 – Last workings Shotton–Connah's Quay: official closure 4th September.

5th October, 1970 – Brymbo–Vron closed.

by October 1989 – Moss Valley Junction–Brymbo, out of use; lifted.

Buckley Junction–Northop Hall

10th September, 1962 – Croes Newydd–Northop Hall trips (two daily)
  reduced to one daily.
5th July, 1965 – Buckley Junction–Northop Hall closed.

[1] 0–4–0ST No. 95 built by Sharp, Stewart & Co. of Manchester in 1857 for the Birkenhead Railway as No. 6 GRASSHOPPER. Rebuilt at Wolverhampton in 1890 with 3 ft 6 in. driving wheels, cut down boiler mountings and cab roof removed, this engine worked the Summerhill length. Similar fourcoupled tank engines, reduced in height for the tunnel, worked this length at other times. (Ref: THE GREAT WESTERN NORTH OF WOLVERHAMPTON (Keith M. Beck) [Ian Allan Ltd.] and LOCOMOTIVES OF THE GREAT WESTERN RAILWAY (Part Three: Absorbed Engines 1854–1921) [The Railway Correspondence & Travel Society].
[2] The portion of Moss Valley line between Moss Valley Junction and the site of Gatewen Colly was relaid to a Coal Disposal Depot by the National Coal Board.

Unless otherwise stated, all above entries refer to ex-WMCQR sections etc.

Appendix Five

WMCQR Employees – 1898

Royal Commission on Accidents to Railway Servants 1900 [Cd.42]

List of Employees at 31st December, 1898

Carriage & Waggon Examiners	5	Mechanics (Boys)	2
Checkers (Men)	5	Number takers (Men)	1
Clerks (Men)	26	Number takers (Boys)	1
Clerks (Boys)	24	Permanent Way men	67
Engine Cleaners (Men)	5	Policemen	1
Engine Cleaners (Boys)	28	Porters (Men)	23
Engine Drivers	30	Porters (Boys)	11
Firemen	28	Shunters	10
Guards (Goods) & Brakesmen	19	Signal fitters	2
Guards (Passenger)	1	Signalmen	29
Horse drivers	1	Stationmasters	16
Permanent Way Inspectors	1	Yardsmen	7
Other inspectors	2	Miscellaneous (men)	17
Labourers	10	Miscellaneous (boys)	1
Mechanics (Men)	20		

Total: 326 adults and 67 boys. Grand total: 393.

Appendix Six

Locomotive Water Supplies and Cranes

Water supplies

Wrexham Central station	1 Water Column
Wrexham Goods Yard	3000 gallon Water Tank & Column
Ffrwd Junction	10,000 gallon Water Tank supported on brick walls (& Coaling Stage)
Hope Village Pumping Station	Buildings, tank & brickwork. 7000 gallon Water Tank. Boiler, Willans' Pulsometer etc. Water Column (Water was pumped from the R. Alyn across which a weir was built: steam power was used)
Buckley	1600 gallon Water Tank on brick support wall (there was no Water Column here)
Connah's Quay	Reservoir storage Water Column beside Engine Shed
Hawarden station	3000 gallon Water Tank on Down platform 3000 gallon Water Tank on Up platform (by Powell Bros. & Whittaker, 1890). Both tanks supported on cast-iron columns.
No. 2 Engine Shed, Rhosddu	14,000 gallon Water Tank on nine cast-iron columns

Cranes

Rhosddu Engine Shed	Derrick Crane with 28 ft jib, to lift 5 tons.
Connah's Quay	5 ton steam travelling crane by Taylor, Birkenhead. No. 2
	3½ ton steam travelling crane with lengthened jib to 19 ft radius (originally 5 tons with shortened jib). No. 3
	Two 3 ton steam travelling cranes by Priestman, Hull. Nos 4 & 6
	Two portable steam cranes 1¼ ton on wooden carriages. Nos 1 & 5.

Appendix Seven

John Summers & Sons Ltd

The opening of the Hawarden Bridge attracted the attention of the Summers family whose clog nail manufacturing business was situated in Stalybridge, Cheshire at that time. Searching for a site for a new works nearer Merseyside, Henry Hall Summers is reputed to have favoured a position on the Sealand marsh on the north bank of the river opposite Connah's Quay ... or thereabouts. Hiring a local boatman, he made an inspection of the place and in 1885, 40 acres were purchased (at a cost, it is said, of 1/- an acre with the option of a further 50 acres) to erect a new factory. £610 was spent on making a junction and sidings with the railway north of the Bridge. (Summers were linked to the MS & LR at Stalybridge and seem to have enjoyed good relations.)

The new works opened in 1896 and was shortly employing 250 persons: by 1901, 30 rolling mills were in operation and labour was recruited from the Stalybridge area, Staffordshire and South Wales. The following year a steelmaking plant and bar mill was installed and from 40 acres the undertaking then embraced 10,000 acres of the marsh. Though much of their traffic was to and from the north of the works, the WMCQR enjoyed a considerable amount of extra business from this establishment. Regrettably this came too late in the life of that Railway to save it from misfortune.*

(There was a Toll on the footway over the Bridge but Summers' employees were given a pass, 'PASS FOR CROSSING FOOTBRIDGE OVER THE RIVER DEE — Persons crossing the Footbridge without a Pass will be required by the Railway Co. to pay a toll of ½d.')

---

*see SHOTTON DEESIDE (published by Shotton Town Council to mark the Centenary of the opening of the Hawarden Bridge: 1989) and TRANSACTIONS OF FLINTSHIRE HISTORICAL SOCIETY: Vol. 25 (1971–72) pp. 103–123.

Appendix Eight

Shipbuilders on the south bank of the Dee

Ferguson & Baird*	Connah's Quay	1858–1910
J. Crichton & Co.	Connah's Quay	c.1910–c.1935
James Boydell	Queensferry	c.1836–c.1840
Abdela & Mitchell	Queensferry	1908–1938
John Rigby	Sandycroft	c.1830–1852
George Cramm	Sandycroft	1852–1856

*Moved from Flint in 1858.
See also CHESTER & THE RIVER DEE (published by City Record Office: 1982).

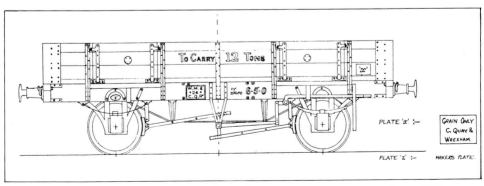

Open wagon for Cobden's Mill traffic (ref. THE LOCOMOTIVE MAGAZINE., Vol.x, 1904 *page 147*).   *Courtesy* RAILWAY MODELLER

Appendix Nine

Ordinary Tickets

(All headed WM&CQR and of Edmondson type)

	1st	2nd	3rd	Parly.
Single	White	Pink	Yellow Ochre	Dark Green or Light Green
Return	White (out) Yellow (ret)	Pink (out) Blue (ret)	Green (out) Orange (ret)[1]	— —

Special Tickets

"Saturday to Monday EXCURSION RETURN Third"	White striped vertical yellow White striped vertical green	(out) (ret)
"HALF DAY EXCURSION Third Class (Parly)"	White: (not known) White: vert. orange bands each side	(out) (ret)
"EXCURSION RETURN Sept. 14. 1874 Wrexham to Longsight for Belle Vue via Hope Jc."	White (out) White: four vertical pink bands	(ret)[2]
"EXCURSION RETURN July 15, 1876 Wrexham to Liverpool Landing Stage via Hope Jn. & Birkenhead"	Blue: three vertical yellow stripes Blue: as out but diagonal green stripe	(out) (ret)
"Saturday to Monday EXCURSION RETURN Wrexham to Rhyl via Hope & Denbigh Cov. Carriage"	Stone: four vertical green stripes Stone: four vertical pink stripes	(out) (ret)[3]
"EXCURSION RETURN Wrexham to Rhyl via Hope Jun. CHILD Cov. Carriage"	Blue with narrow green band top and wider green band at bottom. Single narrow yellow band across waist. Above applies whole ticket but return half has narrow green diagonal stripe.[4]	
"Bicycle"	Brick red	
"Article UNDER 2 CWTS"	Pink upper half: stone lower half	
(Water Closet)	White with name of station and "W.C. Ticket 1*d.*"	

[1] Three horizontal red bands across whole ticket.
[2] Sample ticket number is No. 00 (undated).
[3] Sample ticket number is No. 02 (undated).
[4] Printing error of ticket: outward half is No. 347 and inward No. 346.

Printing errors include "Wrexham (Central) to WREXHAM (Exchang Station) Fare /2*d.*"

[Ticket information kindly supplied by Michael Stewart and Stephen Goodall.]

Above. The Company's Garter crest was carried only by certain of its locomotives. *Courtesy Gerald Hartley*

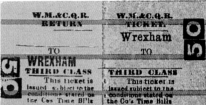
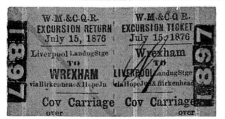
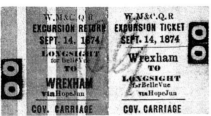

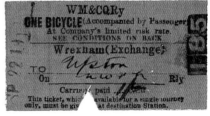
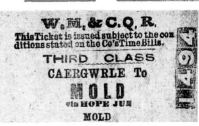

A fine selection of colourful W.M.&C.Q.Rly tickets dating from the earliest times.

Principal documentary sources

Clwyd Record Office
  Birch, Cullimore Mss
  Broughton & Plas Power Coal Co. Ltd. Minute Books
  Catherall & Hancock Mss
  Coppack Bros & Co. records
  Dean, R.J., Deposit
  Grosvenor (Halkyn) Mss
  Hawarden Estate Papers
  Jones, W. Bell, Mss
  Keene & Kelly Mss
  Messham, J.E., Deposit
  National Coal Board Papers
  Penbedw Papers
National Library of Wales
  Piercy Papers (Fraser Group)
  Robertson, Henry, Collection
Public Record Office
  Buckley Railway Minute Books
  Wrexham, Mold & Connah's Quay Railway Minute Books
Miscellaneous
  Bertram Baxter Collection – City of Birmingham Reference Library
  J.M. Dunn Collection
  GW/LNWR Joint Committee Minute Books
  Lawrence Walker Collection
Newspapers
  THE CHESTER CHRONICLE
  THE WREXHAM & DISTRICT WEEKLY ADVERTISER
  THE WREXHAM TELEGRAPH
Paper
  COAL MINING IN HAWARDEN AT THE EVE OF THE INDUSTRIAL REVOLUTION (Rees
    Rawson – 1941)

Periodicals sources

Brymbo Works Magazine
Clwyd Historian
Railway News
Railway Times

The Mining Journal
Trans. Denbighs. Historical Society
Trans. Flints. Historical Society

Bibliography

GREAT CENTRAL	George Dow
HENRY ROBERTSON (PIONEER OF RAILWAYS)	G.G. Lerry
HISTORY OF THE GREAT WESTERN RAILWAY	McDermot & Clinker
THE STORY OF THE CAMBRIAN	G.P. Gasquoine
THE CHRONICLES OF BOULTON'S SIDING	A.R. Bennett
THE RAILWAY FOUNDRY, LEEDS	R.N. Redman
STONE BLOCKS & IRON RAILS	B. Baxter
EARLY WOODEN RAILWAYS	M.J.T. Lewis
COLLIERIES OF DENBIGHSHIRE	G.G. Lerry
MEMOIRS OF HAWARDEN	Willett
THE INDUSTRIAL REVOLUTION IN N. WALES	A.H. Dodd
BUCKLEY & DISTRICT	T. Cropper
EVOLUTION OF THE WELSH COASTLINE	W. Ashton
A SHORT ACCOUNT OF THE BUCKLEY POTTERIES	J. Bentley
TOPOGRAPHICAL DICTIONARY OF WALES (3rd Edit)	Samuel Lewis
A LIFETIME WITH SHIPS	T. Coppack
CAMBRIAN COASTERS	R.S. Fenton

Acknowledgements

Although in the ultimate, this study has far exceeded the work carried out by the late Eric Thomas of Crewe, the writer is indebted to him for his toleration of a young man's interest in the WMCQR following the publication of Mr Thomas's articles in the Journal of the Stephenson Locomotive Society in 1943. His notes of that period subsequently passed to J. Maxwell Dunn and were used in the preparation of a book of that title, published by The Oakwood Press in 1957, and long since out of print.

One day my good friend Geoffrey Platt called and left me all Mr Dunn's research notes to do with as I wished. More recently, Cedric Green handed me all the material he had collected for his own publications and unselfishly suggested I use it as I felt. I also had George Dow's permission to draw on his mammoth work, GREAT CENTRAL. What a fortunate beginning all the afore-mentioned gave to my task!

The finished book has indeed far passed the boundaries which these gentlemen set themselves – at that time no publisher would have accepted a manuscript as detailed as the present one, and we must appreciate the enthusiasm of The Oakwood Press for it – but its inspiration sprang from their kindnesses and I have been conscious throughout of producing a history which their goodwill deserves.

In my fieldwork I have been skilfully educated in local history by the untiring efforts of James Bentley and Ian Jolly, who have been tireless in taking me over the ground of the early tramroads, a subject which has never before been in print on an area basis. The Buckley district is fortunate to enjoy their knowledge.

In terms of draughtsmanship, John Lloyd has seldom been called upon to such extent: he has responded with zeal to my many humble ideas and sketches, questioned my erring knowledge and elevated these pages with his own creativity.

Jeremy Wilkinson, the third member of 'the team' has enhanced my researches in his professionally-competent way and put before me many avenues to follow. We have tramped many miles together and our regular appearance in certain districts has at times, made us feel vulnerable to the new cult of 'Neighbourhood Watch'. However, all's well that ends well.

My wife has been involved at every stage. We have researched, entertained, motored, prepared typescripts, walked, discussed together: it has all been the most tremendous fun yet the tedious side of it all is always her lot. We are agreed that no subject of our previous study has been so enjoyable as has this one.

I have been greatly assisted by the work of others in the preparation of the typescript; not all of those listed are now living, but each has made some special contribution.

Bertram Baxter
Rev. Alan Cliff
W. Noel Davies*
William Davies†
Andrew Dow

George Dow
Mark Hambly
Colin Judge
Dr Michael Lewis
Roger W. Kidner

Michael Morton Lloyd
Mrs Elaine Roberts
Mrs Jean Sharpe
Dr Edwin Shearing

Locomotive, Carriage & Wagon

Alan Brown
David Goodwin
A.M. Gunn

Ian Lloyd
Philip Millard
John Milner

John Quick
Bernard Roberts
Mike Williams

Signalling

Stephen Goodall

T.L. Guest

Local History/Tramroads/Shipping/Industrial

John Bagshaw
Roy S. Fenton
Dr G.I. Hawkes

Ted Mellowes
Dr S. Owen-Jones
Alan Peers

L. Peers
Dr C.B. Waine

The patience and helpfulness of staff at the following venues has been enormously helpful and a thoroughly enjoyable experience:

National Library of Wales
Bersham Industrial Heritage Centre, Wrexham
Broughton District Local History Group
Industrial & Maritime Museum, Cardiff
Clwyd County Record Offices, Ruthin and Hawarden
The Public Record Office
House of Commons Record Office
House of Lords Record Office
Central Reference Library, Manchester
Law Society Library, Manchester
Museum of Science & Industry Record Office, Manchester
Mold County Library
County Record Office, Shrewsbury
Wrexham Public Library (Reference Department)

---

* An interchange of letters between J. Maxwell Dunn and W.N. Davies formed part of the material left for my use by Geoffrey Platt. The collection is entitled The Roseneath Letters and was returned to Mrs Platt after use, at her request. The collection covers a far wider spectrum than the WMCQR alone, and has great value in its references to railway personalities at the turn of the century. W.N. Davies was born on 12th May, 1885: he was a son of William Davies MICE (q.v.) He was educated at Shrewsbury School with a strong classical bias, reflected in the many Latin quotations in his writings. He entered Crewe Works as an apprentice under Francis Webb and left there in April 1910 for the Buenos Aires Great Southern Railway, Argentine. He returned to England and worked in the road motor department of the LMSR, retiring in 1944. He died at Prestatyn age 83 on 16th May, 1968.

† William Davies is mentioned frequently in the text. He was father of the above W.N. Davies and had married a sister of Benjamin and Robert Piercy in 1856. He worked with his brothers-in-law in many situations, especially with Benjamin whom he followed abroad. He was appointed Resident Engineer to the WMCQR in 1884 and resigned in 1890. He continued to live an active and public life in Flintshire until his death.

Index

351